Mirror for the Muslim Prince

Modern Intellectual and Political History of the Middle East
Mehrzad Boroujerdi, *Series Editor*

OTHER TITLES IN MODERN INTELLECTUAL AND POLITICAL HISTORY OF THE MIDDLE EAST

Democracy and Civil Society in Arab Political Thought: Transcultural Possibilities
Michaelle L. Browers

The Education of Women and The Vices of Men: Two Qajar Tracts
Hasan Javadi and Willem Floor, trans.

The Essentials of Ibadi Islam
Valerie J. Hoffman

A Guerrilla Odyssey: Modernization, Secularism, Democracy, and the Fadai Period of National Liberation in Iran, 1971–1979
Peyman Vahabzadeh

The International Politics of the Persian Gulf
Mehran Kamrava, ed.

The Kurdish Quasi-State: Development and Dependency in Post–Gulf War Iraq
Denise Natali

Modernity, Sexuality, and Ideology in Iran: The Life and Legacy of a Popular Female Artist
Kamran Talattof

Pax Syriana: Elite Politics in Postwar Lebanon
Rola el-Husseini

Pious Citizens: Reforming Zoroastrianism in India and Iran
Monica M. Ringer

The Urban Social History of the Middle East, 1750–1950
Peter Sluglett, ed.

Mirror for the Muslim Prince

Islam and the Theory of Statecraft

Edited by Mehrzad Boroujerdi

SYRACUSE UNIVERSITY PRESS

First Edition 2013
13 14 15 16 17 18 6 5 4 3 2 1

An earlier version of part of chapter 13, "God's Caravan: Topoi and Schemata in the History of Muslim Political Thought," appeared previously in *The Times of History: Universal Topics in Islamic Historiography*, published in 2007 by Central European University Press. © Aziz Al-Azmeh.

∞ The paper used in this publication meets the minimum requirements of the American National Standard for Information Sciences—Permanence of Paper for Printed Library Materials, ANSI Z39.48-1992.

For a listing of books published and distributed by Syracuse University Press, visit our website at SyracuseUniversityPress.syr.edu.

ISBN:978-0-8156-3289-4

Library of Congress Cataloging-in-Publication Data
Available upon request from the publisher.

Manufactured in the United States of America

To those who employ the pen
to inscribe ethics in the register of politics

"*Historia est Magistra Vitae*" (History is life's teacher).

—CICERO, *De Oratore*

Contents

Acknowledgments

THE IDEA FOR THIS BOOK germinated during a conference I had organized at Syracuse University in 2006. All the distinguished contributors to this volume presented papers at this event and in the ensuing years revised their papers to make them suitable for publication. The chapter by Shomali and Boroujerdi and the one by Rutherford were not part of the conference but were added later to address certain lacunae in the project. I want to sincerely thank each and every one of the contributors for their graciousness and patience as this manuscript went through the travails of the publication process. Gratitude is also due Zayde Antrim, M. Sükrü Hanioglu, Naeem Inayatullah, Tazim Kassam, David S. Powers, and Robert Rubinstein, whose participation, presentations, and comments enriched the quality of this project.

I would like to thank Syracuse University's "Ray Smith Symposium" and the Maxwell School of Citizenship and Public Affairs for providing financial support for the conference and to Smithsonian Freer Gallery of Art and Arthur M. Sackler Gallery for the book cover. I also would like to gratefully acknowledge *Middle East Journal,* Princeton University Press, and Central European University Press for permissions to use modified and abridged sections from the following earlier texts by Bruce K. Rutherford ("What Do Egypt's Islamists Want? Moderate Islam and the Rise of Islamic Constitutionalism"); Roxanne L. Euben *(Journeys to the Other Shore: Muslim and Western Travelers in Search of Knowledge)*; and Aziz al-Azmeh *(The Times of History: Universal Topics in Islamic Historiography)*.

I owe special thanks to John Fruehwirth for ameliorating this manuscript with his meticulous attention to thorny details as only he can and to Mary Selden Evans for her eagerness to see this volume published. I also owe a great deal to my friend and colleague Alireza Shomali, and to my able research assistants Todd Fine, Joanna Palmer, Nicholas Patriciu, Roya Soleimani, and Kate Vasharakorn for their administrative support and for tracking down missing references in every possible way.

A Note on the Text

EMPLOYING A TRANSLITERATION SYSTEM in a bulky book where some thirteen scholars use more than half a dozen languages to analyze ancient, medieval, and modern treaties proved a formidable task. It soon became clear that adopting a rigid transliteration system can be problematical. Hence it was decided that while we employed—as a heuristic device—the transliteration system laid out by the Library of Congress, certain exceptions had to be made for the sake of accuracy, accessibility, or deference to the respective authors' preferred spelling of names. All the diacritical marks for Persian and Arabic terms were dispensed with—with the exception of *ayn* and *hamza,* which are dropped only at the initial position. However, the full range of diacritics was retained for Turkish names and terms. Anglicized words that appear in the English dictionary (such as A'isha, Ali, Arab, ibn, Umar, and Uthman) have been granted preference where appropriate. Familiar geographical names have been provided in their common spelling. We aimed to have one style convention for punctuation, spelling, capitalization, hyphenation, italicization, numbers, and abbreviations.

In the body of the texts and the notes we have dropped the equivalent Hijrah dates for the sources cited and have only provided the Christian Era dates. Finally, all translations from non-English sources are those of the respective authors unless otherwise indicated.

Contributors

ASMA AFSARUDDIN is Professor of Islamic Studies and Chairperson of the Department of Near Eastern Languages and Cultures at Indiana University (Bloomington). She is the author of *The First Muslims: History and Memory* and *Excellence and Precedence: Medieval Islamic Discourse on Legitimate Leadership* as well as editor of *Hermeneutics and Honor: Negotiation of Female "Public" Space in Islamic/ate Societies;* and coeditor of *Humanism, Culture, and Language in the Near East: Essays in Honor of Georg Krotkoff (with Mathias Zahniser).*

MUZAFFAR ALAM is the George V. Bobrinskoy Professor in South Asian languages and civilizations at the University of Chicago. His main publications include *The Crisis of Empire in Mughal North India; The Mughal State, 1526–1750* (edited with Sanjay Subrahmanyam); *A European Experience of the Mughal Orient* (with Seema Alavi); *Languages of Political Islam: India 1200–1800; Writing the Mughal World: Studies in Political Culture* (with Sanjay Subrahmanyam); and *Indo-Persian Travels in the Age of Discoveries, 1400–1800* (with Sanjay Subrahmanyam).

SAÏD AMIR ARJOMAND is Distinguished Service Professor of Sociology and director of the Institute for Global Studies at State University of New York at Stony Brook. He is the author of *The Shadow of God and the Hidden Imam; The Turban for the Crown;* and *After Khomeini;* and editor of *Constitutional Politics in the Middle East* and the *Journal of Persianate Studies.*

AZIZ AL-AZMEH is university professor in the School of History at the Central European University (Budapest, Hungary). He is the author of *Arabic Thought and Islamic Society; Muslim Kingship: Power and the Sacred in Muslim, Christian, and Pagan Polities; Ibn Khaldun: An Essay in Reinterpretation; The Times of History: Universal Topics in Islamic Historiography;* and *Islams and Modernities.*

MEHRZAD BOROUJERDI is associate professor of political science and director of the Middle Eastern Studies Program at Syracuse University. He is the author of *Iranian Intellectuals and the West: The Tormented Triumph of Nativism* and *Essay on Iranian Politics and Identity* (in Persian).

CHARLES E. BUTTERWORTH is emeritus professor of government and politics at the University of Maryland College Park. He is coauthor of *The Introduction of Arabic Philosophy into Europe* and *Between the State and Islam;* and the editor/translator of *Averroes' Middle Commentary on Aristotle's "Categories" and "De Interpretatione"; Averroes' Middle Commentary on Aristotle's "Poetics"; Alfarabi: The Political Writings: "Selected Aphorisms" and Other Texts;* and *Averroes' Decisive Treatise and Epistle Dedicatory.*

ROXANNE L. EUBEN is the Ralph Emerson and Alice Freeman Palmer Professor of Political Science at Wellesley College. She is the author of *Enemy in the Mirror: Islamic Fundamentalism and the Limits of Modern Rationalism; Journeys to the Other Shore: Muslim and Western Travelers in Search of Knowledge;* and (with Muhammad Qasim Zaman) *Princeton Readings in Islamist Thought: Texts and Contexts from Al-Banna to Bin Laden.*

PETER GRAN is professor of history at Temple University. He is the author of *Islamic Roots of Capitalism: Egypt, 1760–1840; Beyond Eurocentrism: A New View of Modern World History;* and *The Rise of the Rich.*

ŞERIF MARDIN is emeritus professor of political science at Sabancı University (Istanbul, Turkey). He is the author of *The Genesis of Young Ottoman Thought; Religion and Social Change in Modern Turkey;* and *Religion, Society, and Modernity in Turkey;* and editor of *Cultural Transitions in the Middle East.*

LOUISE MARLOW is professor of religion at Wellesley College. Her publications include *Writers and Rulers: Perspectives from Abbasid to Safavid Times,* coedited with Beatrice Gruendler; and *Hierarchy and Egalitarianism in Islamic Thought.*

BRUCE K. RUTHERFORD is associate professor of political science at Colgate University and director of the university's Program in Middle Eastern Studies and Islamic Civilization. He is the author of *Egypt after Mubarak: Liberalism, Islam, and Democracy in the Arab World.*

ALIREZA SHOMALI is associate professor of political science at Wheaton College in Massachusetts. He is the author of *Politics and the Criteria of Truth.*

JAVAD TABATABAI is a former professor of political science at Tehran University. He is the author of *Philosophical Introduction to the History of Political Thought in Iran; Decline of Political Thought in Iran; Essay on Ibn Khaldun: Impossibility of Social Sciences in Islam; Nizam al-Mulk and Iranian Political Thought: Essay on the Continuity of the Iranian Thought;* and *Reflections on Persia* (all in Persian).

Mirror for the Muslim Prince

1

Introduction

MEHRZAD BOROUJERDI

THE STRING OF POPULAR UPRISINGS, commonly referred to as "the Arab Spring," that jolted the Arab and Muslim worlds in 2010 and 2011 came as a shock to most political observers. The toppling of Zine El Abidine Ben Ali (r. 1987–2011), Hosni Mubarak (r. 1981–2011), Ali Abdullah Saleh (r. 1978–2011), and Muammar al-Qadhafi (r. 1969–2011), who collectively had ruled for more than a century, called into question many shibboleths about Arabs and Muslims such as their fatalism and aversion to democratic politics. The Arab Spring has also forced the Middle Eastern scholarly community to reexamine a host of its assumptions and theories.[1] The future of these countries is unknown at this conjuncture. Some may be heading toward a more democratic future, while others may head toward resurrected dictatorships or other uncertain outcomes. Yet one can say with a certain degree of confidence that these societies will inevitably draw on the collective wisdom of their populations. Having seen the debris of the atavistic solutions offered by nativism,[2] and the pitfall of unbridled cosmopolitanism, one hopes that the intellectual elite in these societies will try to reanimate their communities by careful deconstruction and reconstruction of their intellectual traditions. The (re)reading of the Islamic traditions is a part of the responsibility of intellectuals who wish to help future generations of Muslims contemplate a more humane style of

1. For one such example, see Bellin 2012.

2. For a critical discussion of nativism, see Boroujerdi 1996.

statecraft. Contemporary Muslim intellectuals such as Muhammad Abed al-Jabri (1999) have insisted on the need for a "critique of Arab reason," whereas the Moroccan sociologist Abd al-Kabir al-Khatibi has argued that contemporary Arab knowledge that is stamped by the ideology of Islam "should be subjected to deconstruction in order to show that its concepts are historical products that have taken their particular structures in relation to a specific way of thinking and specific events in time and space."[3]

In this volume, a group of distinguished scholars tries to reinterpret concepts and canons of Islamic thought in Arab, Persian, South Asian, and Turkish traditions and to demonstrate that there is no unitary "Islamic" position on important issues of statecraft and governance. They recognize that Islam is a discursive site marked by silences, agreements, and animated controversies (not to mention denunciation and persecutions). There is no shortage of disagreements among Islam's clerical literati and their lay counterparts about the authenticity of hadiths and the partisanship of historiographies. Rigorous debates and profound disagreements among Muslim theologians, philosophers, and literati (and their Western interlocutors) have taken place over such questions as: What is an Islamic state? Was the state ever viewed as an independent political institution in the Islamic tradition of political thought? Is it possible that a religion that places an inordinate emphasis upon the importance of good deeds does not indeed have a vigorous notion of "public interest" or a systematic theory of government (à la Hobbes, Mills, or Rawls)? Does Islam provide an edifice, a common idiom, and an ideological mooring for premodern and modern Muslim rulers alike? Are Islam and democracy compatible?

The volume begins both thematically and historically with Asma Afsaruddin's chapter concentrating on the explicit and implicit invocations of the concept of *maslahah* (translated as "public interest," "utility," or "expediency") in Islamic history. She maintains that even though it was not termed as such, maslahah as a political concept existed from almost the onset of Islam. Grounding her argument on hadith sources and historical/political treaties, Afsaruddin argues that the sociopolitical principle of maslahah

3. Cited in Boullata 1990, 115.

has been utilized in both Sunni and Shi'i exegetical works.[4] She points to Ayatollah Khomeini's theory of *wilayat-i faqih* (the guardianship of the jurist) as one of the latest works in which maslahah serves as the cardinal principle of legislation.[5] The concept of maslahah has profound implications for modern Islamic political thought and for the type of political systems Muslim societies may wish to embrace. Considerations of "public interest" by religious scholars can enhance the effectiveness of democratic discourse and the compromises that are invariably required in any modern state. But what if the theologians were to insist that they were the only legitimate class of interpreters of maslahah or that one among them who was primus inter pares (first among equals) had to serve as an inalienable sovereign?[6] Already in Iran, dissenting voices like those of Mahdi Ha'iri-Yazdi (1923–1999), Mohsen Kadivar (1959–), Muhammad Mujtahid-Shabistari (1936–), and Abdulkarim Soroush (1945–) have complained that the doctrine of wilayat-i faqih is destroying the sacredness of Islam as jurisprudence and theology have become intertwined with state power, material interest, and political considerations.[7] Some have even argued, in a counterintuitive fashion, that the theory of wilayat-i faqih is the last and

4. Two other philosophers not discussed by Afsaruddin whose works implicitly recognize the concept of public interest are Muhammad ibn Zakariya Razi (865–925) and Farabi (ca. 872–951).

5. For an excellent discussion of the mystical influences on Khomeini, see Knysh 1992.

6. Years ago Karl Jaspers (1959, 85–86) wrote, "Theology [which aims at the eternal salvation of the soul through an understanding of religious revelation] touches upon the supra-rational realm but through rational means. Now, instead of rationally developing the meaning of revelation, theology can develop a passion for 'the absurd.' Self-contradiction is then supposed to confirm the very truth of an assertion; the enslavement of reason to confirm the very truth of faith; and arbitrary submission to an authority, even though in reality it exists in the world in the form of judgments and expressions, which are supposed to be the true way of life. Brutality, fanaticism, inquisition, and 'lovelessness'—these make up this theological fury."

7. Ayatollah Ha'iri-Yazdi (1995) has argued that "[g]overnment is representation [wikalah not Wilayah] and nothing else and anytime you feel that your representatives have betrayed you, you can impeach them."

most important attempt at secularization of Shiʿa jurisprudence. The argument goes like this: since the state is the guardian of the national interest and since the protection of national interest requires the acceptance of maslahah as a principle of statecraft, the pragmatist logic of wilayat-i faqih opens the gate for all types of evolution within *shariʿa*. When a religious system moves toward the formation of a state, it becomes incumbent upon it to modify its religious laws in accordance with the new conditions at hand. A prerequisite for doing so is to prepare a strong digestive system to swallow an entity referred to as the "state." Secularization is the catalyst that enables religion to digest the state and, in turn, precipitates the absorption of religion within the machinery of the state (Salihpur 1995, 18).[8]

We then turn our attention to five chapters that discuss the contributions of some of the medieval Perso-Islamicate works on political ethics and statecraft. Goethe referred to Persia as the Land of Poetry par excellence, and the chapter by Shomali and Boroujerdi concentrates on Saʿdi Shirazi (1209–1291), who has earned the accolade of "Master of Prose and Poetry" in Iran. However, instead of concentrating on his poetry, the authors provide a full and original translation of the celebrated poet's *Treatise on Advice to the Kings (Nasihat al-Muluk)*. The chapter also ventures a reconstruction of a number of elements in medieval Persian political

8. On the other hand, Albert Hourani and Aziz al-Azmeh have both criticized the zeal of revivalist Muslims of the ilk of Muhammad Abduh to present such a reading of Islam as to make it look consistent with guiding principles of European thought. Hourani (1983, 344) writes, "Ibn Khaldun's *ʿumran* gradually turned into Guizot's 'civilization,' the *maslahah* of the Maliki jurists and Ibn Taymiyya into the 'utility' of John Stuart Mill, the *ijmaʿ* of Islamic Jurisprudence into the 'public opinion' of democratic theory, and 'those who bind and loose' into members of parliament." Meanwhile, discussing the various forms this "authentication" has taken in the hands of revivalist Muslims, al-Azmeh (1993, 56) writes, "Thus parliamentary democracy is presented as a simple revalorization of the *shura*, a process of consulting clan chiefs in early Islamic times, and rationality becomes a reclamation of the work of Averroes and of Ibn Khaldun, while freedom becomes a repetition of Muʿtazilite theological theses on free will, and socialism is made to stand in direct continuity with peasant rebellions of the tenth and eleventh centuries." According to Hourani, by equating Islam with whatever form of politics that served the public interest, Islamist reformers of the "liberal age" inadvertently opened "another door to secular nationalism."

philosophy that appeared in this work and in Sa'di's other literary opuses. As scholars like Abdullahi An-Na'im (2010) and Bassam Tibi (2012) argue, the ideology of Islamism and the concept of the Islamic theocratic state whose sole purpose is implementation of the shari'a are but modern and postcolonial phenomena in the Middle East.[9] It is philosophically mistaken—and politically dangerous—to commit the fallacy of anachronism and read the history of political thought in the Islamic world in terms of an unfolding of "perennial" ideas such as theocratic statecraft or political Islam. The authors' reconstruction of the political philosophical elements in Sa'di's thought offers a counterexample, which is by no means unique and exceptional, to the radical Islamist claim and also to the oversimplifying generalizations by figures such as Ann Lambton (1981, xiv), who argues that Muslim political theorists never ask why the state exists in the first place since it is taken for granted that it is needed to promote and protect God's law. Far from claiming that Sa'di has articulated a systematically consistent political theory, the authors highlight Sa'di's predominantly pragmatic and secular beliefs about statecraft and situate him within a broad conception of social contract. Sa'di, the authors argue, does ask why the state exists and adopts a language of social contract to formulate his response. In Sa'di's view, the king does not own the people and is not God's representative on earth. Rather, he is an employee hired by the people to protect their welfare and security. The chapter concludes with the point that Sa'di's works reflect "a sketchy conceptualization of a humane type of politics incorporating elements of pragmatism, secular statecraft, and public interest." Sa'di "views governance as a rational contract between the sovereign and the people without having to reject Deity or embrace theocracy."

Saïd Amir Arjomand's chapter takes us into the midst of another serious ongoing debate as to whether we are dealing with "Islamic political

9. Lapidus (1992, 16) writes, "Muslim political theorists, such as al-Baqillani, al-Mawardi, and Ibn Taimiyya, devised a theory of the caliphate that symbolized the ideal existence of the unified umma, while at the same time allowing for historical actualities. The conclusion of their theorizing was that the state was not a direct expression of Islam but a secular institution whose duty it was to uphold Islam."

thought" or "concepts of politics held or advocated by Muslims." The proponents of the latter approach are preoccupied with what they consider the quintessence of Islam and tend to separate Islam as an idea from the social milieu in which it developed. The exponents of the former view contend that political thought and utterances of Muslims should be reckoned Islamic so far as their endeavor is to denote a religious understanding of political praxis. Arjomand—who in his earlier works had rebuffed the thesis that the state is unavoidably illegitimate in Shiʿism—embraces this more expansive viewpoint and calls into question the contention of such scholars as H. A. R. Gibb and Patricia Crone who maintain that the literature on statecraft and political ethics was somehow "un-Islamic" and was implanted upon the more authentic Islamic shariʿa. He does this by providing a reading of some seminal Persian texts on political ethics from the medieval period and advancing the idea that far from being alien to Islamic precepts, the architects of this tradition were able to rest their claims on the scriptural sources of Islamic law. Arjomand's analysis maintains that civilizational encounters allow for intellectual loans and crossfertilization of ideas rather than rigid ideological separations of what is purportedly Islamic and what is not. Hence he writes, "from the tenth century onward, the legal order of the caliphate had two normatively autonomous components: monarchy and the shariʿa."

The political theorist Javad Tabatabai follows in the footsteps of Richard N. Frye and Marshall Hodgson, who before him had challenged the Arabistic bias of Islamic studies by highlighting the significant contribution of Persianate philosophers, mystics, jurists, poets, and statesmen.[10] Tabatabai draws attention to the fact that the Islamic theory of the caliphate never resonated with Iranian thinkers and that indeed in the annals of

10. Among them one can mention Muhammad ibn Zakariya Razi (d. 932), Rudaki (d. 940), Farabi (d. 950), Firdawsi (d. 1020), Biruni (d. 1030), Avicenna (d. 1037), Farrukhi (d. 1037), Nasir Khusrau (d. 1077), Nizam al-Mulk (d. 1092), Khayyam (d. 1131), Ayn al-quzat-i Hamadani (d. 1131), Sana'i (d. 1131), Anvari (d. 1190), Suhrawardi (d. 1191), Nizami (d. 1209), Fakhr al-Din Razi (d. 1210), Attar (d. 1230), Jalal al-Din Rumi (d. 1273), Nasir al-Din Tusi (d. 1274), and Hafiz (d. 1390). For works that deal with some of these authors, see Walzer 1963, Dabashi 1996, and Kazemi 2011.

the history of Persian political thought in the Islamic period, "no treatise on the Islamic theory of politics was ever written by an Iranian political thinker or scribe." Tabatabai, who in an earlier work (1996, 130) had labeled the celebrated Seljuq vizier Nizam al-Mulk's *Siyasat-namah* (Book of Government) as the most important manifesto of an attempt to reconnect with the legacy of Iranian political thought in the Islamic period, here argues that the book has "no trace of the caliphate theory" and that it "follows the tradition of Persian advice literature and criticizes the Seljuq style of governance." Like Arjomand, Tabatabai draws our attention to the continuing infatuation of Persian political thought with pre-Islamic moral codes and conceptual schemes (including the ancient theory of kingship). Arabic might have become the lingua franca of the conquered Persian Empire but the Persian *mawali* (Non-Arab Muslims) continued to write all their political advice treatises in the Persian language. In other words, cultural integration of Persia proved much more difficult than its political domination.

Louise Marlow continues the rereading project of this volume by suggesting that the "Mirror for the Prince" literature should not be merely scrutinized for its "political" content but rather should be valued for its literary expression and historiography as well. The "mirror" genre is not just a branch of political thought but also an important cultural artifact that has enriched the *adab* (belles lettres) tradition. To demonstrate this argument, Marlow examines a work of counsel literature entitled *Tuhfeh* (The gift) that was dedicated to a fourteenth-century Persian ruler, Nusrat al-din Ahmad. Her approach succeeds in making the reader better comprehend the restraints and plasticity of the advice literature.

Muzaffar Alam's chapter introduces us to the Indo-Persianate tradition of statecraft and political ethics between approximately 1550 and 1750. His main claim is that the Mughals managed to create a high political culture in a non-Muslim setting thanks to "Nasirean *akhlaq* norms of governance, traditions of mysticism, and Persian literary culture." Like Marlow, Alam pays ample attention to the significance of the Persian literary dimension, and similar to Arjomand and Tabatabai, he emphasizes the significant role of the ethical discourse of statecraft, this time by concentrating on the teachings of Nasir al-Din Tusi (d. 1274). The period covered by Alam is momentous because the sixteenth century marks a crucial stage in the growth of imperial political culture and ideology in the Indian subcontinent. The sixteenth century was also important in Persia because of the coming to power of the Safavid dynasty that made Shiʿism the country's state religion, as well as in Europe as it marked the emergence of Protestantism. As pointed out by H. R. Trevor-Roper (1959, 42), "the sixteenth century was an age of economic expansion. It was the century when, for the first time, Europe was living on Asia, Africa and America." Trevor-Roper argues that the "Renaissance State" that emerged created a new machinery of government with an ever-expanding bureaucracy. In his discussing of "governmentality," Michel Foucault (1991, 87) writes,

> Throughout the Middle Ages and classical antiquity, we find a multitude of treaties presented as "advice to the prince," concerning his acceptance and respect of his subjects, the love of God and obedience to him, the application of divine law to the cities of men, etc. But a more striking fact is that, from the middle of the sixteenth century to the end of the eighteenth, there develops and flourishes a notable series of political treaties that are no longer exactly "advice to the prince," and not yet treaties of political science, but are instead presented as works on the "art of government." Government as a general problem seems to me to explode in the sixteenth century, posed by discussions of quite diverse questions.

Following a theme developed in his other works, Alam shows how by patronizing Arab, Persian, and Central Asian traditions the predominantly Muslim Mughal elite managed to rule over a largely non-Muslim population. While one cannot speak of a single "Muslim" view of kingship,[11] the Mughals embraced the idea of a just worldly potentate.[12] The Mughal kings

11. The notion of kingship has been rather contested in Islam. While some viewed it as anti-Islamic and deemed courtly power and splendor as contaminating the purity of the ruler's soul, others did not see anything wrong with the sinecures of the state or proximity to the pomp and power of the Muslim king, *padshah, malik,* sultan, and *zil allah* (shadow of God).

12. Mottahedeh (2001, 175) writes, "The role of arbiter, distant from the society for which it arbitrated, known to live largely for its own interest and not for any particular

were able to enjoy such boasting titles as the "Refuge of Islam," "Propagator of the Muslim Religion," and "Shadow of God."[13]

The next three chapters examine the intellectual oeuvre of Islamic intellectuals in the Arab world during the last two centuries. Peter Gran takes a new look at one of the seminal writings of Rifa'ah Rafi' al-Tahtawi (1801–1873), who was the leading Egyptian intellectual of his time. He maintains that Tahtawi's account of his five-year sojourn (1825–31) in Paris as recounted in *Takhlis al-ibriz fi talkhis Bariz* is more an example of a Mirror for the Prince literature than a simple travelogue. Gran, who has a long-standing interest in history and political economy, situates Tahtawi and his text in the body of literature about hegemony in Middle Eastern history. He specifically makes use of the "Italian Road" theory of hegemony—which he had developed in a prior work[14]—and maintains that this theory does a better job than Oriental Despotism in accounting for the development of Egypt during the crucial period from 1760 to 1860 when the contradictions between the North and the South in Egypt were deepened. This, of course, happens to be the period in which Tahtawi was writing and in which the "modern national hegemony of Egypt was coming into being." Gran considers this Egyptian political reformer and scholar as a "Southern Intellectual" who was writing for the khedive of Egypt, Muhammad Ali Pasha. Like many other reformist Islamic thinkers of his era, Tahtawi believed in educational reform as a necessity and

---

interest, was the role of the king. The king who fulfilled this role and saw that each interest got its due, but no more than its due, was 'just.'"

13. On medieval Indian kingly theories, see Richards 1998 and Tripathi 1998, and for discussions of courtly ritual in Mughal India, see Schimmel 2004.

14. Gran (1996, 88) defines the "Italian Road" as a common form of hegemony in which "the ruling class plays off the mass population of one region against the mass population of another to disguise the class conflict existing in the country as a whole. In this hegemony, the ruling class, or at least the part of it that comes from the economically dominant region, not only wants to divide the working classes to weaken them politically but [desires] to gain access on favorable terms to the labor force of the weaker region of the country. To achieve this goal, this part of the ruling class is prepared to share power with the ruling class of the weaker region . . ."

indeed wrote *Takhlis* to awaken his compatriots. As C. Ernest Dawn (1991, 5) has quoted him, Tahtawi described the purpose of writing his book in the following way: "I made it to speak to stimulate the lands of Islam to investigate the foreign sciences, arts, and industries, for the perfection of that in the land of the Franks is a well-known certainty, and the truth deserves to be followed . . . By the Eternal God! During my stay in this country I was in pain because of its enjoyment of that [perfection] and its absence from the lands of Islam."

Charles Butterworth continues Gran's endeavor of rereading a seminal text by examining the travails of another Muslim scholar who sought to reform the religion and politics of the Muslim world: Ali Abd al-Raziq (1888–1966). In 1925, less than a month after John T. Scopes was found guilty in Tennessee on a charge of teaching Darwinism in a state-funded school, Abd al-Raziq was denounced by al-Azhar hierarchy in Egypt for the publication of his *al-Islam wa usul al-hukm* (Islam and Roots of Governance). Leonard Binder (1988, 130), quoting Albert Hourani, writes, "Abd al-Raziq's book . . . raised in a vivid way the most fundamental question involved: is the caliphate really necessary? . . . is there such a thing as an Islamic system of government? Abd al-Raziq grants that 'some sort of political authority is indeed necessary, but it need not be of a specific kind.' And even more far-reaching: 'It is not even necessary that the umma should be politically united.'"

Abd al-Raziq's book did not appear out of thin air. A year earlier the institution of caliphate had been abolished in Turkey and now a man who himself was a shari'a judge was being censured for maintaining that Islam neither requires nor rejects the rule of a caliph or an imam. Moreover, he argued that the annals of Islamic history demonstrate that the institution of caliphate, which was not instituted by the Prophet, has brought horror and disaster to the *umma* and as such there is no need for its reestablishment. Abd al-Raziq insisted that it was the message of Islam that was important and not the form of government that was established. Muhammad was a "'warner' or a 'reminder,' not a 'warden' or a 'guardian'" (Kurzman 2002, 20). He was a "messenger with a religious calling" rather than a "master of a political state," "the leader of a religious group" rather than "the ruler of a government."

Contrary to scholars like Michaelle Browers (2006, 35) who consider Abd al-Raziq to be advocating secularism, Butterworth undertakes a careful reexamination of *al-Islam wa usul al-hukm* and reaches the conclusion that he was writing from within the religious tradition and was trying "to show clearly how much religion has to gain by distancing itself from politics and how politics will gain in justice and wisdom as it distances itself from religion." According to Butterworth, Abd al-Raziq was not calling passionately for secularization but was articulating a case for why religion and politics should be separated.[15] Yet Butterworth is not in agreement with Abd al-Raziq's bold critique and feels that a more conciliatory argument about the contentious issue of how Islam can be enamored or be complicit with political power could have been more politically and pedagogically efficacious. Butterworth also faults Abd al-Raziq for his omission of the ninth-century philosopher Farabi (d. 950) and the eleventh-century jurist al-Mawardi (d. 1058) who should have been central to Abd al-Raziq's argument.[16] As Richard Walzer (1963, 45) has argued, Farabi wished to restore the caliphate through philosophy. Writing more than 1,200 years after Plato, Farabi believed that the shari'a is a subdivision of the practical rationality and that philosophers had a crucial role to play. Fauzi M. Najjar (1958, 102) sums up the gist of Farabi's views on this subject matter as follows: "If the philosopher cannot rule the city, he must act as an adviser to the ruler. Thus Farabi makes the distinction between the 'king of the city' and the 'manager—*mudabbir*—of the king of the city.' The *mudabbir* is none but the philosopher himself."

Abd al-Raziq's dismissal of the caliphate and the imamate did not sit well with his contemporary Rashid Rida (1865–1935), who strongly believed in the need to restore the caliphate to achieve Islamic unity. Rida's

15. A better example of a secularist thinker impugning religious thought was Sadik Jalal al-Azm's *Naqd al-fikr al-dini* (1969), which caused a controversy in the Arab world upon its publication. Alas, sixty-eight years after Abd al-Raziq's case, another Islamic reformist thinker, Nasr Hamid Abu Zayd (1943–2010), found himself in trouble for challenging the writ of established Islamic doctrines.

16. Afsaruddin discusses the important contributions of al-Mawardi in chapter 2 in this volume.

ideas on the Islamic state came to resonate with the Muslim Brotherhood (MB), which is the subject of the following chapter by Bruce Rutherford. On June 30, 2012, Muhammed Morsi (b. 1951) of the MB was elected the first civilian president of Egypt after a long and bumpy ride by his organization to political power. Rutherford's essay, written six years before this watershed event, interrogates the type of political order Egypt's most prominent contemporary Islamic thinkers (clerical and lay) have been striving to create. Through an examination of the writings of Yusuf al-Qaradawi (b. 1926), Kamal Abu al-Majd (b. 1930), Tariq al-Bishri (b. 1933), and Muhammad Salim al-Awwa (b. 1942), Rutherford maintains that they have managed to articulate a distinctly Islamic conception of constitutionalism and that their ideas have left an indelible mark on the political agenda of the MB. These thinkers share with classical liberalism such notions as support for "the rule of law, constraints on state power, and the protection of many civil and political rights." Rutherford argues, however, that there are "decidedly illiberal" aspects to their ideas as vast differences emerge when we examine such issues as the purpose of the state, the role of the individual in politics, and the function of law.

Şerif Mardin draws our attention to a hitherto unexamined question. What happens when the "Jacobin corporate" understanding of the *millet* (populace or nation) as embraced by the political elite of modern Turkey since its inception is forced upon a people who operate on the basis of the notions of "Islamic bonding" or "sociability" discernible among Islamic groups?[17] Mardin maintains that the conception of corporate personality/public domain that was developed in nineteenth- and twentieth-century

17. This problem is not without its precedents in Islamic history. Tribal solidarity may have been frowned upon by the Prophet as an obstacle to Islamic unity, but as Afsaruddin reminds us in her chapter it took all the skills of a "master genealogist" like Abu Bakr to bring the tribes back into the Islamic fold and avoid a catastrophic split asunder in the Islamic umma. Moreover, as pointed out by Walzer (1963, 56) in his magnum opus, *The Muqaddimah,* Ibn Khaldun took "to task Averroes . . . for having been unaware in politics of anything but urbanized life, as it existed in Muslim Spain in his day, and for having neglected the special features of tribal life which make up such a considerable part of the political reality of Islam throughout the centuries."

Turkish history—along the lines of Western European law—was discordant with the notion of "bonding" and "sociability," which is "the deepest foundation of Islamic political theory." Tanzimat-era bureaucrats could have easily penned encomiums about sultanic majesty and authority,[18] as well as fictitious accounts of a "corporate body" that was inherently weak. Here Mardin relies partly on the works of Timur Kuran (2004; 2010), who has argued that the nonrecognition of corporate entities (as both an economic and a legal construct) came to impede the development of capitalism in the Middle East. According to Kuran, such central features of modern capitalism as private capital accumulation, investment, profit sharing, and impersonal exchange were discouraged, blocked, or slowed down by Islamic legal institutions. Mardin ends his chapter by referring to the Gülen movement as an example of an "Islamic Freemasonry" that makes excellent use of the "cementing" mechanisms of Islamic solidarity.

The last two chapters in the book deal with broad isssues of historiography and political theory. Roxanne L. Euben's "Cosmopolitanisms Past and Present, Muslim and Western" more fully addresses the subject of travel previously touched upon in the chapter by Peter Gran. Euben takes to task the literature of "new cosmopolitanism" that maintains that thanks to the deterritorialization of politics human beings now constitute a supranational throng tied by moral, legal, and political commitments transcending the modern nation-state. She maintains that despite its promising scholarship this literature still suffers from a presentist bias and a historical and cultural parochialism since it largely proceeds in European analytical and temporal terms that belie its ideal ecumenicalism.

18. The bureaucratic class, of course, has long been subjected to criticism for their unsavory character, debauchery, and convoluted language. In the medieval Isma'ili "encyclopedia" entitled *Rasa'il ikhwan al-safa wa khullan al-wafa* (Epistles of the pure brethren and the sincere friends), "the bureaucrats *(ashab al-dawawin)* are lampooned for their skill in causing unmatched mischief thanks to their 'acuteness of intelligence, excellence of discernment, subtlety of artifices, length of tongue, and effectiveness of speech'. So by using 'rhymed prose, sweet words and eloquent oration' they deceive the people while conspiring to injure them behind their backs, registering the deeds of confiscation, and finding excuses for the seizure of their properties" (Nasr 1977, 37).

Euben's charge is similar to the one articulated by Dipesh Chakrabarty in *Provincializing Europe,* who argued that "Europe remains the sovereign, theoretical subject of all histories" and that "it works as a silent referent in historical knowledge" (2000, 27–28). Moving beyond the pantheon of Western embedded criteria, exemplars, idioms, and imaginaries is needed if one is to recenter the debate on cosmopolitanism. Euben undertakes the task of divesting the vocabulary and historiography of new cosmopolitanism from its blatant limitations by tracing the alternative genealogy of "Muslim cosmopolitanism." She refutes the arguments of scholars such as Bernard Lewis who argue that whereas the "Westerners" were curious to learn about other people, the Muslims were insular and noninquisitive. Instead, Euben demonstrates that there has been an "Islamic ethos of travel in search of knowledge" that has marked the social imaginary of Muslims past and present.

The last contribution to this volume is by Aziz Al-Azmeh, who scans the field of "Islamic political thought" by closely scrutinizing two important works, namely Anthony Black's *The History of Islamic Political Thought* and Patricia Crone's *God's Rule—Government and Islam.* Al-Azmeh objects to a long list of methodological and epistemological premises and to historiographical narratives in the above books as well as those of other like-minded scholars. He maintains that Black and Crone

(a) have reified the word *Islam* so much so that for them history happens "in Islam" rather than in "territories with determinate characteristics and traditions";
(b) have neglected the fact that Islam is "not a product of the early polity of Muhammad's Arabia" but a product of history and geography;
(c) have narrated Islamic history in terms of "measure of fidelity to origins";
(d) have depicted Islamic political theory as "somehow essentially sui generis" and have thus assigned a "hyperdoctrinaire character" to it;
(e) failed to realize that the principal concern of Islamic political thinking is not "legitimacy" but the problem of public order;
(f) have overstated the "illegitimacy" of sultans;
(g) have presumed that Islam was "the main source" of the state and that the umma was nothing but "congregation and state rolled into one";

(h) have privileged the Arabs and imputed to them a unitary ethos of egalitarianism and anti-statism;

(i) did not recognize that "the *ulama* were not only *ulama*" and that they were not "congenitally opposed to the state."

The above points raised by Al-Azmeh underline a number of methodological and theoretical weaknesses of the scholarship in the field of Islamic political thought that this volume and its contributors have wished to partly rectify. We hope that the erudite scholarship assembled here spawns further studies of the topics covered in this book. After all, like citizenship, history necessitates listening to a multiplicity of voices.

2

Maslahah as a Political Concept

ASMA AFSARUDDIN

THE ARABIC TERM *Maslahah* is usually translated as "welfare," "public interest or utility," and "common good" in various contexts. A single, concise definition is not possible in English, but all the above meanings may be encompassed by the Arabic term. At the basic semantic level, maslahah connotes being the source of what is sound, beneficial, and conducive to peace *(sulh).*

In premodern Islamic thought, maslahah was considered primarily a juridical term. In the early centuries of Islam, the term *istislah* appears to have been more common than maslahah. Istislah was a procedure common among the Medinese jurists, including Malik b. Anas (d. 795), and among the Iraqi Hanafis of the eighth century. These jurists relied heavily on reasoning and discretionary opinion *(ra'y)* in order to devise legal rulings that promoted the public interest in the absence of specific scriptural injunctions (Hallaq 2005, 145). Early sources confirm widespread recourse to istislah to derive legal rulings in the second and third centuries of Islam. Thus Muhammad b. Ahmad al-Khwarazmi (d. after 997) lists istislah in his well-known work *Mafatih al-ulum* as one of the sources of law for the Maliki school (1895, 9). The gifted belletrist and secretary Ibn al-Muqaffa' (d. ca. 757) recommends the use of istislah by jurists in the absence of specific textual prescriptions to derive legal rulings (1966, 360).

By the eleventh century, maslahah appears to have become the preferred term to connote public interest or good and became foregrounded as a juridical principle in relation to the "objectives of the law" *(maqasid al-shari'a).* The impetus for this further development of the principle of maslahah was provided by the Shafi'i jurist Abu Hamid Muhammad al-Ghazali (d. 1111) in his work *al-Mustasfa min ilm al-usul*. Al-Ghazali divides the objectives of the law into two types: religious *(dini)* and worldly *(dunyawi)*. Both types of objectives are concerned with securing *(tahsil)* and preserving *(ibqa')* the public interest or maslahah. Maslahah is thus ultimately what allows for the acquisition of benefit *(manfa'ah)* and the avoidance of harm or injury *(madarrah)* (al-Ghazali 1877, 1:286).

The worldly objectives of the shari'a are distilled by al-Ghazali into "five necessities" *(al-daruriyat al-khamsah)*, which guarantee, for each individual, preservation of religion *(din)*, life *(nafs)*, progeny *(nasl)*, intellect *(aql)*, and property *(mal)*. These primary objectives of the law are followed by supplementary objectives in descending order of importance: "needs" *(hajat)* and "ease" *(tawassu'* and *taysir)* (al-Ghazali 1877, 1:161–62). Al-Ghazali's concept of maslahah and its link to the maqasid al-shari'a proved to be seminal and was discussed by practically every major jurist afterward, especially al-Tufi (d. 1316) and al-Shatibi (d. 1388). These concepts have enjoyed a resurgence in the contemporary period as the notion of the shari'a and its objectives are revisited, particularly by modernists and reformists.

Maslahah as a Political Concept in the Early Period

In comparison with its use as a juridical term, maslahah as a political concept per se receives scant discussion in the early literature. Its pervasiveness as a political concept has to be inferred from various genres of works that discuss the early caliphate as a historical phenomenon and conceptualize legitimate political leadership. The term *maslahah* or *istislah* need not be explicitly used for us to be able to assert that it was a principle broadly recognized in the early period in the sense that al-Ghazali had defined it in the legal context in the eleventh century, that is, as a principle that allowed for the acquisition of benefit *(manfa'ah)* and the avoidance of harm or injury *(madarrah)*.

Three primary types of literature have been consulted in this chapter to determine the importance of maslahah as a general political and social organizational principle in the premodern period: historical works,

Qur'an exegetical works, and political treatises. Some of these works are now discussed in greater detail below.

Historical and Exegetical Works: Sunni Views

Most Sunni historical works present the institution of the office of the caliph as a pragmatic response to the special circumstances that ensued after the sudden death of the Prophet Muhammad in Medina in 632 CE. As the sources inform us, it was clear to a majority of the Companions that no successor had been explicitly designated by the Prophet. The Companions were confused as to how to proceed to select a leader and maintain political stability. A significant number of people converged at a portico in Medina to attend a hastily convened meeting in order to select a leader. The procedure, the sources tell us, entailed debating rather noisily and heatedly the merits of some of the obvious contenders for the office of the caliph, who included Abu Bakr, Umar, and Ali, the Prophet's cousin and son-in-law. The matter was resolved by Umar's offering his allegiance to Abu Bakr, his older friend, and asking the crowd to follow suit. According to several sources, Umar prefaced his offer of allegiance by reciting before the gathered audience an impressive résumé of meritorious deeds that Abu Bakr had performed during Muhammad's lifetime (al-Nasa'i 1984, 55–56). This résumé convinced the assembly of people to recognize Abu Bakr as the Prophet's first successor, and they thronged toward him to offer their allegiance, which he accepted with some diffidence and considerable humility, as the various versions of his inaugural speech testify (al-Tabari 1987, 242–43). When asked later to reflect on the process of Abu Bakr's election, some of the sources report that Umar described it as a *faltah* (al-Baladhuri 1960, 1:581–83; al-Tabari n.d., 2:242).

The Arabic word *faltah* in this context means a "happenstance" or an "unpremeditated event." Umar was essentially describing the process of Abu Bakr's election as something that had happened on the spot, in reaction to the exigencies of the situation. The situation, in fact, was quite serious. Believing that their fealty to the government had lapsed on the Prophet's death, some Arab tribes had risen in revolt against the Medinan government, and they refused to pay the obligatory alms or taxes, known as the *zakat*. These tribes had to be brought back into the fold, and Abu Bakr's skills as a master genealogist—predicated on expert knowledge of tribal relationships and the tribe-based alliances of pre-Islamic Arabia—were greatly in demand.

The broad circumstances of Abu Bakr's election as depicted in the historical sources make it clear that, in these early political deliberations, the Companions resorted to human reasoning and interpretation of general Qur'anic notions such as "precedence" or "priority" in Islam (Ar. *sabiqah*) and "virtue/moral excellence" (Ar. *fadl/fadilah*), as well as the concept of "consultation" *(shura)*. On the basis of such broad, general concepts, they devised the solution regarded as the most apt and in the best interests of the community after the somewhat unexpected death of the Prophet. Faltah in this context is a purely descriptive term and contains no moral valuation (at least in most Sunni sources) of Abu Bakr's selection as the Prophet's successor in such a spontaneous and unpremeditated manner.[1]

Sunni sources are practically in agreement that Abu Bakr's superior and appropriate knowledge about genealogies and religious matters in general contributed to the greater welfare of the polity in this critical period and was, therefore, the most important consideration in his selection as the caliph. In his *firaq* work, the Andalusian jurist Ibn Hazm (d. 1064) states that although Abu Bakr lived a mere two and a half years after the Prophet's death, he transmitted 142 hadiths from Muhammad and issued numerous fatwas. In contrast, Ali, who lived thirty years beyond the Prophet's death, transmitted 586 hadiths, out of which only 50 are *sahih*. If their life spans after the advent of Islam and the number of hadiths related by each are compared, Ibn Hazm maintains, Abu Bakr was far more prolific in the transmission of traditions and in the issuance of fatwas. This comparison establishes beyond a doubt Abu Bakr's greater excellence in this regard because "someone with any degree of knowledge knows that what Abu Bakr possessed of knowledge was several multiples more than what Ali possessed" (Ibn Hazm 1928, 4:108). Furthermore,

1. See, however, al-Baladhuri 1968, 1:584 for a dissenting view.

Ibn Hazm remarks that the Prophet's appointment of Abu Bakr as the prayer leader during his final illness proves that he was so appointed on account of his superior knowledge of the prayer rituals. Similarly, the Prophet appointed Abu Bakr to collect alms *(al-sadaqat)*, to lead the hajj, and to conduct several military expeditions *(al-bu'uth)*, all of which testify to his greater knowledge regarding prayer, alms-giving, the pilgrimage, and jihad, which "are the support *(umda)* of religion" (1928, 4:108). Because of this unique constellation of virtues and aptitudes, Abu Bakr is presented as having been exceptionally qualified to come to the defense of the nascent Islamic polity during one of its most critical periods.

Abu Bakr's success in quelling the *riddah* uprisings is lavishly praised by later authors, who see in it a testimonial to his greater mental acumen and political skills and, consequently, to his greater moral excellence vis-à-vis other Companions. Al-Tabari, for example, relates how Abu Bakr's sound judgment prevailed during the riddah wars when he asserted the necessity of fighting those tribes that were resisting the Medinan government. He reports that Abu Bakr stated, "God will not assemble you in error and, by the One in whose hand is my soul, I do not see a matter more excellent with regard to myself than fighting those who withhold from us a camel's hobble on which the Messenger of God, peace and blessings be upon him, used to take [what was due upon it]."

Al-Tabari continues, "The Muslims acceded to Abu Bakr's opinion, for they saw that it was better than their opinion and thus Abu Bakr dispatched at that time Usamah b. Zayd" (1:119).

In a hadith recorded by al-Muttaqi al-Hindi (d. 1567), the Prophet states, "I am the sword of Islam and Abu Bakr is the sword of the riddah" (al-Hindi n.d., 6:2251), while another, recorded by Ibn Abd al-Barr in the eleventh century, states that Abu Bakr "undertook the fighting of the people of the riddah, and the excellence of his opinion became manifest in that, and his firmness along with his gentleness which was inestimable. Thus God proclaimed His religion through him and slew through his hands and His grace all those who had rebelled against the religion of God until the matter of God became manifest while they were resistant" (Ibn Abd al-Barr n.d., 3:977).

The exegete al-Khazin al-Baghdadi (d. 1341) relates a report from Abu Bakr b. Ayyash,[2] to the effect that there was no one more excellent than Abu Bakr born after the Prophet and that in fighting the "people of rebellion" *(ahl al-riddah)*, Abu Bakr had attained the position of "a prophet from among the prophets" (Al-Khazin al-Baghdadi 1961, 2:54).

Such generous praise by various authors highlights Abu Bakr's specific attributes and skills, which were deemed to be the best suited to the times, resulting in maximum benefit for the people. Here the benefit is clearly construed in a pragmatic, political sense. During the two years of Abu Bakr's caliphate, the unity of the polity was of overriding concern. Secession of the rebellious Arab tribes represented a threat primarily to the political well-being of the people. Even though the uprising was termed riddah and unfortunately translated consistently into English as "apostasy," it had in fact only slight religious overtones. The rebellious tribes refused to pay taxes to the changed government in Medina not because they had "apostasized" from Islam but because they considered their allegiance to the Prophet to have lapsed upon his death. This practice was in accordance with the nature of tribal agreements in this period, which were usually considered to be personal in nature. The rebellious tribes were thus guilty of political disloyalty to the Medinan government. Political stability was held to be the necessary prerequisite for an ordered religious community and, at this juncture in history, restoring harmonious tribal relationships while attempting to replace narrow tribal assumptions of political fealty with allegiance to the supratribal *umma* was the highest priority. Abu Bakr with his intimate knowledge of tribal alliances was clearly the man of the hour.

Following Abu Bakr's brief two-year tenure as caliph, Umar assumed the caliphate, having been designated as such by Abu Bakr. In the

2. See Ibn al-Jawzi 1986, 2:228, #3893, where he is identified as a Qur'an reciter and a *mawla* of Wasil b. Hayyan. His *ism* is listed variously as Shu'ba, Muhammad, Salim, or Abu Bakr itself. Cf. also Ibn Hajar al-Asqalani 1995–96, 7:18, where the author admits ignorance of his true identity.

descriptions of Umar's ten-year tenure as caliph we see maslahah deployed as a broad sociopolitical organizational principle that determined the overall orientation of the Muslim polity. The early literature does not, however, explicitly refer to maslahah or istislah in these sociopolitical contexts. Rather, it maintains that Umar was duly selected as the second caliph on account of his greater precedence in serving Islam in the early period *(asbaq)* and his greater moral excellence *(afdal)* compared to the other Companions.

During Umar's longer tenure as caliph, the broad Qur'anic principles of sabiqah (precedence/priority) and fadilah (moral excellence/virtue) often found reflection in highly pragmatic measures, which reflected a deep concern for the public, political good. For example, Umar's establishment of the *diwan,* the register of pensions, embodied both worldly savoir faire and Qur'anic ideals of religious merit (al-Baladhuri 1866, 448ff.; Yusuf Ya'qub 1985, 140–44; Ibn Sa'd 1997, 3:224; Abu Ubayd al-Qasim ibn Sallam 1988, 266ff.). This institution borrowed from the Persians allowed Umar to recognize the exceptional contributions of the early Muslims to the community on the basis of sabiqah and fadilah and to arrange for an equitable, albeit merit-based, distribution of the revenues pouring into the Medinan coffers.

The establishment of the diwan and its organizational principle met with some initial resistance, but later historians applaud the shrewd intelligence and good sense apparent in Umar's recognition of the religious and praxis-based merit of the earliest and most loyal Muslims in this manner. Abu Yusuf (d. 798) in his *Kitab al-kharaj* mentions that when Umar assumed the caliphate, he refused to place those who had fought against the Prophet on the same level as those who had fought with him and, therefore, awarded larger stipends to "the people of precedences and priority" *(ahl al-sawabiq wa al-qadam)* from among the Muhajirun and the Ansar who had witnessed Badr (Yusuf Ya'qub 1985, 140; Ibn Sa'd 1997, 3:225). Abu Ubayd al-Qasim ibn Sallam (d. 838) states that both Abu Bakr and Ali believed in egalitarianism *(al-taswiyah)* in the disbursement of pensions, while Umar resorted to preferential treatment *(al-tafdil)* "based on precedences and indispensable service to Islam" *(ala al-sawabiq wa al-ghina' an al-islam)* (Abu Ubayd al-Qasim ibn Sallam 1988, 267–68; Ibn Sa'd 1997, 3:225; Hinds 1971, 366). Abu Ubayd further reports that Abu Bakr declined to rank people in terms of their excellences, demurring that "their excellences were with [known to] God" *(fada'iluhum inda Allah)* and that the system of pensions *(al-ma'ash)* was better served by the principle of al-taswiyah (Abu Ubayd al-Qasim ibn Sallam 1988, 267; Yusuf Ya'qub 1985, 140).[3] Abu Bakr's and Umar's divergent views on how state pensions should be disbursed was then a function of their individual understanding of what was in the best interests of the community during their reign. It appears that differentiation on the basis of merit would have proved even more divisive during the riddah wars, prompting Abu Bakr to maintain equality in the disbursement of stipends. With internal unity more or less restored and perhaps even to boost the morale of the most pious Muslims, Umar felt that it redounded to the greater benefit of the community to institute a merit-based system of pensions.

The invocation of "excellence" and "precedence" as essential traits possessed not only by the caliph/imam but also by lesser rulers and administrators is ubiquitous throughout the literature that deals with these issues and establishes their perceived strong connection with effective, pragmatic leadership in various social and political contexts. It appears that in the early period, moral excellence as manifested particularly in mastery of the Qur'an sometimes led to positions of political and social leadership. A well-known hadith is related by the Companion Abu Mas'ud al-Ansari in which Muhammad says, "The best reciter of them [specifically, the people] of the Book of God will lead the people. If they should be equal with regard to [proficiency in] reciting, then the most knowledgeable of them with regard to the *sunna*" (al-Fasawi 1976, 1:449–50; al-Razi 1994, 97ff.). It is not surprising that both Sunni and Shi'i authors cite this report as evidence in favor of the superior qualifications of Abu Bakr and Ali

3. See also Ibn Sa'd 1997, 3:144, where A'isha reports that in his first year as caliph, Abu Bakr distributed the *fay'* equally, giving ten shares to every free man and woman, male and female slave. The following year everyone received twenty shares.

respectively for the caliphate/imamate on account of each being the best reciter of the Qur'an.[4]

Other kinds of expertise in relation to the Qur'an conferred various kinds of authority on the individual. Thus the moral excellence and precedence of the famous Companion Abd Allah b. Mas'ud derived not only from his acknowledged superior exegesis of the Qur'an but also from his status as the first Companion who had publicly propagated the Qur'an *(afsha 'l-Qur'an)* (Ibn Sa'd 1997, 3:112). A broad recognition of his moral excellence and precedence in Islam led to several important political appointments for Ibn Mas'ud. Sabiqah became in fact a highly emotive term in the early period, pregnant with sociopolitical implications for those who possessed it.

Particularly illustrative of this semantic and functional connection between sabiqah and sociopolitical status is a report recorded by the well-known exegete and scholar al-Razi in a work he composed on the excellences of the Qur'an. In the section significantly titled "Chapter regarding those who are the most deserving among the people of leadership on account of their memorization of the Qur'an," we find the following report, according to which Nafi' b. Abd al-Harith[5] met Umar b. al-Khattab, who asked the former, "Whom did you leave in charge of Mecca?" The answer was Ibn Abza. Umar asked, "[Is he] a *mawla* [non-Arab Muslim convert]?" Nafi' replied, "Yes, he is a reciter of the Book of God the Exalted." Umar said, "God enhances [the status] of certain people by this Qur'an and diminishes [that of] others by it" (al-Razi 1994, 100; Ibn Majah 1983, 1:42). This well-attested report underscores unambiguously that a non-Arab could have precedence over an Arab on account of the former's superior knowledge of the Qur'an, which established his greater moral excellence over others. In this report, Umar's true intention in adhering to the principle of sabiqah becomes clear: in the case of a non-Muhajir Arab and a non-Arab, one had precedence over the other only on the basis of moral excellence, gauged by one's superior religious

4. For example, Ibn Tawus 1990, 287.

5. For whom, see Ibn Hajar al-Asqalani 1995–96, 6:226, #8651.

knowledge of the Qur'an in this case. In both this incident and the report cited earlier concerning Ibn Mas'ud, we discern a radical religious egalitarian attitude subversive of socially and culturally constructed superiorities based on ethnic and tribal considerations (Marlow 1997, esp. 114ff.). Such "subversive" appointments drove home in the early period the intimate connection between individual moral virtue and its worldly pragmatic consequences, particularly in the promotion of the public good.

The combination of sabiqah and fadilah was particularly important in the general discourse on legitimate leadership of the polity and in Sunni-Shi'i dialectics on the caliphate/imamate. This leads us next to a consideration of whether the early Shi'a also had similar conceptions of maslahah as a sociopolitical principle.

Shi'i Views

It is generally assumed that the Shi'a have always subscribed to a legitimist view of religiopolitical leadership and have insisted that the ruler of the Muslim polity be a blood relative of the Prophet Muhammad. However, early Shi'i sources sometimes offer a different perspective and suggest that we must be wary of retrojecting later assumptions back into the very early period.

For example, when comparing early and later Shi'i sources, we notice a certain evolution in Shi'i interpretation of the key Qur'anic term *sabiqun,* which has important implications for political thought. Early Shi'i views appear to be similar to the general Sunni understanding of this term while later views (roughly after the tenth century) on the sabiqun became markedly different from the Sunni perspective. The typical (and expected) Shi'i view is that the term *sabiqun* refers only to the Prophet and "his legatee" *(wasiyyihi),* in other words, Ali—and ipso facto excludes all the other Companions. However, in his commentary on Qur'an 46:10, the ninth century Shi'i exegete al-Qummi says that, according to the Companion Hudhayfah b. al-Yaman, the Prophet referred only to himself as "one of those who preceded and who was the best among them" (al-Qummi 1966, 2:347). The tenth century Shi'i scholar al-Kulayni says in exegesis of Qur'an 9:100 that the verse assigns the highest rank to the earliest Muhajirun, second place to the Ansar *(thanna bi-al-ansar)*, and third place to the Successors *(thallatha bi-al-tabi'in)*, a view that is in complete accordance with the general Sunni perception of sabiqah (al-Kulayni 1990, 2:48). Chronology is, after all, the essence of sabiqah.

A well-known report, attributed to the sixth Shi'i Imam Ja'far al-Sadiq and frequently cited in Sunni sources, quotes the Prophet as saying, "The best of people *(khayr al-nas)* are from my generation *(qarni)*, then from the second [generation], then from the third; then will come a group of people in whom there will be no good" (al-Tabarani 1995, 3:339, #3336; for variants, see 2:27, #1122; 8:358, #8868). The people from the Prophet's generation would, undoubtedly, include all his Companions.[6] Another tenth century Shi'i author, Abu al-Qasim Ali b. Ahmad al-Kufi (d. 963), comments that it is possible to interpret al-sabiqun in Qur'an 9:100 as a reference to the Aqabiyyun, the seventy people who came to Mecca one night and pledged their allegiance to the Prophet in the house of Abd al-Muttalib in Aqabah (al-Kufi 1980, 69). This view is also in accordance with that of a number of Sunni scholars, even though the lists of these men and women are sometimes different in the sources.

This early trend in Shi'i political thought concerning the sabiqun has several significant ramifications. A number of early Shi'i exegetical works state that the sabiqun referred to the pious Muslims of the first generation, which signifies that the proto-Shi'a of the early period apparently made no distinction between those Companions who were blood relatives of the Prophet (notably Ali) and those who were not. This perception is further bolstered by the fact that a number of Shi'i authors relate that some of the earliest pro-Alid supporters were vigorous participants in the debates regarding the qualifications of Abu Bakr and Ali for the caliphate/imamate. According to the pro-Alid Mu'tazili scholar Ibn Abi al-Hadid (d. 1257), immediately after the death of the Prophet the partisans of Ali were the first to put into circulation reports that praised their preferred candidate's

6. Cf. van Ess 1977, 4, where he points to an early Shi'i positive attitude toward Abu Bakr and Umar.

unique virtues. In response, Abu Bakr's partisans, the Bakriyah,[7] are said to have come forth with traditions of their own, which espoused the merits of their candidate, thus creating this distinctive *manaqib* genre within the evolving hadith corpus (cited by Juynboll 1983, 12–13 and n10). Other sources, mainly Shi'i, mention that when Abu Bakr entered the mosque at Medina after having been appointed the first caliph, twelve men from among the Muhajirun rose up one after the other to recite the excellences of Ali and proclaim his right to the imamate.[8] Ibn Abi al-Hadid commented on this episode by maintaining that the events of the Saqifa could not have transpired if the Prophet had explicitly designated his successor. The fact, he says, that a debate centered around the key concepts of "precedences, excellences, and relationship [to the Prophet]" did ensue regarding a successor and that there was no mention of *nass* (explicit designation) in this debate logically leads one to conclude that there was no explicit designation either of Abu Bakr or of Ali as Muhammad's successor (Ibn Abi al-Hadid 1963, 2:267).

The retrieval of this early pro-Alid discourse based on excellence and precedence in the context of political leadership makes it possible to remark that the proto-Shi'a also stressed the public good of the polity

7. It should be pointed out that the appellation "Bakriyah" is used with some imprecision in our literature and appears to have been applied to two primary groups of different provenance. The first reference is to an earlier amorphous group from the seventh century and is said to have sprung up immediately after the Prophet's death and proclaimed Abu Bakr's greater precedence in claiming the caliphate, as already indicated. The Shi'a in particular tended to use Bakriyah in this sense; see Watt 1973, 362n19. The same name was applied to a later group that emerged in the eighth century, followers of a man called Bakr b. Ukht Abd al-Wah.id b. Zayd (d. 793); for the Bakriyah in this usage, see al-Ash'ari 1929–33, 273–74; al-Baghdadi 1970, 146; al-Mas'udi 1893, 337; van Ess 1991–97, 2:108–18. See also my article "In Praise of the Caliphs: Recreating History from the *Manaqib* Literature," *International Journal of Middle East Studies* 31 (1999): 329–50.

8. See Razi 1952, 656–64; also cited by Mahdjoub 1988, 54. Ahmad b. Ali b. Abi Talib al-Tabarsi mentions in his *Kitab al-ihtijaj* (1965–67, 1:97), that twelve men divided equally between the Muhajirun and the Ansar repudiated Abu Bakr. Ya'qubi in his *Tarikh* (1883, 2:137) briefly refers to this incident.

as an important consideration in the selection of the first caliph/imam. They maintained, in tandem with the proto-Sunnis, that greater moral excellence and precedence as exemplified in Ali's track record of vigorous service to the polity redounded to the greater sociopolitical benefit of its members. Ali's priority in Islam and his exceptional moral attributes were unmatched by any other Companion, they asserted, and thus uniquely qualified him to be the first successor to the Prophet. An extensive literature developed in the subsequent centuries establishing Ali's repertoire of singular moral excellences greater than those of any other Companion and thus his greater qualifications for the imamate. We see a similar development among the Sunnis in regard to Abu Bakr and Umar.

Among Ali's moral excellences were his capacious learning, wisdom, and eloquence. Since pre-Islamic times, there has been an intimate connection between these attributes and effective leadership in the Arab cultural milieu. The leader of the tribe in the Jahiliyah was frequently selected for his dexterity with words and was often referred to as a *khatib* (orator) or *za'im* (spokesman).[9] Since the Arabic language as the vehicle of divine revelation became the sacralized medium of Islam (cf. al-Sayyid 1993, 126), mastery of Arabic became equated with moral excellence and indicated superior knowledge and, therefore, often superior qualifications for positions of leadership, as we saw earlier in the case of Ibn Abza.[10] The word *za'im*, in fact, remains to this day one of the Arabic words to refer to a leader in various situations.

Ali's exceptional knowledge in fact established his claim nonpareil to the caliphate/imamate according to his supporters. Indeed, many Shi'i

9. See, for example, Lammens 1914, 222; Cantarino 1975, 21–22; "Sha'ir" in *The Encyclopedia of Islam,* new ed., 9:226 (Leiden: E. J. Brill). Al-Razi in his *Mafatih al-ghayb* (1980–89) relates that the Abbasid caliph al-Ma'mun's chief vizier counseled his sons to "learn how to speak well, for man's superiority over all other beings is through speech; and the more skillful you are in speaking, the more worthy you are of humanity" (1980–89, 6:43-44).

10. Ibn Qutaybah, for example, relates an anecdote in which Ibn Hubayra the senior *(al-akbar)* declared that the pious man who spoke Arabic correctly possessed greater merit both in this world and the next than the pious man who did not; see al-Hamawi 1982, vol. 1, 23.

scholars affirm that various branches of learning derive directly from Ali's wide-ranging knowledge. Thus al-Allamah al-Hilli maintains that *kalam* originated with Ali as did Sufism, eloquent speech *(fasahah)*, grammar, *tafsir*, and *fiqh*. Major schools of thought, including the four Sunni legal *madhahib* and Ash'arism, are said to derive from al-Hilli (1986, 1:177–80). Al-Sharif al-Murtada states that the Mu'tazili concepts of *adl* and *tawhid* had been borrowed from Ali b. Abi Talib himself, since Ali is the true founder of the discipline of kalam. This is so because the Mu'tazilah belong to the school of Wasil b. Ata', who was the student of Abu Hashim Abd Allah b. Muhammad b. al-Hanafiyah. Abu Hashim in turn was the student of his father, Muhammad b. al-Hanafiyah, who was a student of Ali. Al-Murtada, like al-Hilli above, similarly states that the learning of the four eponyms of the Sunni madhahib ultimately derives from Ali (al-Murtada 1967, 1:148), while Ibn Abi al-Hadid declared Ali to be the true founder of Ash'arism and Zaydism (Ibn Abi al-Hadid 1963, 1:35–36).

In contrast to the early reports and exegeses that reference proto-Shi'i discourses within the paradigm of sabiqah and fadilah, later Shi'i understanding of certain relevant Qur'anic verses became markedly partisan. The twelfth century Shi'i commentator al-Tabarsi reports that Muhammad himself in exegesis of Qur'an 9:100 and 56:10 commented that these verses referred to the prophets and their legatees; he added, "And I am the most excellent of the prophets and messengers of God and Ali b. Abi Talib, upon whom be peace, my legatee, is the most excellent of legatees."[11] One report quoted in later Shi'i and Sunni manaqib works on Ali is attributed to Ibn Abbas, who states in exegesis of 56:10 that the sabiqun were only three: Yusha'a b. Nun, who was the first to reach *(sabaqa ila)* Moses; the Companion *(sahib)* mentioned in Ya Sin, who was the first to reach Jesus; and Ali, who was the first to reach Muhammad.[12] This kind of "pre-election" of Ali as Muhammad's successor, which these reports convey, became linked over time to the former's blood kinship with the latter.

11. See al-Tabarsi 1965–67, 1:213. For Shi'i invocation of these verses in support of the notion of *sabq/sabiqah*, see al-Kulayni 1990, 2:45–47.

12. See, for example, Ibn al-Maghazili 1974, 320.

Ali's exceptional personal attributes also become a function of his lineal descent, and it is his genealogy (and that of the subsequent imams) that became subsequently advanced as an ontological moral excellence superior to other virtues.

The classic Imami (Twelver) Shi'i belief that only the rightful imam of the age *(sahib al-zaman)* may legitimately rule the polity was challenged and successfully revised only in the twentieth century with the promulgation of the theory of the wilayat-i faqih (the guardianship of the jurist) by Ayatollah Ruhollah Khomeini (d. 1989).[13] This theory is clearly predicated on pragmatic considerations of the public good and political expediency. Because the rightful imam is still in occultation and the earth is, in the meantime, in need of righteous, just rulers, the jurists *(fuqaha')* were the logical and legitimate representatives of the hidden imam. The jurists, after all, can claim to be the most knowledgeable among the faithful just as Ali was among the Companions; thus, they too "inherit" the right to legitimately rule the polity on behalf of the occulted imam.

A full-scale exposition and analysis of this innovative political doctrine is beyond the purview of this chapter. Suffice it to say that by formulating this theory, Khomeini may be regarded as having retrieved an earlier strand of pragmatism that had informed Shi'i political thinking. Maslahah was the cornerstone of this bold new doctrine. In this sense, the doctrine of wilayat-i faqih harks back to proto-Shi'i considerations of the public good, which, as we discerned, undergirded early debates about succession to the Prophet among the supporters of both Abu Bakr and Ali.

Political Treatises

The Arabic word *fitnah* is generally, and particularly in the political realm, understood to connote "disorder" and "chaos."[14] Disorder is to be prevented at all costs because it militates against the peaceful, just, and law-abiding society that the Qur'an envisions for humankind. Apart from

13. For a discussion of this principle, see Khomeini 1981.

14. Among the other meanings assigned to this word are "temptation" and "polytheism."

espousing that disorder be contained and that believers must be continuously engaged in promoting what is right and forbidding what is wrong with a variety of means (cf. Qur'an 3:110; 3:114; 9:71; 22:41, etc.), the Qur'an or the sunna do not prescribe the establishment of any formal mechanism or a specific governing body to achieve this end.

Most of the historical sources inform us that the earliest Muslims perceived the need for a ruler or a ruling council in view of the rather dire circumstances immediately following the Prophet's death, as we have already indicated. This view became encoded as political dictum in the eleventh century by the well-known Shafi'i jurist and political theorist al-Mawardi (d. 1058) in his influential work *al-Ahkam al-sultaniyah*. In this work he described the imamate as necessary both for the "protection of religion" *(hirasat al-din)* and for the proper administration of the world *(siyasat al-dunya)* (al-Mawardi 1996, 13ff.). Considerations of maslahah, both in a religious and a sociopolitical sense, continued, therefore, to be uppermost in the selection and appointment of the imam. Al-Mawardi points to the existence of two camps in his day on the question of the imamate, one of which believed that the office was mandated rationally while the other subscribed to the position that the office was decreed by the revealed law *(al-Shar')*. According to the first, rationalist, camp, all intelligent people conceded the importance of submitting to a leader who would prevent them from oppressing one another and keep them from disputing with one another. In the absence of rulers *(al-wulat)* in general, there would be disorder and general pandemonium. In this context, he cites a line of verse by the pre-Islamic poet al-Afwah al-Awdi, who wrote,

> People without ruling notables will be beset by chaos,
> And they will have no notables if the ignorant among them rule.
> (Al-Mawardi 1996, 13)

The second camp consisted of people who insisted that the imamate was ordained by revelation alone because the imam undertook matters decreed by the religious law. However, even this camp conceded a major role to reason in matters that had to be decided by the imam. Thus, according to al-Mawardi, this second group, like the first group, maintained that human intelligence prevented individuals from wronging one another and helped to enforce the criterion of justice in relations with one another. The revealed law delegated these matters to the ruler according to Qur'anic verse 4:59, which states, "O those who believe, obey God and obey the messenger, and those possessing authority among you" (1996, 13).

Thus al-Mawardi subscribes to a position that emphasizes both religious and rational imperatives for selecting the caliph in order to safeguard the well-being of the community. It is clear from his appeal to pre-Islamic poetry as proof-text that ultimately he believed that there should be a ruler to contain chaos and regulate society on the basis of common sense, reason, and tradition. Once installed, the caliph is deserving of the obedience of his people, in support of which belief he adduces Qur'an 4:59 as proof-text.

Mu'tazili Thought

Al-Jahiz's Views

A number of Muslims in the formative period remained unconvinced, however, that they needed a ruler or any form of government at all to contain disorder. This attitude would become most pronounced among the Mu'tazilah, the rationalist theologians of the eighth and ninth centuries. Among this group of scholars and theologians were several individuals who thought that a caliph was unnecessary as long as the Muslims obeyed the religious law. Most prominent among them were Abu Bakr al-Asamm (d. 816) and Abu Ishaq al-Nazzam (d. ca. 835) (al-Ash'ari 1929–33, 460).

An early Mu'tazili political treatise, the *Risalah al-Uthmaniyah* of the celebrated belletrist Amr b. Bahr al-Jahiz (d. 869), embodies this utilitarian attitude toward the caliphate quite strongly. In this work, written to refute the Shi'i notion of the divinely ordained imamate, the author compares the qualifications of Abu Bakr and Ali for the office of the caliph in the immediate aftermath of the Prophet's death. Al-Jahiz makes his case by emphasizing Abu Bakr's moral virtues and pragmatic qualities, which uniquely qualified him for the caliphate. Among the constellation of virtues that distinguished Abu Bakr from the rest of the Companions were his greater maturity vis-à-vis Ali; his knowledge, both religious and practical; and his courage, both on and off the battlefield. Like the authors and historians mentioned earlier, al-Jahiz praises Abu Bakr's exceptional knowledge of genealogy as well as his religious knowledge, which allowed him to act decisively during this crisis-ridden period.

Al-Jahiz records several other closely related events to drive home this point. For example, he relates that on the day Muhammad died, Uthman b. Affan and Umar b. al-Khattab stood by the door of A'isha's room, loudly proclaiming their disbelief that the Prophet had passed away. The people who had gathered grew agitated, and Umar forbade them on threat of dire consequences to say that the Prophet had died. It was Abu Bakr who took control of the situation and affirmed that Muhammad was indeed dead, "for death spares no one" (al-Jahiz 1955, 80; cf. Ibn Sa'd 1997, 2:205).

Another incident concerned those rebellious tribes who resolved after the Prophet's death to offer the prayers but not the *zakat*. Abu Bakr responded firmly that were the hobble of a young camel *(iqal ba'ir)* to be withheld in payment of zakat, he would fight those dissenters. The Muhajirun and the Ansar protested this decision, saying that Muhammad had declared that he had been commanded to fight people only until they said, "There is no god but God"; the utterance of the *shahadah* alone made their lives and property inviolate.[15] Abu Bakr said, however, that the hadith continued with "*illa bi-haqqiha*" (except for what is due upon it).[16] All then acknowledged that Abu Bakr had spoken the truth; al-Jahiz comments that he thus taught the people what they did not know and steered them toward the correct understanding of the Prophet's statement (al-Jahiz 1955, 81). Furthermore, al-Jahiz continues, Abu Bakr's sound judgment and wisdom are reflected in his appointment of Khalid b. al-Walid to lead the attack upon the false prophets, Musaylimah and Tulayhah, and to conduct the riddah wars, in all of which Khalid met with remarkable successes. These attributes are further affirmed in his selection of Umar, who as his successor subsequently went on to consolidate and expand

15. Cf. Ibn Abd al-Barr n.d., 2:85, 102; Abd al-Jabbar 1966, 227–28.

16. For this version of the tradition, see Muslim ibn Hajjaj 1995, 4:1491, #33; al-Nasa'i 1930, 6:6; al-Marwazi 1970, 145–46, 108.

the territories of Islam (1955, 86–87). All these incidents provide strong examples of Abu Bakr's unique foresight and pragmatism, which stood the Muslims in good stead during his crisis-ridden caliphate.[17]

Like the overwhelming majority of Sunni scholars preceding and following him, al-Jahiz too lays great emphasis on the immediately beneficial consequences of Abu Bakr's mature knowledge of worldly, political matters in the critical period that ensued after the Prophet's death. In contrast, Ali's youth at this time and, therefore, the assumed corresponding lack of political sophistication on his part were perceived by many to be serious impediments to his candidacy for the office of the caliph/imam. Sunni discourses on this topic generally emphasize Abu Bakr's seniority over Ali and the inevitably positive consequences of this basic fact. Thus the well-known exegete Ibn Kathir (d. 1373) cites a hadith ("the soundness of which is agreed upon by the scholars") in which the Prophet states that the best reader/reciter of the Qur'an should lead the people. Should there be several equally proficient readers of the Qur'an, one who was the most knowledgeable of them of the sunna should lead. If there are several candidates equally knowledgeable about the sunna, "then the older of them in age" *(fa-akbaruhum sinnan)* should assume leadership of the community (Ibn-Kathir 1966, 5:236). Umar b. al-Khattab is reported to have said, "Man has ten character traits, nine of which are good and one of which is bad and leads to evil." Then he warned, "Beware of the folly of youthfulness!" (Muslim ibn Hajjaj 1995, 3:310) These reports establish that a very clear equation was thus drawn between mature age and effective political leadership, which ultimately had repercussions for the commonweal of Muslims.

Diversity of Views on the Necessity of the Caliphate

The diversity of opinions in the first three centuries of Islam regarding the office of the caliph/imam is attested to by the rationalist theologian Abd

17. Among modern historians who have emphasized the relevance of this aspect of Abu Bakr's knowledge, especially his prominence as a genealogist, are Shaban 1971, 1:18–19; and Donner 1981, 84–85.

al-Jabbar (d. 1095), who identifies three broad trends of thought in his time on the issue of the caliphate. The first, a minority, held that the caliphate was not necessary; the second believed that it was required on the basis of reason; and the third maintained that it was necessary according to the religious law.[18] This range of thought testifies to the active engagement of many thinkers with the critical issues of sound governance and sociopolitical administration, unfettered by an assumed religious mandate for a specific political institution. Their suggestions and solutions were clearly the product of rational deliberation and philosophical reflection, based on the perception of the public good in their own times and circumstances.

The early literature records these debates matter-of-factly and nonjudgmentally, in contradistinction to the later, particularly heresiographical, literature that tends to treat the Muʿtazili as dissenters,[19] given that a broad consensus *(ijmaʿ)* had developed among the later scholars about the necessity of a (preferably single) ruler for the polity. In fact, it is rather this consensus, which by the fourth century of Islam (tenth century CE) had evolved through natural and deliberative historical processes, that ultimately, and somewhat ironically, conferred on the office of the caliph the imprimatur of a divinely ordained institution. By this time, Muslims (or more accurately Muslim scholars) had developed the conviction that their consensus was reflective of the divine will. In other words, it was the rational and utilitarian necessity of providing for law and order, which in turn was held to ensure the moral and material welfare of the polity, that led to a consensus on the necessity of the caliphate. Once this consensus developed, an alternate situation seemed no longer politically viable or morally desirable, although dissenting voices continued to be heard through the premodern period. Thus the famous tenth-century Sunni theologian al-Ashʿari (d. 935) formulated the doctrine that the caliphate (or the imamate

18. See Abd al-Jabbar n.d., 20:16. I owe this reference to Hayrettin Yucesoy's unpublished paper "Is Political Leadership Necessary? Religious and Rational Morality in Islamic Political Thought," delivered at the annual conference of the Middle East Studies Association, Anchorage, Alaska, Nov. 2003.

19. This attitude is quite evident in the later heresiographical works; see, for example, al-Shahrastani 1995, 1:56ff.

as it was often called) was a requirement of the religious law, but the later scholar Adud al-Din al-Iji (d. 1355) maintained that popular consensus from the time of Abu Bakr onward and social utility, rather than religious doctrine, had established the necessity of this institution (al-Iji 1983, 396–97). Al-Ash'ari's position would, however, be accepted by most Sunni scholars as axiomatic.

Ibn Taymiyya's Views

In the fourteenth century, the Hanbali theologian Taqi al-Din Ibn Taymiyya (d. 1328) in his well-known work *al-Siyasah al-shar'iyah* explicitly invokes the concept of maslahah as a political concept undergirding the era of the Rashidun caliphs. Maslahah as political expediency and public interest is particularly evident in the political appointments made by both Abu Bakr and Umar b. al-Khattab, according to Ibn Taymiyya. The ideal, our author says, is to appoint the individual who is most qualified *(al-aslah)* for a particular position, but such qualifications have to be assessed in view of who would best serve the public interest. This discussion occurs in the context of debating the following question: who among the following two men should be appointed to a public office: the one who is the most trustworthy *(ahaduhuma a'zamu amanatan)* or the one who is the strongest *(a'zamu quwwatan)*? (Ibn Taymiyya n.d., 22). The answer, according to Ibn Taymiyya, is the individual from whose appointment the greatest benefit may be derived and the least harm may occur in a particular position. Thus, for the position of a military commander, the strongest and the most courageous man should be picked, even though he may have moral failings *(wa in kana fihi fujur)*, over the weaker and less capable man, even though he may be more trustworthy. Here he cites the opinion of Ahmad Ibn Hanbal, who had been questioned regarding the appointment of a military commander from among two possible candidates. One was strong but morally deficient while the other was virtuous but weak—who should be selected in this case? Ibn Hanbal replied that the morally inferior individual should be chosen "for his physical strength was for [the benefit of] Muslims and his moral failings were to his discredit only. As for the virtuous but weak individual, his virtue was for the benefit of his soul and weakness to the disadvantage of the Muslims." Thus Ibn Hanbal recommended that the strong but morally deficient man be selected as the military commander (22).

Ibn Taymiyya then goes on to cite a hadith in which the Prophet states, "Indeed God strengthens this religion with the morally deficient man." This report serves as a proof-text validating Ibn Hanbal's opinion. It is for this reason, Ibn Taymiyya affirms, that Muhammad appointed Khalid b. al-Walid as a military commander after his acceptance of Islam, even though the latter was guilty of a number of misdeeds and the Prophet clearly disapproved of them. In spite of this, the Prophet made use of Khalid's martial skills because, Ibn Taymiyya comments, "he was more qualified (aslah) than others in this regard" (23). Thus, Abu Dharr al-Ghifari, who was more trustworthy and truthful than Khalid, was not appointed by the Prophet to any position of leadership because he perceived him to be physically weak. Out of similar considerations for the greater public good *(li-maslahah rajihah)*, Ibn Taymiyya affirms, Muhammad appointed Amr b. al-As and Usamah b. Zayd as military commanders, even though there were others who were more knowledgeable in religious matters and more pious than they (25).

After the Prophet, both Abu Bakr and Umar b. al-Khattab made political and military appointments on the basis of public interest as they perceived it in their own time. Thus, while Abu Bakr deemed it wise to retain Khalid in his leadership position, Umar did not and had him removed and replaced with Abu Ubaydah b. al-Jarrah. One of the reasons for this change was that the formidable Khalid was an appropriate counterfoil to the gentle Abu Bakr while the stern Umar was better counterbalanced by the more lenient Abu Ubaydah (26).

When the objectives of good governance in certain matters were better served through the selection of someone who was trustworthy and honest, such as in financial matters, then a person endowed with such qualities was to be preferred. Ibn Taymiyya also suggests that in military matters, if the ruler were to consult with learned religious scholars, then he would advance the public good even more. In other matters as well, he states, sometimes the public good was more effectively served through a council of administrators rather than through one individual alone (26).

It is in the *al-Siyasah al-shar'iyah* of Ibn Taymiyya that we see the strongest and clearest articulation of maslahah as a political concept, according to which pragmatic, mundane considerations of public benefit and communal welfare take priority over idealized notions of moral leadership.

Modern Discourses

The views on good governance of twentieth-century exegete and scholar Rashid Rida (and of Muhammad Abduh as well)[20] may be derived to a great extent from his treatment of Qur'an 4:59 in the exegetical work *Tafsir al-Manar.* Qur'an 4:59 states, "Obey God and His Messenger, and those possessing authority among you." The early Qur'an commentator Mujahid b. Jabr (d. 720) had understood this phrase as referring primarily to an amorphous group of learned scholars, or more literally, "those possessing critical insight into religion and reason" *(uli al-fiqh fi al-din wa al-aql)* (Mujahid ibn Jabr 1977, 1:62). Rashid Rida expands on this idea and comments that the phrase *uli al-amr* refers to the political rulers *(umara')*, the judges *(al-hukkam)*, the religious scholars *(ulama)*, the chiefs of the army *(ru'asa' al-jund)*, and the rest of the rulers and leaders *(sa'ir al-ru'asa' wa al-zu'ama')* among Muslims, to whom, he says, people resort in their need and for their general welfare (Rida 1999, 5:147). Rida warns, however, that Qur'an 4:59 does not call for obedience to the uli al-amr but only to God and His Messenger, the reason being that the verse continues with "And if you should differ with regard to a matter, then refer it to God and His Messenger." If the uli al-amr rule according to the precepts of God and the sunna, then obedience is due to them; if they do not and in fact resort to tyranny and oppression *(zulm)*, then obedience is no longer an obligatory duty *(wajiba qat'an)*, but is rather forbidden *(muharramah)* (1999, 5:150). He continues by saying that the actions of the temporal political rulers *(al-umara' wa al-salatin)* are bound by the legal opinions *(fatawa)* of

20. Muhammad Abduh, the brilliant rector of al-Azhar University, died in 1905 before the *Tafsir al-Manar* was completed.

the scholars (ulama), for the ulama are in fact "the leaders of the leaders" *(umara' al-umara')*.

In this interpretation, Rida is echoing in part the exegesis of the ninth-century commentator Muqatil b. Sulayman, who had similarly understood the verse as enjoining obedience to God and His Messenger only and not to the uli al-amr as well (al-Balkhi 1969, 1:246). The uli al-amr have primarily a consultative role; their counsel is to be solicited when the Qur'an and the sunna do not provide categorical answers in certain matters. Acting upon the uli al-amr's recommendations is consequently a discretionary option rather than binding. These conclusions are implicit in Muqatil's exegesis but more explicitly formulated in Rida's.

Further on, Rida equates the uli al-amr with the "people who loosen and bind" *(ahl al-hall wa al-aqd)*, thus broadening the description of this group of people in a modernist vein. The "people who loosen and bind" include all those in whom the Muslim community, the umma, have faith: they would include the scholars, the leaders of the army, and the leaders of various sectors of society who promote the general interests of the people *(al-masalih al-ammah)*. Among these sectors are trade, industry, and agriculture. Therefore, labor union leaders, political party leaders, and members of the editorial boards of respectable newspapers and their chief editors are all included in the category of the people "who loosen and bind" (Rida 1999, 5:152). Thus Rida explicitly yokes the concept of maslahah/masalih to the Qur'anic phrase *uli al-amr* and includes within the latter phrase those groups of people with combined specialized expertise, most of which is not explicitly religious but contributes to the overall commonweal of the polity. We may say here that Rida secularizes the concept of uli al-amr to a considerable extent.

Contemporary Modernist Discourses

Muslim modernist political discourses today specifically focus on the issue of democracy and democratization in the Islamic heartlands. A number of modernist scholars and political thinkers today are advocating democratic reform in Muslim-majority countries by invoking the twin concepts of shura and maslahah. The word *shura* occurs in the Qur'an and means "consultation" in general. Two verses specifically refer to this concept: the first (3:158–59) states, "So pass over [their faults], and ask for [God's] forgiveness and consult them in matters; then, when you have made a decision, put your trust in God." The second verse (42:38) runs, "[The believers are] those who answer the call of their Lord and perform prayer, and who conduct their affairs by mutual consultation, and who spend of what We have bestowed upon them." Consultation on various matters has been considered obligatory by many scholars through time while others have tended to regard it as a highly recommended practice. The predominant sentiment in the sources—theological, juridical, ethical, and administrative—is that shura as mutual consultation in various spheres (political, communal, social, military, familial) is the preferred and desirable method of resolving matters because it reflects the public will and results in greater public benefit. As dynastic rule became the norm after the death of Ali in 661, invocation of shura as a desirable and even mandated social and political practice became a way of registering disapproval of a political culture that had progressively grown more authoritarian by the Abbasid period (750–1258).

Qur'an commentaries and certain genres of ethical and humanistic literature *(adab)* continued to extol the merits of consultation in various spheres—particularly the bureaucratic, military, and political—throughout the premodern period. Representing a fairly common perspective on the concept of shura, the Qur'an commentator Muhammad al-Qurtubi (d. 1273), in his exegesis of Qur'an 3:158–59, records that "it is the obligation of the rulers to consult the scholars on matters unknown to them and in religious matters not clear to them. [They should] consult the leaders of the army in matters having to do with war, and leaders of the people in administrative issues, as well as teachers, ministers, and governors in matters that have to do with the welfare of the polity and its development" (al-Qurtubi 1967, 2:1491–92). In the twelfth century, the Andalusian scholar Ibn Atiyya (d. 1146) was of the opinion that consultation was one of the pillars of the religious law and of judicial activity and "whoever did not consult with the people of knowledge and religion should be subject to removal [specifically, from public office]" (1967, 2:1491). Nonconsultative, dynastic rule was regarded in most circles as un-Islamic and as a betrayal of the early Islamic ideal of collective decision-making that was deemed to have contributed to the greater welfare of the populace.

To this day, therefore, the concept of shura resonates strongly with a significant cross-section of Muslims, which they understand as leading the way to just and consultative power-sharing in accordance with Qur'anic precept in contrast to arbitrary despotism (Ar. *istibdad*). In the contemporary period, modernist and reform-minded Muslims have tended to conflate shura with modern notions of democracy.[21] Thus the well-known modernist scholar Fazlur Rahman stated that "Muslim critics are . . . obviously wrong in rejecting democracy, which is positively and patently enjoined by the Qur'an as the moral foundation of the Community's life" (Rahman 1983). A wide range of Muslim scholars and public intellectuals, such as the Tunisian political dissident and activist Rachid Ghannouchi (1993), Muhammad Imara (1979), Sa'id al-Ashmawi,[22] and Azizah al-Hibri (1992) have supported the compatibility of traditional notions of shura with modern democratic ones, emphasizing maslahah as one of the main reasons for doing so. For most reform-minded Muslim thinkers, democracy does not imply full-fledged secularism and a total evacuation of religious values from the public sphere. The prominent Iranian scholar Abdulkarim Soroush has in fact maintained that for a democracy to live up to its name in most Muslim majority societies, it has to be accommodating of religious values and sentiment, if this be reflective of the popular will. "Indeed, in such a society any purely secular government would be undemocratic," he says, voicing the concern that a government that is not reflective of the popular will is not conducive to the public commonweal.

21. Not all those described as Islamists reject the equation between shura and democracy; thus Yusuf al-Qaradawi sees little dissonance between a shura-based government and a democratic one; see his influential tract *Min fiqh al-dawlah fi al-Islam* (1997). For a fairly wide-ranging discussion of this topic, see the published volume of essays *Islam and the Challenge of Democracy,* edited by Khaled Abou el Fadl (2004).

22. His views are primarily expressed in the important work *Al-Islam al-siyasi* (al-Ashmawi 1987).

From a younger generation of contemporary modernist scholars, Khaled Abou el Fadl, Muqtedar Khan, and Tariq Ramadan have been among the most insistent in drawing parallels between shura and some form of a democratic system of government (procedural, constitutional, liberal, and so forth), which through recourse to consultative and collective political decision-making maximizes the sociopolitical well-being of Muslims. Abou el Fadl derives the basis, even the imperative, for democratic governance, not only from a historic and juristic understanding of shura but also from related concepts such as *ijtihad* (independent reasoning); the rights of people *(huquq al-insan)*, which take precedence over the rights of God *(huquq Allah)*; and the responsiveness of the shari'a, contingent as it is upon human interpretation to changing circumstances (Abou el Fadl 2004, 3–36). Ramadan more forcefully establishes a link between good governance, which in the contemporary period means democratic governance, and *al-masalih al-mursalah* (public interest). He refers to the well-known legal maxim "maqasid al-ahkam masalih al-anam" (the objective of legal rulings is the welfare of humankind) and extrapolates from it a broad sociopolitical mandate for effecting reform in Muslim societies. Ramadan remarks, "Muslims have a duty to make an appropriate study of their society in order to determine the features of the common good (al-maslahah), the main achievements to be preserved, the injustices to be fought as a priority, and the means at their disposal and, at the same time, to identify the actors and the key points in the social and political dynamics of their society" (Ramadan 2004, 162).[23] Similarly, Khan makes an explicit connection between shura and the possibility of democratic political reform and emphasizes the flexibility of the shari'a. He states that "for the liberal Muslim theorists, Shura is paramount and Sharia too must be arrived at through consultative processes and not taken as given" (M. Khan 2006, 160). In my own writings, I have similarly pointed to the salience of the concept of shura in Muslim conceptualizations of good governance over time (Afsaruddin 2006, 153–73).

23. For a general, concise discussion of maslahah, see Ramadan 2004, 38–43.

Conclusion

Even from this brief survey it is rather clear that maslahah as an implicit political and social organizational concept was already shaping the decisions of the early leaders of the Muslim community, even when this term was not explicitly invoked as such. In the early period, discourse regarding legitimate and beneficial leadership tended to be phrased in terms of two key Qur'anically inspired concepts: sabiqah and fadl/fadilah. However, when we look at the historical narratives that employ these terms in relation to the first generation of Muslims, it is clear that the authors of these narratives extol the possession of these attributes by the most prominent Companions precisely because the synergy of these two virtues led to the most beneficial consequences for the polity. Both the early Sunnis and the Shi'a subscribed to common standards of moral excellence and precedence, which were invoked to gauge the superior qualifications of their respective candidates for the caliphate/imamate. In this early period, maslahah was not explicitly stated as the intended objective of the various sociopolitical measures adopted in the early period. Rather it was implicitly articulated within the context of describing and eulogizing the manifold beneficial consequences of appointing a specific caliph/imam and other lesser rulers. Even though later Shi'i theological works foregrounded Ali's blood-kinship to Muhammad (and the moral excellences thereby implied) as his supreme qualification for the caliphate/imamate, early Shi'i works sometimes focused more on Ali's personal moral attributes, such as courage and generosity, rather than on his kinship, in supporting his candidacy for the caliphate/imamate. This tendency suggests an early pragmatic emphasis on considerations of communal welfare rather than subscription to a legitimist perspective on political authority in the early period. It was suggested that this early proto-Shi'i perspective on leadership finds amplification in the revolutionary concept of the wilayat-i faqih promulgated by Ayatollah Khomeini in the last quarter of the twentieth century.

Among the authors of political treatises in the premodern period, the Mu'tazili author al-Jahiz in the ninth century placed considerable stress on the practical and religious knowledge of Abu Bakr, which stood the community in good stead in the immediate aftermath of the Prophet's death. In the eleventh century, al-Mawardi referred to two early competing schools of thought, one of which believed that reason decreed that there be a ruler of the polity after the death of the Prophet while the other believed that this was so decreed through revelation. Both schools concurred that in either case social harmony and the public good were served by appointing a ruler who could contain chaos and adjudicate disputes. By Ibn Taymiyya's time we see maslahah specifically cited as one of the main reasons, if not *the* main reason, for considering the rule of the Rightly-Guided caliphs as paradigmatic for later Muslims. In his usage, maslahah is both "public good/interest" and "political expediency," judicious recourse to which enhanced the well-being of the early polity as was the case with the Rightly-Guided caliphs and their successors. In the early modern period, Rashid Rida regarded a wide range of people who possess expertise in traditional fields (such as jurisprudence) to modern sciences (such as horticulture) to share in a broadly defined notion of socio-political-intellectual authority. He maintained that to fail to consult the proper expert at the proper time is to fail in proper administration of the polity. Since the late twentieth century and continuing into the present one, modernist and reformist Muslim scholars, as we saw, have been emphasizing the concept of maslahah and, in conjunction with traditional concepts such as shura and ijtihad, are establishing a theoretical basis for the legitimation of representative and democratic governments.

Interpretations of what exactly constituted the public good/interest and how it was to be achieved remained diverse through time, but that the public good must be served has remained a central and stable concern of Islamic discourses on legitimate leadership and political ethics since the formative period.

3

On Sa`di's *Treatise on Advice to the Kings*

ALIREZA SHOMALI

AND MEHRZAD BOROUJERDI

> Cherish the poor, and seek not thine own comfort. The shepherd should not sleep while the wolf is among the sheep. Protect the needy, for a king wears his crown for the sake of his subjects. The people are as the root and the king is as the tree; and the tree, O son, gains strength from the root. He who has fear of injury to his kingdom should not oppress the people. Seek not plenteousness in that land where the people are afflicted by the king.
>
> —King Anushirvan's deathbed counsel to his son Hormuz (Sa`di's opening remark in *Bustan,* chapter 1)

THE NINTH to the thirteenth centuries AD represent the "golden age" of Iranian culture and Islamic philosophy. Emblematic of an awakening self-consciousness in the Islamic world, which some have referred to as "medieval Enlightenment,"[1] rationalism emerged within this period as a

We wish to thank Ebrahim Khalifeh-Soltani for his valuable comments on an earlier draft of this chapter.

1. See Strauss 1991, 205–6; and Strauss 1995, 152–53. From the ninth through the eleventh centuries, western Iran under the Persian Buyids and eastern Iran—i.e., Khurasan and Transoxiana—under the Samanids witnessed what scholars identify as the "new Persian Renaissance" or the "Renaissance of Islam." See Fry 1965 and Kraemer 1986.

powerful discourse that could capably rival the dominant jurisprudential discourse. Accordingly, a whole range of important philosophers, scientists, historians, poets, and statesmen plunged themselves into new endeavors and contemplated different and novel questions.[2]

Muslih al-Din Sa'di's (1209–1291) opening passage from the first chapter of *Bustan,* where he approvingly quotes counsel from the pre-Islamic King Anushirvan,[3] cleverly embodies elements of the type of rationalism that emerged during this era.[4] Despite Sa'di's extensive training in Islamic theology and jurisprudence, there is a curious absence of jurisprudential language in his deliberations on statecraft. Why, one might ask? In this chapter we will address this question by (a) highlighting Sa'di's predominantly pragmatic and secular beliefs about statecraft, and (b) situating him within a broad conception of social contract. The Sa'di that emerges is one who adopts a language of social contract in which the king does not own the people and is not God's representative

2. To name but a few, Muhammad ibn Jarir Tabari (ca. 841–922), Muhammad ibn Zakariya Razi (865–925/932), Rudaki Samarqandi (858–941), Abu Nasr Farabi (874–950), Firdawsi (940–1020), Avicenna (980–1037), Farrukhi Sistani (960–1037), Abu Rayhan Biruni (973–1048), Nasir Khusrau Qubadiyani (1004–1088), Nizam al-Mulk (1017–1092), Khayyam (1048–1131), Anwari Abiwardi (1126–1190), Shahab al-Din Suhrawardi (1154–1191), Averroes (1126–1198), Nizami Ganjawi (1141–1209), Fakhr al-Din Razi (1149–1209), Attar Nishaburi (1145–1230), Ibn Arabi (1165–1240), Jalal al-Din Rumi (1207–1273), Sadr ad-Din Qunawi (d. 1273/5), and Nasir al-Din Tusi (1201–1274).

3. Anushirvan (surnamed "the Just") (ca. 501–579) was the twenty-second Sassanid emperor of Persia, who ruled from 531 to 579.

4. According to medieval Enlightenment, reason incorporates both theoretical and practical wisdom *(hikmat-i nazari* and *hikmat-i amali)*. Politics, ethics, and economics are the three constitutive elements of practical wisdom. Political philosophy in its original meaning, which embodies Socrates's philosophic life, probes into the nature of good and evil and applies this knowledge in order to make noble life possible in the just polis. Political philosophy, therefore, is based on practical wisdom (for more on this see Bruell 1988). A second meaning of rationalism suggests something that promotes a means to an end. This is also the definition of pragmatic rationality. In this chapter rationalism connotes both practical wisdom and pragmatic rationality, and the expression "secular reasoning" is used interchangeably with it. Secular or practical reasoning should not be confused with *philosophical secularism,* which is a type of metaphysics that belongs to *theoretical* wisdom.

on earth. Rather, he is an employee hired by the people to protect their welfare and security.[5]

Far from claiming that Sa'di has articulated a systematically consistent political theory, we offer a series of observations concerning his seminal work on a manual for the prince, *Nasihah al-muluk,* and suggest a (re)reading of Sa'di as part of the responsibility of intellectuals to revive and refurbish possibilities that are latent in the Islamic tradition. The tradition is pregnant with a whole host of potentialities that might help future generations of Muslims contemplate a nontheocratic statecraft.

On Secular Reasoning and Justice

Sa'di overtly differentiates between the realm of politics and practical wisdom on the one hand and the domain of individual life on the other. He believes that while the individuals must follow the *shari'a* in their daily prayers and interactions, the supplications of the king are qualitatively different from those of clerics and ordinary subjects. For Sa'di, a just king who serves his subjects by protecting them from harm and secures a just society is simultaneously praying to God (see #94).[6] Sa'di's background in Islamic mysticism leads him to differentiate between two types of religiosity corresponding to two distinct modes of a man-God relationship: the shari'a and the *tariqah* [path to God]. While the universal rules of jurisprudence dominate the former, singularity and virtue uphold the realm of the latter. Underscoring this distinction, Sa'di elevates the king's proper fulfillment of his mandate as the king's admission into the realm of tariqah, thereby guaranteeing his ultimate salvation. In contradistinction to mainstream mysticism,[7] Sa'di maintains that the king's application of

5. In the canons of Islamic law and jurisprudence, the concept of *ijarah* also includes the meaning "to hire" or "to employ." This age-old concept plays an important role in shedding light on the idea of social contract.

6. The numbers refer to the 151 articles of Sa'di's *Treatise on Advice to the Kings,* whose English translation constitutes the second part of this chapter.

7. According to different schools within mainstream mysticism, following *tariqah* can be realized through (a) solitude and abnegation of worldly affairs advocated by

secular-practical reasoning in serving the people inducts the king into the realm of tariqah.[8]

One place in which Sa'di makes this point explicit is in the story of Atabeg Tuklah,[9] as narrated in *Bustan:*

It is recounted in the history of preceding kings
That when Tuklah ascended to the throne of the Zangi dynasty,
Under his rule no one harmed a fellow creature,
And his good repute outshined that of other kings.
The king once confided to a sage
That, alas, fruitless have been my years,
May I now sit in the corner of devotion?
To usefully employ the few short days that yet remain to me?
[Since] the throne and positions of power are all but transient
It is only the ascetic Sufi who takes happiness to the [narrow] grave
Upon hearing Tuklah, the sagacious sage burst into rage
And, rebuking Tuklah, cried: Enough!
Tariqah consists solely in serving the people
And finds no place in the prayer beads, or prayer-rug, or tattered garment.
Be a king in sovereignty and simultaneously
A devotee of purity of morals

Bayazid Bastami (804–874), (b) self-control and inward monitoring advocated by Junayd Nahavandi (830–910), and (c) love and compassion championed by Jalal al-Din Rumi (for more information see Furuzanfar 1972).

8. Similar to Sa'di, the Persian mystics Abu Sa'id ibn Abi al-Khayr (967–1049) and Abu Hafs Umar Suhrawardi (1144–1234) also equate the tariqah with serving the public. See Munawwar 1998. Sa'di's novelty, however, resides in the fact that he ties tariqah with *political* service to the people. Badi' al-Zaman Furuzanfar (1904–1970), the renowned scholar of Islamic mysticism, confirms the point that Sa'di moves beyond the above-mentioned interpretations and offers yet a fourth alternative that links tariqah with political service (79–80).

9. Muzaffar al-Din Tuklah ibn Zangi (d. 1195) was one of the sultans of the Salghurid dynasty who ruled from 1175 to 1195. He had a reputation for justice and mystical devotion. See Musawi Bojnurdi 1994, 492.

Act sincerely and in good will
And never rave about piety and creed.
Action, not words, is demanded by *tariqah*
For words without action are void of substance.
The wise who have the wealth of purity
Wear this tattered garment underneath their pristine mantle.[10]

The above poem demonstrates how in the poet's eyes, a wise king who acts justly is striding toward God. Furthermore, following a causal logic, Sa'di believes that the king's justice guarantees the city's well-being and in turn secures the prosperity of his state. In other words, the king's primary self-interest (that is, power and sovereignty) becomes conditional upon meeting the primary interest of the subjects (that is, security and prosperity) (see #95). Sa'di invokes this language of causal relationship when he maintains that a city's reputation for justice and security lures traders to its shores to invest (see #1, 43, 44). And, on the contrary, the king's injustice is tantamount to self-destruction, like a lumber thief who saws a tree's branch while sitting on it. Observing this thief, the "owner of the garden," who is a metaphor for the people, concludes that, more than harming me, this thief is wounding himself (Sa'di 1997, 239–41; also see #103). Furthermore, Sa'di's idea of justice does not derive from any specific religion. Instead, it is imbued with secular/pragmatic (or utilitarian) implications (see #79). The pagan King Anushirvan secures a place in glorious Paradise by choosing justice (Sa'di 1906, 35, 40), that is, by not being kind to criminals or tormenting the innocent (see #29).

In the spirit of the Golden Rule of ethics, Sa'di counsels the king, "Hold sway over others such that if you were one of them, you could tolerate such reign" (#121). And, "rule in such manner that if dethroned you would neither feel ashamed of your track record nor be treated unkindly by people" (#142). In other words, practical reason, including ethics, alone discerns what justice is. Moreover, Sa'di (1997, 228) adds that just kings are

10. Sa'di 1997, 233–34. Parts of this translation were transcribed from *The Bustan of Sa'di* prepared by the Iran Chamber Society (2010).

simultaneously "cultivators of religion," that is, if justice with its metareligious definition is promoted, religion will be shielded. Using this subtle meaning or distinction, Sa'di's king becomes a servant of religion. Such a king serves faith not by establishing theocracy but by addressing the demands of universal and metareligious justice, which human reason discloses. Borrowing Isaiah Berlin's terminology, we may state that Sa'di's king is akin to a "night-watchman"[11] with a clearly defined duty of securing the neighborhood/city and protecting its inhabitants from the wicked inside and outside its boundaries.

In Sa'di's eyes, the otherworldly good is the dependent variable whereas the worldly good (read security and justice in society) is the independent variable. The happiness in the afterlife for the king and his lieutenants follows the worldly happiness of the people;[12] that is, their consent, security, and prosperity—the very secular measures of affluence in the city—are the sign of the otherworldly redemption. Accordingly, God's consent—that is, the warranty of the king and his subjects' salvation in the hereafter—naturally follows the execution of justice.

Sa'di on Social Contract

The king's service to the people entitles him to receive a wage for his service. The compensation he receives is indeed what empowers the king to perform his duty in the first place. Sa'di calls this reward *authority*, which demands the subjects' actual obedience (see #89). Let us lay out the logic of protection/obedience in Sa'di's treatment of authority at greater length (see #93). This logic is the rationale that underwrites the tacit contract between the king and his subjects. The king guards (see #12) the latter against harm, provided that he receives obedience from

11. See Berlin 2000, 75 and 199.

12. Article #96 reads, "The king's emissary must consider God's consent over the king's command so as to truly benefit from his vicinity to him/Him." Obeying God's commands, as stated in the preamble of *Nasihah al-muluk*, and obtaining God's consent are conditional upon acting justly and not obeying the king blindly.

them, and in their turn people offer obedience to the king on condition that they receive security. For Thomas Hobbes, such rationality of exchange results in a covenant among the people (and not between the people and the king). According to this covenant, the people relinquish all of their rights before the state and unreservedly obey the Leviathan, which, consequently, emerges as the Absolutist State (Hobbes 1966, 157). In contradistinction to Hobbes, Sa'di's works harbor an implicit contract-based concept of governance that does not result in the absolute authority of the king. Perhaps the difference can be attributed to, among other things, the presence of a third factor in Sa'di's worldview (and its absence in Hobbes's), that is, God.

There is a philosophy hidden behind Sa'di's application of the famous metaphor of king as shepherd. This age-old metaphor can be understood in at least two different ways. First, the king is the shepherd and the subjects are *his* sheep, akin to a master who *owns* his slaves. The shepherd unilaterally decides what is best for the sheep while the latter have no say regarding their own well-being. The shepherd-king thus is a master who has the right to command, establish the law, and demand obedience while the subjects have no right but the duty of compliance.[13]

Sa'di presents the shepherd-king metaphor in a second way, one in which the king is a shepherd who is *hired by* the people to protect their life and belongings. As he emphatically states in *Golestan* (Sa'di 1997, 52), "the sole purpose for having kings is protection of people":

> The sheep is not for the shepherd
> It is the shepherd that is for serving the sheep.

And on another occasion, he continues (Sa'di 1949, 27), "the king is more needful of having subjects than the subjects are in need of a king. The subjects can live with or without a king while kingship is not imaginable

13. This viewpoint is discernible in the medieval theory of the divine rights of king as well as in modern secular dictatorships where the ruler sits on the throne vacated by God.

without subjects." To further assert his position, Sa'di immediately adds, "An apt analogy for the king and the subjects is that of the shepherd whose wage would be *haram* should he fail to take proper care of the herd" (Sa'di 1949, 27).[14] In this more humane and rational interpretation of the king-shepherd allegory, the central point of analogy is not ownership but employment; the shepherd does not own the sheep; rather, he is merely a hired agent. In the presence of someone of the stature of Sultan Abaqa Khan, the representative and son of the Mughal emperor Hulagu Khan, Sa'di recites the following lines:

> A righteous monarch who protects his subjects from harm
> Receives tax that is *halal* for his shepherding wage
> And if he is not a true shepherd *of* the people, may that wage change
> into poison
> Since what he receives is poll tax illegitimately achieved.[15]

What emerges as a recurring theme in Sa'di's conception of statecraft is a contract whereby the king is the employee[16] and the people are the employers. In other words, Sa'di's expression "the shepherd *of* the people" denotes a servant *of* the people who is hired to protect the latter's security/property (that is, the herd).[17] The shepherd's income (authority) is considered *haram* (illegitimate) if he is (a) unable to perform his job in protecting the flock, (b) capable of protecting the sheep but refuses to do so, or (c) the wolf in the cloak of the shepherd (see #33). In all of the above scenarios, the king has violated his obligations toward the people

14. In general, the term *haram* implies what is sanctioned as illegitimate by God. In the lexicon of Islamic jurisprudence, it is the opposite of *halal.*

15. Sa'di 1997, 1182. Abaqa Khan (also spelled Abaga) (1234–1282) reigned over the Tabriz principality from 1265 to 1282.

16. In other words, he is the "shepherd *of* the people."

17. Compare Sa'di's to Nietzsche's lines: "*On the sovereign types.*—The 'shepherd' as opposed to the 'master' (—the former a *means* of preserving the herd; the latter the end for which the herd exists)" (Nietzsche 1968, 479).

by depriving them of their right to be protected. Such conduct is not only illegitimate but also unvirtuous (see #97).

Sa'di's Realism

As a man of the world, Sa'di is not a utopian thinker necessarily intent on changing it. Having probed into the *nature* of man and society, he is aware that human nature, unlike molding clay, cannot be radically altered. Sa'di acknowledges that man is motivated by self-interest and that politics cannot be understood without taking this fact into consideration. Almost two centuries before Machiavelli (1469–1527) and three hundred years before Hobbes (1588–1679), he acknowledges that kings are first and foremost interested in their own well-being and self-preservation. In *Nasihah al-muluk*, he devotes the lion's share of his advice to the reason of the state and the type of conduct that the sovereign should undertake to preserve his throne. Consider the following:

On statecraft, see #7, 21, 40, 48, 54, 70, 135.
On staffing the state, see #8, 10, 14, 24, 25, 59, 104, 106, 150.
On dealing with enemies, see #38, 39, 55, 72, 83, 87, 102, 105, 132, 133, 134, 149.[18]
On political economy, see #15, 17, 37, 43, 44, 88, 103, 110, 120.
On judicial affairs, see #14, 16, 26, 27, 35, 41, 46, 58, 65, 67, 74, 75, 81, 107.

As a further sign of realism, Sa'di's state administers the city and regulates peoples' lives based on secular human intellect; not by religious provisions. His city flourishes and collapses from material, not metaphysical, causes (see #1). Article #30 indicates human experience and

18. Furthermore, in Sa'di's advice to Sultan Ankiyanu (1949, 27), it reads, "Make strong allies to weaken your strong enemies." This same statement can also be interpreted as follows: "Strengthen your allies in order to weaken your strong enemies."

rational consultation should steer the machinery of the state.[19] Furthermore, as stated in the advice treaty to Sultan Ankiyanu, once the king has articulated the state interest in such a fashion it is incumbent upon all to follow it. Sa'di immediately adds that, on issues pertaining to the interest of religion, however, the verdicts of [clerical]-judges take precedence. "Otherwise both will ruin." This last sentence can be interpreted in two radically different manners. One interpretation implies that, if the citizens were not to follow the commands of kings and [clerical]-judges in their respective domains of authority, chaos would ensue. A second interpretation warns that mixing the mandates of religion and state will result in ruin to both.[20]

Within the universe of Sa'di's realism, self-interest is not given free rein. He articulates at least three arguments that admonish the king against turning self-interest into a destructive force. Sa'di's method of taming the sovereign is to warn him about worldly and otherworldly losses. He reminds his king of the following points:

The Mutual Self-interest of the King and the Public. "Under a king totally preoccupied with securing his self-interest, the public interest is not realized. Accordingly, the interest of all parties including the king will perish" (#95). In other words, Sa'di reminds the sovereign that the durability of office is contingent upon mass consent more than the state's coercion. In *Golestan* he writes,

> A true king never adopts injustice as his vocation
> Since a wolf is not fit for shepherding
> A king who inaugurates failure of justice
> Strikes at the foundations of his own sovereignty. (Sa'di 1997, 32)

19. Similar to Sa'di, Iran's national poet Firdawsi (940–1020) considers secular practical reasoning as the crux of statecraft. See Parham 1998, 88–125.

20. The exact text reads, "The king's decree on what constitutes State interest must necessarily be followed. And, the [clerical]-judges' decree on what constitutes the interest of religion must necessarily be followed. Otherwise, both will [end in] ruin" (Sa'di 1949, 27).

The Requisite of Good Repute. Appealing to the human desire to master death by immortalizing one's reputation, Sa'di writes to the king, "Among your possessions it is only your good repute that lasts with you after your departure; poor is he who does not leave a good repute behind" (#111; see also 113, 114, 119, 129). Invoking Prophet Abraham's prayer narrated in the Qur'an,[21] Sa'di reminds the statesman, "Life may leave you with but two achievements: good repute and spiritual reward. Beyond these two, everything else shall perish" (Sa'di 1997, 930). In other words, injustice is the corrosion of a good reputation while justice is the adornment of loyalty.

The Weight of the Day of Judgment. Perhaps more than any other Persian thinker, Sa'di conjures up the theme of Judgment Day for a blatantly political purpose. His works are filled with references to death, afterlife, and perdition in order to plant fear into the heart of the sovereign lest he commit injustice (see #80, 82, 124, 125, 130). He intermittently counsels the king to read the chronicles of earlier kings and to commit to memory those passages about the transitory nature of power (and how everything scatters to the winds) (see #21, 116, 131).[22]

But what happens if the king is not tamed by the above three provisions? Can the people then rise up against him? The Hobbesian theory of social contract leaves no room for legitimate rebellion and overthrow of the Leviathan because the people have relinquished a priori all their citizenry rights. However, one can deduce a notion of legitimate rebellion within the confines of a non-Hobbesian contract such as Sa'di's. If one side of the contract, that is, the king, fails to meet his obligation of protection, the subjects have the right to withhold his payment, that is, their obedience. Moreover, because the contract is sanctioned by God, a

21. "Grant me honorable mention on the tongue of truth among the latest [generations]." Qur'an 26:84.

22. For examples of Sa'di's emotive depiction of death while counseling the king, see the odes and exhortations section, especially the ode addressed to Sultan Ankiyanu (Sa'di 1997, 912–14).

king who breaks his covenant with the people simultaneously garners the wrath of God.[23]

Sa'di's nonutopianism, however, prevents him from enthusiastically embracing a theory and practice of rebellion. If confronted with the above questions, Sa'di would probably have maintained that the three aforementioned provisions are the only choices left to the public and that prudence does not permit more. There is no guarantee that through revolution people will not make their condition even worse.[24] Moreover, God may vanquish an unjust king through the might of an adversary or exact his justice in the afterlife.

As mentioned above, the presence of God is one of the ways in which one can distinguish Sa'di's contract from that of Hobbes. According to the theistic worldview that dominates Sa'di's era, God has created the cosmos and has entrusted human beings with a social nature. The God-created nature of humans calls for collective life, security, and governance. If in response to this call the people enter into a contract that helps them fulfill the above requirements, God will bestow his sanction on them because the contract is rational and accordingly in harmony with the state of nature. Moreover, the omnipotence of God precludes entrusting the king with as much absolute power as Hobbes's Leviathan enjoys (see #2, 3, 35, 151). Within the universe of Sa'di's theistic weltanschauung, the king *and* the subjects must all be God-fearing creatures (see #101).

While *Nasihah al-muluk* contains numerous articles about the king-public relationship, only a few articles address the king-clergyman liaison. Sa'di states that the king must act and speak respectfully in the presence

23. This same logic is also applicable to people whenever they fail to fulfill their part of the contract in obeying a just king. Such conduct disappoints God, the guarantor of the contract. A contract-based interpretation, therefore, sheds new light on the traditional divine dicta about following the king: people should obey the king and please God not because the king is His representative on earth but because they have signed a contract.

24. In *The Revival of Religious Sciences (Ihya' ulum al-din),* Sa'di's intellectual mentor, Abu Hamed Ghazali (1058–1111), states in a jurisprudential decree that the people may at best softly admonish the unjust king and shall never draw swords against him to cause bloodshed (see Ghazali 1982, 2nd quarter, bk. 19).

of religious leaders (#20), exalt and dignify them (#136), and recognize the sovereignty of the jurist's jail as a parallel judicial organ (#41).[25] While the above three articles are still compatible with a secular reading of Sa'di's notion of statecraft, the article that seems most pertinent is article #4: "The ruler must treat religious leaders and clergymen with reverence and offer them a prominent seat, and rule as they deem it advisable so that kingship is in compliance with the shari'a and not vice versa."

The above article is open to a number of different interpretations. One can view it as yet another manipulation by Sa'di to curtail the emergence of absolutist kings. A second interpretation suggests that "compliance with the shari'a" does not necessarily rule out the practicality and desirability of a wide range of secular undertakings, which do not fall under the jurisprudential label of *haram*.[26] In this sense, kingship is not theocratic but still in compliance with the shari'a. Yet a third interpretation is one that calls for the establishment of a theocracy.[27]

The reading of Sa'di presented in this chapter does not present him as a modern thinker with a well-developed political philosophy or a champion of revolutionary politics. Sa'di, living in the thirteenth century, did not develop a systematic political theory of statecraft akin to the yet-to-emerge school of social contract represented by Thomas Hobbes, John Locke, and Jean-Jacques Rousseau. Indeed, the intellectual paradigm of his time could not have found the modern theory of social contract relevant simply because the latter is "modern" in its *philosophically* secular and nonreligious worldview. In other words, Sa'di is not the forefather of the modern school of social contract. And this is entirely appropriate for the time.

Nevertheless, what makes Sa'di's deliberations so intriguing is a sketchy conceptualization of a humane type of politics incorporating

25. The jurist's jail was used to hold civil law offenders while the king's penitentiary incarcerated those guilty of penal offenses. See al-Mawardi 1996.

26. Islamic jurisprudence has a notion of the discretionary sphere of the law *(mintaqah al-firaq)*, which can host the secular and practical reasoning of the State.

27. The same ambiguity is also present in article #77. In light of our interpretation of all the other articles of *Nasihah al-muluk*, we prefer the first and second interpretations when addressing articles #4 and 77.

elements of pragmatism, secular statecraft, and public interest. He views governance as a rational contract between the sovereign and the people without having to reject Deity or embrace theocracy.

Sa'di's *Treatise on Advice to the Kings*

Translated by Alireza Shomali and Mehrzad Boroujerdi

Introduction

Sa'di, a celebrated Persian poet and writer, was born in Shiraz. His poetical nom de plume, Sa'di, was derived from Atabeg Sa'd ibn Abu Bakr ibn Sa'd ibn Zangi.[28] As a young man Sa'di studied Islamic theology and jurisprudence in the prestigious Nizzamiya school in Baghdad. He reportedly traveled extensively through such regions as Anatolia, Arabia, Caucasus, the Fertile Crescent, North Africa, and South Asia. In addition to his worldly excursions *(sayr-i afaq)*, Sa'di also undertook inward sojourns *(sayr-i anfus)* into the realm of the human mind and mysticism. These travels endowed him with a wealth of practical wisdom and deliberation on the economic, political, and social experiences of those with whom he rubbed shoulders. *Bustan* and *Golestan*,[29] which exhibit Sa'di's intellectual maturity in his most eloquent manner, provide the reader with a treasure trove of practical advice concerning morality, politics, and humane living.

Sa'di's *Nasihah al-muluk* (Treatise on advice to the kings) encapsulates his lifetime deliberations on the above themes succinctly and lucidly. Although it is not clear exactly when this treatise was penned, its content demonstrates the maturity of thought that is evident in Sa'di's *Bustan* and

28. Atabeg Sa'd bin Abu Bakr ibn Sa'd ibn Zangi (1223–1260) was one of the sultans of the Salghurid dynasty, who officially ruled for only eighteen days before succumbing to illness. See Musawi Bojnurdi 1994, 495.

29. Sa'di started writing these two books respectively in 1257 and 1258.

Golestan. Rather than directed at any particular ruler, the treatise provides a set of broad moral-political insights and instructions for present and future rulers. These instructions are also consistent with his other shorter advice treatises dedicated to Sultan Ankiyanu (Sa'di 1949, 27–28)[30] and to Sultan Abaqa Khan (Sa'di 1997, 1181–82).

Convinced of the canonical role of *Nasihah al-muluk* in illuminating Sa'di's political philosophy, we have undertaken a full translation of this treatise from Persian into English. In translating this text we relied upon Sa'di's primary text (1997, 1117–37) as our main source. This version is meticulously edited by the erudite scholar and politician Muhammad Ali Furughi (1878–1942), who based it upon more than twelve of the earliest editions dating back to the fourteenth century (see Sa'di 1997, viii–ix).[31] In addition to Furughi's version, we examined four other editions of this treatise and took note of the minor differences between them inasmuch as they could alter the meaning of some of the statements.[32] These differences are highlighted in the footnotes.

Treatise on Advice to the Kings

May all praises be to God who alone and self-sufficiently watches over His creatures. May all thanks be to Him for His grace. I beg for more of His grace and declare that there is no God but He who is known as the absolute and eternal and that Muhammad is His servant and messenger who traversed the heaven.

After paying tribute to the lord of existence and commending the best among Adam's progeny—God's blessing and peace be upon him—we begin

30. The Mughal-era governor of Fars province from 1268 to 1272.

31. Furughi confirms both the authenticity of *Nasihah al-muluk* and its conformity with the scroll of wisdom that unfolds in *Golestan* and especially in *Bustan* (Sa'di 1997, 876).

32. See citations under Sa'di in the Works Cited section of this book. In addition, we also consulted Sa'di 1906 to find equivalent terms for a few Persian expressions.

to offer advice to statesmen, responding to a dear friend who requested a lucid treatise on this subject. I wrote to this friend—may the noble moments of his life be sustained by God's grace and sanctioned by serving the Almighty Lord—that God in the Holy Book states, "[God orders you] when ruling over and judging among the people, to do it justly," and on another occasion, "God orders you [the people] to act toward others based on justice and grace." God Almighty phrased it succinctly, and yet the elaboration of God's words exceeds books. However, within the capacity of our intellect, we shall offer a few words on justice and grace, and we trust God in this task because our success is in His hands.

1- Kings who attend to their subjects are, in fact, guardians of their own state and status because the kings' justice, grace, and fairness result in security and harmony among his subjects, breed civil prosperity, and boost productivity. Consequently, the excellent repute of the king and of his subjects' comfort—together with news about the security and affordability of major staples within the territory—travels around the world. The travelers and traders, therefore, will be encouraged to trade fabrics, grains, and other goods. The State and the country will subsequently thrive. The State coffers will be filled; soldiers and State servants will prosper; worldly goods will abound, and [hence] otherworldly salvation will be obtained. The king who follows the path of injustice forfeits all these achievements at once.

The unjust departed and left their wicked customs behind
The just departed and left their good name as a memorial.[33]

2- One of the chief qualities of the kings should be that, in their nightly solitude, they beg at the Almighty's doorsill, while during the day,

33. In Sa'di 1876, 27, the poem reads instead,

Look at the mistake [or the mischief] of the unjust
The world [that he conquered] survives, yet he departed carrying but the burden of his ill-repute.

they resume their statesmanship. It is said that Sultan Mahmud-i Sabuktakin[34]—may God's blessing be upon him—removed his attire every sunset and assumed the garb of the dervish and humbly prostrated to God, crying, "O Almighty Lord! authority and State are truly yours, and I am your servant. Authority has not come to me by my might and sword; you blessed me with this kingdom, and I pray that you empower me and assist me since you are the compassionate." Umar ibn Abd al-Aziz[35]—may God's blessing be upon him—also prayed to God each dawn, while praising God's grace and requesting from Him his subjects' security and harmony. He would say, "O Almighty Lord! you have entrusted this weak servant with an arduous task that exceeds his capacity. Pray, assist me to be just, gracious, and fair; and save me from treating people unjustly; pray, relieve me from the vice of people and relieve people from my vice. Pray, do not let my behavior injure a heart or let an indignant heart curse me."

3- The king must continuously contemplate God's omnipotence and permanence [as opposed to man's ephemeral power]; be cautious about the sport of fortune; and, finally, ponder the frequent transition of power from one group to another, lest [the king] deceive himself by the fleeting moments of his worldly sojourn or take solace in his short-lived status.

One of the caliphs requested advice from Bohlul.[36] The latter replied, "Thou canst bear nothing with thee from this world to the next, save a recompense or a punishment, and the choice rests with thee."[37]

34. Sultan Mahmud Ghaznavi (971–1030) was the most prominent ruler of the Ghaznavid dynasty, who ruled from 998 to 1030 and died in Ghazni, in today's Afghanistan.

35. Umar ibn Abd al-Aziz (ca. 682–720) was an Umayyad caliph who ruled from 717 to 720 and died in Halab, in today's Syria.

36. Abu Wahib Bohlul ibn Amr al-Seyrafi al-Kufi (died ca. 806), also known as Bohlul the Majnun, was a wise man pretending to be mad. He is famous for his clever remarks.

37. Translation taken from Sa'di 1906, 19–20.

4- The ruler must treat religious leaders and clergymen with reverence, offer them a prominent seat, and rule as they deem it advisable so that kingship is in compliance with the shari'a and not vice versa.
5- Among the most important tasks of the State is the construction of mosques, houses of dervishes, bridges, water reservoirs, and roadside wells.
6- Cater to the needs of God-fearing people and consider your service as an opportunity, for the prayers of the pious assist government and nourish the State. The sages have advised that durability of the State and the augmentation of its power depend on the king's attendance to the destitute and assistance to the desolate.
7- An astute king should keenly probe the disposition and temperament of his companions and subsequently win them over in proportion to their merit, and not as to what the greedy expect. Otherwise, the State's reserves dwindle before the thirst of those fallen into greed's snare is quenched. Self-respecting souls would never engage in self-promotion or send an advocate to negotiate on their behalf. Therefore, those who truly deserve the king's esteem will receive it without having to demean themselves by uttering their needs. Consequently, the dignified will not solicit, and the greedy will not submit to avarice.

> If a man possesses a worthy art,
> It is that worthy art, and not his utterance, which reveals itself.

8- The king should provide for the aged servants of the State and not expect further service from them since their dawn prayer exceeds their daytime service in value.
9- To ensure that his own achievements live on posthumously, a newly minted ruler should not demolish the worthy relics of past kings.
10- The associate of the court must be wise, handsome, pious, of noble birth and good name, propitious, experienced, and competent so that his conduct is nothing but praiseworthy.
11- A minister worthy of the designation is concerned first and foremost with the king's salvation and not with his property. He should consider

the king's maltreatment of his subjects as a more severe problem than the king's being wronged by his subjects.

12- The king should incessantly attend to the weak and aged, to widows, orphans, the needy, and strangers. As advised by the sages, the king who does not care for his subjects is not worthy of the name of master, and his mastery will not last.

13- The king is the father of the orphan. He should care for the orphan better than his own biological parents so that one can clearly see the difference between having a poor father and having the king for a father.

It is reported that someone left behind a child and a bag of gold. The ruler sent an envoy to the guardian to confiscate the gold. The guardian placed the gold next to the child and took them to the ruler's court. "This gold is not mine," said the guardian, "as it belongs to this orphan. If you are taking it away, take it from him so that you know to whom it should be returned on the Day of Judgment." The ruler was in tears, and kissing the eyes of the orphan, said, "How can I defend myself against the charges of this orphan on the Day of Judgment?" The ruler handed over the bag of gold to the guardian and provided for the livelihood of the orphan until he reached adolescence.

14- The openly corrupt must not be embraced or appeased by the ruler because the companion of the criminal is a criminal too and deserves punishment.

15- Generosity when your expenses exceed revenue is blameworthy; squandering and stinginess are equally culpable. Find the path in between.

16- Benevolence and noblesse oblige have limits; too much clemency may empower the wicked and kindle their avarice. Earning a reputation for magnanimity does not imply tolerating the transgressors' injustice. The wise do not find such tolerance virtuous, only fatuous.

17- Generosity is praiseworthy as long as it does not weaken state power or cause it harm. Reducing state expenditures is prudent as long as the soldiers and state servants do not suffer financially.

18- The king's manifest wrath and obduracy are effective as long as they do not plant the seeds of hatred in people's hearts. His jubilance and jesting are permissible as long as they do not suggest that the king's behavior is frivolous.
19- Piety and abstinence are commendable so long as they do not hamper life for the sovereign and his associates. Relaxation and joy are acceptable so long as such practices do not distract the king from attending to his religious obligations or upholding the interests of the citizenry.
20- The king should observe prayer times and, out of respect, refrain from drinking or other indecent acts during such times. [Similarly], in the presence of the pious and religious leaders, he should speak and act in accord with their view.
21- The king must immerse himself in the history of former kings so that he may imitate their noble practices, ponder the vicissitudes of their times, and not be deceived by status, prestige, and power.
22- The king should not always preoccupy himself with entertainers, chess and backgammon players, performers, poets, storytellers, magicians, and the like. Although entertainment is occasionally permissible to lift the king's spirits, excessive leisure can have its toll on the king's judgment. It is reported that Shibli—may God's blessing be upon him—entered the court and saw the king and his vizier playing chess.[38] "Bravo," Shibli remarked sarcastically, "you are placed here to act [seriously] and righteously. Instead you are playing chess?"
23- The administration of the State is a tremendous responsibility. It requires vigilance and prudence and, also, continuous prayer to God so that what happens by the king's will, tongue, hands, and pen will be productive to the dominion and to religion and [thus] accord with God's consent.

38. Abu Bakr Shibli (861–946) was a renowned pious and Sufi master. Of Persian background, he was born in Samarra (present-day Iraq), became a governor of the Damavand region in Persia, and later left office to follow the path of asceticism.

24- Do not entrust the novice and the untested with crucial tasks if you do not wish to regret your decision later.

25- Do not enlist those branded as impious among your companions because their vicious temper can spoil your soul. Even if it doesn't, such companionship encourages people to reproach you, and it takes away your justification to penalize those who choose to have wicked companions.

26- Do not listen to the accusation of treason from a claimant whose piety you have not ascertained. Nor issue a verdict unless you have carefully established the nature and magnitude of the alleged treason.

27- Do not allow your friends to intercede in matters pertaining to the execution of murderers and the dismemberment of thieves.

28- There are two types of thieves: those with bows and arrows in deserts and those with scale and standard in bazaars. It is imperative to vanquish them both.

29- King Anushirvan the Just,[39] who was reputed to be irreligious, is said to have been seen in a dream residing happily in a paradise-like garden. "How and on what basis have you received this status?" the dreamer asked Anushirvan. The king responded that he was never kind to the criminal or a tormentor of the innocent.

30- When an idea that sounds beneficial to the country percolates in the king's mind, he should not rush to action. Rather, the king must first ponder it and then consult about it, and only then, if his intellect deems it reasonable, should he enact it with trust in God and in His name. [As the Qur'anic verse goes], "when you resolve to do it, then trust God [and enact your will]."

31- The king should expect contemplation and foresight from the sagacious elder as he would expect nothing but ill-considered demands for war from the imprudent youngster.

32- Respond positively to a wronged subject's plea for justice so that transgressors are not encouraged. As the saying goes, the sultan who does not vanquish the thieves is, in reality, the thief of the caravan.

39. See footnote 3.

33- The king's joy [of power] and ambition [for authority] are halal only if he manages to protect his people against the wicked, like a shepherd who effectively shields the sheep against wolves. If the shepherd was unable to guard the flock and, consequently, did not save the sheep from harm, the wage he had received would be haram. Now consider how much more illegitimate his wages would become had the shepherd been indeed capable of protecting the flock but did not rescue them from harm!

The sage Zunnun al-Misri complained to a king that an agent he had dispatched to a certain province acts unjustly toward the subjects and illegally appropriates their property.[40] The king said that he would punish the agent someday. "Yes," the sage replied, "you will punish your agent when he has already appropriated all of the subjects' possessions, and then through torture and confiscation, you will expropriate these possessions and add them to your own treasury. Tell me, what benefit would the poor subjects receive from such an act?" The king was embarrassed and put an end to the abuses of the agent at once.

The shepherd shall behead the wolf at the outset
Not when the beast has already torn apart the people's sheep.

34- The king's punishment of the debauched and the corrupt is praiseworthy only if he inwardly resists the impulse to commit the same mischief.

It is reported that a king ordered the destruction of a wine cellar and the same night ordered his servants to crush the grapes in one of his gardens. The news reached a connoisseur who observed, "O you! who forbid the vice, follow your own bid."

35- It is unbecoming a king to express unjustified wrath. When rightfully angry, the king should exact fair revenge because, should he exceed

40. Zunnun al-Misri (796–859) was an Egyptian Sufi sage and a follower of Gnosticism.

what is prudent, the king would become the offender—and the punished person the claimant.

36- Follow the path of beneficence in treating your friends and foes alike. Favors bestowed on friends augment sympathy and when transferred to enemies will diminish hatred and hostility.

37- The State coffer should be kept filled at all times. Refrain from [a torrent of] improper expenditures, and keep in mind that unforeseen incidents do occur and that enemies are always ready to take advantage of your vulnerabilities.

38- Never feel impervious to conspiracy and disloyalty. Meditate upon your affairs in order to undercut the sinister plots of the envious.

39- The king should investigate his lieutenants' servants and associates. He must know their names and scrutinize their lineage so as to acquire meticulous and reliable information about them all, lest the enemy manage to infiltrate spies and assassins into the court.

40- The king shall appoint undercover informants to every high-ranking State official so that he may discover each official's vice and virtue and detect potential conspiracies.

41- The king should command the chief of police to review the prisoners' files every other month or so, release the innocent, and pardon those guilty of petty crimes who have served a few days of incarceration. The chief of police will also ensure that the same procedure is followed in the jurists' prison.

42- If the borrower is incapable of repayment and the lender's livelihood does not depend on timely repayment, command them both to be patient and work out an installment plan. If both sides are desperate and the state coffers are full, consider paying the loan out of the State's funds. On the surface, it appears that soldiers and financial wealth protect the State while, in reality, it is the prayers of the disenfranchised.

43- One of the most crucial obligations of the ruler is to provide for those [merchants] whose caravan has been raided, whose ship has sunk, and whose wealth has suffered, no matter how large or small their loss may be.

44- The contractors who work on court properties [such as farmers and gardeners] and whose income does not rise to the level of profit promised to the court should not be pressured for payment. Rather, the king may compromise in closing the case and indeed offer them a more lucrative contract the next time around.

45- The king should pay tribute to the erudite and the artisan so that those deficient in such qualities feel inspired and will patronize art and science. Consequently, learning will spread and boost the glory of the country.

46- The king may reappoint an employee with a positive record of service who has been dismissed due to some shortcoming and who has already been punished by eviction from the court. Providing occupation for the unemployed is as worthy as releasing innocent prisoners.

47- The king may call to service those who have suffered hardship. Such people will sincerely and tirelessly serve the State, lest their destitution recur.

48- Attend to the welfare of the soldiers and win over their hearts through your affability expressed in different ways. Since all your enemies are united in their enmity toward you, your friends should not be divided in their friendship.

49- The soldier who runs away from the enemy in the battlefield should be executed since he has already received his blood money from the king in advance. The bread [livelihood] that the king gives the soldier is the latter's blood money; hence, if the soldier absconds with it, the king has the right to demand his blood.

50- Remove the unjust official from office and entrust him with no more responsibility, for the complaints and curses of those who have been wronged do not extend to such an official alone. And you know what I mean by being accursed!

51- One of the responsibilities of a newly crowned heir is to value his predecessor's friends and companions and provide for them.

52- The kings owe their throne to their subjects. Sovereigns become enemy of their own throne once they ill-treat people.

53- Kings are to subjects as heads are to bodies. Only a truly stupid head would tear apart its body with its teeth.

54- A secret that should not reach the public should not be communicated to even your closest associates. For, close associates have close associates ad infinitum.

55- Do not reveal everything about yourself to your friends because friends can turn into enemies.

56- Do not ignore the agonizing accounts and distressing appeals from the poverty-stricken. Address them tenderly and listen to them sympathetically.

57- A ruler should carry the burden of his subjects so that their interests are preserved. Inquire about their aspirations and needs and gratify the desires of your subjects as you deem it conducive to their interest. A quick-tempered and morose ruler does not deserve a leadership position.

A ruler endowed with authority, wisdom, and glory
Should not be made impatient by the crowd's clamor.

Once a plaintiff petitioned Hajjaj ibn Yusuf and was ignored by him.[41] The frustrated man walked out muttering that Hajjaj is more arrogant than the Almighty. Hajjaj heard the grumbling and asked the plaintiff to explain why. "Because," the man replied, "the Almighty conversed with Moses and you cannot make yourself talk to one of God's creatures." Hajjaj accepted the comment and treated the man fairly.

58- If someone accuses another without proof, the ruler should hand over the claimant to the accused so that the latter may take full vengeance on the former. Let the accuser's ill-fate be a lesson to others.

59- Relocate or assign a state clerk periodically to a new office so that if he has embezzled, his fraud will be discovered.

60- The sultan should reward those who bring him gifts, offerings, and young servants, and he should reciprocate with gifts in kind—and do so promptly.

61- Before strangers, the king must appear majestic and display severity. Yet, in private and in the midst of intimate companions, the same king is advised to appear cheerful, amicable, and blithesome.

41. Hajjaj ibn Yusuf al-Thaqafi (661–714) was reportedly a cruel governor of Iraq during the Umayyad dynasty.

62- Appoint two agents who are not friendly toward each other as partners in the same office so that they will not conspire.

While the wolves attack one another
The sheep stays safe and secure.

63- A wise king[42] shall not torment his subjects because he will forfeit their support vis-à-vis his domestic rivals in the midst of an attack by his foreign enemies.
64- Command the border guards not to plunder the residents of the adjacent territory so that the country is safe within and without.
65- If, because of gross misconduct, the tenure of a State servant must be terminated, [the king] should not further abolish the servant's entitlements that are warranted by his previous services.
66- Considering the lineage and dignity of a [public] servant's ancestors, the king is justified in pardoning the servant's multiple transgressions and flaws.
67- When issuing a death warrant for a felonious public servant, the king must provide for the criminal's wife and children so that they will not be left without livelihood.
68- The king should unreservedly provide for the spouse and children of his soldiers who died on the battlefield.
69- As much as possible be modest and friendly toward foreigners and acquaintances, strangers and citizens alike, so that you may endear yourself to them. Friendship will not harm your rule [and helps you apprehend how the subjects really think].
70- When the king decides to forgive a wrongdoer, he should delicately reveal hints of grace so that the astute nobleman comprehends the king's true wish and intercedes. Having considered the mediator's pledge, the subject's penitence, and the overall merit of the case, the king may pardon the subject.

42. In Sa'di 1876, 28, the word used is *farehmand* [charismatic] rather than *khiradmand* [wise], which better indicates Sa'di's emphasis on mass consent as a pillar of the king's charisma.

71- When a man of high status is imprisoned, the king should hold the detainee in esteem and provide him with the clothing, food, drink, spouse, servants, and other necessities of life commensurate with his status. Such is expected from the principle of magnanimity.[43] And remember your life is but two days; one auspicious and the other ominous [lest you experience misery in your second day].

72- A wise king does not provoke a mighty foe, nor will he perpetrate injustice toward a weak enemy. It is not prudent to clash with a greater power, nor is it virtuous to harass the weak.

73- Breaking the heart of your friends is tantamount to fulfilling the wishes of your enemy.

74- Blatant injustice is when the king refuses to punish a courtier for his transgressions yet beheads a layman for the very same offense.[44]

75- A just ruler/judge is like a fortified wall; if it leans toward one side [of a quarrel], know that the wall is failing.

76- Exhort your close associates to be virtuous before reprimanding others. Your most intimate associate is your own self. Your words do not have an effect on others if your deeds belie your words.

> Have you contemplated how to preserve the State?
> By you controlling your Self and following God's commands.

77- He whose inner self does not abide by the commands of shari'a is not worthy of leadership and his State will not endure.

78- Forbearance and not acting hastily are commendable at all times except on those occasions when delay can cause irreversible damage, such as rescuing people from fire or drowning.

79- Religion without knowledge and governance without moderation will fade away.

43. This sentence is added in Sa'di 1876, 29.

44. Sa'di 1876, 29, reads, "Blatant injustice in the eyes of a layman occurs when the king beheads a subject arbitrarily whereas in the eyes of the courtiers the king's ignorance of them constitutes blatant ignorance."

80- Avoid sin as much as possible and if—God forbid!—you succumb to iniquity, pay alms to the destitute so that God may forgive you.
81- Pardon a condemned person whose release will be met with grateful prayers by all rather than the sole prayer of the offender.
82- Tomorrow, on the Day of Judgment, all will be fearful except those who fear God today and haven't caused harm to people.

It is reported that the Caliph Harun al-Rashid[45]—may God bless his soul—used to invoke this prayer: "O Lord! don't let any day that I have committed a sin come to an end without me asking for forgiveness from you and sending alms to the needy." His wife, Zubaydah,[46] would constantly pray to God and ask him to forgive and conceal her flaws.

A righteous official of Alexander the Great engaged in an argument with the latter. Alexander asked him, "Are you not afraid of me?"

"Why should I be afraid?" responded the official. "One who does right won't fear God because you fear either your own mischief or your Lord's injustice, and my mind is at ease about both."

A king confided to a pious man his deep angst about his destiny on the Day of Judgment. The man advised, "Be fearful of God Almighty today, and don't fear tomorrow."

It is reported that a caliph dismissed an official because of embezzling only one dinar. After a few days some noblemen pleaded with the caliph not to deprive the official of service because of such a meager misappropriation. The caliph responded that what is at stake is not the amount but the fact that an officer who dares to steal money dares to shed the subjects' blood with no remorse.

83- Do not feel secure before the one whose mind is not at peace with you; the snake attacks when fearing for his life. It is unwise to excavate the

45. Harun al-Rashid (763–809) was the fifth Abbasid caliph, who ruled from 786 to 809.

46. Zubaydah bint Ja'far (d. 832) was a descendent of the Abbasid caliph al-Mansur and married Harun al-Rashid in 781.

base of a wall and still sit in its shadow, or to kill the baby snake and leave its parents alive.

84- Avoid the one who gives accounts of others' misdeeds in their absence. Such a person will flatter you in your presence and reveal your defects behind your back.[47]

85- The saying "the statements of kings are the king of statements" should not be trusted. Speak judiciously, reflectively, and meaningfully so that if your statement is recited in your absence, the taunter cannot scoff at it. Make utterances that, if voiced by others, you too would find appropriate.

86- A dervish of inward repose looks down at the king's wealth and power. However, a king of meager soul covets his subjects' property.

It is not virtuous to torment the weak
The wicked bird robs the ant of its grain.

It is reported that a merchant had a chest full of jewelry for sale. The sultan dispatched an envoy and asked the merchant to bring his merchandise to the court whereupon he demanded the goods at a cheap price. The merchant responded, "I have been away from my abode for more than a year and upon my departure my spouse pleaded that I transact only with one who is fearful of God, faithful, and trustworthy." The sultan was receptive to his point and told the merchant to leave. "I will buy these jewels only when I see myself in possession of these three virtues," the sultan vowed.

87- It is considered a weakness for the king if he downplays the potential danger of his weak enemy or grants his friends so much latitude that, if tempted to harm the king, they prove capable.[48]

47. Sa'di 1876, 30, reads, "Do not feel safe from, do not socialize, and do not consult with whoever speaks ill of others in their absence. Whoever mentions others' fault to you will no doubt reveal your fault to others."

48. Sa'di 1876, 30, reads, "It is wise for the king not to unnecessarily preoccupy himself with his weak enemy or to grant his friends so much latitude that if tempted to harm the king, they prove capable."

88- Prudence demands that you reap profits tomorrow by planting seeds today and not postpone today's tasks to tomorrow.[49]

89- A master has the right to demand obedience and service from his servants. However, a virtuous master is appreciative of his subjects' obedience and service and does not hold them in servitude.[50]

An unjust king asked a pious man what is the fate of kings on the Day of Judgment. The pious man responded, "A just sultan who is fair, who does not mistreat his subjects, and who does not desire the riches of his wealthy subjects is king of both realms."

The just king is the king of both realms
Otherwise, he is but a beggar in both worlds.

90- So long as the enemy's harm can be forestalled by gold, war is not recommended because blood is nobler than gold. As the Arabic proverb goes, "Sword is the last resort," that is, war is justified only when all other options are exhausted. Turning one's back [in flight] on the enemy is better than fighting the enemy without a sword.

91- A true aficionado of the king discloses the king's defects to his face—so that rectification may follow his master's dismay—and conceals the king's defects in his absence so as to preserve the sovereign's reputation.

92- The dignity of the wealthy and those of rank emanates from the fact that they may use their affluence to serve the people. Acting to the contrary divests them of their dignity.

93- The king and the army exist for the protection of the public so that the strong may not wrong the weak. Hence, if the king failed to prevent

49. Sa'di 1876, 30, reads, "Prudence demands that you neither spend tomorrow's income today nor postpone today's tasks to tomorrow."

50. Another possible translation of this advice reads, "A master has the right to demand obedience and service from his underlings. However, a virtuous master is one who appreciates the opportunity of serving his subjects and does not hold them in servitude."

such a transgression or he himself transgressed, such a king would then be useless. Consequently, his reign would necessarily decline.

94- Each and every blessing calls for its corresponding type of appreciation. The gratitude for wealth is benefaction; for kingship, it is service to the people; for being an elite, it is advocating the public's interest; for bliss, it is compassion for the wretched; and for power, it is assisting the powerless.

95- Under a king totally preoccupied with securing his self-interest, the public interest is not realized. Accordingly, the interest of all parties including the king will perish.

96- The king's emissary must consider God's consent over the king's command so as to truly benefit from his vicinity to him/Him.

97- Virtue demands that, when receiving a favor, the recipient acknowledge the right of the benefactor to be praised and also recognize his duty-bound obligation to reciprocate the favor. Kings owe their State and status to their subjects because without a people there would be no governance. Therefore, it is utterly unvirtuous if a king does not acknowledge the rights of his subjects and his resulting obligation to provide for their well-being.

98- Whoever sets a bad precedent inadvertently brings about his own destruction.

99- The [smiting] swords of the enemy battalion are less perilous to the king than the anguished sighs of children and the cries of the aged.

100- The king should not belittle the moans of the destitute when a single blaze may burst the whole city into flames.

101- Considering that a State official can always betray the king's trust without the king realizing the treachery, the State official's heartfelt fear of the almighty God is a necessity [for the well-being of the State and society].

102- To chastise the wicked briefly and then to set him free is tantamount to capturing a wolf and releasing it upon the beast's oath!

103- The king who makes trouble for the merchants closes the door of prosperity and prominence on his own city and territory.

104- As a general principle, do not trust the neophyte.

105- If wickedness is discovered in a man, the king should execute, and not exile, him; it is unwise to capture a snake or scorpion and toss it into the neighbor's house.

106- Entrust with a mission those who are equipped with power, wealth, and the wherewithal. Otherwise, you will not see any real progress, only empty promises.

107- Graciousness demands that the sovereign pardon a misdemeanor done unintentionally. However, if the transgressor committed the offense intentionally, the ruler should frighten the criminal over his first transgression and execute him if he dares to repeat it. The rotten root does not fruit.

108- Do not hasten to make judgments while angry. It is always possible to put the living to death; however, it is not possible to revive the dead. You are able to smash a precious stone but incapable of restoring it.

109- Virility is not aggressiveness. It is about the ability to hold yourself in check at times of wrath and not violate the parameters of fairness.

110- Leave to the orphans what they have inherited. It is unbecoming of a king to take possession of such assets. It is inauspicious too.

111- Among your possessions it is only your good repute that lasts with you after your departure; poor is he who does not leave a good reputation behind.

112- Wealth, if spent, can turn foes into friends. Yet, if kept, it can turn friends into enemies. Even one's son, if deprived of the father's wealth, may wish his death.

113- A ruler who is unjust and expects his name to be remembered for his goodness is like he who plants barley and expects wheat.

114- Oh, you who desire wealth for the sake of glory adopt the path of magnanimity and modesty because there is no glory higher than being loved and praised by the people.

115- Hunger is nobler than enriching yourself by feasting on the desolate.

If 'Anqa is on the verge of dying from lack of food
She will not feast on sparrows.[51]

51. 'Anqa was a fabled bird.

116- You occupy the throne of those who came before you and of those who are yet to come. Such short-lived existence between two nonexistents is not worth much.

117- Virility is not conquering new lands but properly administrating your own territory. The wise take over the world and administrate it, and the unwise ruin the world.[52]

118- The king should position himself such that he can directly hear the pleas of his subjects because courtiers and officers do not always transfer the public's concerns and pleas to him.

It is reported that Anushirvan the Just extended a cord between his bed and the city square so that people could ring the chamber bells and demand the king's attention when they had a concern.

It is reported that an Arab monarch would patrol his city incognito so that he could correct wrongs, and he would also dispatch agents to various villages and neighborhoods for the same purpose.

119- Those from whom people do not receive benefits are all but dead, even if they still breathe. On the other hand, those who do good works may die, but their good name remains.

120- The requisite gratitude for opulence is to support the populace and to refrain from stealing from the poor.

121- Hold sway over others such that if you were one of them, you could tolerate such a reign.

122- The accumulated grievances of the helpless wound more severely than the elbow of champions.

123- The elapse of time makes remorse for missed opportunities futile. Seize every chance to attend to the wronged and pull out the teeth of the unjust.

124- O you who are enjoying your slumber should think of those who are homeless; O you who can move should accommodate the handicapped; O you who are prosperous should assist the needy. Did you

52. The last sentence is taken from Sa'di 1876, 33, and Sa'di 1917, 23.

see what the ancients accomplished and what they took with them? They departed and their injustice against the innocent is now over, but the burden of injustice is on their shoulders. It is better to be a dervish with a clear conscious than a sovereign chastised for injustice.[53]

125- If you are enlightened, you will hear dead bones speak to you: "I was once a human being like you; yet I did not realize the value of my days and threw my life away."

We spend our life negligently
Unlike us, avail yourself of your moments.

126- One who does not torment others fears no soul. The scorpion flees and fears everyone because of its own wicked conduct; the cat is safe within the confines of the house because it is harmless; the wolf is not safe in the desert owing to its bad behavior; the minds of city beggars are at ease because of their decency; and the thieves hide in mountains and deserts because of their roguery.

127- Be cautious against a frail foe who, fearing his life, will resort to the most extreme measures against you. Although weak, the feeble cat wrestling a lion will not shy away from injuring the lion's eyes.

128- The king's confidant should befriend the nobleman and the commoner alike. He should not assume that, being under the king's patronage, no one will defy him. If a wicked person killed the reckless confidant and the vengeful king set the country on fire, this action would not bring the confidant back to life.

129- Behave in such manner that people praise you in absentia, because in your presence they will eulogize you out of fear or avarice.

130- While alive, take every effort to precede others in good deeds, prudence, and generosity; in death, kings and paupers are the same. Open the graves of a king and a dirt farmer, and witness that one cannot differentiate between the two bodies [enveloped in the earth].

53. In translating this sentence we followed Sa'di 1917, 27, which uses the term *malamat* [chastising] instead of *alamat* [sign] in Sa'di 1997, 1134.

131- Happy are those sages who, upon realizing that in death one has to leave the world to others, did so while still alive.

132- The king cannot divide his united enemies without making friends with some among them.

133- Instigate one enemy against another so that, following either one's conquest, you emerge as the true winner.

134- Do not let the enemy grow and emerge out of childhood, and don't let the feeble *piyadeh* [pawn] of chess reach the other side to become *farzin* [queen].

135- Win over hearts during easy times so that they are useful to you in times of hardship.

136- Exalt and dignify the great figures and leaders of all different religions.

137- A king will soon witness the downfall of his country if he spends all in lust and license, neglects the interest of the State, and delegates the important matters of statecraft to various secretaries who in turn privilege their own personal interests over the public's.

138- Do not blame those who highlight your vices because you are the guilty one. Why don't you change your ways so that your virtues are highlighted?

> One who commits injustice can't expect
> People to honor his name.

139- Celebrate your enemy's death on condition that your own death is surely postponed forever!

140- Eat only when the appetite is fully ripe, speak only when necessary, go to bed only when sleepy, and engage in feasting and drinking only when utterly craving.

141- Take seriously the pain that is inflicted upon people's hearts during your watch. United, a community of tiny ants can frustrate the lion, and a swarm of mosquitoes can kill the elephant.

142- Rule in such manner that if dethroned you would neither feel ashamed of your record nor be treated unkindly by the people. Remember that the bee is trampled upon once it is seen as frail and fallen.

143- Be as vigilant against the inner pain and sighs of the wounded and broken-hearted and the curses of the maltreated as you are against poison, conspiracy, betrayal, assassins, and night assaults. The Sultan of Ghazni used to say, "I don't fear the spear of men as much as I fear the spindle of women," that is, the desolation in their hearts.

144- Do not be troubled so much by the [mythical] demons under the earth as by the real demons on earth, that is, vicious men.

145- If you dislike being reprimanded by others, scrutinize and contemplate your actions before undertaking them.

146- Do not inquire about your defects from your friends because they may refuse to point them out. Discover what your enemies say about you instead.

147- In circumstances where tenderness is called for, do not invoke harsh language, because the noose is appropriate for taming only the wild. And where roughness is required, do not resort to using a delicate tone because sweet sugar is no substitute for bitter scammony when only the latter helps the patient.

148- If you are fearful of God, who is your true commander, be nice to whomever you command.[54]

149- Always be seated on your throne as though the enemy is at your doorstep [that is, an attack is imminent] so that if they entered [your domain], you won't be caught off guard.[55]

150- Do not trust anyone unless you have subjected them to multiple tests.

151- If there is a threat that is causing you anxiety, ask God for assistance and victory at night when the people have fallen asleep. Then pay a visit to the pious to seek their prayers and attend to their requests from you. Then visit the holy shrines and request absolution. Show special mercy toward orphans, the weak, the disenfranchised, and

54. The original text can also be interpreted in the following manner: "If you are concerned about your commander's loyalty, try to win over the hearts of his inferiors directly."

55. Sa'di 1949, 24, reads, "Always be seated on your throne as though the enemy is at your doorstep [i.e., an attack is imminent] so that if they entered, you are already standing on guard!"

the needy. Release some prisoners, vow and distribute charity, further oblige the soldiers and promise them more perks. Then take measures to handle the threat through deliberation and consultation with wise and loyal friends. Once you have attained your aim, thank God for his mercy, and do not attribute your success to your own efficiency and power. Finally, fulfill your vows and give thanks so that, when faced with the next threat, the people are desirous and hopeful for your victory.

The king should apply Sa'di's advice truthfully and cordially so that, with the help of God Almighty, his State and faith remain safe, his soul and offspring stay healthy, and his wishes for this world and the next come true. And God knows what is best, and to Him returns everything.

4

Perso-Islamicate Political Ethic in Relation to the Sources of Islamic Law

SAÏD AMIR ARJOMAND

THERE IS AN ALARMING TENDENCY in the conventional wisdom to identify what is "Islamic" in the Persianate, and more generally the Islamicate,[1] culture and civilization by deriving it from Islamic jurisprudence *(fiqh)*. This practice is true for what is usually called Islamic political thought but should more accurately be considered Perso-Islamicate political ethic and public law. For centuries, the readings for moral education in Iran began with *Kalilah wa Demnah* and the *Golestan* of Sa'di, and this continued to be the case after the educational reforms and the establishment of the modern national schools under Reza Shah in the 1920s. Excerpts from these books were accordingly included in literature textbooks for the new high schools, as were selections from the *Four Essays (Chahar maqalah)* of the Seljuq secretary, Nizami Arudi Samarqandi. Anyone who read the fiqh books in Arabic would not have expected to find a section on Islamic government for his or her moral education; even if they had intentionally sought such a section, they would not have found one.

I began my academic career by rejecting a thesis on the allegedly inescapable illegitimacy of the state in Twelver Shi'ism as elaborated by A. K. S. Lambton and Hamid Algar and affirmed by Nikki Keddie (Arjomand

1. I use these terms as conceptualized by Hodgson 1974.

1979). It did not occur to me at the time that some Orientalists also came close to considering all historical and actual states "un-Islamic" and virtually illegitimate in Sunni Islam as well. The Abbasid accusation against the Umayyads that they had degenerated the caliphate into kingship *(mulk)* was implicitly or explicitly taken to have essentialist, transhistorical reality, ignoring not only the ruler's regular titles *(malik, sultan, shah)* but also the lavish overlay of such imperial titles as *padshah, shahanshah, khaqan,* and finally *khalifah.* Only the idealized picture of the caliphate was considered "Islamic" and therefore truly legitimate. The implication of this view is that not only the subjects of the Safavids but also those of the Mughals and the Ottomans—and just about any Muslim government in the preceding half-millennium—considered them illegitimate! Such flight from history and sociology was made possible by the Orientalist privileging of a narrow genre of "Islamic" juristic writing that was completely marginal to the fiqh corpus itself, not to mention the literature on ethics, evident most notably in H. A. R. Gibb's 1955 essay on "constitutional organization," and following him, A. K. S. Lambton (1981). More recently, Patricia Crone (2004a), the erstwhile Orientalist enfant terrible, decided to mark her return to the fold by introducing an element of diversity into Islamic political theory of "God's government." She has done so by extending Gibb's privileged body of texts, which she considers Sunni "constitutional law," by adding "sectarian" doctrines of the imamate as their presumed counterparts, that is, as statements of theories of government. The result has been a completely distorted and ahistorical picture of the political ethic and public law of the Muslim world in this new thesis of the inescapably un-Islamic character of all Muslim governments. The situation is exacerbated by the discovery of the same marginal genre, namely the *al-Ahkam al-sultaniyah* and a small number of works on *al-Siyasah al-shar'iyah*[2] by the contemporary Islamists who consider secular governments illegitimate.[3]

2. This genre developed in certain western Muslim lands but not much in the eastern lands.

3. Aziz Al-Azmeh 1997 has done much to inject a dose of historical reality into the conventional wisdom with his *Muslim Kingship,* but much more remains to be done.

I have tried to show in my own work of the last few years on this subject that the idea and normative principles of monarchy were elaborated on in the literature of ethics and statecraft—called advice literature in Louise Marlow's chapter in the present volume—and they were fully integrated into Islam by the time of the development of the ethicolegal order based on the *shari'a* around the tenth century CE. Of the two normative systems, monarchy and the ethicolegal order, monarchy developed faster by absorbing the Persian political tradition. The idea was firmly established that God had chosen two classes of mankind above the rest, the prophets to guide mankind to salvation and the kings to preserve order *as the prerequisite* for the pursuit of salvation. This idea allowed for the legal pluralism of the Islamic Empire. One could pursue salvation under a just ruler through the Islamic shari'a or the Christian shari'a, or the Jewish shari'a, or those of the Zoroastrians, Sabians, and other honorary "peoples of the Book." I have called this a "theory of the two powers," with deliberately provocative intent (Arjomand 2003). I would readily admit that the institutional framework of Muslim polities did *not* show the same dualism, except much later and only in Iran with the emergence of an independent Shi'ite hierocracy in the late eighteenth century. But this historical condition will not, I think, affect the particular argument I want to make in this chapter. Monarchy as temporal power rested on the fundamental conception of a circle of justice, which predated Islam, and reflected the dependence of the agrarian state on its taxpaying subjects and the corresponding need to deliver justice to them (Darling 2008).

Independent royal dynasties were established in Iran and in Egypt in the latter part of the ninth century. The Shi'ite Buyids, who captured Baghdad in the mid-tenth century, became the first of a series of secular independent rulers to assume the title of sultan and, in Iran, shahanshah. The bifurcation of sovereignty into caliphate and sultanate was a dramatic expression of the autonomy of the political order in the form of monarchy from the caliphate (Bartold 1963). But this autonomy had in fact existed since the last quarter of the ninth century, that is, about the same time as the consolidation of the normative autonomy of the shari'a. In other words, from the tenth century onward, the legal order of the caliphate had two normatively autonomous components: monarchy and the shari'a. I have referred to these as the political order and the shar'i order, respectively. This duality is reflected in the medieval literature on statecraft and kingship as a theory of the two powers: prophecy and kingship. This, I maintain, is the common framework within which geographical variations and inflections occur from India to Morocco.

The absorption of Perso-Indian political ideas is evident in the opening chapter (entitled the "Book of Sovereignty" [sultan]) of *Uyun al-akhbar* by Ibn Qutaybah al-Dinawari (d. 889–90), which reproduces many of the political aphorisms of Ibn al-Muqaffa' and quotes very extensively from the Persian and Indian books on statecraft. Ibn Qutaybah devotes the aforementioned chapter to "the ruler, his *sirah* [manner, way], and his policy *[siyasah]*" (al-Dinawari 1986, 1:53). This is typical of the works on statecraft and customs of the ancient kings, which used the same normative vocabulary as the works of the early jurists, the two key words being *sunna* (custom or tradition) and *sirah*.[4] With the eventual triumph of Muhammad b. Idris al-Shafi'i and his school of law, these terms were exclusively appropriated for the Prophet. But the customs and the traditions of the ancient kings were given a similar normative status by the use of identical vocabulary. The title of "History of the Prophets and the Kings" ("Tarikh al-rusul wa' l-muluk") is attested several times, the most notable instance being the great universal history by Abu Ja'far Muhammad b. Jarir al-Tabari in the early tenth century. Abu Rayhan Biruni (1879, 108) mentions five early books on the Persian kings with the title of *siyar al-muluk*.

The theory of the two powers was a consequence of the reception of the Indo-Persian tradition of statecraft and political ethic. Before long, it was amplified by the selective reception of the Greek political science.[5] In the great synthesis of these traditions as "eternal wisdom" *(javidan*

4. Among the early jurists, Abu Yusuf used *sunna* in the sense of approved tradition and urged the caliph to institute good ones; Ibn Ishaq, Shaybani, and others use *siyar* as normative models. Streusand 2006 shows how Gibb is misreading Abu Yusuf's celebrated work of jurisprudence, *Kitab al-kharaj*, which is in fact fully consistent with mirrors for the princes in statecraft.

5. The most glaring omission in this reception, I have argued, was the neglect of Aristotle's *Politics* (Arjomand 2001).

khirad), Ibn Miskawayh (1952, 179) presented a key maxim of the Persianate political ethic as a tradition of the Prophet:

> The ruler is the shadow of God on earth, with whom the oppressed among his creatures take refuge. If he rules with justice, for him is the reward and, upon the subjects *[ri'aya]*, gratitude. If he is oppressive, for him is the punishment, and upon the subjects, patience.

It is true that Ibn Miskawayh relativized the traditions of the Prophet by including them in "the Arab wisdom," alongside the Persian, the Indian, and the Greek (Ibn Miskawayh 1952, 101–208). But he is exceptional in this respect, and others continued to privilege the words of God and His Prophet over the wisdom of the other nations and, thus, remain in line with their colleagues in Islamic jurisprudence. A key figure in the latter group, which sought to integrate the Greek wisdom into the theory of the two powers, is Abu al-Hasan al-Amiri (d. 991). He diverges from Farabi in differentiating prophecy and kingship, which, incidentally, allowed for a more harmonious reconciliation of Islam and philosophy. In the chapter on "the excellence of Islam in relation to kingship" in his *Virtues of Islam (Kitab al-i'lam bi-manaqib al-Islam)* (1967, 152), al-Amiri backs his statement of the theory of two powers with verse 5:20 of the Qur'an: "Remember the favor [God] bestowed upon you when He made prophets appear among you, and made you kings." He considers prophecy and kingship the two institutions fundamental for the preservation of the world: "There is no authority in learning and wisdom higher than prophecy. There is no higher authority in power and majesty than kingship. . . . It is related from Moses when addressing his people: 'Remember the favor [God] bestowed upon you when He made prophets appear among you, and made you kings'" (Q.5:20).[6]

In this chapter I will examine the role, in the normative hermeneutic of Persianate political ethic, of the two scriptural sources it shares with

6. Al-Amiri goes even further (1967, 119) and tries to reconcile religious jurisprudence and statecraft based on political science in view of the overlap between the religious and the political spheres.

Islamic law, namely the Qur'an and the hadith. My evidence will be drawn from two sources of medieval Persianate political ethic and public law: (1) books on ethics and statecraft written for the education of the princes and officials of their chanceries, and (2) actual and model royal decrees collected for the education and training of the bureaucratic class of secretaries and administrators. I think the model and actual decrees of the royal chanceries presented in the *insha'* literature of the twelfth and early thirteenth centuries are valuable additions to the works on statecraft and ethics.[7] My main focus will therefore be on this literature in order to rectify the current misconceptions and paint a more accurate picture of the medieval Persianate political ethic and public law. But let me first turn to the literature on ethics and statecraft and examine Persian texts on the subject from the Seljuq and Il-Khanid period, the formative period of Persianate Islam.

Literature on Political Ethic and Statecraft

I have argued that the Indian concept of punishment *(danda)* was transmitted through Persian translations and became central to the Muslim conception of government, so much so that the same term *siyasah* came to mean "policy" as well as "punishment." This transmission is evident in the collections of tales on statecraft from the mid-twelfth and early thirteenth centuries, which I have cited elsewhere (Arjomand 2001), the most important being the translation of the above-mentioned *Kalilah wa Demnah.* In an elaborate preface on the theory of government to his amplified translation of this work, Nasr Allah Munshi (the scribe), an official of the late Qaznavid state, typically integrates the idea of punishment into the theory of kingship based on justice as a commentary on Qur'an 57:25: "Indeed, we sent our Messengers with clear signs, and We sent down with them the Book and the Balance so that men might uphold justice. And we sent down

7. The historical as distinct from pedagogical value of this literature has been highlighted by a number of scholars (Roemer 1971 and Paul 1995) but does not concern us here.

iron, wherein is great might, and many uses for men." He affirms that the book, the scale, and the sword are brought into unity through the function of kingship because "the explanation of the laws *[sharayi']* is through the book, the passing of the gates of justice and equity through the scale, and the inspection and enforcement of the above through the sword. As it is established that the interests of religion are not observed without the majesty of the kings, and the putting out of the fire of rebellion is impossible without the dripping sword, the incumbency of obedience to the kings . . . becomes evident" (Nasr Allah Munshi 1998, 20). Nasr Allah Munshi follows this affirmation with the central maxim of Persian statecraft, which was also represented as "the circle of justice" and is attributed to the founder of the Sassanian Empire, Ardashir: "there is no kingdom except through men, and no men except through wealth, and no wealth except through cultivation *[imara]*, and no cultivation except through justice and punishment *[siyasah]*." Munshi explains that wealth is the means for conquering the world, and justice and punishment are the elixir of wealth. Peace and security of roads and the preservation of the realm depend on punishment, hence, the priority of justice and punishment in the ethic of the kings (1998, 21). This is followed by another maxim, "religion and kingship are twin-born." Once again, Munshi is careful to offer a synthesis of Islam and statecraft with a number of citations from the Qur'an, including "the authority verse" 4:59, and from the Traditions of the Prophet to prove that "the kings of Islam are the shadow of the Creator" (1998, 21).

In *Makarim-i akhlaq,* a book on ethics from the second half of the twelfth century, Razi al-Din Muhammad Nishaburi (d. 1201–2) alternates between the Qur'anic verses with their traditions of the Prophet and the Persian and Greek wisdom and the tradition of kings in their normative hermeneutics. His key chapter "On Justice and Its Opposite" (Nishaburi 1962, 125) begins with three Qur'anic verses, interspersed with two traditions of the Prophet: "I was born in the age of the just king, Anushirvan" and "Kingdom will remain with infidelity but not with tyranny!" A somewhat unusual feature of this work is the inclusion of the early Turkish figures among the exemplary kings. In fact, "the circle of justice" maxim is put in the mouth of a queen of Turkistan visiting the last Umayyad governor of Khurasan, Nasr b. Sayyar (Nishaburi 1962, 126), and an interesting implicit social contract is attributed to Afrasiyab: "I have not written this covenant explicitly, but whoever undertakes the covenant of kingship *[bay'at-i padshahi]* . . . has made a covenant to obliterate injustice *[jawr]*" (Nishaburi 1962, 73).

In the second quarter of the thirteenth century, Nasir al-Din Tusi was much more systematic in ranking the scriptural and wisdom sources as the fundamentals of ethics. His *Akhlaq-i Muhtashami* is a collection of Qur'anic verses, traditions, and maxims from the wisdom literature arranged in order of priority in each of the forty topical chapters and translated into simple Persian. Some revealed verses are also integrated into the maxims of wisdom. An interesting example (Tusi 1960, 141) is Qur'an 57:25, and it is cited in exactly the same context as in the preface to Nasr Allah Munshi's *Kalilah wa Demnah:* "The foundations of justice and policy *[siyasah]* are three: The law *[namus]*, the ruler and the scale; or in other words, the pen and the book, the sword, and the scale. The divine book has confirmed this in His words, 'Indeed, we sent our Messengers with clear signs, and We sent down with them the Book and the Balance so that men might uphold justice. And we sent down iron, wherein is great might and many uses for men'" (Q.57:25).

The "shadow of God" tradition is cited (Tusi 1960, 137) exactly as in Ibn Miskawayh, from whom a number of other traditions attributed to the Prophet were taken, with a variant cited as a maxim of the wisdom literature (Tusi 1960, 23). These variants are supplemented by the response of a Greek sage to Alexander: "When the subjects obey their king and the king exercises punishment/policy and justice, the kingdom will indeed stand firm and kingship be rectified" (1960, 400). None of these traditions and maxims, as is well known, allows the right to rebellion if the ruler deviates from justice and is tyrannical. "Oppression *[zulm]* is the darkness of the Day of Judgment; [and] there is no appeal from prayer of the oppressed" (1960, 136). Dire punishment may await the oppressive ruler in the other world, but in this world patience and prayer are the subjects' only remedy. The *Akhlaq-i Muhtashami* is also very interesting for demonstrating, as does the reception of Tusi's greater classic *Akhlaq-i Nasiri,* that there is absolutely no sectarian difference between the Shi'ite and the Sunni conceptions of statecraft and political ethic. The normative hermeneutic is identical in both cases. As an Isma'ili, Tusi simply extends the tradition of the Prophet with those of Alid imams and, at the lower level of normativity, with the wisdom of the Greeks and the Persians to include a few directives from the Fatimid caliphs and Isma'ili missionaries.

The absence of sectarian difference is evident if we take a Sunni book on ethics from the late-Timurid period, which was similarly presented as a hadith collection and commentary, with frequent backing by Qur'anic verses. The chapter on monarchy begins with Qur'an 16:90 as the backing for the shadow of God hadith, with the word *just* added to the ruler, making *"al-sultan al-adil"* the shadow of God, which is followed by another famous hadith, "an hour of justice is better than sixty years of worship." The author then moves on to other hadiths and then to political maxims, citing, among other things, Anushirvan's testament to his son as versified by Sa'di, including the maxim "the subjects are the root and the ruler the tree" (Kashifi Bayhaqi 1965, 240).

The author of a book on the vizierate to be discussed later tells us that he fled from strife and calamity in his beloved Isfahan to Fars, "the abode of justice *[adlabad]*" (Isfahani 1985, 22). He arrived there early in the long reign of Atabeg Sa'd ibn Zangi, a half-century or more before Sa'di dedicated *Golestan* to the same ruler (1258), a book on ethics that begins with the chapter "On the Tradition of Kings" *(dar sirat-i padshahan)* and aims, among other things, to "increase the eloquence of the secretaries *[mutarassailan]*." The Mongol devastation had intervened, making the prosperity and political stability of Fars and the just rule of Atabeg Sa'd even more exceptional. Sa'di typically calls his royal patron "the king of Islam" and praises him as "the lieutenant of Solomon's kingdom and the helper of the people of Iran, the great shahanshah and the magnificent Atabeg, Abu Bakr Sa'd ibn Zangi," through whose justice God will protect the blessed territory of Shiraz until the end of time:

> The land of Pars will fear no earthly injury
> So long as upon its head is such shadow of God as thee.

Like earlier and less distinguished books on ethics, such as *Makarim-i akhlaq*, Sa'di's normative hermeneutics combines the Qur'anic verses and the traditions of the Prophet eclectically with the Persian and Greek wisdom and the tradition of kings, albeit with his distinctive and exceptional genius for highlighting the paradoxes and moral ambiguities in statecraft and political ethic.

Some of the most important works in the Persian literature on political ethic and statecraft, including Munshi's *Kalilah wa Demnah* and the *Jawami' al-hikayat* of Sadid al-Din Muhammad Awfi, were produced at the courts of the later Ghaznavids and the Ghurids who succeeded them. This Perso-Islamicate political thought and ethic was disseminated by the sultans of Delhi in India in the thirteenth century. A key work in this transmission, the *Adab al-harb wa al-shuja'ah* of Muhammad ibn Mansur Mubarakshah, written in the early decades of the thirteenth century in Lahore and dedicated to Sultan Iltutmesh of Delhi (d. 1235–36), merits special attention.

Mubarakshah's preface contains a half-dozen Qur'anic verses and as many traditions of the Prophet, including Qur'an 57:25 on the book, the sword, and the scale (Mubarakshah 1967), which is reinforced later by a hadith to reemphasize the link between justice and punishment (Mubarakshah 1967, 15). But the tradition of the mythical Persian kings is also fundamentally normative and is reported especially to highlight the link between justice and economic/urban development (Mubarakshah 1967, 6–7, 12) and the institution of the social hierarchy (by Jamshid) (Mubarakshah 1967, 7–8). The "circle of justice" maxim is also duly attributed to Ardashir (Mubarakshah 1967, 120). The most important chapters on political ethic begin with a scriptural citation, preferably a revealed verse.

The distinctive feature of this work, however, is the integration of military organization and its normative regulation into statecraft: "As the reins of world-conquest *[jahangiri]* and rulership *[saltanat]* and military campaigns and punishment and justice and kindness are entrusted to kings, and such critical task cannot be ordered and rectified except through men and horse, the world-conqueror and army leader must know [the organization of] the army *[lashkar]* military organization and warfare" (Mubarakshah 1967, 19).

What is more remarkable is that here too supportive traditions abound, and traditional precedents are sought wherever possible in the practice of the early prophets, beginning with Adam (Mubarakshah 1967, 240).

Two-thirds of this book is in fact about the Prophet and the rightly guided commanders of the faithful, Abu Bakr, Umar, Uthman, and Ali (Mubarakshah 1967, 265, 294–95, 336–38), while other nations and practices are also included. This ample reference to the practice of the Prophet and the rightly guided caliphs makes for the properly "Islamic" normative regulation of military action and organization. Of particular interest is the grounding of his chapter 8 on the horse in two traditions from the Prophet, followed by a very extensive one from Ali (Mubarakshah 1967, 176–77).[8]

The transmission of Perso-Islamicate political ethic to India continued beyond and after the Delhi sultanate into the Mughal Empire. The old historian and bureaucrat from Timurid Herat, Ghiyath al-Din Khwandamir, who had remained there to record the fall of its last Timurid ruler and the rise of the new Safavid dynasty in Iran, migrated to India, a year after it was conquered in 1527 by the Timurid Babur, and was received at his court. In Herat, he had composed a *Dastur al-vuzara'* in 1500 (and updated it eight years later) and had abridged his great history, *Habib al-siyar,* under the significant title of *Athar al-muluk wa al-anbiya'* (Traditions of kings and prophets) in 1525. He must have taken these works with him to India. More important, he composed a special book on the rule of statecraft for Babur's successor, Humayun, which was appropriately entitled *Qanun-i humayuni* (also known as *Humayun-namah*). This work is particularly emphatic on the Qur'anic legitimation of monarchy and in resting the theory of the two powers firmly on the word of God. Khwandamir describes his last royal patron, Humayun, as the embodiment of the saying "the ruler is the shadow of God" (Khwandamir 1993, 272). After the death of Babur, "the messenger angel of the absolute 'possessor of kingship' [God] whispered the delightful call of 'verily I have appointed thee a deputy [*khalifah]* upon the earth' (Q.38:25) in the inner ear of the deserving king, . . . and clad this land-conquering Khusrau with

8. Curiously, Mubarakshah's first chapter on the generosity and clemency of kings consists mainly of the stories about the Prophet, the descendants of Ali, Hasan, "the commander of the faithful Hussein" [*sic*], and Muhammad al-Baqir (Mubarakshah 1967, 28), and those of Hajjaj, Abu Muslim, and the Abbasids.

the august garment of 'Thou givest kingship to whom Thy wilt'" (Q.3:26) (Khwandamir 1993, 258). As for the two divinely sanctioned powers, Khwandamir tells us that, among the humankind, God

> has honored and made powerful two classes. . . . First, the messenger prophets by whom those close to the divine court and the wayfarers along the path [of salvation] are guided. . . . Second, the kings and rulers whose command is legitimate for the ordering of the conditions of groups of people. . . . He distinguished and made exceptional those charged with the ordering of the matter of prophethood by election, according to the miraculous [divine] words, "Verily God has elected *[istafa']* Adam and Noah and the House of Abraham and the House of Imran (Moses) upon the worlds" (Q.3:3) . . . and made those elevated to the office of monarchy and Caliphate the cause of order in all that is produced and renovated, according to the vouchsafing Verse, "then we appointed you deputies upon the earth." (Q.10:15; Khwandamir 1993, 251)[9]

Literature from the Chanceries *(Insha')*

The three typical components of the epistolary collections of the period are (1) the actual and model decrees of the chancelleries of Seljuqs and Khwarazmshahs, or *manshurat;* (2) the diplomatic correspondence with the other rulers, or *sultaniyat;* and (3) the secretaries' letters to individual dignitaries and petitioners, or *ikhwaniyat* (Paul 1995; Foruzani 2000). The first component has constituted a major source for administrative history (Horst 1964; Lambton 1988), and Jürgen Paul (1995) has effectively drawn on the third component to throw light on the conditions of the administered, the subjects. Here I want to query the important collection of decrees by Baha' al-Din Muhammad ibn Mu'ayyad Baghdadi, head of the chancellery of Ala' al-Din Takash Khwarazmshah (1172–1200), which was compiled in the last quarter of the twelfth century (in 1182–84, according

9. Here, as with Abu al-Hasan al-Amiri five centuries earlier, there can be no question about an invidious contrast between prophets and kings, as the same class of persons happen to be holders of both offices by God.

to Rypka 1968b, 621) and recognized as a model by contemporaries *(Marzban-namah; Lubab al-albab).* These decrees contain elaborate statements of the principles of statecraft, which I equate with the pre-Mongol Persianate public law and the political ethic in which it was embedded.

Mu'ayyad Baghdadi opens his collection with a decree he had drafted early in his career (Baghdadi 1937, 13). It is the decree issued by Takash,[10] appointing his son, Malikshah, to the governorship of the city of Jand, and it contains a concise mirror for the prince (Baghdadi 1937, 13–38), instructing him in statecraft in order to "revive the firm tradition *[sunna]* . . . of the martyred Lord *[khudawand-i shahid]*" (Baghdadi 1937, 15), whom I take to be the prince's namesake, the Seljuq Malikshah. Other statements in the insha' collections from Khwarazm leave little room for doubting that the chancellery of the Khwarazmshahs saw itself as belonging to the administrative tradition of the Great Seljuqs founded by Nizam al-Mulk.

The instructions to the prince on the art of government begin with the praise of God as the grantor of kingship (Q.3:2) and source of authority (Q.4:59), who bestowed upon the king the status of the shadow of God [upon the earth] for the maintenance of order on the basis of justice and the observance of the interests of the subjects *(masalih-i ri'aya)* (Baghdadi 1937, 13). Protection of religion and the reading of the Book of God to ascertain the shari'a and Islam's commandments are a necessary means for royal government based on justice. But the core of royal justice is the maintenance of the social hierarchy, and its chief instrument the exercise of the sword for punishment *(siyasat)* (Baghdadi 1937, 17–26). It is evident from all the insha' collections, as from the books on ethics (Marlow 1997), that the maintenance of the social hierarchy meant the acknowledgment of the priority of the notables' established families for administrative and judiciary appointments.

Punishment, to be carried out by the royal sword, is the *danda* of the Indian statecraft, transmitted through the Sassanian political lore

10. An added reason for the significance of this decree was that the conquest of Jand marked the ascendance of Takash to the throne (Baghdadi 1937, 14). The city was completely destroyed by the Mongols and never rebuilt.

(Arjomand 2001) and reinforced by the Qur'anic verse 2:179 (175): "In retaliation there is life for you" (Baghdadi 1937, 26). Another decree, granting the *iqta'* of Nesa, instructs its holders to make sure their subordinates observe the "laws of punishments" *(qawanin-i siyasat)* and applies a different verse to highway robbers, Q.5:33 (37): "This is the recompense for those who fight against God and His Messenger, and hasten about the earth, to do corruption there: they shall be slaughtered, or crucified" (Baghdadi 1937, 35–36).[11]

The mirror contained in the decree enumerates eight classes of the social hierarchy, the maintenance of whose status and position in society is required by justice: the descendants of the Prophet *(sadat)*, the imams and ulama, the judges *(quzat)*, the Sufi masters, the elite of the subjects, the farmers, the craftsmen, and finally, the tribesmen and/or the military (Baghdadi 1937, 20–22). The maintenance of justice among these classes requires both punishment and economic development *(imarat)* according to the above-mentioned fundamental maxim of Persianate statecraft: "No kingdom except through men, and no men except through wealth, and no wealth except through development, and no development except through justice by means of punishment" (Baghdadi 1937, 22).[12] In *Jami' al-ulum,* the Khwarazmshah's protégé Fakhr al-Din Razi represents this maxim in a more elaborate graphical form, taken from the tenth-century pseudo-Aristotelian *Secret of Secrets,* as a circle with eight segments.

Furthermore, justice is equated with the Aristotelian [golden] mean and opposed to tyranny or wrongdoing *(zulm).* Tyranny is highlighted in another decree by citing another maxim of statecraft: "The kingdom will last with infidelity but will not last with tyranny." The decree of appointment of a viceroy and judge of (the Persian) Iraq, included in a different collection, defines the maintenance of order by kings and rulers as "putting everything in its place *[wad' al-shay' fi mawdi'ihi]*, which is the

11. The same verse is adduced to justify the punishment of highway robbers in Juwayni 1950, 25, 79.

12. The maxim is cited again in a slightly abbreviated form in another decree (Baghdadi 1937, 110).

opposite of tyranny/wrongdoing (zulm)" (Nur al-Din Munshi 2002, 49). The king's need for the advice of his counselors is backed by one of the Qur'anic "Consultation Verses," Q.3:159 (Baghdadi 1937, 27). Other notable aphorisms of statecraft cited in the collection are "Religion and kingship are twins" (Baghdadi 1937, 102) and, in a curiously corrupt form, "The kingdom *[mulk]* is the foundation and religion *[din]* is its guardian; and what has no guardian is destroyed!"[13] (Baghdadi 1937, 57, 102). The one principle of Persianate statecraft not specifically mentioned in the mirror is the importance of the use of spies, which is mentioned in other decrees (Baghdadi 1937, 41), notably in a decree of appointment to the *diwan-i arz,* which was responsible for the royal intelligence service (Nur al-Din Munshi 2002, 99).

Mu'ayyad Baghdadi does not explicitly claim the authority of the Prophet for the title of "shadow of God," as does Nur al-Din Munshi after him by citing the hadith—"the ruler is the shadow of God upon the earth" (Nur al-Din Munshi 2002, 14)—nor does he explicitly claim religious authority for his royal patron, as Rashid al-Din Watwat had done for Atsiz b. Khwarazmshah, whom he had called "the shadow of God upon the earth and the deputy of the Prophet" (Watwat 2004, 9) and also "the commander of the faithful" (Watwat 2004, 68).[14] Nevertheless, he considers the royal charisma *(farr-i padshahi)* and significantly also the charisma of the [dynasty's] turn in power *(farr-i dawlat)* to be a divine emanation (Baghdadi 1937, 29). He also considers the temporal authority of the king absolute and his decrees "enforced by God" (Baghdadi 1937, 78). A vizierate decree in a different collection shows that the authority delegated by the king was equally absolute, as all the officials of the realm were urged "to recognize [the authority of the vizier] as absolute on behalf of our majesty *[az hazrat-i ma mutlaq shenasand]*" (Nur al-Din Munshi 2002, 44).

13. In the correct form, religion is the foundation and the king *(malik)* the guardian.

14. It should be noted that this appropriation of the caliphal title of "the commander of the faithful" occurred long before the clash between the Khwarazmshahs and the caliph.

The principles of statecraft stated fairly comprehensively for the instruction of the prince-governor of Jand are elaborated separately in other decrees, as appropriate to the function of the appointed official. The vizierate comes next in importance, and it seems fruitful to examine the norms and rules the viziers were instructed to observe in their appointment decrees. The two such decrees included in *al-Tawassul ila al-tarassul* underscore that the craft of the vizier is based on reason, in contrast to that of the judge, which rests on tradition. I have argued that this conception shows the influence of the Greek political science as the rational art of government (Arjomand 2001). The primary function of the vizier is the maintenance of the body politics' well-being through the "operational laws of royal government *[qawanin-i kar-i padshahi]* and the rules for the well-being of the kingdom." It is exercised by "the methods of justice, punishment, and through the path of reason and acuity *[madhahib-i adl wa siyasat, wa shari'at-i aql wa kiyasat]*" (Baghdadi 1937, 75). The second decree, appointing a vizier to the above-mentioned Prince Malikshah, considers the foundations of monarchy and the stability of the state crucially dependent on "a vizier adorned with the manifestations of reason" (Baghdadi 1937, 70). His action should be based on "a firm principle and comprehensive law *[qanun-i rashad]*, leaving the derivation of such acts from principles and the varieties of their conditions to reason and the intellect *[aql wa khirad]*" (Baghdadi 1937, 83). Malikshah is urged to make no decision "without consultation with the perfect reason and the comprehensive intellect," meaning the vizier (Baghdadi 1937, 84).

A decree of vizierate in a different collection underlines the importance of the maintenance of the social hierarchy by offering the following justification of it that stresses the interdependence of the elite and the masses:

> The wisdom of our divine Lord ordained that the population should not sit in equal degrees but be ordered in different ranks, and that different classes should appear; . . . one group to enjoy wealth and maximum of prosperity, another to be afflicted with penury; one class be ensconced at the height of honor, another be isolated in the lows of squalor and abjection, so that they would always be interdependent through need . . . and the path of cooperation among them thus be kept open. The shepherds

> cannot neglect the flock/subjects as the stability of their position and fulfillment of their comportment depend on the latter, and the common masses will not disobey the elite because the currency of their affairs and prosperity of their crafts depend on that class. (Nur al-Din Munshi 2002, 40–41)[15]

Embedded in the political ethic of Persianate patrimonial monarchy that is centered on justice and the welfare of the subjects[16] are two concepts that can be translated as "public law": *dastur* and *qanun*. The first term is much vaguer and more abstract, referring to a general constitutional principle as well as to the person of the vizier, probably on account of his turban *(dastar)*. The second term is used both abstractly in the sense of public law and concretely to refer to fiscal regulations. In the above-discussed mirror for Prince Malikshah, the term *qanun* appears in connection with the land tax,[17] but the term is also represented as the expression of justice and the mean *(hukm-i ma'dalat)* (Baghdadi 1937, 28). In either case, the legitimacy of the qanun is enhanced if it is old, reflecting ancient, unaltered custom. In an iqta' grant from the crown lands in favor of another prince, the latter is instructed to make sure his agents do not deviate from the "customary regulations" *(qawanin-i muta'arif)* and "ancient rules of transaction" *(qawa'id-i mu'amilat-i qadim)* (Baghdadi 1937, 93).

15. One of Watwat's decrees provides a contrasting political division of the population into three classes, those loyal to the dynasty, the dissidents engaged in opposition and conspiracy against it, "and the third class which are called the 'commoners of the city' . . . This class consists of the masters of the crafts and the people of cultivation; they know neither loyalty to kings, nor treachery . . . The short of their preoccupation is with the provision of livelihood and the management of their family [wife and children], and they therefore always keep away from trouble, and are close to [political] health" (Watwat 2004, 45).

16. Here, as elsewhere, I find Max Weber's (1978, 2:1006–69) ideal type of patrimonialism applicable to Persianate monarchies. His characterization of its ethos in terms of concern for substantive justice (Weber 1978, 2:856–57), i.e., fairness to the subjects and promotion of their welfare, is particularly apposite.

17. The precise expression is *"qanun-i mu'ayyan wa mal-i muqannan"*; cf. *"qanun-i mu'ayyan wa kharaj-i mubin"* in Baghdadi 1937, 35, and *"dasturat-i . . . mu'amilat wa qawanin-i muhasibat"* and *"dasturat-i qadim wa qawanin-i muta'arif"* in Watwat 2004, 79.

In a decree of appointment of a chief judge to the position of his father, who had resigned, the judge is also instructed to make certain that the agents administering the land and endowments belonging to the judiciary *diwan* observe "the customary dues *[marsum]* and the customs *[rusum]* that were included in the ancient law *[qanun-i qadim]*" (Baghdadi 1937, 74). The decree is appropriately couched in the need for the observance of the sharī'a and independent legal judgment *(ijtihad)*. The term could also denote public law in the abstract, as in the hyperbolic claim made by the last Khwarazmshah, Jalal al-Din, while retreating south from the Mongol onslaught in an advance proclamation to secure the province of Kirman, that "the secretaries of the chancellery of the heavens *[diwan-i falak]* have inscribed the law *[qanun]* of his kingdom *[mamlakat]*" (Nur al-Din Munshi 2002, 74).[18] His chief secretary, who accompanied him during his long flight from the Mongol army, Shahab al-Din Muhammad Nasawi, who had interspersed his account of his desperate flight with Qur'anic verses as much as literary citations, saw the collapse of religion and statecraft as the one and the same consequence of Mongol victory: "the laws *[qawanin]* of Islam have been completely shaken, . . . the rules of the kingdom have fallen into disorder and the contracts of the state *[dawlat]* have totally disappeared" (Nasawi 1991, 94).

Taking all the decrees collected by Mu'ayyad Baghdadi in part 1 of *al-Tawassul ila al-tarassul* (13–125),[19] it can be said that, alongside the

18. It must be emphasized that the concern for the well-being of the subjects is conspicuous in all these decrees, where the mention of the subjects/flock *(ra'iyah, ri'aya)* is frequently qualified by the phrase "may God be their shepherd" *(ra'ahum Allah)* (Baghdadi 1937, 94, 109, 121; also Juwayni 1950, 71). They are frequently addressed in the decrees, and as Paul notes (1995, 544–45), some appointments were made upon their request. The paper can be expanded by a section on the subjects, drawing on the *ikhwaniyat* sections of the *insha'* collections, and put in the context of my contention (1999) that the relative strength of civil society in relation to the patrimonial state should be treated as a historical variable and that it was considerably greater in the Qaznavid and Seljuq Iran than after the Mongol invasion.

19. For the purpose at hand, I am excluding the two proclamations of victory *(fathnamah)* and an oath of loyalty by a local ruler to Khwarazmshah Il-Arslan included in part 1 (Baghdadi 1937, 125–44).

authority verse (Q.4:59) and just as frequently if not more,[20] we have verse Q.3:26, "Thou givest the kingdom to whom Thou Wilt" and its variant (Q.5:54, 57:21, and 62:4),[21] and verse 3.159, "And consult them in the affair." Also conspicuous in these decrees, and even more so elsewhere (Juwayni 1950, 70, 74, 80), is "Surely God bids to justice and good-doing" (Q.16:90 [92]). This verse, and on occasion (Baghdadi 1937, 19, 53) verse Q.38.26, "David, behold, We have appointed thee a viceroy in the earth; therefore judge between men justly," are adduced to highlight justice as the cardinal principle of statecraft. Finally, verse Q.4:58, "God commands you to deliver trusts back to their owners" is adduced to establish the officials' duty to return what they are entrusted with to the people (Baghdadi 1937, 70). Other Qur'anic verses, as we have seen, are cited ad hoc for normative as well as stylistic purposes. The most frequently cited and significant hadith is "You are all shepherds, and all of you are responsible for your flock" *(kullukum ra' wa kullukum mas'ul an ra'iyatihi)* (Baghdadi 1937, 40, 98). Another important cited tradition is "The people have the religion of their kings" (Baghdadi 1937, 116). Other sayings of the Prophet are adduced ad hoc.

It is evident from the insha' literature surveyed above (see also, Nur al-Din Munshi 2002, index of Qur'anic verses, 373–93, and of traditions, 394–97) that the secretaries were eager to establish the principles of statecraft as their own normative tradition *(sunna)* and that, like the jurists, they drew extensively on the Qur'an, and to a lesser extent the hadith, in their elaborations of the maxims of royal government and justice. The same bureaucratic class was engaged in creating a tradition of administration with generally accepted grounds for legitimation and shared principles of normative hermeneutics. In this way, the main sources of Islamic law were added to the tradition of kings and the maxims of statecraft to complete the normative hermeneutic of Persianate political ethic.

20. In Nur al-Din Munshi 2002, Q.3:26 and its variant are cited more than Q.5:49.

21. Yet another variant, "[God] grants wisdom to whom He wills" (Q.2:269), is also quoted twice (Baghdadi 1937, 52, 101) but with reference to a member of the religious elite, the ulama.

Formation of an Administrative Tradition and Obstacles Thereto

In his *Mafatih al-ulum* (Keys to the sciences), written in the latter part of the tenth century by Muhammad b. Ahmad Katib Khwarazmi, the craft of the secretaries, alongside jurisprudence (fiqh), is included among the six "sciences of the shari'a," in contrast to the nine sciences emanating from the Greeks and other nations.[22] The two bureaucratic and clerical professions were still not completely separated three centuries later: Nur al-Din Munshi, the secretary to the last Khwarazmshah and the compiler of *Wasa'il al-rasa'il wa dala'il al-faza'il,* was a cleric, as had been the famous Qur'an commentator Zamakhshari, from whom Rashid al-Din Watwat had hoped to learn the craft of the secretary (Watwat 2004, intro.). The differential success of the jurists and the scribes in legitimating their respective crafts and professional identities was far from evident, especially in light of the serious challenge of the Sufis to juristic authority. The formation of a juristic tradition in Islam is well studied, while the attempt to create a parallel administrative tradition has received scant attention.

The great Seljuq vizier, Nizam al-Mulk Tusi, took a major step toward the formation of an Islamically legitimated administrative tradition by integrating the vizierate into the dual theory of power. Nizam al-Mulk, whose Nizamiyah colleges throughout the Seljuq Empire were the main agency of "the Sunni restoration," was certainly aware of the value of traditional legitimation, as was demonstrated by his symbolic gesture of holding a session to personally dictate hadith in the library of the Nizamiyah during his last visit to Baghdad in 1091 (Arjomand 1999). In his trailblazing *Siyar al-muluk* (Nizam al-Mulk 1978, 233–34), he was careful in his choice of words to adduce *both* traditions of the kings and the prophets to legitimate the authority of the vizier: "Every king who has attained greatness . . . has had good viziers, as have had the great prophets." Great kings such as Khusrau I Anushirvan and the Ghaznavid sultan Mahmud

22. He also significantly defines *insha'* as the draft prepared by a secretary for submission to the diwan.

have appointed great viziers and "the *sunna* [custom or tradition] of the prophets and the *sirah* of the kings have thus become well-known tales."

Nizam al-Mulk's project of creating an administrative tradition of the secretaries alongside the legal tradition of the ulama gave birth to a new genre in Persian literature, the history of the viziers, modeled on the earlier Arabic *kitab/akhbar al-vuzara'* (for a bibliographic survey by M. T. Danish-pazhuh, see Qumi 1985, 18–24). In the following century Najm al-Din Abu al-Raja' Qumi wrote an extremely detailed history of the Seljuq viziers in the fifty years preceding the publication of his *Tarikh al-vuzara'* in 1188.[23] Qumi's concern is not so much with the normative hermeneutics but with actual administrative history, which could serve as a reliable record of precedents to guide administration. In *Dastur al-vuzara'*, written in the following decade, a major concern of the author, by contrast, is the legitimation of administrative authority in terms of the traditions of the kings on the one hand and of the Prophet and his caliphs on the other. To justify a tradition of vizierate on the basis of the tradition of kings, Mahmud ibn Muhammad Isfahani equates the turban of the vizier with the crown to signify the delegation of royal authority to him, and he sees it as adorning the head of "the lord of vizierate and the *mufti* of the seat of the *shari'at*" (Isfahani 1985, 40). What is more interesting from my point of view is that Qur'anic verses and traditions from the Prophet and his disciples *(sahabah)* are cited very frequently and given normative priority over the maxims of statecraft and poetry. Of some fifty-five verses cited (listed in Isfahani 1985, 246–48), Q.3:26 ("Thou givest the kingdom to whom Thou wilt, and takest away from whom Thou wilt!") occurs most frequently (four times). Perhaps the most pertinent of the cited traditions is the saying of the Prophet: "For him who institutes a good tradition *[man sanna sunnah hasanah]*, there is a reward, and a reward for whoever acts according to it" (Isfahani 1985, 29). The goal of this solid traditional backing is, however, to justify and elaborate an autonomous administrative tradition with whose foundation he credits Nizam al-Mulk (Isfahani 1985, 67). The norms of giving gifts to the

23. A similar work was written a half-century earlier but is no longer extant (Qumi 1985, 24).

king, for instance, are said to amount to "an approved tradition *[sunna]*" with respect to which the viziers have made "the law of their predecessors *[qanun-i aslaf]* their own regulation *[dastur]*." Several traditions from the Prophet, one from Abd Allah ibn Abbas and one from Ali, are cited in support of this (Isfahani 1985, 110–11).

Nizami Arudi begins his book, written around 1154, with "the authority verse," Q.4:59 (1962, 3), and inserts the caliph/imam into the chain of derivation of kingship from God to enhance its legitimacy, but in substance it only affirms the theory of the two powers. The Prophet needs a deputy *(na'ib)* "to sustain his law and tradition *[shar' wa sunna]*" who is called the imam and in turn needs a deputy with executive power "who is called *malik*, meaning *padshah* [king]."

> Therefore the king is the deputy of the imam, and the imam is the deputy of the Messenger and the Messenger is the deputy of God Most High. Firdawsi has said this well: "Know that kingship and prophethood are two stones in the one ring."
>
> And as the Lord of the sons of Adam [i.e., Muhammad] himself says, "Religion and monarchy are twins." (Nizami 1962, 10–11)

His four essays in the book are devoted to justifying the four crafts whose practitioners are the counselors of the kings and pillars of the kingdom: the secretaries, the poets, the astronomers, and the physicians. The first and most important, the craft of the secretary *(dabir)*, on whom depends the establishment of the kingdom *(qawam-i mulk)* (Nizami Arudi 1962, 11), requires dexterity in the citation of the Qur'an and traditions (Nizami Arudi 1962, 14, 25). It is interesting to note in passing that Nizami Arudi, who practiced all the four crafts (Nizami Arudi 1962, 87), claims that his master in astronomy, Umar Khayyam, who dutifully performed his function of casting horoscopes for his royal patrons to determine auspicious hours, "did not at all believe in horoscopes/astral determination *[ahkam-i nujum]*, and I have not seen or heard of any of the great men who believes in them!" (Nizami Arudi 1962, 63). Great men, at any rate, are not cultural dupes.

Mubarakshah also has an important chapter (5) on the vizierate, in which the vizierate is given revealed and traditional sanction and indeed derives from prophethood. God's appointment of Aaron as the vizier (helper) of Moses (Q.25:35) is paraphrased as a request: "Make him my partner in whatever task you ordain for me, meaning prophecy. This would be right because the vizier is the partner in kingship and his transactions (binding and loosening) in the kingdom are more current than those of the king because the well-being of the kingdom is entrusted to him."

Muhammad is also reported to say, "I have two viziers in heavens [Gabriel and Michael] and two on earth [Umar and Abu Bakr]" (Mubarakshah 1967, 129), and the chapter ends with a citation from Ali (Mubarakshah 1967, 139).

From the Il-Khanid period, too, we have a number of histories of the vizierate that fortify administrative history and legitimate administrative practice with occasional, apposite adducing of supportive Qur'anic verses and prophetic traditions. Hindushah Nakhjavani, known as Sahibi, wrote a greatly expanded translation/adaptation of Ibn al-Tiqtaqa's book on the caliphs and viziers, *Kitab al-Fakhri* (written in 1301–2),[24] barely a quarter-century later in 1324. Sahibi, who belonged to an old bureaucratic family and served as deputy governor of the city of Kashan on behalf of his brother, is the father of the author of the best-known fourteenth-century manual on administration, *Dastur al-katib*. He was a graduate of the Mustansariyah college in Baghdad and had also studied with the masters of the Nizamiyah of that city. He was evidently aware of the importance of building a well-legitimated tradition in the ethics of statecraft, especially the norms of vizierate. He begins with the Prophet and his caliphs, and offers a history of the viziers who served them, taking care to adduce some twenty-five Qur'anic verses in addition to the usual smattering of traditions and maxims. It should be noted that he does not deal with pre-Islamic kingship, although he has no hesitation about including the viziers of the Fatimids, the Buyids, and the Seljuqs.

In another, more original book on the history of the vizierate written in 1325, *Nasa'im al-ashar min lata'im al-akhbar* (Kermani 1959, 136), dedicated to "the shadow of the merciful God, Sultan son of Sultan

24. It is nearly three times the size of the original.

Abu Sa'id Bahadur Khan," Nasir al-Din Munshi Kermani cites the same Qur'anic verse and tradition as Mubarakshah as well as a few others to legitimate the vizierate (Kermani 1959, 2–4). He explains the goal of his historical research as "the collection of the traditions *[akhbar]* and works of the class of viziers . . . and investigation of their biographies and exploration of their customs *[siyar]* . . . since the dawning of the vanguard of the army of the Muhammadan reign *[dawlat]* and the sunrise of the nation *[millat]* of Ahmad" (Kermani 1959, 5). He begins his treatise with the viziers of the rightly guided caliphs and emphasizes that the greatest of the viziers, Nizam al-Mulk, was the vizier of the caliph and the sultan at the same time (Kermani 1959, 12, 31). More than once, this valuable historical record of the Gaznavid, Seljuq, and Il-Khanid vizierate offers an important insight to the stunted growth of the administrative tradition of the viziers in comparison to the legal one of the ulama. Surveying the long history of the caliphate that had been overthrown seven decades before his writing, our Munshi from Kerman offers the following reflection: "During those four hundred years, only these four viziers died in office, and all the rest were either put to the sword or, after dismissal, incurred the wrath of kings or in jail succumbed to fate and were trodden down by fear and danger" (Kermani 1959, 31).

Conclusion

Expressing his horror at what he took to be the pollution of an Islam born fully formed into history by the non-Arab clients *(mawali)* (who were in fact its chief architects as a world religion), Gibb (1962, 72) asserted that the reception of the Sassanian political tradition, which evolved into the Perso-Islamicate political ethic examined in this chapter, "introduced into Islamic society a kernel of derangement" because the strands thus "woven into the fabric of Muslim thought were, and remained, foreign to its native constitution." Echoing the same sentiment of horror at the corruption of pristine, "tribal" Islam in her recent restatement of the Orientalist conventional wisdom on the illegitimacy of government in Islam, Patricia Crone has this to say about the "men who styled themselves amirs, kings, and sultans": "Devoid of legal status and moral significance, they were rulers of the type that the Muslims had initially seen themselves as called upon to eliminate, and though they learnt to live with them, they could never see them as intrinsically Islamic" (Crone 2004b, 146).

The very short preface to Khwandamir's *Qanun-i humayuni* is grounded in eight Qur'anic verses that are universally recognized by all Muslims as the word of God and ultimate source of authority. What right do Gibb and Crone have to consider it deranged and not "intrinsically Islamic"? Neither Crone nor I have any direct evidence for what "the Muslims" really thought, and we both must infer such evidence from a body of texts assumed to have been read by the literate. My opening remarks about the texts read in Iranian schools down to World War II was a statement about the wide, inferred readership of the texts chosen as my sources. The evidence I have presented on the care taken by the architects of the Perso-Islamicate tradition of political ethic and statecraft to justify that tradition as Islamic by resting it on the two scriptural sources of Islamic law suggests that the proponents of the thesis of the inescapably un-Islamic character of all Muslim governments are barking up the wrong tree. Rather than taking comfort in the Islamists' tendentious neglect of history, they should have the humility to let the Muslim historical subjects speak for themselves, or at any rate through the texts catered for their readership.

5

An Anomaly in the History of Persian Political Thought

JAVAD TABATABAI

THE HISTORY of Persian political thinking is generally considered to be an integral part of the study of Islamic political thought. By generalizing the specificities of so-called Islamic political thought, historians of Islamic studies tend to focus on the dominance of the Islamic paradigm in Persian political thinking. According to this approach, Persian society became increasingly Islamized as a result of the Arab conquest, and it was organized and ruled by Islamic law with a political theory drawn from the Qur'an and Islamic tradition. Although Persia, along with many other regions of the Islamic Empire, formally became Islamized to some extent, this Islamization was a much more complicated process than is often assumed. For this reason, general studies of Islamic political thought must be examined using a country-specific analysis. Thanks to many careful studies of Islamic political thought produced over the past two centuries, we not only know much about this subject's sources, representatives, and trends, but we also have a thorough understanding of its intellectual arguments. However, most of our knowledge about the varieties of political thought in different regions of the Islamic world is still contingent on Islamic studies in the broader sense.

Before I begin this discussion, I would like to draw the readers' attention to the history of the Persian historiography in the Islamic period. Indeed, pre-Islamic "advice literature" and historical writings were closely associated, and following Islam's advent, the main sources of Persian historiography also constituted sources of political thought. Between Franz Rosenthal's classical study *A History of Muslim Historiography* (1968) and Chase F. Robinson's *Islamic Historiography* (2003), much research has been conducted, but it is astonishing that there is little or no mention of the Persian school of historiography from the tenth century to the Mongol invasion. Most of these works by historians are in Arabic, and Persian historians attract little attention if they do not write in Arabic. The Persian histories written in Persian such as Bayhaqi's and Juwayni's works (1989 and 1958 respectively) remain a *corps étranger* among the general scholarship in Islamic studies.[1] By confining their research to works in Arabic, these scholars are limiting themselves to a partial perspective or view of their subject. Indeed, in the Persian school of historiography (especially in the writings of Ibn Miskawayh and Bayhaqi), the influence of traditionalism was held in check, and reason became the foundation of their approach. These two historians do not include prophecies, miracles, or nonfactual events in their examination and analyses. Bayhaqi's commitment (1989, 149) to write a "fundamental history," in contrast to histories that use fictional sources, and Ibn Miskawayh's attempt (1990, 1:51–53) to purge all imaginative or nonrational events from his history indicate important steps taken toward achieving what has been called "the renaissance of Islam" or "the golden age of Persia" (Frye 1975a). In my view, this "golden age" was made possible by the reemergence of "reason" as an explanatory paradigm and with its line drawn against traditionalism in modern scholarship.

Even if political thought had had quite a different evolution in Persia, one can observe the same distancing of Islamic traditionalism in the elaboration of a new political discourse independent from the Qur'an and the traditions. I do not contest the assertion that Islam is an eminently political religion, but I would like to draw attention to the fact that the first treatise on politics drawn from the Qur'an and the traditions was not

1. There are some exceptions: Marilyn Robinson Waldman's book (1980) on Bayhaqi is an interesting one. Juwayni's Mongol history is translated in English (1958). Also, Holt and Lewis 1962 is useful on some aspects of Persian historiography.

written until the mid-eleventh century when the caliphate was in deep crisis and an efficient political institution in the Islamic Empire was about to vanish. The history of Persian political thought, which cannot be reduced to an epiphenomenon, reflects a different approach for the early centuries of Islam. Before internal conflict among different religious sects was understood in terms of political theory, the practice and theory of governance were important and necessary parts of the Persian legacy. Of all the prophets in the Qur'an, it is significant that only the Israeli king-prophets, like David and Moses, are depicted as kings, while Muhammad is only depicted as God's messenger. In the language of Islam's primary sources, such as the *shari'a* and the positive law, statements having a political connotation are less frequent than those found in the language of ethical-civil law. I will demonstrate, however, that the Sassanid legacy was eminently political, and this legacy survived until the collapse of the Persian Empire.

The Arab military conquest of the Persian Empire was completed rather early, in the middle of the seventh century, and for about two hundred years Persia was dominated by the caliphs and merged into the Islamic Empire. Persia lost its national identity for a significant period of time and its religious identity permanently. Considering the scale of the military defeat, the complete collapse of the Persian Empire, and its total absorption into the Islamic fold, the Persian elite were expected to assimilate rather than exile themselves. Although the elite were integrated at the earliest moments into the fabric of the Islamic Empire, the complete annihilation of all aspects of Persian culture was not as easy to achieve. However, until the restoration of the Persian monarchy, some political integration occurred, although outbreaks of cultural tension flared up and served to block efforts to annihilate completely the Persian Empire. The actual cultural integration of Persia into the Islamic fabric turned out to be more difficult than its political domination. In addition to the massive presence of Persian elite, who eventually took part in a revival movement of Persian culture, some of the cities of the Sassanid Empire, which had been important cultural centers, were located in the eastern regions of the caliphate, including the capital of the Sassanid Empire and its administrative center.

The first step in the resistance against the Islamic Empire's cultural domination was an attempt to save Persian as the national language. Soon, especially under the auspices of the *dihkans,* "the lesser feudal nobility of Sasanian Persia" (Lambton 1984b), these cities became the focus of Persian cultural revivalism. The collapse of the Persian Empire during the massive conversion of its population had made it impossible to organize religious resistance, and the contentious relationship between Persians and Arabs remained and intensified. This conflict facilitated the preservation of a new Persian as the first national language within the Islamic world and acquired more national character through the restoration of the Persian monarchy. The emergence of a new Persian language and the restoration of the Persian form of government are well-known events of Persian history. But of utmost importance is the fact that the restoration of the Persian monarchy and the maintenance of the Persian language were not possible without a renewal of some aspects of Persian culture. Even though Islamized Persia was under the domination of the caliph's authority and it is difficult to separate the historical evolution of Persia from that of the Islamic Empire,[2] the cultural battles began to use and promote Persian as the second language of Islam. The battle to save the Persian language was not mere resistance against speaking Arabic; it was more a battle to save Persian culture under the guise of language.

The emergence of the new Persian language was the first step toward Persia's independence within the Islamic Empire, and it was considered the vehicle of Persian culture. In the first three centuries of the Islamic era, several important attempts at Persian cultural revival were made, specifically, the rewriting of the lost Sassanid Pahlavi texts and their translation, thus facilitating their use for a new generation of Persian scholars and scribes. At the end of the ninth century, considerable work to restore Persian culture had begun, and important efforts toward its full elaboration were under way. Thus there was interest in not only refining the newly elaborated synthesis of what one could call the new Persian culture but also in creating from it a paradigm for the interpretation of the Islamic precepts on ethics and politics. In this respect, the Abbasid revolution

2. "The period of Iran's history from the Arab conquest to the Seljuq expansion is very difficult to separate from general history of the Islamic oecumene" (Frye 1975b, xi).

could be considered a turning point. In addition to the attempts to formulate a political framework drawn from the Islamic precepts, the Persian tradition of advice literature began increasingly to dominate reflections on governance after the Abbasid revolution and especially from the restoration of the Persian monarchy onward. In fact, the Persian Empire came into the Islamic Empire to carry out its own cultural legacy. The importance of this cultural continuity has been studied in some areas of Persian culture, but the persistence of the Persian political thought can be used to illustrate the significance of this cultural continuity as an important component of Persian culture, although Islam was the official religion.

The Islamic version of Greek political philosophy as founded by Farabi lost its importance from the late tenth century onward, and some Persian political philosophers, including Abu al-Hasan al-Amiri, made an attempt to create a synthesis of Greek political philosophy and Persian advice literature. Although the influence of Greek political philosophy was long-lasting, especially in Persia where it had an influence even into the nineteenth century, it existed more as part of traditional scholarship than as a reflection of political reality. The fate of that other major trend in political thought, the theory of the caliphate, was quite different and also deserves to be examined in detail. The constellation of the triple "Persian legacy," namely, the new Persian language, Persian kingship, and the renewal of advice literature, stood in the way of the "islamization" of Persian politics. In the mid-eleventh century, Ali ibn Muhammad al-Mawardi (1973) developed his theory of the caliphate. At the same time in Persia, the advice literature had not only acquired a dominant role in political thought, but "persianate" thought also became the principal content of almost all scholarly works in Persia.[3] The case of Firdawsi's *Book of Kings* is too well known to be invoked here, but the fact is that Firdawsi's work, in which he articulated a deep-rooted sentiment of national identity,

3. "Most of the more local languages of high culture that later emerged among Muslims likewise depend upon Persian, wholly or in part, for their prime literary inspiration. We may call all these cultural traditions, carried in Persian or reflecting Persian inspiration, 'Persianate' by extension" (Hodgson 1974, 2:304).

gathered and presented a synthesis of all "persianate" thought, especially the Persian conception of ideal kingship. Firdawsi's *Book of Kings* is not only the "Persian national epic" (Nöldeke 1920), it is also a compilation of all the sources of Persian political thought and historical records of the Sassanid kings that were accessible in the late fourth century. Although the *Book of Kings* is clearly a literary masterpiece, as a history of Persian political thought it is also more revealing than any other advice book. In fact, the *Book of Kings* gives an overview of the non-Islamic nature of Persian political thought through a literary presentation of Persian mythology and history of the Sassanid Empire. Even if the general tone of the *Book of Kings* is not anti-Islamic, Firdawsi's attempt to sustain the Persian advice legacy barely concealed his intentions to prepare the groundwork for an anticaliphal system of political thought, which could serve as the missing ideology for the restored Persian monarchy.

Firdawsi was not only a poet belonging to the *dihkan* families of Khurasan and imbued with the Persian, anti-Arab elements of Shu'ubi ideas (see Mottahedeh 1976); he was also a member of the Persian revivalist movement, and his poetry was considered an act of political resistance to caliphal domination. The case of Firdawsi is not isolated in the history of Persian political thought. More revealing is the case of Nizam al-Mulk's *Siyasat-namah* (Book of government) (1962). As I mentioned before, Firdawsi was more a "political" opponent, if not a resister, belonging to the crypto-shi'a milieus, while as the grand vizier, Nizam al-Mulk was an orthodox Sunni in the service of the Seljuq sultans and not in political opposition to the caliphate authority. As the founder of the Nizamiyah theological seminaries tasked to propagate the orthodox version of Islamic faith, Nizam al-Mulk was closer to the caliph's polity, but nothing in his internal polity or in his political thought was drawn from canonical texts or from the caliphs' tradition of government. Apart from some accounts of the caliphs, no trace of the caliphate theory can be found in his *Book of Government*. Elaborating a theory of ideal kingship, his work closely follows the tradition of Persian advice literature and criticizes the Seljuq style of governance. I shall now examine some preliminary subjects before I return to this point.

Until the Abbasid revolution, the principal organizing idea of the Islamic Empire during its first two centuries was the vicegerency of the Prophet. But, with the advent of the first Persian royal houses and the context of the Persian political reality, many Islamic views on politics gave way to a theory of Persian kingship alien to the Islamic ideal of government.[4] Thus, the Persian advice literature, by acquiring a dominant role in discussions on governance, became not only a mere component of the Islamic synthesis of a new political thought, but also, at least for the Persian cultural arena, the paradigm for interpretation. Despite the importance of the early discussions on the vicegerency of Muhammad and the persistence of Greek political philosophy after the ninth century, Persian advice literature remained the conceptual framework for the renewal of the Persian kingship. Increasingly, from the tenth century onward, the conceptual framework of Persian advice literature extended to the two other trends of political thought. In Persia, with the restoration of the monarchy, the caliphal institution no longer played the role it was supposed to according to the theory of caliphate. On the other hand, with Farabi, Greek political philosophy had taken up a prominent place in the new Islamic scholarship, although it remained alien to both the caliphate tradition and Persian kingship.

While examining the continuity of Persian political thought, a nuanced approach is needed for the first historical attempt, which only touches the surface of events. In the history of Persian political thought, one needs, as Oleg Graber states about the prominence of Persian art in the Islamic world, "some sort of hypothesis about what happened during the first centuries."[5] In the history of Persian political thought, the historical—and philological—approaches have prevailed so far, and almost all of

4. We have to distinguish three trends in the history of political thought in Islam prior to the nineteenth century: the juristic theory, political philosophy, and "mirror for prince." Cf. Erwin I. J. Rosenthal 1948 and 1971; Lambton 1974.

5. "The later importance of Iran in Moslem culture and especially in Islamic art is so great as almost to demand some sort of hypothesis about what happened during the first centuries of Moslem rule" (Grabar 1973, 9–10).

the research remains predominantly descriptive, mere philological study of the related themes with variations. What one could expect from the history of Persian political thought and its place in the Islamic arena is no more than a political theory subordinated to Islamic theology. In addition to Ann Lambton, Erwin Rosenthal has asserted that "an independent political theory cannot . . . be expected in Islam" and that in all three trends of political thought in Islam, especially in juristic theory, "the connection with theology is close" (1971, 17). According to Lambton (1962, 92), "political science did not exist as an independent discipline in Islam; and so far as it exists at all it was a department of theology." In her survey of the three trends in Islamic political thought (especially of what she calls "juristic theories"), Lambton says in a very confusing assertion, "of all the constitutional theories the juristic theory is the most purely Islamic; and to a greater or lesser degree it moulded and influenced the thinking of all Muslim political thinkers" (1962, 92).

In this context, the label "Muslim political thinkers" is extremely confusing for the three major trends in the history of Islamic political thought; neither political philosophy nor advice literature is "a department of theology," and neither was molded by the "juristic theories." By reasoning this way, Lambton trusts the appearance, according to which "the ideal in each of the three formulations . . . was inspired by Islam," and claims that "all assumed the ultimate source of power to be divine, and to come from God through the ruler, be he caliph or king, which made the problem of tyrannical ruler insoluble" (1974, 422). Lambton takes the unity of Islamic political thought for granted and believes that "[p]ower was not a central problem for any of them" for "the keyword of all these formulations was justice, which medieval Islamic political thought understood to be harmonious relationship of society in a divinely appointed system, the component parts of which were in perfect equilibrium" (1974, 422). In view of our sources and in the light of this new hypothesis, all these assertions are unconfirmed and contested.

Despite the advent of Islam in the Persian cultural arena, the Islamic theory of the caliphate was never taken seriously. From the very beginning of the Islamic era, a new synthesis of rescued sources was made possible, and a new Persian political discourse emerged. In this respect, it is surprising that, throughout the long history of Persian political thought in the Islamic period, no treatise on the Islamic theory of politics was ever written by an Iranian political thinker or scribe. With the restoration of the monarchy, all the resources of the ancient theory of kingship were embodied in a new theory of kingship. Moreover, although during the early Islamic period the scholarly lingua franca in Persia was Arabic and the first generations of scribes, such as Ibn al-Muqaffaʿ, wrote in Arabic, from the tenth century onward, most texts in the tradition of advice literature and political treatises on kingship were written in Persian and in a newly developed style.

In order to understand the specificity of Persia within the Islamic Empire, one must examine the emergence of this new Persian political discourse and analyze the reasons Persian remained the sole language of this theory of kingship. From a purely Islamic point of view, these two facts seem to be an "anomaly," but they can also be considered as the key to some salient aspects of Persian history. The hypothesis I propose is that the political discourse that emerged during the Islamic period of Persia cannot be considered a component of so-called Islamic political thought. Instead, it was elaborated through the blending of materials of the Sassanid era written in middle Persian and should be considered as a continuum of pre-Islamic political thought. As paradoxical as it may seem, it was only in the aftermath of the Mongol invasion and under the impact of the predominance of mystical ideas that this political discourse became increasingly imbued by some "Islamic" themes.

Before returning to the theoretical aspects of the Persian kingship, I have to point out one of the most important aspects of the Persian cultural revival. During the first and second centuries, especially after the Abbasid revolution and prior to the emergence of the new Persian, texts of the Persian advice literature were translated into Arabic as a part of Iranian national revival. This safeguarding of the texts, which made the transmission of Persian political thought possible, was an important step in its development during the Islamic period. Even during the Arabic phase of transmission and under the concealment of overlapping Islam, the spirit of the political treatises remained essentially Persian, and this was of utmost importance. The striking example for this period is Ibn al-Muqaffa''s treatise, *Risalah fi al-sahabah,* which is "a memorandum on government" (Goitein 1968, 150) to the caliph al-Mansur, and apparently an Islamic document.[6] But, as Shaul Shaked had shown comparing the treatise to the Pahlavi texts written before and after Islam and placing their ideas in context, major motifs coincide with the Sassanid ones. Affirming that "human endeavor has been established by God to revolve about two concepts, religion and reason" *(al-din wa al-aql),* Ibn al-Muqaffa' uses the Arabic *din.* But, as Shaked (1995, 35–36) points out, referring to the similar contexts in Pahlavi texts where the term *den* occurs, this use of *din* as a "notion relating to the psychology of the individual" is "somewhat unusual in Islamic writing." According to Shaked, in the context of al-Muqaffa''s treatise the coupling "religion and reason" renders *den* and *xrat* of the Pahlavi texts, which "designate powers of the human soul." Hence the meanings of these words should not be understood in an "institutional sense."[7]

Ibn al-Muqaffa' asked the caliph to write and publish an *aman* for the military corps (Ibn al-Muqaffa' 1976; Arabic text, §11ff.). The Arabic term was translated into French as *catéchisme* or *règlement clair et succinct* (1976, 6, 24), but, according to the context, the corresponding terms for *aman* in the middle Persian and Sassanid models, as Shaked suggests, translate Pahlavi *zinhar* as "security, pact, and pledge," which is very close in sense to the Arabic word *used* and which seems to have been used in a much broader range of meaning than that usually assigned to *aman* in Arabic (1995, 34–35).

Another revealing fact in Ibn al-Muqaffa''s treatise, which was written for a caliph, is the dominant use of *imam* to designate the "chief of community"—nineteen times—in place of *caliph,* which is used no more than four times (Ibn al-Muqaffa' 1976, 8). The use of the term *imam* in this context is important because in Islamic political philosophy, this term is

6. Arabic text is in Ibn al-Muqaffa' 1966; French translation by Charles Pellat (Ibn al-Muqaffa' 1976).

7. Shaked (1995, 36), citing a passage of the *Dinkart,* states, "*Den* and its Arabic rendering *din* is not 'religion' in the institutional sense of the term, but rather a disposition of the soul."

considered by Farabi to represent inter alia the "king in the sense used by the ancients [Persians]" (Farabi 1987, 152).

The Persian political discourse, in its inner structure as elaborated after the advent of Islam and even in its early treatises, is not only quite different from the theory of caliphate but is fundamentally its opposite. It is understood that in all premodern political theories all power comes from God. But, while in the Qur'an there is no specific mention of the transmission of political power from God to His messenger, in Persian political discourse kings are mentioned as chosen by God himself. In the Qur'an, Muhammad is the messenger of God, but it does not tell us if he is also the political guide of the community as well. The fact that the Qur'an remains silent on this important issue, as it does about what political power entails, is very significant to the theory and practice of the caliphate. Even more ambiguous is the problem of the vicegerency of God's messenger that gave rise to the first religious schisms. While some verses about the Jewish prophets qualified them as "kings," in verses concerning Muhammad there is no explicit mention of the kingship as a supplementary dimension of the prophecy. Because political Islam has prevailed as the sole authorized interpretation of Islam, less and less attention has been paid to this fact. But, even in the tenth century, the philosopher Abu al-Hasan al-Amiri, referring to the above-mentioned verses, distinguished two kinds of supreme mastership, true prophecy and true kingship. According to al-Amiri, kings are the masters of "authority," and prophets are the masters of "science and wisdom." These masteries can only be granted by the will of God (al-Amiri 1988, 254).[8]

In his interpretation, al-Amiri follows the commonly accepted opinion of the *adab* literature in which kings and prophets are ontologically at the same level in creation. All adab literature, especially historiography and the mirror for princes, shares the principle that "religion and kingship

8. The verses to which he refers explicitly are the following: "So Moses told his people: my people remember God's favor towards you when He planned prophets among you and set you up as kings; and gave you what no one else in the Universe had ever been given" (Qur'an 6:20; Cf. also "great kingdom" or ملكاً عظيماً in 5:54).

are twins," and, according to Hamzah al-Isfahani, acts "of the kings of the earth and the prophets" should be valued equally (Tabari 1879–1901; al-Isfahani 1921–22). This vision had prevailed in the Eastern countries of Islam, but Persian advice literature goes further and, by emphasizing that kings are elected directly by God, confers higher dignity on the king. Nizam al-Mulk, a grand vizier but also a very strict Sunni and founder of the Nizamiyah madrasa for the defense of Sunni orthodoxy, describes the king as a prophet. Nizam al-Mulk follows precisely the Persian theory of kingship, which is obviously in contradiction with Islamic precepts. He says, "In every age and time God . . . chooses one member of human race and, having endowed him with godly and kingly virtues, entrusts him with the interests of the world and well-being of His servants" (Nizam al-Mulk 1978, 9).[9] Prophets are elected as God's messengers; they command for good and forbid the prohibited, but they do not necessarily possess the *majestas* that is indispensable for a king's mission. In other words, according to the advice writers, kings and prophets both have *auctoritas* but only kings have *potestas.* Nizam al-Mulk continues, "He [God] charges that person to close the doors of corruption, confusion, and discord, and He imparts to him such dignity and majesty in the eyes and hearts of men, that under his just rule [he] may live in constant security and ever wish for his reign to continue" (Nizam al-Mulk 1978, 9).

Nizam al-Mulk's *Book of Government* considers all editions of pre-Islamic advice literature and develops a new theory of Persian kingship that, despite some references to Islam, the Qur'an, the traditions, and the records of the caliphs, remains essentially alien to the caliphate. By definition, the caliphate is a rule of shari'a and thus a rule of law; a caliph himself is nothing but the vicegerent of Muhammad, who supervises the former's praxis. Even Muhammad himself is not a lawmaker but only the messenger. In advice literature, the king is elected by God and in his ambiguous ontological status he is the incarnation of law if not of God himself. Nizam al-Mulk emphasizes this aspect of Persian kingship by declaring that his subjects and the continued existence of the kingdom are dependent on the

9. Persian text reads بدو باز بندد where Hubert Darke translates "entrusts."

king's actions. God "entrusts the king with the interests of the world," said Nizam al-Mulk, but if any disobedience or disregard of divine law occurs, the good kingship disappears, and in its absence a civil war is launched. Later, when the evil times have passed, God elects a just and good king, giving him the power to vanquish his enemies (Nizam al-Mulk 1978, 139). The mystical version of the Persian advice literature is more revealing, especially concerning the status of the kingship. An Iranian Sufi master of the thirteenth century, Najm al-Din Razi (known as Dayeh) emphasized that, according to Muhammad, a king is a "shadow of God upon earth," stating that "kingship is vicegerency and lieutenancy of God" (Najm al-Din Razi 1986, 412).

Obviously, Najm al-Din Razi's paradigm for the interpretation of kingship is his theory of the prophecy. According to Razi, it can be argued that, following the closure of the cycle of prophecy, the cycle of kingship begins. Hence the vicegerency of God on earth is always necessary, and the vicegerent is viewed as the manifestation of God's glory and dominant attributes. In other words, a king is the prophet of the times when prophets no longer exist. As Razi says, "[O]ne could only be king with the status and dignity of the prophets" (Najm al-Din Razi 1986, 416).[10] Quoting verse 38:35 in which Solomon asks God to give him "a kingship," Razi adds that he asked God for a kingship and not "the wisdom of prophecy" (1986, 417). Razi's exegesis of verse 2:30 ("I am placing a vicegerent on earth") sums up his opinion on the relationship between prophecy and kingship: "He [God] said 'I am placing a vicegerent on earth and nominating a lieutenant in the kingdom of world,' rather than say 'I am creating a prophet or man of science or ascetic.' He also said to David, 'I am placing you as vicegerent on earth' rather than say 'a prophet or messenger or man of science, for the kingship includes caliphate'" (1986, 417–18).

We can understand why, in the advice literature, there is no room for caliphs. Nizam al-Mulk's theory of kingship is certainly the most elaborate one, but his interpretation is confirmed by all of the other Persian sources that are at our disposal. Although Nizam al-Mulk refers to the

10. "پادشاهی خلق با مقام و مرتبه نبوت می توان کرد."

acts of caliphs and cites them, he never depicts a caliph as having both auctoritas and potestas. The caliphate, as an actual institution, is tolerated de facto because "religion and kingship are twins," but its theory is missing in advice literature. Except for al-Ghazali's treatise against Shi'a sects in which he includes a defense of the caliphs' dignity, there is no treatise on the caliphate in the history of Persian political thought.[11] So far, this aspect of the Persian "anomaly" has not drawn much attention from historians.

There is also another aspect of this "anomaly" worthy of comment. Beginning with the Mongol invasion, there is yet one more important period in the history of political thought. Mysticism became a refuge for the rescued population, and, after the conversion of the Mongol khans to Islam, a syncretism of Sunni Islam, mysticism, and elements of Mongol popular beliefs replaced the official religion. Mir Sayyid Sharif, one of the great *ulama,* claimed that, according to the Prophet's tradition, Tamerlane was not only a king of Islam on earth but also the renewer of the fourteenth century (Sharif 1963, 18–20). Sharif was a jurist and Sufi master, and, moreover, he was Tamerlane's own mentor. In a letter to Khan, which is cited by Tamerlane himself, Sharif compares "the fabric *(karkhaneh)* of kingship to the fabric of God," asking him to imitate God's direction in governing the kingdom (Sharif 1963, 200–202).

With the fall of Baghdad to the Mongols and the collapse of caliphate, the political situation in the Eastern lands of Islam became more complicated. Al-Ghazali's synthesis of legalitarian Islam and Sufi principles prevailed, and, with the conversion of the Mongols to Islam, the idea of harmonization of the caliph and the kingship functions became a central trope of political theory. Few political treatises were written during the Mongol period, but political theory gained favorable ground through the historiography of the period. Some of the most important histories of the era contain a full chapter on political thought and give an eclectic overview of Persian advice literature, along with elements of caliphate theory and of the mystical idea of the king-caliph. Mongol historians, using ambiguous word choice, attempted to harmonize a new concept of ruler

11. Arabic text and German commentary in al-Ghazali 1956.

in which Mongol rulers were depicted as "king-caliphs"[12] elected by God to rule Persia as well as Turkistan (Shami 1984 [1937], 171). Kamal al-Din al-Samarqandi (1946, 6), speaking about Shahrukh Mirza, compares the king-caliph to the sun and adds, "Since the throne of kingship was illuminated by the glory of the kings, such a felicitous sun had never shined at the zenith of the firmament of the caliphate."

Between the Mongol invasion and the advent of the Safavids, the Persian theory of kingship increasingly lost its idealism. The synthesis of three major trends of political thought, with Islamic elements preeminent in this synthesis, occurred in the aftermath of the caliphate's collapse, while the Persian theory of kingship was integrated within a toned-down version of caliphate theory. This new synthesis was part of a body of scholarship and unrelated to the reality of Iranian politics. Eclectic philosophers from Qutb al-Din Shirazi to Jalal al-Din Dawwani in the sixteenth century, along with other treatises in the Qajar period, scrambled all the genres. Advice literature became caliphate theory and caliphate theory became political philosophy. This evolution created a void in which the theory of Islamic revolution was bound to emerge and develop. This remains another aspect of the Iranian anomaly.

12. "سلاطین خلافت مکان"

6

Teaching Wisdom

A Persian Work of Advice for Atabeg Ahmad of Luristan

LOUISE MARLOW

NUSRAT AL-DIN AHMAD (r. 1296–1330 or 1333)[1] of Greater Luristan (Lur-i buzurg) was known, like earlier members of the Hazaraspid or Fazlavi dynasty to which he belonged, by the title of Atabeg.[2] In contrast to some of his predecessors, and in particular his brother Afrasiyab, whose reign immediately preceded his own, Ahmad was almost uniformly portrayed as an exemplary ruler, praised for his wisdom and justice by his contemporaries and by posterity. This chapter is concerned with the distinctive political culture in which Atabeg Ahmad participated, the historical conditions that shaped it, and the literary forms that sustained it,

1. The uncertainty of Ahmad's regnal dates reflects a lack of unanimity in the sources regarding the overall chronology of the Hazaraspid dynasty. According to Shabankarah'i (n.d., 209), Ahmad died in 732; Bidlisi (1994, 209) states that he died in 733; as do Mirkhwand (2001, 7:3635) and Khwandamir (1973, 3:328). Among modern scholars, Iqbal (1962, 447–48; 1999, 504) adopts the date of 730; Spuler (1971, 337; 1985, 897) records both 730 and 733, as does Minorsky (1986, 827). Other publications give 733 alone (Spuler 1985, 135; Zambaur 1927, 234).

2. Abu Tahir, the founder of the dynasty, is reported to have adopted the title Atabeg after establishing himself in Lur. The Hazaraspids were not, in fact, tutors to princes, as the term *atabeg* would imply; they adopted the title in a nominal fashion *(ja'li)*, as Bidlisi puts it (1994, 46–47). Additionally, the rulers of the dynasty sometimes used the title *malik* (see, for example, Rashid al-Din 1945, 255).

especially as exemplified in the *Tuhfeh* (The gift), a little-studied Persian work of counsel dedicated to him.

In order to situate the *Tuhfeh* as fully as possible in its historical and cultural context, I shall begin with a discussion of the book's recipient, Atabeg Ahmad, as he is depicted in contemporary accounts, especially those written in the regions of western and northwestern Iran. Next, I shall address the cultural forms that Ahmad promoted, as far as they can be reconstructed from the surviving literary works that bear his name. In the second half of the chapter, I shall discuss the *Tuhfeh* itself, with attention to its functions and significance in the environment of the Atabeg's court, and to the author's careful use of certain literary strategies in order to communicate most effectively with his audience. I shall be especially concerned with the close relationship between advisory and historiographical types of writing, and with the common representation of Ahmad as a model ruler across this literary continuum.

The Atabeg Nusrat al-Din Ahmad

In a variety of literary sources dating from the period of his lifetime and after his death, the Atabeg Ahmad is depicted in conformity with the established Perso-Islamicate image of the model ruler. He is praised in effusive terms for his personal piety and devotion to ethical conduct, as well as for his political choices and actions. Hamd Allah Mustawfi Qazvini completed his *Tarikh-i guzidah* in 1329–30, toward the end of Ahmad's long reign; the historian dedicated his work to Ghiyath al-Din Muhammad, the vizier of the Il-Khan Abu Sa'id (r. 1317–35), who knew Ahmad well and held him in high esteem. Mustawfi described Ahmad as "a king of pleasing conduct" (Qazvini 1983–84, 548; cf. Mirkhwand 2001, 7:3634). Among other contemporary admirers of Ahmad was Ibn Battuta (1304–68), who visited the regions of the Atabeg's kingdom in approximately 1326–27 and made a second visit on his return in 1347.[3] In his

3. There is, as Gibb has noted, some confusion as to which Atabeg(s) Ibn Battuta encountered on his visit(s) to Luristan. The traveler reports that at the time of his initial

subsequent narrative Ibn Battuta reports that Ahmad was a righteous king *(malik salih)* and a self-denying and upright man *(zahid salih)* (Ibn Battuta 1992, 210–11). Strikingly, even after his eventual return to his own land of Morocco, and having encountered and heard about countless rulers in the course of the thirty years of his travels, Ibn Battuta (1992, 671) remembered Atabeg Ahmad with undiminished admiration and invoked him in his encomium to his own ruler and patron, Abu 'Inan. The poet and historian Muhammad b. Ali Shabankarah'i (d. 1358), as his *nisba* implies, hailed from Shabankarah in Eastern Fars. Well acquainted with conditions in his own region, on which he provides information derived from oral sources, Shabankarah'i observed the political life of the Il-Khanid camp from a provincial vantage point (Aubin 1981; Aigle 2005, 66).[4] In an allusion to the Atabeg's reputation for piety, Shabankarah'i (n.d., 208–9)

---

arrival in the Hazaraspid capital of Idhaj, the city was ruled by the sultan Atabeg Afrasiyab, whom he describes as the son of Atabeg Ahmad. Yet if his visit occurred in 1326–27, as seems likely, Ahmad himself would have been the reigning Atabeg, despite the fact that Ibn Battuta's remarks regarding Ahmad are reported as hearsay. Ahmad was succeeded by his son Rukn al-Din Yusufshah II, then by Muzaffar al-Din Afrasiyab II. It is possible that it was Afrasiyab II whom Ibn Battuta encountered on his return journey. See Gibb 1959, 288n59 and below; and for a full discussion, see Hrbek 1962, 427–33.

4. The *Majma' al-ansab* has survived in several manuscripts, many of them partial, and only the second half of the work, covering the period from the Saffarids onward, has been published. The published section reflects the author's second redaction, completed in 1337. According to Shabankarah'i's account in the published edition of the text, he had dedicated the initial version, composed in 1332–33, to Abu Sa'id and entrusted the work to Abu Sa'id's vizier Ghiyath al-Din, but before the latter had been able to convey it to the Il-Khan, Abu Sa'id died. The book was subsequently lost, but in 1342–43, Shabankarah'i rewrote the work and added an account of the reign of Abu Sa'id. This later, surviving version of the work includes in its preface much praise of Ghiyath al-Din, the author stating also in his text itself that the vizier's accomplishments eclipsed those of his illustrious predecessors the Sahib-i Abbad and Yahya the Barmakid (see Shabankarah'i n.d., 272–73, 279–80). Later still, Shabankarah'i created a further version, dated 1342–43, which survives in full and in abridged forms (see Aubin 1981). Storey, on the basis of other manuscripts, states that the first version of the *Majma' al-ansab* was dedicated to Ghiyath al-Din and that it was lost when the vizier's house was pillaged in 1336 (Storey 1953, 85; Bosworth and Jackson 1997, 158). See further Aubin 1981.

refers to Ahmad as Pir-i Ahmad, and describes him as of "angelic conduct." He asserts that in no age had Iran seen a ruler to equal him in his disposition to kindness and his sound religious conviction (n.d., 208).[5]

According to many sources, including the *Tarikh-i guzideh* composed during the Atabeg's lifetime, among the most celebrated accomplishments of his reign was his support of the religious law. Mustawfi reports that on his accession, the Atabeg took great pains to enact the commands and prohibitions of the shari'a. His efforts were so effective that thirty-five years later, at the time when Mustawfi was composing his history, the historian reports that he found nothing contrary to the religious law in the Atabeg's domains (Qazvini 1983–84, 548–49; see also Shabankarah'i n.d., fol. 144b; Mirkhwand 2001, 7:3634; Khwandamir 1983, 3:32). Sharaf al-Din Bidlisi (1543–1603), whose *Sharaf-namah,* a history of the Kurds, broadly follows the account of Mustawfi in this section, likewise reports that Ahmad "opened the gates of justice and equity" by his efforts to run affairs according to the shari'a throughout his reign of thirty-eight years (Bidlisi 1994, 55). Shabankarah'i (n.d., 208) similarly refers to the Atabeg's justice and equity, and compares him to the caliph Umar in this regard.[6] Natanzi describes Ahmad's skill, justice, and compassion, by which he quickly restored the land after his brother's depredations and brought it into better condition than before (Natanzi 1957, 48).

A further mark of the Atabeg's devotion to religious values, for his contemporaries, was his exceptionally generous support of scholars, shaikhs, members of religious (mystical) organizations, and the institutions

5. Shabankarah'i describes him as *niku-i'tiqad.*

6. According to Minorsky (1986, 827), Spuler (1971, 337), and Iqbal (1962, 447), Ahmad also introduced some Mongol customs *(a'in-i mughul)* into Luristan. Minorsky's account suggests that this information, which does not appear in the printed edition of the *Majma' al-ansab,* derives from the manuscript preserved in the Royal Asiatic Society, one of the abridged forms of Shabankarah'i's third redaction. The manuscript, like others that preserve the abridged version, includes an account of the atabegs of Luristan in a section appended to the end of the main text (fol. 142b–145b). Its treatment of Ahmad (referred to as Pir-i Ahmad and Qurrat al-ayn of the Lur) is highly laudatory. Ahmad is credited with the introduction of certain Mongol customs *(a'in-i mughulan)* (fol. 144b).

associated with them. On his first visit to Luristan, Ibn Battuta stayed at the capital, Idhaj, also called Mal al-Amir, where he was received graciously by the leading shaikh.[7] The traveler was greatly impressed by the evidence of the Atabeg's extraordinary expenditures on public works, especially on madrasahs and *zawiyah*s (hospices). He reports having heard that Ahmad had established 160 hospices in his territories, 44 of them in Idhaj (Ibn Battuta 1992, 210; Gibb 1959, 288).[8] Ibn Battuta himself observed that of the Atabeg's public works *(min atharihi al-saliha)*, the majority were amid lofty mountain ranges but had been made accessible through roads, wide enough for transport animals, hewn out of the rocks. At each station in these mountains there was a hospice where travelers were given food and fodder for their animals, whether they asked for it or not. All of these facilities were supported by the Atabeg's endowments *(awqaf)* (Ibn Battuta 1992, 210).

By other contemporary accounts, the Atabeg's generosity was by no means restricted to religious institutions and their personnel. He was also exceptionally liberal toward his notables, administrators, officials, courtiers, and servants. Invoking another attribute of the model ruler, Shabankarah'i praises Ahmad's fairness and generosity toward the noble and humble, nomads and settled alike (Shabankarah'i n.d., fol. 144b–145a), and witnessed firsthand the lavishness of Ahmad's stipends, charitable donations, and gifts. He likens the Atabeg to the Barmakids in his liberality, manliness *(muruwwat)*, and generosity and claims that

7. According to Natanzi, it was Atabeg Shams al-Din Alp Arghun who had, to the benefit of the soldiery and subjects alike, adopted the Mongol custom of designating winter and summer pastures; accordingly, Idhaj and Shushtar constituted the Lurs' winter quarters and Mt. Zardak, the source of the Zendeh-Rud, became their summer quarters (Natanzi 1957, 44).

8. Reading, with Iqbal and Minorsky, 160 for 460: Iqbal, whose account follows that of Ibn Battuta quite closely, states that Ahmad constructed nearly 160 zawiyahs in various areas, of which 34 were in the capital (1999, 507; 1962, 447); Minorsky (1986, 827), also citing Ibn Battuta, reports 160 madrasahs, of which 44 were in Idhaj. (According to Ibn Battuta, in this region the customary term for a zawiyah was *madrasah*.)

Ahmad eclipsed the reputations of those paragons of largesse Hatim [al-Ta'i] and Ma'n ibn Za'idah. The historian was especially impressed by Ahmad's custom of bestowing greater gifts on persons of eminent families whose position had declined to a lowly and impoverished status *(az dawlat bi mihnat wa az tawangari bi darwishi)*. As examples of Ahmad's exceptional generosity, Shabankarah'i reports that it was the Atabeg's custom to record the names and districts of all persons who had served him for a year as eligible for permanent stipends; if they returned the following year to collect their allowances, they would receive them; if they did not appear, these allowances were sent on to their districts. Once a stipend had been delivered to the appropriate district, if the individual entitled to it were alive, he received it; if he had died, it went to his heirs and relatives. The Atabeg, according to Shabankarah'i, employed over five hundred secretaries to maintain the accounts of his disbursements in gifts and charitable donations, which were never worth less than five hundred dinars and were sometimes worth as much as ten thousand dinars (n.d., 208–9; see further fol. 144b–145a).[9]

The idealizing depiction that emerges from contemporary and later sources regarding Ahmad is thrown into greater relief by the contrasting models of rulership associated with other Atabegs of the Hazaraspid dynasty. In particular, Atabeg Ahmad's exemplary leadership is contrasted with the oppressive and capricious exercise of power said to have been exhibited by his brother Afrasiyab. Afrasiyab had acceded to the throne on the death of their father Yusufshah (r. ca. 1274–88) and had immediately sent his brother Ahmad in attendance *(mulazim)* to the Il-Khanid court of Arghun (r. 1284–91) (Qazvini 1983–84, 546; Bidlisi 1994, 52).[10] Such arrangements, whereby tributary rulers sent their sons or other

9. Fazl Allah Qazvini, a contemporary writer who, as will be seen below, enjoyed the Atabeg's patronage, similarly remarks on the Atabeg's liberality, especially toward scholars, mystics, descendants of the Prophet, and specialists in the Qur'an and hadith (Qazvini 2004–5, 25–26).

10. According to Natanzi, Afrasiyab himself had been in attendance at the Il-Khanid camp, while Ahmad had been with his father (Natanzi 1957, 45).

close relatives to the Il-Khanid court, were intended to consolidate the ties between the two houses and to guarantee the cooperation of the subordinate dynasty. Mustawfi characterizes Afrasiyab's reign as one of injustice and oppression *(jawr* and *zulm)* and notes especially the ruler's (false) suspicions of former officials, "like Yusuf's wolf" (Qazvini 1983–84, 546 [the reference is to Q.12:13–17]; see also Mirkhwand 2001, 7:3632; Khwandamir 1973, 3:327). Bidlisi (1994, 52) similarly states that Afrasiyab pursued a disagreeable path of oppression (zulm) and hostility *('udvan)*. According to Mustawfi, following his accession, Afrasiyab set about mistreating his subjects near and far and mulcting officials who had served the dynasty since the days of their eponymous founder Hazarasp, during whose reign in the first half of the seventh/thirteenth century large numbers of tribal groupings had migrated to Luristan (Qazvini 1983–84, 540–42; Bidlisi 1994, 47–48; Natanzi 1957, 40–41). Several relatives of those afflicted in this purge sought refuge in Isfahan, where Afrasiyab sent Qizil, his father's cousin, in pursuit (Qazvini 1983–84, 546; Bidlisi 1994, 52–53; Natanzi 1957, 46). By such conduct, Mustawfi comments, Afrasiyab brought ruin to his own kingdom. He also challenged the Il-Khanid state. On hearing of the death of the Il-Khan Arghun, Qizil executed Baydu, the Mongol *shahna* of Isfahan, and Afrasiyab took the opportunity to extend his territories. He dispatched various relatives to take control of regions stretching from Hamadan to the Persian Gulf, and at Darband, his forces defeated a Mongol garrison and plundered Mongol houses. The Mongol retribution was swift and severe: it was said that a single woman killed ten men of Lur (Qazvini 1983–84, 547; Bidlisi 1994, 53; Natanzi 1957, 46). Afrasiyab fled but was brought to Arghun's successor, Gaykhatu Khan (r. 1291–95). Two women of the khan's household, Uruk Khatun and Padshah Khatun Kirmani, remembering the services of Afrasiyab's father Yusufshah, successfully interceded for the Atabeg. In consequence, Afrasiyab was reinstated over Luristan, while his brother Ahmad remained in compulsory attendance at the Il-Khanid court. Afrasiyab ordered the execution of several of his own relatives and administrators, all of whom possessed sound judgment in matters of administration (Qazvini 1983–84, 547–48; Bidlisi 1994, 53–54). Finally, Ghazan Khan (r. 1295–1304) had Afrasiyab put to death in 1296 or 1297 (Qazvini 1983–84, 548; Bidlisi 1994, 54–55; Natanzi 1957, 47).[11]

In Mustawfi's narrative, Afrasiyab is portrayed according to the paradigm of royal injustice: he is oppressive, acquisitive, disloyal, opportunistic, poor in judgment, ungrateful to his overlords despite their repeated clemency and to his servants despite their years of loyal service.[12] His brother Ahmad, by contrast, is depicted according to the image of the just, generous, and magnanimous ruler. Despite the damage done by Afrasiyab, Mustawfi reports that Ahmad quickly returned affairs to their best condition, the kingdom was brought under cultivation once again, the subjects were treated kindly, and the treasuries were filled (Qazvini 1983–84, 548). Ibn Battuta also drew explicit contrasts between Ahmad's virtuous rule and the corruption of other members of the Hazaraspid dynasty. Ibn Battuta, presumably on his return journey in 1347, reproached one of Ahmad's successors (possibly Muzaffar al-Din Afrasiyab II, grandson of Ahmad), whom he describes as a notorious drinker, with the words "You are one of the sons of the sultan Atabeg Ahmad, who was celebrated for self-restraint *[zuhd]* and piety *[salah]*; yet there is nothing that impairs your authority [as much as] this," and he indicated two goblets (Ibn Battuta 1992, 212–13).[13]

11. For other accounts of these events, see Rashid al-Din, *Jami' al-tawarikh,* 1994, 2:1270–72; Hafiz-i Abru 1999, 2:193–94.

12. By contrast, Natanzi describes Afrasiyab as having rendered pleasing service and having won the favor of Arghun Khan and his leading commanders prior to his father's death and his own accession (Natanzi 1957, 45–46). In this instance and in some others, Natanzi diverges from the perspective carried in the accounts of Mustawfi, Bidlisi, and other historians, whose depictions of Afrasiyab evoke the archetype of the unjust ruler.

13. As noted in footnote 3, it is not entirely clear which Atabeg Ibn Battuta encountered in this episode. If the Atabeg in question was indeed a son of Ahmad, the traveler's poor opinion was not shared by Shabankarah'i, who described each of Ahmad's sons as a "Faridun of the age." Shabankarah'i (n.d., 209) remarks that Rukn al-Din, who succeeded his father, was no less skilled than Ahmad himself and that he strived to maintain his father's principles and effectively maintained his standards of justice. Natanzi, in his account of the reigns of Ahmad's two sons Yusufshah and Afrasiyab, ascribes a territorial acquisitiveness to

According to these laudatory portrayals, a central factor in Atabeg Ahmad's successful and popular rule was his maintenance of excellent relations with the Il-Khanid court. As mentioned above, Ahmad had been brought up at the Il-Khanid court, having been sent there by his brother Afrasiyab following the death of their father, Yusufshah. In the cordiality of his relations with his Il-Khanid suzerains, Ahmad recapitulated his father's mode of conduct. Yusufshah had also been in attendance at the court of Abaqa Khan (r. 1265–82), who had invested him with a *yarlıgh*, a decree or rescript, for the government of Luristan. Furthermore, Yusufshah had supplied troops to assist the Il-Khan in his campaigns and distinguished himself in battle, for which Abaqa Khan had rewarded him with additional territories (Qazvini 1983–84, 545; Bidlisi 1994, 50–51; Mirkhwand 2001, 7:3631–32; Natanzi 1957, 44–45). After Abaqa's death, when Ahmad Khan (r. 1282–84) and Arghun Khan were struggling for supremacy, Yusufshah, according to Mustawfi's report, out of loyalty sent troops to assist Ahmad Khan in response to the latter's request (Qazvini 1983–84, 545–46; Natanzi 1957, 45; cf. Hafiz-i Abru 1999, 2:182–83). After Ahmad Khan's defeat and Arghun Khan's accession, however, Yusufshah presented himself to the new Il-Khan, who instructed him to bring to the court the Khwajah Shams al-Din Muhammad Juwayni, the Sahib-Diwan under Abaqa. Shams al-Din had assisted Ahmad Khan against Arghun and had since taken refuge in Luristan; he duly accompanied Yusufshah to the Il-Khan's presence and married the Atabeg to one of his daughters.[14] Yusufshah attempted to intercede for Shams al-Din, although the latter,

Yusufshah and great good works and generosity to Afrasiyab and his vizier (Natanzi 1957, 48–49). Hrbek's analysis suggests that as far as the dating of Ibn Battuta's travels is concerned, the Atabeg in question would indeed have been Afrasiyab, whom the traveler would have encountered on his return journey in 1347 (Hrbek 1962, 429–30).

14. For other accounts of the demise of the Sahib-Diwan Shams al-Din, see Rashid al-Din 1994, 2:1110–15, 1158–59; Khwafi 1962, 2:354–56; Natanzi 1957, 45. According to some of these accounts, Shams al-Din was in Qum, and according to Natanzi, Yusufshah had to bring him to the Il-Khan's court by force, an act that met with Arghun Khan's approval. See further the discussion in Aubin 1995, especially 29–36, and Melikian-Chirvani 1997, especially 160–63.

apparently unable to raise the necessary ransom for himself and his family, was subsequently executed in 1284. Yusufshah himself was permitted by Arghun Khan to return to Luristan, where he died soon after, following a bad dream (Qazvini 1983–84, 546).[15]

In conformity with his father's pattern of cordial relations with the Il-Khans, Ahmad, after his accession as Atabeg, maintained his personal connections with the court through frequent visits and the sending of tribute and lavish gifts. According to Ibn Battuta, he used to send a gift to the Il-Khan every year and often went to visit him in person *(wafada alayh bi nafsih)*. He divided the revenue from his territories into three parts, one-third of which he allocated for the upkeep of the zawiyahs and madrasahs, one-third for his troops' salaries, and one-third for the maintenance of his own household; from these funds he sent a large annual tribute to the Il-Khan (Ibn Battuta 1992, 210–11).[16] Again following his father's custom, Ahmad and the Lurs sometimes provided the Il-Khan with military support, such as their joining a campaign in Kirman under Ghazan (Hafiz-i Abru 1999, 3:92). As C. E. Bosworth points out, the dynasty managed to survive through a combination of "skillful diplomacy, submission to superior force, and the timely payment of tribute to stronger neighbors" (2004, 93).

It is reported that the Il-Khan Abu Sa'id, like other contemporaries, held Ahmad in high esteem. Abu Sa'id was noted for his own cultivation of poetry, music, and calligraphy, and for the respect and favor that he extended toward scholars and artists (Natanzi 1957, 142). The Il-Khan's respect and affection for Ahmad are portrayed as deriving in considerable measure from the Atabeg's reputation for personal probity and his consistent devotion to high moral values. Ibn Battuta relates how the Atabeg used to wear a hair shirt for purposes of self-mortification. On one occasion when he arrived at the Il-Khanid court, the Il-Khan's attendants caught

15. According to Mustawfi, Yusufshah died in 680. Bidlisi (1994, 50–52) gives substantially the same account as Mustawfi but dates Yusufshah's death to 684. Natanzi records the year of the Atabeg's death as 685 (1957, 45). See also Iqbal 1999, 506.

16. Spuler specifies that Ahmad's annual tribute amounted to 91,000 dinars (1971, 337; 1985, 273; see also Iqbal 1999, 507; 1962, 447). On the position of subordinate kingdoms and their rulers during the period of the Il-Khans, see Spuler 1985, 297–99.

sight of the garment and mistook it for a cuirass. When they informed the Il-Khan of their suspicions, Abu Sa'id instructed them to look into the matter. It emerged that the Atabeg was wearing a hair shirt. The Il-Khan was deeply moved, embraced him, and said to Ahmad, "You are [as] my father" *(sen ata)*. Furthermore, the Il-Khan returned to him the value of his gift many times over and wrote him a *yarlıgh* to the effect that neither he nor his descendants should henceforth be required to render tribute to the Il-Khanid court (Ibn Battuta 1992, 210–11).

Ahmad's cordial relations with the Il-Khanid court brought a number of rewards to his subjects. Bertold Spuler observes that Ahmad's avoidance of conflicts with the Mongols, together with the insignificant military role played by Luristan during his reign, allowed for a quieter development of "the inner life" of the kingdom (Spuler 1985, 135). Furthermore Ahmad, by reputation, was a ruler who administered justice in his domains, treated his administrators and servants with generosity, and was liberal in his support of institutions, and his kingdom in Greater Luristan attracted numerous scholars, contemplatives, poets, and men of letters. Mustawfi remarks that in Ahmad's reign, Luristan became "the envy of the multitudes" (Qazvini 1983–84, 548), and Shabankarah'i reports that people flocked to Ahmad's court from all directions and were never disappointed (Shabankarah'i n.d., 208–9).

As these descriptions indicate, the depiction of Atabeg Ahmad that predominates in the historiographical literature and in the narrative of Ibn Battuta is shaped to a considerable degree by prevailing ideals of leadership and governance. Invocations of such paradigmatic figures as Hatim al-Ta'i and Umar and the selection of anecdotes that demonstrate accepted virtues constitute overt allusions to these ideals. The somewhat divergent point of view conveyed in the *Selected History* of Natanzi highlights the exemplary nature of the accounts of Mustawfi, Ibn Battuta, Shabankarah'i, and Bidlisi.

Atabeg Ahmad and Persian Literature

As Abbas Iqbal observes, the Atabeg Ahmad is remembered favorably in Persian literary history on account of three works dedicated to him

(Iqbal 1962, 447; 1999, 524). The first of these works is the *Tajarib al-salaf* of Hindushah b. Sanjar (also known as Hindushah Nakhjavani), a history of the Islamic era, from the life of the Prophet to the end of the Abbasid caliphate in 1258. This history, composed in the first quarter of the eighth/fourteenth century, is based loosely on a version of the Arabic work known as the *Kitab al-Fakhri* of Ibn al-Tiqtaqa, expanded to include considerable supplementary material.[17] The second work, also a history, is the *Muʿjam fi athar muluk al-Ajam* by Sharaf al-Din Fazl Allah Qazvini (d. 1339). The third work dedicated to Atabeg Ahmad is the *Miʿyar-i Nusrati* of Shams-i Fakhri, a work on Persian prosody composed in about 1313 (Iqbal 1999, 507, 524; 1962, 337). To these titles provided by Iqbal may be added the *Tuhfeh*, the work of counsel that forms the focus of the second half of this chapter.

The three compositions noted by Iqbal provide context for an exploration of the *Tuhfeh*. Together, the *Tajarib al-salaf*, the *Muʿjam fi athar muluk al-Ajam*, and the *Miʿyar-i Nusrati* suggest the cultural milieu in which Ahmad participated. In particular, they indicate an emphasis among the elites that surrounded Ahmad on the writing and reception of history and the skillful use of Persian artistic prose.

As has long been recognized, the writing of history in Persian assumed a high level of importance in the Il-Khanid era as a whole; the *Tarikh-i jahangusha* (completed 1260) of Ata Malik Juwayni (1226–1283) and the *Jamiʿ al-tawarikh* (completed 1310–11) of Rashid al-Din Fazl Allah

17. There is disagreement among scholars regarding the date of the *Tajarib al-salaf*'s composition. Abbas Iqbal, on the basis of the manuscripts used in the preparation of his edition of the text (Nakhjavani 1965), dates its completion to 1324 (see Iqbal 1981, 341–54), a dating followed by Danishpazhuh in his introduction to the *Tuhfeh* (1962, 13-14). Rawzati (1981, 14-15), who published a facsimile of an earlier manuscript, adopts the date of 1314, a dating followed in Melville 1998, 58. Hindushah, it is important to note, does not refer to the *Kitab al-Fakhri* but to the *Munyah al-fuzala' fi tawarikh al-khulafa' wa al-vuzara'*, a later, considerably revised version of Ibn al-Tiqtaqa's work, the first version of which had been completed in 1302 and dedicated to Fakhr al-Din Isa of Mosul. The *Munyah al-fuzala'*, according to Hindushah, was written by Ibn al-Tiqtaqa for Zangishah b. Badr al-Din Hasan of Damghan (Nakhjavani 1965, 4). On the relationship of the *Kitab al-Fakhri* and the *Tajarib al-salaf*, see Iqbal 1981, 342–44.

(d. 1318) are only the best known examples of Persian historiography in the period. Ahmad himself was shaped by a culture in which the value attached to history and its lessons served to consolidate the standing of the courtly elite. The Atabeg, as already noted, was related to the family of Juwayni through his father Yusufshah's marriage to the historian's niece, a daughter of Shams al-Din, the Sahib-Diwan.[18] It is also highly likely that Ahmad, through his long-standing presence at the Il-Khanid court, was acquainted with Rashid al-Din and his son Ghiyath al-Din (d. 1336), both of whom served as viziers to the Il-Khans and were great patrons of scholarship, including historical writing and other literary and artistic activities. The two works of history known to have been dedicated to Atabeg Ahmad, the *Tajarib al-salaf* and the *Mu'jam fi athar muluk al-Ajam*, attest to his cultivation of an environment in which the preservation and transmission of historical knowledge and an appreciation of the instructiveness of the past flourished. It might be added that according to the predominant portrayal of Ahmad, discussed above, the Atabeg heeded the lessons of history in his decision to follow his father's path of accommodation with and loyalty to the Il-Khans as opposed to his brother's reported opportunism and disloyalty (cf. Spuler 1985, 897).

The third work known to have been dedicated to Ahmad, the *Mi'yar-i Nusrati* of the poet Shams al-Din b. Fakhr al-Din Fakhri Isfahani, suggests an appreciation of the Persian literary arts. A keen interest in the adept and subtle use of the Persian language is suggested by the Atabeg's patronage of several poets and literary specialists. Shams-i Fakhri himself lived in his youth at the court of the Atabeg and completed his book on the art of prosody in Luristan in 1313.[19] Another eminent poet who wrote

18. Such marriages among local dynasties and vizieral families were not uncommon in this period; for an example of marriage ties between the Inju dynasty of Shiraz and the family of Ghiyath al-Din Muhammad, son of Rashid al-Din, see Aigle 2005, 159.

19. Shams-i Fakhri moved subsequently to the court of the vizier Ghiyath al-Din and later still entered the service of Shaikh Abu Ishaq Inju (1321–59), the patron of Hafez. He also wrote, while in Qum in 1331–32, a celebrated ode in praise of Ghiyath al-Din, and in 1344–45 a work on prosody, the *Mi'yar-i jamali wa miftah-i Abu Ishaqi*, dedicated to Abu Ishaq Inju (Nafisi 1984, 1:148–49).

panegyrics for Atabeg Ahmad as well as for Ghazan Khan and Öljeitü (r. 1304–17) was Sa'd al-Din Sa'id Haravi (d. 1364–65), a few of whose poems survive, although his diwan has been lost (Nafisi 1984, 1:175). Furthermore, Sharaf al-Din Fazl Allah Qazvini, author of the history *al-Mu'jam fi athar muluk al-Ajam,* also wrote panegyric poetry for the Atabeg, as well as for the viziers Shams al-Din Bughal and Ghiyath al-Din Muhammad (Jajarmi 1959, 1, chap. 11).

This group of works shows Atabeg Ahmad to have been fully engaged in the cultural production of his time and region and to have shared in the role of patron with the major sponsors of cultural activities of the age, among them the vizier Ghiyath al-Din. The books written for Ahmad exhibit a combined interest in historiography and the literary arts, a trend represented in many works of the Il-Khanid period. As M. G. S. Hodgson noted, "History was felt to be fine literature and was expected to be artfully constructed and adorned, after the increasingly elaborate style that had already made an appearance in the Earlier Middle Period" (Hodgson 1974, 2:486). The popularity of versified histories, such as the *Zafar-namah* (1334–35) of Mustawfi (Qazvini 2001), the *Shahanshah-namah* (commissioned by Abu Sa'id, completed 1337–38) of Ahmad-i Tabrizi (Tabrizi n.d.), and the *Ghazan-namah* (ca. 1357) (Nur al-Din 2001) of Nur al-Din b. Shams al-Din is a particularly striking feature of the period under discussion in this chapter. But even works of historiography written in prose in this era often displayed, in places, an adept use of the artistic style associated with the literary production of the chancery.[20] Probably the best known example of this form of Persian prose in a historiographical context is the *Tajziyah al-amsar wa tazjiyah al-a'sar,* known as the *Tarikh-i Vassaf,* of Vassaf al-Hazrat (1264–1334), widely considered among modern scholars to be at once an invaluable source of historical information and virtually impenetrable in its use of language (Browne 1928, 3:67–68; Rypka 1968b, 314; Hodgson 1974, 2:486; Spuler 1985, 7; Iqbal 1999, 524). Significantly, the *Tarikh-i Vassaf* bears some resemblance to one of the historiographical

20. On artistic prose in Arabic, see Meisami 1998, 1:105–6, and references there cited; and see further Roemer 1971; Paul 1998, 455–57.

works dedicated to the Atabeg, the previously mentioned *Mu'jam fi athar muluk al-Ajam* of Fazl Allah Qazvini. E. G. Browne describes the *Mu'jam* as "a highly rhetorical account of the ancient Kings of Persia," "a quasi-historical work similar in style but far inferior in value" to the work of Vassaf (Browne 1928, 3:67–68). Perhaps reflecting earlier perceptions of similarities between the two works of history, the great Ottoman bibliographer Katib Çelebi Hajji Khalifa (1609–1657) reported, without endorsing, the opinion that Qazvini was Vassaf's father (Çelebi 1943, 1:1736).[21]

While the involved, often highly figurative prose of the era's chancery style may lack appeal for many modern readers, it was greatly prized in the Atabeg's time. Hodgson situates the popularity of this ornate Persian style not only in the context of cycles of literary preference but also in the context of Persian's function as a lingua franca, a second language to many persons who wrote and read it, and who were conscious of using "a more or less artificial instrument for delimited social purposes. The language was expected to conform to the canons of courtly civility" (Hodgson 1974, 2:487). The development of the cultivated style was linked, as it had been in earlier periods, to the specialized character of the bureaucracies of the Il-Khanid and tributary states,[22] and perhaps also to the important role of poetry, especially panegyric, in gaining access to the court and to the ruler: it is noticeable that Vassaf, Shabankarah'i, Fazl Allah Qazvini, and other writers who employed the chancery style in their prose also composed panegyric poetry. Artistic prose was appreciated as a kind of literary display that engaged its audience through its apposite citations, allusions, tropes, and metaphors and evoked pleasure by means of particular literary effects.[23] In social and cultural terms, the production and appreciation of artistic prose was closely linked to the

21. Katib Çelebi dates the composition of the *Mu'jam* to around 1256–57, a date that, in view of the book's dedication, cannot be correct. On the ascription to Vassaf, see further Futuhi Nasab 2004–5, xviii–xx. The *Mu'jam* is listed as the work of Fazl Allah b. Abdullah al-Shirazi in al-Baghdadi 1951–55, 2:821.

22. Luther 1990; Meisami 1992. On this aspect of premodern belletristic prose in Arabic, see al-Musawi 2006, 101–33.

23. Cf., with reference to Arabic prose in an earlier period, Hamori 1994, 99.

affirmation of a set of cultural-ethical ideals and constituted a mark of belonging to the courtly elite.

In this context, it is no surprise that the Atabeg, like other patrons of his time, was the recipient of works composed in the ornate chancery style. A prime example, as Browne noted, was the *Muʿjam fi athar muluk al-Ajam* of Fazl Allah Qazvini. This history draws attention to its stylistic virtuosity in its title, which, as Muhammad Taqi Bahar indicated, alludes in a conscious gesture of deference and imitation to the celebrated *Muʿjam fi maʿathir ashʿar al-Ajam* (completed in neighboring Fars in about 1232–33) of Shams al-Din Muhammad b. Qays Razi, known as Shams-i Qays.[24] Another example of the conscious employment of the decorated style for particular purposes is the *Tuhfeh,* which forms the subject of the remainder of this chapter.

The *Tuhfeh*

Authorship and Genre

The book known simply as *Tuhfeh,* or *The Gift,* was dedicated to the Atabeg by an author whose name does not appear in the text. In the single known manuscript of the *Tuhfeh,* the space in which the author's name would have been inscribed has been left blank (*Tuhfeh,* 6).[25] Consideration of the book's relationship to works of known authorship also written for Ahmad has allowed for some conjectures regarding the *Tuhfeh*'s possible authorship.

M. T. Danishpazhuh, who edited and published the text of the *Tuhfeh,* has proposed that it may be the work of Sharaf al-Din Fazl Allah b. Abdullah Qazvini, whose *al-Muʿjam fi athar muluk al-Ajam,* as indicated above, was likewise dedicated to the Atabeg Ahmad (Danishpazhuh 1962,

24. Bahar 1958, 3:105–6, cited in Futuhi Nasab 2004–5, vi–vii.

25. Such lacunae appear not infrequently in manuscripts of advice literature in cases in which, presumably, the authorship of the work was not known to the copyist. In fact, many mirrors were written for whom the authors are not known; for several examples in Arabic, Persian, and Turkish, see Levend 1962, 181, 183, 188–89.

12–14).[26] Danishpazhuh advanced this proposal in part on the basis of suggestive remarks in Qazvini's introduction to the *Mu'jam*. The proposition finds further support in the occurrence of certain metaphors and allusions in both works, especially in their introductory sections, where the same phrases occasionally appear.[27]

Danishpazhuh has also pointed to the relationship between the historical section of the *Tuhfeh,* which will be discussed below, and the *Tajarib al-salaf,* similarly dedicated to Ahmad. For instance, in one place the author of the *Tuhfeh* refers to an individual, apparently a poet, as "a dear one" *(azizi)*; the poem in question appears in the identical location in the *Tajarib al-salaf,* and may be assumed to be by Hindushah himself (*Tuhfeh,* 174; Nakhjavani 1965, 81). On the basis of these textual commonalities, Danishpazhuh has proposed that both the *Mu'jam* and the *Tuhfeh* must have been written after Hindushah completed his *Tajarib al-salaf* but before the Atabeg's death (Danishpazhuh 1962, 13–14).[28] A closer examination of the *Tuhfeh* suggests a relationship with the *Kitab al-Fakhri* (or rather, its later adaptation, the *Munyah al-fuzala' fi tarikh al-khulafa' wa al-vuzara'*), perhaps independently of the *Tajarib al-salaf,* and Danishpazhuh also proposed that in certain places the *Tuhfeh* and the *Tajarib al-salaf* may have drawn on a common source (Danishpazhuh 1962, 14). Whether or not Sharaf al-Din Fazl Allah Qazvini wrote the *Tuhfeh,* the intertextual relationships and similarities among the various works dedicated to Atabeg Ahmad illuminate the context that gave rise to them all.

The author of the *Tuhfeh* refers to his book as a *mukhtasar,* that is, a short work or abridgement. The ninth and longest chapter of the book, which constitutes a summary of the history of the caliphs, indeed resembles an abridgement, possibly of the *Tajarib al-salaf* or of a common source, the previously mentioned *Munyah al-fuzala'*. If Danishpazhuh's

26. Cf. Nafisi 1984, 2:760, where the work is listed as anonymous.

27. For example, in both texts, the author introduces his reasons for writing with the expression *az muddati madid wa ahdi ba'id;* see Qazvini 2004–5, 28; *Tuhfeh,* 6.

28. Danishpazhuh takes 724 as the date of the completion of the *Tajarib al-salaf* and thus places the composition of the *Tuhfeh* between 724 and 733, when the Atabeg died. As mentioned above, however, there is some uncertainty surrounding both dates.

suggestion that the *Tuhfeh* is the work of Fazl Allah Qazvini is correct, it is possible that the writer composed it as a brief companion to the longer and more elaborate, and apparently more widely circulated, *Muʿjam fi athar muluk al-Ajam.*[29] The *Tuhfeh* complements the longer work in that the *Muʿjam* deals with the history of Iran from Gayumarth to Anushirvan (531–79), whereas the *Tuhfeh,* in its historical section, addresses only the Islamic era, beginning with the birth of the Prophet in the reign of Anushirvan. The two works thus draw on different historiographical repertoires, a contrast that is perhaps reflected in slight differences of emphasis in other aspects of their composition as well. Whereas the preface to the *Muʿjam* draws heavily on poetic quotations, the preface to the *Tuhfeh,* while citing some lines of verse, gives precedence to Qur'anic texts. In the *Muʿjam,* Ahmad is referred to as "the greatest sovereign, the ruler of the Persian kings, the Chosroes of Iran, heir to the Kayanid sovereignty, the Jamshid of the age, the Darius of the time, eraser of the traces of the Barmakids" *(padshah-i aʿzam wa shahriyar-i muluk-i Ajam, khusrau-i Iran wa varith-i mulk-i Kayan, Jamshid-i zaman, Dara-yi dawran, nasikh-i athar-i Barmak)*—all epithets that emphasize the Iranian cultural context and are in keeping with the history of Iran that constitutes the subject of the book (Qazvini 2004–5, 18). The *Tuhfeh,* on the other hand, is dedicated to the Atabeg as "the Emperor of Islam *[padshah-i Islam],* the refuge of the people of faith, the mighty sovereign, shadow of the favor of God, the most perfect guardian among the Sons of Adam, caliph of the Ajam, heir to the kingship of Jam[shid], an Alexander in judgment, a sun with regard to the lawful, a Buzurgmihr in administration, a luminary in mind, of finest qualities, exalted aspiration, a Chosroes among kings, Nusrat al-Dunya wa al-Din, supporter of the Muslims"—epithets that draw on multiple cultural traditions and place greater emphasis on Islamic categories than was

29. Whereas only one manuscript of the *Tuhfeh* has been found, the *Muʿjam* survives in many copies (Futuhi Nasab 2004–5, xli–xlii). Furthermore, Katib Çelebi reports that the *Muʿjam* was translated on the order of Mahmud Paşha, vizier to Sultan Muhammad Khan (Mehmed II, r. 1444–46, 1451–81), under the title *Tarjuman al-balagha* (Çelebi 1943, 1:1736). On the high regard in which the Persian histories of the Mongol period were held among Ottoman writers and patrons, see Fleischer 1986, 240.

apparent in the dedication in the *Mu'jam* (*Tuhfeh,* 5). The dedication in the *Tajarib al-salaf,* it may be noted, invokes the Kayanids, Jamshid, and Darius, and addresses Ahmad as "supporter of the Muslim foundations, protector of the area of certainty, guardian of the heartlands of religion" *(mu'ayyid-i qawa'id-i musalmani, hami-yi hawzeh-i yaqin, ra'i-yi bayzeh-i din)* (Nakhjavani 1965, 2–3). The difference in emphasis among these dedicatory passages is likely to be related to the different subject matters of the books being introduced, serving to situate the royal patron in the traditions of Iranian kings and Muslim rulers alike.

The title *Tuhfeh* reveals nothing of the book's contents, nor of the genre to which it might belong; it suggests only that it was written with a presentational function in mind. At the beginning and end of the manuscript, the copyist referred to the work as *Kitab Nasihat al-muluk,* "Book of counsel for kings" (*Tuhfeh,* 15, 239), an indication that in his view, the work's central purpose was to provide counsels and instructions regarding royal conduct. A perusal of the work reveals that, as the copyist's description would imply, it contains many counsels and instructions regarding the conduct of rulers and viziers. But the book's contents are not limited to these topics. As already mentioned, an especially striking feature of the work is a chapter entitled "On Islamic History," significantly placed in the penultimate position among the ten chapters that comprise the book. Probably noting this feature, a later owner, librarian, or reader has inscribed the manuscript with the descriptive label *Kitab al-Tuhfeh fi al-nasa'ih wa al-tawarikh* (The gift: moral counsels and historical narratives) (Danishpazhuh 1962, 15).

THE TOPICS of the ten chapters are as follows:

(1) The virtues of just rulers;
(2) The close ties between kings and their subjects;
(3) Justice and injustice;
(4) Knowledge of the qualities on which the order of the state depends, and with which felicity in this world and the next is bound up, such as forgiveness, force, resolve, and vigilance;
(5) The accomplishments *(ma'athir)* of kings in their sovereignty;

(6) The fine sayings and witticisms of kings;
(7) The conditions of viziers and a portion of the choicest stories concerning them;
(8) The consequences of viziers' reflections and their wise sayings;
(9) On Islamic history;
(10) Exhortations for kings (*Tuhfeh*, 7).

The *Tuhfeh* thus belongs to the genre of the work of advice for rulers. It is a "mirror for princes," but, this genre being characterized by considerable fluidity, it readily accommodates the particular interests of author and patron. In this case, the role of history is assigned a prominent position. Of equal importance and inseparable from the author's communication of moral instruction through historical narrative is his deft use of the chancery style, or artistic prose. In fact, the *Tuhfeh* combines the prevalent interest in history and the attention to style, already noted in connection with the Atabeg, with a third element, an emphasis on moral counsel for holders of political authority. I shall consider these various dimensions of the text with particular reference to its preface and its distinctive ninth chapter.

The Preface

The *Tuhfeh*'s preface, composed in rhyming prose, employs Qur'anic quotations as units of reference and lines of poetry chosen to heighten the import of or comment on the author's points. Meanings are rendered more complex, for purposes of accentuation or nuance, through the dexterous use of homonyms, synonyms, and antonyms. The work opens as follows:

> Most abundant thanks, that in the places where the robe of "If you are grateful, then I shall increase you" (Q.7:14) is graciously accepted, He increases life in the excellence of existence; and richest praise, that when He breathes from the most precious heights He makes the horizons [of the created world] and the souls [of humankind] resplendent—are due to the sacred presence of the Possessor of Sovereignty, who is the Creator of the World and the Holder of the Earth and the Heavens. A countenance of fresh petals, its rose-colored beauty at the top of the branch, is

the ornament of His creation, and the lustrous curling ringlet from the bridal attire of the wind in spring is the adornment of His power. Every [being] that steps onto the desert of existence, out of the concealment of non-being into the world of generation and corruption, releases its tongue in praise and reverence for the ineffable Originator, "For there is nothing but that it sings His praises" (Q.44:17).

A Wise One who illumined the hardness of the sky of [humanity's] inner nature *[fitrat]* with the jewel of the planets of prophecy, and gave beauty and adornment to the gardens of the earthly globe through the flowers of the trees and the varied lights of the equity *[ma'dalat]* of just kings *[muluk-i ba-dad]*, and perfumed the minds and lives of those on earth with the gentle breezes of the favor of their justice, and made their rank to follow that of the guides on the paths and the leaders among the prophets, so that by the signs of right guidance and the ornaments of the stars of prophecy they deliver the path of those wearied in the wilderness of confusion to the safe haven of faith, and the straying of corrupters remains banished to the extremities of the world by the bright tips of the life-taking spears of sultans.

The best of wishes and purest of prayers be upon the purified grave and perfumed place of martyrdom of the choicest of beings and the epitome of existent beings, the possessor of the highest portico of prophethood, the most exquisite couplet of the ode in the diwan of greatness, Chosroes of the kingdoms of prophecy, the traveler on the routes of generosity *[futuwwat]*, the Seal of the Prophets, Muhammad the Chosen, God's prayers be upon him, who delivered those drowning in the seas of (humanity's) innate nature *[fitrat]* from the shipwreck of aberration to the shore of guidance by the ship of following him, and quenched the thirst of those parched in the desert of waywardness from the living fountain of his message by the pure water of his generosity; and on the members of his Family and his Friends, who are the stars of the firmament of Islam and the keys to the doors of faith, [as in the] verse:

On their souls, the gifts of blessings
From God, who created all beings.

For the masters of perspicacity it is confirmed with evident signs, and for the possessors of knowledge it is confirmed by clear proofs that the human species, in accordance with "And We have ennobled the Sons of Adam" (Q.70:17), are the noblest of creatures and the most eminent of beings fashioned (by God); and the maintenance of humankind's livelihoods and the contract for their provision would be prevented and impossible were it not for the justice-spreading sultan.

Thus, the choicest and noblest of existent beings may be the persons of kings endowed with justice. Authority *[saltanat]* and dominion *[dawlat]* depend on the worldly and the other-worldly, and the just ruler by dispensing mercy and spreading equity possesses the reins of these two realms *[dawlat]*; and whoever embraces the dominion of these two kingdoms, of necessity his virtue will be higher than that of all existent beings except for prophets.

Justice is a fragrant tree: its roots lie in the meadow of power *[qudrat]* and might *[kamgari]*, and its branches reach up to the mountain-peaks of authority *[saltanat]* and sovereignty *[jahandari]*. Every king who, in his appreciation of this state and his nurturing of this young seedling, sets an example in the path of perfection and the law of equilibrium *[qanun-i i'tidal]*, must make obligatory the seeking of permanence for the principles of good fortune and the stability of unceasing dominion from the presence of the Possessor of Glory, the source of religious obligation.

Today, by the praise of God Almighty, the ear and neck of fortune are adorned with the gem of justice and the compassion of the Emperor of Islam *[padshah-i Islam]*, the refuge of the people of faith, the mighty sovereign, shadow of the favor of God, the most perfect guardian among the Sons of Adam, caliph of the Ajam, heir to the kingship of Jam, an Alexander in judgment, a sun with regard to the lawful, a Buzurgmihr in administration, a luminary in mind, of finest qualities, exalted aspiration, a Chosroes among kings, Nusrat al-Dunya wa al-Din, supporter of the Muslims, the Most Mighty Atabeg Ahmad, son of the Exalted Atabeg Yusufshah, son of the Ennobled Atabeg Shams al-Din Alp Arghun b. Hazarasp, may God make eternal his dominion and elevate his estate in the East and the West. And the desire of the life of the world is sweetened by the taste of noble characteristics.

> The days have increased in excellence and joy
> Since Islam has supported the reign *[dawlat]* of Ahmad.
> (*Tuhfeh*, 3–5)

These opening sections of the preface are shaped by a vision of royal authority in which the ruler plays a central role in the divinely designed, hierarchically structured order of the world. Within this order, just kings occupy a station immediately after prophets, both of them being divinely chosen. The author employs a rich vocabulary of Persian and Arabic words to convey the notions of ornament and adornment, which he applies in close succession to prophets and just kings. His vivid language evokes the pleasures of the senses, especially the olfactory delight given by fragrance and the visual delights of jewels and the sky at night. He produces these evocations not by direct or explicit means but through the use of rhetorical figures, including a variety of metaphors: justice is evoked by the image of a fragrant tree; the prophets are linked to planets and stars that decorate and illumine the sky; parallel to them, just kings are associated with perfumed breezes in the earth. The author employs figurative language to convey right guidance and rectitude on the one hand and loss of direction and moral confusion on the other. His images are drawn from the flourishing beauty of the divinely made natural world and the sensory delights it affords to humankind, contrasted with the parched conditions of the desert and the disorienting vastness of the wilderness, and from the orderly perfections of architectural forms and literary compositions, contrasted with the peril of being lost at sea.

Later in his preface, the author, having established his facility with the production of artistic prose, moves from his praise of God and the Prophet to address his personal situation and to introduce his book. He praises the Atabeg Ahmad for having transformed the city of Shushtar (Ar. Tustar), the major town in Khuzistan, from a place of hostility into one of security:

> The author . . . [lacuna] . . . of this brief work writes as follows: For a long period and an extended period the workings of [my] mind were searching for the intermediacy of an expedient that would attain the honor of an audience in the elevated presence of that exalted one of the court. The hindrances of the age of the concealment of veils were not lifted by way of my desire, and connections without number showed negligence in realizing this goal, until the time came when the place of Shushtar was honored by the right flank of the august legions of that religion-nurturing

and justice-spreading king, and its localities and environs, that had been the stopping places of the saddle bags of hostility, became the campground of safety and security and the envy of the garden of contentment. Then this greatly desired bride showed her face from the veil of fortunate opportunity and by that dominion *[dawlat]*, which is the most highly praised objective of the intelligent and the most delightful gift of the virtuous, found happiness. I said to myself [in verse]:

> You have no horses to give, nor any money
> So may a favorable omen bring happiness, even if your condition is unfortunate.
> (*Tuhfeh*, 6)[30]

In this passage, the author again employs figurative language to evoke the ruler's inaccessibility, which is likened to the remoteness of the beloved, until by good fortune the author gains an audience with the hitherto secluded ruler just as the bridegroom finally comes face to face with the bride. These metaphors, it should be noted, were well established, familiar to and even anticipated by the author's audience. It was their skillful use that demonstrated the author's fluency in the literary arts and his ability to communicate effectively in the particular courtly milieu to which, as his preface indicates, he sought entry.

Like Fazl Allah Qazvini in his evocative naming of his *Muʿjam fi athar muluk al-Ajam*, the *Tuhfeh*'s author, whose awareness of literary devices has already been suggested, drew attention to its style. Further still into his introduction, like other writers in the tradition of *adab*, the author of the *Tuhfeh* listed the literary materials that he intended to include in his work.[31] More than this, however, the author of the *Tuhfeh* proceeds to identify a number of literary techniques, for which he uses the appropriate technical terminology:

30. The final verse (reading *al-fa'l* for *al-qal*) is again in Arabic.

31. The itemizing of materials occurs in prefaces to works of many genres. For a discussion of this feature in the geographical work of Ibn al-Faqih, see Miquel 1967, 154.

> [The author of this brief work] . . . has written a few sections on the ways of kings *[siyar-i muluk]*, the histories of the caliphs *[tawarikh-i khulafa']*, pieces of advice *[nasa'ih]* and admonition *[mawa'iz]*, a portion of choice materials related to the conditions of viziers and their eloquent sayings *[zarf]*, witticisms *[lata'if]* and memorable utterances *[ma'athir]*. He has called this brief work *[mukhtasar] The Gift*, and has embellished *[muwashshah gardanid]* it with the ornaments of beautiful Qur'anic passages *[ayah]*, reports *[akhbar]*, wise sayings *[hikam]*, stories *[hikayat]*, proverbs *[amthal]*, poems *[ash'ar]*, and verses *[abyat]*. As far as his ability allows and in accordance with his capacity and capability, he has adorned the bride of the word *[sukhan]* with a range of beautiful ornaments, and with the garments *[hulal]* of internal rhyme *[tarsi']*, paronomasia *[tajnis]*, rhymed prose *[saj']*, brevity *[ijaz]*, concision *[ikhtisar]*, metaphors *[isti'arah]*, pleasing qualities *[mahasin]*, and unusual allusions *[ghara'ib-i kinayat]*: "And he whose sustenance is abundant, let him spend of that which God has given him" (Q.65:7). (*Tuhfeh*, 6–7)[32]

As has been suggested, the author indeed employs these rhetorical devices in many instances throughout his text. In the passages already cited, several instances of specific literary techniques may be noted. Among these strategies are the use of *saj'*, rhyming prose, throughout much of the preface; *iqtibas*, that is, references to Qur'anic verses that are not explicitly identified as quotations (as in *malik al-mulk* [Q.3:26]); sequences of words in which similar letters are juxtaposed *(anwa'-i anwar)*; rhyming words used in immediate succession *(kakh-i shakh, adam qadam, azhar-i ashjar)* and other forms of internal rhyme *(bar marqad-i mutahhar wa mashhad-i mu'attar-i khulasih-i ka'inat wa zubdih-i mawjudat; iwan-i risalat // diwan-i jalalat, mamalik-i nubuwwat masalik-i futuwwat; qawa'id-i iqbal // dawlat-i bi zawal az hazrat-i dhi al-jalal)*; alliteration *(zib wa zinat, ma'dalat-i muluk, nujum-i nubuwwat, gush wa gardan-i gardun)*; the use of lexical items derived from the same Arabic root *(anfas // anfus //*

32. On these literary devices, many of which are adopted from Arabic, see van Gelder 1998; Heinrichs 1998a; 1998b; Rowson 1998.

tanaffus; lata'if-i lutf-i ma'dalat-i ishan; bi barahin-i qati'-i mubarhan); and the quotation of lines of poetry, as well as Qur'anic verses.[33]

These features of the preface, however, are not employed in a uniform manner throughout the book. The *Tuhfeh* exhibits a range of literary styles, depending on the subject matter under discussion and its position in the structure of the composition. In prefaces, the use of the ornate, often quasipoetic chancery style was common, even expected, in this period. In Arabic, the use of rhymed prose in prefaces dates from the ninth century,[34] with authors writing in Persian following the Arabic model from about a century later. The principal medium of expression for most works of advice literature is prose, but *saj'* is often adopted in prefaces to works of advice as to works of so many other genres, and poetry is interwoven with prose throughout such works. From the tenth and eleventh centuries and later, prose and poetry are interlinked in a close, cross-referential relationship in many Persian writings, including advice literature.[35]

In the *Tuhfeh,* the author's preface prefigures and prepares the reader for the main body of the work.[36] The vision of order and authority indicated in the preface has already been mentioned. For the Atabeg and his court, it was a familiar order, in which just kings occupied a station just below that of prophets; unjust kings, by contrast, awaited eternal punishment for the sufferings they had inflicted on, or failed to avert from, their subjects. These themes, alluded to in the author's preface, did not require full explication, but they are reiterated in the body of the work. The author links the themes of divine reward and punishment with the pivotal role of the ruler, who is responsible for maintaining justice in his kingdom by preserving balance and harmony among the different groups of his subjects. He expresses this vision, with which his audience was already

33. For an analysis of the use of these rhetorical features in the *Mu'jam,* see Futuhi Nasab 2004–5, xxxiii and following.

34. For the use of rhymed prose in Arabic prefaces, see Freimark 1967, 16–17, 20–21.

35. For an insightful exploration of prosimetrum in Persian literature, see Meisami 1997, 295–319.

36. Among numerous parallel examples, see Schimmel 1975, 163, for a discussion of the role of the poem of invocation in prefiguring the themes of epic poetry.

conversant, more explicitly in the opening section of his first chapter, "On the Virtues of Just Rulers." He writes,

> God Almighty has said, "Were it not for God's defense of some people against others, the world would fall into ruin" (Q.2:251). The Prophet, peace be upon him, said, "Were it not for authority (sultan), some people would consume others." The Glorious and Almighty Truth raised the foundation of the pillars of kings' sovereignty by the execution of commands and prohibitions in order that they should adorn the heartland *[bayzeh]* of the kingdom and the core *[hawzeh]* of the sultanate with the ornament of the goodness of equity and the felicity of justice, and that they should provide a refuge for the weak among the subjects from the assault of the strong, and nurture [them] in the fortress of compassion and the cradle of mercy, just like a tender mother; that they should keep the vicinities of the roads and the regions of the realm free of the wickedness of tyrants and the onslaught of fearless rebels *[bughat]*. For if the rose garden of the kingdom remains devoid of the gusts of the breeze of the ruler's justice, the rose of the heart of the weak will become, like the heart of the rose, a part of the thorn of the oppressors' cruelty. And if the water lily of the dazzling sword of just kings does not raise its head above the pool of the gardens of governance, they will draw forth the arm of the oppression of the lily-tongued rebels like a violet from the nape of the neck. For this reason He has manifested their existence on the stage of favor to the world's people, as He said, "But God is possessed of goodness over the people" (Q.2:251), that is, by the establishment of authority the people will thrive. (*Tuhfeh,* 8)

Like the preface, this opening passage of the first chapter contains many rhetorical figures, including *tabdil,* the inversion of terms (heart and rose); the use of metaphor, here drawn especially from a variety of flowers; the repetition of sounds *(bi nawafidh-i avamir wa nawahi; zawahi-yi masalik wa nawahi-yi mamalik)*; and the balance of phrases that are virtually synonymous. Also evident is the copious use of Arabic lexical items, a prominent feature of the cultivated prose of the period (Rypka 1968a, 220, 317).[37] The passage depicts more fully the political culture of the court that

37. On the extensive use of Arabic in the *Mu'jam* as well, see Nafisi 1984, 1:144.

was implicit in much of the preface. It does so by extending the metaphors already encountered in the introduction, where the kingdom is likened to a rose garden and the ruler's justice to a gentle breeze, the cultivation of the garden's blooms and the judicious pruning of its thorns alike dependent on the sovereign's equity.

The Ninth Chapter

Among the most striking features of the *Tuhfeh*, as noted above, is its inclusion of a disproportionately long chapter "on Islamic history" *(dar tarikh-i islami)*; this penultimate chapter is more than three times longer than any of the others. The inclusion of historical material in works of advice was by no means unusual, especially in this period (see further F. Rosenthal 1968, 115, 118). The interplay between historiography and moral instruction allowed for the image of the ideal ruler, explored in mirrors, to inform works of history, which sometimes incorporated entire advisory texts, and for the explication of moral lessons through historical narratives in works of advice. In this way, single works quite frequently brought together one or more "genres" in structural combinations that attested to the widespread conception of history as exemplary. As Julie Scott Meisami has demonstrated in a number of publications, from the eleventh century onward, if not even earlier, many Persian historiographical works display an emphasis on the moral dimensions implicit in the unfolding of history (1992, 1995, 1999; see also Busse 1968, 18).

Just as historians frequently composed their narrative accounts to didactic effect, authors of advice literature related historical episodes in ways that conveyed their discursive intentions.[38] Furthermore, as in the case of the *Tuhfeh*, some authors of mirrors incorporated substantial chapters devoted to historical subjects. For example, as Danishpazhuh has noted, the *Nasihat al-muluk* ascribed to al-Ghazali includes a section devoted to "the genealogies, conduct, and histories of the kings" *(dhikr*

38. For a skillful demonstration of Nizam al-Mulk's shaping of historical narrative in the *Siyasat-namah*, see Simidchieva 2004.

ansab al-muluk wa siyarihim wa tawarikhihim) (Danishpazhuh 1962, 12).[39] This "historical" section of the *Nasihat al-muluk* differs considerably, however, from the ninth chapter of the *Tuhfeh*. The former provides a sketchy account of the pre-Islamic Iranian past only, whereas the *Tuhfeh* supplies a comprehensive treatment of the history of the Islamic era, from the birth of the Prophet to the end of the Abbasid caliphate. The two authors' approaches to their historical materials are also quite different. (Pseudo-) Ghazali's account is relatively brief and provides little detail. After reaching the point of the Muslim conquest, the author abandons his roughly chronological approach for a series of anecdotes and aphorisms concerning various exemplary rulers of the Islamic and pre-Islamic eras; as F. R. C. Bagley has put it, his purpose appears to have been "only to recapitulate the moral character traditionally assigned to each king" (al-Ghazali [Bagley] 1964, 47n2). The author of the *Tuhfeh,* by contrast, follows in his much fuller account the clearly structured, sequential pattern of a caliphal history. He treats the reign of each caliph, and in each section he includes, as well as narratives of events, particular kinds of information, such as the dates of the beginning and end of the caliph's reign, the caliph's age at his accession and when he died, the duration of his reign in years and months, and the names of his viziers (see further Robinson 2003, 74–79).

In a format that recapitulates the model established by the *Kitab al-Fakhri* (or the *Munyah al-fuzala'*) and the *Tajarib al-salaf,* the author of the *Tuhfeh* begins his historical section, the ninth chapter of his book, with the birth of the Prophet in the Year of the Elephant in the reign of Anushirvan. He narrates the life of the Prophet, with the genealogies of his parents, including his father's genealogy through Ishmael and Abraham back to Adam, his divine inspiration in his fortieth year, with Abu Bakr being the first man, Khadija the first woman, and Ali the first child to recognize his prophecy. He explains how, as long as Abu Talib was alive, Quraysh were unable to hurt him, and how, following Abu Talib's death, his uncle Abbas protected him against Quraysh; after the *hijra* to Medina, "Islam became manifest and strong." He lists the battles with Quraysh and

39. See al-Ghazali 1972, 84–99.

the Prophet's wives, children, and secretaries. He describes the Prophet's physical appearance and the impact of his beauty on those who beheld him. He describes in detail the disagreement among the Prophet's Companions surrounding the leadership of the community after his death and the negotiations that ensued (*Tuhfeh,* 130–33).

The author then asserts that there are two kinds of dominion (dawlat): "original" or "principal" *(asli)* and "subsidiary" *(far'i)*. "Original" dominions have themselves been of three kinds only: first, that of "the five caliphs": Abu Bakr, Umar, Uthman, Ali, and Hasan b. Ali; this dominion came to an end with Hasan b. Ali's peace settlement with Mu'awiyah (the author cites an Arabic verse at this point); second, the dominion of the Umayyads; third, the dominion of the Abbasids, which ended with the martyrdom of the caliph Musta'sim. The "subsidiary" dominions have also been of three kinds: first, that of the Alavis in Egypt; second, that of the Buyids; third, that of the Seljuks. The author explains his treatment of history in this fashion by observing that other than these three dominions, no other dynasty succeeded in gaining predominance over the caliphate, even if their territory was extensive (*Tuhfeh,* 133–34). The author's typology of rulership, together with his decision to conclude his historical narrative with the demise of the Abbasid caliphate, precluded the inclusion of an account of his patron's dynasty, yet his description provides a referential framework for and a prefiguration of contemporary conditions.

The author then provides an account of the caliphates of Abu Bakr, Umar, Uthman, Ali, and Hasan b. Ali. (The fluidity or perhaps irrelevance of sectarian boundaries suggested in the author's reading of Islamic history is consistent with the impression conveyed in other sources for the region in this period.) A Persian poem, to which I shall return shortly, on the fourteen Umayyad caliphs concludes the section and anticipates the upcoming treatment of the Umayyad dynasty (*Tuhfeh,* 134–54).

The author asserts that the Umayyads were despised by Muslims, all of whom longed for their passing. He details the rule of Mu'awiyah, whom he describes, evoking the lapse from *khilafa* (caliphate) to *mulk* (sovereignty), as a "sovereignty-holding king" *(padshahi mulk-dar)*; he narrates Mu'awiyah's advice to his son Yazid as his death approached, noting that he had built a foundation and warning him to preserve it against ruin, and specifically warning him against strife with four persons, the last of whom is Hussein; this "testament" foreshadows the disasters and tragedies of Yazid's caliphate (*Tuhfeh,* 154–57).[40] The author also records how Yazid tricks Amr b. al-As into pledging allegiance to him, as well as other accounts concerning Abu Sufyan at the conquest of Mecca. He provides a dramatic narrative of the caliphate of Yazid. Next, he treats Mu'awiyah b. Yazid, Marwan, Abd al-Malik, Walid, Sulayman, Umar b. Abd al-Aziz, Yazid b. Abd al-Malik, and so on down to Marwan "the Donkey." At this point he cites the Persian poem of "a dear one," apparently Hindushah, in which the names of the Abbasid caliphs are recorded (*Tuhfeh,* 157–75).[41] He then recounts the caliphates of each of the Abbasid caliphs, from Abu l-Abbas to Musta'sim. After stating the length of Musta'sim's caliphate and the names of his viziers, the author concludes "God knows best" and narrates nothing further (*Tuhfeh,* 174–218).

In much of this chapter, the structure and even wording of the *Tuhfeh* resemble those of the *Tajarib al-salaf.* Notably, Hindushah's *dawlat-i awwal* consists of the same five caliphs, and he too uses the phrase *dawlat-i Alawiyyan* in connection with the Fatimids (Nakhjavani 1965, 174). The author's style in this chapter is simple and for the most part unadorned, quite different from the complex and allusive prose of the preface and from the varied styles employed in earlier chapters. One of the few literary devices employed in this historical narrative is the insertion of poems, which are cited to serve specific purposes. For example, as mentioned previously, an unattributed poem (in Persian) precedes the account of the Umayyads:

> There were fourteen commanders among the Umayyads
> They seized the kingship *[mulk]* [and extended it] up to the courtyard
>   of the horizons
> The first was Mu'awiyah, the son of the faithless Hind
> After him, Yazid, the cruelty-working and wicked-hearted
> Then Mu'awiyah, then Marwan, and after him

40. For the words of the dying Mu'awiyah (r. 661–80) to his successor Yazid (r. 680–83), see also al-Jahiz 1985, 2:131.

41. The poem appears in the *Tajarib al-salaf* (Nakhjavani 1965, 81).

Abd al-Malik, Walid, Sulayman and then Umar
Then Yazid, and then Hisham, and next Walid
After him, Yazid, and Ibrahim in his tracks.
Marwan b. Muhammad, he whose *laqab* is the "Donkey,"
Was the last. And other than these fourteen, there was none.
(*Tuhfeh*, 154)[42]

Like the other complete poems that appear between major sections of the narrative, this example serves as a transitional device that marks the end of the author's discussion of one of his three "principal" dominions and the beginning of the next. The poem functions as a mnemonic and, at the same time, stresses the author's central moral point regarding the Umayyads: that their seizure and exercise of power was usurpatory and unjust. To render this point entirely explicit, the author concludes this section, after his relating of the poem, with the final sentence: "It should be known that the Umayyad state was detested *[mabghud]* among the Muslims, and the entirety of the people anticipated and looked forward to the demise of that state" (*Tuhfeh*, 154).[43]

The author's use of history to point moral lessons is perhaps particularly evident in his account of the ending of the Abbasid caliphate. In this narrative, which in several places resembles the account of Ibn al-Tiqtaqa more closely than that of Hindushah, the author emphasizes the personal failures of al-Musta'sim in the face of the advancing Mongol armies:

> He [al-Musta'sim] was a fine-souled and religious man *[mardi nik-nafs wa mutadayyin]*, but he possessed no judgment, and was inclined toward pleasure and amusement. Most of the time he went to his library and sat there, but not in such a way that he benefited in knowledge by so doing. . . .

42. Danishpazhuh has observed that the same poem appears in the *Athar al-vuzara'* of Sayf al-Din Aqili ('Uqayli) 1958, 22–23 (*Tuhfeh*, 154n1). A different Persian poem appears at the comparable point in the *Tajarib al-salaf* (Nakhjavani 1965, 74).

43. The word that appears as *mahfuf* has been left untranslated. On the use of poetry in Arabic historiography, see van Gelder 2004.

After [receiving the *bay'ah*] he remained neglectful of the administration of the realm, and took to the path of diversion. The vizier [Ibn al-Alqami, d. 1258] sometimes told him that the Mongol army had seized the entire world, and that their numbers were too great for the Commander of the Faithful to be able to confront them. But however much the vizier talked in this fashion, it was to no avail. The pillars of the state said, "The vizier is trying to frighten you," and behaved in such a way that he [the caliph] paid no attention to his [the vizier's] words and considered the matter unimportant. They behaved [in this way] until the moment when Hülegü took Baghdad and the caliph stood in the presence of the Sovereign. Hülegü said, "What kind of man are you, and what intellect and experience of affairs *[tadbir]* do you possess, that you neither gathered an army to confront us, nor pursued [a policy of] graciousness and moderation with us?"

In sum, day by day his negligence grew. Mu'ayyad al-Din, the vizier [Ibn] Alqami, when he saw that the matter was hopeless, sent an embassy in secret to the presence of the Sovereign of the World: "If the Blessed Emperor sets off on the march for Iraq, I will arrange for half of Iraq to fall under the rule of the Sovereign, and half under the rule of the caliph." And he made it clear that the caliph would not listen to advice. The Sovereign was pleased by Ibn Alqami's overture, and said, "He is an intelligent man; he attends both to our interests and to those of his own master."

Then, in accordance with a *yarlıgh* from the World-Conqueror, Bayju-Noyan reached Takrit with thirty thousand cavalry, and came to Baghdad from the western side. They approached the capital by way of Raqqa [?], and an army arrived in uninterrupted order from the eastern side. On Thursday [the fourth of Muharram] in the year 656, a great cloud of dust arose from the road to Ba'quba. The people climbed onto minarets and roofs to watch. The victorious banners of the Sovereign of the World Hülegü Khan arrived, and Nasir al-Din Tusi, Ala' al-Din, and Shams al-Din, his brother, were in attendance on the Sovereign.

When the troops of the Sovereign reached the outskirts of Baghdad, [the city] was surrounded by the army on all sides, and the caliph commanded that the army of Baghdad, which amounted to all of 11,000 cavalry, climb the ramparts of the city, and fight, until the nineteenth of Muharram. All at once the army of the Sovereign seized a tower, and

> the army entered Baghdad from that side. There was so much killing and plundering that no heart could bear even a brief explanation of it, and as for the details (they were beyond what could be endured). A *yarlıgh* was issued to the effect that they should bring the caliph, with his women and children, outside Baghdad, and a decree was then promulgated that Musta'sim, with two of his sons, Abu al-Abbas Ahmad and Abu al-Fada'il Abd al-Rahman, should be executed. The three were martyred on Thursday, the fourth of Safar, and the state of the Abbasids was cut off, after 520 years. Glory to Him whose dominion never ends. (*Tuhfeh*, 215–18)[44]

This narrative, clear and direct in its use of language and generally favorable in its portrayal of Hülegü and the Ilkhans, conveys the tragic results of a ruler's unwillingness to pay attention to affairs or to heed advice, even in the face of impending disaster for himself, his family, and his subjects. Of the various protagonists in the narrative, it is the vizier Ibn Alqami alone among the caliph's entourage who is portrayed as reasonable, sagacious, and loyal.[45] The author's interpretation of events is expressed forcefully through his poignant references to moments when the worst might yet have been averted, had the caliph behaved sensibly and responsibly in his decision-making.

Without drawing explicit parallels, the author's account of the caliph's dealings with Hülegü are likely to have carried particular meanings in the context of Atabeg Ahmad's court. Drawing on relatively recent events, the author's narrative serves to affirm the path of accommodation that had been pursued by Ahmad and his father Yusufshah when faced with a

44. For fuller accounts of these events, see Boyle 1968, 345–49; and Boyle 1961, 145–61. Compare Ibn al-Tiqtaqa 1980, 333–36, and Nakhjavani 1965, 317–23, where the narrative diverges considerably from that in the *Tuhfeh* from p. 321. The dates supplied in the *Tuhfeh* differ from those found in other accounts (e.g., Boyle 1961; Rashid al-Din 1994, 2:1004–21), but they appear in Ibn Tiqtaqa's account.

45. For other accounts in which Ibn al-Alqami is portrayed in a similar manner, see Boyle 1961, 152–53; Ibn al-Tiqtaqa 1980, 337–39. Ibn al-Alqami's role has been presented far less positively elsewhere; see Browne 1928, 2:464–66.

similar situation of asymmetrical power in their relations with Hülegü's descendants. The account casts an appreciative light on the wise and pragmatic conduct of Atabeg Ahmad himself, who cultivated close relations with the Il-Khans, who were now *padshahan-i Islam* (among the epithets used of Atabeg Ahmad himself) as well as *padshahan-i jahan*. Additionally, the narrative implies strongly that the caliph's perdition was largely owing to his failure to heed the advice of his sagacious and loyal vizier. This aspect of the story evokes the contrasting behavior of Ahmad's brother Afrasiyab, who, presented in conformity with the topos of ill-judged, impulsive, and excessive punishment, had mulcted and executed families of administrators who had served the dynasty loyally, and was eventually executed himself. By inference, the account of Musta'sim's final weeks serves to reinforce the generous and forbearing conduct of Ahmad toward servants of the state. It is worth noting that other viziers or vizierlike figures, such as Nasir al-Din Tusi and the Juwayni brothers, are depicted in the company of Hülegü and, like Ibn Alqami, emerge as men of intellect and judgment who had accepted and adjusted to the new historical circumstances. To make these points still more evident, this account appears at the very end of the long ninth chapter. Accordingly, it is followed immediately by the tenth and final chapter, "Admonitions for Kings."

Conclusion

As these various, contrasting sections of the *Tuhfeh* illustrate, the relationship of history and counsel is a very close one in the cultural setting to which the book belongs. In this environment, the categories of historical narrative and moral counsel constitute less distinct genres than variants of a single literary continuum that served to define, consolidate, and perpetuate a distinct cultural-political elite.

As the *Tuhfeh* demonstrates, authors of works of advice seek to communicate their counsels through the effective use of rhetorical techniques. A deft demonstration of literary skill established the writer's claim to participation in the maintenance of the courtly elite and might secure for him the practical benefits of a generous reward or an offer of employment.

The *Tuhfeh,* whose author sought access to the Atabeg's court, provides an example of such attention to literary strategies.

As literary texts, works of advice fulfilled social and cultural as well as intellectual functions. Written as complete works, they follow generic patterns adapted to suit the author's own purposes and were usually intended for presentation as books, that is, in their entirety. The literary qualities of works of advice literature have long been recognized among modern scholars. Indeed, in their pioneering studies of "Mirror for the Princes" literature, Gustav Richter (1932, 35), Erwin I. J. Rosenthal (1962, 77), and A. K. S. Lambton (1970, 419)[46] all acknowledged the genre's affinities with the broader literary category of adab. The same scholars chose, however, to emphasize the "political" content of mirrors in their work; as Lambton put it, her interest lay not in "the literary aspect of mirrors" but rather "the political ideals put forward in them" (Lambton 1970, 419).[47] In their focus on the political perspectives that shaped the writing of mirrors, these scholars followed the predominant approach among scholars of the corresponding literary forms of the European Middle Ages: several of the most extensive and foundational studies of European mirrors stressed above all the image of the ideal ruler and conceptions of the ethics of kingship as they were presented explicitly or implicitly in the literature (Berges 1938; Anton 1968; Hadot 1972; see also Skinner 1987, 1:88–128).

In both the medieval European and West Asian contexts, this approach has been a productive one. It has brought advice literature from a marginal to a more widely valued position in the study of intellectual and cultural history and has greatly enriched the scholarly conceptualization of "political thought," the construction of which, in the Islamic

46. Lambton opened her article "Islamic Mirrors for Princes" with the statement "Mirrors for princes are an important and characteristic branch of Persian belles lettres. Many of them are written in elegant and pleasing prose and illustrated by anecdotes and stories which, at their best, are graphic and revealing pictures of contemporary society" (Lambton 1970, 419).

47. See also Lambton 1981, xvi–xvii; 1984a, 55–66.

context, has otherwise tended to bestow an especially privileged status on the writings of jurists and philosophers.[48]

In recent decades, scholars of the European and West Asian mirrors have paid renewed attention to their functions as integrated literary artifacts in which the "political" content is inseparable from the literary vehicle that conveys it.[49] In the preceding discussion of the *Tuhfeh,* I have attempted to demonstrate that each complete work of counsel constitutes an integrated whole that, to a greater degree in some cases than others, is somewhat artificially dismantled in the process of extracting its "political" content. The *Tuhfeh* attests, as much through allusion as explication, to a cultural vision that supported royal rule, confirmed the ruler's role and responsibilities, assured him of earthly appreciation and eternal rewards for his justice and generosity, and encouraged and admonished him to virtue. Like other works of adab, the *Tuhfeh* seeks to offer moral instruction and to entertain and delight. It emanates from and addresses a courtly elite whose culture it serves to reinforce and perpetuate.

At the same time, the *Tuhfeh* reflects and responds to a highly specific historical context. The Atabeg Ahmad, whose kingdom was situated relatively close to the Il-Khanid capital, was obliged to balance a number of objectives: the maintenance of his relationship with the Il-Khanid court, the preservation of his own authority, and the fulfillment of the requirements of legitimacy in his own regional and cultural context. Toward these goals, Ahmad is reported to have cultivated personal relations with the Il-Khans and those around them, supported the religious and cultural elites within his domains, created generous endowments for the institutions associated with them, distributed gifts and stipends to all persons who participated in his administration, maintained justice, and rewarded liberally the scholars, poets, and men of letters at his court. The reports of these efforts, conveyed in the image of the model ruler, earned Ahmad the

48. For a recent treatment of medieval political thought that encompasses a particularly wide range of materials and perspectives, see Crone 2004b. See also the comments of Senellart 1999, 244.

49. Examples include Jonsson 1987; de Fouchécour 1986; Meisami 1991; Senellart 1995; Yavari 2004.

lasting praise and admiration of his contemporaries and successive generations. The historiographical and advisory writings that reflect and promote this image constitute a continuous cultural seam. In an example of this continuum, the *Tuhfeh* contributed to the building and maintaining of a complex culture in a specific set of circumstances—a project in which author and audience, historians and counselors, courtiers, administrators, and the Atabeg all participated.

7

A Muslim State in a Non-Muslim Context

The Mughal Case

MUZAFFAR ALAM

IN THE SIXTEENTH CENTURY with the ascendancy of the Mughals, an important step in the development of imperial political culture and ideology occurred in South Asia. Power in the Indian countryside was mostly in the hands of large and small Hindu family and kin groups. These groups had emerged as the great consolidated Rajput caste, spread over a very large part of northern India and incorporating the various erstwhile ruling elements and the newly brahmanized tribal/pastoral chiefs. They enjoyed claims over the surplus produced by the peasants and were masters of their respective territories. The Mughals referred to them as *zamindar,* a generic term whose earliest reference occurs in the fourteenth century. Caste cohesion and caste affinity had encouraged conditions in which members of a subcaste lived close to each other in a cluster of villages, known in Mughal India as *pargana.* Caste, zamindari, and pargana boundaries often coexisted (Habib and Raychaudhuri 1982, 244–49; Habib 1965).

The conditions created by the expansion of the Mughal state after 1560 enabled a new set of assumptions to emerge from political questions that had been debated in South Asia since at least 1200 and the founding of the sultanate of Delhi. In particular, how was one to resolve the demands of an imperial center with powerful local and regional traditions? How could the existing ideas deriving from Arabo-Persian and Central Asian traditions be adapted to a situation in which a predominantly Muslim group ruled over a largely non-Muslim population? Political management in the Mughal Empire, thus, required the integration of very diverse cultural groups into a political community.

This problem of cultural diversity was by no means unique to the Mughals, but it was somewhat exaggerated because as a Muslim ruling group they were a distinct minority in a realm predominantly Hindu among significant other minority groups. In the thirteenth and fourteenth centuries, Muslim authors such as Fakhr-i Mudabbir and Ziya' Barani had written treatises on how Muslims should govern non-Muslim peoples.[1] Since Tughluq times (fourteenth century) Hindus had begun to appear in state service. Sikandar Lodi (r. 1489–1517), generally remembered otherwise for his bigotry, did encourage the Hindus to learn Persian high positions in the state, and the rise to power of the Sur sultan Sher Khan (r. 1540–45) depended considerably on his ability to integrate the Rajputs into his army (Hasan 1963, 311–39; Kolff 1990, 71–116). By the time of the early Mughals (Babur, r. 1526–30, and Humayun, r. 1530–40 and 1555–56), Hindu presence in the Muslim state was so pronounced that it began to threaten some sections of the Muslim notables *(shurafa')* (I. A. Khan 1977). Furthermore, much of the strength of the regional sultanates seems to have depended on the sultans' ability to coordinate their relations with the territorial Hindu magnates.[2]

Under Akbar and his successors, the Mughals reinforced this coordination and developed a new political vocabulary and syntax to legitimate it. Indeed, so successfully did the Mughals wed existing political discourse with innovations that many of the local Hindu elites began to identify

1. Fakhr-i Mudabbir, also known as Fakhr al-Din ibn Mubarak Shah (d. early thirteenth century), and Ziya' al-Din Barani (d. ca. 1360) were among the early Muslim thinkers and historians in India. Fakhr-i Mudabbir's major works included *Adab al-harb wa al-shuja'ah,* while Ziya' Barani is best known for his history, *Tarikh-i Firuz Shahi* (1860–62[2005]), and a treatise on political theory, *Fatawa-i Jahandari* (1972). Cf. Aziz Ahmad 1969, 79, 80.

2. For some relevant references, see Sherwani, Yazdani, and Joshi 1973, 1:289–490; and Sheikh 2006.

themselves, to a certain degree, not simply with the Mughal state system but also with the Mughal Persian culture. There were three important idioms, namely, the Sufi ideology and practice, the Nasirean *akhlaqi* norms, and a Persian cosmopolis. The Mughals used them to articulate and reinforce their political management. This chapter is an attempt to understand these idioms, focusing in particular on how Nasirean *akhlaq* shaped and influenced the course of Mughal politics.

Pre-Mughal Beginnings

Early in the thirteenth century, after the establishment of the Turkish sultanate in northern India, a delegation of eminent theologians approached Sultan Iltutmish with a demand to implement the *shari'a* in his sultanate. The infidels, according to the theologians' shari'a, were to be given the option of "Islam or death" *(imma al-Islam, imma al-qatl).* In the assessment of the sultan and his nobles, the theologians' demand was clearly impossible to carry out. It was, however, also difficult to simply set it aside. His response was somewhat evasive.

The sultan realized the nature of the conflict between the narrowly defined shari'a and the demands of governance. He feared he might lose the support of the *ulama.* There was little help in the manner in which Fakhr-i Mudabbir and Ziya' Barani, the early two Muslim political theorists, carried the *siyasah al-shar'iyah* discourse from the Islamic lands. Indeed, Barani's plea was for repudiating outright all that he saw as non-Islamic. In his *Fatawa-i Jahandari,* he sketches a rather impractical framework for governance and insists that the ruler who does not follow it does not deserve to be called a Muslim (Barani 1972; Habib and Khan 1961, 40). The Muslim king should not be content with merely levying the *jizyah* and *kharaj* from the Hindus. He should establish the supreme position of Islam by overthrowing infidelity and by slaughtering its leaders *(imams),* the Brahmans (Barani 1972, 165–66; Habib and Khan 1961, 46). There is a place for exceptions by the ruler *(zawabit)* in Barani, but he makes it very clear that zawabit were to be justified on grounds of political expediency in a situation when Muslim rulers were unable to implement the regulations of the shari'a in full. The aim of framing the zawabit was to reinforce the shari'a, to recuperate and complement it; the zawabit were not to work separately from or contrary to the shari'a (Barani 1972, 217; Habib and Khan 1961, 64).

We may also consider here briefly the work by Sayyid Ali ibn Shahab Hamadani (d. 1384) titled *Zakhirah al-muluk* (Hamadani n.d., fol. 2a, 6a, 19b), even though it is not strictly an Indo-Islamic text. Hamadani's name, however, is often associated with the history of Islam in Kashmir (Rafiqi 1972, 28–85).[3] Hamadani wrote the *Zakhirah* with an aim to discuss and elaborate the principles of both the form and the substance of power and governance *(lawazim-i qawa'id-i saltanat-i suwari wa ma'nawi)* for the Muslim rulers and state officials who wish to set right the affairs of religion *(istislah-i umur-i din).* The thrust and the contents of the passages on principles of *saltanat,* the qualities and duties recommended for the king, and the categories of the people or *ri'aya* are all discussed with reference to shari'a. He divides the ri'aya into *kafir* and *Muslim* and dwells only on the category of the latter *(ahl-i iman)* (Hamadani n.d., fol. 19b, 92). The rights of the ri'aya, according to Hamadani, should follow their religions. The Muslims and the kafirs both enjoy the Divine compassion *(rahmat-i Haqq).* Nonetheless, they have to be treated differently by the Muslim rulers. The kafirs living in a Muslim territory are *ahl-i zimmah;* the Muslim rulers should protect their lives and properties, provided they (ahl-i zimmah) maintain the conditions laid down in the agreement *(ahd-namah)* that the Second Pious Caliph Umar made with the People of the Book and the fire worshippers *(majus wa ahl-i kitab)* (*Zakhirah al-muluk,* fol. 99, 91a).

For Barani, kingship with all its attendant attributes was a sin for which the king must make compensation *(kaffarah)* (Barani 1972, 277). In the process, bigotry and narrow religious sectarianism became integral to his political theory. Hamadani's prime concern, wherever he discussed statecraft, was to advise a Muslim ruler to ensure the welfare of the people of the Faith. They all saw the king as a Muslim ruler, to manage in the first

3. For a different view of the spread of Islam in Kashmir, see M. Ishaq Khan 1994, 1–21.

place the interests of the Muslims. Besides the kharaj, jizyah, and jihad, there was not much in their writings to help the ruler to negotiate a political settlement with his non-Muslim subjects.

The Sufis and the Sultans

The sultan thus looked for legitimacy from the Sufis, who by then had amply demonstrated that truth, the Islamic truth, was not confined to the pages of a book on shari'a alone. Sufism was now growing into a system and had its own social mission. Sufis had now their own paths and orders *(tariqah)* and had also served the sultans outside India in their political missions (Trimingham 1971, 1–30; Eaton 1978, xiii–xxxii). In India, they encouraged and promoted many things held in common by local communities and the Muslims. Besides, even among those Sufis who were puritanical in their attitudes and uncompromising on questions of adherence to shari'a in purely juridical terms, there were examples of general charity and tolerance. They shunned ritualism and ceremonialism, spoke the language of the commoners, and gave impetus to linguistic and cultural assimilation. All this represented a deliberate Sufi intervention in politics and an attempt at defining its direction. Later, the sultan tried to establish his links with the Sufis in a rather exaggerated way. Soon the Sufis' support to the sultan acquired a clearly articulated ideological basis as Sufic beliefs and practices centered around the doctrine of *wahdat-i wujud* (Unity of being).

In the sixteenth century, the influence of the ideology of wahdat-i wujud was very strong in northern India. For example, Muhammad Ashraf Simnani, the ancestor of the famous saintly family of Kachhauchha (in the modern district of Faizabad), was an eloquent defender of the doctrine. Besides writing a number of treatises to explain it, Simnani popularized the use of the expression *Hamah Ust* (All is He), thus emphasizing the belief that anything other than God did not exist. Rudauli (in the modern district of Barabanki, Uttar Pradesh) was another major Sufi center where the doctrine received unusual nourishment. The *khanqah* of Shaikh Ahmad Abd al-Haqq (d. 1434) has been mentioned as the "clearinghouse" of Hindu yogis and *sanyasis*. Shaikh Abd al-Quddus Gangohi (d. 1537) was among the eminent Sufis who later became associated with this khanqah. Among his significant writings is listed *Rushd-namah* (Gangohi n.d.), a treatise on *tawhid* (monotheism) that consists of his own Hindavi verses and those of his preceptor *(pir-i dastagir)*, together with the Persian and Hindavi verses of other saints including the noted twelfth-century Persian saint and poet Shaikh Farid al-Din Attar. The *Rushd-namah* identified Sufi beliefs based on wahdat-i wujud with the philosophy and practices of the Hindu Shaivite Gorakhnath and received inspiration from the "syncretistic" religious milieu of Rudauli. Some of these verses with slight variations often appear in the Nath poetry as well as in the *doha* verses of the weaver-mystic Kabir. Several important issues are discussed in this treatise. These include the origins of the universe, the purpose of the creation of Man, the "path" or "direction" *(nahw, samt)* to the Truth, the real nature of life, the *sama*ʿ or spiritual music, the Truth *(haqq)* as it is illumined in the heart of a mystic, and the justification for prostration *(sijdah)* before one's spiritual master—all adumbrated as illustrations of tauhid.[4]

Rushd-namah represented an important Sufi trend. The sentiments and philosophical approaches enumerated therein found a fascinating expression in the mid-sixteenth century in another Chishti treatise, *Haqa'iq-i Hindi* of Mir Abd al-Wahid Bilgrami (d. 1608), in which Bilgrami sought to reconcile Vaishnava symbols and the terms and ideas used in Hindu devotional songs with orthodox Muslim beliefs. According to Bilgrami, Krishna, a Hindu deity, and other names used in such verses symbolized the Prophet Muhammad, or "Perfect Man," or even sometimes the reality of human being *(haqiqat-i insan)* in relation to the abstract notion of oneness *(ahadiyat)* of the Divine Essence. Krishna's female devotees, the *gopis*, sometimes stood, Bilgrami wrote, for angels, sometimes for the human race in relation to the relative unity *(wahidiyat)* of the Divine attributes. Braj and Gokul signified the different Sufi notions of the world *(alam)* in different contexts, while the Yamuna and the Ganga stood for the sea of unity *(wahdat)* and the ocean of gnosis *(ma*ʿ*rifat)*, or otherwise the river

4. Compare *Rushd-namah* (Gangohi n.d.), fol. 2a, 35b, 39a–43a, 43b, 45b, and 49a, for instance. See also Digby 1975, 1–66; Rizvi 1978, 1:335–40.

of *hads* (origination) and *imkan* (contingent or potential existence); the *murali* (Krishna's flute) represented the appearance of entity out of nonentity and so on (Bilgrami 1957; Rizvi 1965, 60–62).[5]

All this became acceptable in the context of the Sufi doctrine of wahdat-i wujud, popular then with the Chishtis. There is an unmistakable imprint of the doctrine on the ideas of Abu al-Fazl (d. 1602), the noted ideologue of the Mughal emperor Akbar (r. 1556–1605), as well (Nizami 1972, 33–44; Rizvi 1975, 339–73; Habib 1998, 332–53). It is not necessary for us to go into the details of the influence of these mystic developments on Abu al-Fazl. A number of measures and innovations of the time of Akbar and his successor Jahangir (r. 1605–27) were inspired by this doctrine. Akbar had shown a keen interest in local culture and mystic traditions. He invited some Hindu scholars to his court and inquired about their religions and philosophy. He is reported to have organized a separate quarter for the yogis in Agra (Bada'uni 1865–69, 2:324–25; Engl. trans., 334–35). The support for the doctrine of wahdat-i wujud or the unity of being, and the associated philosophy and practice of generous accommodativeness to the local social beliefs and customs, continued through the seventeenth century. Following the example set by Akbar, Jahangir also had close contacts with Hindu scholars and yogis (Mubed 1983, 1:94; Engl. trans. Shea and Troyer 1843, 164). Jahangir often held discussions around spiritual and religious matters with Jadrup, the noted Vaishnavite divine at Ujjain and Mathura. The result of all these discussions was a belief that the Vedantic philosophy of the Hindus and Sufi ideas were more or less identical among the Muslims (Jahangir 1864, 250–51, 252–53, 279, 280, 281; Jahangir 1968, pt. 2, 49, 52–53, 104, 105, 108; Mubed 1983, 1:184–86, 1:159; Engl. trans. Shea and Troyer 1843, 2:159; Mu'tamad Khan 1865, 543–44, 556–57).[6]

It is well known that the Sufistic leanings of the seventeenth-century Mughal prince Dara Shukoh led him to explore the depths of Hindu religion. By his patronage and partly through his own efforts, several Sanskrit works were translated into Persian (compare Hasrat 1953, 174–292; and

5. For Bilgrami's biography, see Azad Bilgrami 1910, 3:65–66.

6. Jadrup died in AD 1637.

Qanungo 1952, 241–68). These works include *Bhagavadgita, Yoga Vasistha,* and *Prabodhacandrodaya.* Dara himself is reported to have translated the Upanishads, and to emphasize that the Hindu scriptures are also sacred and divine, he named the translation *Sirr-i Akbar* (Divine secret). After a critical examination of Hindu religions, he found that all religions are identical and lead to the same goal. His work *Majma' al-bahrayn* is devoted to highlighting the similarity between the beliefs and practices prescribed in Islamic *tasawwuf* and those of Hindu Yoga.[7] The author of the *Dabistan-i mazahib* prepared a new translation of *Amrit Kund* and named it *Khawas al-Hayat* (Mubed 1983, 182). The celebrated seventeenth-century savant Chandra Bhan "Brahman" compiled a treatise known as *Mukalmah-i Dara Shukoh wa Baba Lal,* focusing on the discussion the prince had had with the saint of that name.[8]

Among the best interpreters and defenders of the doctrine of wahdat-i wujud during this century were Shaikh Muhibb Allah (d. 1648) and Shaikh Abd al-Rahman Chishti (d. ca. 1683). The reputation of some of the treatises Shaikh Muhibb Allah wrote to expose and elaborate on the doctrine brought him into close contact with Prince Dara Shukoh. His *Risalah-i taswiyah* (Treatise on equality) (Muhibb Allah n.d.) evoked a storm of opposition in orthodox circles and later under Aurangzeb (r. 1658–1707), who is reported to have taken strong exception to its contents. The text was ordered to be burnt in public. Shaikh Muhibb Allah also laid emphasis on the acquisition of mystic knowledge from Hindu yogis. One of his eminent disciples, Shaikh Muhammadi, undertook study and training in yoga from Brahmans after he had perfected his grounding in Islamic Sufism under Shaikh Muhibb Allah (Rizvi 1965, 340).[9]

In another case, Shaikh Abd al-Rahman Chishti, a descendant of Shaikh Abd al-Haqq of Rudauli (d. 1434), commented on the text of the *Yoga Vasistha* and other materials in a treatise he wrote under the title of *Mir'at al-makhluqat* (Mirror of the creatures), framed as a conversation

7. For a critique of Dara Shukoh's approach, see Omar 2005.

8. For a discussion on this text, see Kinra 2006.

9. For an interesting discussion on the theme, see Muhibb Allah, n.d.

between Mahadev, Parvati, and the sage Vasishta. Abd al-Rahman sought to explain at some length the Hindu legends and, as Rizvi points out, made a plea for them to be adapted to Muslim ideas and beliefs. He also prepared a recension in Persian of the *Gita* entitled *Mir'at al-haqa'iq* (Mirror of realities), presenting it as an ideal exposition of the doctrine of *Hamah Ust* (Rieu 1885, 3:1034).[10] Abd al-Rahman's attitude in these texts is somewhat complex, however; if his translations show appreciation for Hindu scriptures, they also read like a kind of polemic (Alam 2012).

In the early eighteenth century, the implication of these doctrines and the Sufi endeavor to define the larger political and social trajectory is well illustrated by the career of Shah Abd al-Razzaq Bansawi from the province of Awadh. Aurangzeb's bigotry and the association of the Mughal state with Sunni orthodoxy then threatened a serious rupture in the relationship between the communities in the province. The clashes of Rajput zamindars with the Muslim revenue-grantees were a major source of tension in the countryside. The keepers of the symbols of Islam *(sha'a'ir-i Islam)* and the shurafa' encountered serious threats from the "infidels" surrounding their habitats. Strong-arm tactics in the handling of the "rebel" zamindars had further aggravated the problem (Alam 1996). This tension was to be resolved only by a policy of adjustment of the claims of the dominant Rajputs on the one hand and the Muslims and non-Rajput Hindus on the other. This political balancing received strength from the prevailing Sufi ideology of the region, which, even if it had received a temporary setback (in the seventeenth century), was repeated with remarkable dexterity by Sayyid Shah Abd al-Razzaq Bansawi, the founder of a Qadiri Sufi center in Bansa, a small town near Lucknow.

Nasir al-Din Tusi and His *Akhlaq* in Mughal India

However, while the doctrine of wahdat-i wujud continued to support accommodation between the sections of Hindus and Muslims, a tradition

10. For a discussion on the *Mir'at al-makhluqat*'s translation, see Vassie 1988; 1999.

within the Sufi circle also emerged in the seventeenth century that contested the legitimacy of the doctrine of wahdat-i wujud. During the century, Shaikh Ahmad Sirhindi (d. 1624), the noted disciple and the *khalifa* of Khwaja Baqi Billah (d. 1603) and the founder of the Mujaddidiya branch of the Naqshbandiya *silsila,* is said to have commanded considerable reputation in Mughal Muslim society. He rejected the doctrine of wahdat-i wujud and rearticulated Shaikh Ala al-Dawlah Simnani's (d. 1336) doctrine of *wahdat-i shuhud* (Friedmann 1971, 23–31). His influence on Mughal politics, however, was of little consequence until the end of Shah Jahan's reign (1627–58) (Friedmann 1971, 77–86; Habib 1960, 209–23). The participation of the Hindus in state management remained unprecedented. This participation, I would suggest, became possible in part because the mythic code of normative behavior among the Mughals, the *Tura-i Chengizi* or *Yasa-i Chengizi,* weakened the determining role of the shari'a. But more important, it was the tradition of the akhlaqi norm of governance *(mamlikatdari),* as reflected in Nasir al-Din Tusi's *Akhlaq,* that influenced and shaped state building under the Mughals. *Akhlaq-i Nasiri,* as we know, drew on Ibn Miskawayh's *Tahzib al-akhlaq* or *Kitab al-taharah.* But the book was much more than a mere translation. Besides the first discourse, which was a summary of Ibn Miskawayh's *Tahzib* arranged anew, Tusi added two new discourses, one on household and family management *(tadbir-i manzil)* and another on politics *(siyasat-i mudun),* as parts of practical wisdom *(hikmat-i amali)* drawing on the Greco-Hellenic philosophical writings and blending them with his own "Islamic" view of man and society. In his discussion on the categories of social order, Tusi followed the classification of the noted tenth-century Muslim philosopher Farabi. The civil society *(tamaddun),* according to him, is first to be divided into two categories: (1) the ideal or excellent city and state *(al-madinah al-fazilah)* and (2) the bad or unrighteous city. The second type was again divided, this time into three categories: the astray-going or misguided city *(al-madinah al-zallah),* the evildoing city *(al-madinah al-fasiqah),* and the ignorant city *(al-madinah al-jahilah)* (Sharif 1966, 1:704–14). Like Farabi, Tusi also suggested that it was possible for the ideal city to be composed of peoples with diverse social and religious practices.[11] The leader of the ideal city was ideally to be the philosopher-king under whose care and protection each member of the society, secure in the place best suited for him, was to aspire and struggle to achieve perfection (Tusi 1976, 286, 288).

The *Akhlaq-i Nasiri* is a work of theory, idealistic and normative in character. It is difficult to take the text as evidence of the circumstances that actually prevailed when it was prepared. Still, one is tempted to point to the fact that the book was composed at a time when the kings' religious views did not correspond with those of a large number of their subjects. In 1235, Tusi dedicated the book to an Isma'ili prince of a region that in Nizam al-Mulk's *Siyasat-namah* was identified as an especially disturbed and misguided one (Tusi 1964, 262–67). Later, when the Mongols' power increased within the world of Islam, Tusi wrote a new preface without changing its contents and dedicated it to the pagan Mongol king of Maraghah. The region was in such turbulence that Tusi envisaged an ideal ruler to ensure uniformity, harmony, and a coordination of the conflicting interests of the diverse social and religious groups in the state. The crisis the Muslim world encountered in the face of the Mongol disaster created conditions for the acceptability of Tusi's idea.

There is not much in available medieval Indian intellectual and literary history to indicate the exact time and the place of the first entry of Tusi's *Akhlaq* into the subcontinent. The book was, however, widely read in Mughal India. The Mughals received and appropriated Nasirean ethics as part of the legacy of Babur, the founder of their rule in India, who in turn inherited it from the Timurids of Herat after their extirpation at the hands of the Shaybanis. Sultan Hussein Bayqara (r. 1470–1506), the last great Timurid in Herat, even though a Sunni, seems to have disapproved of his government's being run exclusively on narrow Sunni Islamic lines.[12] This

11. "The People of the Virtuous City, however, albeit diversified throughout the world, are in reality agreed, for their hearts are upright one toward another and they are adorned with love for each other. In their close-knit affection they are like one individual." Cf. Tusi 1976, 286–87; 1964, 215.

12. According to S. A. A. Rizvi, Sultan Hussein Bayqara had decided to have the *khutbah* read in the names of the Twelve Imams, but his prime minister Mir Ali Sher

attitude is supported by his policy that at least two versions of Tusi's work, *Akhlaq-i Muhsini* by Mulla Hussein Wa'iz al-Kashifi and *Dastur al-vizarah,* better known as *Akhlaq-i humayuni,* by Qazi Ikhtiyar al-Din Hasan bin Ghiyath al-Din al-Husseini, were prepared at his behest.[13] Of these two, a tour of Ikhtiyar al-Husseini's treatise helps us, in particular, to identify some reasons for Tusi's special status in Mughal Persian reading lists.

Akhlaq-i humayuni was first titled as *Dastur al-vizarah* and is a book of modest size on ethics and politics. The author claims he has described in tabulated form and summed up in an "elegant" Persian the subtle, abstruse, and complex discourses on human nature, family, household, and governance *(ba ikhtisar rashahat-i masa'il ra dar mashari'-i jadawil jaryan dad)* that he had read in numerous books including, and in particular, the works by Ibn Miskawayh and Nasir al-Din Tusi. The purpose of writing this book was to provide a manual for day-to-day activities *(dastur al-amal-i ruznamah-i ayyam)* for state officials *(ashab-i riyasat wa arbab-i siyasat)* as a means to manage their religious and worldly fortunes as well as to promote the stability of the state *(sabab-i salah wa falah-i suwari wa ma'nawi wa ba'is-i dawam wa khulud-i mulk wa dawlat).*

The author, Ikhtiyar al-Din al-Husseini, the chief *qazi* of Herat and a vizier in the time of the Timurid sultan Hussein Bayqara, came from an eminent family of the ulama of Turbat-i Jam, who held high positions in Timurid Central Asia (Khwandamir 1973, 4:355–56, 311, 376, 377, 382, 298, 514, 685; see also Blochet 1905–34, 2:37). He prepared the earlier version of the book in the time of Sultan Abu Sa'id Mirza (r. 1459–69) for

Nawa'i (d. 1501) and some other authorities stopped him from doing so. Compare Rizvi 1986, 1:165–66. Rizvi cites Nur Allah Shushtari's *Majalis al-mu'minin.* Using several contemporary chronicles, Jean Calmard has recently shown that Bayqara discouraged strict legalistic Sunni Islam, had Shi'ite leanings, and also proposed to proclaim Shi'ism as the state religion. See Calmard 1993, 113.

13. Hussein Wa'iz Kashifi's *Akhlaq-i muhsini* is available in print; among its several editions is the one published from among its early editions from Newalkishor, Lucknow, in 1774/AH 1291. Husseini's *Akhlaq-i humayuni,* also known as *Dastur al-vizarah,* has not been published; a manuscript copy (no. 768) is preserved in Bibliothèque Nationale de France, Paris. See Blochet 1905–34, 2:37–38.

the young prince Hussein Mirza (later Sultan Hussein Bayqara), who was then the chief prop and support of the saltanat and acted virtually like the vizier (*Akhlaq-i humayuni,* fols. 4a–6b). Later, after the collapse of Timurid power in Herat, al-Husseini—lucky to escape the fate of many of his contemporaries (imprisonment and execution)—chose a life of retirement in his hometown, Turbat, "accompanied and favoured there by the souls of the great saints and of his ancestors."[14] Then a day came when he heard that "the lamp of the illustrious Timurid house" was again alight in Kabul with the valiant efforts of Zahir al-Din Muhammad Babur. Subsequently he arrived at the court of Babur, accompanied by several princes.

The young Babur impressed al-Husseini with his unusual accomplishments, specifically his support for learning and his active participation in learned debates. Ikhtiyar himself had long discussions with Babur on diverse branches of sciences and on the laws and forms *(qawanin wa adab)* of government. The result, as the author claims in the second preface to the book, was a treatise with the title that he thought very appropriately should be *Akhlaq-i humayuni* because it represented the high ethical ideals of the king Babur *(chun in risalah partawist az nataij-i akhlaq-i humayuni-i hazrat-i ali, an ra Risalah-i Akhlaq-i humayuni nam nihad).* We know that this treatise was the same as the one that the author had earlier compiled for Prince Hussein Mizra. At any rate, al-Husseini was very conscious of the value of his work, and, just as he had earlier advised Hussein Mizra to keep it always with him, he now hoped it to be a source of strength for Babur, as well as later for his "illustrious descendants" in running the government (*Akhlaq-i humayuni,* fols. 2a–6a).

The main part of akhlaq texts generally begins with a discussion on human dispositions and the necessity of disciplining and sublimation. The discussion is interspersed with the Qur'anic verses and the traditions of the Prophet, with a bearing on universal human values. Thus the reference points are unequivocally the man *(bashar, insan, bani adam),* his living

14. Khwandamir says that Abu al-Fath Muhammad Shaybani retained him in the office of qazi. But after his death he was dismissed. Husseini then retired to Turbat to lead the life of an agriculturist (Khwandamir 1973, 4:355).

(amr-i ma'ash), and the world *(alam, afaq)*. The perfection of man according to the authors of these texts is to be acquired through admiration and adulation of Divinity, but it is impossible to be achieved without a peaceful social organization where everyone could earn a living though cooperation and mutual assistance.

The goal of discourse on political organization in akhlaq literature is thus "cooperation," to be achieved through justice *(adl)* administered in accord with law, protected and promoted by the king, whose principal instrument of control should be affection and favors *(ra'fat wa imtinan)*, not command and obedience *(amr wa imtisal)*. The shari'a here refers to an elaboration not strictly based on the Islamic law. The reader here is reminded of the Qur'anic verse that there is a single God who has sent prophets to different communities, with shari'as to suit their times and climes.

Justice (adl) emerges as the cornerstone of the social organization. But how the "cooperation" was sought as a valuable destination could be gauged from the fact that Tusi initially suggests mutual love *(mahabbat)*, a much higher and nobler means, as the ultimate and the most powerful guarantor of this cooperation. Justice occupied second place in the order of Tusi's preferences; it was an artificial way to create social balance, as it could be attained only through the king's exercise of power and through the coercive means of government machinery.

Justice leads to artificial union, whereas love generates natural unity, and the artificial in relation to the natural is compulsory, like an imposition. The artificial comes after the natural, and thus it is obvious that the need for justice, which is the most accomplished human virtue, is because of the absence of love. If love among the people were available, *insaf* (justice) would not have been needed. "[The word] *insaf* comes from *nasf* [which means taking the half, reaching to the middle]. The *munsif* [the dispenser of justice] is called so [because he] divides the disputed object into two equal parts *[munasafah]*; division into halves *[tansif]* implies multiplicity *[takassur]* whereas love is the cause of oneness" (Tusi 1976, 258–59).[15]

15. For further elaboration and a discussion on different categories of love, see Tusi 1976, 251–74; and Tusi 1964, 196, 195–211.

The akhlaq literature recommends the evaluation and treatment of man on the strength and level of his natural goodness or his malady *(khair wa sharr-i taba'i)* (*Akhlaq-i humayuni,* fols. 37b–38b). The rights of the ri'aya do not follow their religions. The Muslim and the kafir both enjoy Divine compassion *(rahmat-i Haqq).* For that reason, categories such as kafir, *kufr, zimmah,* and discrimination find no place in akhlaq treatises. The true representative, the shadow of God on earth, is the king who could guarantee the undisturbed management of the *affaire* of His (God's) "slaves," so that each could achieve perfection *(kamal)* according to his competence and ability. This pattern of governance is called *siyasat-i fazilah* (the ideal politics), which establishes on firm foundation the leadership *(imamat)* of the king. There is also a flawed and blemished politics *(siyasat-i naqisah),* against which the ruler is warned to guard himself, because faulty and perfunctory politics leads eventually to the ruination of the country and its people (*Akhlaq-i humayuni,* fol. 28b).

The man of ideal politics is always on the right path and considers the ri'aya as his sons and friends. His intellect enables him to refrain from greed and lust *(hirs wa shahwat).* The man of faulty politics resorts to coercion, regards the ri'aya as his slaves (even as women), while in actuality such a man is himself a slave of greed, lust, and desire for wealth (*Akhlaq-i humayuni,* fol. 29a).

In akhlaq texts justice is defined as social harmony, the coordinated balance of the conflicting claims of the diverse interest-groups that may as well adhere to more than one religion in an ideal state. The ruler, like a good physician, must know the disease of the society, its symptoms and its correct treatment. Because society is composed of groups of diverse interests and of individuals of conflicting dispositions, the king must take all possible care to ensure justice (adl) and a balance of their interests *(i'tidal)* in the society. This is how all parts of the body politic are held together into a healthy single unit. Divergence from adl causes conflict and eventually destruction. No one should get less or more than what he deserves in terms of his class. Excess, shortage, or defect *(ifrat wa tafrit)* dislocate the union and the relations of companionship (*Akhlaq-i humayuni,* fols. 30a–b). The emphasis in akhlaq texts was on the maintenance of balance in society and not on the eradication of infidelity and idolatry. One of the primary items of advice to the king was to consider subjects as "sons and friends" irrespective of their faith. Against this background, it was a matter of considerable significance that these treatises began over time to be taught at the Sunni madrasas in Mughal India.

Nasirean Ethics and Mughal Politics

Babur's "illustrious descendants," however, did not relish much of Ikhtiyar al-Husseini's simplified recension of the works of Ibn Miskawayh and Tusi. Introduced as they were now through *Akhlaq-i humayuni,* they preferred to read and understand by themselves the fuller, even if "convoluted," original texts. Akhlaq digests were among the most widely read and cited texts in Mughal India. Tusi's book was not simply among the five most important books that Abu al-Fazl wanted to be read before the Emperor Akbar regularly: it was among the most favorite readings of the Mughal political elites. The emperor issued instruction to his officials to read Tusi and Rumi in particular.

Furthermore, in the discourses on justice, i'tidal, harmony, siyasat, reason, and religion, the influence of akhlaq literature is unmistakable in a large number of Mughal edicts and texts (Rizvi 1975, 197, 355–56, 366–69). To illustrate this influence, I quote an extensive passage from an imperial order from the collection of Abu al-Fazi's *insha'* (epistolography). The order is referred to as a proclamation of the royal code of conduct and a working manual *(Manshur al-adab-i ilahi wa dastur al-amal-i agahi)* issued by the Emperor Akbar to the managers *(muntaziman)* and officials *(karpardazan),* including the princes, the high nobles, the *mansabdars,* the *amils,* and the *kotwals* in charge of the towns and the villages throughout the empire. It runs as follows:

> In all works, from the routine and mundane duties to prayers, they should endeavor to please God. . . . They should not seek solitude *[khalwat-dust]* like the recluses, nor should they mix freely with the commoners as the people of bazaar do; they should always adhere to the balanced middle and should never abandon the path of equipoise [*miyanah-rawi, sarrishtah-i i'tidal*]. . . .

When they are free from the public work, they should read books written by the pious and saintly, like the ones on *akhlaq* that cure moral and spiritual ailments. . . . They should appreciate what religion *[dindari]* in truth is so that they do not fall into the impostors' trap *[arbab-i tazwir wa khud'ah]*.

The best prayer is service to humanity. They should welcome all with generosity, whether they are friends, foes, relatives, or strangers; in particular, they should be nice to the recluse and seek the company and advice of the pious.

They should investigate judiciously the nature of the crimes and offenses of the people *[ba mizan-i adalat]*, and they should assess which of these offenses is worth punishing *[saza-dadani]*, which one is forgivable and is to be ignored *[pushidani wa guzashtani]*. Most of the crimes which look to be of lesser magnitude require to be dealt with drastically, while most others, which appear large and serious, should just be ignored. They should first try to admonish and reprove the culpable, should resort to tying, beating, severing of limbs, and execution only after they fail to correct them by admonition and reproof. They should never encourage killing and should refer the cases of execution to the royal court, even if they fear mischief [due to delay in execution caused] by their dispatch and imprisonment. They should refrain from skinning and trampling the offenders under the feet of the elephant and from the other practices of the barbarous rulers. The punishment should be commensurate with the nature of the offender, for an angry look *[niqah-i tund]* works better on the good than killing, while for the ignoble even a severe blow *[lakad]* is ineffective.

They should not encourage flattery; most of the works are left undone because of [the evil influence of] the flatterers. They should personally look into the grievances of the people, should note the names of the aggrieved, and should not allow delay in providing them with redress. . . .

In moments of anger they should not give up the thread of reason *[sarrishtah-i aql]*. They should instruct the wise among their servants to check them when they are full of rage or are overwhelmed with grief *[dar zaman-i hujum-i gham wa ghussah]*. They should not swear habitually, as this inspires lack of trust *[saugand khurdan khud ra muttaham dashtan ast]*; they should not resort to abusive words which behove only the ignoble. Their troopers should not occupy the houses of the people without their consent.... They should ever be watchful about the conditions of the people, the big and the small. Leadership or rulership means to guard and protect [the people] *[sardari ibarat az pasbani ast]*.

And they should not interfere *[muta'arriz]* in any person's religion *[din wa mazhab]*. For, wise people in this worldly matter, which is transient, do not choose a thing that harms. How can they then choose to inflict losses on themselves in matters of faith which pertain to the world of eternity? If he is right, they [the state officials] would oppose the truth [in case they interfere]; and if they have the truth with them and he is unwittingly on the wrong side, he is a victim of ignorance *[bimar-i nadani]* and deserves compassion and help, not interference and indignation *[mahall-i tarahhum wa inayat ast na ja-i ta'arruz wa inkar]*. They should be fair, well-disposed, and friendly to all *[neku-kar, khayr-andish wa dustdar-i har guruh]*....

They should not eat like an animal, beyond the necessary limit. They should not indulge in jocularity and frivolousness. They should regularly receive information through more than one purveyor of intelligence and should never rely on the information given by one person, because people are generally not absolutely honest and free from greed. The intelligence people should follow and check each other without their knowing that each of them is under surveillance *[bar har amr chand jasus ta'y'in kunad ki az yek digar khabardar nabashand]*. They should not let the wicked and ill-natured men come close to them, even as such men are useful and could be utilized in chastising the other evildoers. They should be careful that those who are close to them should not be oppressive, and they should refrain from the company of the unsound and glib-tongued *[charb-zaban-i nadurust]* who are dangerous and who are an enemy in the guise of a friend. There should be adequate arrangement to disseminate and promote learning, to encourage generously the learned and the accomplished, and to tutor and train [the scions of] the reputed, literally, "ancient" families.

The expenditure should always be less than the income. Those who spend in excess of their income are fools, while those whose expenses equal their income are neither fools nor wise. And they should not lie and should always honor their word. They should go hunting only occasionally to pass time and for the drilling and exercise of the soldiers.

> In each town *[qasabah]*, city *[shahr]*, and village *[dih]*, the officials should work in tandem to find out the number and the kind of the inhabitants there, depute the *mir* [chief] of the *mahallah* [quarter, locality] to supervise the local business, and appoint intelligence persons to supply news of daily developments. They should see that, in case of mishap or fire, the neighbors should help each other; in case of theft, that goods stolen should be recovered and that if they fail in this, they should lose their job. They should see that the property of deceased and missing persons goes to their rightful heirs or else is deposited in the treasury. The sale, distillation, and drinking of wine should be allowed only as a medicine. They should try to ensure a reasonable price *[arzani-i nirkh]* for goods and should not allow the practice of repricing. (Abu al-Fazl 1863, 57–67)

Clearly, this imperial *dastur* is inspired by the akhlaq texts. A close examination might possibly show that even the wording, language, and style of the Mughal political writings bear the impact of the akhlaq texts. The following passage from *Akhlaq-i humayuni* (fols. 37b–38b), which relates to the manual for the king, demonstrates the nature and extent of such influence:[16]

> In each matter which the king takes up, he should regard himself as a subject and the other as the king. He should not tolerate for others what he considers improper for himself. He should not wait for the time for the needy to approach his court. He should not be given totally to bodily joys and pleasures. Benevolence and favor and not force and violence should be the cornerstone of his activities.
>
> He should endeavour to please his people for God's sake. He should not disobey God for people's sake. He should be just and fair when people ask from him his decision, and be forgiving when they expect mercy from him.
>
> He should seek the company of the pious and thus obtain peace of heart. Each should be kept within the limits of his ability. It is not enough that he is not a tyrant. He should manage the country in a manner that none in his territory can afford to be cruel.

16. al-Husseini n.d., fols. 37b–38b.

The Mughals' concern for akhlaqi norms is also reflected in their extraordinary interest in facilitating conditions for their subjects *(jumhur-i anam)* to appreciate each other's religion and tradition. It is interesting to note here the terms in which Abu al-Fazl accounts for Akbar's encouragement of the translation of the Hindu scriptures. In his introduction to the Sanskrit epic *Mahabharat*'s Persian translation, he writes,

> The generous heart [of His Excellency] is naturally inclined toward the well-being of all the classes of the people *[islah-i ahwal-i jami'-i tabaqat-i baraya']*; friend and foe, relations and strangers are all equal in his farsighted view. This [consideration for all] is the best method for the physicians of bodies, should be highly appropriate for the physician of the soul [as well]. Why should this beneficence then not be the [distinctive] feature of [His Excellency], the chief physician of the chronic ailments of the human soul *(pashima-i karima-i sar-i daftar-i mu'alijan-i amraz-i muzmanah-i nufus chira nabashad)*? He noticed the increasing conflict *[niza']* between the different sects of the Muslims *[farai'q-i millat-i Muhammadi]*, on the one hand, and the Jews and the Hindus *[Juhud-wa Hunud]* on the other, and also the endless efforts to deny each other's [faith] among them. The sagacious mind [of His Excellency] then decided to arrange the translations of the sacred books of both communities *[fariqayn]*, so that with the blessing of the most revered and perfect soul [the emperor] of the age, they both refrain from indulging in hostility and disputes, seek truth, find out each other's virtues and vices, and endeavor to correct themselves. Also in each community *[ta'ifah]* a group of illiterates, fanatics, and petty-minded people have gained prominence. Pretending to be leaders of religion, they have misguided the people with their frauds and fallacies *[tazwirat wa talbisat]* to treat as significant those matters which are far from the path of wisdom and prudence. These inauspicious impostors *[muzawwiran-i bi sa'adat]*, because of their ignorance or dishonesty, hankering after their carnal desires, misinterpret the ancient scriptures, the wise sayings and doings of the sages of the past. When the books of both these communities are rendered into simple, clear, and pleasant style, simple-hearted folks would appreciate the truth and be free from the [traps of] trivialities *[fuzuliyat]* of the fools who go around pretending to be learned and wise *[nadanan-i dana-nama]*. It was therefore ordered that a translation in

> a plain style of *Mahabharat,* which consists of most of the basic principles and rites of the Brahmans of India and is their most honored, most sacred, and most detailed book, be prepared in collaboration with the experts of [both the Persian and the Sanskrit] languages and under the judicious scrutiny of the learned and the wise of both the communities. (Qazvini 1979, 18–19)

It is difficult to measure the exact impact of the translations of such books on the manner in which the two communities viewed each other. It is noteworthy that in seventeenth-century Mughal India, a number of Muslim scholars included the pre-Muslim Indian past in the histories they wrote and thus instructed their readers to appreciate and appropriate Indian tradition as part of human history. Indeed, Abu al-Fazl stated that this too was one of the objectives of the translation of *Mahabharat.* He wanted the Muslims in general, who believed that the world is only seven thousand years old, to know the age of the history of the world and the people *(kuhnagi-i alam wa alamiyan).* Further, he wanted the kings, who loved to listen to histories, to learn from the experiences of the past (Qazvini 1979, 19).

Among such histories is *Rawzah al-tahirin,* compiled in 1603 by one Tahir Muhammad Imad al-Din Hasan Sabzawari. The book is divided into five chapters. The first chapter deals with the histories of the pre-Islamic prophets, the Greek philosophers, and the Persian and Arab kings. The second chapter then describes the histories of the Pious Muslim caliphs and the subsequent developments in the lands of Islam. The third describes the history of the Turks and the Mongols. The fourth gives the histories of the pre-Islamic Indian rulers; a summary of the *Mahabharat;* lineages of the Surajbansi and Chandrabansi (solar and lunar) kings and their successors; an account of Nandghosh, Gautam, and their sons; an account of Kamdev; and the histories of Bengal, Pegu, Ceylon, Martaban, and other islands. The fifth and final chapter is a history of the Muslim rulers in India down to the age of Akbar with an account of the contemporary nobles, scholars, and poets (Sabzawari 1603, author's preface). It is noteworthy that all those whom Sabzawari included in his history were, as the title suggests, intended to be among the *tahirin,* that is, the pure, clean, and holy. Sabzawari's book was a history of mankind, and the author saw himself as an inheritor of the heritage of all of humankind.

Thus the tradition of Nasirean ethics contested the norms of governance mentioned earlier in Barani's *Fatawa (1972);* it proved to be an important support to facilitate stable and enduring Mughal rule in the complex religiocultural conditions of India. The Mughals took pride in the fact that the followers of different religions lived in peace in their empire. Jahangir (1864, 16) contrasts this peaceful coexistence boastfully with the conditions of "intolerance and bigotry" in the territories in control of the Uzbeks and the Safavids in Central Asia and Iran. In the assessment of a noted religious divine and Chishti Sufi, Shaikh Abd al-Rahman, the Mughals ensured the supremacy of *din* with their exaggerated concern for social harmony *(mashrab-i i'tidal).* In Mughal India, he noted, unlike in Uzbek Central Asia and Safavid Iran, the followers of all religions *(adyan wa mazahib)* lived in peace and performed their rites and social practices freely. And yet the Mughals acted in complete accord with the injunctions of their faith *(nusus)* (Chishti n.d., fol. 507a).

The manuals on Nasirean ethics contributed significantly to the making of an intellectual milieu in which nonsectarianism and a serious concern for justice and harmony among the elite were desired, especially noticed, and highlighted. The seventeenth-century noble Shayistah Khan, according to the compiler of the author of a Mughal political treatise, *Intikhab-i Shayistah Khani,* rose head and shoulders above his contemporaries because he was totally free from bigotry, was a man of *sulh-i kul* (universal peace), and saw all as his friends and possible allies, whatever their personal faiths and religions (*Intikhab-i Shayistah Khani,* fol. 3a). Shayistah Khan's *din* (faith) was thus not in conflict with his liberal and open-ended approach.

Also noteworthy here are two contemporary observations on the existing atmosphere of the high Mughal period. They help us understand the extent to which the Mughal state either followed or disregarded the demands of narrow religious considerations. An example of this extent is a remark of Abd al-Qadir Bada'uni, the noted historian of Akbar's time, about the reception accorded in India to Mir Muhammad Sharif Amuli, the Iranian scholar and leader of the deviant Nuqtawi sect, who had to flee

Iran for fear of persecution. Bada'uni, as we know, was narrow-minded and an orthodox and conservative Sunni. He detested the nonorthodox ideas of Amuli and disapproved of the prevailing situation in which deviants like Amuli were welcome. He writes, "Hindustan is a wide place, where there is an open field for all licentiousness, and no one interferes in another's business, so that every one can do just as he pleases" (Bada'uni 1865–69, 2:253). Relevant for us are also the observations of the French traveler François Bernier, who visited India decades later in Aurangzeb's time. After commenting disapprovingly on "strange" Hindu beliefs and rituals regarding the eclipse, he remarks, "The Great Mogol, though a Mahometan, permits these ancient and superstitious practices; not wishing, or not daring, to disturb the Gentiles in the free exercise of their religion" (Bernier 1972, 303). Even in matters such as *sati* (the immolation of widows), the Mughals intervened only indirectly; Bernier writes that "[t]hey [the Mughals] do not, indeed, forbid it [sati] by a positive law because it is a part of their policy to leave the idolatrous population, which is so much more numerous than their own, in the free exercise of its religion; but the practice is checked by indirect means" (1972, 306).

The Mughal Persian Cosmopolis

The Persian cosmopolis was the third important idiom to reinforce the Mughal political discourse. The resources for the development of this Indo-Muslim imperial idiom, which we will consider briefly, came from the world of Persian literary culture. The Mughals showed a rather unprecedented interest in patronizing Persian literary culture under their rule. Mughal India has hence been particularly noted for its extraordinary achievements in poetry and a wide range of prose writings in Persian. In terms of sheer profusion and variety of themes, this literary output was probably incomparable with that under any other Muslim dynasty. The Mughals were, of course, Chaghatay Turks by origin, and we know that, unlike the Mughals, the other Turkic rulers outside of Iran, like the Ottomans in Asia Minor and the Uzbeks in Central Asia, were not quite so enthusiastic about Persian. Indeed, in India too, Persian did not appear to occupy such a position of dominance at the court of the early Mughals.

It is noteworthy that Babur recounted the story of his exploits in Turkish (the *Babur-namah*) and that Turkish poetry enjoyed an appreciable audience at his son Humayun's court even after his return from Iran (Reis 1975, 47, 49–51, 52–53).

Nonetheless, it was not Turkish but Persian that came to symbolise the Mughal triumph in India. One may conjecture that in matters of language, the Mughals had no other choice and that they simply inherited a legacy and continued with it. Such a conjecture sounds somewhat plausible. Persian had established itself in a large part of northern India as the language of the Muslim elite (Ghani 1941, 152–233, 381–485). The famous line of Hafiz of Shiraz (d. 1398), "All the Indian parrots will turn to crunching sugar with this Persian candy which goes to Bengal" (Hafiz [Shirazi] 1967; 1972), was a testimony to the receptive audience that Persian poetry had in India. However, there seems to have been a setback in the subsequent trajectory of Persian. India had hardly any notable Persian writers in the fifteenth or early sixteenth centuries,[17] while in Hindavi, texts such as Malik Muhammad Jayasi's *Padmavat* represented the best expression of Muslim Sufi ideas. Use of Persian did not appear to be very strong under the Afghans from whom the Mughals assumed the reins of power. Most of the Afghans, Babur writes, could not speak Persian. Hindavi was recognized as a semiofficial language by the Sur sultans (1540–55), and their chancellery scripts even bore transcriptions in the Devanagari script. This practice is said to have been introduced by the Lodi sultans, who had been the Mughals' immediate predecessors (Mohiuddin 1971, 28).[18] For the extraordinary rise of Persian under the Mughals, the explanation may be found more in a convergence of factors within the Mughal regime than in the Indo-Persian heritage of earlier Muslim regimes.

17. For the history of Persian in the period, see Husaini 1988; Schimmel 1973, 21.

18. Mohiuddin cites from Maulavi Muhammad Shafi's article in *Oriental College Magazine* (Lahore), May 1933, for a reference to UP State Archives Document no. 318, an edict of Sher Shah dated AH 947. For Babur's remark about the Persian of the Afghans, see Babur 1970, 459–60. (Also see John Leyden and William Erskine's 1921 edition [Oxford, UK: Oxford Univ. Press] and W. M. Thackston's 1996 edition [Washington DC: Smithsonian Institution, and New York: Oxford Univ. Press]).

The Mughals were not content with establishing a mere paramount and imperial authority over the numerous local and regional power groups. They aspired also to evolve a political culture, as we have seen earlier, arching over the diverse religious and cultural identities. Persian in the existing circumstances promised to be the most appropriate vehicle to communicate and sustain such an ideal. Persian was known to the Indians, from the banks of the River Sind to the Bay of Bengal. If Amir Khusrau (d. 1325) is to be believed, as early as in the fourteenth century "Persian parlance enjoyed uniformity of idiom throughout the length of four thousand leagues *[parasangs]*, unlike the Hindavi tongue, which had no settled idiom and varied after every hundred miles and with every group of people" (Khusrau 1950, preface, 173). As late as the eighteenth century, Hindavi had not evolved a uniform idiom even in northern India. Siraj al-Din Ali Khan Arzu (d. 1756), a noted eighteenth-century poet, writer, and lexicographer, mentions Gwaliyari, Braj, Rajputi, Kashmiri, Haryanavi, Hindi, and Punjabi as diverse authentic forms of Hindavi in addition to the dialects of Shahjahanabad Delhi and Akbarabad Agra (cited in Abdullah 1968, 75). Sanskrit, or *Hindi-ye kitabi* (Hindi of the Book) as Khan-i Arzu calls it, might have been a candidate to replace Persian as the empire's language. But Sanskrit, as Mirza Khan, the author of *Tuhfah al-Hind,* noted in Aurangzeb's time, was not taken as an ordinary human tongue; it was a *deva-bani* (language of the gods) and *akash-bani* (language of the firmament). The language was too sacred, too divine. No *mlechha* (polluted outsider) would perhaps have been allowed to contaminate it by choosing it as a symbol and vehicle of his power. The mlechha could not have used it to create the world of his vision. On the contrary, Prakrit, which was a *patal-bani,* the language of the underground and of the snakes, was considered too low by the Mughals to be appropriated for lofty ideals. Braj or Bhakha, the language of this world, was also a regional dialect. Furthermore, in the Mughal view, Bhakha was suitable only for music and love poetry (Muhammad 1977, 1:51–52).

Persian poetry had integrated many things from pre-Islamic Persia, and poetry had already been an important vehicle of liberalism in the medieval Muslim world, as illustrated earlier in the verses of Amir Khusrau and Hasan Sijzi Dihlawi (d. 1336). In Mughal India, Persian poetry helped significantly in encouraging and promoting conditions to accommodate diverse religious and cultural traditions. Among the Persian books that Akbar had read aloud to the emperor every night was the *Masnawi* of Jalal al-Din Rumi (d. 1273). The emperor's nonsectarianism must have been inspired by Rumi's verses such as the following (Rumi 1976, 2:173):[19]

Tu baray-i wasl kardan amadi
ney baray-i fasl kardan amadi
    Hindiyan ra istilah-i Hind madh
    Sindiyan ra istilah-i Sind madh
(Thou hast come to unite,
not to separate
    The people of Hind worship in the idiom of Hindi
    The people of Sind do in their own)

The echoes of these messages and the general suspicion of mere "formalism" of the faith are unmistakable in the Mughal Persian poetry as well. Faizi (d. 1595), the Mughal ideologue, poet laureate, and brother of Abu al-Fazl, had the ambition of building "a new Ka'ba" with stones from the Sinai:

Biya ki ruy be mihrab-gah-i nau benahim
Banay-i Ka'ba-i digar ze sang-i Tur nahim
(Come, let us turn our face toward a new altar
We shall take stones from the Sinai and build a new Ka'ba)
    (Faizi 1983, 470)

The idol *(but)* to the poet was the symbol of Divine beauty; idolatry *(but-parasti)* represented the love of the Absolute. The Brahman deserves a high stature because of his sincerity, devotion, and faithfulness to the idol. Furthermore, the poet is also delighted to be privileged with a love for the idol that made him embrace the religion of the Brahman (Faizi 1983, 53).

19. For Akbar's administration and fondness for the *masnawi* of Maulana Rumi, see Abu al-Fazl 1873–86, 1:271.

Shukr-i Khuda ki ishq-i butan ast rahbaram
bar millat-i brahman-o bar din-i Azaram
(Thank God, that the love of idols is my guide,
I follow the religion of the Brahman and Azar)

The temple *(dair, but-kadah)* and the wine house *(mai-khanah)* were the same to the Mughal poet Urfi (d. 1591) as the mosque and the Ka'ba. The Divine Spirit pervaded everywhere (Urfi Shirazi 1915, 445).

Chiragh-i Sumanat ast atish-i Tur
buwad zan har jihat ra nur dar nur
(The lamp of Somnath is [the same as] the fire at the Sinai,
from which light spreads all around)

This feature of Persian poetry remained unimpaired even when Aurangzeb tried to associate the Mughal state with Sunni orthodoxy. Nasir Ali Sirhindi (d. 1696), a major poet of his time, echoed Urfi's message with real enthusiasm (Ali Sirhindi 1872, 15).

Nist ghair az yek sanam dar parda-i dair-o haram
key shawad atash du rang az ikhtilaf-i sangha
(In the temple or in the Ka'ba, the image is the same behind the veil.
With the change of flints, where does the color of fire change?)

In fact, neither the mosque nor the temple was illumined by Divine beauty; it is the heart *(dil)* of the true lover wherein lies its abode. The message was thus to aspire for the high place that lovers occupy. Talib Amuli (d. 1626) called for transcending the difference in names (Amuli 1967, 688):

Na malamat-gar-i kufr am na ta'assub-kash-i din
khanda-ha bar jadl-i Shaikh-o Barhaman daram
(I do not condemn infidelity, I am not a bigoted believer,
I laugh at both, the Shaikh and the Brahman)

In this milieu the plea to the conqueror was for conquest and dominance without staining the victor's skirts with the blood of the vanquished (Urfi Shirazi 1915, 3):

Zakhm-ha bardashtim-o fath-ha kardim lik
hargiz as khun-i kasi rangin nashud daman-i ma
(We have suffered wounds, we have scored victories,
but our skirts were never stained with anyone's blood)

The desire to build an empire where both Shaikh and Brahman could live with the least possible degree of conflict also necessitated the generation of adequate information about the diverse traditions of the land. Akbar's historian, Abu al-Fazl, is not content in his *Akbar-namah* with a mere description of the heroic achievements of his master; he concludes his book with what he calls the *A'in* (institutes) of Akbar. The A'in contains a survey of the land, the revenues, the peoples of the empire, and, above all, an empathetic treatment of the social conditions and the literary activity, especially in philosophy and law, of the Hindus, who "form the bulk of the population, and in whose political advancement the emperor saw the guarantee of the stability of his realm" (Abu al-Fazl 1965, v–ix). Moreover, in order to make the major local texts accessible to the Muslims and thus to dispel their ignorance about the local traditions, Akbar took special care in rendering the Indian scriptures into Persian. The translations of these religious texts were followed in Akbar's own time and later in the seventeenth and eighteenth centuries by Persian renderings of a large number of texts on "Hindu" religion, law, ethics, mathematics, medicine, astronomy, romances, moral fables, and music (Rizvi 1975, 203–22; Mujtabai 1978, 70–91).

Persian thus promoted conditions in which the Mughals could build a class of their allies out of heterogeneous social and religious groups. While this class cherished universalistic human values and visions, the emperor was seen, in the words of the noted late sixteenth–early-seventeenth-century Hindi poet Keshavdas, as *duhu din ko sahib* (the master of both religions), possessing the attributes of Vishnu, the Hindu god (Keshavdas 1969). *Din* in this atmosphere assumed a new meaning; the king could blend "Hindu" social practices and Rajput court rituals with his Islam at the Mughal court. These practices ranged from applying *tika* (the vermilion mark) on the foreheads of his political subordinates, to *tuladan* (the weighing ceremony), and to *jharoka darshan* (the early morning appearance of the emperor on the palace balcony) (Sharma 1972, 30–74). Again, as Abu al-Fazl emphasized the legendary origins of the Mughals from light, he intended perhaps to highlight their affinity with new local allies, the Rajputs, in whose legends fire and light occupied a special position (compare Abu al-Fazl 1873–86, 1:122). True, the influence of the illuminationist philosophy of Shihab al-Din Suhrawardi Maqtul (d. 1191) on Abu al-Fazl cannot be underestimated (Richards 1998). The Mughals married Rajput princesses and allowed them to observe their rituals ceremoniously in their palaces. However, the alliance also received nourishment from the local Hindu culture in Rajputana and developments within the Rajput society. The Rajput saw the Mughals as a subcategory of their own *jati.* In their tradition, the Mughal emperor held a high rank, was held in high esteem, and was often equated with Ram (Zeigler 1998), the prominent Kshatriya cultural hero and ideal and exemplary king of Hindu tradition. The Rajputs began to identify themselves with the Mughal house, to be defended in the same way as their own families and houses.[20]

Conclusion

My purpose in this chapter has been to touch upon a number of resources that the Mughals mobilized to construct and extend their notion of an inclusive polity in a society that had a high potential for conflict and was outside the conventional domain of Islam. These included the Nasirean akhlaqi norms of governance, traditions of mysticism, and Persian literary culture. All these were seen, both in Mughal times and later—when historians and others looked back on the Mughals—as part of the peculiar political synthesis that helped constitute imperial identity under their rule. In stressing elements of accommodation and creative synthesis, it

20. This identification is best illustrated in Raja Ram Singh Hara's reported response to the anxiety expressed by Prince Muhammad A'zam's wife (a Safavid princess), who asked what the Raja was planning to defend her with against the Marathas who were threatening her party. The Raja, who was then escorting the princess from the emperor's camp to the camp of Muhammad A'zam, exclaimed, "the honor of the Chaghtais is one with the honor of the Rajputs." Cf. Sarkar 1919, 4:302.

has not been my intention to claim that no conflicts took place under the Mughals, whether in the towns or in the countryside. Such conflicts were many, whether in the time of Akbar or under later rulers. However, the existence of such conflicts should not lead us to neglect the fact that the Mughals built a high political culture that was meant to incorporate and extend, that is, to draw the riʿaya in, rather than to control them by mere force. The Mughals, as much as any other early modern dynasty, wanted to be seen by their very diverse subjects as legitimate rulers. The long period between the actual seizure of power by the English East India Company in 1765 of an important region of the empire and their displacement of the Mughal emperor in 1857 suggests that they did succeed in good measure in this difficult task.

8

Al-Tahtawi's Trip to Paris in Light of Recent Historical Analysis

Travel Literature or a Mirror for Princes?

PETER GRAN

RIFAʿAH RAFIʿ AL-TAHTAWI'S *Takhlis* (al-Tahtawi 1834) is traditionally studied as travel literature not so much because of its contribution to that genre but because of its content.[1] Its importance rests on the fact or, more precisely, on the scholarly assumption of its being an early if not the first example of the Arab discovery of modern Europe. This assumption affects how the book has long been read. The present chapter, basing itself on recent developments in Egyptian studies, proposes that the *Takhlis* might be better understood as an example of Mirror for Princes literature or advice literature with the travel dimension being a subordinate feature.

Postscript: Two recent publications of interest are Tageldin 2011 and Coller 2011. The former sheds further light on the life and work of Joseph Agoub, who influenced al-Tahtawi's translation theory during his stay in Paris. The latter discusses the Marseille Arabs of that period.

1. This chapter is based on several previous pieces of work and on some ongoing research (Gran 1979; 1996). Articles I drew on here were Gran 1999 and Gran 2001, which present a map of specific hegemonies, the countries they illustrate, and why. "Tahtawi in Paris," *Ahram Weekly,* no. 568, Jan. 10, 2002, 14, presents a revisionist reading of al-Tahtawi. Articles on state formation include Gran 2002 and Gran 2004. For articles of a more general and comparative nature, see Gran 2006 and Gran 2005. For a sketch of an outline of world history going beyond Hegel, see Gran 2007.

Modern historical analysis of al-Tahtawi's period in Egyptian history (1801–73) suggests that Egyptians and Europeans were acquainted with each other and that therefore al-Tahtawi would not have been traveling into the unknown as has long been claimed. Rather he would have been making a trip (1826–31) to a fairly familiar destination on behalf of a ruler whom he, of course, supported but about whose policies he nonetheless had some criticisms. This is why the "mirror for princes" characterization of the *Takhlis* is more useful than the *rihlah* (trip or book of travels) one. It allows us to understand why certain aspects of France were of interest to him and not others, why, for example, Paris and not other cities, why the parliamentary tradition and not the Bourbon Restoration. It was all related to his perception of Muhammad Ali's policies in Egypt.

To pursue this line of interpretation, one needs to make a number of claims about Egyptian history, claims about what kind of system was emerging in Egypt at this time as well as claims about what al-Tahtawi's position was in it and therefore what sort of advice he would have been likely to give and why. This chapter spells these out. Egypt, it is suggested, is not an example of an Oriental Despotism as has generally been assumed, but rather an example of an "Italian Road" regime, a description that makes use of a model of political analysis developed by the Italian writer Antonio Gramsci. Al-Tahtawi's place in this regime was that of a "Southern Intellectual," the *Takhlis* becoming a Sa'idi (Upper Egyptian) Mirror for Princes, one that was written for Muhammad Ali Pasha.

To pursue this line of interpretation, this chapter is divided into sections. Following an opening section introducing the subject of hegemony analysis as it would relate to Egypt, the second section turns to the economic and political dynamics of Egypt in the period of al-Tahtawi's life. The third section then proceeds to consider Egyptian cultural history and al-Tahtawi's place in it within this set of dynamics. The next sections examine the wider implications of adopting an Italian Road model for the study of Egyptian history by addressing the period after 1860 and the institution of the Southern Intellectual as a part of that wider history. Once this "groundwork" has been laid, al-Tahtawi's *Takhlis* will best be understood, I propose, as a mirror for princes of the sort just mentioned. The chapter concludes with a consideration of the existing historiography on al-Tahtawi.

What I establish is that, over the past century, there has been a rise and then more recently a decline of the traditional *rihlah* (book of travels) paradigm. This article can be understood as a part of the latter trend.

Hegemony Analysis with Reference to Egypt

Hegemony analysis is an approach to analyzing political dynamics that brings together insights from politics, sociology, and history. Hegemony analysis differs from the traditional study of government in fields such as political science not only by including the dialectic of ruler and ruled but including the strategies employed by both. Writers who have worked with the concept of hegemony have produced a considerable body of writing (Bocock 1986). Traditionally, the subject has had a liberal center of gravity owing much to the work of Max Weber and a Marxist one owing much to the work of Gramsci. With the rise of globalist and transnationalist analysis in recent years, writers have attempted to fuse these approaches, doing so, for example, in fields such as neo-Gramscian international relations.[2] My work follows this tack in a general way, but it is centered in the discipline of history and political economy and not international relations. Despite the existence of transnational linkages as a part of the world system, it is assumed that the nation-state remains the political backbone of capitalism. Therefore, one needs to inquire into the particular form of the nation-state at hand. Al-Tahtawi's trip to France, one might understand, does not have the same significance as those of his Moroccan and Lebanese contemporaries, individuals who also wrote about Paris, in part at least because the form of hegemony of Egypt was different from those of Morocco and Lebanon.

I spell all this out because the study of hegemony in the subfield of Middle Eastern history remains a fairly new endeavor. Until now, the study of hegemony is more commonly found in the study of Europe and in parts of the Third World other than in the Middle East. In the study

2. For neo-Gramscian international relations, see, for example, Bieler and Morton 2001 and Morton 2007.

of Egypt, scholars have generally assumed that hegemony simply meant Oriental Despotism. Overwhelmingly, scholarly writing on modern Egypt follows the Oriental Despotism model. Following the Oriental Despotism model, the later eighteenth century in Egypt becomes a period of chaos and decline followed by a partial awakening with the coming of Napoleon in 1798. This in turn is followed by the reconstruction of a modernized version of the Oriental Despot system. The study of hegemony in the sense intended here, which is termed "Italian Road" hegemony, calls this tradition into question.

Following an Italian Road approach, the study of Egypt (1760–1860) witnessed a deepening contradiction between the North and the South in Egypt, one that would play an even larger role in the years that were to follow. It is this point that leads to the characterization of Egypt as Italian Road. In other words, in this period, the strategy of maintaining order by playing class against region had come into being. Eventually it would become a fully developed system based on playing the Northern worker off against the Southern peasant. This is the main feature of the Italian Road form of hegemony. By 1860 the outlines of a system of this sort were apparent with the coming of Khedive Isma'il.

Economic and Political Dynamics in Egypt in the Period of al-Tahtawi's Life

Al-Tahtawi was born in 1801 in the midst of considerable changes in Egypt. The state that had existed in the last years of the eighteenth century based on the indigenous mercantile capitalist sector had suffered a blow as the world market forced its way into the country and redefined its economics and politics. As this took place, there was a protracted social crisis; many individuals were driven into poverty. As this crisis grew, it gradually reached threatening proportions, and the existing political system lost its legitimacy. As a result, Muhammad Ali, an Albanian adventurer, was able to rise to power. Growing up when he did, al-Tahtawi had no real choice but to work for Muhammad Ali.

As late as the middle of the eighteenth century, this dramatic series of events could hardly have been anticipated. Up to that point, artisanal production, a strategic location on trade and pilgrimage routes, renowned institutions of learning, and the potentiality of producing products sought in Europe and elsewhere had supported what might have been a transformation from mercantilism to modern capitalism of a very different sort—had circumstances allowed.

The leading sector of the economy, scholarship shows, was that rooted in the artisanal guilds and merchant groupings, the two often linked together through their overlapping memberships in Sufi *turuq* (mystical confraternities or orders). These were dynamic institutions; they were continuously adjusting to market conditions, continuously in motion. Some stayed in a single location; others spread through Egypt and beyond. In modern scholarship, religionists lead the way in analyzing these developments. In their scholarship, the spread of the Sufi orders has been observed as an "Islamic Enlightenment."[3] Certainly for historians, the spread of the orders over vast distances, such as the Khalwati order, draws one's attention. For example, at one point in the eighteenth century, the Khalwatis expanded all the way from Cairo to Upper Egypt. Upper Egypt was opening up; there were new opportunities. Ali Bey al-Kabir (1728–73), the ruler in Cairo, had recently defeated the leader of Upper Egypt, the Hawwara chief Shaikh al-Arab Hammam (1709–69). The region as a whole could therefore potentially be exploited by the North of Egypt (Ahmad 1987). Sufis, local merchants, and others all began to arrive.

As this North-South dynamic was progressing, a deepening struggle among groups seeking to dominate the Egyptian market in the North (Haridi 2004) was also occurring. The outcome of that struggle, as earlier noted, was one that would bring in world market forces and new political actors. In effect, as the indigenous capitalist sector fought it out and lost and the Mamluks went into crisis, commercial minorities allied to European powers became the indispensable middlemen benefiting from the fact that Europe opposed the formation of Muslim merchant establishments not

3. Concerning the main reaction to the hypothesis of an Islamic Enlightenment as propounded by Reinhard Schulze (1996), see the special issue of *Die Welt des Islams* 36, no. 3 (Nov. 1996).

only in Europe but even in Egypt. As a result, the Greek, Jewish, Armenian, and Syrian Christian communities in Egypt grew in importance. From this period of the later eighteenth century onward, it might also be noted that rulers in Egypt chose to play or were forced to play a facilitating role in these developments as well. They allowed the indigenous production and trade to wither away; they allowed artisanal workshops to collapse, leaving many workers unemployed. Foreign goods were allowed to flood the markets.

A question that the scholarly literature has never adequately addressed is that of "why?" Moving beyond older explanations of decline on cultural grounds, it seems that what took place can be better understood in material terms. In this period in history, rulers were becoming a part of the worldwide phenomenon of the "Rise of the Rich." With the new options created by the world market at this point, rulers stood to gain handsomely by collaborating with other rulers worldwide against even their own people. Through this system of mutual cooperation, each ruler could finally introduce a system of capitalist relations and, in doing so, derive far more wealth and power than they could from the older mercantilist system of tribute and taxes prevailing up to that point in time. To effect this transformation, rulers made available to each other sophisticated weapons and technology, loans, and credit, not to mention luxury goods useful as bribes. Progressively from this period, rulers worldwide appear to grow richer and more powerful in relation to their own people, a trend continuing until our own day. This was the case in Egypt. If the Ottoman Walis of the sixteenth century lived in barracks in the Citadel in Cairo, the leading eighteenth-century Mamluks built lavish private homes. Later, the nineteenth-century rulers built palaces; twentieth-century rulers added to the palaces a variety of villas, chalets, and foreign residences.

Capitalist development has always been by its nature uneven. In the case of Egypt, political and economic factors favored the development of the Delta (North Egypt) over that of the Sa'id (the South of Egypt, also called Upper Egypt). In the second half of the eighteenth century, the Delta exported rice and wheat to France; France in turn sold Egypt finished cloth and luxuries. The balance of trade favored the Egyptians to an extreme degree, and this imbalance led to crises when the French could not pay. Partly as a result of these crises, France invaded Egypt in 1798 under the command of Napoleon Bonaparte. Upon their arrival, the French set out to gain access to the rice fields of the Egyptian Delta. To this end, Napoleon had one of his generals convert to Islam and marry the daughter of an influential local farmer from that region. While the invasion itself only lasted a short period of time, the French managed to establish enduring links to the local power structure. Through an agent, Bernardino Drovetti (1776–1852), France was able to influence the course of events that followed (Ridley 1998). For example, France helped Muhammad Ali come to power in 1805. France helped Muhammad Ali defeat all his potential rivals, even Muhammad Alfi Bey, the Mamluk known for his ties to Britain and to Upper Egypt. This was obviously to the detriment of the Upper Egyptian region from which al-Tahtawi hailed.

And while France played a role, the dynamics in Egypt itself were decisive. Thus what actually lay behind Muhammad Ali's rise to power was the social crisis in the Delta, the one that had begun back in the 1780s. In other words, there was a lot more than simply the growth of poverty that we had mentioned before. Peasants were protesting the breakdown of village life as the Delta region was integrated into the market. As a result, the interests of dominant groups, both regional and national ones, were threatened. Landlords dreaded peasant protests. Ulama rushed to the area from Cairo to intercede. The conflict, however, would not go away; soon it spread to Cairo itself, attracting artisans whose world was also threatened by the rise of the open market. As this occurred, a local political "Jacobinism" arose. In the 1790s, it was spearheaded in Cairo by the followers of Shaikh Ali al-Bayyumi, the late shaikh of the guild of the water-carriers, along with various other workers and artisans. Later, this political radicalism carried over into the resistance to the French occupation (1798–1801) and into the movement in support of Umar Makram (1755–1822) in the early nineteenth century. Umar Makram, it appears, would have been the popular choice for ruler of Egypt over any Ottoman nominee and even over Muhammad Ali himself. It was not to be; Jacobinism in Egypt as elsewhere went down to defeat. Muhammad Ali was politically more adroit than was Umar Makram. He was able to build relations with Drovetti and to play the fears of the Egyptian landlords against their sympathy for their peasants, splitting any potential alliance in the making that might have emerged to unify these groups against him. Thereafter, Muhammad Ali was able to overwhelm the remaining Mamluks and to capture the entire country. Umar Makram ended up in forced retirement in the Delta far from his native Asyut; most of the Mamluks wound up dead.

Muhammad Ali was a notable figure in modern world history (Batou 1991; 1993) in the view of contemporary scholars. Not only did he seek to wipe out the tradition of Egyptian radical protest just referred to, he set out to have Egypt escape from the periphery of the world market, which was the fate of all late joiners. To this end he worked closely with the French to build up his army and industry. In return, he supplied the market with long staple cotton, which was quickly becoming the principal export crop of Egypt. As was noted before, Muhammad Ali rose to power by benefiting from the unrest in Egypt. Once in power, however, he quickly set out to try to bring an end to this unrest, first by drafting large numbers of landless peasants and poor artisans into his army and shipping them abroad in wars of expansion from which many never returned, and then by using direct repression. Thus, for example, he crushed a number of peasant uprisings, and he brutally punished draft resisters and tax evaders. The upshot for our purposes is that Muhammad Ali wound up dealing with or papering over the existing political problems. He did so chiefly by concentrating Egyptian industry in the Delta and leaving Upper Egypt to stagnate, in other words, deepening the already-existing divisions of North and South.

Muhammad Ali attracts the attention of most scholars today largely because he progressed so far toward his goal. Few of the dozen or more other attempts on the part of rulers from the periphery met with the same success as did his. It is thus not surprising that his regime had an almost magnetic appeal for various highly skilled European technicians who were frustrated by the policies of their own countries and who as a result were willing to go abroad and to serve foreign governments such as that of Muhammad Ali's for the sake of promoting technical development. Chief among these skilled technical people who came to Egypt were the Saint-Simonians. A number of Saint-Simonians worked in Egypt at least for a short period of time. Had the Saint-Simonians stayed in Egypt for a longer period of time, history today might have been different. But they could not. All this is duly noted in the scholarship on Muhammad Ali and is generally explained as follows. The problem for Muhammad Ali, it is frequently claimed, was ultimately a problem with England. England saw no need to weaken the Ottomans who were holding Russia at bay, nor to allow the development of a power that blocked the way to India, nor to develop a rival for its own textile industry. For all these reasons in the later 1830s, England turned against Egyptian development. It had become a potential threat.

At this point (1838–40), however, one comes perhaps to a clearer understanding of the Pasha's true motivations. Egyptian development was for him a means to an end. When he could not reach that end by pursuing Egyptian development, he pursued it in other ways. At that point, Muhammad Ali's behavior represented what one could term an example of the "Rise of the Rich." With an undefeated army in the field, one that had crushed the Ottomans in battle, he ordered a retreat and a policy of deindustrialization and demilitarization, doing so in return for a promise from the Ottomans and the English to recognize himself and his family as the legitimate rulers of Egypt in perpetuity. Personal power and, to a lesser extent, class interests trumped dreams of national development.

As some have noted, with this shift in strategy came the end of his support for industry and education. And as other have noted, Egypt at this point had taken another step toward a free market economy. Left unexplained in the critical literature, however, is how this dissolution and shrinkage of the army, factory system, and educational system were achieved without major incident. One possible explanation might lie in Muhammad Ali's success in inducing a number of Egyptians and Europeans to join with him prospecting for mineral wealth in the Sudan. This undertaking required a certain military presence, and it occupied many Egyptians through the nineteenth century, imperialism coming to serve as a substitute for national development. Many Egyptians served in the lower echelons of the armies of exploration and occupation. Some of them even came from the tribal levies of the South.

What is also noticeable is that, from this point onward, Egyptian rulers tried to deepen market relations in the country. Whether or not this resulted in development became a secondary issue. What the market brought was increased profit for those who could benefit from it. It also brought social unrest. To the extent possible, the rulers in this period in Egypt as elsewhere tried to ignore this unrest and even tried to speed up the full and complete introduction of private property in land. And this sometimes succeeded at least part of the time up through the 1850s. In the 1850s, however, much of the Sa'id arose in a movement led by Ahmad al-Tayyib, a leading figure of the Hawwara Confederation. This movement could not be ignored. The Hawwara were the dominant group around Minya and Asyut. The government had to attack them, and this it did. Crushed militarily in a battle in 1865, Al-Tayyib was forced to flee for a time to Libya. More unrest, however, followed; political order would take a long time to reestablish. Ultimately, it required concessions to the southern ruling class. Ahmad al-Tayyib eventually returned in triumph. As this took place, the regime in Cairo seemed to solidify itself, taking its particular hegemonic form with the rise to power of the Khedive Isma'il (1863–79). This one could term an example of "Passive Revolution."

Egyptian Cultural History: Al-Tahtawi's Place within It

In this section, I discuss al-Tahtawi's place in Egyptian cultural history and argue that the old interpretation is clearly inadequate and that a new one is required. The old interpretation was one that pictured Egypt as a static Oriental Despotism, that is, a country with little or no cultural activity. The only hope for change would depend on the arrival of the West. According to this old interpretation, al-Tahtawi was among the first Egyptians to appreciate the significance of the West and to avail himself of the new opportunities it afforded. The newer interpretation of al-Tahtawi is one premised on the assumption of a continuing vitality of the existing cultural dynamic. Al-Tahtawi found himself a Southern Intellectual, by virtue of his background in the intellectual class of Upper Egypt and by virtue of his success at finding his way into and then out of al-Azhar and then into government service. This success meant that he gained an opportunity to be quite influential in Egyptian affairs, but at a certain price. He would have to defend the regime and not directly acknowledge that it was oppressing the people of his home region. In return, he would be honored for his services. Al-Tahtawi accepted the offer but did so conditionally.

Scholars have long wondered why al-Tahtawi emerged as such a dominant figure. His background reveals the answer. Al-Tahtawi had grown up in a well-known family spread between Tahta and other towns of Upper Egypt. Following the early death of his father, he was raised by relatives and given a good education by them in the years before he and his mother moved to Cairo in his late teens. This is an important point because conventional wisdom would scarcely lead one to think of Upper Egypt as a center of culture. Yet, in Ottoman times, it was. During al-Tahtawi's youth, its center was the city of Girga. Girga was the southern capital of Egypt and, at that time, had become a cosmopolitan city with links to the Hidjaz and to the Sudan and Cairo. While Girga has not been well studied, we know some things about it from the books of a local historian, Muhammad al-Jirjawi, one of which was edited and published in 1998 (al-Jirjawi 1998). From this book, it is obvious that the city produced many writers, including poets and theologians; we can also infer that al-Tahtawi was exposed to such works during this formative period. When al-Tahtawi moved to Cairo and began as a student in al-Azhar, he was thus not surprisingly considered a very advanced student. We know, for example, that al-Tahtawi tutored students who were ahead of him in age to earn money.

It should also be noted that al-Tahtawi's al-Azhar education, along with what may have occurred before it, often gets ignored in the studies of al-Tahtawi because he is so often associated in scholarship with secular culture, and many scholars seem to doubt—and I believe without good reason—that al-Azhar offered secular culture. The Fahrasah then in use clearly included a number of examples of such subjects (Shalash 1981).

The traditional view is not entirely wrong because at the particular time that Al-Tahtawi arrived it is true that secular culture was less in evidence than it had been in the late eighteenth century. For the late eighteenth century, the picture we have of the al-Azhar is one of a precocious, frustrated, and ultimately defeated group of intellectuals who were promoting a pragmatic modernizing approach to culture. During this late eighteenth-century period, significant works in lexicography, grammar, literature, and history appeared. These works underlay the new journalism and the translation movement, which were to arrive during the Muhammad Ali period. They may have some features of religious learning in them but they are essentially secular. By the early nineteenth century, al-Azhar's repertoire, however, seems more limited.

Scholars are thus correct in their observation that much of the cultural production in the eighteenth century was largely derivative of what had come earlier. Dozens of works of the era, for example the glosses or the textbooks, were simply copies of what went before, leaving us with the question of how one should characterize the more scholarly works that were produced. Until the 1990s, there was no easy way to answer that question. In *Islamic Roots of Capitalism,* I had experimented with the use of the term "neo-classical revival" as a kind of "low-level" descriptor (Gran 1979).

In the 1990s, students of the eighteenth-century Enlightenment in different countries began to point out that the Enlightenment had many varieties and patterns and that, for example, the well-known instance of the French Enlightenment was simply one among them. Thus while Enlightenment remains a fusion of middle-class and elite production of culture in contrast to the fusion of middle-class and popular culture found in the seventeenth century, what the recent developments in scholarship demonstrated were that there existed a number of different versions.

Because of this recent scholarship, one can provisionally characterize Egyptian cultural history as a part of the Italian Road. The Egyptians' concern was not in playing off secularism against clericalism (as occurred among the French) so much as a recognition of a scholastic modernism (as seen among the Italians). Put in other terms, it was not a question of rejecting what France could offer but of how to integrate it. It was how the new knowledge of the Muhammad Ali period was to be integrated that was so controversial with the Azharites, less so the knowledge itself. To summarize, it appears that Egypt went through a long period of enlightenment of this integrative sort first under the later Mamluks and then under Muhammad Ali.

In analyzing Egyptian culture of the nineteenth century, the Italian model is influential for yet another reason, namely, that of regionalism and regional culture. Regionalism, it appears, played a distinctive role in Egyptian culture as it did in politics. Again, as with Italy, the cosmopolitan belletrists and linguists of Egypt seem to come mainly from the South. Thus, for example, in the new institutions of the 1820s and 1830s, such as the *Egyptian Gazette,* the Bulaq Press, and the Language School, one encounters several Upper Egyptian belletrists working as writers and linguists. The technical cadre, however, which would serve the army and the factories, appears to have come from elsewhere, either from the Ottoman Diaspora or from the Delta.

A few years earlier during the late eighteenth century, regionalism was not that pronounced, and the language question had not become that political. From the earlier period, one encounters the last main attempt in Egypt at a dictionary of classical Arabic as a living language; it was the *Taj al-arus* of Muhammad Murtada al-Zabidi (1732–1791). What stands out concerning this work compared to others that appeared even earlier was the author's concentration on actual word usages instead of possible or potential word usage, that is, a preference for useful, empirically based knowledge of a living language over speculative usages or over classicism. To acquire this knowledge, al-Zabidi traveled around Egypt sampling actual usages. As some have noted, he tended to resist the colloquial he encountered although some of that is registered as well. The main point is that such data collection was something that was still possible to do; the boundaries between city and town, town and village, and Upper and Lower Egypt were still not that rigid. As one finds with a number of other eighteenth-century reference books worldwide, Italy included, the *Taj* was not just a dictionary; it was an encyclopedia as well. For our purposes here, al-Tahtawi was quite familiar with the *Taj,* as was his contemporary Edward Lane, who was working on his own classically oriented dictionary.

The late eighteenth century also saw the production of a great history book, one also rooted in much empirical knowledge. This work was Abd al-Rahman al-Jabarti's *Aja'ib al-athar* (1754–1822?). Still read with admiration as the greatest work on modern Egyptian history, it represents a high point of the Enlightenment, one of the relatively few works in the history of history-writing on Egypt in which the author succeeds in discussing both the power of the state and, at the same time, the power of civil society (see al-Jabarti 1880). In his later years, the author al-Jabarti, the historian just referred to, became alienated by the policies of Muhammad Ali, especially by the latter's confiscation of the wealth of the *ulama*. And, while his life is not known in great detail,[4] it is believed that he may have met with Wahhabi sympathizers at a time when Muhammad Ali was at war with the Wahhabis. Later, al-Jabarti was murdered by unknown persons, and no one investigated this crime. Some have speculated that Muhammad Ali may have had him killed. In any case, there is no doubt that his history of Egypt was another influence on the *Takhlis,* and no doubt that al-Tahtawi took cognizance of what befell al-Jabarti in the crafting of his own work. Al-Tahtawi would be less direct in his criticisms than was al-Jabarti.

A major figure in grammar and literature from the late eighteenth-century period was Hasan al-Attar (1766–1835). Al-Attar achieved many things in his career in the area of language and grammar. Historians have not given him his due. Al-Attar has often been identified simply in terms of his influence on al-Tahtawi. This, however, is less than accurate. As was noted before, al-Tahtawi's major formative influence was his own extended family. According to his own words, his relationship to al-Attar was, first, that he read a number of books with al-Attar in the latter's home (they were not taught at al-Azhar at that time), and second, al-Attar supported his career, recommending that Muhammad Ali appoint him as the imam-translator for the Paris Translation Mission. It might also be noted that al-Tahtawi did not study the subjects that al-Attar generally taught, such as Arabic language and grammar. Those subjects he already knew. Exactly how one would characterize the relation of al-Attar to al-Tahtawi is, therefore, a bit more ambiguous. "Junior colleague" might be a better characterization than "major formative influence," the phrase most commonly invoked.

As I have suggested in this chapter, the century of 1760 to 1860 was one of transition for Egypt into an Italian Road–type regime. It contained two overlapping phases of enlightenment. The Muhammad Ali period represents the second phase of the Enlightenment, the one that was more directly inspired by contact with Europe than was the first. During it, Muhammad Ali sent student missions to Paris to learn science and to

4. The main biography of al-Jabarti is still Shaybub 1948.

translate European language texts into Arabic. These works Muhammad Ali then published in the new government printing press at Bulaq. The most famous individual associated with the missions and with the translations was al-Tahtawi. From 1835 onward following his return from Paris, he ran the school for translators in Cairo.

Al-Tahtawi, one needs to make clear, was a supporter of Muhammad Ali. His first position after al-Azhar was that of an army imam, a government appointment. The nature of this appointment needs to be underscored because in al-Tahtawi's time al-Azhar was a major center of opposition to the government. Not all shaikhs were against the government, but most of the leading ones were. And this reaction was not surprising because Muhammad Ali, as mentioned earlier, had confiscated most of al-Azhar's wealth. As a result, al-Azhar opposed many of the government's initiatives, which denied them the ordinary rewards they would have otherwise received. Given al-Tahtawi's desire for a career in government, it is obvious why he did not seriously consider at the same time a career as an al-Azhar shaikh.

From what is known, although al-Tahtawi appears to have always planned to make his career in the service of Muhammad Ali, he also had hoped that the reformist party in the government would remain influential. This, however, was not destined to be the case, and, as a result, in the period extending from the 1840s until the 1860s, al-Tahtawi's career suffered. He could neither work for the government nor for al-Azhar.

The Italian Road Form of Hegemony in Egypt from al-Tahtawi's Time Onward (An Aside)

The argument for Egypt as an example of the Italian Road form of hegemony is one based primarily on a consideration of the country's history during the period 1860 to the present. To do the argument of this chapter justice, therefore, it is necessary to consider at least parts of that wider history. This section attempts to do that. I begin with some general points applicable to many countries in modern times and then progress to some specific features of Egypt that support this hypothesis.

While it is true al-Tahtawi happened to live into the early part of this later period, that is, into the 1860s and beyond for some years, the purpose for including this section, I repeat, is more to show how the Italian Road approach would work than to show the course of al-Tahtawi's later years, as my focus in this chapter is on the *Takhlis*, which was written earlier in al-Tahtawi's life.

For historians today, Egypt 1860 to the present is the account of Egypt as a modern capitalist nation-state. Some of its dynamics were those of most other states of the period, and some were not. On the economic level, Egypt passed through the same three economic phases that most other countries in the world did and in the same sequence: classical liberalism lasted from 1860 to 1952, corporatism from 1952 to 1970, and neoliberalism from 1970 onward. Like most other countries, Egypt has had to depend on one main crop, cotton.

Cotton in the Egyptian case produced immense wealth, but its production brought many problems. Cotton was a product that required an immense infrastructure as well as an immense labor force, and it also required a specialized system of finance. It is this latter system that attracts one's attention in particular. Up to the 1952 Revolution, bankers and moneylenders were a conspicuous part of the structure. Farmers could not farm without credit; they needed this credit because of the vagaries of the growing season and of the actual market itself. Even the state had its debts. As a result, bankers and moneylenders occupied center stage when it came to economic power and to policy-making in Egypt, and this position was scarcely in Egypt's national interest. Under such conditions, it was difficult to escape from debt, much less to forge a national economic policy. It was difficult as well for the country to adjust to the declining position of cotton in the world market, which occurred after the rise of synthetics, a situation making it all the more difficult to justify the continuing investments needed for the infrastructure. But to change the economy from agriculture to industry, which was one solution, would have required extraordinary political change. The middle classes and the workers would have had to play a role in politics. Would this have been possible given the obligation to pay off the debts? The answer is probably in the negative. Italy faced some of the same problems during this period and resolved them through fascism.

Under classical liberalism, which was what prevailed during the nineteenth century in both countries, the approach to politics was that of the minimal state, the state as a "night watchman." In this type of arrangement, there was little room for middle strata to develop. There was in effect no need for it. Thus, on the one hand, one finds a small ruling class, on the other, a large peasantry. Typically, however, periods of classical liberalism led fairly rapidly to social crises. For governments to cope with these crises, they needed to be able to smooth over the rough edges left by the market, and this typically led to their bringing elements of the middle strata and upper working class into the political system at least for awhile. The entrance of these classes and strata into the dominant bloc strengthened it politically and brought it the skills it needed for its survival. The entrance of these classes and strata also allowed for new directions in politics and economics. Scholars use the term *populist* or *corporatist* or simply *cross-class* to characterize this shift in strategy. A large body of scholarship drawn from the study of Latin Europe examines these phenomena in considerable detail. As for countries that were colonized, such as Egypt, the development of populism and cross-class alliances were also important. They simply reached this phase in political economy more slowly than did the others. In the wake of the 1919 Revolution, there was little question that Egypt was ready for populism, but populism actually only fully arrived some thirty-three years later in the 1952 Revolution. The probable reason for the delay was colonialism.

Egypt was a colony for much of its modern history. Even in al-Tahtawi's time there was already a semicolonial dimension affecting Egypt's development. It is this factor among others that adds to the complexity of interpreting the *Takhlis*. How does one read the political writing of semicolonialism? Did M. Jomard, the Savant,[5] and the other French with whom al-Tahtawi associated kibitz in the writing of this book, and if so, to what end? This cannot be known without pursuing the career of these individuals through

5. On M. Edme-François Jomard, see Laissus 2004.

state papers and private papers and without considerably more theorizing. All this has yet to be done.

Colonialism, it was observed, bolstered the existing structure, making the classical liberal age last longer in Egypt than it did in most of the countries that were not colonized. Rather than relying on the local middle classes, which was what commonly took place, rulers in colonies such as Egypt often relied on Europeans who made their careers serving the local bureaucracy. Europeans became a surrogate middle-strata service structure. As a result, what was insidious about colonialism was not that a country like Egypt would be left undeveloped but that Egyptians would not be involved in that development. In the particular case of Egypt, this trend was exacerbated by the sheer size of the European communities resident in Egypt, communities fully possessing the skills needed to manage the country's business and professional life. While, in some cases, these communities had actually been a part of Egypt for centuries, the conjunction of circumstances that came with the modern nation-state and with colonialism encouraged their growth and made them suitable allies of the British, and thus by extension made them appear as antinational to most other Egyptians. This alliance was beginning to become noticeable much earlier, even when al-Tahtawi wrote the *Takhlis*.

As I noted, crises in classical liberal regimes were common. It was a very unstable type of system. This instability was certainly the case for Egypt and one might add for Italy among many other countries as well. In the case of Egypt, the introduction of classical liberalism led to the rise of a nationalist movement. This movement in turn triggered fears on the part of the European bondholders for their investments. This fear gave the Egyptian ruling class and the European residents in Egypt (the so-called "Men on the Spot") a certain leverage to bring about a colonial regime. And this leverage they used. Egyptian nationalism was a threat to the bondholders, they claimed; the Great Powers must send an army. Such statements no doubt contributed to the decision of the English prime minister, Gladstone, to take action. From sending a few senior advisors to the Egyptian government over the years, suddenly the English government progressed to sending an army to occupy Egypt, and occupy the country it did. Soon a second "threat" developed, this one apparently contrived by various interested parties as well, perhaps out of a fear of a British withdrawal from Egypt. The Mahdi of the Sudan, it was declared, had now become a threat to the Nile Valley. It would be necessary for the British and the Egyptians to invade the Sudan and to overthrow him. And this too came to pass, with verbal threats leading to actual policy decisions and these in turn leading eventually to the creation of the Anglo-Egyptian Sudan.

Here one sees the completion of a process that had been going on through much of al-Tahtawi's life. In the course of a century, the Sudan had gone from being a major trading partner with Girga, to being a hinterland, and then to being a colony of the Egyptians and the English. This transition had been facilitated by people such as al-Tahtawi, who threw in his lot with the government in Cairo. When by chance he was exiled for a period to the Sudan, he was miserable, feeling out of place.

Anglo-Egyptian Sudan, as the name suggests, serves as one example of what were a number of unequal partnerships among ruling classes in the period of the late nineteenth and early twentieth centuries. It required of Egypt, the weaker partner, an immense contribution in manpower and service to the British, and this was rendered. Not much was given in return. Britain in fact took much of the Middle East for herself more or less as she took the Sudan. This extreme exploitation of Egypt not surprisingly produced a reaction. Even segments of the ruling class could not abide by what was happening. The Wafd Party led by Sa'd Zaghlul Pasha (1859–1927) created the 1919 Revolution. This time, England was left in a weak position. Except for the royal family, British colonialism in Egypt at that point had few defenders compared to the situation from 1879 to 1880. To hold onto their overall position, the British were thus finally obliged to acknowledge the rights of Egyptians to sovereignty and to an eventual timetable of decolonization. Once again the regional factor stands out. The bulk of the nationalist movement was in the Delta. Perhaps, as a result, it was not altogether accidental that the king, who supported the British, seemed to relish his honorific title *Amir al-Sa'id* (ruler of Upper Egypt). In the 1930s, he made a famous tour of that region. In the Italian case, colonialism was not taken away from them by a stronger power but rather they were left to shoulder the responsibilities themselves, and this they did. In both cases, one could tell the monarchy was on its way out.

When one arrives at the twentieth century, the conventional historiography of most countries, Egypt and Italy included, emphasizes change and progress. This change is the case even where one finds historians making use of the Oriental Despotism model. In the case of Egypt, however, a deeper look suggests that the country had reached the age of Isma'il in the 1860s with a severe regional imbalance between North and South. As we come to the twentieth century it became clear, at least to Upper Egyptians, that the maintenance of regional inequality was a part of the strategy of the hegemony. One could go from ruler to ruler and from colonialism to independence as political historians do with whatever change that might entail, but still there was a system based on region. What seems likely is that the ruling class found it useful to exploit the regional inequality to split the mass population of the country, making it difficult for opposition movements to arise. What seems likely as well is that for a long time, the maintenance of regional inequality assured the dominant region a supply of migrant labor *(tarahil)* for harvest seasons. Still, as more recent history bears witness, with or without this cheap labor, the system I term Italian Road would live on. Until today, one finds its presence on all levels, not just in economics but in politics, in law, and even in the humor of daily life. The proverbial jokes about the Sa'idi's stupidity and his accent remain until today as a part of the culture of regional oppression, a culture contributing to keeping the system in place. For details about the Italian case, the reader need only turn to the life and writings of the Italian communist Antonio Gramsci.

Exploitation requires desensitization. It demands a desensitizing of the general population of the North in regard to the well-being of the Upper Egyptians, and there is evidence to show this desensitizing had happened. As far back as the 1870s, for example, starvation appeared in Upper Egypt. For a period of several years, this starvation was left to progress around Asyut with no help coming from the central government or from the Delta. This neglect suggests a fairly considerable desensitization. Was it surprising that the British and Egyptian ruling classes could fear a possible pro-Mahdist orientation concentrated in that region a few years later? Nor was this neglect an isolated occurrence. When a cholera epidemic broke out in Upper Egypt in the 1940s—no doubt also related to the widespread malnutrition—the American Rockefeller Foundation became involved, as did even the Egyptian royal family, but not the rank-and-file Egyptian nationalists of Cairo. Egyptian nationalists of the period were busy beating the drum for Egyptian independence from the British.

In 1952 independence came and with it land reform and the nationalization of industry, but still Upper Egypt continued to suffer as most of the reforms were carried out in the Delta. Later in the 1960s, Nasir placed the High Dam in Aswan, disrupting the lives of thousands of Nubians there. In the 1967 War, many Upper Egyptians served in the infantry of an army whose officer corps was trained in the Delta. Mortality, it might be added, was very high in that war on the level of the infantry.

Still later with neoliberalism in the ascendancy, Upper Egypt became a place for foreign chemical waste sites. At least once, a chemical waste dump created a poisonous flood emergency around the city of Suhaj in Upper Egypt. In recent times, the struggle of the Sa'idis has taken the form of mass out-migration from the South to such cities as Cairo and Alexandria. The population of these cities has mushroomed as a result. In recent times, radical Islamism emanating from Upper Egypt suggests yet another level of struggle.

The Southern Intellectual as an Institution of the Modern Egyptian Political Economy

This section—a continuation of the preceding one—shows that while al-Tahtawi may be considered to have been the first of what I term the Southern Intellectuals, there were quite a few other Upper Egyptian intellectuals who followed him, all of whom served the regime in similar capacities. Why has this fairly obvious point been ignored? The biographical details of the famous figures are widely known.

This question brings us back to interpretation. Many of the great analysts of Egypt in modern times have been Marxists. And, although Marxists are very interested in the role of the intellectual in history, in general their interpretation is drawn from Lenin, not Gramsci. From a Leninist perspective, intellectuals are an elite; they are the bearers of the high culture, which gradually trickles down to the lower level of the rural mass. Here, by way of contrast, the spotlight is shone on the issue of region. Intellectuals are assumed to be tied to power blocs, some of which are regionally based.

Identifying a few examples of these prominent intellectuals in terms of their regional background will make this contrast clear. Following al-Tahtawi, in the twentieth century, came the legal reformer Ali Abd al-Raziq, the literary critic Mahmud Abbas al-Aqqad (1889–1964), and the educator and litterateur Taha Hussein (1889–1973). These talented individuals, all of Upper Egyptian background, were given a seemingly virtual free hand in their areas of specialization, apparently in return for their political stance on the question of region. As a result, it was they who influenced the development of the secular education system, for example the law and the shape of modern Arabic culture in Egypt more generally. The point here is that the country had many other talented individuals, but it is these men whose lives and writings we study, hence the idea of the Southern Intellectual. Lenin did not use this term, presumably because it was not compatible with his approach.[6] He preferred terms such as "internal colonialism" and "comprador."

In the 1920s, Gramsci characterized the philosopher Benedetto Croce and his role in Italian society (both as an individual and as a set of institutions that supported him) as that of a Southern Intellectual. At the time, Gramsci was trying to explain why Croce, who was a liberal, was given an opportunity to deflect the radical critics of fascism, especially those of the South, by turning their criticism toward liberalism. What Gramsci wanted to understand was why Croce's liberal values were praised by politicians who did not share them, for example, Mussolini. The answer lay, he decided, in the Italian Road system. As an aside, but a fairly important one, Gramsci's theory even in the Italian left was not widely accepted. The Italian left, like the Egyptian left, on the whole preferred Leninism.

6. On the Southern Intellectual, see Gramsci 1978.

There is a possible second reason for why the term "Southern Intellectual" is so little used, be it for al-Tahtawi or more generally, one more technical than philosophical. In Gramsci's own writings, the Southern Intellectual as a subject is treated as a part of the study of many fields, fields such as philology, folklore, the philosophy of education, and others. This mixture makes it difficult to reduce it to one thing or another, which would be needed were it to have a wide circulation. This chapter picks up one small piece of the subject, that is, the use the Southern Intellectual makes of the ideology of secular culture (for example, cosmopolitanism) as a foil against the narrow nationalism and business orientation of the dominant northern region. And while this is only one piece, it is a significant one and not just for al-Tahtawi or the others who have been referred to. For, if one were to pursue the matter of the social origins of Egyptian professional communities, one could show that many diplomats, translators, media personalities, and multilingual cosmopolitan people arose in the South or came from Southern families resident in the North and then gained national prominence. What one understands from this is that the Italian Road type of power structure predictably creates a certain niche for Southerners in these areas while on the whole retaining a monopoly of the political and economic decision-making in the hands of Northerners. In this regard, what Gramsci wrote about Croce thus serves to allow us to return to the subject of al-Tahtawi, an Upper Egyptian, one who emerged as the leading Egyptian intellectual of his time, as a major translator, writer on subjects French, and cultural emissary of Egypt to France in the period when the relationship between Egypt and France was most important. Al-Tahtawi was thus a cosmopolitan in Gramsci's sense, as were others who came later.

As many others were as well, al-Tahtawi was a belletrist. He translated a number of works including literary ones into Arabic from French. And there were others too, for example, Taha Hussein. Taha Hussein wrote that Egypt was a part of the Mediterranean, this at a time when many especially in the North of the country looked at Egypt as Arab Islamic. He was perhaps the quintessential example of a cosmopolitan belletrist in modern Egyptian history.

Al-Tahtawi's *Takhlis al-Ibriz* as an Upper Egyptian Mirror for Princes

In taking the *Takhlis* as a Mirror for Princes,[7] this article overlaps partly with the received interpretation, but it goes beyond it. It overlaps with it—to give credit where credit is due—inasmuch as most modern commentators note some element of advice with regard to educational reform. There was more behind the *Takhlis,* however, than educational reform; there was a regionalist agenda, even one including a veiled threat.

Al-Tahtawi was a political reformer. From the *Takhlis* it is clear that al-Tahtawi stood for republicanism, for the educated citizen, and for modern liberal education for boys and girls. The *Takhlis* was among the first works to take up these subjects in Arabic. As a result, it is not surprising that it has been closely read by scholars for a long time. It is also not surprising, given the influence of the Oriental Despotism model, that a great deal of the scholarly commentary on this book has dwelt on what was understood to be France's role in his education. The problem with this—repeating earlier points—is not about this emphasis per se but about the assumption accompanying it—that al-Tahtawi was being modernized by going to France. More likely what was happening was al-Tahtawi's use of his visit to France to point to certain empirical details about France in a discussion that was actually about Egyptian policies. He was not simply learning new things and reporting on them.

Given the conventional reading, several important points as a result have drawn little if any attention. This omission is unfortunate as these points appear to bear directly on what al-Tahtawi actually intended to convey. The first of these points is inserted in his description of his arrival in Marseille on his way to Paris. Here, near the very beginning of the book, he tells us that he unexpectedly met some Egyptians, among them a member of his own extended family from Upper Egypt, a man who claimed to have become adjusted to life in France. The most plausible

7. On the Mirror for Princes genre, see Ferster 1996 among others.

reason for why one would find this point placed at the beginning of the book is to eliminate the expectation that this was going to be a book about the unknown. The fact that al-Tahtawi encountered a relative from Upper Egypt who had adjusted to life in France seems like a deliberate way to make this clear. A second point, again one that has generally been ignored in the commentary literature, is of a similar sort. I refer to one particular comment about democracy and republicanism. In dealing with the subject of democratic and republican forms of government found in France, one might have expected al-Tahtawi to categorize them as something new or foreign. Most writers who were not French or English tended to do so. Al-Tahtawi's approach was a bit more cosmopolitan. He began by making reference to the experiment of Shaikh al-Hammam, understanding it to be an Upper Egyptian example from the 1700s of a republican and democratic sort (al-Tahtawi 1973, 2:201).[8] To the Egyptian reader who had heard about the Tahtawi family, this would bring to mind a time and place when that family was prominent. While these references leave much unresolved, it is clear and unambiguous that when al-Tahtawi used terms like *jumhuriyah* (republic), he was thinking in Upper Egyptian as well as in global terms. Here was Egyptian cosmopolitanism.

Al-Tahtawi was no doubt hoping to bring about actual reforms in Egypt. The *Takhlis* was in this sense a reformist tract. Education, he more or less said, would bring change, political and otherwise. Moreover, al-Tahtawi makes clear he was thinking here of the education of both men and women. What is certain is that when al-Tahtawi came back to Cairo, he championed the idea of founding a university, but as is also well known, the Madrasah al-Alsun (his translation school), which was to serve as a basis for the proposed university, did not become one for another century when Ayn Shams University absorbed it. In fact, there was no serious contemplation of the idea of any university in Egypt for many years to come. Had a university been founded in this period, many

8. This sentence is missing from the edition published by the Ministry of Culture and National Guidance in 1958, edited by Anwar Luqa, Mahdi Allam, and Ahmad Badawi. In Imara's 1984 biography of al-Tahtawi, there is still a bit of his socialism (299ff.).

Upper Egyptians might have found positions in it. This is the regionalist implication in what he wrote. Another implication, a historiographical one, is that, despite the considerable amount of scholarship on the subject of education in the Muhammad Ali period, it is still not exactly clear what Muhammad Ali's concerns about education were. One wonders as well if al-Tahtawi had a strategy in place for when Muhammad Ali might resist the further development of education. The answer to this question is uncertain.

One other point stands out in this book, that of the advice or threat dimension. Many authors have given advice and even warnings to rulers if they had the standing to do so. Few books written by a relative outsider and addressed to a ruler, however, contain threats. If the people want something, al-Tahtawi wrote, they could overthrow a ruler who denied it to them. This belief can be found in his comments on the Revolution of 1830 in France and the French invasion of Algeria of the same year. The Algerian ruler, he observed, left with his personal wealth while King Louis XVIII (Louis the Last) did not.[9] Here al-Tahtawi was taking chances. He was not an adviser of the ruler, nor was he a social intimate. Furthermore, he knew what had befallen al-Jabarti.

The Rise and Decline of the Traditional View of Rifa`ah al-Tahtawi in Scholarship

The traditional approach to al-Tahtawi as the author of a rihlah outlined above appears in recent years to be slowly breaking down. A review of the scholarship from the past century suggests this. Although the process has been a gradual one, the groundwork has clearly been laid for the development of a more complex view of this remarkable figure.

Apart from reference works, nineteenth-century writing about al-Tahtawi was confined to a single, somewhat hagiographic work written by a former student, al-Sayyid Salih al-Majdi (1827–1881), in his *Hilyah*

9. On the dignity of the Algerian ruler leaving with his personal wealth versus the French ruler leaving without his, see al-Tahtawi 1973, 219.

al-zaman bi manaqib khadim al-watan; sirah Rifa'ah Rafi' al-Tahtawi (1958). Between the 1940s and the 1980s, al-Tahtawi was incorporated into the scholarship of the *Nahda* (or Arab Renaissance), and he became an icon of the rising corporatist culture. In this period, what has been termed the dominant paradigm solidified itself. It seems clear that al-Tahtawi's work in education, language, translation, and modernization clearly resonated with the concerns of many of the important scholars. One could mention as examples the work by the late Alexandria professor Jamal al-Din al-Shayyal (1945) and the work of Cairo University professor Mahmud Fahmi Hijazi (1974). Still later, the well-known Nahdah writer Hussein Fawzi al-Najjar (b. 1918) issued his *Rifa'ah al-Tahtawi, ra'id fikr wa al-imam nahdah* (1987). With the coming of neoliberalism in the 1970s, one finds subtle shifts in the scholarship reflecting changes at that point. For example, more specialized works appeared, works on his poetry and then even on his contribution to language development, for example, al-Badrawi Zahran (1983). The idea of the Nahdah was by this time in disarray, and al-Tahtawi's putative relationship to it was starting to be downplayed.

Before pursuing these more recent developments in the historiography, one needs to make mention of the work of one major Tahtawi scholar in particular, that of Muhammad Imara. In the 1970s, Muhammad Imara tried in a five-volume collection of texts to bring together the main works of al-Tahtawi. He may not have entirely succeeded because Al-Tahtawi wrote a good number of books, which could not be located easily, but what Imara did achieve was to make the general reader aware that al-Tahtawi had a profound interest in religion and religious history and not simply in Europe and in secularism. Imara's work represented a turning point in the historiography. The conventional approach to reading al-Tahtawi in terms of his two most European-oriented and secular books would not suffice. Thus it is not surprising to find that in 1990 came an edited edition with comments on al-Tahtawi's work on the Islamic state (al-Tahtawi 1990). This edition was followed two years later by Sulayman Khatib's *Al-Din wa al-hadarah fi fikr al-Tahtawi: qira'ah Islamiyah* (1992). The most important recent publication on al-Tahtawi is the three-volume manuscript catalog of his private library in Tahta (now in Suhaj) prepared by Yusuf Zaydan

(1996). As one can see from a perusal of this work, the library is made up entirely of Islamic heritage books. If one pursues the books listed by Zaydan, a more complex picture of al-Tahtawi should emerge. As for the currently dominant *tanwir* paradigm, it goes back to *Rifa'ah al-Tahtawi: ra'id al-tanwir* (Imara 1984).

To sum up, I have set out in this chapter to offer a somewhat revisionist reading of al-Tahtawi's famous travel work the *Takhlis* with the suggestion that it might be looked at profitably not simply as rihlah literature but also as an example of Mirror for Princes literature, a genre that was still being composed at the time when the modern national hegemony of Egypt was coming into being. This chapter then examined what advice was being conveyed and concluded that there was a dimension of regionalism involved. I argued that this detail was probably one of the real keys to the text because, as I postulated, Egypt was an Italian Road regime and not, as is commonly supposed, an Oriental Despotism. To pursue this line of thought, the chapter went on to consider in some greater detail whether Egyptian history could be treated as Italian Road and found that it could. On this basis, I conclude that the *Takhlis* is best understood as a Mirror for Princes written by a Southern Intellectual and not in the more conventional way as a voyage to the unknown by a young author from a backward country.

9

Law and the Common Good

To Bring about a Virtuous City or Preserve the Old Order?

CHARLES E. BUTTERWORTH

THERE IS NO AVOIDING IT. Once the name of Ali Abd al-Raziq is mentioned today, one immediately associates it with the idea of secularism or, at least, the secular interpretation of politics in Islam. For most people interested in contemporary politics in the world of Islam, something is fundamentally problematic about Ali Abd al-Raziq's—or anybody else's for that matter—attempt to separate Islam from politics. To do so is to introduce a nonreligious, a secular perspective. The criticisms, even the legal accusations Abd al-Raziq had to face immediately upon the publication of his famous book *al-Islam wa usul al-hukm* (Islam and the roots of governance),[1] are well known. And they continue until this day. So learned a scholar as Parvez Manzoor thinks it perfectly reasonable to refer to Abd al-Raziq's book as a "scandalous work" insofar as it called for "a separation of religion and state in Islam" (Manzoor 1990, 84). Indeed, such an argument appears to be the height of secularism—of bringing

This chapter is dedicated to the memory of Louis J. Cantori, fellow teacher and scholar, dear friend, and constant advocate for truth and justice.

1. Note that "roots of governance" far more accurately renders "*usul al-hukm*" than "bases du pouvoir" (Abd al-Raziq 1933–34), "fundamentals of government" (Enayat 1982, 62), "bases of political authority" (Hourani 1983, 183), "sources of political authority" (Binder 1988, 129), "fondements du pouvoir" (Abd al-Raziq 1994), or even "foundations of political power" (Abdel Razet 2012).

the standards of the temporal, limited world to bear upon the eternal precepts of revealed religion.[2]

It is usual, moreover, to take Abd al-Raziq's silence about such matters after the travails following his book's publication as a sign that he decided to abandon his standing as a religious scholar, as an *alim*. To be sure, he was forced to resign from his position as a judge in the shari'a court by the August 12, 1925, decision of al-Azhar—a decision rendered a mere four months after the book had first been published. Talk about critical reviews!

But is that perspective of the book's teaching and the consequences to which it led correct? Is not Abd al-Raziq, much like a medieval predecessor of whose writing he seems to have no idea, merely trying to speak about the obvious limits of religion from within the religious tradition? Would it not be more accurate to speak of him as following in the steps of Marsilius of Padua (not to mention Jean of Jandun and John of Salisbury) by trying to show why it is better for religion to be limited to spiritual concerns and for politics not to intrude on the sphere of religion? If so, does such an undertaking not contribute more to the defense of religion and to its spiritual enhancement by setting firm limits on religion's political role?

These are the questions to be addressed in what follows. They have been ignored by those who have attempted to analyze Ali Abd al-Raziq's fascinating little book heretofore, primarily because most interpreters are intent upon determining what the book contributes to the contemporary fascination with Islamic governance. Whether one looks at Muhammad Imara, Albert Hourani, or Leonard Binder, the response is the same: such obvious and textual lines of inquiry are cast aside so that those promising political relevance may be pursued. The same holds for the analysis set

2. Fauzi Najjar characterizes Abd al-Raziq and his book as follows: "The first Muslim religious scholar to advocate secularism was Shaykh Ali Abd al-Raziq (1888–1966) in his *al-Islam wa usul al-hukm,* published in 1925. In that famous and controversial work, Abd al-Raziq asserted that Islam was a religion and not a state, a message not a government, a spiritual edifice not a political institution, a proposition that led to his defrocking by the Azharite Committee of Ulema" (Najjar 1996, 1). Najjar's subsequent analyses of the way different thinkers return again and again to Abd al-Raziq are especially important.

forth by Hamid Enayat, even though he pays more attention to the particulars of Abd al-Raziq's book. Indeed, he begins by noting that it "marked the highest point in the debate" and showing some of its major arguments. But he then turns away from a consideration of what Abd al-Raziq actually said in order to focus on the reactions it provoked (Enayat 1982, 62–68). Given the responses and vociferous debate the book has engendered among so many people, including those not familiar with Arabic, it is all the more striking that the only Western European language into which it has been translated is French—and this twice in almost six decades.[3] The introduction by the most recent of these two translators, Abdou Filali-Ansary, rich and nuanced though it is, carries on the same tendency to focus on what the book contributes to the contemporary political scene (Abd al-Raziq 1994, 7–30).

Abd al-Raziq's desire to question the tradition from within and to fathom its meaning on its own terms is evident from the emphasis he places on traditional terminology in the very title of the book. It is, after all, *Islam and the Roots of Governance.* Any number of his fellow *ulama* or clerics (that is, certified scholars in the Islamic sciences of jurisprudence or theology) habitually wrote about "roots of jurisprudence." The term, central to the traditional Islamic presentation of Islam as a religion, is precisely the one Abd al-Raziq chooses to situate his argument. And the titles he assigns to the books, chapters, and sections of his treatise evoke religion as well.

Far from seeking to distance himself from religion, Ali Abd al-Raziq aims in this work to show clearly how much religion has to gain by distancing itself from politics and how politics will gain in justice and wisdom as it distances itself from religion. Separation, then, for love and preservation, as well as because it has become clear to Abd al-Raziq that governing is not now and never has been a proper concern for religion.

3. See Abd al-Raziq 1933–34 and Abd al-Raziq 1994. Of the two, the Bercher translation is the most reliable. Although Filali-Ansary's translation (2003) is often inaccurate to the point of misleading, his footnote explanations of Abd al-Raziq's sometimes opaque references are quite helpful. Recently, an English version of Filali-Ansary's has been published (Abdel Razek 2012).

What Is Islamic Governance?

Abd al-Raziq was at his provocative best in an interview with an unnamed journalist from the *Bourse Égyptienne* on the day after the senior clerics of al-Azhar had expelled him from his position of shari'a court judge as well as from that of cleric in al-Azhar and from any other future state-sponsored employment, "religious or nonreligious." Asked to provide the substance of his book, Abd al-Raziq replied, "The basic point of the book, on account of which I was judged, is that Islam did not determine a precise order of government; nor did it impose a particular order on Muslims by the requirements of which they must be governed. Rather, it left us with absolute freedom to order the state according to the conditions of thought, society, and economy in which we find ourselves, taking into account our social development and the requirements of the times."

He went on to note how he had maintained that the caliphate had no basis in religion, being neither commanded nor counseled by the Qur'an. For him, there was no doubt but that Muslims were free to found government as they saw fit. The caliphate was not set in place by the Prophet, for he "was not a king in any way at all and had not tried in any way at all to found a government or state; he was a messenger sent by God and not a political leader" (Abd al-Raziq 1972, 92–93; see also Binder 1988, 131–32).

And Abd al-Raziq was equally direct in the opening lines of his book. After a traditional, but nonetheless pointedly pious, declaration of allegiance to God and an equally traditional, but still effusive, homage to Muhammad, Abd al-Raziq comes to the main issue. As a judge, he is necessarily concerned with Islamic government. Though the judiciary is only one branch of government, it is still the primary mainstay of Islamic government. "The foundation of all governance in Islam is the most august Caliphate and Imamate," he says, but then quickly adds, "according to what they say" *(ala ma yaqulun)*. This, then, must be investigated. To that investigation, acknowledges Abd al-Raziq, he has already devoted several years. He speaks at some length about his toils in writing the book and notes how he laid it aside several times for long periods. Yet something kept drawing him back to the task, that something most likely being the importance of the subject. After all, it is most important for every Muslim to know whether the caliphate and the imamate are the foundation of governance in Islam or not.

The treatise itself is divided into three books, each book into three chapters, and each chapter into several sections. The first two books are aimed at showing that nothing in Islam allows for the particular instance of rulership—the caliphate—and, more important, for rulership or government in general. Once these points have been settled on theoretical grounds, Abd al-Raziq returns to consider how such an error could ever have arisen among the faithful. He enumerates the fateful steps taken at various periods that inevitably led to the error he is now combating.[4]

To be sure, Abd al-Raziq's exposition is at times repetitive, and his penchant for castigating those whom he opposes by returning again and again to snippets of their arguments heightens that sense of repetitiveness or redundancy. This style may have tempted commentators such as Enayat, Hourani, and Binder to ignore the formal structure of the book and seek instead to capture its overarching argument in a sentence or two.[5] That is a pity, for Abd al-Raziq has quite clearly organized his argument with a view to addressing distinct sets of opinions about the caliphate and to moving

4. Here is a summary outline of the book according to its different formal parts:

Book One: The Caliphate and Islam

- a. Chapter One: The Caliphate and Its Nature
- b. Chapter Two: Governance of the Caliphate
- c. Chapter Three: The Caliphate from the Social Perspective, Completion of the Investigation

Book Two: Government and Islam

- a. Chapter One: The Organization of Governance During the Era of the Prophet
- b. Chapter Two: The Message and Governance
- c. Chapter Three: Message, not Governance—and Religion, not State

Book Three: The Caliphate and Government in History

- a. Chapter One: Religious Unity and the Arabs
- b. Chapter Two: The Arab State
- c. Chapter Three: The Islamic Caliphate

5. Filali-Ansary stands alone in noting the passionate argument that is almost completely obfuscated by the terse, juridical language in which it is presented (Abd al-Raziq 1994, b).

the reader from the more general to the more particular. Moreover, to guide the reader and facilitate understanding through each step of his argument, while discerning its different threads, Abd al-Raziq provides a short indication at the head of each chapter of the subjects to be discussed in the sections to come and numbers each of the sections. Finally, at the conclusion of every chapter but two, he summarizes the chapter's basic argument.[6]

However, the introductory list of topics does not always correspond to those treated in the chapter, nor does the concluding summary fully state the chapter's argument and implications. At the beginning of chapter 1 of book 1, "The Caliphate and Islam" *(al-Khilafah wa al-Islam)*, for example, Abd al-Raziq enumerates six short phrases about the caliphate. Many have to do with the way the caliphate is understood by the jurists. But he actually begins the chapter with a short discussion of what the term "caliphate" *(khilafah)* means in Arabic and the various senses of the verb on which it is based. The bulk of the chapter focuses on the way "caliphate" has been understood or interpreted by jurists through the ages as well as by the famous Ibn Khaldun. At the very end of the chapter, he says nothing about the term's linguistic features and merely expresses the hope that the reader will discern now that the misunderstandings attaching to the way the caliphate and the imamate are viewed must be traced back to the jurists. It is they who have made these offices a "general rulership with respect to religion and this world, a caliphate from the Prophet."[7] As we shall see subsequently, he will show the many errors in this interpretation foisted upon the Muslim community by the jurists and their cohorts.

The Argument of Book One

Abd al-Raziq begins by pointing to the manners in which the caliphate and the imamate resemble kingship, then attempts to show that they, like kingship, have no place in a well-governed polity. Above all, they are like

6. Bk. 1, chap. 3, and bk. 3, chap. 3, are the exceptions.

7. See Abd al-Raziq 1972, bk. 1, chap. 1, sec. 11, 120:20–22 (these last numbers refer to the pages and lines of the book). The first chapter of book 1 is entitled "The Caliphate and Its Nature" *(al-khilafah wa tabi'atuha)*.

kingship with respect to the way they are constituted. That, for Abd al-Raziq, is their nature, and he notes in passing how fully and accurately Ibn Khaldun depicted them, treating him as merely another jurist, albeit a somewhat more famous one. Yet, when referring to Ibn Khaldun and citing passages from his *Muqaddimah,* Abd al-Raziq neglects or overlooks that Ibn Khaldun was presenting a portrait of the caliphate and imamate and contrasting them to kingship in order to explain the way social organization develops, rises to a certain level of complexity, and then declines. His critical portrait of the caliphate and the imamate was intended as a clear indication that even these forms of government, however highly revered by the community of Muslims and in spite of whether they are inspired by God or not, also necessarily fell prey to the tendency of solidarity *(asabiyah)* to grow old and then weaken. The portrait is not intended as praise or indictment of rule by one, for Ibn Khaldun argued that all forms of political organization wax and wane. In this respect, such constructed organisms follow very much the same rules as natural ones. Indeed, the reader approaching Ibn Khaldun's text without predispositions will find the analysis maddeningly dispassionate. Ibn Khaldun was interested in showing how civilization functions, not in identifying which forms of it are better or worse. Abd al-Raziq is not, however, that kind of a reader and thus depicts Ibn Khaldun as a partisan of kingship, then blames him accordingly.[8]

Abd al-Raziq focuses special attention on two sections in chapter 3 of the *Muqaddimah,* sections in which Ibn Khaldun explains first what considerations justify an institution such as the caliphate and then painstakingly notes how those charged with carrying out its goals have transformed and distorted it so that it no longer performs its proper function of

8. The way Abd al-Raziq refers to sources is almost cavalier, a vestige perhaps of the approach he uses for citing juridical sources. The latter are so well known and the texts so familiar that normal scholarly conventions can perhaps be ignored. Even though that cannot be the case with Ibn Khaldun and his text, Abd al-Raziq approaches it as though it were. Worse, he drops words from passages quoted, runs phrases together without indicating that he has omitted words and clauses, and adds formulaic religious phrases or references. It is possible, all the same, that these errors originate in the text on which he relies and are not of his own making.

helping people abide by the religious laws that will help them achieve their best interests in the life to come (Ibn Khaldun 1958, 1:385–88, 414–28; 1970, 1:342–44, 364–76). Even so, he reads them all too loosely and thus misses an important point on which they both agree, namely, the inevitable decline of the caliphate into unjust monarchical rule. Apparently, agreement on that point is too minor an issue. Whatever the merit of Ibn Khaldun's understanding of the way rulership degenerates, his acceptance of the notion that the Prophet Muhammad was a ruler—as were all other prophets—and his ready identification of caliphs as substituting for prophets to look after the welfare of the people is not acceptable (1958, 1:387/22–23, 388/4–6; 1970, 1:344/1, 8–9). Worse, it is precisely the premise that Abd al-Raziq vehemently and repeatedly contests.

Abd al Raziq cites the writings of the jurists about the character of the caliphate and the imamate along with verses of the poets who attempted to portray different rulers continuing the task assigned to the Prophet Muhammad, and he demonstrates the way these rulers have exaggerated the qualities of the office. For him, the caliphate and the imamate can be justified in only two ways. They must either be based on something like divine will or on something like popular will. And here, what is supposedly unique about Islam and the rulership exercised over Muslims becomes very similar to what has occurred among the Europeans with respect to kingship. If justification for these political institutions is to be traced back to divine will, then it becomes very similar to the one used by Thomas Hobbes with respect to kingship. The only other ground for such institutions is something akin to popular will. Were recourse to be had to the notion that the rulers derive their being from the will of Muslims as a community, then they can be defended by arguments like those used by John Locke (Abd al-Raziq 1972, bk. 1, chap. 1, sec. 11, 120:15–19).

Abd al-Raziq refers only obliquely to Thomas Hobbes and John Locke here. He does no more than note the parallel, even larger, argument with the debate over kingship in Europe and then identifies each thinker as the source for one or the other approach. Nor does he explain why he deems such a digression relevant. He says nothing to suggest the incorrectness of either argument or that the position of one defender is to be preferred over the other. The footnote that ostensibly identifies where Hobbes and

Locke set forth such arguments sheds no light on this question either, for the book referenced in support of what is said about Hobbes and Locke is one written by neither. Rather, it is a general textbook about the history of philosophy.

In chapter 2, Abd al-Raziq narrows his focus in order to address the matter at hand: Islamic governance. No matter where one turns, there is no source for either the caliphate or the imamate in Islam. It is not to be found in the Qur'an, nor in the sunna, and certainly not in consensus. There are no verses that can be found in the Qur'an to justify either institution, and those that tell people to obey the authorities are not to be understood as telling people to obey the caliph or to institute a caliphate (1972, bk. 1, chap. 2, secs. 4–5, 122:7–10, 11–24, plus 123:4–5 with special reference to the Qur'an, 4:59 and 83).

At this point, the tone of the exposition changes dramatically. Proclaiming his thorough familiarity with all of the traditional sources—that is, the very ones to which a cleric should turn to figure these things out—Abd al-Raziq asserts that there is nothing solid in them. His tone is aggressive and peremptory. He is audacious in his categorical rejection of any argument that fellow jurists might bring forth, but he shows beyond a doubt that he has given thoughtful consideration to the arguments of his opponents. For him, their defense of the caliphate rests either on the notion that it has come about through consensus on the part of the early Muslims or is derived from some kind of syllogistic reasoning that is based on intellectual judgments.

Clearly it is now imperative to ask why such an error has arisen. Why has the *umma* been subjected to rule by one when there is no textual or valid traditional justification for it? And why has taking care of religion been identified with taking care of political well-being? In an almost exasperated tone, Abd al-Raziq notes that anyone desiring further evidence of what he has been claiming need only look at the book on the caliphate by the noted Sir Thomas Arnold.[9] Even more, were one to study carefully the

9. Thomas Walker Arnold (1864–1930) taught at the Muhammedan Anglo-Oriental College, Aligarh, from 1888 to 1898, then became professor of philosophy at the Government

Qur'an from the first *surah* to the last, there would be found "no mention of this general imamate or caliphate" (1972, bk. 1, chap. 2, sec. 5, 123:13–16).[10]

Those such as Rashid Rida who rely upon the sunna to defend the caliphate and the imamate are also in error. Seizing upon a tradition about the Prophet urging people to give allegiance to a ruler, they draw the false conclusion that this signals the Prophet's endorsement of the caliphate. Conceding—at least for the sake of the argument—that the tradition is perfectly sound, Abd al-Raziq denies the significance Rida and others attach to it. To be sure, the Prophet may well have urged Muslims to give the allegiance in question. But he did nothing more. And he certainly did not urge the early Muslims to institute a caliph to rule over them any more than Jesus endorsed the rule of Caesar or called for the institution of that kind of rule when he spoke of rendering unto Caesar what is Caesar's and unto God what is God's (1972, bk. 1, chap. 2, sec. 7, 125:11–21; see also 123:22–125:10).

That dismissal—although too quick, almost to the point of glibness—points to where Abd al-Raziq's argument must go. By distinguishing between what belongs to divine and what to earthly power, Jesus relinquishes the latter to concentrate on the former. This is precisely what Abd al-Raziq thinks Muhammad sought to do, and this is what he must eventually prove. In doing so, he must also contend that the whole history of Islamic civilization until now has rested upon an error. Moreover, it is incumbent upon him to show what kind of rule can replace the old, mistaken one.

For now, however, it is sufficient for him to insist on the importance of the caliphate and the imamate and the consequent necessity for their

---

College, Lahore, and eventually dean of the Oriental faculty at Punjab University. After various governmental positions associated with the India Office, he served as professor of Arabic and Islamic studies at the School of Oriental Studies, University of London, from 1921 until his death. His book, *The Caliphate,* had been published only the year before Abd al-Raziq's own. At Abd al-Raziq 1972, bk. 1, chap. 2, sec. 5, 123:4–5, Abd al-Raziq urges the reader to consider chapters 2 through 3 of Arnold's book, those dealing with how the caliphate came about and the putative sources for it in the Qur'an and *sunna.*

10. He adds, "about that, there is matter for discussion."

proponents to adduce proofs of their conformity with Islamic doctrine superior to the rhetorical ones he has now refuted. The problem is that there are no such proofs. About that, Abd al-Raziq is categorical. Arnold is equally firm about there being no Qur'anic justification for the caliphate and about the Prophet's having died without providing for a successor. But he does offer reasons for the opinions he sets forth. Thoroughly conversant with the historical studies of nineteenth- and early twentieth-century European Orientalists as well with the writings of several Arab and Muslim historians from the early years of Islam, he traces the choice of Abu Bakr as Muhammad's successor to Arab tribal practices and deems the explanations offered by his successor, Umar, for his own appointment to be without foundation. Moreover, his skepticism about the reliability of tradition or hadith keeps him from accepting arguments based on it.

Chapter 3 begins on what seems at first to be a more conciliatory note, for Abd al-Raziq agrees that there was some consensus among Muslims to have someone like Abu Bakr take the place of Muhammad as leader of the religious community. But he then notes adamantly that to be leader of the religious community is not the same as being leader of the political community. Nor can the silence and acquiescence of the first followers be cited to support the claim that they held Abu Bakr to be the duly appointed political leader. Neither silence nor acquiescence to a status quo is equivalent to consensus (1972, bk. 1, chap. 3, sec. 12, esp. 133:5–9). The denial, adamant as it is, nonetheless reveals that Abd al-Raziq is thoroughly familiar with the arguments based on history and precedent in favor of the caliphate. And this position explains his embrace of Arnold; although coming to the subject from quite different perspectives, both Abd al-Raziq and Arnold reach the same conclusions about what the history of Islamic civilization says concerning this institution.

For Abd al-Raziq, part of the problem facing the Muslim world at the time he is writing is that Muslims have always tended to accord politics—that is, the study of politics—too little attention. The reason is that caliphs and other rulers, who maintain their status by force, discourage such study (1972, bk. 1, chap. 3, secs. 6 and 12, 128:12–18, 132:19–134:4). In this sweeping generalization, Abd al-Raziq neglects al-Farabi and all those who succeed him. He even fails to mention al-Mawardi. Along the way, he makes a most interesting—albeit misleading, even false—observation, namely, that political philosophy flourished in democratic Greece. If truth be told, it did not. Perhaps in oligarchic Greece and certainly, at least with respect to Aristotle, in a tyrannically ruled Greece, but not in democratic Greece. To the contrary, it was the people of Athens who in solemn assembly sentenced Socrates to death.

Still, the more salient point for his argument is his insistence on how the caliphate, imamate, and kingship in general depend upon coercion and domination. To make this argument, he speaks openly and most critically of the king of Egypt. Whatever stifling effect rule by one is supposed to have upon the general body of the citizens, it is patent that Abd al-Raziq fears the royal authority of his day not in the least (1972, bk. 1, chap. 3, sec. 7, esp. 129:15–28; see also sec. 19, 137:10–138:5).[11]

He raises the issue about coercion and domination as mainstays of rule by one in order to contrast those forms of governance with Islam. It differs from them insofar as its primary features are brotherhood, equality, and freedom (1972, bk. 1, chap. 3, sec. 8, 130:1–25).[12] Consequently, to link Islam with the caliphate and the imamate is a fundamental contradiction in principles.

Finally, even though it is obvious that all people need government, Abd al-Raziq notes that the caliphate is not the only form of rule. And he closes the chapter by reiterating the earlier claim that there is no proof of the caliphate and the imamate being God's will for Muslims. No Qur'anic verses back it up. Nor can any sayings recorded in hadith be cited to favor it. And there is no consensus for such rule. In sum, the caliphate is without

11. All the same, Abd al-Raziq's penchant for openly challenging royal authority was surely misguided. His book follows upon Mustafa Kemal Atatürk's abolition of the caliphate on March 3, 1924. Had Egypt's King Fuad been thinking of claiming title to the caliphate, Abd al-Raziq's book posed a hurdle to be overcome. The trial and judgment against Abd al-Raziq succeeded in blunting the challenge posed by the book.

12. Abd al-Raziq does not elaborate on his choice of these three characteristics or attributes. Witting choice or not, they call to mind the key themes of the French revolution—*liberté, égalité, fraternité*—and thus to the way others have distanced religion from politics.

religious foundation. Worse, it is an unmitigated disaster for Muslims (1972, bk. 1, chap. 3, sec. 16, 136:4–10, esp. 136:7–10).

There is another feature of the conclusion to chapter 3 of part 1, and thus to part 1 as a whole, that is worth noting. Throughout this chapter (as, indeed, throughout the preceding chapters and the book as a whole), Abd al-Raziq addresses himself to an unspecified reader in the first person singular. Now, in closing the chapter as well as the first book of the treatise, he engages that reader in a long peroration:

> Perhaps you will be persuaded by what we have advanced that what they call caliphate or the great imamate is in no way based on a foundation taken from upright creed or sound intellect and you will find, when you reflect upon it, that what they claim as proof for it is anything but a proof.
>
> It may be that you have a right to ask now about our particular opinion with respect to the caliphate and its origin. And it falls upon us to accede to you in explaining that, relying upon God, may His undertakings be magnified, for fine assistance, guidance, and success. (1972, bk. 1, chap. 3, sec. 20, 138:10–15)

Having shown why the claims of those who seek to defend the caliphate or the imamate are inadequate and false, Abd al-Raziq now intends to show how government functioned in the early days of Islam—that is, during the life of the Prophet—and what that says about the way it should have continued after his death. The reader addressed in such familiar terms is every concerned Muslim wishing to understand better the roots of governance within Islam.

The Argument of Book Two

Calling on studies he has undertaken previously in order to learn about the status of the judiciary at the time of the Prophet, Abd al-Raziq begins chapter 1 of book 2 by noting how much confusion and obscurity there is about the events that occurred then. Many sources offer reports of the Prophet's sending one person or another to settle a problem in a distant area. And while it is well known that at the beginning he was the sole person to whom Muslims turned to adjudicate disputes, it is equally well known that he soon found it necessary to enlist the assistance of distinguished fellow Muslims both at home and in the more distant areas inhabited by Muslims. It is also beyond doubt that all those involved in disputes were accustomed to seeking out an adjudicator, a task that most often fell to a tribal chief.

But these sources provide no clear explanation of what extrajudicial tasks the Prophet assigned these adjudicators, if any, or whether he instructed the adjudicators to settle some particular disputes and then return or to remain where they were sent and carry out other duties (1972, bk. 2, chap. 1, secs. 1–7, 139:8–143:13). Given such difficulties, Abd al-Raziq despairs of gaining clarity about the Prophet's precise intention in dispatching individuals to one place or another and thus of discerning what political objectives he might have had in mind. Yet any attempt to claim that the caliphate and the imamate originated with the Prophet must show clearly that he did have a precise political vision for the community of Muslims. That has not yet been done, nor does Abd al-Raziq think it can be done. Too little is known about the way the fledgling community of Muslims functioned in Mecca, Medina, and elsewhere, that is, about whether or how they governed Mecca and interacted with the rulers of other cities and provinces. Abd al-Raziq does not belabor the point. Instead, setting aside the difficulties of piercing through the muddled historical record—if any even exists—and his doubts that any single individual could do so, he poses the basic question with respect to Muhammad in as clear and uncompromising a fashion as he possibly can: "[W]as he the master of a political state and the ruler of a government in the same way that he was the messenger with a religious calling and the leader of a religious group, or not?" (1972, bk. 2, chap. 1, sec. 9, 144:11–12).

So posed, one might well answer in the manner of Ibn Khaldun that the Prophet was both. That is an opinion held by almost all Muslims, and they can point to several things the Prophet did and spurred others to do as signs of its veracity. Moreover, they can point to Joseph and Jesus as being messengers as well as political leaders of their respective Jewish and Christian religious communities. Yet it is also known that Joseph allowed his interest in politics to eclipse his spreading of the message, and Jesus explicitly turned away from political rule (1972, bk. 2, chap. 2, secs. 1–8,

144:23–148:25). In other words, the difficulty, perhaps the impossibility, of knowing with certainty what the Prophet was intent upon accomplishing with his little community of believers cannot be evaded.

It is known, however, that he led the newly formed Muslim community in military encounters, or acts of jihad. So, too, did he establish ways to raise money through different kinds of taxes and encourage charity as well as appoint judges and assign them to precise places in Yemen and Saudi Arabia. All the same, notes Abd al-Raziq, these kinds of activities might well have been undertaken in order to protect the fledgling community of the faithful, not to expand it. Thus one might urge that they are to be viewed not as political acts, but rather as actions a religious leader carries out in the course of his religious stewardship.

Still, the absence of precise knowledge about what was happening at the time of the Prophet prompts Abd al-Raziq to refrain from embracing that notion. It also keeps him from siding with those who insist on viewing the Prophet as the founder of a political regime. Given what Abd al-Raziq eventually had to endure, the gentleness is striking as he turns away from this opinion and explains that its proponents are not to be considered as any less faithful Muslims. A final possibility is also rejected by him, namely, viewing the absence of formal offices and other details of rule as signs that the Prophet sought to establish only a simple and natural political order. In the end, it is clear to him that the lack of prescriptions and of organization are signs not of Muhammad's desiring simplified government, but rather of his not wanting to countenance government of any sort (1972, bk. 2, chap. 2, secs. 9, 10–17, and 18, 148:26–149:12, 149:13–153:12, and 153:13–26, esp. 13–15).[13]

13. His September 3, 1925, letter to Abd al-Aziz Fahmi, minister of justice, contesting the decree issued by the Commission of Senior Clerics of al-Azhar University that removed him from his position as a cleric and judge is also worth considering with respect to this question. In calm, measured tones, Abd al-Raziq (1972, 100–101) notes, first, that the decision is null because al-Azhar University has no authority over the Ministry of Justice of which Abd al-Raziq is a functionary; and, second, that it is unconstitutional because it seeks to stifle the expression of opinion, a right guaranteed by the Egyptian constitution.

The gentleness of tone comes to an abrupt halt in the final chapter of book 2, when Abd al-Raziq balances his earlier denial that any Qur'anic verse or reliable hadith could be adduced in favor of Muhammad's having been designated a ruler by God with a plethora of citations from these two sources to prove that he is definitely never identified as a ruler. No obedience is due him, nor is there any indication that he ever sought the trappings usually associated with temporal rule. Similarly, he never focused on the issues that so preoccupy ordinary political rulers. To the contrary, Muhammad's greatest concern was for the spiritual well-being of those to whom he brought his message (1972, bk. 2, chap. 3, secs. 3–4, 156:6–10 and 157:12–17).

Throughout this chapter, Abd al-Raziq insists on setting Islam and its messenger apart from ordinary rule and those who assume its tasks. Thus Islam is portrayed as speaking first and foremost to the ultimate happiness of human beings, to their religious desires, and not to their material well-being except insofar as this is necessary for them to attain eternal bliss. Whereas the whole world might fall under the sway of a single religion, it is not conceivable that a single government would ever be able to rule over all human beings or satisfy their needs (1972, bk. 2, chap. 3, sec. 8, 164:14–17 and 165:9–11). Yet it cannot be denied that some of the activities undertaken by the Prophet are similar to those undertaken by secular rulers, and chief among these is armed combat or jihad. As in the preceding chapter, so here, this is an issue to which Abd al-Raziq must respond. He does so by pointing out that all of these apparently political actions, even warfare, are means for the Prophet to establish the religion and promulgate his religious call. Thus, because "evil is sometimes necessary for good" to come about and destruction is needed in order to complete civilization, war is justified (1972, bk. 2, chap. 3, sec. 9, 166:10–16).

That argument and the many citations from the Qur'an and hadith notwithstanding, one begins to wonder whether Muhammad's rulership is really the issue. After all, even if Abd al-Raziq is perfectly correct in his insistence that Muhammad was not a ruler and was never designated as one by God, his successors were. Caliphs, or rulers who sought to combine religious and secular concerns, arose almost immediately after

Muhammad's death. How did this happen? That is the question Abd al-Raziq must address in the final book.

Before turning to that exposition, it seems appropriate to reflect upon the way the people of the two other Abrahamic faiths have responded to this question of rulership. In four of the five books attributed to Moses, that is, the Torah or Pentateuch, he is portrayed as the ruler of the Jews. He first comes to notice for standing up to Pharaoh's tyranny and then for leading the Jews out of Egypt, both under divine prompting and guidance. First and foremost a spiritual ruler, Moses is also the one who organizes the Jewish people during their days of wandering in the Sinai, keeps them in line, and establishes laws by which they conduct their affairs and lead their lives, always acting in response to divine instruction. The books of scripture following the Torah relate how the Jews rebelled against the successors whom Moses appointed to carry on his precepts after his death and how they cried out for a king. Not heeding the advice of other prophets who warned how much they would suffer under kingly rule, the people prevailed. Long, detailed accounts of evils wrought by the kings of Israel follow. They are interspersed with records of the way yet other prophets harangued those kings and the people, all to little or no avail. Indeed, even such revered figures as David and Solomon were guilty of major infractions against the laws first established by Moses. Eventually the Jewish people fell into a new servitude, saw their homes and places of worship destroyed, and were driven from their promised land. Even when some were subsequently able to return to it and rebuild their places of worship, especially the great temple in Jerusalem, the egregious wrongs of their rulers once again brought them into subjection. This time, however, those who had returned to that land were allowed to remain, albeit as subjects of others.

Although Abd al-Raziq might have made a powerful argument against the notion that kingly rule is part of divine order by pointing to the sad experiences of the Jews, he does not. Nor does he draw the most salient lesson from the experience of Jesus, namely, that he did not have to contend against Jewish kings; they were past history. And since his focus was on the life to come, he could ignore Caesar. Differently stated, Jesus could ignore secular rulership with impunity. So, too, could Muhammad.

Had Abd al-Raziq pointed to the parallel between Jesus and Muhammad, had he argued that the successors to Muhammad erred in seeking to replace the guidance of the Prophet by lessons rooted in statecraft—as some groups of early Muslims did argue—Abd al-Raziq might have been more successful in persuading his fellow religious scholars that Islam has nothing to do with secular rule.

Let it also be said here in passing, for anything more would take the argument too far afield, that Abd al-Raziq could also have learned much about these matters from Marsilius of Padua. In the first chapter of his famous *Defender of the Peace,* Marsilius sets peace down as the greatest good and urges that discord, the opposite of peace, leads to great evils in civil regimes or states. He then identifies a new cause of discord and strife, one not foreseen by Aristotle or any other philosopher of earlier times, namely, the belief of the Roman prelates that they have plenitude of power, that is, power over all kings, princes, communities, and groups (Marsilius 2001, discourse 1, chap. 1, secs. 1–3 and 6–8; also discourse 1, chap. 19, secs. 9–12 and 13). This is the opinion he rails against throughout his book, seeking to prove that the clergy should follow the example of Jesus and focus their thoughts as well as their actions solely on the spiritual well-being of Christians. So intent should they be on ministering to the spiritual needs of the faithful that they have no leisure for political activity.

The Argument of Book Three

Clearly Abd al-Raziq holds an opinion about the mission of Muhammad and thus of his true successors or representatives that accords with the opinion of Marsilius about the mission of Jesus and the proper task of his representatives. The whole of chapter 1, book 3, is devoted to showing that Muhammad's goal was the spiritual well-being of those who accepted his message, that there is nothing in his actions or speech nor in the revelation he received to suggest he had a political role or goal of any kind. To be sure, the Prophet did bring Arabs of many tribes and backgrounds together. But he brought them together into a unified religious group, not a unified political group. Nothing in his teaching directs believers to change their political ways or to adopt new ones. Indeed, so focused was the Prophet on forming a religious community—one he alone was qualified to form insofar as he alone had been designated as the messenger of God to the Arabs—that he named no successor. This fact alone ought to indicate that Muhammad had no intention of forming a political entity that would continue his call after his death (Abd al-Raziq 1972, bk. 3, chap. 1, secs. 3, 4, 6–7, and 9, 169:23–26, 170:18–31, 171:20–24, 172:6–9, and 173:16–19).[14]

If the Prophet's success in bringing the previously dispersed and opposing Arab tribes and peoples together as a community of believers gave rise to political aspirations, that success was merely by accident. Nothing that Abd al-Raziq can point to in the Prophet's speech or actions provides the slightest indication that this was Muhammad's goal. Only with Abu Bakr, and then only owing to the aspirations of a few of those originally closest to the Prophet, did the notion of forming a political entity arise. For Abd al-Raziq, the request that members of the Muslim community take an oath of allegiance to Abu Bakr is the first sign that a political goal has come to replace the religious one that had so consumed all of Muhammad's time and efforts. Indeed, what is known of the discussions that occurred then and of the refusal by some to declare such allegiance to Abu Bakr without thereby wishing to separate from the community of Muslims is for Abd al-Raziq powerful evidence that political considerations had come to replace religious ones. Equally important as evidence is Abu Bakr's own declaration, as reported by al-Tabari, that he had no intention of replacing Muhammad in any of his spiritual functions (1972, bk. 3, chap. 2, secs. 2–4, 174:22–26, 175:13–23, and 176:11–14 and 20–25).[15]

For Abd al-Raziq, there is no good reason that any particular significance should have been attached to Abu Bakr's nomination as the

14. In peremptorily rejecting the Shi'ite arguments for Muhammad's having designated Ali as his successor, Abd al-Raziq cites Ibn Khaldun with approval for the first, but not the only, time; see Abd al-Raziq 1972, bk. 3, chap. 2, sec. 8, 172:18–20 and 21–23 with Ibn Khaldun 1958, 1:403:3–10; and 1970, 1:355:10–14.

15. Even more telling is Abu Bakr's declaration, at least according to Ibn Khaldun—that he was the successor or representative (khalifah), not of God, but of Muhammad. See Abd al-Raziq 1972, bk. 3, chap. 3, sec. 3, 177:27–178:1 and Ibn Khaldun 1958, 1:389:11–14; and 1970, 1:345:4–5.

successor or representative *(khalifah)* of Muhammad. To be sure, among all of those closest to the Prophet, he was clearly the most prominent. And that he was so designated must have been in recognition of the esteem in which he was held by both the Prophet and his companions. But in principle, things should have gone no further. Abu Bakr should merely have focused on keeping the community together as a group of believers following out the tenets of Muhammad's revelation. Instead, once that title was accorded Abu Bakr and he began to rule the fledgling community of Muslims, what can only be described as political considerations came to the fore. These are most evident in the refusal to tolerate those who balked at accepting his rule, especially in their coming to be viewed and then castigated as apostates. The politicization of the community was a fatal and unnecessary, even a wrong, step. All that has ensued as the successorship or caliphate developed into simple, unjust, and despotic monarchy could have been avoided. "In truth, the religion of Islam is exempt from this caliphate that Muslims have become acquainted with, exempt from the desires, fears, might, and power that have grown up around it. The caliphate has nothing to do with religious precepts, no more than do judges or others employed in government and state institutions" (1972, bk. 3, chap. 3, sec. 12, 182:1–4; see also secs. 1–2, 6–7, 10 and 11, 177:7–16, 179:3–5, 12–14, 21–23, and 171:6–11 and 22–26).

Without the caliphate, without dependence on a corrupt form of rule, Muslims could be free to use their reason and thus to vie with the other nations of the world as they develop their social and political life in new ways. "Nothing in their religion prevents Muslims from vying with the other nations in all of the social and political sciences or from destroying that antiquated order that has debased them and held them down. Then they might found principles of rulership and an order of government based on the most recent conclusions from human intellects as well as what has been proven through the experience of nations to be the best sources of governance" (1972, bk. 3, chap. 3, sec. 12, 182:10–13).

Holding out this promise of a brilliant future, Abd al-Raziq concludes his book with a pious declaration of gratitude for the divine guidance he has received. It, like the pious invocation with which he opens the book, is to be taken at face value. Whatever shortcomings the book may have in terms of intemperately expressed arguments and even arrogant displays of knowledge about Islam and its sources, there is no reason to suspect its author of insincerity. The issue, rather, is whether he is correct in his understanding of the Prophet and the ultimate goal of his mission. Alas, that issue has never been properly addressed.

Conclusion

In sum, Ali Abd al-Raziq has made here a passionate, heated attack upon the notion of the caliphate and the imamate. He has shown that they are not required, that in many respects they are an aberration. And he goes on to explain that Muhammad's sole concern was for the well-being, the religious well-being, of those to whom he came with a distinct message about how to live to merit a good life on the day of judgment. By no means is this call for religion and politics to be separated tantamount to speaking on behalf of secularization, but—as is made ever so clear in the closing words to the book—it is a passionate call for reform and modernization.

Not only did no one respond to the call, it spurred almost everyone who heard it to attack its author. Founded in error or not, the caliphate and the imamate are institutions central to the history of Islam, ones with which Muslims identify and in which they trace the glorious days of Muslim might. Caesar and all that Caesar stands for remain distinct from Jesus and Christian religion, whereas caliphs and imams—all caliphs and all imams, regardless of their personal or political qualities—are never separate from Islam nor from Muhammad. That is a simple fact Abd al-Raziq should have noted and in awareness of which he should have constructed a much more conciliatory argument.

Had he simply started from the major event of his day, the abolition of the caliphate, and spoken to the modernizing reforms he wished to introduce, he would most likely have achieved his goal and would have found supporters as well as allies rather than detractors and enemies. The change he wishes to effect is in no way dependent upon understanding whether rule in bygone eras was legitimate or not. Rather, it depends on identifying the opinions and practices that stifle modernization and then on removing or otherwise neutralizing them. Abd al-Raziq failed to pay sufficient attention to the opinions of his fellow Muslims and to the origins of those opinions.

The change, reform, and modernization he calls for are, as he rightly notes, quite in keeping with the Prophet's understanding of Islam. Abd al-Raziq could have urged regime change, even the replacement of particular rulers. And he would have had a very good chance of succeeding in such a politically oriented call, at least as long as he kept that call distinct from time-honored opinions and beliefs about the Prophet's uniquely just form of rulership. His failure has had grave consequences insofar as it has inspired critics who deny the wisdom of separating politics from religion and inadvertently make it appear that a call for separation is nothing more than a plea for secularism or for a politics rooted in it.

Those critics have had an easy time largely because Abd al-Raziq is so vague about what he means by change, reform, and modernization. At no point does he identify the kind of political or social organizations he desires or thinks Muslims now need. It seems that all he really desires is an end to the tyranny of monarchical rule, whether it be by a caliph or a king. That, after all, is the only kind of rule he explicitly criticizes. Nor does he insist on a point that is central to his whole analysis, namely, that separating religion and politics is beneficial to both. Here, as noted, greater familiarity with the argument of Marsilius of Padua would have been useful. Or he could simply have pointed to the reforms initiated by Muhammad as he brought his message to fellow Arabs and helped them improve their lives as individuals and members of families as well as tribes.

But Abd al-Raziq is not solely to blame for the failure of his important undertaking. As he so correctly notes in his letter to Abd al-Aziz Fahmi, he has been wronged insofar as he has not been accorded the simple privilege of expressing his own opinion with impunity. There is nothing in that opinion and certainly nothing in the careful, generally respectful way in which it is expressed that threatens religion, casts aspersion upon the character of the Prophet, or denigrates any of the revered sources of spiritual guidance. Just as the Prophet and the early adherents to Islam suffered for expressing new and unsettling opinions, so does Ali Abd al-Raziq suffer for his daring critique of the way those opinions seem to have been misinterpreted throughout the history of Islam.

10

What Do Egypt's Islamists Want?

Moderate Islam and the Rise of Islamic Constitutionalism in Mubarak's Egypt

BRUCE K. RUTHERFORD

IN RESPONSE to both external and internal pressures, many Arab regimes undertook reforms in the 1990s and 2000s that allowed greater political competition. The primary beneficiaries of these reforms were Islamist groups. In the 2000s, Islamists achieved unexpected success at the ballot box in countries as diverse as Morocco, Egypt, Palestine, Iraq, and Lebanon.

As Islamist groups gained more political power, an obvious question arose: what type of political order did these groups seek to create? The Egyptian case provided particular insight into this question. It offered the best-developed discourse on Islamic law and governance of any country in the Arab world. This discourse was led by a vibrant and vocal group

An earlier version of this chapter was published as "What Do Egypt's Islamists Want? Moderate Islam and the Rise of Islamic Constitutionalism," *Middle East Journal* 60(4): 707-31. This earlier version was written while the author was a research fellow in the Islamic Legal Studies Program at Harvard Law School. He is grateful to Frank Vogel and Peri Bearman for their encouragement and support. He is also grateful to Ismail Fayed and Naseema Noor for research assistance and to Nathan Brown for comments on an earlier draft. In addition, it should be noted that this chapter does not attempt to study the development of Islamic Constitutionalism (IC) since the removal of Hosni Mubarak. Rather, it focuses on the rise of IC in the last two decades of Mubarak's rule.

of Islamic thinkers whose ideas were influential throughout the region. In addition, Egypt had a popular and well-organized Islamist movement, the Muslim Brotherhood (MB), that sought to translate the theoretical principles of Islamic governance into a practical political platform. The MB showed considerable flexibility and originality in its efforts to develop a viable conception of Islamic governance.[1] Thus a close analysis of the Egyptian experience allows us to study both the theory and the substance of Islamic constitutionalism.

This chapter begins with an assessment of the conception of constitutionalism articulated by Egypt's most influential contemporary Islamic thinkers. It then examines how these ideas were translated into a specific political agenda by the Muslim Brotherhood, particularly during the 2005 parliamentary elections. It concludes with a discussion of the likely impact of Islamic constitutionalism on democratization in Egypt.

The Theory of Islamic Constitutionalism in Contemporary Egypt

For well over a century, Egypt has been an important center for legal thinkers seeking to adapt Islam to the challenges of contemporary governance. This effort began in the late nineteenth and early twentieth centuries with the works of Jamal al-Din al-Afghani, Muhammad Abduh, and Rashid Rida. It moved forward with Abd al-Razzaq al-Sanhuri's remarkable synthesis of Islamic and French law in the Egyptian civil code. It continued during the Mubarak era with a new generation of Islamic thinkers.

The most important figures in this effort were Yusuf al-Qaradawi, Tariq al-Bishri, Kamal Abu al-Majd, and Muhammad Salim al-Awwa.

1. This flexibility did not extended to its foreign policy. The Muslim Brotherhood remained highly critical of the status quo in the Middle East. For example, the Brotherhood's leader, Muhammad Mahdi Akif, called for sending ten thousand MB fighters to Lebanon to assist Hizballah in its clash with Israel during the summer of 2006. See Muhammad Salah, "Murshid al-Ikhwan al-Muslimin: musta'iddun li-irsal 10,000 Mujahid ila Lubnan" (Guide of the Muslim Brotherhood: We are prepared to send 10,000 Jihadists to Lebanon), *al-Hayat,* Aug. 4, 2006. For further discussion of the Brotherhood's foreign policy, see Hamzawy and Bishara 2006.

These writers have varied backgrounds. Al-Qaradawi received formal training in Islamic law at al-Azhar University in the 1950s and 1960s, eventually earning a doctorate in 1973 with a thesis that examined the legal and social foundations of *zakat.* He worked briefly at the Egyptian Ministry of Religious Endowments before moving to Qatar, where he established the faculty of *shari'a* and Islamic studies at the University of Qatar. He has authored more than fifty books and is one of the most widely read contemporary Islamic thinkers in the Arab world. He also hosts a weekly call-in show *(Islamic Law and Life)* on the satellite channel al-Jazeera, which further broadens his reach and influence.[2] Tariq al-Bishri's background is somewhat more eclectic. He was trained as a lawyer in the early 1950s and began public life as a secular intellectual with leftist leanings. He embarked on a successful career in the judiciary where he eventually rose to the post of first deputy president of the State Council, one of the most senior positions in the administrative judiciary. While pursuing these judicial duties, he also found time to write several highly regarded books on Egyptian history. His best-known books deal with the emergence of Egyptian nationalism and the historical significance of the 1952 Revolution (al-Bishri 1983; 1991). These works return constantly to the themes of reviving Egypt's cultural identity, building national unity, and increasing the country's independence. Al-Bishri argues that strengthening the role of Islam in Egyptian society is essential to achieving each of these goals.[3] Most of his scholarly works since the early 1990s have focused on this issue, with particular emphasis on the question of how to apply Islamic law to contemporary Egyptian society and politics.[4]

Abu al-Majd also has a strong legal background. He earned a PhD in law from Cairo University and an MA in comparative law from the University of Michigan. He served as minister of youth and minister of

2. For further information on al-Qaradawi, see the websites that he helped to found: http://www.islamonline.net/arabic and www.qaradawi.net. Also see the entry about him in *Encyclopedia of the Modern Middle East and North Africa* (Mattar 2004).

3. Al-Bishri (1983, 1–68) explains this point in greater detail in the introduction to the second edition of his book on pre-1952 Egyptian politics.

4. For further detail on al-Bishri's background and views, see Ghanim 1999.

information in the early 1970s before moving to Kuwait to serve as legal advisor for the crown prince. He returned to Egypt in the late 1980s and entered private practice. He has been appointed to several prestigious public bodies, including the Institute of Islamic Research at al-Azhar University and the government-sponsored Egyptian Society for Human Rights.[5] Al-Awwa followed a similar path of advanced legal training in Egypt, supplemented by doctoral studies in comparative law at the University of London. He served as a law professor in Saudi Arabia from 1974 through 1985, then returned to Egypt and joined the law faculty at Zagazig University. He is well known for his lengthy book on Islamic criminal law (al-Awwa 1979), which established his reputation as one of the leading academic specialists on shariʿa. He has also been active in efforts to create a moderate Islamic political party in Egypt. Toward this end, he helped to build the al-Wasat party in the mid-1990s and remains one of its most important advocates.[6] After Hosni Mubarak's removal from power, he announced his candidacy for the presidency but lost badly in the first round of the presidential election in May 2012.

Each of these authors has written extensively on Islam and governance. Their works are widely read in Egypt and throughout the Islamic world. They are also influential among the leadership of the Muslim Brotherhood, particularly the "new guard" of younger leaders who have grown more powerful within the organization in recent years. Nathan Brown observes that these four thinkers are part of an "emerging consensus" regarding the application of Islamic law and tradition to contemporary governance (2002, 161–93). Raymond Baker argues that they constitute

5. For further information, see the brief biography of Abu al-Majd at http://www.un.org/Dialogue/Aboulmagd.html. Also see the biography of him posted on the website of the Egyptian state information service at http://www.sis.gov.eg/. Both sites accessed June 27, 2007.

6. For further details on al-Awwa's background, see his official website: http://www.el-awa.com/. Also see Baker 2003. In addition, al-Awwa was the driving force behind a new nongovernmental organization, the Egyptian Society for Culture and Dialogue. The group had close ties with al-Wasat and aimed to "support the culture of dialogue in a society in which violence prevails" (Rosefsky Wickham 2002, 220).

a distinctive school of Islamic reformist thought that he calls the "New Islamists" (2003, 1). As noted below, these thinkers do not march in lockstep. However, their works are sufficiently similar that they collectively define a coherent view of Islamic constitutionalism.

In order to understand this view, the following analysis will focus on these writers' treatment of four topics: the source and purpose of law; constraints on state power; public participation in politics; and protection of basic civil and political rights. This is certainly not an exhaustive list of issues relevant to a discussion of constitutionalism. However, these topics define the core features of a political order. They allow us to delineate the essential characteristics of Islamic constitutionalism and its philosophical foundations.

The Source and Purpose of Law

Islamic constitutionalist thinkers emphasize that the Islamic faith is based upon the revelation and enforcement of law. Muhammad's primary mission was to convey laws and norms through the Qur'an and the *sunna*. These legal principles became the shari'a. Obedience to shari'a is the key to a righteous life and admittance to paradise. Al-Awwa is particularly clear on this point, writing that "[r]eligion is law in practice" (1999, 2) and "[t]he government of Islam is the government of law" (1999, 6).

In this view, the state is created in order to implement shari'a. Its primary function is to enforce divine law and, by so doing, to create a community of believers under the governance of Islam *(hukm al-Islam)*. This social and legal community is essential to the full practice of the faith. Al-Qaradawi, for example, writes that a believer must live within a community governed by Islamic law in order to fully integrate the principles of the faith into his life. In his opinion, "Muslims are sinners until they live within *hukm al-Islam*" (al-Qaradawi 1997, 15).

From the perspective of the Islamic constitutionalists, the Islamic world is in decline because rulers have wavered from the shari'a and the community of believers has failed to set them back on the correct course. These problems began when non-Arabs (particularly Persians and Turks) assumed positions of leadership in the Islamic world, starting in the ninth century. These non-Arabs lacked sufficient knowledge of the Arabic language to fully understand the divine obligations embodied in the shari'a. In some cases, they also lacked a moral and spiritual commitment to Islam. Instead of implementing shari'a, they manipulated it to serve their personal ambitions for wealth and power. Their machinations led to the steady distortion and corruption of shari'a. This problem was aggravated by the influx of European culture in the nineteenth century. Reformist leaders in Egypt and elsewhere tried to modernize their societies by emulating European institutions in fields such as education, medicine, and government. This process included a widespread effort to transfer European laws to Islamic countries, which had profound repercussions for Islamic societies. As al-Bishri writes, emulation of European laws "drove a wedge between governments and their peoples" as citizens increasingly felt that the laws of the land failed to reflect their values and their sense of justice. This situation produced a demoralized and fragmented society that was unable to resist the continued onslaughts of Europe (al-Bishri 1987, 174–75; 2003, 32–35).

Islamic constitutionalists argue that the renewal of shari'a is essential for reviving the dignity and strength of the Islamic world. The starting point for this effort is the realization that Islam contains two types of laws: those that are clearly stated in the Qur'an and the sunna (the shari'a); and those that apply the principles of shari'a to specific problems and contexts. There is no room for man-made law in those areas where the Qur'an and sunna are clear, such as the performance of prayers five times a day, fasting, and the payment of the zakat (poor tax). But on all other issues, the theorists under discussion favor the creation of man-made laws that are compatible with shari'a.

The Qur'an and sunna are silent on many specifics of running a state, and thus man-made law is needed to manage the details of day-to-day governance. The skillful practice of *ijtihad* is the key to this lawmaking process. Those who exercise ijtihad and draft laws should aim to serve the best interests of the community *(al-maslahah)* while not directly contradicting the shari'a. New laws should respond to the needs of the community *(darurah)* and the distinctive circumstances *(zuruf)* of a particular moment in time (Abu al-Majd 1962, 4). The primary tools for generating law are the same tools used for exercising ijtihad, including consensus *(ijma')* among believers, analogy *(qiyas)* to legal principles clearly presented in the shari'a, and the synthesis *(talfiq)* of ideas from multiple schools of law. The persons drafting law should draw on whatever sources serve the best interests of the community. These include any of the four schools of Sunni law, as well as Shi'a thought (al-Bishri 2003, 48). In addition, Abu al-Majd (1962, 2, 4) and al-Awwa (1989, 141) call for utilizing those elements of non-Muslim law that do not contradict shari'a.

The theorists also discuss the question of who should be empowered to draft man-made laws. There is agreement that it should not be the ruler alone. Abu al-Majd (1962, 7) particularly stresses that the leader of the Islamic community has no special relationship with God and, thus, no special capacity to interpret the shari'a and create law. Religious scholars *(ulama)* should play a role, but they should not be the primary drafters of law. Indeed, several of the theorists have serious reservations about the ulama, owing to their closeness to political power and their willingness to legitimate autocratic rulers. Furthermore, the ulama have failed to educate the people fully in Islam and, as a consequence, bear some responsibility for the weakness of the Islamic world (al-Qaradawi 1997, 98).

As a result of these concerns, each of the theorists calls for including persons other than the ulama in the drafting of laws. There is agreement that the drafting process should involve those with the most relevant knowledge. This may be a person with formal religious training. Or depending on the topic, it may be a person with secular technical training who has the most appropriate expertise regarding the issue at hand. If the law in question deals with the well-being of the entire community, the public as a whole should be involved (Abu al-Majd 1962, 20–21; al-Bishri 1991, 154; al-Qaradawi 1997, 38–39). The specific institutions for drafting laws will vary depending upon the distinctive characteristics and needs of each community.

This approach to law and its role in society essentially restates the views of earlier Islamic reformist thinkers, particularly Muhammad Abduh and Rashid Rida. As Malcolm Kerr notes, it is not a fully developed theory of law (1966, 209–23). However, it delineates several fundamental premises: the state is defined and constrained by law; citizens participate in producing at least some of this law; and law applies equally to ruler and ruled. These principles provide a conceptual foundation for Islamic constitutionalist thinkers, which they build upon in their analysis of the three other dimensions of constitutionalism.

Constraints on State Power

As the preceding discussion indicates, Islamic constitutionalists emphasize a fundamental constraint on state power: the shari'a. If the ruler violates shari'a, citizens are free to disregard the ruler's edicts and, under certain conditions, remove him from office. Abu al-Majd argues that shari'a plays the same role in Islamic legal thought that natural law plays in the Western constitutional tradition. It defines the purposes of state power and delineates its boundaries (Abu al-Majd 1962, 13–14; al-Qaradawi 1997, 38). Within these boundaries, rulers and citizens are free to develop specific laws that respond to the needs of their community.

The Islamic constitutionalists point to several other features of classical Islamic thought that constrain the power of the ruler. They make frequent reference to the concept of *aqd* (contract), which dates to the earliest days of Islamic government in the seventh century. This concept held that an individual could assume power only after reaching a firm understanding with the senior members of the community *(umma)* regarding the style and goals of his leadership. Once this agreement was reached, the senior members of the umma swore an oath of allegiance *(baya'ah)* to the leader that was conditioned on the leader's fulfilling the terms of the Aqd. Abu al-Majd observes that these principles were used in the formation of the first Islamic state by Muhammad in Medina. The Prophet negotiated a "Constitution of Medina" that defined the relationship among the Muslims, the residents of Medina, and the other communities in the area. The document also specified the procedure for reconciling disputes among these groups. Abu al-Majd argues that this document constitutes "the first example in human history" of a political community's being created through a contract (Abu al-Majd 1962, 14; al-Awwa 1989, 61). Similarly, al-Qaradawi writes that the concept of baya'ah embodies the principle that believers join an Islamic state through a voluntary expression of allegiance. Their obedience to the state is conditioned on the ruler's acting in accordance with the law and the community's will (al-Qaradawi 1997, 30–32). The institutional details of how these constraints on state power actually operate are left undefined in classical Islamic thought. However, the theorists argue that these ideas provide doctrinal support for the principle that the leader is chosen through the consent of the people and that he is accountable to them.

Several of the theorists also discuss the Islamic foundations for governmental accountability. They stress that *shura* (consultation) is the guiding precept of Islamic governance. Shura is mentioned in the Qur'an and stipulates that the leader consult with senior members of the umma on issues of importance. The theorists argue that, unlike in the classical period, shura is an obligation *(fard)* of both the ruler and the ruled. They often quote the Qur'anic passages that call on Muhammad to consult with the community. They note that if a leader with the stature of the Prophet was required to consult with his followers, then the average Muslim ruler bears an even stronger obligation to do so. They also cite statements by the first four rightly guided caliphs that demonstrate the importance of consultation in Islamic governance. A quote from Abu Bakr is particularly common, to the effect that he would "gather the people together and consult them" (Abu al-Majd 1962, 19; al-Qaradawi 1997, 34) on any issue where the Qur'an and sunna are unclear. He further stated that "I have been given authority over you, but I am not the best of you. If I do well, help me. If I do ill, put me right" (al-Awwa 1989, 233; al-Qaradawi 1997, 34, 59). A quote from the caliph Umar is also mentioned, which states that "all Muslims have the right to be consulted on matters that affect them" (Abu al-Majd 1962, 19).

The concept of governmental accountability is also derived from the principle that "political authority *(sulta)* lies with the community (umma)" (al-Qaradawi 1997, 62). The people create the state in order to more fully implement the law, both divine and man-made. This state is accountable to them and serves them. Al-Qaradawi, for example, writes that the ruler is the "agent" *(wakil)* of the umma. The people hire him, and he has the same obligations toward the people as an employee toward his employer (1997, 35). If a ruler becomes corrupt, the community may remove him through legislative action, the use of armed force, or the mobilization of the masses (1997, 117).[7] In order to give this principle greater practical force, the theorists argue that each Muslim has an obligation to monitor the behavior and policies of the ruler. This obligation is derived from each Muslim's duty to "enjoin good and forbid evil" among all members of the community, including the ruler. As al-Awwa puts it, "The right of shura . . . and the obligation of each believer to enjoin good and forbid evil constitute a duty by every member of the umma to question the ruler" (1989, 232).[8]

The Islamic constitutionalists also support the creation of an independent judiciary that can constrain state power. Al-Bishri argues that judicial independence is a fundamental and immutable feature of an Islamic political order. Although judges may be appointed by the executive, they are obligated to interpret the law in accordance with shari'a. The shari'a, in turn, is separate from the executive and cannot be altered by any human ruler. As a consequence, judges enjoy a structural separation from executive power that is divinely sanctioned and unchangeable (al-Bishri 1987, 166, 170, 184–90; al-Bishri 2005, 63–64). Abu al-Majd makes a similar argument and adds that independent judicial institutions should be created to constrain the power of the legislative branch and ensure that the laws adopted by the majority still conform with the principles of shari'a (1962, 26–27; al-Qaradawi 1997, 31). Al-Awwa agrees, concluding that the judiciary has an obligation independent of the executive to enjoin good

7. If these options are not available, the believers should wait, resist the leader by whatever means are available, and gradually build the broad public support needed to change the regime. They should be careful not to overthrow the leader if this action is likely to lead to civil disorder *(fitnah)*.

8. Al-Qaradawi makes a similar point (1997, 36). Al-Awwa invokes additional evidence from the period of the Rashidun caliphs to support this position. He observes that the caliphs sought the opinion of the people regarding the appointment and performance of provincial governors. If the people of a region were dissatisfied with their governor, the caliphs replaced him. Al-Awwa argues that this principle was soon extended to the caliphate and constituted the basis for some Muslims to demand the dismissal of the caliph Uthman for alleged corruption (al-Awwa 1989, 87–88).

and forbid evil through its interpretation and application of law (1999, 7; 1998, 10, 35).

In addition, several of the theorists endorse the creation of civil society organizations that constrain the state. Al-Qaradawi advocates a multiparty political system in which each party offers a different view regarding the best strategy for serving the interests of the umma and implementing shari'a (1997, 151, 153).[9] Al-Bishri (1987, 229–31; 2005, 51–54) calls for a rich network of syndicates and other associations that coordinate the actions of individual citizens and enable them to challenge executive power more effectively.

Public Participation in Politics

The theorists of Islamic constitutionalism emphasize that political authority lies with the people. In their view, the Qur'an, the sunna, and the historical experiences of the Rashidun caliphs all confirm that the people are entitled to select their ruler. Al-Qaradawi argues that this idea lies at the foundation of the faith. It is most clearly captured in the Prophet's statement that Muslims are empowered to choose who will lead them in prayer (al-Qaradawi 1997, 132). Al-Awwa writes that the public's right to choose the ruler can be traced back to the selection of Abu Bakr as the first successor to Muhammad. The history of this event states that Abu Bakr ascended to power through the following process: two prominent members of the community (Umar and Abu Ubaidah) showed their support for him by expressing an oath of loyalty (baya'ah); then, the community showed its support through its expression of baya'ah. Al-Awwa argues that the first baya'ah constituted a nomination, while the second was a referendum (1989, 71). He concludes that "one of the most significant results of this event was the decision that a ruler can be chosen only by consulting Muslims" (al-Awwa 1989, 79).

9. He stresses that these parties should not represent competing interests of individuals. Al-Awwa holds a similar view (1999, 13–14).

The theorists further propose that the public should participate in day-to-day governance. They develop this argument by returning to the concept of shura (consultation). They also invoke ijma', or the building of consensus among believers on those matters where the shari'a is unclear. In the view of the theorists, these ideas are best realized in contemporary political life through democratic institutions. These institutions include:

Elections. Each of the thinkers expresses support for selecting public officials through free elections. Al-Qaradawi develops this point in the greatest depth. He writes that voting is analogous to testifying in a court of law, since it entails expressing one's personal witness to the moral and professional suitability of a candidate. He then cites a Qur'anic passage to the effect that each believer is obligated to testify in court if he has information relevant to a case. Thus, by analogy, each citizen has a religious obligation to vote, since he has a religious duty to convey his knowledge of the candidate for office (al-Qaradawi 1997, 138). Al-Awwa holds a similar view, invoking the Qur'anic proclamation "Do not conceal testimony, for he who conceals it has a sinful heart" (1999, 209).[10]

Political Parties. As noted earlier, the theorists also endorse the creation of multiple political parties. For al-Qaradawi, they resemble the multiple schools of law within Islam that reflect different perspectives on understanding and implementing the Qur'an and the sunna. He assumes that all political parties share the goal of deepening the religiosity of the community. Their different perspectives ensure that the community achieves this goal, while also preventing the emergence of tyranny (al-Qaradawi 1997, 142–43, 151).[11] For al-Bishri, multiple parties reflect the varied interests that naturally emerge in society. Social order and harmony require that these interests be given expression through parties as well as through other civil society institutions (al-Bishri 1987, 225–26). Al-Awwa adds that the

10. See also Abu al-Majd 1962, 20–21.

11. Al-Qaradawi adds that all parties must acknowledge Islam and work to strengthen it. He would not allow areligious or atheistic parties or parties that "contradict Islam" (1997, 154).

presence of multiple parties reflects the principle of tolerance of dissent, which he considers fundamental to the faith. He notes that the caliph Ali tolerated the Kharijites, despite their sharp differences with him (al-Awwa 1989, 105–6). He proposes that God intentionally created differing groups and views in order to better serve his will (al-Awwa 1999, 9, 13–14). He concludes that "the existence of political parties . . . is necessary for the advancement [of Islamic societies] and for freedom of opinion within [them], and to ensure the absence of oppression" (al-Awwa 1999, 14).

Parliament. The Islamic constitutionalists argue that a parliament is the most effective institution for enabling the public to participate in the drafting of laws in those areas where the shariʿa is silent. Al-Qaradawi observes that Parliament may legislate in any area where multiple opinions are possible (1997, 142). The range of topics is vast, from traffic laws to taxation to the decision to wage war.

These institutions are clearly borrowed from Western democracies. However, this borrowing is carried out in a highly selective manner. Al-Qaradawi's view is typical when he writes that the Islamic world must "take the best elements of democracy without seeking to duplicate it" (1997, 36). The central goals of an Islamic state are to enhance justice and oppose tyranny. At this moment in history, democratic institutions are the best means for achieving these goals and, thus, democracy "is the form of government that is closest to Islam" (1997, 9). However, democracy in an Islamic context must operate within the ethical framework defined by shariʿa. It must not lead to laws that allow what is forbidden in Islam (such as adultery or alcohol consumption) or prohibit what is required (such as prayer, zakat, or pilgrimage) (1997, 138).

Protection of Civil and Political Rights

When discussing the issue of individual rights, the theorists begin by stressing the importance of justice in Islam. According to al-Qaradawi, the Qur'an's emphasis on justice enabled Islam to assert the basic rights of individuals "1000 years before [these rights] appeared in the West" (al-Qaradawi 1997, 37, 49). A wide range of rights are derived from this principle, including the right to "life, dignity, and property" (Abu al-Majd 1962, 23); "security and sufficiency" (al-Qaradawi 1997, 49); and "consultation, justice, freedom, equality, and the accountability of the ruler" (al-Awwa 1989, 179).

Beyond these general rights, the Islamic constitutionalists elaborate several specific liberties that are protected by Islam. Freedom of choice is considered particularly important. Al-Awwa notes that the very first human being whom God created, Adam, was given the power to choose between obeying God and not obeying. In his view, this fact shows that freedom of choice is a fundamental feature of humanity that has been part of each human being's character since the dawn of creation. Furthermore, the Qur'an stresses that each believer must voluntarily choose to submit to the will of God. In order for this choice to have meaning, believers must also be free to choose not to submit. Thus, choice is at the core of what defines an Islamic community (1989, 211–12). However, al-Awwa adds an important caveat: the freedom to leave the Islamic faith is restricted. The Qur'an clearly declares that apostasy is a sin, although it does not specify a penalty (1998, 65–72).[12]

Al-Awwa further argues that each Muslim is obligated to exercise ijtihad, which he defines as a personal struggle to understand Islam. This struggle requires reason, reflection, and dialogue with fellow believers. As a consequence, freedom of thought, inquiry, and speech are essential to the full expression of each Muslim's faith (1989, 210–25). In addition, Al-Awwa proposes that each Muslim bears an obligation to "enjoin good and forbid evil" within the community. In order to fulfill this obligation, each Muslim must be free to speak out against evil and corruption. Speaking out against these transgressions is a religious duty, and thus freedom of speech is divinely sanctioned and mandated.[13] Al-Awwa concludes that freedom of speech and thought are "commandments in Islam . . . [they are] inviolable basic rights of man (1989, 211, 213)." Al-Qaradawi holds a similar view. He observes that Islam has a long history of multiple schools

12. This book consists primarily of al-Awwa's views on the case of Nasr Hamid Abu Zayd, a controversial scholar of the Qur'an who was accused of apostasy by some Islamic thinkers.

13. In al-Awwa's view, "public declaration of opinion is obligatory and not simply permitted" (al-Awwa 1999, 11).

of law, jurisprudence, and interpretation. Dialog and debate among them are essential to the functioning of a devout community (al-Qaradawi 1997, 49–50, 151–54).

Each of the theorists also addresses women's rights. Al-Qaradawi offers the most detailed discussion of this topic. He stresses that women have the same duties as men and that they play an important role in the life of the community. Trying to exclude them from public life "is like trying to breathe with one lung or fly with one wing" (1997, 82). In his view, women should be allowed to vote and to hold public office. They should also be permitted to hold positions of authority, including the posts of judge and head of state (al-Qaradawi 1997, 165–66, 175–76; al-Awwa 1999, 7). However, these rights are bounded by a traditional view of a woman's role in society. A woman's first duty is child rearing. She should embark on public life only if she has no children or if her children are grown (al-Qaradawi 1997, 173). Also, al-Qaradawi makes no effort to challenge the discrimination against women found in the Qur'an and the sunna. This discrimination includes assigning less weight to a woman's testimony in court, granting women less right to inherit than men, and prohibiting women from leading prayer or leading the umma (1997, 161–63).[14]

The theorists also advocate protecting the rights of non-Muslims. They argue that differences in religion were created by God and, as such, should be respected and protected. Al-Bishri (2004) pays particular attention to this topic in a lengthy book on the relationship between Muslims and Copts in Egypt. He argues that Egypt's unique historical experience has produced a national identity that embraces both Muslims and Copts. Islam is part of this Egyptian identity, but it does not dominate it and does not define Copts as second-class citizens.[15] A strengthening of Islam's role

14. However, in al-Qaradawi's view, a woman's testimony on matters related to child rearing should carry the same weight as a man's. And, a woman is permitted to serve as head of state of a country. Women are only prohibited from leading the entire religious community of Muslims (umma).

15. Al-Bishri writes that many Copts in the past have embraced the Islamic tradition as part of their Egyptian identity. He notes with particular approval a prominent scholar of shari'a, Shafiq Shehata, who was a Copt (2003, 47).

in society need not threaten Copts, so long as the country's shared Egyptian identity is preserved. Copts are further protected by the Qur'an's respect for religious difference and its commandment that there is "no compulsion in religion" (2:256) (al-Bishri 2004, 161–92, 803–86). Al-Awwa makes essentially the same argument, and proposes that sectarian strife has risen in recent years because of political opportunism by troublemakers on both sides. These tensions do not reflect any fundamental incompatibility between Muslims and Copts and can be resolved through "dialog and popular action" (al-Awwa 1987, 62). Al-Qaradawi holds a similar view. He writes that Muslims and Copts constitute a shared "national brotherhood" that is grounded in respect and tolerance. He argues that Copts are equal to Muslims before the law on civil and criminal matters and that they are entitled to practice their own laws on matters of creed, worship, and personal status. Copts may also hold senior positions in government, serve in the bureaucracy, and participate in Parliament. However, the post of president must always be held by a Muslim in order to ensure that the polity remains an Islamic state. For the same reason, Muslims must also hold a majority in Parliament (al-Qaradawi 1997, 32, 195).[16]

The works of these theorists define a conception of Islamic constitutionalism that shares many characteristics with classical liberalism.[17] They support the rule of law, constraints on state power, and the protection of

16. Al-Awwa agrees that non-Muslim judges may preside over cases involving Muslims in all areas of law except personal status (1999, 8).

17. It should be noted that these thinkers do not describe their ideas as "liberal." In contemporary Egyptian discourse, this term is often associated with Western political thought and, particularly, with the British colonial presence in the interwar period. It is also associated with the relatively lax moral standards of the West. The Islamic constitutionalists emphasize that their ideas are derived entirely from Islamic sources and are not drawn from any Western inspiration. Nonetheless, the specific institutional reforms that they advocate can be usefully described as "liberal" in the sense that they incorporate the key features of classical liberalism. These key features include a clear and unbiased legal code, the separation of powers, checks and balances among these powers, an independent judiciary, and the protection of many civil and political rights.

many civil and political rights. They also advocate broad public participation in politics. However, the theorists are vague on many of the details of how Islamic government should function. For example, they answer the question "who is sovereign in an Islamic state" by proposing that God is sovereign but that authority (and thus some law-making power) resides with the umma and its representatives. This view provides a clear doctrinal foundation for man-made law. However, it does not specify who holds the power to determine which topics are subject to man-made legislation. Similarly, they accept that laws should be written by an elected Parliament. But, they are unclear on the specific procedures for electing members of Parliament (MPs), how long these MPs should serve, and the extent of their power. The theorists also do not spell out the institutional relationships that create an effective balance of power among the branches of government and constrain the executive. In addition, they frequently write that laws should serve "the best interests of the community." However, they provide no criteria or procedures for determining the community's interests at a given point in time. Furthermore, they write that the ruler is accountable to the people and that an unjust ruler should be dismissed. But, they fail to specify how this accountability occurs or the procedures for removing a ruler.[18]

Several of the theorists acknowledge that their work is unclear regarding these details of governance. They consider this vagueness unavoidable and argue that the institutional characteristics of Islamic governance will vary depending on the specific features of each Islamic polity. Al-Qaradawi's view is typical. He writes that Islam offers the essential principles of democratic governance, but it leaves the details of how it will work "to the ijtihad of Muslims . . . to be worked out according to time and place and determined by the conditions of mankind at that moment" (al-Qaradawi 1997, 137). Al-Awwa agrees: "The Prophet left the matter of

18. Al-Qaradawi writes that if a ruler acts improperly, the "people who loose and bind" should meet, discuss the matter, and issue their opinion. The ruler should then heed their opinion. He provides no further detail on who convenes the "people who loose and bind," how their deliberations unfold, or how their opinion is enforced if the ruler refuses to comply (al-Qaradawi 1997, 66).

choosing the ruler and determining the system of government to Muslims to decide according to their interests and the requirements of time, place, and circumstance . . . nothing decreed is binding on them, except the general rules of Islamic law and the high moral values that the Prophet exhibited . . . during the Medinan period" (al-Awwa 1989, 67).

In essence, one cannot gain a clear understanding of contemporary Islamic constitutionalism by simply reading the works of theorists. One must examine how these ideas are given substance by Islamic political actors in a specific context. With this goal in mind, we turn to the political agenda of the movement in Egypt that tries to give practical meaning to the abstract ideas articulated by these theorists: the Muslim Brotherhood.

Adapting Islamic Constitutionalism to Contemporary Egypt: The Muslim Brotherhood's 2005 Electoral Campaign

After suffering fierce repression during the Nasser era, the Muslim Brotherhood began to reorganize in the 1970s. Its members won seats in Parliament through alliances with the Wafd, Liberal, and Labor parties in the 1980s. It dominated elections for university student unions throughout the 1980s and 1990s. Its activists also won control of the governing boards of most of the major professional syndicates in the 1980s and 1990s.[19]

As its power grew, the Brotherhood remained reluctant to state its political objectives. Leaders of the organization claimed that this vagueness was a logical response to the country's harsh political climate. In their view, a clear Brotherhood political agenda would be interpreted by the regime as an immediate threat to its power and would lead to a vigorous crackdown. Others argued that the MB's ideological haziness was a product of internal divisions along philosophical, generational, and family lines. According to this perspective, the Brotherhood refrained from developing detailed plans for political reform in order to avoid the divisive internal debates that would undoubtedly ensue (Baker 1990, 243–70; al-Awadi 2004).

19. For more detailed discussion of these developments, see Rosefsky Wickham 2002.

The Brotherhood began to articulate its political goals more clearly in the mid-1990s. This shift partly reflected the rise of a younger generation of activists who were better educated and more pragmatic than their elders (el-Ghobashy 2005, 381–85). They authored pamphlets on several controversial topics, such as the rights of women, the role of Copts in Egyptian society, and the importance of political competition. These documents presented a moderate and conciliatory political agenda. However, the regime was not in the mood to listen. The distribution of these pamphlets was tightly restricted. Many of the leaders who wrote them were imprisoned. The student unions and professional syndicates where the Brotherhood enjoyed such success were either closed or crippled through legal and extralegal measures. As the repression intensified, the internal tensions within the Brotherhood sharpened, and the efforts to define a clear political agenda came to a halt.[20]

This situation began to change slowly in 2001 and 2002, when several younger MB leaders imprisoned in 1995 were released and resumed their positions in the organization. Another turning point occurred in 2004, when the eighty-four-year-old General Guide (Ma'mun al-Hudaybi) passed away. The General Guide holds considerable power. He is the senior leader of the MB and its most prominent spokesman. He also plays a critical role in the appointment of leaders at all levels of the organization. Al-Hudaybi used this power to ensure that the old guard controlled the MB. His death marked the beginning of a transition toward a new generation of leadership. While the younger generation was not permitted to take the top spot, two of its most respected leaders, Muhammad Habib and Khayrat al-Shatir, were promoted to the position of Deputy General Guide. The new General Guide, Muhammad Akif, publicly endorsed the moderate political views articulated by the younger generation (el-Ghobashy 2005, 389).

These internal changes in the Brotherhood coincided with the regime's decision to allow a relatively free parliamentary election in 2005. The

20. El-Ghobashy provides a thoughtful overview of this period (2005, 385–87). Also see Rutherford 2008, 91-99.

campaigning phase of the election unfolded with far less repression than in previous contests.[21] The Brotherhood was allowed to compete openly using its own name and to support a group of independent candidates. It was able to publish a "Reform Initiative" (in March 2004), issue a campaign platform (in October 2005), publicize its agenda through pamphlets and newspaper articles (particularly in its de facto newspaper, *Afaq Arabiyah*), and explain its views in numerous interviews to the media. These documents provided an unprecedented opportunity to examine how the Brotherhood adapts the general principles of Islamic constitutionalism to the specific conditions of contemporary Egypt.

According to the MB's reform initiative, the organization sought to create a "republican system of government that is democratic, constitutional, and parliamentary and that conforms with Islamic principles" (*Mubadirat al-Ikhwan al-Muslimin hawwal Mabad' al-Islah fi Misr* 2004, 12–13). The MB's campaign documents elaborated on the details of this regime by addressing each of the four aspects of constitutionalism discussed above:

Law. Like the theorists discussed earlier, the Brotherhood's 2005 campaign documents stressed the centrality of law to the political order that they hoped to create. Law applies equally to ruler and ruled and is the primary means for achieving a more just society. Mahmoud Ghazlan, a senior leader of the MB, wrote that Parliament should draft laws that are "within the framework *[itaar]* of Islamic shari'a" (Ghazlan 2005, 5).[22] This framework was to be delineated by elected representatives of the people. These representatives may consult with religious scholars (ulama), but the ulama had no authority to issue legislation or to declare laws invalid. The only body with the authority to oversee legislation was the Supreme

21. The 2005 parliamentary election consisted of three rounds. The first round was relatively clean. The subsequent rounds suffered from substantial violence and vote rigging. When the dust settled, the Brotherhood had won eighty-eight seats, roughly 20 percent of the total. See Independent Committee for Elections Monitoring, "A Testimony for History: Monitoring the Egyptian 2005 Parliamentary Elections" (Cairo: ICEM, Dec. 2005).

22. Mahmoud Ghazlan was a prominent member of the Brotherhood's governing body, the Guidance Office (Maktab al-Irshad).

Constitutional Court, which evaluated laws based upon their conformity with the Constitution (2005, 5). Parliament may not adopt legislation that "sanctions what is prohibited *[haram]* or prohibits what is permissible *[halal]*" (Akif 2005). As examples, the MB specified that the Parliament may not issue laws that allow adultery or that interfere with prayer or with the performance of the Haj.[23] The elected representatives of the people were free to legislate in all other areas. The MB's campaign literature placed particular emphasis on adopting laws that strengthened the protection of civil and political rights because, in the words of the General Guide, respect for these rights "is shari'a . . . which considers freedom a religious obligation" (el-Hennawy 2006, 32).

Constraints on State Power. The Brotherhood's 2005 campaign documents asserted that governments are formed through a contract between ruler and ruled that is "established by the umma and carried out by the civil institutions of the state" (*Al-Barnamaj al-Intikhabi lil-Ikhwan al-Muslimin* 2005). Within this arrangement, the ruler functions as an agent (wakil) of the people (*Al-Barnamaj al-Intikhabi* . . . 2005; Ghazlan 2005, 5). The MB provided no further details on how this contract would be drafted under current conditions or whether the existing constitution was considered a contract. However, there was extensive discussion of the need to constrain and regulate state power. The Brotherhood placed particular emphasis on limiting the power of the president. It called for converting the presidency into a largely ceremonial post with no executive power in order to ensure that the president was "a symbol for all Egyptians and not the head of any political party" (*Mubadirat al-Ikhwan al-Muslimin* . . . 2004, 16). It proposed that the president be chosen through multicandidate elections and that he be prohibited from serving consecutive terms (2004, 16).[24] The MB also called for replacing the emergency law with a new law that placed sharp restrictions on the executive. In the MB's view,

23. The Brotherhood's General Guide stated that the organization would not seek the adoption of strict Islamic criminal punishments *(hudud)* (Akif 2005).

24. The Brotherhood's stand regarding restrictions on the president's term in office varied. Akif (2005) and Ghazlan (2005, 5) said that he should be limited to two four-year terms.

a state of emergency should be declared only in response to an active war or a natural disaster. The period of emergency should be limited and its renewal should be subject to clearly specified and stringent conditions. The law should prohibit the president from suspending the constitution during an emergency and from compromising the basic rights of citizens (Ghazlan 2005, 5).

The MB also sought to restructure the executive branch in order to limit its power. For example, the MB advocated an end to state involvement in the operations of al-Azhar University. In its view, the president should no longer have the authority to appoint the shaikh of al-Azhar. Rather, the shaikh should be elected by senior clerics. Revenue from religious endowments *(awqaf)* should no longer be channeled through the state budget but should pass directly to al-Azhar. And, the executive should cease its practice of telling imams and preachers what they should say to their followers (*Mubadirat al-Ikhwan al-Muslimin* . . . 2004, 31–32). The MB also insisted that the military remain uninvolved in politics and that all ministers be civilians. Similarly, it stressed that the police and the internal security forces should be civilian and that they "not be used by the government to secure its stay in power or suppress the opposition" (2004, 16). These agencies should be "barred from intervening in public activities and elections" (2004, 16). In addition, the MB wanted to decentralize power by granting provincial governments the authority to impose taxes and to make local policy decisions (*Al-Barnamaj al-Intikhabi* . . . 2005).

The MB placed considerable emphasis on strengthening the autonomy of the judiciary. In its view, the judiciary was the "safety valve" that allowed for the resolution of disputes before they led to violence or social disorder. The judiciary must be independent in order to play this role effectively. The MB supported the revised judicial law proposed by the Judges Club in 1991 and reissued in 2004, which aimed to strengthen the judiciary's budgetary independence and give it complete control over the hiring and promotion of judges. In the words of the General Guide, this proposed law would "give these noble men their independence so they can perform their duty to defend justice, truth, and honor" (Akif 2005). In addition, the Brotherhood supported two reforms long advocated by the Judges Club: a firm guarantee that citizens will be tried before their "natural judge," which effectively means an end to the use of exceptional courts and military courts to try civilians, and a clear separation between the office of the prosecutor *(niyabah)* and the Ministry of Justice to ensure that the prosecutorial process is not tainted by political considerations (*Mubadirat al-Ikhwan al-Muslimin* . . . 2004, 18).

In addition to these measures, the Brotherhood sought to strengthen the Parliament and make it a more effective check on executive power. The MB supported increasing the Parliament's budget and staffing, as well as expanding its power to initiate laws, review the state's budget, and investigate the decisions and conduct of ministers (Akif 2005). The Brotherhood also called for dramatic expansion of civil society, which it considered a "strategic partner" in its efforts to achieve reform and development (*Al-Barnamaj al-Intikhabi* . . . 2005). In pursuit of this goal, it advocated repealing laws that interfere with the formation, funding, and operation of civil society groups.

Public Participation in Politics. In this arena, the MB reiterated the broad themes mentioned by the theorists above: the people are the source of political authority; free elections are the only legitimate method for selecting a leader; leaders are required to consult with the people or their representatives; and citizens can dismiss a ruler who fails to heed their wishes (*Mubadirat al-Ikhwan al-Muslimin* . . . 2004, 12–17; Ghazlan 2005, 5). The MB's 2005 electoral program stated that "Shura is a fundamental concept in Islam, and democracy is its most appropriate mechanism within the modern state" (*Al-Barnamaj al-Intikhabi* . . . 2005). The representatives of the people should be chosen through free elections that are organized by a neutral agency (*Mubadirat al-Ikhwan al-Muslimin* . . . 2004, 15). Each citizen has a right to vote and to run for office (2004, 15). Beyond these broad principles, the Brotherhood called for specific reforms that would render elections freer and fairer. Security agencies and the Ministry of Justice should be barred from any involvement in elections. The judiciary should supervise the entire electoral process, from the drawing up of voter lists through balloting, counting the ballots, and declaring the results. And there should be no restrictions on campaigning. Candidates should be free to hold rallies, distribute leaflets, and hang posters without interference (*Mubadirat al-Ikhwan al-Muslimin* . . . 2004, 19–20).

The MB also advocated greater use of elections within al-Azhar, including the creation of a "senior clerics council" whose members would be elected by all clerics. This council would, in turn, elect the shaikh of al-Azhar from among its members. The Brotherhood further called for reducing the power of senior clerics at al-Azhar and granting greater freedom to imams and preachers to explain the principles and values of Islam (*Mubadirat al-Ikhwan al-Muslimin* . . . 2004, 30–32).

Finally, the MB sought to strengthen political parties by removing impediments to the formation of parties and ending government interference in their operation. Toward this end, it supported the creation of a Coptic political party.[25] However, the Brotherhood's leadership was divided over whether to create their own political party. The General Guide stated during the parliamentary campaign that the organization should wait until all the existing laws that interfere with the operation of parties were repealed (el-Hennawy 2006, 32). The Brotherhood's spokesman, Isam al-Iryan, wanted the MB to move more quickly to establish a political party with a "civil character" that would be open to membership by all citizens (including Copts). This type of party would mobilize more citizens into the political process, build trust between Muslims and Copts, and strengthen national unity.[26]

Civil and Political Rights. The Brotherhood's 2005 campaign documents addressed a wide range of individual rights. They supported freedom of speech "within the limits of public order, social decorum, and society's constants" (*Mubadirat al-Ikhwan al-Muslimin* . . . 2004, 14). The freedom to own and use different forms of media was also advocated. Freedom of assembly was supported "within the limits of the safety of society and public security" (*Mubadirat al-Ikhwan al-Muslimin* . . . 2004,

25. Personal interview with Isam al-Iryan, Cairo, Dec. 21, 2005.

26. Al-Iryan wanted the Brotherhood to separate its religious and political activities. Its religious *(da'wah)* activity would focus on education and seek to spread the faith, in cooperation with al-Azhar University's da'wah programs. The political party would pursue a conservative social agenda that would appeal to both Muslims and Copts. Al-Iryan argued that the party should be modeled on similar Islamic parties that have emerged in Jordan, Morocco, Pakistan, Malaysia, and Indonesia (personal interview, Dec. 21, 2005).

14). The MB further advocated "canceling all laws that restrict freedom," including the emergency law and the laws dealing with political parties, the socialist public prosecutor, political rights, the press, and professional syndicates (*Mubadirat al-Ikhwan al-Muslimin* . . . 2004, 16–17; *Al-Barnamaj al-Intikhabi* . . . 2005). It called for reviewing all the past verdicts issued by military courts and exceptional courts and, where necessary, ordering new trials before ordinary tribunals. It also supported the release of all political prisoners and a firm ban on torture.[27]

The Brotherhood's 2005 campaign literature discussed the rights of women and Copts in considerable depth. It stressed that men and women hold the same spiritual and moral value in the eyes of God. Women should be treated equally in criminal, civil, and financial matters. They should also be allowed to participate fully in Parliament and other elected institutions (*Mubadirat al-Ikhwan al-Muslimin* . . . 2004, 35–37; *Al-Barnamaj al-Intikhabi* . . . 2005). They can be appointed to all public posts except the presidency, so long as the post does not compromise a woman's "chastity, morality, or honor" (*Mubadirat al-Ikhwan al-Muslimin* . . . 2004, 36). In an interview, the General Guide claimed that the Brotherhood wanted to run twenty-five female candidates in the 2005 parliamentary elections. However, the husbands of most of these women would not allow their wives to enter the elections for fear they might be injured or otherwise mistreated by the security forces (Akif 2005).[28]

The MB's 2005 campaign literature showed a similar degree of attention to the rights of Copts. The Reform Initiative stated that Copts are an integral part of the social fabric and "partners in the nation *[al-watan]*"

27. The General Guide also stated that the furtherance of basic rights should be the primary focus of the MB's parliamentary delegation. More specifically, the MB should concentrate on "freedom . . . abolition of the emergency law, military courts, limiting the president's power, and amending articles 76 and 77 of the Constitution (which dealt with the election and term of the president)." Muhammad Mahdi Akif, "Interview: We Take Nobody's Permission," *al-Ahram Weekly,* Dec. 15–21, 2005.

28. This fear of violence had a solid factual basis, as the security forces had used violence against MB candidates and their supporters in the past. The Brotherhood ultimately ran only one female candidate in the election. She lost her race.

(*Mubadirat al-Ikhwan al-Muslimin* . . . 2004, 37). The electoral platform stated that the MB considers all Egyptians to be equal as citizens, regardless of religion (*Al-Barnamaj al-Intikhabi* . . . 2005).[29] As a consequence, Copts have the same rights and duties as Muslims. They have full freedom of belief and worship and may utilize their own religious law in matters related to personal status. They are also permitted to engage in conduct that is forbidden to Muslims, such as consuming alcohol and pork (Ghazlan 2005, 5). The Brotherhood's electoral platform also cited a passage from the Qur'an that reaffirms freedom of religious belief (*Al-Barnamaj al-Intikhabi* . . . 2005). During the campaign, MB candidates stressed that their organization sought to represent the entire nation and that the Brotherhood would provide services to all citizens, both Muslim and Coptic.[30] Brotherhood leaders also supported the formation of a Coptic political party that would defend and promote the interests of Copts.[31] Some Coptic leaders were skeptical of these promises.[32] However, the Brotherhood's campaign documents went to considerable lengths to reassure the Coptic community that it respects their rights.

As this discussion suggests, the Brotherhood's political agenda in 2005 incorporated many of the principles of Islamic constitutionalism. The organization articulated this moderate view with remarkable consistency throughout the 2005 campaign. It was stated clearly in the official

29. One of the members of the Brotherhood's Guidance Office, Abd al-Mun'im Abu al-Futuh, wrote after the election that "the citizen is considered the foundation of society, regardless of religion or color." He added that the *jizyah* (tax on non-Muslims) and the concept of *dhimmi* (separate legal status assigned to non-Muslims) were "historical terms only, which have been replaced by the concept of citizenship-based democracy in a nation of justice and law" (al-Futuh 2006).

30. This theme appeared repeatedly in the coverage of the MB's campaign by its de facto weekly newspaper, *Afaq Arabiyah.* See the issues from Nov. 10 through Dec. 29, 2005.

31. Personal interview with Isam al-Iryan, Dec. 21, 2005.

32. See, for example, Majdi Khalil, "Al-Ikhwan fi al-Barlaman al-Misri" (The Brotherhood in the Egyptian parliament), *al-Watani,* Dec. 4, 2005.

campaign documents that were approved by the MB's governing body (the Guidance Office [Maktab al-Irshad]). It was also presented in myriad interviews and editorials by the organization's leaders. The MB maintained a similarly united front during the May 2007 Shura Council elections. Although the regime worked vigorously to exclude the Brotherhood from these elections, the MB still issued a campaign platform that reiterated almost word-for-word the documents from the 2005 parliamentary campaign (*Al-Barnamaj al-Intikhabi lil-Ikhwan al-Muslimin fi Majlis al-Shura* 2007). Observers sometimes wondered whether this moderate posture reflected the views of the entire organization. However, if there was dissent, the Brotherhood's leadership concealed it from public view.

The first evidence of internal disagreements within the MB emerged in the summer and fall of 2007. The Guidance Office formed a committee to draft a preliminary party platform, in preparation for formally declaring an MB political party. The large majority of this 128-page document was a faithful restatement of the positions put forward in the 2005 campaign materials. It expressed the MB's support for the rule of law, constraints on state power, and protection of basic civil and political rights. In many areas, it used language identical to that employed in the 2005 documents.[33] However, it contained several passages that reflected the reservations of some Brotherhood leaders toward unrestricted democracy. For example, the Brotherhood's documents from 2005 spoke in general terms about MPs consulting with religious scholars in order to ensure that legislation did not violate the principles of shari'a. The 2007 draft party platform gave this concept greater specificity by proposing the establishment of a "council of senior religious scholars."[34] Members of this council would be selected by their fellow ulama in "free and direct elections" (*Bar-*

33. This is particularly the case for the portion of the document that discusses political institutions (*Barnamaj Hizb al-Ikhwan al-Muslimin: al-Isdar al-Awwal* 2007, 11–24).

34. The precise phrase is *hay'ah min kibar ulama*. As noted earlier, a council of religious scholars was mentioned in the 2004 Reform Initiative in the context of reforming al-Azhar. In this earlier document, the council was to be selected by a vote among all the ulama. It would then be responsible for choosing the shaikh of al-Azhar from among its members (*Mubadirat al-Ikhwan al-Muslimin . . .* 2004, 31).

namaj Hizb al-Ikhwan al-Muslimin: al-Isdar al-Awwal 2007, 10).[35] The council would study proposed legislation and offer opinions on whether it conformed to shari'a. However, the draft platform was vague regarding the degree of influence that these opinions would carry. It suggested that the council's views would be binding on legislators in those areas where the meaning of shari'a is "certain and unchanging" (*Barnamaj Hizb al-Ikhwan al Muslimin: al-Isdar al-Awwal* 2007, 10). These areas were not spelled out.[36] On all other topics (i.e., those where devout Muslims can disagree), the council's opinions would be nonbinding. The legislature would be required to consider the council's views, but it would be free to reach its own decision based on majority vote. The clause's imprecision regarding the scope of the council's powers provoked a sharp response within the Brotherhood and in Egyptian society as a whole. There was particular concern that the council would be empowered to veto legislation that it deemed incompatible with Islam. In subsequent interviews, the presumed author of the passage—Muhammad Habib, the Deputy General Guide of the MB[37]—emphasized that the council's powers would be only advisory.[38]

35. The Parliament would define the general qualifications for participation on the council. It would also determine the council's precise responsibilities (*Barnamaj Hizb al-Ikhwan al-Muslimin: al-Isdar al-Awwal* 2007, 10).

36. The idea that shari'a contains core principles whose meaning cannot be disputed by devout Muslims is mentioned in the 2004 Reform Initiative. In that document, the five pillars of Islam are identified as definitive components of shari'a (the statement of witness, prayer five times per day, alms-giving *[zakat]*, participation in the pilgrimage *[haj]*, and fasting during Ramadan). An Islamic government could not take any action that restricted a Muslim's capacity to perform these duties. In addition, an Islamic government could not adopt legislation that allowed Muslims to consume alcohol or engage in adultery. The draft party platform did not explicitly state any additional definitive features of shari'a. However, subsequent discussion of the platform indicated that some of the Brotherhood's members believed there was at least one other issue in which shari'a is definitive: women and non-Muslims may not hold the most senior political posts in an Islamic state.

37. Other MB leaders who supported this passage include Muhammad Morsi and Mahmud Izzat (Brown and Hamzawy 2008, 7).

38. Abdo Zina, "Ikhwan Misr y'atarifun bi-Ikhta' fi Barnamajhum lil-Hizb al-siyasi hawwal Hay'ah al-ulama al-muqtarahah" (Brotherhood of Egypt admit mistake

It would provide "expert advice" on issues of Islamic law, which legislators could then utilize during their deliberations. This view was shared by the General Guide, Muhammad Akif, who stated that the council of religious scholars would only issue advisory opinions to the Parliament. He further stressed that the Parliament should have unrestricted power to draft and adopt legislation.[39]

The issue at stake here was quite fundamental: how would the principles of shari'a be translated into specific legislation? The theorists discussed earlier argue that this important task is accomplished through the deliberations of an elected Parliament that functions as the modern-day counterpart to the "people who loose and bind" in classical thought. The Brotherhood adopted this view in its 2005 campaign documents. It reiterated this view in the portion of the draft platform that deals with political institutions, in a discussion that runs over thirteen pages (*Barnamaj Hizb al-Ikhwan al-Muslimin: al-Isdar al-Awwal* 2007, 11–24). However, the passage inserted by Habib, which consisted of only four lines at the beginning of the document, demonstrated that some Brotherhood leaders were not entirely comfortable with this formulation. This brief passage clearly was not an effort to reject the lengthy and detailed support for an elected Parliament that appeared later in the draft platform and was emphasized in subsequent interviews with senior MB leaders. However, the passage reflected an underlying concern about democracy that persists within parts of the leadership and the rank and file. They fear that elected representatives may adopt legislation that is at odds with the core principles of the faith. As noted earlier, this concern was also expressed by some of the theorists of Islamic constitutionalism—particularly al-Qaradawi and

---

in their political party platform regarding the suggested board of scholars), *al-Sharq al-Awsat,* Oct. 16, 2007; "Nass Hadith Dr. Muhammad Habib ila Ikhwan Web" (Text of Dr. Muhammad Habib's conversation with Ikhwan Web), www.ikhwanonline.com, Nov. 11, 2007; "Nass Hiwar Dr. Muhammad Habib" (Text of dialogue with Dr. Muhammad Habib), www.ikhwanonline.com, Dec. 6, 2007.

39. "Hiwar ma'a Murshid al-Ikhwan al-Muslimin Mahdi Akif" (Dialog with the Guide of the Muslim Brotherhood, Mahdi Akif), *al-Misri al-Youm,* Nov. 24, 2007.

Abu al-Majd. The council of religious scholars would provide expertise and advice that addressed this concern.

The draft platform contained another feature that further demonstrated the reservations of some Brotherhood leaders toward unrestricted democracy. While the draft platform reiterated the MB's long-standing view that Copts enjoy "full rights and duties" as citizens, it added an important caveat: a non-Muslim should not hold the post of president or prime minister (*Barnamaj Hizb al-Ikhwan al-Muslimin: al-Isdar al-Awwal* 2007, 15).[40] It explained this stance by arguing that the country's most senior political leaders play an important role in ensuring the Islamic character of the state and society. A non-Muslim lacks the religious knowledge and personal convictions needed to perform this role effectively. This issue was discussed by some of the theorists of Islamic constitutionalism analyzed earlier. Al-Qaradawi, for example, writes that the president should be Muslim and that the majority of Parliament should be Muslim (al-Qaradawi 1997, 32, 195). However, this view had not appeared previously

40. The draft platform did not propose the adoption of legislation that prohibited Copts from holding these posts. Rather, it simply expressed the MB's view that only Muslims should hold these positions. Habib and other Brotherhood leaders indicated in subsequent interviews that, while they would not support a Copt for these posts, they would accept this outcome if it was the result of a free election. Ahmad al-Khatib, "Al-Ikhwan yattajihun lil-muwafiqah ala tarshih Qubti lil-ra'asah fi al-nuskhah al-niha'iyah li Barnamaj al-Hizb" (The Brotherhood leans toward agreeing on nominating a Copt to presidency in the final draft of the platform of the Party), *al-Misri al-Youm,* Oct. 23, 2007; "Hiwar ma'a Murshid al-Ikhwan al-Muslimin Mahdi Akif" (Dialog with the Guide of the Muslim Brotherhood, Mahdi Akif), *al-Misri al-Youm,* Nov. 24, 2007; Islam Abd al-Aziz, "Al-Ikhwan: La iqsa li Iryan wa hasamna wilayah al-Qubti" (The Brothers: No firing of al-Iryan and we settled the ruling of a Copt), www.islamonline.net, Nov. 7, 2007; Adil al-Darjali, "Sa'ah harrah . . . Abu al-Futuh: Al-Masihi istahal an yakun ra'is . . . wa Jama'ah al-Ikhwan istiqrrat Ala huqq al-mawatinah" (Heated hour . . . Abu al-Fatuh: Impossible for a Christian to be president . . . and the Brotherhood settles on the right of citizenship), *al-Masri al-Youm,* Aug. 22, 2007; "Representatives of the Brotherhood: We Agree to the Candidacy of a Copt for the Presidency of the Republic So Long as He Fulfills the [Constitutional] Requirements," *al-Misri al-Youm,* Sept. 13, 2006.

in the MB's political documents. In a like vein, the draft platform reiterated that women have full legal equality and the right to vote and to run for office. However, it added a similar caveat: a woman should not serve as president (*Barnamaj Hizb al-Ikhwan al-Muslimin: al-Isdar al-Awwal* 2007, 103). This position was justified through reference to a woman's primary role as mother and wife, which renders her unsuited for the demanding responsibilities of the presidency. Significantly, this was a deviation from the views of the theorists discussed earlier. Al-Qaradawi, in particular, emphasizes that women are prohibited only from serving as head of the umma (the entire community of Muslims). He argues that an individual nation-state is only a small subset of the umma, and therefore the prohibition on women serving as leader of the umma does not apply (al-Qaradawi 1997, 165, 175–76). Despite al-Qaradawi's view, the Brotherhood expressed its opposition to a woman's holding the presidency in the 2004 reform initiative. While some MB members claimed that this position was required by shari'a, most of the organization's leaders explained that this stance was a reflection of the values that prevail in contemporary Egypt.[41] Patriarchy is a well-entrenched norm in Egypt, particularly among the socially conservative segments of society that support the Brotherhood. The MB's leaders were responding to this sentiment among the rank and file.

It should be noted that this draft platform was not endorsed by the leadership body of the MB (the Guidance Office).[42] It also was not endorsed

41. "Nass Hiwar Dr. Muhammad Habib" (Text of dialogue with Dr. Muhammad Habib), www.ikhwanonline.com, Dec. 6, 2007; Muhammad Gharib, "al-Iryan: Al-Waqi' la yasmah illa bi 4 sayyidat wa 4 Masihiyun fi al-Barlaman" (Al-Iryan: The reality does not allow more than four women and four Christians in Parliament), *al-Misri al-Youm*, Oct. 29, 2007. Also, Khalil al-Anani, "Khilafat dakhiliyah tathayyar takhminat hawwal mustaqbal al-Jama'ah: Ikhwan Misr wa hikayah hakimiyah al-mar'ah wa al-Aqbat" (Internal differences stir predictions about the future of the group: The Brotherhood of Egypt and the story of rule of women and Copts), *al-Hayat*, Nov. 7, 2007.

42. The leader of the Brotherhood stated that the organization would analyze the many comments on the draft party platform and then issue a final platform that reflected the official views of the Guidance Office. "Hiwar ma'a murshid al-Ikhwan al-Muslimin Mahdi Akif" (Dialog with the Guide of the Muslim Brotherhood, Mahdi Akif), *al-Misri al-Youm*, Nov. 24, 2007. However, this final version of the platform was not issued. After

by the General Guide, Muhammad Akif, who emphasized that the draft platform was only a means to air ideas and to gain feedback from intellectuals and others on the best political direction for the organization.[43] Furthermore, the draft platform clearly was not a renunciation of the moderate views articulated in the 2005 campaign documents. Indeed, one of the striking features of the draft platform is the extent to which it incorporates these earlier documents. Rather, the three controversial positions mentioned above were adopted in order to affirm that a democratic political order would still respect and defend the core principles of shari'a. These positions were also designed to demonstrate that the Brotherhood's leadership still shares the conservative social values held by many of the organization's members, particularly with regard to the role of women in society.

The Uniqueness of Islamic Constitutionalism: The State and Social Transformation

The Brotherhood's 2005 campaign literature and 2007 draft party platform indicate that the organization conceptualized Islamic constitutionalism in a manner that resembled classical liberalism. The MB advocated the adoption of laws that apply equally to ruler and ruled, the creation of institutions that regulate and constrain state power, and the protection of many civil and political rights. Yet there were some features of the MB's agenda that were decidedly illiberal. These features were most apparent in the frequent references to the transformational character of the Brotherhood's political mission. In the MB's view, Egypt was weak because Egyptians had abandoned the principles of Islam (*Mubadirat al-Ikhwan al-Muslimin* . . . 2004, 11). This moral and spiritual decline could be reversed only by "transform[ing] the individual from within" (Ghazlan

---

the fall of Hosni Mubarak in February 2011, the Brotherhood formed the Freedom and Justice Party. This party issued a platform in June 2011.

43. "Hiwar ma'a murshid al-Ikhwan al-Muslimin Mahdi Akif" (Dialog with the Guide of the Muslim Brotherhood, Mahdi Akif), *al-Misri al-Youm,* Nov. 24, 2007; Islam Abd al-Aziz, "Al-Ikhwan: La iqsa li Iryan wa hasamna wilayah al-Qubti" (The Brothers: No firing of al-Iryan and we settled the ruling of a Copt), www.islamonline.net, Nov. 7, 2007.

2005, 5). This process did not simply entail self-reflection and deeper personal spirituality. The Brotherhood believed that an individual's character was shaped by the community in which he lived. In order to transform the individual, one must transform every dimension of communal life—cultural, economic, legal, and political (*Mubadirat al-Ikhwan al-Muslimin* . . . 2004, 9–10; Ghazlan 2005, 5). A truly Islamic community would emerge only through the purposeful construction of the Muslim individual, home, and society (*Mubadirat al-Ikhwan al-Muslimin* . . . 2004, 9–10).

Furthermore, the state plays the central role in this process of transformation. It is the mechanism for ensuring that people "worship, practice good manners, and act honorably" (*Mubadirat al-Ikhwan al-Muslimin* . . . 2004, 12). It protects the morality of individual Muslims by "purging the media of material that runs counter to the rules of Islam and the values that it instills" (*Mubadirat al-Ikhwan al-Muslimin* . . . 2004, 12; *Al-Barnamaj al-Intikhabi* . . . 2005). It achieves "godliness and religiosity in society" by "constructing an individual with Islamic principles and values that are deeply rooted in his character" (*Mubadirat al-Ikhwan al-Muslimin* . . . 2004, 34, 38) and by "protecting values, ethics, and manners" (Akif 2005).

This conception of the state as a moral actor received its clearest statement in the Brotherhood's call for reviving the doctrine of *hisba.*[44] This is an ancient principle in Islam that dates back to the earliest days of the faith.[45] It mandates that each individual has a duty to strengthen the religiosity of his fellow Muslims and, thereby, to build a stronger and more pious community. As Michael Cook points out, the obligation of hisbah became grafted onto the duties of the state during the early decades of Islamic history. The state assumed the obligation to "enjoin good and forbid evil" in

44. This call is present in the Reform Initiative (*Mubadirat al-Ikhwan al-Muslimin* . . . 2004, 34) as well as in the Brotherhood's campaign platform (*Al-Barnamaj al-Intikhabi* . . . 2005).

45. The obligation to enjoin good and forbid evil appears in eight Qur'anic verses: 3:104; 3:110; 3:114; 7:157; 9:71; 9:112; 22:41; and 31:17. However, the use of the term *hisbah* to describe this obligation was adopted only in the eleventh century. Al-Ghazali was the first to utilize it (Cook 2000, 13, 449). For a useful summary of al-Ghazali's conception of hisbah, see Cook 2000, 428–59.

each member of the community (Cook 2000, 470–79; Cook 2003, 65–72). This obligation involved not only the obvious task of enforcing a wide range of laws governing personal behavior. It also included designing the education system, selecting judges, and appointing officials at all levels of society with the goal of enhancing the piety of the community. In order to perform these tasks, the Islamic community required a state that was far more invasive than that found in classical liberalism or democratic theory.

The theorists discussed earlier also address the concept of hisbah and the type of state that implements it. Al-Bishri (2005, 72) writes at some length about hisbah as an "obligation of the entire community." However, each person is permitted to delegate this obligation to another. He notes that, in practice, it has been delegated to the state (al-Bishri 2005, 74). He adds that many rulers created a specific post, *muhtasib,* to carry out this duty (al-Bishri 2005, 74).[46] Al-Qaradawi argues that the state in Islam is "not simply a state that maintains order" (al-Qaradawi 1997, 19–20). Rather, it is "an intellectual creedal state," a state based upon a creed that it promotes by "creating an atmosphere that converts the teachings of Islam into tangible reality" (1997, 19–20). In his view, the state "represents the justice of God on earth" and, through its actions, "deepens the Islamic character of the people and spreads Islam" (1997, 51, 41). Al-Awwa adds that the state creates the Islamic community by enforcing Islamic law. It gives the abstract moral precepts of Islam practical substance that shapes the lives of individual Muslims and deepens their conviction to the faith (al-Awwa 1989, 137–38).

The fact that both the theorists and the Brotherhood place the concept of hisbah alongside the institutions of constitutionalism is quite striking. In essence, they make a long and detailed case for creating institutions that are normally associated with constraining and limiting state power. Then, in the next breath, they invoke the concept of hisbah and its dramatic expansion of the state's power to interfere in the private lives of citizens.

46. Cook translates *muhtasib* as "official censor" (2000, 448). The root meaning is derived from the term for keeping an account—in this case, an account of the moral shortcomings of one's fellow Muslims.

How can we explain this juxtaposition of seemingly contradictory ideas? One possibility is that the Brotherhood and the theorists were trying to deceive their audience. They invoked the rhetoric of liberal institutions and procedures, perhaps to calm the fears of domestic and international critics. But, at heart, they were actually committed to an autocratic form of rule based upon a powerful state that enjoys divine sanction and few constraints on its power. If this was their strategy, it was executed with remarkable clumsiness. The Brotherhood made no secret of its goal of transforming Egyptian society. This objective was stated in the first paragraph of its reform initiative and appeared repeatedly in its 2005 campaign platform and its 2007 draft party platform. Similarly, the central role of the state in carrying out this transformation was presented openly and repeatedly. The theorists also presented their views on hisbah and the transformational role of the state clearly and explicitly.

There is a certain inconsistency to the claim that the liberal rhetoric of Islamists was merely a smokescreen for an underlying autocratic agenda. On the one hand, it implies considerable intelligence and skill among Islamist leaders. They presented well-crafted arguments, complete with numerous Qur'anic citations and references from the hadith, that articulated a plausible case for liberal political institutions derived from Islamic sources. They repeated this case consistently in many different settings, with minor adjustments to address the concerns of specific audiences. This conceptual sophistication and coherence suggests that the leaders of the movement were smart, disciplined, and well organized. And yet, if the "smokescreen" theory is correct, these same individuals were also capable of remarkable ineptness. They revealed their supposedly secret agenda of transforming individuals and society in every public forum available to them. They also openly made the case for a powerful state that guides this process. In order to conclude that the Islamists discussed above were engaged in an elaborate charade, one must believe that they were capable of great cleverness and great stupidity at the same time. This is certainly possible. However, it is unlikely. We need to look for a more plausible explanation.

The other possibility is that the institutions of constitutionalism play a different role in the thinking of Islamists than they do in classical liberalism. In classical liberal thought, constitutionalism begins from the assumption that the state is a threatening institution. Its control over vast resources and personnel gives it enormous potential to trespass on the rights and liberties of citizens. The purpose of constitutionalism is to create institutions that limit state power in order to protect individual rights, private property, and the private sphere.[47]

For the Muslim Brotherhood and the theorists discussed above, the nature of the state is fundamentally different. From their standpoint, the state is a good institution. Through its enforcement of shari'a, it brings the Islamic community into being and ensures that this community remains pious. Through its implementation of the doctrine of hisbah, it strengthens the morality and spirituality of individual Muslims. It also performs other functions fundamental to Islam such as the collection of zakat, the reconciling of tensions within the community, the protection of the umma from external threats, and the spreading of the faith. From this perspective, constraints on state power play a different role than they play in classical liberalism. The institutions of constitutionalism are not intended to erect a barrier that prevents the state from interfering in the private lives of citizens. Rather, their purpose is to direct state power toward the goal of transforming individual Muslims and society.

Phrased differently, the metaphor for classical liberal constitutionalism is a wall built around the state. This wall constrains the state, limits its power, and protects citizens from unwelcome intrusions into their private lives. In contrast, the metaphor for Islamic constitutionalism is a carefully maintained path that directs state power toward the transformation of individual Muslims and the creation of a more pious community. Within this framework, the institutions of constitutionalism ensure that the state stays on this path and fully achieves its potential to change individuals and society.

If the Islamic constitutionalism described above were fully implemented, it would probably include many of the institutions of Western

47. For a useful summary of the classical liberal conception of constitutionalism and its role in democracy, see Murphy 1993.

democracy such as an independent judiciary, a Parliament with considerable power and autonomy, and an executive accountable to at least part of the citizenry. However, the net result of these constitutional features would be a state that is far more invasive than that found in Western liberal regimes. The purpose of law, police, and courts would not be simply to maintain order. They would also be tasked with monitoring and changing the moral character of the community. The state would play an active role in shaping educational curricula to convey a specific set of moral and religious values. It would also monitor publications, scholarship, the arts, and other forms of expression that shape the morality of the community. In addition, there would be less protection of civil and political rights in some areas. For example, freedom of speech with regard to religious and moral matters would be constrained. Freedom of religious choice would be limited, to the extent that Muslims would not be allowed to choose a different faith. Non-Muslims would probably face some discrimination in economic life and in politics. And women would probably enjoy fewer rights than men.

It should be noted that Islamic constitutionalism is not a doctrine that supports a totalitarian conception of the state. It does not assert that the state holds a monopoly on truth and that it imposes this truth on the citizenry. Rather, Islamic constitutionalism is based on a collaborative relationship between state and society. It is grounded in the premise that both state and society seek to create a pious community. Individual citizens, as well as the state, carry the obligation to improve the moral character of the community. As a consequence, society constrains and monitors the state in order to ensure that it plays its role as effectively as possible and stays "on the true path of Islam" (al-Qaradawi 1997, 30). The resulting regime is participatory and bound by law. But it serves different objectives than in the West.

Furthermore, it would be inaccurate to conceptualize this moral role for the state as simply the "unification of church and state." The Islamic constitutionalists argue that their goal is a "civil state governed by Islam" (1997, 30). To a reader grounded in Western political thought, this phrase is self-contradictory. However, the Islamic constitutionalists use this formulation to emphasize that their goal is not a religious state in the Western sense of the term. They do not call for the state to act on behalf of a religious body or class, nor do they support empowering the state to implement the conception of religious law adopted by the ruler.[48] Rather, they advocate a "civil state" in the sense that it is created by citizens to serve their goals and is accountable to them. The state is not divine, nor does it exercise divine power. However, its fundamental goal is to implement shari'a and, thereby, to create a more pious community. Thus it serves a religious purpose. A state with a religious purpose is not a divine state that is beyond criticism and constraint. To the contrary, the fact that the state has a religious mission in which society also participates means that the state faces two fundamental constraints: the religious law that it is created to enforce, and the public's understanding of this law, which is ascertained through the mechanism of shura (consultation). The institutions that create this form of government are spelled out in broad terms: an executive elected through popular vote, an elected Parliament that issues legislation, and an independent judiciary that monitors whether man-made law conforms to the prevailing understanding of the Qur'an and the sunna.

An obvious question to consider is whether Islamic constitutionalism can support democracy. If democracy is a set of institutions that constrain the state, enforce law, and allow public participation in politics, then Islamic constitutionalism is fully compatible with democracy. However, if one views democracy as the adoption and promotion of a set of values—such as individual liberty, freedom of choice, popular sovereignty, and a minimalist state—then the conclusion with regard to Islamic constitutionalism is more ambiguous. The Islamic thinkers discussed above place less emphasis on individual rights than one finds in the West. The individual is not the center of the political and legal universe. Rather, the focus is on building a pious community. In pursuit of this goal, the state assumes an invasive role in the lives of its citizens. The purpose of the

48. Al-Qaradawi argues that secular observers of the Islamic world often have this misperception owing to their misunderstanding of the term *al-hakimiyah al-Islamiyah*. He emphasizes that this term does not mean the rule of God. Rather, it means rule in accordance with God's law. This law constrains the ruler as well as the subject (al-Qaradawi 1997, 61–62).

institutions of constitutionalism is to enhance and refine this invasive role rather than to limit it.

Finally, it is important to realize that many key aspects of Islamic constitutionalism have not yet been fully articulated. This conception of political order is still under development and is shaped by a wide range of political ideas in contemporary Egypt. It is particularly influenced by liberal conceptions of constitutionalism, which are advocated with growing force and clarity by the judiciary and some prominent political actors. As the Egyptian political system becomes more open and as the autocratic institutions of the current regime erode, we are likely to see increased interaction between advocates of liberal constitutionalism and Islamic constitutionalism. This interaction is likely to produce a distinctive form of democracy that resembles Western democracy in institutional terms but differs with regard to the purpose of the state, the role of the individual in politics and society, and the character and function of law.

11

The Body Corporate and the Social Body

ŞERIF MARDIN

TODAY, the leader of the Turkish Adalet ve Kalkınma Partisi, Prime Minister Recep Tayyip Erdoğan, often refers to his legislative initiatives as legitimized by the party's control of a large majority in Parliament and the popular support he detects behind it. He thereafter goes on to state that his policies are based on the will of the people, or *millet*, the *populus* an ambiguous concept that is also used in Turkish for "nation." Opponents see this type of legitimation as taking its strength from a tacit compact with the mass of the voters as an undemocratic use of the majority postulate to steamroll issues through Parliament. Notwithstanding Erdoğan's often needlessly defensive swagger, his outrage at such accusations seems to have an element of sincerity that needs explanation. I think what we can detect here is a real misunderstanding: Erdoğan refers to millet as representing a society composed of Islamic bonding and sociability among Muslims;[1] his opponents see millet as a corporate entity. The confusion is understandable when one recollects the means by which, in Turkey, the republican, Jacobin corporate understanding of the nation has been repeatedly forced into a different "nation" operating on the basis of what in the most general sense can be named a sociality made up of "Islamic

Postscript: This paper was written in 2008.

1. On bonding, see Shils 1957.

solidarity groups."[2] The difference is that in the latter case the central social "cement" consists of a series of social bonds rather than a single, large corporate legal framework. Although the contrast is important, it is usually not spelled out and is kept a tacit, unexplained component of Turkish politics. The recurring salience of this tacit element of Turkish political ideologies reminds me that long ago I had already encountered another version of such conceptual ambiguity in my study of the Young Ottoman movement.

In fact, one conclusion of my book *The Genesis of Young Ottoman Thought* (Mardin 1962) has never attracted the importance I gave it personally, namely, that the Young Ottoman democratic theory lacked a key political instrument, which I described at the time as the "corporate nature of the state" (Mardin 1962, 399).

In the book I elaborated the idea as follows:

> Paradoxically enough, while the Young Ottomans ran into difficulties because they had no room for atomistic individualism, they also ran into difficulties because they did not dispose of a theory as to the corporate nature of the state. For in some respects liberal thought rested on non-individualistic conceptions. This is particularly true of the theory of representation. Otto von Gierke traced the theory to Roman conceptions which were taken over in Europe in the Middle Ages, specifically to the Roman theory of corporate personality. [That] thesis was advanced by Gierke as part of the general theory that the medieval world was on the way to, but never quite achieved, an organic theory of society. (Mardin 1962, 400)

What Gierke saw as a missing link in medieval history did, however, develop in the field of private and commercial law but also, beginning in the sixteenth century, in the European theory of politics.

2. See Roy 2002, 126. According to Presnjit Duara, these solidarity groups perpetuated themselves through traces left in history by large-scale communities (Duara 1995, 72). For solidarity groups, see also Ritter 1948. See also Fustel De Coulanges 1956 for "fraternal associations."

In modern Turkey, the difference between Islamic bonding and *kamu,* the corporate *staatsrecht,* a product of the nineteenth-century Ottoman reform policy, has had at least two consequences: one related to private law and the second related to conceptualizations of state authority, political representation, and constitutionalism. The problem is made even more difficult by the hybrid nature of Ottoman state practice.

We may place my argument about corporateness into the contemporary Turkish everyday environment by referring to a point made by Ayşe Saktanber (2006) in an article. The major issue underlined in that article is the current proscription of the headscarf in the Turkish "public domain." Saktanber shows a caricature of a woman wearing a scarf and riding in a minibus anxiously asking the driver to let her off because the bus is entering the public domain. The situation described in the caricature underlines not only the confusion created by the abstraction (public domain) among ordinary Turkish citizens but also the use of a concept by republican zealots that has entered Turkish law only recently, in the late nineteenth century and early twentieth century. It reminds us that such abstractions are not part of the ideas available to a Turkish citizenship that still has much to learn about authority and power. Rather than explained as fitting within the framework of a systematic theory, Kemalist views of public law have to be hunted for in the interstices of a brackish ideology. In fact, the concept of the public domain (kamu) stands in stark contrast to basic Islamic political conceptualizations. I shall argue that sociability is the deepest foundation of Islamic political theory and that the minibus, along with the lady's anxiety, also reveals a popular yet amorphous meaning substantiating and validating the idea of law and political theory.

Halil İnalcık (1998) has shown that in the Ottoman Empire all agricultural lands were available for redistribution by the state. This practice is considerably different from the Jacobin elaboration of an abstract area of forbidden practices, a sacralization of political space.[3] It is true that the Ottomans used a mixture of religious and secular laws and that they

3. For Miri lands, see İnalcık and Quataert 1994, 105–13.

promoted a conception of the state *(devlet)* that had a number of secular connotations. Nevertheless, by 1839, the date of the inception of political reform in the Ottoman Empire, there still was no clear concept of an abstract public domain in Ottoman state law although the right of eminent domain was an age-old Ottoman practice.

The best way to introduce this issue is to refer to the detailed article by Timur Kuran in which he describes the Islamic, Western European, and Ottoman practices regarding the concept of a public domain in its interrelation with the concept of corporate personality, an element he shows to be missing in Islamic legal theory.

In the following pages, I shall also elaborate on Timur Kuran's argument by bringing in a number of extant analytical distinctions concerning the history of the concept of corporate personality in the West. Finally I shall attempt to describe how a conception of corporate personality/public domain was very gradually developed in Turkey during the era of reforms (Tanzimat) and was finally brought to light at the very end of the nineteenth century by Ottoman jurists who took their inspiration from Western European state law. This concept was paralleled by a neglect in theory and practice of the "bonding" elements in Islamic practice.[4]

The first point to be retrieved, an argument developed by Harold Berman, is the peculiarity of the Western concept of corporate personality. This peculiarity has important consequences regarding the character of the modern European state (Berman 1983).[5] Quentin Skinner's work, by contrast, allows us to retrieve the steps by which, in parallel to the development of the concept of corporate personality in private law, the idea of the state as a corporate unit was developed (Skinner 1978; Kuran 2004). The point is that, if we follow Skinner's argument, we achieve an understanding of modern politics as the forging of a new conceptual space, that of the state in its ultimate secular-transcendental version. Hanna Fenichel Pitkin

4. I use four sources to study the development of corporate theory in the West and to contrast it with the Islamic deficit I underline: Pitkin 1967; Berman 1983; Skinner 1978; Kuran 2004.

5. Berman is a pioneer in the history of medieval corporatism.

gives us a detailed description of the various meanings attributed to political representation in Europe, some of which derive from corporate ideas. I shall first summarize Kuran's thesis. Kuran explains the ways in which the concept of corporation was developed in the West in civil law and the reasons why it never developed in the framework of Islamic culture.

Kuran begins by describing how in 1851 the first predominantly Muslim-owned joint-stock company of the Ottoman Empire, Şirket-i Hayriye, was founded (Kuran 2004, 1). This step was taken because "the political elites of the mid-nineteenth century had come to consider partnerships based on classical Islamic law ill-suited to the emerging banking, mass transportation and manufacturing sectors" (2004, 1).

This change, however, did not go as far as creating a business corporation, that is, "a profit-seeking legal entity whose standing before the law is independent of the natural individuals who enter in relations with it" (2004, 2). This difference meant that where Islamic culture and its law prevailed, foreigners and non-Muslim subjects were better equipped "to constitute large and durable enterprises" (2004, 2). In Europe, however, "as early as the twelfth century a key difference involved the scope of personhood. [The] Western legal system came to differentiate between a 'natural person' and a 'legal person'—the former a flesh-and-bones individual, the latter a collectivity or organization considered an individual fictitiously for purposes of the law" (2004, 2–3).

To recapture the dynamic of the difference between Islamic–Middle Eastern and Ottoman views, Kuran uses the concept of "historical" paths, earlier developed by Alexander Gerschenkron (1962) for the study of capitalism. In the Middle Ages, although there existed a Roman legal tradition, some facets of which could be used to promote corporate personality, no use was made of it in early medieval times. The growth of private associations in the medieval West eventually led to the vesting of such corporate rights on the firm, the city, and commercial enterprises; all gained recognition as corporations (2004, 4). Between 1075 and 1122, even the Roman Catholic Church began to call itself a corporation. This was part of the construction of a "systematized central body of law" (2004, 5). Thousands of towns followed suit, and commercially flourishing Italian cities bolstered their emerging prestige by forcing the recognition of a legal personhood by the city fathers. I skip the extremely detailed history of business concerns in Italy presented by Kuran and simply highlight his conclusions.

> The innovations of profit-making enterprises fed on advances in corporate governance within the broader social system. In a large organization, insisting on unanimity will usually paralyze governance. Requiring only majority approval, or the decision of a representative body, enhances organizational responsiveness to changing opportunities and group needs. Parliamentary democracy, the crowning political achievement of Western Europe, rests on a separation between the electoral rights of the voters and the legislative and executive rights of their elected representatives. Revealingly, the papal assemblies and parliaments of the thirteenth century were considered corporations. The emergence of parliamentary democracy moved European citizens away from the Roman maxim, *Quod omnes tangit ab omnibus approbetur* [*sic*]—what touches all must be decided by all. (2004, 10)

A new development in the business history of the West was the establishment "of large and effectively permanent companies specializing in trade with a specific region outside of Western Europe" (2004, 11). In a number of instances the state "implicitly" granted them legal personhood. A number of sequences intervened in the expansion of this process. "As the Industrial Revolution unfolded, the corporate form proved useful. In fact, it gave entrepreneurs the means to pursue commercial and financial ventures once unimaginable" (2004, 16).

Kuran then analyzes the Islamic historical process. Although "during the seventh through tenth centuries, the period when classical Islamic law took shape, the idea of a corporation was available to the Middle East, even if in rudimentary form the concept never developed" (2004, 18). In Islam a bifurcation set the Middle East on a different course. According to Kuran this course was the result of a strategy targeted to eliminate tribal strife and "the weakening of real or imaginary kinship bonds" (2004, 19) by promoting "a concept of community based on religion rather than descent" (2004, 19). He elaborates this insight as follows:

> Islam's initial emphasis on community building is reflected in the duties enunciated in the Qur'an. Eight of its verses call for "commanding right and forbidding wrong." Four of these assign this obligation to individuals, the remainder to the collectivity of Muslims *[umma]*. None imposes the duty on a subgroup of the community, such as an assembly of elites or elders. In fact the Qur'an contains no reference to the internal organization of the Muslim community. Although it does not ban associations formed to pursue legitimate ends, it intimates that all Muslims, provided they are sane, are to participate in the regulation of public conduct, in all spheres of activity. But they must do so as individuals, except as they act as a community." (2004, 19; *sura*s 3:104; 3:110; 3:114; 7:157; 9:71; 9:112; 22:41; 31:17)

Kuran goes on to retrieve a number of items in the legal and economic history of Islam such as the "unfulfilled potential of the *waqf*" (Kuran 2004, 28) that set up a path in Islam diverging from the socioeconomic history of Western Europe.

According to Kuran, a key cumulative factor leading to a similar bifurcation was the policy of the Ottoman state. "A path to organizational modernization was blocked by a state focused on protecting sources of revenue and unconcerned with organizational opportunities, except insofar as they affected its own ability to govern in transparent ways" (2004, 36).

Altogether, Kuran's argument is solid with regard to history. Pitkin's enables us to translate Kuran's intimation about medieval representation into the history of modern representation.

Here we may, as a first requisite of a comparison between Islam and the West, proceed from the point at which Kuran left us, that is, from the European thirteenth century to ideas of virtual representation in sixteenth-century England as studied by Pitkin:

> Both the formalistic sense of representation and its substantive correlate, "acting for," emerged during this period [i.e., 1650s] apparently by the way of the idea that Parliament represented the whole realm, which, in turn began in the notion of a mystic or symbolic "standing for . . ."

> The etymological development of this period is confused, and the available evidence is not conclusive, but it suggests that terms like "represent" were first applied to the Parliament as an image of the whole nation.
>
> This entire development took place when the individual member of Parliament was becoming less and less an agent of his constituency. The individual member is sent to "represent" only after he has come to be thought of as acting for the whole nation. (Pitkin 1972, 250, 251)

An additional aspect of corporateness is the image of the "mystical" nature of the nation. This concept was developed further in the political thought of nineteenth-century German idealists such as Fichte and has a tacit residue in our present idea of representation.[6] This abstraction of representation sets the stage for transcending the simpler idea of a proxy and the elaboration of a secular transcendental space for politics. The simpler idea of a proxy becomes so complex and contradictory that Rousseau comes to the conclusion that representation is impossible (Pitkin 1967, 207). But Rousseau has a substitute for the old idea of corporateness—a new concept of corporateness emerges from his ideas in the form of the "general will." Surveying the wider of scope of Rousseau's ideas, however, we find an additional element in his theory: the unity suggested by corporateness is also deconstructed to bring in a more "organic" element, that is, the social bond as one of the foundations of society (Bloom 1987). Rousseau's theory may therefore be seen as embodying two levels: first, a level of abstraction, that is, the general will is not something material. At a second level, the bond reconstituted is an actual emotional-bodily attachment. Joseph de Maistre picked up this element in Rousseau in his explanation of the foundation of society as sociability.[7] This second aspect of group formation, the nature of the bond and its projection into social movements, is an emphasis that contemporary sociology has brought back to the study of social movements (Bayat 1997; Benford and Hunt 1995;

6. Johann Gottlieb Fichte (1762–1814) in Miller et al. 1991, 164. For later developments, see also Meinecke 1924 and Friedrich 1992. "Droit public" was only gradually constructed in Germany with 1871 as a key date.

7. See "Joseph de Maistre," in Miller et al. 1991, 310.

Joas 1996; Hetherington 1998; Urry 2000, McDonald 2002). This approach is a groundbreaking development that sheds much light on the organizational potential of sociability and sociality compared to corporateness, one I shall use throughout this chapter.

We may use the dual system we see in Rousseau, that is, abstraction versus bonding, to gauge some of the developments that characterize the modernization of the Ottoman Empire.

"Traditional" Ottoman political theory did not address the idea of clear representation of a population, but it approached the idea through the status it gave to such units as tribes and religious minority groups, all of these components cemented by Islam, the sultanic idea, and the three "orders" of the Ottoman Empire. What is important in this synthesis is that Islam does not participate as a corporate element. Rather its role is to provide leadership for organized political activity, the role of the imam providing not only leadership but constructing the bond of sociability. "*Without the imam social institutions stop functioning*" (Crone 2004b, 22, my italics).

When we look at the reforms of the Tanzimat era, we see from the beginning an attempt to construct a new fictive Ottoman social body, the foundational base of the reform policy of the Tanzimat. Somewhat of an idea of a public is introduced during the Tanzimat by the 1851 creation of the position of a public proscenter (Bozkurt 1996, 99–100), which was almost impossible to fill because of the specific ways in which public law was conceptualized in the Ottoman world. The unstated premise of the Tanzimat reforming thrust was taken over by Young Ottomans in the 1860s who went on to give it a new definition through the concept of *vatan* (the fatherland). The representation they imagined was a representation of vatan in which Islam was seen as the deeper foundation of political legitimation and the foundation of political ethics. In other words, what they achieved was an artful way of combining the principle of bonding (that is, Islam and its social institutions) with a demand for the representation of the vatan. Namık Kemal stated, "Man is naturally endowed with freedom *[hürriyet]* by God and therefore has to profit from this gift. The freedom of all *[hürriyet-i âmme]* is preserved in the community (*cemiyyet* spelled without an *elif,* i.e., not *cemaat,* i.e., the society; in other words, the community as the public, a linguistic improvisation to introduce a new concept, that of society). The continuity of humanity *[beşerin bekası]* depends on the community because the [only] dominant force *[kuvve-i galibiye]* that keeps individuals from hurting each others is found in the public *[âmme]*."[8]

Notice first of all the subtle shift in Kemal's vocabulary from *umma* (the religious community) to *âmme* ("public" in the sense it acquired after the sixteenth century in Europe). Even while using an Islamic foundation, Namık Kemal feels the need to secularize umma: "Since the majority *[umum]* has no means of undertaking those obligations *[vezâif]* which are part of its natural rights *[hakk-ı mükteseb]*, the appointment *[tayin]* of a community leader *[imam]* and the constitution of a government *[teşkilat-ı hükümet]* become necessary. And this simply means that to enable the *cemaat* (the community) to perform [its] duties, it has to give its procuration *[tevkil]* to certain persons."[9]

In the meantime, the Tanzimat went on to develop national institutions that acquired their theoretical legitimation from the fiction of a corporate body. Included were the new institutions such as province administrative law, a new legal framework for schools and for the reform of the judicial apparatus—again, a change based on new statute law (İnalcık 2006; Akyıldız 1993). As in Europe, within the Ottoman Empire the "intendants" were also taking over, and in their wake raison d'état was assuming a new form (see Downing 1992, 124). Often the direction of reforms destroyed former mechanisms of bonding and emotional attachment. One young officer sent to Urfa as an enforcer of the Tanzimat fiscal reforms described these traditional (political) bonds as they operated around Urfa (Karal 1942). In his case, however, he did not use the traditional mechanism of assessing taxes by bargaining with the leaders of groups, such as the tribes, but was able to extract some taxes due by means

8. "Wa Shawirhum Fi'l-'Amr," *Hürriyet,* 30 Temmuz 1285 (1868), in *Külliyyat-ı Kemal,* Birinci Tertip (3) *Makalât-ı Siyasiye ve Edebiye* Cüz 2 (Istanbul, Selanik: Selanik Matbaası, 1327 [1911]), 165–75, here 165–66. The study of public law later came under the heading of *âmme hukuku*. See Okandan 1950 and Okandan 1949.

9. See footnote 8 for complete documentation.

of his sympathetic appeal. Martin Van Bruinessen (1992) has shown how the elimination of traditional patterns of Ottoman solidarity groups and their leadership by a newly invasive state resulted in anarchy in the Kurdish region of the Ottoman Empire.

At various junctures the Young Ottomans did understand the distinction between the mechanism of social bonding and corporateness and commented on it (Mardin 1962). However, they seem to have believed that, with Islam once pigeonholed as a foundation of the fictitious state, the new value of patriotism that they introduced would make up for the loss of bonding. Selim Deringil (1998) has shown that Sultan Abdülhamid once again concentrated on the creation of a unitary Ottoman state by various means. Although the sultan clearly dismissed formal representation, he seems to have believed, just as in the case of the Young Ottomans, that a unitary Islam, shorn of its warts, could promote both representation and the bonding aspect of unity he was pursuing. Within thirty years, representation was once again taken up by the generation that succeeded the Young Ottomans, that of the Young Turks as their major aim in politics. In the meantime, in the 1890s the social structure of the empire had once again changed. The success of administrative reforms required that administrative law should exist for the settlement of disputes of an administrative type. The centralization derives from the Tanzimat, and its innovations demanded that a central administrative mechanism be established. Reforms had been carried out on the basis of semiconstitutional edicts (the Hattı Humayun of Gülhane and the reform of 1956) (Findley 1989). The first theoretical unifiying statement was the book of Ibrahim Hakki Paşa on the foundations of administrative law.[10] The central process of integration within a unified empire was very gradually being undermined by emerging separatist currents in the empire. Although it has been argued that the dissolution of the principle of bargaining with blocs of Ottoman society (that is, solidarity groups, such as tribes and religioethnic parties) was the work of Young Turks in

10. Hakki 1889. Here Ibrahim Paşa also explains the European concept of "droit publique," p. 6.

power, a contrary argument now seems to have considerable merit. It is not entirely true that the fanaticism of the Young Turks led to the separation of such elements from the Ottoman Empire. As shown by David Dean Commins, in Syria Islamic reform was itself promoting new centers of identity and bonding around the Arabic language.[11] The dual emphasis on tacit corporateness versus bonding can also be observed in Sultan Abdülhamid's policies and in the plans of his successors, the Young Turks, and the Turkish Republic. At this time, the representation of a corporate entity (of sorts) was part of the foundation of the republican regime. The element of bonding, on the other hand, was to be achieved by Turkish nationalism. What had been neglected in this equation was the impressive power of a rival bonding institution, the Nakshbandi Order and its Islamic revivalism in Anatolia in the nineteenth century.[12] The policy of the Republic placed this bonding element in the position of the underground "Other." And that "Other" now had new organizational resources, which were opened up by the relative modernization of the Turkish social structure in the early twentieth century.

I once described the struggle between the two principles of corporateness and bonding as showing itself in a struggle between the center and the periphery (Mardin 1973). I admit that nowadays there may be better explanations, especially in terms of some of the new theoretical developments in social theory. Observers of Turkish Islam who never seriously subscribed to the long-term history of Islam's revival in Turkey now seem faced with a new dual task: they will not only have to take up the study of Turkish Islam, as the result of a path-directed past with all the historical knowledge that such an approach requires, but, in addition, they will also have to study sociability as a bonding element, exploring its similarity with the internal solidarity one finds in the Falun Gong (Keith and Lin 2003) in China or the Chiapas movement in Mexico. The theoretical

11. Commins 1990. Ibn Arabi's mysticism was another indication of the attempts at creating an Arab renaissance. See Weismann 2001.

12. Yücer 2003. See also Algar 1990. Also as a basic reference, see "Tarika" in the 2nd edition of *Encyclopedia of Islam* (Gibb et al., 1960–2005, 10:243–57), where the more organizational active Tarika structure is described as "energetic colonization" (254).

insights about these bonding mechanisms made by the scholars we have discussed will have to figure in future surveys of Turkish Islam.

Mr. Erdoğan's invocation of the bonding mechanism in order to legitimate his policies and its lack of fit with the republican corporate framework demonstrate an element that is repeatedly observed in Islamic "fundamentalist" movements, namely, the firmer foundation of their Islamically inspired solidarity and an ability to better use basic "cementing" mechanisms compared to those legislative initiatives that, in a democratic or quasidemocratic system, are linked formally to a corporate understanding of lawmaking in Parliament. This foundation of sociability and bonding appears in much clearer outlines in an organization that may be best described as an Islamic Freemasonry with a mission to build an educational empire. I have in mind Fethullah Gülen, a somewhat mysterious personage who has attracted attention for the last decade through his achievements as the head of an international educational empire.

Who then is Fethullah Gülen and how shall we form an estimate of the size of his movement? Available biographies stress his background in a family that was not only pious but also part of the loose Islamic structure of prayer leaders and Sufis so often found in provincial towns in East Turkey. As a prayer leader, Gülen was for many years an employee of the Turkish state's Directory General of Religious Affairs. Eventually he was appointed to İzmir, Turkey's second commercial metropolis after Istanbul. There Gülen was assigned to teach Qur'anic courses and went on to organize groups of young Muslims in "schools, dormitories, summer camps," attracting a number of devotees who eventually established what amounted to a religious community. His courses, known as "lighthouses," also brought in a number of university students. Gülen's reputation as a preacher with a score of disciples enabled him to tap into local, unofficial sources of financial support using the opportunities created by the new law on charitable foundations. The sympathetic response he received from the then leader of the Motherland Party, Turgut Özal, allowed him to expand the scope of his activities and go on to establish his own secondary-level, private educational institutions (Acar 2002; Sezal and Dağı 2001).

Today this undertaking, much expanded and diversified, has become an enormous educational federacy comprising university, secondary, and primary schools, reaching to Albania, the Balkans, Brazil, Uzbekistan, and Kazakhstan. The Gülen enterprise sponsors seventy-nine university preparatory courses (the door to success in Turkey's university entrance examination system) as well as fifty secondary schools and many private dormitories for university students. Core courses in these institutions emphasize science and are in English; religion is less conspicuous in the curriculum. Students of such Gülen colleges have won many prizes in international competitions in science.

Especially because he has distanced himself from party politics, Gülen can stress his role as a teacher primarily interested in expanding the knowledge of science to all. In this respect he appears paradoxically to have adopted the fundamental motto of the secular Turkish Republic, "science is the only true guide in life." However, his promotion of science has more complex origins, which will become evident in the next sections.

The End of the *Ulama*

The most important preliminary consideration in the evaluation of the Gülen movement is a very simple one, namely, that Turkey has no ulama, no religious establishment using Islamic law to cover such civil institutions as marriage, divorce, or economic transactions. This unusual phenomenon immediately distances Turkey from almost all other countries with a majoritarian Islamic culture—and that includes ironically the former Soviet Union, which, after the revolution, had kept the Islamic religious hierarchy of its Muslim minority with some modifications. In Turkey a law was passed on March 3, 1924, that did four things simultaneously: it abolished the caliphate, it abolished the Ministry of Religious Affairs, it established the monopoly of the state over all educational activities, and it vested the power to rule on religious matters to a General Directorate of Religious Affairs, which functioned under the prime minister's office. This law, known as the Law on the Unification of Education,[13] resulted in

13. Law on Unification of National Education No. 430 was put into force on Mar. 3, 1924.

the historical religious establishment's ceasing to exist and in religion and education completely controlled by the state. However, in time new opportunities became open to religious associations created under the Turkish Law of Associations. Some Turkish Islamists bewailed the disappearance of the *medrese,* the Islamic seminary and site where both legal and religious issues could be adjudicated within the frame of Islam. The Muslim population's liturgical needs were now to be met by a new institution, the General Directorate of Religious Affairs. There was a positive outcome of this secularization introduced by the March 3, 1924, law. If a religious association could show that under Turkish law it did not pursue a political objective or endanger the foundation of the Republic, it could organize more freely than if it was subject to control as a full-fledged religious establishment. The expansion of the scope of the statute on charitable and other foundations in the 1990s opened up additional opportunities for groups like those of Gülen's.

We may state then without exaggeration that under the present circumstances the various republican statutes governing private education associations, publications, and the benefaction of students paradoxically can be interpreted as veritable gifts of the secular republic to Gülen's association. The value of the gift is not diminished by Gülen's well-known support of the state. His pro-state position probably resulted from a necessary cautiousness. I believe, however, that Gülen's position regarding the state is much better understood as an aspect of his "Ottomanism." One of the central themes in Gülen's ideas is the uniqueness of an Ottoman-Turkish construction of Islam. Gülen seems to have attained these ideas or beliefs after spending some time in the Hijaz, possibly in Mecca. As someone who has published an article on this subject, I can only say that such an Ottoman-Turkish variant of Islam seems to have some substance, although we still need more research to fill in the gaps. Gülen's religiosity is inspired by the difference between what he would describe as the narrow provincialism of the Arab-Wahhabi interpretation of Islam and what we see as the relaxed, tolerant, multifaceted Ottoman Empire. Usually Gülen's Ottomanism is seen as a retrieval of Ottoman culture, but I would propose that his movement also has a structural foundation that rests on what I have described as the Islamic social "cement" that is made up of a number of elements working as traces of Ottoman history (Duara 1995). Connected to this view of Islam is Gülen's use of a mystical Islamic approach based on the many dimensions of love, an idea that he often echoes.

A Few Words about Structural Elements

All the constituent elements that enter into the extraordinary expanse of the Gülen movement point to some internal structure, but the real nature of this structure is difficult to fathom. Despite the manifest activism, organizational competence, and leadership his endeavor shows, Gülen has repeatedly and vehemently rejected the attribution of being the leader of an Islamic *tarika*, or brotherhood, and he also denies being vested with shaikhly authority, or *barakah*. His followers' use of *hoca* or "teacher" to refer to him reinforces this persona of a teacher. It is here that the Ottoman principle of sociability, still a latent element in Mr. Erdoğan's thought, emerges once again.

A Peaceable Kingdom

Studying the internal dynamic of the Gülen movement, however, involves a reconsideration of how an extraordinary number of Turks from all classes embraced him in the mid-1990s. A first step in reconstructing the origins of Gülen's kingdom (an approach that has *not* been pursued) is the exploration of Turkey as a "chip on the shoulder society" (as the late anthropologist A. P. Stirling [1965] has stated). Turkey can be seen as a society in which the love of handguns exceeds even that of the American West. Another anthropologist, Michael Meeker, has underscored the special role of the hero in Turkish society (see Mardin 1978). Much has been written about the way in which Mustafa Kemal Atatürk fits into this role of the eponymal hero. But an aspect of his charisma less often investigated is his role in *overcoming conflict*. In reality, the lineaments of the social habitus in Turkish society allow for a perpetuation of incipient conflict only held in abeyance by structures of authority. We may, at this point, recall the recent autobiography of the former Turkish Islamist activist Mehmet Metiner. Metiner (2004) paints an extraordinary picture of his birthplace,

Kâhta, where the only means for a fifteen-year-old adolescent to integrate himself into the culture of this provincial town—in other words, to play—was to join one of two existing conflict groups, either the Muslims who were the conservatives or the Communists who represented the secular republicans. One is reminded here of Lewis Coser and his study *The Functions of Social Conflict*.

One of the elements in Coser's thesis is the idea of nonrealistic conflict, conflict that does not pit opposing interests against each other. Here is how Coser explains this type of conflict: "Nonrealistic conflicts . . . are not occasioned by the rival end of the antagonism, but by the need for tension release of one or both of them. In this case conflict is not oriented towards the attainment of specific results. Insofar as unrealistic conflict is an end in itself, insofar as it affords only tension release the chosen antagonist can be substituted for by any other 'suitable' target" (Coser 1956).

One reason why this disposition toward conflict in Turkish society has been considered very little in the scholarly literature centers on the optimistic assessment of Turkey's being placed in the stream of "civilization," and this view has had priority over other judgments. Even the role of the so-called "deep-state" in Kurdish disappearances has been chronicled as a failure of the structure of the Turkish state and *not* as the cumulative product of deep-lying social structural elements of conflict *and* politics.

Again, the overwhelming explanation for the anti-Alevi "defenestration" of Sivas in 1993 (Büyüktanır 2006; Kaleli 1995) has been about Sunni "fanaticism," once more an assessment based on interfaith conflict and not on the shared disposition to social conflict that precipitated the frenzy of the crowd. Yet Turks have much to remember about conflict. Between 1975 and 1980 about four thousand Turks lost their lives in left-right, Alevi-Sunni, Turk-Kurd conflicts. The military intervention of September 1980 was a convenient way to end the conflict by incarcerating many more men than had died. It is no coincidence that the rise of Gülen's movement and the support he received coincides with those years: in reality Gülen was seen as a *peacemaker* by a society that was riddled with conflict, with maiming and death, and this attribution endures today. This image is where the often overly sweet discourse of Gülen functions as some kind of social balm. And this example once again shows an aspect of the Islamic ideological mechanism of social integration that I have attempted to highlight here. The attempt to contravene deep-lying elements of social conflict with reference to Islamic solidarity seems to be at the real core of Gülen's contribution. However, hope, faith, and charity, prominent as they are in Gülen's peace offering, do not exhaust the questions that are raised by his success. Other elements have to be brought in to understand the deeper foundation of his praxis and what Hans Joas (1996) has described as the "creativity of action." Once again, this example in the study of "bonding" as an aspect of structure underscores the theme I have pursued throughout this chapter.

Let me approach somewhat obliquely an element that has always made me uncomfortable, the impression of insubstantiality in the bonds that keep the Gülen group together—and Gülen's own repeated claim of faith and love as the only elements of internal cohesiveness. I believe this is a true description of *at least one layer* of the element of "bonding" of the Gülen crowd. Max Weber, writing on mysticism, charisma, and the exemplary prophet, provides us with a clue to the force of compact involved:

> Wherever genuine mysticism did give rise to communal action, such action was characterized by the acosmism of the mystical feeling of love. Mysticism may exert this kind of psychological effect, thus tending—despite the apparent demands of logic—to favor the creation of communities *(gemeinschaftsbildend).* The core of the mystical conception of . . . brotherly love, when sufficiently strong and pure, must necessarily lead to unity in all things, even in dogmatic beliefs. In other words, men who sufficiently love one another . . . will also think alike and, because of the very irrationality of their common feeling, act in a solidary fashion which is pleasing to God. (Weber 1968, 283)

Here we can find an explanation of Islamic revival that today we would place within "social theory." For the study of Islam, we need to be receptive to these new ideas by promoters of social theory with an emphasis on bonding and consider them in tandem with political theory.

12

Cosmopolitanism Past and Present, Muslim and Western

ROXANNE L. EUBEN

IT HAS BECOME almost common scholarly wisdom that the progressively dizzying flows of people, knowledge, and information characteristic of the contemporary world have inaugurated an unprecedented deterritorialization of politics. We are now said to live in a world in which "borders have stopped marking the limits where politics ends because the community ends," our identities not only shaped by particular places and spaces such as nation and domicile, but also subjected to the multiple crosscurrents and exposures created by rapid economic globalization and cultural hybridization (Balibar 1998, 220). As is often noted, such developments have not only rendered national borders increasingly permeable but have also called into question the preeminence of the modern nation-state as the dominant frame and unit of political analysis. In turn, such changes have precipitated a reevaluation of the spatial and conceptual parameters that have governed most scholarly inquiries into statecraft, sovereignty, citizenship, identity, and rights since the seventeenth century.

Such a reassessment is particularly evident in the wide array of political and social theorists who have engaged in debates about the "new cosmopolitanism," a protean category that signals an attempt to rethink the

An earlier version of part of this chapter appeared previously in my book *Journeys to the Other Shore: Muslim and Western Travelers in Search of Knowledge,* published in 2006 by Princeton Univ. Press and reprinted here with permission.

scope and scale of moral, legal, and political obligations among human beings whose identities and loyalties are no longer—if they ever were—coextensive with the modern nation-state. This scholarship may register as just one among many by-products of the rapid transfigurations in culture and knowledge brought about by globalization. Yet arguments about the new cosmopolitanism are establishing many of the scholarly terms in which the deterritorialization of politics is defined, and delineating the range of moral, political, and economic practices that do or should flow from it. Consequently, such debates are significant not only because of the way they reflect this historical moment but also because they are helping to determine how and in what terms we come to understand it.

This chapter is an analysis of how this otherwise promising scholarship often enacts a cultural and historical parochialism that inadvertently conceals cosmopolitan genealogies located beyond a series of "Western" figures and philosophical touchstones.[1] As a partial antidote to this provincialism, I sketch the outlines of an Islamic ethos of travel in search of knowledge. The contours of this ethos, I argue, illuminate a genealogy of Muslim cosmopolitanism, one woven from a variety of doctrinal sources as well as from disparate practices, moments, and ideas that punctuate the history of Muslim societies. This countergenealogy, as it were, brings into focus the historical and normative resources that inform and transform the ways in which the *umma* (Muslim community) is continually reimag-

1. Oppositions such as West/non-West and West/Islam carve up the world in ways that obscure the fissures within each category, erase their mutual historical indebtedness, and deny the cross-pollination of the present. Given the frequency with which these terms are invoked by people all over the world and the very real allegiances and enmities they evoke, however, scholars engaged directly or indirectly with the dilemmas of contemporary politics cannot simply dispense with such categories by reference to all that they miss, distort, or exclude. As the current political climate attests, there is much more at stake here than whether or not categories such as Islam and the West are *accurate,* in the sense of corresponding, more or less precisely, to actual geographic, political, historical, and/or normative borders in the world. I will thus retain references to these terms without quotation marks, but they should be understood as political constructions rather than historical, cultural, or territorial descriptions.

ined as a moral, political, and now even virtual *oikoumene* (Greek for the word *ecumene,* meaning "entire world").[2]

In a geopolitical landscape that has been reshaped by a War on Terror, such a genealogy has a particular political import. It not only underscores the unnecessarily narrow parameters of the current debate about the new cosmopolitanism, but it also brings into sharp relief the range of cultural, historical, and political forces that collude (intentionally or unintentionally) to erase these more ecumenical precedents and practices from view. At the same time, this genealogy helps disrupt Manichean narratives about a world divided into "us" and "them," "the West" and "Islam," by disclosing significant moments of cross-cultural commonality, as well as many of the intracultural dynamics that continually transform the contours and political purchase of Muslim cosmopolitanism.[3]

Cosmopolitan Itineraries

In the last twenty years, there has been a virtual explosion of scholarship on the "new cosmopolitanism."[4] This scholarship is simultaneously a response to the economic and cultural transformations associated with rapid globalization and the renascence of an ancient idea with a very uneven career in Euro-American history. As is often noted, the word *cosmopolitan* comes from the ancient Greek for "citizen of the world," and its elaboration as a

2. *Oikoumene* in Greek originally referred to the inhabited as opposed to the uninhabited world, an opposition that corresponded roughly to the distinction between the Hellenic world and the world of "barbarians." The term eventually came to include both Greeks and some non-Greeks as part of the "inhabited world" and would later denote an even more expansive understanding of "the whole." It is the etymological precursor to "ecumenical," meaning "belonging to the whole world."

3. These arguments are drawn from Euben 2006.

4. The literature here is too extensive to list, but those that have informed my account include Martha Nussbaum's argument for cosmopolitanism and responses to it initially published in the *Boston Review* (19[5] [Oct./Nov. 1994]), subsequently published as Nussbaum and Cohen 1996; P. Mehta 2000; Waldron 1995; Pollock 2000; Robbins 1992; Breckenridge 2002.

way of being is usually traced to the Stoics (although at least one scholar traces it to ancient Egypt).[5] Yet from the time of the Romans to that of Rousseau, cosmopolitanism has been construed quite differently in different epochs, serving at one moment to valorize the aspiration to love strangers as one's own, at another to vilify various undesirables as deracinated parasites, and at yet another to cloak in politically palatable garb a universalism "tainted" by association with Western imperialist ventures.

At once derived from and critical of this uneven past, the new cosmopolitanism is itself difficult to pin down, as it has been debated, restated, and endlessly qualified by a dizzying array of modifiers—discrepant, rooted, comparative, vernacular, critical, and actually existing, among others. As Pratap Mehta (2000, 621–22) points out, these proliferating cosmopolitanisms have many valences—aesthetic, existential, moral and legal—but at the very least they express a "suspicion of closed horizons . . . a willingness to engage with the 'Other' . . . [and] an aesthetic and intellectual openness to diverse strivings, cultures, and forms of reasoning." Convinced that cosmopolitanism is "the sensibility of our moment," most proponents are concerned with the extent to which proliferating experiences of displacement may be mobilized for the kind of dialogue productive of genuine engagement with unfamiliar cultural forms as well as critical purchase on one's own commitments (Robbins 1992, 183). Despite—or perhaps because of—the ways in which increasing contact among peoples has produced as much hostility as hybridity, scholars of cosmopolitanism also tend to nurture the hope that politics itself can be transformed by way of such engagements, "stretched" to meet the challenge of the times by being "forced to include the variable power of sympathetic imagination to define collectivities of belonging and responsibility in the absence of that long history of face-to-face interaction that Dewey thought was necessary to

5. Harris refers to inscriptions at Tell-el-Amarna that indicate that Akhnaton, pharaoh of Egypt from 1375 to 1358 BCE, viewed "himself as owing the same duties to all men, irrespective of race or nationality." Harris quickly concludes, however, that "this was an isolated phenomenon, without any apparent influence on the subsequent history of human thought. . . . the ancient Greeks were the first of Europeans to promulgate this idea, and it is from them that Western civilization has directly inherited it" (Harris 1927, 1–2).

community. . . . [t]he opportunities for turning distant economic interdependence into conscious political cooperation have never been so promising. The time for cosmopolitics is now" (Robbins 1998, 8–10).

It is beyond the focus of this chapter to track the shifting fortunes of cosmopolitanism over time, survey the various understandings of cosmopolitanism currently in vogue, or adjudicate among the complex claims for and against it. Instead, I approach the proliferating meanings of the new cosmopolitanism as symptomatic of a moment in which increasing awareness of contact among peoples, cultures, and ideas has engendered new efforts to theorize the politics of mobility and the mobility of politics. In this light, the new cosmopolitanism is perhaps most usefully understood as signaling entry into a debate about the actual or desirable relationship between the local and the global, rootedness and detachment, particularism and universalism, rather than as a consistent set of empirical claims and normative arguments. The debate itself is, however, animated by some common concerns, including the need to keep apace of the speed of current structural and cultural transformations and to develop conceptual tools capable not only of recognizing but of theorizing new identities, interstitial public spaces, and deterritorialized cultures. The stakes of such concerns, moreover, are simultaneously intellectual, moral, and political: for many participants in these debates, there is an urgent need to summon any and all ethical practices and precedents capable of countering "dramatic nostalgia politics" unleashed by globalization, ranging from ethnic cleansing to revanchist nationalism to violent strands of religio-political fundamentalism (Nederveen Pieterse 1995, 62).

While poised to meet the multiple challenges of what appears to be an unprecedented level of contact and exchange among peoples and information, however, current "analyses of cosmopolitanism are themselves rarely cosmopolitan," simultaneously enacting and disavowing a provincialism that is at once historical and cultural (Pollock 2000, 596). To begin with, the parameters of the debate are decidedly "presentist," not only in the sense that those engaged in these debates are animated by a concern with the world as it currently is, but also in the ways localism and globalism, particular and universal, vernacular and cosmopolitan, are largely rendered coextensive with what happen to be their contemporary expressions. Discussions about the reach and limits of local and translocal attachments, for example, are almost entirely organized in terms of the nation-state, a distinctively modern invention, however "modernity" is defined.[6] Some participants in these debates seek to shore up the centrality of the nation-state and the "societal culture" it is said to demarcate; others aim to document or facilitate its decline (Kymlicka 1995, 76ff.). But in either case, politics, identities, allegiances, and communities under pressures conjured by the globalization of capital are invariably transnational, subnational, postnational, international, or multinational. Whether conceptualized as a way of being in the contemporary world, an array of moral obligations to those beyond our national borders, or a set of legal relationships among sovereign nations, cosmopolitanism in this way becomes a continual comment on the state of the nation-state. This is why, despite a variety of translocalisms and cosmopolitanisms of earlier epochs, one scholar would describe modernity, globalization, and cosmopolitanism as "concepts whose meanings and projects . . . largely overlap and coincide at the level of procedures and operational modes" (Diouf 2000, 679).

Yet the dynamics of fragmentation and unification, antagonism and mélange so closely associated with the whirl of contemporary life represent an extension, not a replacement, of the structural globalization of earlier epochs, those in part constituted by "long-distance cross-cultural trade, religious organizations and knowledge networks" (Nederveen Pieterse 1995, 46). The fluidity of identities and attachments now associated with the postcolonial world thus has a long history and is not merely the product of the spread of Western cultural and economic power throughout the globe. In a sense, then, "globalization is a very old story that is yet to be fully remembered" (Bamyeh 2004, 218; Reichmuth 1998, 37–38). This is not to deny that technological innovations in travel, communication, trade, and exchange have brought about mobilities and exposures

6. There are, of course, various accounts of the precise "origins" of the nation that presuppose different national ontologies. Here I rely on Benedict Anderson's account of nations as "imagined communities" initially consolidated in Europe by the emergence of print capitalism and the decline of belief in divine providence characteristic of a post-Enlightenment world, and often established elsewhere by colonial fiat (B. Anderson 1992).

that are most certainly new at least in terms of scope, scale, and speed.[7] Yet a longer view draws attention to historical precedents that, when they register at all in the current scholarship, largely serve as evidence for the radical break in space and time wrought by globalization.

Just a quick view across history reveals that collective experience "has been in motion all along and the fixities of nation, community, ethnicity, and class have been grids superimposed upon experiences" too complex and subtle to be accommodated therein (Nederveen Pieterse 1995, 64). While the ahistoricism characteristic of many analyses of cosmopolitanism might appear to be an expression of what Norbert Elias once called the social science "retreat into the present" (1987), the disciplines of political and social theory are unusually attentive to ideas of the past. In this case, such ahistoricism does not derive from a preoccupation with the present but rather from a somewhat Eurocentric genealogy in which the thread that begins with the Stoics, proceeds through the usual suspects such as Rousseau and Kant, and culminates in the work of scholars such as Nussbaum, Waldron, and others to become the history of cosmopolitanism tout court.[8]

The presentism of the current debate thus expresses and compounds a cultural provincialism that has several dimensions. First, it tends to be organized around an exclusively Western pantheon of figures and touchstones—or touchstones and figures rendered "Western" after the fact.[9] Second and relatedly, as Sheldon Pollock points out, the new cosmopolitanism debate largely proceeds within "European analytical and temporal frameworks. . . . [D]iscussion typically takes place on a highly localized

7. Some go so far as to argue that the current conditions have produced the "death of distance" (van der Veer 2001, 3).

8. It also erases the many fissures within this tradition. See, for example, U. Mehta 1999, 20–23; and Kleingeld 1999.

9. In this connection, it is instructive to recall that the West is a category of relatively recent provenance through which history and geography have been retroactively organized. The ancient Greeks, for example, understood themselves as geographically west of the barbarians but not Western in the contemporary sense. See, for example, Gillespie 1999, 7–10.

conceptual terrain and in a very vernacular idiom constituted by European culture" (Pollock 2000, 595–96). Such a vernacular idiom both expresses and reinforces the valorization of skepticism toward certain modes of belonging and knowing, particularly those that conjure the ghosts of a premodern European "dark ages" associated with religious superstition and ecclesiastical power. Both the presumptive value of skepticism and the allegiances said to be particularly suspect thus derive from a genealogy rooted in a specific culture and religious tradition.[10] So understood, the universalization of this skeptical stance as a way of being in the world particularly appropriate to our time entails a double move: it renders as a model to all a mode of self-understanding that emerged out of historically specific conditions and erases cosmopolitan precedents that transpire beyond the coordinates of Euro-American time and space.

Most advocates of the new cosmopolitanism seek to enact a stance of openness in their own work. Among other things, this means that they tend to ground openness to "diverse strivings" in a dialectic of local and attenuated attachments and generally avoid the claim that such ecumenicalism can or should be predicated on relinquishing all forms of belonging.[11] Yet cosmopolitanism, as it is currently articulated, privileges a particular form of belonging over others, one that enacts a stance of ironic distance toward one's own community and commitments. It does this often without taking serious account of the inequalities of power that make such a stance a luxury rarely enjoyed by those whose place and identity is historically marginal or continually in jeopardy. The crux of the problem here is not the celebration of openness to others per se, for this often (although not always) expresses the aspiration to extend to all humans qua humans a certain imaginative generosity it would be

10. Van der Veer (2001, 15) points out, for example, that nineteenth-century European cosmopolitanism was "always complemented by a Christian cosmopolitanism of both the Catholic and Protestant kind . . . Liberal cosmopolitanism and Evangelical cosmopolitanism developed side by side in the colonial era."

11. For arguments that do imply such relinquishment and strenuous claims to the contrary, see Martha Nussbaum (1996). For an adjudication between two positions often portrayed as antithetical, see Waldron 1995.

churlish to impugn and distasteful to disavow. The problem is, rather, that this celebration is rarely accompanied by close attention to how history, culture, and power inflect the very meaning and value of "openness" in ways that can render it politically suspect or untenable, even or especially to those whose mobility is extensive and encounters with what is unfamiliar are many.

"Western" Curiosity versus "Islamic" Insularity

Questions about the context and content of "openness," to what and to whom, become particularly salient whenever the topic turns to Islam and Muslims. For despite the fact that large numbers of Muslims live in Europe, that Islam is one of the fastest growing religions in the United States, and that there is a mutual cultural and intellectual debt between Europe and Islam dating back centuries, Islam is consistently associated with a world "over there," home of an explosive anti-Western rage, the front line of conflict in a post–Cold War world increasingly defined by a clash of civilizations between "the West and the Rest" (Mahbubani 1993; Huntington 1996). In the post–September 11 world in particular, the most ubiquitous image of Muslim travel is the mobile *mujahid* (one engaged in *jihad*) who moves from Saudi Arabia to Pakistan to Africa to the United States and back with terrifying speed and ease. Such an image sharpens the anxiety that when non-Westerners—and Muslims in particular—travel to unfamiliar cultures and places, it is less to learn about the world than to disrupt or destroy it.

The claim that Muslims are captured by a particularly insular and mythic worldview has a particularly long and distinguished pedigree (Renan 1883). In recent years, it has enjoyed a new prominence among policymakers, scholars, and journalists who regard the commitment to unfettered intellectual curiosity as a predominantly Western cultural trait.[12] Such claims can even be found in the work of experts on Muslim

12. The examples are too numerous to list, but it is perhaps worth noting here that ideologues and political pundits do not have the monopoly on such assumptions. They are

societies. A case in point is Bernard Lewis, whose arguments about Islam have found a particularly sympathetic audience among the architects of post–9/11 U.S. foreign policy. As first outlined in depth in *The Muslim Discovery of Europe* almost a quarter of a century ago, Lewis argues that Europeans sought to acquire knowledge of the languages, politics, culture, and economics of Muslim lands not only to fulfill the practical demands of commerce and diplomacy but also to "gratify the boundless intellectual curiosity unleashed by the Renaissance" (Lewis 1982, 80).[13] By contrast, Lewis repeatedly notes a lack of Muslim curiosity or desire for knowledge about languages, literatures, religions, or cultures beyond Islamic lands, a narrowness attributable to the Muslim world's "belief in its own self-sufficiency and superiority as the one repository of the true faith and—which for Muslims meant the same thing—of the civilized way of life" (1982, 280). It was only under duress that a Muslim world in the shadow of Western power began to show interest in matters European, Lewis contends, but then only for purely practical purposes. Thus it "was not until Renaissance and post-Renaissance Europe that a human society for the first time developed the sophistication, the detachment and, above all, the curiosity to study and appreciate the cultures of alien and even hostile societies" (1982, 75, 87).

Lewis here appears to equate curiosity about Europe with curiosity per se, yet his claims about Muslim parochialism past and present can be challenged on several different grounds.[14] At the point in history when

also evident in the work of well-respected scholars, from Jürgen Habermas's contention (1998, 162) that "[t]o gain distance from one's own traditions and broaden limited perspectives is the advantage of Occidental rationalism" to Richard Rorty's assertion (Rorty and Vattimo 2005, 72) that "the idea of dialogue with Islam is pointless."

13. Lewis reiterates versions of this thesis in many different places, including various essays in Lewis 2004.

14. Said, among others, has taken aim at Lewis's repeated insistence that "the western quest for knowledge about other societies is unique, that it is motivated by pure curiosity, and that in contrast Muslims neither were able nor interested in acquiring knowledge about Europe, as if knowledge about Europe was the only acceptable criterion for true knowledge" (Said 2000, 351).

European interest in Islamic cultures was particularly unrequited, for example, scholars point out that Muslims were, in fact, borrowing from China (Hodgson 1974, 2:362). Moreover, Lewis's argument that a sense of Muslim superiority prior to the nineteenth century meant that the "question of travel for study did not arise, since clearly there was nothing to be learnt from the benighted infidels of the outer wilderness" is belied by recent studies of Muslim travels and travel narratives (Lewis 2004, 132). Nabil Matar's work on sixteenth and seventeenth-century Arabic travel texts shows, for instance, that while travelers to non-Muslim lands often felt the need to "temper exhilaration with denunciation" for the consumption of Arab rulers, such strategic gestures often went hand in hand with a keen appreciation of non-Muslim societies and practices (Matar 2003, xxxvi).[15] Indeed, such texts reveal not only the largely unrecognized extent of Arab travel writing about Europe but also an intense curiosity about it on the part of the travelers themselves. These documents show Arab travelers eager to record, measure, and evaluate their observations about Europeans and quite able to differentiate among, rather than essentialize, the peoples of *bilad al-nasara* (lands of the Christians).[16] Ironically, given Lewis's claims, Matar suggests that it was often Christian antipathy to "Mahumetans" that deterred or constrained the mobility of Muslims who wished to travel to Europe, ranging from English seamen unwilling to transport "infidels" on their ships to the fear of violence regularly unleashed by Christians against Muslims (Matar 2003, xxv–xxviii).[17]

15. See also Matar 1999 and 2008.

16. Other scholarship further challenges Lewis's assertion that as "Islam was conceived as a single entity, it was natural to think of the House of War in the same terms. The subdivisions among the infidels, particularly those of them who lived beyond the Islamic frontier, were of no interest or significance" (1982, 202). A case in point: E. M. Sartain (1996) discerns in twelfth to fifteenth-century Muslim officialdom an understanding of Europe less as a coherent entity and more as a conglomeration of warring and culturally and linguistically distinct kingdoms.

17. This observation affirms anthropologist Mary Helms's argument that curiosity about cultural others, along with an emphasis on the intrinsic value of knowledge gleaned from travel to "geographically distant places," is common to a remarkably wide array of preindustrial cultural traditions and practices (1988). See also Subrahmanyam 1997, 737.

Further complicating Lewis's arguments, encounters with what is foreign have been accompanied as much by anxiety and ambivalence as by curiosity *within* Western traditions past and present.[18] But what is perhaps most striking in Lewis's argument is the almost offhand remark in which he draws a distinction between an "appetite for wonders and marvels" and genuine knowledge. Here the line between history-as-knowledge and fiction-as-fantasy is fixed and bright, a reiteration of the age-old epistemological distinction Cicero drew between history, which aims at truth, and poetry, the purpose of which is pleasure (Cicero 1928, 301). For Lewis, this epistemological distinction maps onto a civilizational divide between modern Islam and Christendom in particular.[19] Muslims gather factual information about the unfamiliar for purely instrumental purposes, but their curiosity is reserved for the realm of fantasy and imagination. By contrast, the pursuit of knowledge about others for its own sake—knowledge that is, to borrow from James Clifford, scientific and ennobling—is a distinctively European phenomenon (Clifford 1992, 105).[20]

A Cosmopolitan Ethos of *Talab al-ilm*

In contrast to such presumptions about a uniquely Western openness to and curiosity about what is unfamiliar, there is a fair amount of scholarship on non-Western cultural traditions demonstrating that a more capacious understanding of cosmopolitanism is long overdue. For example, Sheldon Pollock has drawn on his knowledge of South Asia to argue that cosmopolitanism should be understood as an "action rather than idea,

18. Nigel Leask shows that there are multiple valences to "curiosity" within the West, and travel in the name of curiosity occasioned a diversity of responses, not all of them celebratory (2004, 4, chap. 1).

19. Lewis does not attribute any inherent superiority to Europeans, yet he goes on to note that while Europe had "shared the general lack of curiosity concerning strange peoples," the combined impact of the discovery of the New World, the Renaissance, and the Reformation produced a spirit of "intellectual curiosity and scientific inquiry" in direct contrast to the Muslim world (1982, 300–301).

20. Clifford is being ironic in this description.

as something people do rather than something they declare, as practice rather than proposition (least of all, philosophical proposition)" (2000, 593). Such a shift in the conceptualization of cosmopolitanism from "professions of moral commitment" to particular practices that transpire under specific circumstances makes visible a variety of ways of being and moving in the world that are cosmopolitan without explicit justification or systematic articulation (Pollock 2000, 602). This shift, in turn, makes possible an inquiry into the presuppositions and political import of a variety of cosmopolitanisms that can—and in many ways already do—serve as resources for the reworking of contemporary social imaginaries.[21]

As "religious communities are among the oldest of the transnationals" (Rudolph and Piscatori 1997, 1), the networked nature of Muslim travel throughout history reveals a particularly rich set of precedents and normative resources for contemporary cosmopolitan imaginaries. Indeed, recent scholarship on Arab and Muslim travel amply demonstrates that the association of curiosity, travel, and knowledge is particularly prevalent in both Muslim doctrinal sources and historical practice.[22] The religious imprimatur for such travel is grounded, in part, in the now legendary peregrinations punctuating the highly contested life of the Prophet Muhammad, from his nocturnal journey *(isra')* to Jerusalem in the company of the angel Gabriel to the *hijrah,* the migration from Mecca to Medina that inaugurates the Islamic calendar. In a general sense, as historian Franz Rosenthal (1997, 54) points out, the "ancient use of travel as a metaphor to describe man's sojourn on earth was widely accepted in Islam" and is

21. Here I draw upon Charles Taylor's definition of social imaginaries as the "ways people imagine their social existence, how they fit together with others, how things go on between them and their fellows, the expectations that are normally met, and the deeper normative notions and images that underlie these expectations" (Taylor 2004, 23).

22. In addition to Matar's work, see, for example, Euben 2006; the work of Abdenbi Daker as well as Eickelman and Piscatori 1990; Miquel 1967; Chejne 1962; el-Moudden 1995; Hammam 2003; Qadduri 1995; Netton 1993; Subrahmanyam 1997; Tavakoli-Targhi 1998 and 2001; the series on Muslim and Arab voyagers called *Irtiyad al-Afaq,* jointly published by Dar al-Suwaydi lil-Nashr wa-al-tawzi and Al-Mu'assasah al-Arabiyah lil-Dirasat wa al-Nashr 2009; and al-Ghashi 2003.

evident in several Qur'anic verses, including one that states that "Allah's is the Sovereignty of the heavens and the earth and all that is between them, and unto Him is the journeying *(masir)*."[23] Some Sufi mystics would even transform the metaphorical rendering of life as a journey into an embrace of perpetual homelessness, an exhortation to live as a stranger through constant travel (F. Rosenthal 1997, 42, 54, 58).[24]

The specific association between travel and knowledge is evident in several Qur'anic verses that exhort readers to "travel on the earth and see" both how the end comes to the unjust and "how He originated creation."[25] As Qur'an 22:46 asks, "Have they not traveled in the land that they could have the heart to understand, and ears to hear?" The hadith literature, the reports of the words and deeds of the Prophet, elaborates on this Qur'anic thread. Al-Suyuti (d. 1505) relates a now famous narrative in which Muhammad is said to have exhorted his followers to seek knowledge as far as China (al-Suyuti 1979–81, vol. 1, 3207, 3208, 618). Several hadiths link travel to God's pleasure, including three related by al-Tirmidhi (d. 892), one in which the Prophet characterized the search for knowledge as expiation for past deeds and two others in which Muhammad reportedly said that "those who go out in search of knowledge will be in the path of God until they return" and "wisdom is the lost property of a believer, it is his, wherever he may find it" (al-Tirmidhi 1965, vol. 4, 2:2785, 137; 2:2786, 138). Yet another hadith related by Ibn Majah (d. 886) states, "God makes the path to paradise easy for him who travels a road in search of knowledge, and the angels spread their wings for the pleasure of the seeker of knowledge. All those in heaven and earth will seek forgiveness from those who pursue knowledge, even the serpents in the water. The learned person is superior to the worshipper just as the moon has precedence over the rest of the stars" (Ibn Majah 1972, vol. 1, hadith no. 223, 81).

23. Qur'an 5:18. See also Q.2:156; 50:43; 42:53 (Pickthall 2000).

24. See, for example, Ibish 1977. For the particular significance of networks of Sufi *turuq* to the practice of travel and the emergence of Muslim interregional unity in the wake of the Abbasid caliphate, see Voll 1994, 221–22. See also Reichmuth 1998.

25. Qur'an 3:137; 6:11; 12:109; 16:36; 29:20; 30:9; 30:42; and 29:20 (Ali 1984).

The knowledge *(ilm)* here is unquestionably religious, but a hard and fast distinction between secular and religious knowledge misses the scope of ilm.[26] Within the terms of Islam, all things in the world are themselves aspects of divine creation, and thus all human knowledge—whether of things divine or purely mundane—ultimately derives from God (F. Rosenthal 1970, 28–32).[27] The scope of what humans can know is, of course, clearly delimited by the Qur'an, which repeatedly invokes God's omniscience and cautions believers to remember that "God knows, but/and you do not know" (3:66). Yet when joined to the exhortation to travel and learn, the invocation of God's omniscience serves not to arrest human inquiry but to insist upon its limits; it prescribes humility rather than ignorance.[28] The insistence that only God knows the secrets of the universe presupposes the finitude of human understanding and suggests, much as Socrates had argued, that specifically human wisdom lies not only in what one knows but also in recognizing what one does not know.

Both the translation of *ilm* as knowledge broadly understood and the connection between learning and mobility are suggested by the very etymological commonality between ilm (knowledge) and *ma'lam* (road sign), both derived from the same Arabic root *(ayn-lam-mim).*[29] Such connections and connotations are reflected in historical practice. As one scholar

26. Even among Euro-American political theorists, the divide between the religious and the secular is increasingly permeable, from William Connolly's *Why I Am Not a Secularist* (1999) to the rediscovery of Walter Benjamin's interest in the Kabbalah to the Old Testament sources of Emmanuel Levinas's work.

27. Rosenthal (1970, 2) goes as far as arguing that "there is no other concept that has been operative as a determinant of Muslim civilization in all its aspects to the same extent as *ilm,*" which is "something of supreme value for Muslim being."

28. As Carlo Ginzburg (1976, 28–30) shows, there was a similar tendency to read the Pauline warning against moral arrogance in his Epistle to the Romans (xi. 20) as a condemnation of intellectual curiosity.

29. *Encyclopedia of Islam,* CD-ROM ed., vol. 1.0 (Leiden: Brill, 1999), "*ilm.*" According to Rosenthal (1970, 10), the etymological connection is rooted in pre-Islamic Arabia, where such signposts were "characteristic marks in the desert, which guided [the Bedouin] on his travels and in the execution of his daily tasks" and thus constituted "the kind of knowledge on which his life and well-being principally depended."

of the *rihlah* (trip or book of travels) in Andalusia demonstrates, Muslim travelers were concerned with secular and religious disciplines alike: "far from being restricted to the search and study of Tradition . . . [the rihlah] was a many-sided intellectual endeavor, true 'Wanderjahre' spent with the best scholars in various parts of [the] Islamic world." As a motive for travel, then, talab al-ilm "surpassed in significance all other incentives including the pilgrimage itself . . . [T]he seeking of knowledge is a lifetime mission rather than a short term goal motivated by practicality" (Lenker 1982, 189, 194–95, 224).[30]

The scope of ilm in the exhortations to travel in search of knowledge is further expressed in the many formal categories of Muslim travel, any one of which may entail both physical movement and spiritual transformation: the hajj (pilgrimage to Mecca, one of the pillars of Islam), *hijrah* (emigration, modeled on the Prophetic journey), *rihlah,* and *ziyarah* (visits to shrines). These categories encompass many kinds of Islam, from what is often called orthodox to mystical, popular to elite; thus a single journey may well incorporate all four of these purposes and traverse different religious expressions. This mobility suggests, of course, that such carefully differentiated terms can never fully capture the varieties of historical experience, for "the practice and significance of Islamic faith in any given historical setting cannot readily be predicted from first principles of dogma or belief" (Eickelman and Piscatori 1990, 18). Like any other people, Muslims have traveled for a wide array of reasons, including job-seeking, trade, diplomatic missions for sultans, desire for status, or just plain curiosity, and wanderers throughout the *Dar al-Islam* have included beggars, slaves, soldiers, crooks, and entertainers, as well as pilgrims, merchants, students, poets, and fortune hunters.

Yet it is also the case that the plural purposes of Muslim travel can be usefully understood in terms of a vast web of transnational networks

30. Lenker's study is particularly useful in challenging Ignaz Goldziher's restriction of ilm to the study of hadith and sunna (Goldziher 1971, 2:164–80). Goldziher himself (1971, 178–79) seems to recognize the wider scope of ilm when he notes that an *ijazah* (authorization or license) was often given no matter "whether the book concerned belonged to the class of religious or profane literature."

whose content and reach have been established through "trade, language, Sufism and scholarship but above all . . . common moral ideals and social codes" that at once facilitate and are themselves reshaped by mobility (Cooke and Lawrence 2005, 5). Such common codes and norms range from the religious imprimatur for travel in search of knowledge to the Islamic exhortation to extend protection *(ijarah)* and hospitality to strangers and travelers, an exhortation captured in a hadith stating that "Islam began as a stranger and it will return as it began, [as] a stranger. Blessed are the strangers" (Wahidi and al-Farmawi 1994, 1:253; Watt 1999).[31] As Miriam Cooke and Bruce Lawrence (2005, 1–28) argue, Muslim networks can be understood simultaneously as a medium of travel, a method for analyzing the constant refiguring of the transnational umma, and a metaphor for the fluidity, contingency, and variety of exchange among Muslims across time and space, from traffic along fourteenth-century trade routes to cybernauts engaged in virtual hajj.[32]

Understood in these terms, Muslim networks are particularly evident in the mobility of those, such as Ibn Battuta, whose fourteenth-century travels proceed along well-established routes of trade, study, and pilgrimage. Ibn Battuta's voyages were punctuated by the many brotherhoods *(turuq)*, associations, and hospices *(manazil)* dedicated to extending travelers hospitality, and his emergence as a *qadi* (Muslim judge) initiated him into a "shared and longstanding language of discourse and meaning, of shared ideas about what constituted valuable knowledge and how such knowledge was articulated, preserved, transmitted" (Zaman 2003, 84). Yet the networked nature of Muslim mobility extends well beyond such

31. Indeed, drawing on the sunna, Qadi al-Nu'man (d. 974) distinguishes between two kinds of etiquette *(muru'ah)*, one that governs "settled habitation," the other that governs travel. The latter consists of "generosity in spending provisions, abstaining from discord with fellow travellers and transmitting reports from them" when they part ways (Nu'man ibn Muhammad 2002, 1:431–32). I am grateful to Ali Aslam for bringing this to my attention.

32. For the usefulness of a "network model" of Islamic societies, see Lapidus 1975; Allievi and Nielsen 2003; Levtzion and Weigert 1998; Voll 1994; and Reichmuth 1998 and 2004.

established routes and purposes to "privilege travel of all kinds to many places," as is evident in the nineteenth-century voyage of Rifa'ah Rafi' al-Tahtawi to Paris in search of knowledge abroad (al-Tahtawi 1834; Cooke and Lawrence 2005, 3; Euben 2006).

Viewed through the prism of Muslim networks as medium, method, and metaphor then, travel in pursuit of knowledge may be said to constitute a central component of mainstream and popular Islam past and present. Talab al-ilm is thus best characterized as an ethos, an ethical practice more ordinary and elastic than a doctrine, yet more continuous and systematically articulated than either a recurrent theme or an occasional activity of Muslims. Sanctioned by divine exhortations, tied to the promise of *barakah* ("blessings" but also charisma), and nourished by a complex and cosmopolitan civilization "which in the fullest sense owed its vibrancy to constant movement" (Gellens 1990, 51),[33] this ethos captures the ways in which the exhortation to seek knowledge informs Muslim social imaginaries even as it is, in turn, reshaped by contemporary Muslim travel within, along, and beyond the borders of the umma.[34]

What I am calling an Islamic ethos of travel in search of knowledge does not presuppose an essential "Islam" constituted by fixed and self-evident truths located in texts insulated from power, history, and human interests—a presumption shared, paradoxically, by many Orientalist and Islamist narratives. There is no doubt that a singular Islam captures and organizes the subjectivities of millions who self-identify as Muslim (among other things). Yet much like "the West," what travels under the rubric of Islam is inescapably diverse, multiethnic, and defined as much by disagreement as by consensus. Just as the Torah and the Bible lend

33. *Barakah* is a complex term with multiple valences that are beyond the focus of this chapter. In connection with Ibn Battuta, Charles Beckingham (1977, 267) describes it as "the blessings both in this world and the next which would come from visiting holy places and obtaining the blessings of saintly men."

34. Importantly, as Eickelman and Piscatori (1990, xvii, 5) note, "Muslims share more explicit doctrinal tenets enjoining movement than do the followers of other major religious traditions . . . [but] such phenomena need not be seen as unique to the Muslim world in order for their significance to be affirmed."

themselves to at times radically divergent interpretations of what it means to be Jewish or Christian, the Qur'an and hadith are complex and indeterminate, susceptible to even contradictory enactments. In this light, Islam is less a fixed essence than a living tradition that captures what is imagined as continuous and unitary in dialectical relationship to those concrete articulations and practices by which it is transformed and adapted in different contexts for plural purposes.

So understood, this elaboration of an Islamic ethos in search of knowledge does not depend upon establishing, for example, the authenticity of the hadith encouraging travel "as far as China." Nor does it presume, in the absence of such evidence, that such an ethos nevertheless expresses "the true Islam." In fact, my arguments here are a deliberate attempt to shift the focus from unresolvable questions about what Islam "really" is to an investigation of how and under what conditions particular narratives and practices reflect and sustain such an ethos; this approach, in turn, enables an inquiry into the actual or potential relationship between Islam and cosmopolitanism.

Toward this end, I want to suggest that an Islamic ethos in search of knowledge expresses a particularly rich countergenealogy of cosmopolitanism to the one that currently prevails, one woven from a variety of doctrinal sources and historical practices. The threads of this genealogy include the array of exhortations to Muslims to seek wisdom wherever it resides. It also includes the emphasis on the moral significance of the diversity of mankind in the Qur'an exemplified in verse 5:48–49: "To each of you We have given a law and a way and a pattern of life. If God had pleased He could surely have made you one people (professing one faith). But He wished to try and test you by that which He has given each of you. So try to excel in good deeds. To Him will you all return in the end; it is He that will show you the truth of the matters in which you dispute."[35] This emphasis is echoed in the hadith in which Muhammad was said to

35. Also Qur'an 49:13: "We created you from a male and female and formed you into nations and tribes that you may recognize each other. Verily, the most honored of you in the sight of God is he who is the most righteous."

have characterized difference of opinion *(ikhtilaf)* within the umma (community) as a source of mercy *(rahmah)* (al-Jarrahi 1979, 1:66–68).[36] Along with the humility commanded by the reminder that "God knows, but/and you do not know," such sources encourage what Sohail Hashmi calls a "maximalist ethic of tolerance," one that not only entails respect for plural perspectives but also a willingness to engage with them (Hashmi 2003, 82).[37] Hashmi further argues that, in the context of an integrated reading of the Qur'an as a whole, verse 5:48 in particular encourages Muslims to see in such plurality both God's creative hand and His inscrutable design:

> Though each community advances along its own path toward a common goal, it is not the goal but the journey that is the real focus of this verse. The journey is the test, and this test is not only of conflict among rival and competing faiths struggling for hegemony. Nor is it a religious cold war, a journey of the deaf and mute. In this verse, the Qur'an affirms that the problem of religious and moral diversity is not a hindrance to be overcome, but an advantage to be embraced—a necessary facet of God's unknown plan for humanity. The journey can be meaningful only if there are a number of travellers, for just as human beings urge each other toward evil, so human beings urge each other toward the good. (Hashmi 2003, 100–101)

Such doctrinal sources inform and are themselves reinterpreted in and through a variety of practices, moments, and ideas that punctuate the history of Muslim societies and continually shape collective memory. A countergenealogy of cosmopolitanism might thus include, for instance, the cosmopolitan context of the Abbasid Dynasty in which Islamic law

36. Joseph Schacht traces this expression to Abu Hanifa and argues that it was attributed to the Prophet only later. "Ikhtilaf." J. Schacht, *Encyclopaedia of Islam*, CD-ROM ed., vol. 1.0 (Leiden: Brill, 1999). For a discussion of *ikhtilaf* and counterveiling impulses toward consensus, unity, and uniformity among Muslim scholars, see Abou el Fadl 2001, esp. 24–25.

37. This, of course, entails an interpretation of the Qur'an at odds with what Hashmi calls the prevailing "master narrative" rooted in a primarily chronological reading of the revelations.

can itself be understood as a response to a fluid, syncretic milieu; the specific cultural, linguistic, and religious mélange of Umayyad Andalusia; the interconnectivity of the transhemispheric oikoumene of the Islamic Middle Periods; and the interchange among the multiethnic Ottoman, Safavid, and Mughal empires (Gallois 2005, 59–109; F. Robinson 1997, 151–84). It would also encompass the work of those Hellenized Muslim philosophers insistent that the Qur'an itself is a spur to philosophical reflection, the interest in and preservation of aspects of Stoic cosmopolitanism in Middle Period Arabo-Muslim thought, and the emergence and dissemination of particularly ecumenical interpretations of Sufi theosophy. Finally, such a genealogy would attend to the ecumenical possibilities of practices ranging from an intensely cosmopolitan hajj past and present to a virtual umma at once enacted and refigured electronically by Muslims around the world (Levtzion and Weigert 1998; Reichmuth 1998, 21ff.; Zubaida 1999, 19; Averroës 2001, 2; Bianchi 2004; Gallois 2005).[38]

I deliberately use the term "genealogy" here, for all genealogies are by definition selective and contingent rather than exhaustive or inevitable.[39] These eclectic precedents do not, for example, erase the bloodshed that often accompanied the expansionist ambitions of various Muslim states throughout history any more than the new cosmopolitanism can efface the marks of violence from the rise and fall of Western empires and nation-states. Even now, the potential of the Internet to mobilize virtual communities of Muslims in the struggle against radical Islamist violence is continually offset by transnational cyber-networks committed to deeply xenophobic versions of political Islam. What this genealogy does do is

38. See also Hassan M. Fattah, "Islamic Pilgrims Bring Cosmopolitan Air to Unlikely City," *New York Times*, Jan. 20, 2005, A4. Rosenthal (1990, 3:473n1) points out the popularity of Diogenes in particular at the time, as well the "disproportionate amount of space" devoted to the Epicureans, Sceptics, and Cynics in the introductions to Arabic translations of Aristotle. For an extensive treatment of this subject, see Gutas 2000, 475–518. There is a burgeoning literature on "digital Islam"; see, for example, Karim 2002 and Mandaville 2002; Bunt 2003 and 2005; J. Anderson 2005; and Shichor 2003.

39. Here I rely upon the understanding of genealogy as articulated by Foucault and Nietzsche. See, for example, Foucault 1977.

foreground a cosmopolitan social imaginary perhaps best captured by the image of crisscrossing networks of mobile Muslims with multiple nodes serving plural purposes. Such an image is quite different from that, for example, of empire, whether defined in terms of the domination of the periphery by the center or as a deterritorialized, impersonal, and homogenizing world market (Hardt and Negri 2000).

The threads of this genealogy thus sustain the image of an umma in which extensive Muslim social networks largely flourished independently of territorially based state power, where institutions of the state constituted but one of "the dense knots where many network lines crossed" (Lapidus 1975, 34, 40). This is an umma whose preeminence in the Middle Periods was secured less by the systematic consolidation of political power than by the extensive social and cultural mobility of Muslims bearing a moral code at once fixed and flexible enough to apply "wherever Muslims were to be found in sufficient numbers, being dependent upon no territorial establishment nor even on any official continuity of personnel, but only on the presence, among Muslims committed to it, of someone at least minimally versed in it to see to its application" (Hodgson 1974, 2:349). Here is a "global civil society" before the age of globalization, one constituted in part by a principle of free movement that simultaneously confounded state aspirations to total control and conferred legitimacy upon those empires willing and able to safeguard routes of trade and pilgrimage (Bamyeh 2004, 220–22).[40] And here is an organizing image of "networks" that actually corresponds to the "conceptual world of Islamic culture . . . [where] society is an ever living, never completed network of actions" (Lapidus 1975, 40–41).

The Politics of Cosmopolitanism

These are just a few threads of one possible genealogy of cosmopolitanism counter to the one that currently prevails; one might "begin" earlier, later,

40. Richard Bulliet (1989, 147) similarly suggests that a "standard indicator of the strength and prosperity of an Islamic state is the remark that the routes were so secure that travelers could move wherever they wished without molestation. . . . [u]nhindered travel appears to have been a goal of medieval Islamic government."

or elsewhere.[41] Yet wherever one begins, such historical precedents are not merely matters of antiquarian interest, reducible to the plaint that "there are Muslim cosmopolitanisms too." These touchstones and precedents are the terms in which the umma has been and continues to be reimagined as a moral, political, and even virtual oikoumene, a cultural imaginary undimmed and in some ways even intensified (albeit in complex ways) by the advance of European colonialism, the rise of the nation-state, and now the march of globalization.[42] Such an imaginary informs a range of current practices and discourses, from transnational Sufi networks to those virtual communities constituted by Muslims from all over the world engaging in interpretive debates on-line *(e-ijtihad)* (Masud 1990; Werbner 1999; Mandaville 2002; Bunt 2005).

What is at stake in recuperating such countergenealogies is the very possibility of recognizing a more capacious cosmopolitanism, one that makes room for ecumenical practices and exhortations to engagement derived from cultural imaginaries located beyond the unnecessarily narrow temporal and analytic parameters of the current debate. Such recognition challenges the ways in which ecumenicalism is often implicitly understood in terms of openness to the West by foregrounding how Muslim cosmopolitanism is continually defined and reworked by way of *intracultural* encounters across time and space. A case in point is the fourteenth-century *Dar al-Islam* of Ibn Battuta, whose travels reveal what historians characterize as a transhemispheric Afro-Eurasian civilization

41. In his macrohistory of the dynamic of cosmopolitanism and vernacularism in South Asia, for example, Sheldon Pollock (2000) traces another countergenealogy, and there are others still. See also Holton 2002.

42. David Gilmartin, for example, argues that this gap between state power and a moral community "defined by networks and cutting across political systems and political boundaries" became more rather than less marked with the advance of European colonialism and the rise of the nation-state, but in complex and distinctive ways (Gilmartin 2005, 54). In a similar vein, Paul Lubeck (1999) delineates a correlation between globalization and the strength of transnational Islamic movements. Research on Muslim transnationalism in Europe is particularly revealing in this regard. See, for example, the special issue "Islam, Transnationalism and the Public Sphere in Western Europe," *Journal of Ethnic and Migration Studies* 30(5) (2004).

in almost continuous intercommunication by way of an extraordinary fluidity of people and knowledge across political, cultural, and linguistic boundaries. This was a time in which the religious community was almost completely liberated from dependence on any territorial state, a development rooted in the mercantile, metropolitan, and cosmopolitan tendencies of an "Islamicate culture" in the process of expanding to become an "intercivilizational entity" encompassing both urban-based and pastoral nomadic communities (Voll 1994, 217).[43] In this context, cross-pollination was not solely the product of Muslim/non-Muslim exchange but also of literal and imaginative interaction among Muslims located in different cultural milieus, encounters that at various moments articulated and occasioned a reworking of racial, religious, and geographic frontiers.

Such an intracultural dynamic is also evident at later moments in Islamic history. Concentrating on the period up to the nineteenth century, for example, Francis Robinson (1997) points to the cosmopolitanism of a Sunni world in part constituted by itinerant scholars, individuals, and families whose mobility not only forged channels of interconnection but produced in communal institutions a shared body of knowledge across the Ottoman, Safavid, and Mughal empires. Here, then, is another instance in which a continuous Islamic cosmopolitan imaginary is at once enacted and reworked by Muslims committed implicitly or explicitly to "the initial creative events and to the succeeding dialogue" about both the meaning of those events and methods reworking them (Hodgson 1974, 2:336).

Taken together, these moments are particularly instructive points of comparison to what some are calling this current, "postnational" epoch. This is because they disclose ways of being, acting, and encountering others in a deterritorialized world in which engagement with others flows from deeply held local attachments and sodalities that travel and are themselves reworked by mobility, rather than requiring or producing a stance of ironic distance from too much—or the wrong kind of—belonging. As Mohammed Bamyeh aptly puts it, here cosmopolitanism is "not a product of induction from the comforts of a sedentary hiding place but an

43. The term "Islamicate Culture" is Hodgson's; see Hodgson 1974, 349–50.

outcome of conducting one's life on a route to a number of destinations" (2000, 103).

These instances also suggest that the channels of such mobility, the paths by which such attachments are reworked, and the knowledge such itinerants carry, acquire, and rearticulate by way of human exchange are intimately related to the experience of cultural power or its perceived loss. In this connection, it is instructive to consider Tarif Khalidi's argument that an early confidence in the providential significance of the Islamic umma "gave medieval Muslim civilization an unparalleled capacity to learn from other cultures, an open and oft-expressed willingness to acknowledge its cultural debt to Indians, Persians, and Greeks" at odds with the current tendency to read all of Islamic history through the juridical distinction between *Dar al-Islam* (Abode of Islam) and *Dar al-Harb* (Abode of War) (Khalidi 1995, 35–36). Here a willingness to learn actively from, rather than merely coexist with, diverse cultural formations is derived from a cultural confidence in Islam as "the final heir of the world's cultures" (Khalidi 1995, 35) rather than from, for example, a Lockean principle of toleration.

The connection between knowledge and ascendant large-scale cultural imaginaries is further illustrated by Robinson's analysis of how shifts in the political power of Muslim empires contributed to the wax and wane of ecumenical forms of knowledge. In his study of knowledge in the Ottoman, Safavid, and Mughal empires, Robinson tracks the balance among the rational sciences (logic, philosophy, mathematics, many derived from ancient Greece), those "transmitted subjects" concerned with authenticating and interpreting the meaning and implications of the sacred texts, and, finally, the resources for esoteric understanding (for example, mysticism). Robinson is careful not to overstate his conclusions and notes that "great scholarly traditions might have a life of their own regardless of the political context" (1997, 173). Yet he persuasively argues that when "Muslims were confidently in power" during the growth and consolidation of these empires, a Sufism conducive to discerning divinity even among non-Muslims flourished. Under these circumstances, the rational subjects also flourished and, in turn, often served as a bulwark against a congealing orthodoxy grounded in the transmitted subjects (Robinson 1997, 163, 172).

By contrast, when Muslim power and ascendance were felt to be in jeopardy, either from within or without, these moments coincided with the suppression of these ecumenical knowledges in favor of renewed emphasis on transmitted subjects seen as conducive to "socio-moral reconstruction" (Robinson 1997, 172).

It is well established that empires and states at the height of power—Roman, Christian, and Muslim alike—frequently demonstrated an insular refusal to tolerate "diverse strivings" beyond or within their borders, at times inventing a sense of crisis for political purposes, just as in contemporary American politics the religious right has repeatedly mobilized followers with the specter of a Christianity imperiled from all directions.[44] Yet the extent to which propensities toward ecumenicalism reflect and are reshaped by shifts in cultural confidence depends upon the *experience* of loss or threat, regardless of whether this sense can be corroborated or measured by empirical indices. The connection I am suggesting between ecumenicalism and power is thus speculative rather than causal, culturally and historically contingent rather than predictable.

Yet even such tentative connections can help illuminate a geopolitical landscape in which the legacy of specific historical asymmetries and current global inequalities continually reproduce a sense of Muslim powerlessness relative to the West. Indeed, a radical disparity in awareness of the Other is itself a symptom of such global inequalities: while those who live in postcolonial societies have long contended with the universalization of "Occidental" culture, it is only recently and as a result of acts of horrific

44. There is, moreover, a crucial difference between the ebb and flow of ecumenical *attitudes* on the one hand and, on the other, cosmopolitan *practices* that persist in spite of, and in some cases because of, shifts in political and cultural power. As Sami Zubaida (1999, 21) points out, for example, particular aspects of the rise of European power and dominance in the nineteenth century actually produced rather than inhibited "the formation of social milieus and personalities which may be identified as cosmopolitan" in Ottoman societies. Indeed, even in the current climate of what some characterize as neoimperialist globalization, cosmopolitan practices—virtual and physical—proliferate like wildfire under the radar or beyond the coercive control of embattled Middle Eastern regimes.

violence that grievances rooted in poorly understood historical narratives of marginalization and persecution have come to press upon European and American political consciousness in unprecedented ways. It is precisely these narratives that help determine how the inexorable forces of globalization are experienced by those on "the periphery"; constrain the terms in which questions about openness can be asked and answered; and inflect how purportedly ecumenical calls for a "cosmopolitan sensibility" are received by those for whom hybridization looks more like a cultural invasion than a proliferation of restaurant options.

Coca-Cola–ization?

In an article in *Al-Ahram,* Egyptian journalist Fahmi Huwaydi argued that Coca-Cola is only the most visible sign of a much more corrosive phenomenon: "Is the goal Coca-Cola–ization of the world, such that Coca-Cola becomes the pre-eminent drink among human beings, leading the roster [of what is] imposed on everyone, from hamburgers to jeans and the songs of Madonna and Michael Jackson? In other words, is this the meaning of globalization: that Western taste and its [entire] way of life be imposed on the world?!" (Huwaydi 1995). Huwaydi's view is echoed by many for whom, as Sami Zubaida (1999, 15–16) puts it, the connotation of cosmopolitanism is "not the fact of multi-cultural coexistence, but the development of ways of living and thinking, styles of life which are deracinated from communities and cultures of origin, from conventional living, from family and home-centredness, and have developed into a culturally promiscuous life, drawing on diverse ideas, traditions and innovations." The very language of "deracination" and "promiscuity" already suggests a view of cosmopolitanism and its multiple attachments less as an ecumenical way of being in the world than, in Jeremy Waldron's words, "a shallow and inauthentic way of living . . . [an embodiment of] all the worst aspects of classic liberalism—atomism, abstraction, alienation from one's roots, vacuity of commitment, indeterminacy of character, and ambivalence toward the good" (1995, 102).

In the contemporary political climate, such objections and perspectives are easily assimilated into an ongoing narrative about an essential

Muslim insularity and reflexive xenophobia. This brief discussion of Muslim cosmopolitanism points to a different conclusion. It suggests that whether cosmopolitanism denotes imaginative generosity or inauthentic deracination depends less on the religion to which one belongs than on the range of available narrative scripts produced by the dialectical interplay between a discursive religious tradition (Asad 1986) conducive to diverse enactments and specific historical, political, and economic relations of power. In the post–September 11 world in particular, coerced and inescapable hybridization from the "outside" conjures new emphases on authenticities and purities that never were. Such emphases render the costs of publicly advocating openness to aspects of Western culture in particular increasingly high—where costs are measured not in hard currency but in lost livelihoods and lives. This condition grants an outsized voice to those who seek to erase the ecumenical practices and precedents constitutive of Muslim cosmopolitanism in favor of an ahistorical "authentic" Islamic umma vigorously demarcated and vigilantly policed by highly mobile *mujahidin* moving with ease across and within communal borders.

Even attempts to reconcile the counterveiling pressures of global engagement and communal closure reveal how thoroughly anxieties about cultural corrosion have set the terms of the debate. Just as some Euro-American scholars argue that "the only way to be universal now is to be national," for example, there are many Muslim thinkers for whom reclamation of certain kinds of Islamic authenticity is "not only a prerequisite for self-development, but also a precondition for dealing with the West on an equal footing . . . [T]rue contact can only be attained through authenticity" (Pollock 2000, 622). Taken together, these arguments suggest how and why the path to, and course of, reflective dialogue so dear to proponents of the new cosmopolitanism are ragged and contingent rather than linear and inevitable (P. Mehta 2000, 631, 632). They further confirm what ought to be by now self-evident: the causes and consequences of intensifying contact among different peoples are irreducibly unpredictable, a complex and mercurial interaction of the personal, political, cultural, historical, and institutional more suggestive of loose patterns than of scientific paradigms capable of predicting which journeys and conditions will produce a critically reflective or tolerant "attitude."

The previous discussion brings one pattern into particularly stark relief, however: the extent to which ecumenical forms of knowledge reflect radical shifts in the relative confidence of large-scale social imaginaries. Such a pattern underscores the intangible yet powerful ways contemporary inequalities between and within regions and nations compound the legacy of historical asymmetries to continually frame and constrain the possibility of deriving "sympathetic imagination" from diverse experiences of displacement. Given these conditions, the very future of "reflective dialogue" requires attending to the complex nexus of power, history, and culture that differentially constrains potential participants to any "cosmopolitan conversation," and establishes the grammar in terms of which such engagement at least initially proceeds. It also requires critical reflection on exclusions at once enacted and concealed by the current parameters of the cosmopolitan debate.

Such reflection, in turn, makes possible a more capacious cosmopolitanism. It does so, in part, by bringing into view ecumenical practices and exhortations to engagement derived from many cultural imaginaries—whether it is the revitalized Stoicism of Martha Nussbaum; the insistence by Tariq Ramadan that European Muslims inhabit not *Dar al-Harb* [Abode of War] but rather *Dar al-Shahadah* (Abode of Testimony), a "space of responsibility" requiring "permanent involvement and an infinite self-sacrifice for social justice, the welfare of mankind, the environment . . . good and equity through *human brotherhood*"; or the argument by Hasan al-Turabi that global engagement and partnership between Muslims and non-Muslims is a duty not only sanctioned by Allah but presaged by a long Islamic history of "intercivilizational dialogue" (Nussbaum and Cohen 1996; Ramadan 1999, 149–50, emphasis in the original; Sadiki 2004, 362). The actual or potential commensurability of such understandings of ecumenicalism and the conceptions of moral obligations said to flow from them cannot be determined a priori, just as questions about to what and to whom, precisely, we must be open or obligated cannot be specified in the abstract. Ultimately, these are inescapably *political* questions, the answers to which can only be elaborated through sustained political engagement.

13

God's Caravan

Topoi and Schemata in the History of Muslim Political Thought

AZIZ AL-AZMEH

IT IS LITTLE SURPRISING that conceptions of power and political thought elaborated in the course of Muslim histories, in modern times no less than in the classical and medieval periods, are fields of study that have continued to attract attention in recent years in this field of scholarship, which had rarely entertained the idea of a world disenchanted.[1] Yet these conceptions have not been generally well served by scholarship except within the rather narrow constraints of political history and of the dogmatic history of Muslim sects and insofar as a small number of individual thinkers have been the objects of particular interest. Basic research and monographic studies in this field have generally been rather sparse and, partly as a consequence, systematic and synthetic studies—as opposed to summary statements—have been few and far between. Such studies as are available have, moreover, generally been incomplete, often appearing

An earlier version of part of this chapter appeared in my collection of essays *The Times of History: Universal Topics in Islamic Historiography,* published in 2007 by Central European University Press, and reprinted here with permission.

1. I am most grateful to a number of friends and colleagues who have read and commented upon an earlier version of this chapter: Saïd Arjomand, Nadia al-Bagdadi, János Bak, Yehuda Elkana, Garth Fowden, Wael Hallaq, Almut Hoefert, Janet Nelson, David Powers, Walid Saleh, and Hayden White.

to drift toward formulations and inflections that tend to reconfirm unreflected and untested general assumptions and presumptions held by the general public about the course of Islamic history.

It is therefore to be welcomed that two general and systematic studies in English, by Anthony Black and Patricia Crone, have appeared in print.[2] They provide the opportunity to consider and assess the state of the field in the study of the history of Islamic political conceptions and to consider what progress might have been made since the appearance almost forty years ago of a book also intended as a teaching manual, by the veteran scholar William Montgomery Watt (2003), and what avenues of research might be thereby opened or foreclosed.

Correlatively, the discussion to follow will attempt to clarify issues, attempt to set and reset research questions, and help to define or redefine the field of Islamic political thought. It will describe, first of all, some generative historiographic parameters—narrative, conceptual, institutional, and public—that act as a grid for the study of Islamic political thought. These parameters yield thematic elements that are regarded to be of central relevance, and exclude others, thereby orienting the perspectives adopted in the two books, which are taken here as describing the state of the field. One assumes that a field of research gains a specific consistency and coherence when set in general treatments and works meant as textbooks. This assumption does not deny that the field has not been otherwise approached; but general statements of the kind treated in this chapter represent a different degree and manner of diffusion and accessibility.

The pages that follow will then go on to examine substantive historical and conceptual themes that arise from the frames of reference discussed. It will doubtless be noted that this article will be constrained by the structure and thematic content of the two books discussed here, and that an alternative approach cannot be adequately articulated. Finally, the

2. The following works will be discussed in the course of this chapter: Anthony Black, *The History of Islamic Political Thought from the Prophet to the Present* (2001); and Patricia Crone, *Medieval Islamic Political Thought* (2004a). A U.S. edition of the Crone book was published as *God's Rule: Government and Islam* (2004b).

thematic and conceptual dimensions of an object of study, which we might term "Islamic political thought" and necessitating clear definitions of the field of the political and how such might be delimited as "Islamic" (with the kinds of sources that would be appropriate for its study), are matters that will be taken up at a variety of points. This treatment is an important issue. Civilizations preceding the periods of modernity, including classical and medieval Arabic and Islamic civilization, produced discourses on matters that in early modern and modern times came to be seen as those pertaining to political science and political thought. Yet the domains of politics and political thought as understood today were not absent, albeit conceived hitherto as belonging to other discursive genres, such as philosophy, political theology, law, history, mythology, and works of advice for princes, and it would not be illegitimate to assume that a distinctive domain called "political thought" as it came to be constituted later already existed, anywhere, in classical or medieval times.

Historiographic Schemata: *Chronotopoi* of Singular Origins, Rise and Decline

Substantial progress has doubtlessly been made in some respects since the publication of Watt's book. It is clear that the range of themes treated by Black and by Crone and the historical and geographical parameters the authors adopt enhance Watt's slender empirical base very substantially. Crone's is a work of substantial erudition and range. The command of her material is much firmer and the coherence of her arguments is far firmer than Black's, whose chronological range is nevertheless longer, she stopping with the thirteenth century and he, with considerable learning, following up the matter until today.[3]

3. There are few, but not insignificant, technical, linguistic, and factual errors in Crone's book; Black's publishers have clearly not served their author as well as they might and allowed the book to appear with an unusual body of errors. These lapses, with respect to both books, are discussed in the appendix to the longer version of this chapter, published in Al-Azmeh 2006.

Unfortunately, it is equally clear that this treatment in the Crone and Black works is unmatched by progress of historiographic import. Crucial assumptions relative to periodization, to thematic divisions and conceptual configurations, and to topics identified as salient to Islamic political thought remain largely the same, unresponsive to the enhanced empirical base. These assumptions derive seemingly from the once-standard tropes, habits, and historiographic presumptions that constituted, until recently, inertial energy of the Islamic Studies institution in Western universities, and from more demotic assumptions as well. Watt's book consists of a sequence of brief and often simplistic stereotyped outlines of selected historical moments, organized by an implicit but substantive periodization according to a simple pattern of sudden rise and protracted decline. This is a narrative structure, an historiographic schema, familiar alike from textbooks and from popular treatments of and pronouncements on Muslim history, and is largely repeated, far more elaborately, in Crone's and Black's construals of the history of Islamic political thought.[4]

Both works postulate a pattern of Muslim history and a correlative pattern of political thought that begins with defining a history utterly apart and singular, ex nihilo in structural terms. This approach then is seen to lead to the uncommonly rapid elaboration of a religious culture that settles into patterns, which are to last for centuries and which prescribe the mainsprings of cultural production, including political thought. But this approach is chronologically correlated with a decline in historical energy and the entry of entropy into a structure fully energized at its beginning. From this perspective, Islamic political thought is constituted whole, coterminously with its moment of origin, and subsequent political thought devolves to devising ways of coping with political atrophy and with the incommensurability between original religiopolitical

4. This historiography, with variants, is generally repeated in German scholarship as well. See Tilman Nagel, *Staat und Glaubensgemeinschaft im Islam* (1981), whose title already announces a historiographic program. Scholarship in French is generally more adventurous. See, for instance, Dakhlia 1998, which has broader anthropological and thematic orientations and a greater methodological sophistication, despite a certain furtiveness and an incomplete control of historical material.

ideals henceforth sustained in the imagination and the realities of political life. The ex nihilo character of this beginning, and the self-enclosed, sui generis character of the "culture" it produces, are thus reinforced by the elision of the geographical dimension in historical analysis and the conditions obtaining in the territories where Islamic political conceptions were conceived—the eastern territories of Late Antiquity—are obscured from view and overdetermined by their Arabian-Muslim origin. Things happen not in territories with determinate characteristics and traditions, but "in Islam," here become an extraterritorial substitute for space, just as "beginnings" are a substitute for historical time. Consequently, one might characterize this historiography as proceeding not with the diachronic comparativism generally called periodization, but with the succession of Chronotopoi—slices of time responding more to prior patterned narrative exigencies than to the desiderata of history.

Assumptions of Singularity

That Black is neither an Arabist nor a Persianist and that he is rather a scholar of medieval European political thought is signally courageous and particularly welcome. This circumstance arouses in the reader the reasonable anticipation that the history of Islamic political thought might at last have attracted the attention of the mainstream in medieval studies and in the history of political thought and that the history of Islamic political thought might at last have been conceptually naturalized, subjected to the standard methods and conceptual equipment of the historical sciences, beyond presumptions of exoticism, of Muslim exceptionalism, and of historical self-enclosure.

But, on the whole, such anticipation is unfortunately thwarted. For all the range of his reading, Black seems at once to defer uncritically to once-common Islamic Studies institutional and demotic clichés. In all, the books under discussion constitute conceptually congruent variants on a number of common standard themes and historiographic orientations, with some technical differences and variations of emphasis. All share the assumption that Islamic political theory, and Islamic history more generally understood, is somehow essentially sui generis, that it derives from a definitively constituted, predominantly scriptural and to a smaller extent Arabian "core," that it is fundamentally self-referential, and that it is *sans pareille* and therefore ultimately admits of no truly systematic or systemic comparisons with other histories of political thought. Commonalities are reduced to influences, to survivals, to vicarious concordances, not to affinities, generic conceptual unities, or historical continuities, accculturations, contrary to evidence.[5] Black's ingenuous expressions of surprise at finding in Islamic political thought ideas to be encountered in medieval Latin political thought arise from this.

Our authors present their overpatterned histories as books put before an equally overpatterned reader, explicitly called "the Western reader." This reader is offered details and specifications on themes and arguments that may often be unfamiliar, but hardly anything is offered that might appear counterintuitive even to the average reader of newspapers or to the spectator of television programs. It is therefore perhaps unsurprising that some distinguished modern scholarship in Arabic on the topics treated, some quoted below, has not been taken into account.

This target reader is enjoined, in different individual tonalities, to access a history that differs "completely" (Watt 2003, 64) from that of Europe, including Byzantine and medieval Western Europe. He or she is advised that Islam "comprises a distinct and self-contained cultural unit" with "a coherent . . . tradition, separate from the West and with a logic of its own" (Black 2001, 1), which nevertheless, and perhaps not too incongruously in a mood of political correctness, might elicit a benign regard for "the kinship of the different" (1). Islam, though not a place, is put forward as "the paradigmatic alternative to Europe" (3). It resulted from an event, Muhammad and his Qur'an, that marks "a decisive break in human thinking about politics and society" (9), and that sets the scene for the formation of "a type of society" that is "generically different from

5. See Crone (1987, 2ff., passim) for a good argument, empirical and conceptual at the same time, against these institutional habits in the field of the emergence of Islamic law, both generally and with specific regard to law governing patronage, refuting claims for its "parthenogenesis." The overall thesis has attracted criticism; see Hallaq 1990.

Greek, Roman, or Euro-Christian civilization" (12). The consequence is that "our" political language "equips us poorly" to understand it (13).

More concretely, the difficulty "the Western reader" would have in understanding political thought in medieval Islam arises partly from the entirely unquestioned presumption that the religion of Islam was "the main source" of the state (Crone 2004a, viii), as this strange historical itinerary "began with the Qur'an" (Black 2001, 10). Of course, if that were indeed the case, if Islamic history and the political thought it produced were indeed spawned by a book as Eve emerged from Adam's rib, it would be truly peculiar and out of line with human history overall, and would confirm the claims to uniqueness propounded by Muslim religious traditions. It is proposed that the "fusion"—the term implies indistinction, yielding vagueness and indeterminacy, and the rhetorical occasion for asserting everything and nothing—of religion and politics is not only complete but also in its consummateness unique among complex societies, and that there were no precedents for this in the Near East prior to the advent of Islam (Crone 2004a, 14f). This presumption of exceptionalism is a matter that will be addressed presently in broad perspective, and I must rest content here with further specifying the presumed title to singularity attributed to Islamic history.

This singularity is grounded in a basic assumption, what Crone (2004a, 396) calls the "perfect identity" of religion, state, and society.[6] It is of course extremely difficult to envisage such a "perfect identity" in the course of any history. Moreover, Crone's justifiable source-critical skepticism about what knowledge of this "beginning"—in Crone somewhat more extended and more complex than Black's but still nevertheless brief, and a germinal repository of the future—may admit of empirical reconstruction (2004a, 21) that would itself vitiate the very possibility of making assertions about an initial condition retained as the mainspring of

6. The locus classicus is von Grunebaum 1953. On the trope of such "perfect identity"—an alias for indistinction—in scholarship on Islam, see Laroui 1976. This rhetorical trope is, of course, an important component in the culture-morphological approach to history that predominates in the writing of Islamic history.

what followed. The Muslim community, or *umma,* is nevertheless seen as having been ab initio an "all-purpose community," congregation and state rolled into one (13, 15), related by disjunction to the actually existing imperial Arab-Muslim state, the substrate of its history.

In a way, this all-purpose community—this *ekklésia*—is more reminiscent, in its claim for sociohistorical collectivities without functional and other internal differentiations, of the self-conception of radical Protestant communities, and their modern Muslim fundamentalist ideological analogues, than of Late Antique and medieval Muslim empires. Clearly, the late antique aspect would have been crucial to the historiography of Muslim political conceptions, as they took shape in the central territories of Late Antiquity. Yet the fairly standard presumption of such "perfect identity"[7] and the correlative procedure of reading history from texts and other forms of ideological expression and discursive sublimation (to derive the latter from political events)[8] are crucial components implicit in the historiographic approach of the books under discussion. The identification between text and event, their consubstantiality, makes it very difficult to specify the parameters of "political thought" as a specific topic of study distinct from other enunciations made in the course of addressing political events.

Scripturalist Assumptions

A comparison between aspects of the Reformation and ostensibly Muslim conceptions of all-purpose community might have been interesting for the history of religions had it not been for the two important facts that render

7. Perhaps most systematically, see Levy 1930–33 (2nd ed. published by Cambridge Univ. Press as *The Social Structure of Islam* in 1957 and reprinted in 1962). In the field of Islamic political and social thought, with an almost sentimentalist appreciation energized by distant echoes of St. Augustine, see Gardet 1967.

8. For a very clear warning about these excesses of such a reductive procedure in which the world is stood upon its head, and for an exemplary historical sense, see "Considérations sur l'utilisation des ouvrages de droit musulman par l'historien," in Cahen 1977, 81–90.

such an approach anachronistic, and this becomes the first general comment to be made on the historiography of Islamic political thought. For one thing, Calvin and other figures of the Reformation had a well-defined scripture. They also had well-established textual, Patristic, and ecclesiastical traditions. Early Muslims at the "beginning," in contrast, had a fragmentary scripture to which no definitive tradition of practice or interpretation had yet crystallized as tradition. Yet to this uncertain beginning much of Western and Muslim scholarship has ascribed a stupendous, logocentric internal coherence and a sense of definitive accomplishment, buttressed by what is generally taken as an ab initio monocratic order of Levitical resonance called *shari'a.* Ultimately, this monocratic reading of Islam and the Qur'an is modeled on a strand of nineteenth-century scholarship on Judaism in general and Rabbinism in particular, despite the fact that there is no Qur'anic equivalent for the legislative sweep of Leviticus, Numbers, or Deuteronomy and that Muslim jurisprudence *(fiqh)* is in decided measure extra-Qur'anic and noncanonical, despite its haggadic form.

More important is an anachronism of broader sweep, which would concern not only "the beginning" but also the entire course of Muslim history up to the nineteenth century and Christian history to the Reformation. This anachronism has to do with the conception of the canonical text and the techniques of reading and handling scriptural traditions in the context of considering the common assumption that the Qur'an is not only the fount of Muslim political theory but also an integral "blueprint for life." Together with the Reformation, the antiquarian humanism of the sixteenth and seventeenth centuries produced a philological notion of text that allowed for scriptures to be regarded as definitive and unmediated repositories of sense, to be approached integrally with the slogan *ad fontes,* accessible to a person, not so much lay as initiated, eschewing all but *sola scriptura sancta.* Yet Late Antique and medieval Muslim or Christian veneration for scripture did not allow for a meaningful Procrustean management of this ubiquitous slogan as would be required by what might broadly be termed fundamentalism. Like other seemingly simple principles, the *sola scriptura* slogan itself and the appeal *ad fontes* were in practice, and beyond an almost cultic bibliolatry (the term is Lessing's) highly polysemic and multivalent, textually and historically, reflecting the vast complexity of the Reformation itself.[9]

Premodern rhetorical and philological techniques of reading precluded treating texts as monological, and this fact is underlined by recent studies of canonicity. Texts, including scriptures, were determinedly regarded in practice as intertextual, densely woven through the unflinching prism of commentary and of tradition, replete with different possibilities of reading yielded by linguistic, semantic, and conceptual elements internal to different commentarial traditions that, like interpretive traditions overall, covered a vast range varying between the kerygmatic and that which assumes an inherent objectivity of sense (Ricoeur 1970, 26–27),[10] usually seen as lexical, grammatical, syntactical, and more generally proto-philological, but also as historical, as in the exegetical genre of *asbab al-nuzul* (circumstances of Revelation, *circumstanciae scribentis*).

It is not surprising in these circumstances that no medieval Muslim divine [cleric] was driven to claim that the Qur'an, for all its exemplary force, is a total "blueprint for life"; this would have meant nothing to him. No medieval Muslim divine derived the state, political thought, or an entire blueprint for society from the canon—this was possible only for modern fundamentalism building upon modern historiographic possibilities. The derision of commentaries, glosses, summaries, exegeses, and similar textual procedures of aggiornamento is, in religious discourse, associated with the Reformation, and, in historical scholarship, with nineteenth-century positivism, in which text-critical procedures sought original documents and ostensibly the original meanings deposited therein.

9. The literature on these matters is very large. See especially Stierle 1971 for a review of issues and McGrath 1987, chaps. 4–7. For overall historical considerations, see especially Kemp 1991, 81ff. For analytical studies, see in particular Todorov 1978, pt. 2, B; Jacob 1999, and the special issue of *Speculum* 65, no. 1 (1990) [on the New Philology]. For Muslim texts, where research into this matter is in its infancy, see particularly al-Haddad 2003, 78ff.; and Smith 1980.

10. See the interpretation of this passage with regard to medieval European letters in Stock 1990, 39–40.

What mattered to medieval Muslim divines was what a canonical text might yield for a variety of genres, purposes, and contexts; in short, the Qur'an was invoked, not "applied." The crucial matter was not the simple announcement of some notion of *ad fontes,* ubiquitous in Islam, Christianity, and Judaism, but the recognition that such an announcement would be either meaningless or inconsequential if unaccompanied by an hermeneutical or pragmatic program. In the case of the Qur'an, these contexts and purposes of the canon might be devotional, ritual, dogmatic, oracular, recitational, homiletic, incantatory, commentarial, exegetical, magical, apotropaic, fetishistic, linguistic, literary, rhetorical, ideological, legal, theological, pseudohistorical (legendary, mythological, and genealogical), salvation-historical, political, and ethical, and for the sumptuous display of precious manuscripts. Each of these posed and still poses specific problems of interpretation.

Moreover, the Muslim canon also comprised prophetic traditions, both canonized and uncanonized or "apocryphal," related to the Qur'an in a variety of complex ways, including the possibility that such traditions might override the Qur'anic text by means of the complex concept of *naskh,* usually rendered as "abrogation." There were also various layers of consensus. No effort at summary simplification is thinkable in this regard, or in regard to the relation between prophetic traditions, the Qur'an, and traditions of consensus.

What mattered about the Muslim canon for medieval authors, then, was not a notion of semantic objectivity inherent in the canonical text and disembodied from textual transmission, recitation, commentary, and use; such required a notion of semantic objectivity that was unavailable to Muslims before the nineteenth century.[11] Hence, skeptical statements made by

11. See Graham 1987; Wheeler 1996; Yunis Ali 2000; Madigan 2001; Saleh 2004. Yet, despite this practice and despite the techniques of reading the canon through a variety of traditions, many modern scholars impatiently seem to deride these contexts and techniques of interpretation, blaming medieval Muslim exegetes for not having had proper instruction in nineteenth-century positivist philology, taking such simplistic summary styles for intellectual robustness. Thus, see Crone (1994, 2) for an example of missing the point of medieval techniques of reading and notions of foundational text: "Given that the

medieval Muslim divines about the veracity of traditional accounts relating to early Islam went uncontested. The literal veracity of prophetic traditions, for instance, was subject to healthy skepticism, but it was thought unwise to mount cognitive challenges to matters that had become components of a Great Tradition and had acquired practical consequence, which necessitated the practical suspension of skepticism.[12] Hence also the probabilistic character of Sunni legal traditions and their conception of legal judgment, the contention that, contrary to the possibility and necessity of certainty in matters of dogma, legal judgments can only be probable, and liable to contestation (Al-Azmeh 1994, 180ff.; Al-Azmeh 1986, 87ff.).

This said, one might proceed further and state that, in the books under scrutiny, there are three sources of canonical status attributed to Islamic political thought: the Qur'an, prophetic actions and pronouncements (the hadith), and historical experience. The Qur'an is indeed ubiquitously quoted by Muslim authors on matters political as on other matters, and thus topologically used like all other scriptures, as proof-texts. But it is a seldom appreciated fact that political exegesis of the Qur'an, that is, reading the Qur'an as a whole for the purpose of constructing political theory, is a twentieth-century phenomenon associated with integralist Islamic fundamentalism, without precedent in the classical and medieval periods, just as today's ubiquitous slogan that Islam is at once "religion and state" is a product of the twentieth century. In classical and medieval Muslim traditions, the Qur'an was not the object of sustained political meditation;

---

entire exegetical tradition is characterized by a proliferation of diverse interpretations, it is legitimate to wonder whether guesswork did not play as great a role in its creation as did recollection."

12. See Al-Azmeh 1998a, 202–3. For similar skepticism on the part of a modern Muslim reformist transiting to the philological from the prephilological notions of text, see Dunya 1958[1873], 1–29. This uncertain manner of dealing with incompatibilities between the rational and the traditionally doxographic is not unique to Islam, but it is ubiquitous in traditionalist discourse. For the workings of this manner in Judaism, see Halbertal 1997, 29ff. For an example of a similar disjunction between the cognitive and the traditionally normative in Christianity, see Fraenkel 1961, 312ff. and passim. For this disjunction more generally formulated, see Deconchy 1980, 35ff.

Qur'anic proof-texts with their extraordinary standing and weight were interpreted to support very contradictory political views, and solicited for authority and support. This practice is, of course, also the case with all solicitation of and appeal to the biblical scripture in other monotheistic religions in premodern times (Buc 1994, passim).

The same approach would apply to the second component of the Muslim canon, the hadith: this is not so much a "source" of Muslim political thought as a quarry for quotations that sustained positions arising from the conceptions and practices of Muslim kingship and political thought associated with it and spawned by it and, in large measure, persisting in continuity with Late Antique notions of kingship and ecumenical monarchy. In these quotations, the caliphate was an historical and a technical legal specification, to be discussed below (Al-Azmeh 1997, 163ff.).

The third canonical component is history: The construal of sectarian differences as crucial points of departure for the genesis of political theory is questionable for parallel considerations. Although there is some truth to Watt's statement that Muslims tend to express political theory in the form of history (Watt 2003, 36–37), this statement is true only in the sense that present differences and political ideas in place sometimes tend to be recast in or to be associated with the form of elegiac or revanchist recollections of and meditations upon ancestral justices and injustices. Thus, as with the solicitation of and appeal to the canon, past events are quoted in support of or in opposition to this or that position, and a line of filiation is made into a justificatory argument. One would certainly have wished that scholars dealing with the political teachings of Muslim sects were aware of the distinctions it makes between the sociological and the historical on the one hand and the dogmatic and the theological on the other (Troeltsch 1912).

The readiness to tolerate anachronism and other departures from the standard requirements of historical scholarship overall in studies of Islamic history arises from the exigencies of a particular narrative construction and conceptual apprehension of this history. The coherence of this approach requires the often counterfactual and implausible reiteration and reassertion of certain motifs and patterns for conceiving the succession and concatenation of major historical events. It occasions the correlative marginalization of central facts and patterns of events—broadly conceived, in all manner of duration—and will become readily apparent from what follows. "Islamic" history is generally construed as the sudden, unearthly explosion of a religion and a massive movement of conquest upon the face of a very large part of the world, comprehended by "religion" lodged in a Book and other canon and, in lesser proportion, "Arabian traditions," both components acting as a kind of genetic program arising from the moment of origin. Being complete at its bibliocentric and Arabian tribal beginning, and having been entirely constrained by the conditions of its scriptural and geoethnological genesis, its subsequent history is implicitly seen to be a series of glosses on these beginnings, a drama with predetermined roles, and sometimes an almost self-parodic psychodrama, resulting in an historical narrative structured along the lines that mirror the epic genre, as an antiepic—very much like satire, caricature, and polemic. Epic and its negative double operate by an exaggeration in the scale of selected episodic elements and fragments, which are then taken to stand for the whole (cf. Olrik 1965, 137).

Snares of Origins

What was said above in the course of sketching the chronological narrative components of the books under consideration devolves therefore, more substantively, into the following. "Islamic" history is seen to have been born somehow complete, its early energies spent within a short time, with little to sustain them along the course of time but with various forms of repetition that, with the effects of entropy, can then be comprehended by categories of disorientation ("coping"), decrepitude, sclerosis, and decline.[13] Thus typically, in commonly used textbooks such as in the

13. The unreflected trope of decline has been subject to much analysis, contestation, and precision in the past half-century, not least in the context of imperial histories and particularly the paradigmatic case of Rome, which led to the recent flowering of Late Antique historiography. It will suffice here for purposes of general orientation to mention Starn 1975; Koselleck and Widmer 1980, 214ff., passim; Chaunu 1981, passim; Cowgill

books under consideration here, a skeletal narrative structure with much uneven flesh is put forth as a chronotopical backbone from which political theories, like religious and other histories, are elicited in corresponding sequence, as direct manifestations and epiphenomena. This structure is in turn grafted upon two unreflected periodizations woven together, the one dynastic and the other a scheme of rise and decline. The former is common in the writing of political history, the latter in sketching cultural and religious histories that are not often distinguished enough.

According to this image, diagrammatically represented in structural outline, Muhammad and his immediate successors appear, Book in one hand and Bedouins towed by the other. They explode upon the vista of world history, set up a polity in Medina and ultimately a tribal state in Damascus, enter into internecine bloody conflicts that spawn sects with attendant politico-religious views; these views come to serve as "political thought" in works such as those under discussion here. Then the Abbasids appear, reckon unsuccessfully and ambivalently with the mixed heritage of their Medinan and Umayyad epigones, lose control of both Book (to the ulama and their shariʿa) and tribal muscle (to Turkic Praetorians and foreign dynasts). They thus come rapidly to occupy a world of make-believe, while the original genetic impulse, which is Islam, congeals ponderously into unworldly, pious malaise and is played out on the street, now that people have become Muslims led by the ulama who, by virtue of speaking for the Book, husband the imprint of Muslim origins upon the masses, setting

---

and Yoffe 1988; Tainter 1988; Demandt 1984, esp. 431ff., 586ff. for a discussion of the culture-morphological notions of decline under discussion here; and pt. 4, passim, for a systematic consideration of this paradigmatic case overall—the other, not unrelated theme of Ottoman decline would repay systematic and detailed consideration. For the "decline of Islam," the classical repertoire of studies is still Brunschvig and von Grunebaum 1957, with papers and discussions on this topic by scholars who reacted with incomprehending horror to the suggestion by the representative of a more developed field of scholarship, H. I. Marrou, that "decline" might be a complex matter and that popular conceptions of Roman history may not be used as an exemplary case in point (109–23). See Al-Azmeh 2004a, 68ff. For the theme of decline and the rise of the historiography of Late Antiquity, see Peter Brown et al. 1997.

Muslims against the state, or at the very least disconnect them from it, and propound an outlook of autocephalic disengagement. Politics wallows in bloody, un-Islamic vainglory, greed, injustice, and hubris, while what the books under discussion describe as "Islamic political thought" devolves rather into what might more appropriately be likened to a carping, apolitical ecclesiology.

From this narrative scheme of the history of Islam derives a particular specification of Islamic political thought: its topics are derived from the worldly misadventures of the Muslim religion over time. Starting with dogma and legal institutes ostensibly associated with it, Islamic political thought at once emanates from and is spawned by sectarian impulses and by what religion is presumed scripturally to require, and it rapidly and determinedly settles into largely apolitical morosity on the part of the ulama, while tyrannical praetorian parvenus and conquering princes from the east luxuriate in un-Islamic theories of kingship and suspend the caliphate in an ethereal unreality. In response to this, some of the ulama again try to recover what might be salvaged of the imprints of origin, by producing for the caliphs wildly dreamy and ultimately opportunistic theories about the public order, with their imagination the only means they have of "coping" with new circumstances. It is clear that this pattern of the history of Islamic political thought, following on the heels of the broader historical narrative skeleton outlined, is fully reflected in the books under discussion here.

Albert Hourani had many years ago made the link, however implicitly, between periodization in terms of the chronotopoi of rise and decline and conceiving the historical category "Islam" as a persistent "culture" (Hourani 1976, 114–15), commonly reduced to religious beliefs and summary commands and prohibitions, with the history of Muslims overdetermined by the full amplitude of their religion's definitive beginning. This link was confirmed and made in more explicit detail by other writings subsequent to Hourani (Olender 1992, 54ff.; Al-Azmeh 2004a, 72ff.). In this perspective, historical causality, being endogenous to Islam as such and governed by a genetic imperative, devolves to what biblical scholarship knows as typology, and the history subsequent to the moment of genesis stands as so many diminished figures of this very beginning. Thus one of our authors quotes with approval V. S. Naipaul's insistence on "the flow of origins" throughout Islamic history (Black 2001, 341), what the renowned scholar H. A. R. Gibb, with exquisite censoriousness, called the "kernel of derangement [in] Islamic society" (Gibb 1962, 14). If one wished to investigate genealogies of this perspective, one would need to look closely into positions developed in the nineteenth century, very well exemplified by Wilhelm von Humboldt and Ernest Renan, in which racial stock, language, and religious characteristics are coterminous and deterministic, with germinal origins playing a very decidedly predestinarian role with respects to terminal outcomes.[14] Paradoxically, this perspective construes the ethnogenetic beginnings of Islam and the course and outcomes of Muslim history to be conceptually equivalent; historical developments embody at best the unstable results of clashes and of maladroit adjustments to ambient reality, but they have no consequence for the construal of the impulse of origins or its imprint.

Unsurprisingly given the hypercoherence attributed to Islam ab initio, its condition of perpetual decline, when no allowance is made for the complexity of historical periodization, can only be catastrophic or alternatively long-drawn and pathetic. In the schema under discussion, the former applies to politics, the latter to political thought and to culture more generally, and it appears on close scrutiny to be less a process than a permanent condition.

Historiographic Lineages and Methodological Commonplaces

There is indeed a very distinguished lineage to views of Islamic history just outlined, in which heroic moment of the beginning rapidly becomes the antiheroic narrative of misadventure stretching over many centuries. We find such views expressed by Voltaire, Herder, and Hegel, who ought

14. There is much interesting scholarship on this subject and on the correlation between Islam and its Arabian moment of inception. See, most recently, Masuzawa 2005, 171ff., 186ff., 192ff., and chap. 5, passim. Friedrich Max Müller had already most thoroughly questioned such views, not least the poetical obscurantism they subtend (Masuzawa 2005, 218ff.).

not to be underestimated as historians, and by Ranke, Renan, and Burkhardt, among many others. In terms of historical doctrine, what we have in the books under discussion is the implicit restatement of the romantic, vitalist philosophy of history out of which emerged, most rigorously in Germany from the late eighteenth century, variants of politico-historical scholarship on cultural morphology known as *Kulturkreistheorie* and *Weltanschauungslehre.*[15]

Each such "cultural sphere," such as "Islam" or "the West," is essentially homeostatic and possesses a constant culture-morphological pattern. Its history is essentially the measure of fidelity to origins, here the Qur'an and the Muhammadan example, allied to tribesmen, with history replaced by an ethnology of "cultural patterns." History is construed endogenously, chronologically and geographically adjacent histories being adjudged incommensurable. History becomes a vast space of ethnological classification (Al-Azmeh 1998b, chap. 1). That which is out of conformity with supposed primal impulses and energies lodged in the culture-morphological pattern is taken for being merely exogenous, the corrupting or otherwise complicating "influence" of heterogeneous impurity, and historical transformations are denuded of their specific gravities and taken for variations on an invariant origin, or otherwise as what Spengler termed *pseudomorphism*, Hellenism in medieval Islam and "Westernization" in modern times.[16]

That this deeply conservative theory of history should form the renewed basis of writing the history of Islamic political thought is perhaps to be expected at a time of neoconservatism of various hues—neoconservatism being here understood as the recuperation of concepts

15. See, in particular, Hourani 1980, chap. 2; Hourani 1991, chap. 1, 7–61; Rodinson 1988, 85ff.; Anidjar 2003, 120ff.; Al-Azmeh 2004a, 75ff.

16. The latter is seen typically as provoking a "crisis of identity" leading to a "return" to Islam of which fundamentalism is an extreme but adequate manifestation—heedless of the problems attendant upon using transhistorical notions of identity, or of the fact that Islamic civilization, like the Greek or the Roman, no longer exists except as a bookish memory. It is such a conception that renders Black's (2001) (and others') treatment of modern "Islamic political thought" very questionable.

discredited until recently and their tart and sometimes almost festive reassertion—as if this were a triumph for what had always been obvious but had been in abeyance because of the deleterious impact of leftists, antiorientalists, and other assorted sources of mystification. Neoconservatism in Western Islamic studies is here the reassertion of an older inertia internal to the Islamic Studies establishment after a period of experimentation, often innovative if sometimes with dubious cognitive results, that followed the publication in 1978 of Edward Said's *Orientalism* against the backdrop of a culturalist and civilizational turn in the humanities, a turn not unrelated to conceptions (and some practices) of international politics.

In this culturalist and civilizational perspective on history, in which both xenophobia and xenophilia mirror one another in their claim for generic differentiation between Islam and West, the related notions of incommensurability and immemorial incompatibility are figures of the imagination, which often structure conceptually both the multiculturalist and the exclusivist or social-Darwinist parties (of the latter, for instance: Professor Bernard Lewis and assorted Evangelical ministers and neoconservatives in the United States[17]) to this civilizational turn (Al-Azmeh 2001). For the latter, a martial or potentially martial perspective on present-day international politics (clash or war of civilizations) is correlated to an historical narrative of perennial adversarialism born of generic incompatibility, in the form of an historical account of "Islamic" civilization so radically exotic, irrational, and menacing as to require a very special effort to render it comprehensible to the "Western reader."

One last observation concerning this neoconservatism is in order before going further. This concerns the general antipathy of venerable vintage, still persisting among some scholars of Islam, to what is vaguely

17. Professor Lewis is one of very few academics singled out for approval by a shrill and denunciatory U.S. neoconservative politico-academic lobby on Middle East studies (www.campus-watch.org/recommends.php). Among the few others singled out for approval on grounds of reliability is Professor Crone. See the clarion-call of Kramer 2001 and Lewis 2004 (which contains the notorious "The Roots of Muslim Rage"). See also the comments of Lockman 2004, 130ff., 173ff., 251ff., chap. 7, passim; Salamé 2005, 440ff.

known with disparagement and alarm as "theory." This attitude demonstrates an insular inclination to, and a preference for, a cherished marginality arising partly from the undemanding comforts of institutional marginality in which Islamic Studies had for long found itself, recently encouraged by demands from the public for knowledge of the apparently strange phenomenon of Islam, appearing to this general public as daily becoming more and more eccentric and perplexing.

The effects of conceptual and institutional marginality had already been noted by Hourani and others. Such marginality yielded work by scholars of Muslim history who, in Hourani's words, "other historians would [not] recognize as historians sharing in their historical culture," taking over the "commonplaces of the general culture and information of their age" (Hourani 1976, 98ff., 113; Rodinson 1988, 117ff.)—what Marcel Mauss (1930, 94) had long ago termed a "sociologie inconsciente qui encombre l'histoire vulgaire." Thus, common demotic assumptions about Islamic history, and particularly assumptions of incommensurable exoticism, are still given expert voice by some representatives of Islamic Studies institutions, and they make their way into the mainstream of scholarship, even of usually discerning and critical scholarship, deferentially content with unexamined certainties emerging from this particular field of study and general expertise.[18]

A corollary, crucial for the purpose of this chapter, of the romantic historical doctrine that has just been discussed is that the categorization of empirical materials whose history is written, that is, the construction of historical objects and topics, is still seen by some, despite recent advances in orientalist scholarship, to yield a unique culture called Islam, from which follows the implicit proposition that the history of political thought must spring from this culture—just as did "Islamic society," "Islamic

18. Even discerning, erudite, and conceptually aware scholars seem to be almost automatically susceptible to such demotic commonplaces and move imperceptibly from summary statements to the summary dismissal of entire histories, their designation as irrelevant for conceptual or comparative purposes, as if by a scoffing legerdemain in the guise of recognition. For some examples, almost at random, see Assmann 2000, 27n41; Lambert 1995, 245ff.; Little 2004, 928.

economics," and the "Islamic city" in a previous time of scholarship. All of these outcomes, and their cognates, are habitually deduced from texts of a religious character, which come to stand in for the history implicitly thought to mirror them. Histories of this kind are endogenetic, with outcomes decided by geneses yielding continuity and repetition, consideration of which replaces historical causality. This approach amounts to anachronism and reflects more the conceptual apparatus that structures traditions internally than the historical concepts that are called upon to explain these.[19]

One final point of method needs to be addressed briefly at this stage. This point concerns the way in which the history of political thought, and intellectual history more broadly considered, are approached in the books under consideration. We find that the history of Islamic political thought as expressed in the books discussed here is written according to canons of intellectual history that prevailed before the discovery of historical anthropology, the history of religions, the sociology of knowledge, the techniques of textual analysis (conceptual and rhetorical), and the pragmatics of discourse beyond what the elementary positivistic philology that predominated in Islamic studies permitted (Rodinson 1988, 85ff.). Thus the contextualization of political ideas in this respect might be termed lazy contextualization, generally done with implicit reference to a very "soft" conception of ideology as the simple mechanism of instrumentalization and justification, without recourse to the more elaborate and more effective manners of approaching this important topic.[20] Little deliberate attention is paid to the complexities of intellectual history or

19. For instance, see Skinner 1969, 10ff.; Foucault 1972, 3ff., 11ff., 21ff., 141ff.; al-Arwi 1992, 283ff. For "radical anteriority" as a principle of order in the history of religions, of considerable relevance to the structure of traditions religious and otherwise, see, in particular, Gauchet 1985, xvff., chap. 2, chap. 3, passim. On the notion of tradition overall, see most especially Wiedenhofer 1992; Boyer 1990, 2ff., 10, 32ff., 79ff., 118.

20. In the cognate fields of Late Antique and medieval European political thought, for instance, see work as rich and as different as that of Georges Duby (particularly 1978), Janet Nelson 1976; 1977; 1994; and 1999; and Averil Cameron 1983 and 1987.

the history of ideas in general, or to correlative techniques of reading,[21] with little distinction made between topoi, articulated concepts, symbolic notions used as ritual refrains, and stock phrases; hardly any attention is directed to historical-anthropological approaches, to notions of mentality, to the import of political ritual, and much more. Little distinction is made between ideas of seemingly uniform propositional content that may be expressed in different settings and discursive locations. The complex discursive and sociopolitical relation between descriptivism and prescriptivism in medieval Muslim writings on politics is simplified to the polarity of identity and contradiction. One need not hold a particularly abstruse view of textuality in order to realize that a text (including a text discussing matters political) is more than the sum of its discrete statements and that it is more than an archive.

The self-presentation of a group holding particular ideas is thus taken as an adequate study of these ideas, in keeping, in this particular case, with the perfect correspondence of "Muslim society" to the political ideas it spawned, to the extent that the statements of Watt and Crone that they seek to read ideas into political practices and to uncover implicit assumptions (Watt 2003, x; Crone 2004a, ix) transpires to be less the reading of practice than radical simplification of the relationship between theory and practice, by postulating correspondence between them. Black expresses such implicit assumptions well when he states that, with respect to Muhammad's polity, "the irony was that the Muslims had little in the way of political theory to inform what they were doing" (Black 2001, 10). What remains is religion, articulated in this kind of historical writing as an imperative and unvarying cultural pattern closer to instinct than to deliberative action in political, social, cultural, doctrinal, and imperial contexts.

21. The literature is substantial and rich. See, for instance, Krieger 1973 and crucially Burke 2002. For a balanced view of recent developments, see Spiegel 1990. Of course, these concerns are not entirely new and not confined to poststructuralist notions of text and textuality; see, for instance, Marrou 1983, 665ff.; and Stock 1996, 138ff.

In light of the above, we might usefully move on to the categorization of an historical object called "Islamic political thought." The key to this categorization lies in the Islamic character attributed to it as its constitutive differentia. Islam thereby not only constitutes historical objects but also renders them self-explanatory qua Islamic. Islamic political thought starts with Islam, not with the history of political ideas nor from political practices, almost as if the name, Islam, conjures up a history. "Theologocentrism" had for long been a common preference in Western studies of Islam (Rodinson 1988, 104). Now Islam is, of course, indubitably a religion. But it is also a name attributed, often as shorthand or for some other convenience, including ideological convenience, to a certain historical order, to a presumed culture and civilization, to a presumed form of social organization, to certain peoples, and to much else. Moreover, religion, including Islam, is not only canon and interpretation (and not merely catechism and simple litany) but also bespeaks cult, devotional styles, dogmas over which discord is lively, social institutions, forms of authority, ethical precepts, myth, magic, and much else, all of which vary greatly over time, place, social group, and according to a variety of other criteria.

All these distinctions are to a considerable degree effaced if Islamic history, culture, and society were to be reduced to the religion whose name they are made to bear—and most particularly effaced if this religion is in turn reduced to its canon, heedless of Arnold Toynbee's prescient proposition that the Qur'an is but "stony ground" for institutional and legal development (1951, 2:53). This interpretation is also heedless of Albert Hourani's gentle warning that "words like Islamic history do not mean the same things in different contexts . . . in no context are they enough in themselves to explain all that exists. In other words, 'Islam' and the terms derived from it are 'ideal types,' to be used subtly, with infinite reservations and adjustments of meaning, and in conjunction with other ideal types, if they are to serve as principles of historical explanation." He adds with approval, as a corrective, the suggestion made by Claude Cahen that historical categorization in terms of concrete geographical or temporal qualifiers such as medieval, preindustrial, Mediterranean, or Near Eastern would be far more adequate than "Islamic" (Hourani 1976, 117). Clearly, careful consideration of the complexity of large-scale historical units is an essential desideratum that is not met with sufficient frequency.[22] After all, one rarely reads of Christian political thought, except for certain theologically focused political writings of the Church Fathers, but rather of Late Antique, Byzantine, and medieval political thought, even with reference to the political writings of monks writing for other monks, and one reads not of religion constituting imperial political thought, but of religion and the rhetoric of empire (for instance, Cameron et al. 1992).

In light of the above, a more precise orientation in the accounts of Islamic political thought might have been obtained had their subjects been properly constituted, not of putative continuities with and variations on canonical texts but in terms of spatial or temporal parameters: political thought under the Baghdad caliphate in its various phases and places, for instance, or notions of worldly authority propounded by various Muslim sects, or concepts of royalty in relation to ceremonial. In the books under discussion, the political thought of Muslim sects is put forth as "Islamic political thought" tout court, in distinction to un-Islamic influences on "Islamic" political thought. The chance to constitute the topics in political thought properly speaking in social, discursive, political, and other contexts of their deployment—power, order, monarchy, empire, authority, and allied topics—is thereby lost.

As in medieval Latin political thought (Buc 1994, 19), Islamic "political thought" is not defined and delimited in terms that came attached to it with its constitution as an academic discipline, awaiting scholars of the twenty-first century to summarize it. Medieval Muslims' political notions and the topics they treat need to be reconstructed from a wide variety of writings, not all political nor necessarily religious, but comprising also belles lettres, epistolary literature, poetry, legal works, philosophy, historical writings, official documents, courtly ceremonial, numismatic evidence, and much more. Out of these can emerge notions of the state *(dawla)*, of politics as statecraft, as *politikē technē*, of hierarchy, of order, of empire, all of which would be truncated if they were not regarded as

22. On this complexity, see especially "Reich," in *Geschichtliche Grundbegriffe*, ed. Koselleck et al. 1972–2004, 5:423–24 and passim; and Fischer 1957.

transversal themes cutting across sectarian divisions and as being born of political conceptions properly speaking in connection with practices. "Political thought" is not as apt in this regard as political conceptions or political enunciations (Al-Azmeh 1997, chap. 5 and pt. 2, passim).[23]

This reductive, origin-obsessed approach to political thought, schematizing by repeating the refrains of the Sunni mainstream and of various sectaries, has as a most significant result, then, the obscuring of overarching and transversal themes: conceptions of power, of order, of ecumenical empire, of authority. While sectaries dwelt at length on ancestral disputes, on themes of legitimism, on various instances of justice and injustice that might be the subject of works of social, political history and religious history, the more interesting topics pertaining to political thought properly so called are not generally given the centrality due to them in the works giving occasion to this discussion: themes of monarchy, of universal salvation history, of imperialist universalism, of social order, generally treated in the books under discussion simply as functions of sectarian difference or of religious thought without proper systematic consideration in terms of political thought. The theme of monarchy in relation to salvation history is especially crucial for the proper appreciation of classical and medieval Muslim political conceptions, as of the Christian, in which *imitatio Christi* or *Christomimesis,* the Imitation of Christ, plays an important role. This is a scheme in which caliphal monarchy stands for, and figures prophecy in, the medium of historical time, all the while deriving direct sustenance and election from God. But this theme of typology is almost virtually absent from standard scholarship.

As has been suggested, this kind of treatment of historical materials pertaining to Islamic political thought is to some extent related to a direct and fairly elementary philological approach to reading medieval texts, generally eschewing textual and conceptual analysis in favor of paraphrase or lexical explication. Thus, for instance, with respect to the all-important

23. This book is the source of much of what will be said in what follows on Islamic political conceptions.

notion of *dawlah,* a politico-historical notion indicating "dominion," "reign," "Reich," "dynasty," and generally translated as "state," the very first citation in Crone's book (2004a, 4), in what is perhaps appropriate homage, follows Professor Lewis in giving this crucial notion short shrift by blithely deferring the matter of meaning not so much to the history of usage but to the senses conveyed by the Arabic trilateral root *d-w-l,* which yields the sense of "a turn of fortune," among many others. Thus resting content with vague semantic associations rather than closer scrutiny of the complex relation between Arabic morphology and the Arabic lexicon in effect empties the term *dawlah* of determinate historical sense or conceptual shape, much like scrutinizing the notion of revolution in the political thought of the nineteenth century by baldly stating it "meant" return to a point of departure. But the history of concepts, or indeed of institutions, cannot be derived from the history of words, let alone in facile manner from Arabic trilateral roots.[24] An analysis of the historical, discursive, institutional, and political uses of this term, as a bearer of semantic fields, as a concept of order, as a technical administrative term, as an historiographic category inserting politics in the medium of time, would have yielded far richer material for the analysis of medieval Islamic political thought, both at certain crucial junctures (Al-Azmeh 1997, passim; Al-Azmeh 1982, 27ff., passim; Al-Azmeh 1995, 71ff.) and with reference to notions of the state, of monarchy, and of dynasticism. Conceptions of the state are, partly as a result, conspicuously absent from Crone's book, and indeed from Black's, who does however use the word "state" in entitling a major portion of his book. Full treatment of the term *siyasah,* politics and statecraft, would have been another desideratum.

24. There is a general assumption, often simplistically conceived, that semantic elements are intrinsically embedded in Semitic consonantal trilateral roots into which various vowel patterns are interdigitated, rather than considering the idea that the semantic treatment of the trilateral scheme might have been a device for the learned lexical and morphological elaboration of Semitic languages. For a crisp classic expression of the standard position, see, for instance, Cantineau 1949, 93–95. See also the arguments of Larcher 1995.

Thematic Commonplaces and the Frames of History

Egalitarian Arabs and Muslim Empires

It has been suggested that works on Islamic political thought under discussion habitually start their solicitation of Muslim origins' indelible mark with the paleo-Islamic polity of Muhammad and his immediate successors. In terms of supposed Arabian traditions, these are usually characterized as communitarian and egalitarian, with the polity headed by a primus inter pares. It is also presumed that this polity answered to the social patterns of nomadic tribesmen, despite the well-known antipathy of Muhammad and his companions (townsfolk to the man) toward nomads, regarded as fractious and congenitally godless.

Thus the conditions that made for the genesis of Islamic political thought are confined to vaguely conceived religious precepts and to "Arabian traditions," deleting in effect the crucial salience of the apparently "foreign" Persian norms and practices and universalist notions of the *Panbasilea* and its historical and political theology. This position is crucial to the formation of the narratives of Islamic political thought under scrutiny and necessarily precludes the scrutiny of historical growth, interaction, and transformations, great and small, apart from the contrastive register of the supposedly native and autochthonous and the influence coming from "outside." Historical scrutiny properly conceived would by contrast regard Islam and Islamic political thought as historical movements occurring wherever Muslim polities took root, rather than as autarchic phenomena emanating from a book and the desert.

In this process of adaptation, acculturation, growth, and transformation, out of which Islamic political thought emerged, ab initio in forms and by conceptual means not specifically Islamic, history has none but symbolic loyalty to origins, particularly as interaction and acculturation was as intense as it was in the case of the Arab conquests and their imperial aftermath. History rather voraciously acquires and digests unfamiliar matters and elements that are not "original" and, with time (with the passage of centuries in the case of Islamic political thought [Al-Azmeh 1997, 101ff.]) endows them with homely genealogies. There is much more to the name "Islam" than a few vaguely defined marks of origin. Furthermore, apart from the bare text of the Qur'an and some prophetic traditions of ascertainable authenticity, there is little in Islam as an historical phenomenon that is uniquely Arabian, Arab, or "original." Rather, a more historical model of interpretation would be one in which an imperial and royalist koine was commandeered to construct Islamic political concepts, much like the koine of Roman provincial law that led to the formation of certain legal traditions (Crone 1987, 93, 99, passim): conceptual Islamization was retroactive, a work of the imaginary, and a telescoped political genealogy.

Where the much-vaunted Arab traditions are concerned, scholars of Islamic political thought have clearly preferred to share with their readers an implicit cliché of the proud and frugal egalitarian Arab (Henninger 1989, 26ff.) than to consider more exact ethnographic and historical studies of Arab tribalism. The Arabs of Muhammad's time were various, with city-dwellers, nomads, and tillers, with different forms of social and political organization, extending over a vast geographical zone. Some groups were relatively autarchic, isolated, and primitive; others divided among aristocrats and a variety of lower orders; while yet others had lived under elementary monarchical regimes and sustained royalist and quasiroyalist arrangements, notions of kingship of various descriptions, phylarchies, and many other polities. To impute to them all a unitary ethos and an idyllic and vigorous egalitarianism is implausible. When and where this confluence of tribalism and sectarianism occurred, as with the marginal Kharijites who have been a favored object of study for European scholars of Islamic political thought, it was the result of competition for resources and influence within the state, without which tribes as political actors would be inconceivable, rather than of continuity with a supposed initial condition of origin.

It is worth repeating that sectarianism was less the result of congenital "egalitarian" behavioral patterns than of balances of political forces and alliances within the state—alliances of "tribes" whose names may have been ancient but whose alliances, and sometimes whose very existence as specifically named political entities and certainly their genealogies, were subject to shifts, internal differentiation, adjustments, and telescoping in the context of changing conditions. Genealogies connected with the reconfiguration and consolidation of politico-genealogical groups were a function of migrations associated with the Arab conquests and resultant changing alliances, the formulation of which is perhaps inconceivable and irretrievable "in the wild," outside the ambit of state histories and particularly of the state register of soldiery and of pensions *(diwan)* and the context of genealogical literature, as recognized by both classical Arabic and modern scholarship. Genealogies are performative texts in the form of aetiological tales, like other denominators of identity, including "Islam."[25] It should be stressed, moreover, that it was not "tribes" that became Kharijites, but certain clans and sections thereof, according to geographical location, political involvement, socioeconomic position, and much else, that constitute the social elements of sectarian movements, without a serious consideration of which sectarianism would not be amenable to the historical understanding.[26] Yet this topos of tribesmen fulfills a specific function in the construals of Islamic political thought under discussion here, where it appears as a refrain much too often, without regard to time or place. This discursive function is one of simplification upon which is premised the attribution to Muslims of a congenital communalist ethic, and to flatten out Islamic political thought in general and endow it with a core of declamatory pietism.

It is therefore important to realize that a perspective such as that outlined obscures, in the name of originality and autochthony, the mainsprings of the historical elaborations of the Muslim religion and, by the

25. The literature is considerable. Suffice it in this context to refer to Bräunlich 1934; Henninger 1989, 54, 49–82, passim; Caskel 1953, 11ff.; 1962; 1966, 1:19ff., 27ff., 31ff., 38ff., 57ff., 64ff.; 2:417, passim. For very useful general considerations, see Szombathy 2002. Also see M. Saʿid 2005 for a painstaking and most perceptive investigation, at once historical and historiographic, of Arab genealogical literature, with results of salience for much broader fields of early Islamic history and early Arab historical writing. For not dissimilar conditions in barbarian Europe, see Geary 2002, the Arabian equivalent of which is still to be written.

26. For a proper consideration of some of these elements, see al-Bakkay 2001, 74ff. and passim. One might very well, *mutatis mutandis* and for comparative orientation, refer to more general anthropological and historical studies. Of the former, see, most notably, Evans-Pritchard 1949.

same token, the mainsprings of the political thought spawned by Muslim polities. According to the normal conceptions one would associate with historical writing, political thought under the Islamic signature would be sought rather in the widening circles of acculturation and the elaboration and interpretation of the emergent canon in light of political practices and ideas in place, rather than in contracting the remit to Arabia: this place being not so much Medina and Mecca as Damascus and Baghdad, heirs to very ancient royalist and monarchical traditions, institutional, symbolic, and discursive, in the light of which later developments were construed as original.

Thus for example political and gnomological literature attributed to Greek and Persian sages came with time to be attributed to Muslim authorities, in the same way as prophetic traditions generated in the eighth century were attributed to earlier times, and in which the persons of Muhammad, Ali, and others themselves became topoi to which were attached current practices, and indeed as hadith itself is a mass of exempla attributing to Muhammad later practices, dogmatic statements, and myths. There is a strong case for looking at Islamic political thought as an *interpretatio Islamica* of Late Antique kingship and at classical Islamic culture as *interpretatio Islamica* of cultures in place, just as in the process of acculturation natural to human societies as they change, triumphant Christianity produced an *interpretatio christiana* of what was in place, including exempla and political arrangements.[27] That very many aspects of Arab imperial culture and society, Umayyad and Abbasid, are in fact an *interpretatio islamica* of Late Antiquity is a line of research that has reached critical mass and now requires an initial systematic statement.[28]

It is not so much constraint within a poor and rather primitive original scheme of tribalism and elementary monotheism that is crucial, but

27. See Inglebert 2001, 326ff. for the Christianization of pagan exempla. For the Islamization of exempla in Islamic political thought, see Al-Azmeh 1997, 104ff.

28. The work of Peter Brown has, of course, been a prime inspiration for opening out the notion of Late Antiquity and assimilating some crucial aspects of Islamic history to its vast swell (see footnote 13). See, in particular and by way of example, G. Fowden 1993; 2004; E. K. Fowden 1999, chap. 6; Morony et al. 1995; Cameron, Conrad, and King 1992.

the way in which traditions, and most particularly royalist, absolutist traditions and traditions of sacral kingship in place came to be symbolically inserted in an Islamic textual and historical genealogy, and came to constitute "memory," and historical "memory," itself has a history, constituted of practice, fancy, desire, interest, abbreviation, oblivion, and the imaginary. This is the case with all traditions with their telescoping and rhetorical procedures and indeed with their invention, a theme that has become standard in modern historical scholarship. And although it be true, as books under discussion would have it insistently, that some Muslim divines did execrate kingship, this remained largely a pietistic polemical motif for use in jeremiads and does not constitute political thought any more than does the execration of kingship in the Bible (for instance, and very famously, 1 Samuel 8) found Byzantine or Latin theories of kingship. But what this means and implies seems altogether to have escaped discussions of this theme: what was the target of antiroyalist polemic for a variety of reasons was the title *malik,* usually translated as "king." But this title was infrequently used before it became rather common in Syria and Egypt from the twelfth century—it might be interesting to note that the title of the famous pietistic and eminently Sunni *Fürstenspiegel* of al-Turtushi (d. 1126 or thereafter) is generically and unapologetically addressed to *muluk,* the plural form of *malik,* as was that of al-Ghazali, much quoted by Crone. One might note, moreover, that the kings of Saudi Arabia and their Wahhabi ulama, rigorously pietistic and traditionalist, inflexibly Sunni and not given to self-irony, have no problem with kingship or with the term *malik.*

Nevertheless, some modern scholarship has taken the facile but entirely illegitimate route of making the term *malik* cover all supreme instances of political authority, thus misdirecting the gaze and entirely misconceiving the whole question, and indeed unconscionably proposing a false question, inferences from which went on to cast a mystifying historical argument that permeates and in many ways structures the books under discussion. The anti-malik polemic by no means vitiated the construal and veneration of Muslim monarchy and royalty, of caliphism and sultanism, both forms of *mulk,* royalty and royal authority, nor does it justify downgrading or otherwise rendering marginal or "inauthentic" the producers of political thought other than that of some Muslim divines. Equally unjustifiable is it to ride roughshod over the fact that caliphs, though sometimes referred to individually as *sultan*, were not regarded merely as kings, but as sovereign emperors of a universal state whose royal dominion is a legacy they received from God, the Prophet, and their own ancestors. Not dissimilar controversies took place over the title *Basileus* as applied to Christ in the Patristic period, the New Testament being replete with royalist epithets of Christ. But he did ultimately become, quite uncontroversially, the *Pantocrator* (Beskow 1962, 173ff.).

This tendency to prejudge historical developments is perhaps most explicitly evident in Black, in a manner that, if applied to medieval Europe, might have proceeded by quoting the New Testament (for instance, Acts 5:29: "we must obey God rather than man," or Rom. 13:1: "for there is no authority except from God") in order to demonstrate that kingship was merely a polemical topos with no salience to political thought and except insofar as it kept the clergy in a position of radical social, political, and intellectual separation from the exercise of power. But such a procedure is evident in both books under consideration and leads to the almost irrepressible inclination to ignore material evidence that speaks against such prejudgments and against the overpatterning and the stereotypes to which it gives rise or reconfirms. For instance, as already mentioned, Black frequently expresses surprise at finding in Islamic political thought matters he would have expected only in what he takes to be generically distinct "Euro-Christian" traditions. He asserts, for instance, that in contrast to Europe, Islamic political theory did not develop an organismic conception of the state (2001, 53). Yet the texts he quotes and lists in his bibliography, perhaps most notably the writings of Ibn Khaldun, are replete with this organismic conception: metaphors abound in which different functions of the state are compared to different parts and organs of the body, more systematically discussed in the medical terms, with the state giving coherence to the body-social organism, just as the predominant humor of a particular body may be described as choleric or sanguine and give that body a particular humoral consistency (Al-Azmeh 1997, 119ff.). Furthermore, Black finds in the conception of human society of Ibn al-Muqaffa' (d. 759) a view that is "strangely Hobbesian" (2001, 21). Yet all Muslim theories of the state and of order generally speaking, almost without exception, were explicitly based on such a bleak view of human nature.

Black's surprise and his denial alike sustain an a priori understanding of Islamic political thought that, as we have noted, is seen to arise from "Muslim societies," having themselves "emerged out of the Islamic faith" (2001, 15), in a history that "began with the Qur'an" (9), in which perspective it is unthinkable that certain crucial ideas in political thought might be shared by other histories. For "Islamic society" is "dedicated to the pursuit of religious knowledge" (26), and Islam developed as a "stateless praxis" in a revolt against Roman and Persian etatism (10). In the case of Islamic history, norms developed "from below," thus, against all historical evidence, undermining the project of monarchical authority (33) and vitiating the possibilities of historical comparison.

There are in this conception distinct echoes of Walter Ullmann's portrayal of medieval European political thought as structured along "ascending" and "descending" schemes, bracketing for the moment the points from which these schemes are said to commence their ascent. Quite apart from the fact that Ullmann's conception itself is somewhat summary and in need of serious revision,[29] although it might be of didactic value and to some extent of heuristic value, it is interesting that the denial of commensurability to Islamic political thought should be accompanied with implicit conceptual comparison with the "ascending" medieval European scheme. One might, if Medieval Latin cognates were to be sought, have more appropriately looked in another, more Platonic direction, and looked rather at the political-theological scheme proposed by Carl Schmitt.[30]

29. There are echoes of other Ullmannesque conceptions elsewhere in Black's treatment of Islamic political thought—the emphasis on legal texts, on church-state relations, the contention that the "lag" between theory and practice reflects incoherence in political theory itself rather than a consideration of political theory's politico-discursive complexity and the locations and complexities of its social embeddedness and reception. See Oakley 1973; 1996, 96, 106–7; Nelson 1997; Ullmann 1966.

30. These two views reflect, of course, like the scholarship under discussion, historiographic orientations, Romantic and otherwise, and associated ideological drifts. See the perceptive remarks of Stock 1990, esp. 63ff. These are clearly associated with political

Without begging the question of how such antistatist Muslim societies managed to produce far-flung absolutist empires and a formidable succession of vigorous absolutist dynasties, some of extraordinary longevity, it can be noted that these assumptions simply do not stand up to historical examination. Furthermore, having dissipated the possible leads to the core of political thought produced under Muslim polities provided by Ibn al-Muqaffa''s "strangely Hobbesian" perspective, Black clearly dissipated the possibility of examining clearly, seriously, and deliberately the theories of state, authority, patrimonialism (which cannot be reduced to tribalism), and royalty, whose connections underpin the main thrust of Islamic political thought and constitute its lynchpin, the point around which it coheres.

Such counterfactual assertions as Black's arise from a desire to construe Islamic political thought as at once sui generis and, captive to religious belief very vaguely conceived, as determined by the canon and to a smaller extent Arabian and supposedly nomadic origins that survived as "Islamic post-tribalism," which, in the view of Black and in keeping with desiderata of widespread clichés about nomads, were adventitiously tempered by patrimonialist ideas and practices (2001, 20). Thus, according to this conception, Muslim empires and dynasties, caliphal and sultanic, in view of their presumed sui generis propensity to decline, were based on societies communally strong but with weak and transient political structures, characterized more eloquently by Hegel as "destitute of the bond of an organic firmness: the kingdoms, therefore, did nothing but degenerate," devolving to what he so felicitously termed "ease and repose" *(Gemächlichkeit und Ruhe)* admixed with abstract violence and fanaticism (Hegel 1956, 358, 360).[31] Politics being inexistent in such circumstances, it is not surprising that Black—and others—embark upon writing a history not especially of political thought, but of apolitical and counterpolitical thought.

inclinations. For Schmitt, Peterson, Kantorowicz, and the overall problematic of medieval political theology, see Buc 2001, 212, 229ff.; Geréby 2004.

31. For this trope, see Grosrichard 1979.

As might be expected, this entire history, for all its complexity, is that of a Muslim nation "transcended at the moment it was created," which continued in the project of transferring power "from empire to Prophet," such that a community was created based on the shari'a designed "to determine morals, law, religious belief and ritual, marriage, sex, trade and society" (Black 2001, 9)—a mirror-image of Ullmann's image of the medieval papacy. Hence Black's contention that "the irony was that the Muslims had little in the way of political theory to inform what they were doing" (2001, 10).

Against such a common view, one would argue that Islamic political thought cannot really be said to have emerged before state formation or outside of it, and that the state in question is not Muhammad's but that of the Umayyads and the Abbasids: remote historically, geographically, culturally, and socially from Muhammad; inheritors of great empires; continuators of imperial ecumenism; legatees of a relatively short time-span of intensely accelerated history, despite their Arcadian idyll of desert Arabhood. Its idyll rather demonstrates nostalgia and underlines distance. For though the Umayyads and Abbasids were Arab Muslims, their Islam, unlike that of Muhammad, for centuries incorporated imperial peoples along with the territories, polities, and cultures of erstwhile empires, the Sassanid and the Byzantine that Black scarcely ever mentions and that he tends to dissolve into a "Euro-Christian" tradition. Behind both lay the whole antique and Late Antique ecumenical imperial tradition, without which no consideration of Byzantine or medieval Latin political thought is thinkable. It will not do to search for the roots of "theocracy" in the Bible or in the Qur'an,[32] although one will surely find textual support for it. It should come as no surprise that, being in the business of ruling, Arab dynasties first incorporated the administrative and ideological appurtenances of kingship left behind by retreating or defeated empires. "Stateless practice," if such were to be thinkable, only came in under circumstances when imperial authority receded, as in tenth- and eleventh-century Syria, for instance, when local urban patriciates, which included ulama, often

32. This is signally missing from Ullmann. See Oakley 1973, 24ff.

in alliance with plebeian fraternities, ruled briefly in urban political systems not unlike those of contemporary Italian city-states (Cahen 1958–59; Sabari 1981).

Black does acknowledge that the Umayyads tapped into the Middle Eastern rhetoric of monarchy, but he claims that this had little support outside court circles and that the Islamic mainstream remained anti-monarchic (2001, 18–19). It is very odd to write off "courtly circles" in this fashion when speaking of politics and of political thought. Indeed, if popular conceptions of political order were to be pursued, it is most likely that they will appear to be not populist but rather patrimonialist, rising from the local to the ultimate instance of patrimonialism, this last being monarchy, sacred and profane, with notions of justice and equity allied to concepts of honor and manliness reflected in popular culture, rarely implicating shariist notions and ending in divine justice and retribution dispensed by the monarch. There is no evidence that popular movements of protest (some, but certainly not all sectarian movements) carried a notion of polity and of political leadership that was conceptually at variance with the absolutism of the caliphate, most particularly of the sacral character of supreme leadership and the status of the supreme office as the fount and guarantor of justice and equity and the instance of last resort (al-Najjar 1981, 90ff., passim). Caliphs were the real and the imaginary, proximate or distant instance of appeals for justice, favor, and much else, very much like the Roman emperor (Millar 1992, chap. 7). If anything, this was accentuated by Shi'ite sectaries of all hues.

Black's argument that an imperial state ideology could not develop under Muslim polities, and that the caliphate therefore "failed" from the mid-ninth century (2001, 29–30), when the age of praetorian anarchy began, is clearly at variance with historical fact. This is so not only because there were periods of caliphal reassertion following the age of praetorian anarchy, some of them quite vigorous and effective, but also because, with the exception of short periods of eclipse and humiliating control, caliphal authority was exercised at a number of levels and in a variety of ways, some symbolic and some institutional, and yet others military and political. This authority was no less real for having receded during periods of relative military powerlessness (Al-Azmeh 1997, 131ff., chap. 7, passim), and bears comparison with certain moments in the history of Byzantine emperors besieged by vigorous Bulgar and Serb kings or indeed of various Augusti in fifth-century Ravenna and Constantinople threatened by Germanic princes like Stilicho, Arbogast, Alaric, or Ricimer who wanted to be incorporated into *Romanitas*, an accommodation eventually successful under Theodoric and his immediate successors. No moment in the history of the caliphate was nearly as chaotic and anarchic as during certain periods of the history of Rome East and West, but this circumstance is not considered by historians to be sufficient reason to decree the Roman Empire and its imperial ideology a sham; instability does not necessarily imply atrophy except in the perspective of the trope of rise and decline.

The source of this imperialist authority was precisely what scholars so often deny: that the Abbasids had an hegemonic universalist and arguably theocratic imperial ideology and sustained a presumption of the sacral character of the caliphate that with time was elevated to ever more hallucinatory heights, ceremonially and in terms of courtly culture expressed in a variety of genres, reproduced in independent and semi-independent provinces, some very remote, in imitation of and in the name of the caliphate, and down the line of social hierarchy. Caliphal authority was not confined to "tacit consent" for the application of penalties and the validity of contracts under caliphal control (Black 2001, 30). Caliphal control over legal institutions was never contested, despite attempts to diminish its extent in practice by overpowering princes.

In short, the situation was neither monochromatic nor melodramatic; it was dynamic and rapidly changing, and is clearly resistant to being cut to Procrustean measure as required by the scholarly vulgate under discussion. The caliphate was a most resilient institution; it is this that is interesting and salient to political thought, not the vagaries of events. Ecumenical, imperial caliphal ideology, moreover, was not only disseminated in court, but also in the marketplace reflected in popular literature, and its expression involved the very ulama whom the vulgate takes as the mainsprings of antistate, "post-tribalist" communitarianism. All evidence points to the fact that the ulama bought into caliphal authority and that, rather than emerging "from below," which some undoubtedly did, they were not outside the ambit of caliphal institutions and lines of patronage. Crone proposes that the ulama came into their own against the state with the early Abbasids, and particularly with the famous persecution *(al-mihna)* of al-Ma'mun and his immediate successors, in which the divines were compelled to embrace the doctrine of the createdness of the Qur'an in time and to abjure the thesis that it is coeternal with God.

Autocephalic Hierocracts?

But this common assertion is surely vitiated, not only by the fact that this was not a persecution of "Sunnis" who then came to the fore, but also because the mihna was put into effect by the ulama themselves, notably by Ibn Abi Du'ad (d. 854), against other ulama. There is no reason, apart from retrospective heresiographic assumptions and contemporary scholarship, which often tends to embrace them uncritically, to adjudge Ibn Du'ad and his associates any less "Sunni" than Ibn Hanbal (d. 855) and others victims of this persecution; historical accounts of these events have tended to be stylized, dramatized, with decidedly legendary elements.[33] Neither is there reason to attribute to Sunnism of the time a distinctiveness it acquired only later, a distinctiveness that nonetheless did not prevent it from being very much a broad church, ultimately not so much "orthodox" as catholic in outlook. What might arguably be described as proto-Sunnism came in many hues, among which Hanbalite literalism and pietism was for long a minority position, which only crystallized much later and remained a minority position throughout the classical period and the Middle Ages of Islam. That pietists sometimes refused payment for acting as judges or prayer leaders or teachers, or even refused official appointment altogether, is incontestable; there was indeed, throughout the classical and medieval Muslim periods, a pious genre of lamentation with reference alienation *(ghurba)* in an impious world buttressed by a prophetic Tradition of uncertain provenance, but it was by no means central to any social or

33. See comments of van Ess 1991–97, 456ff., 481, 486, 502ff. This persecution is generally treated very summarily, despite its great complexity. For an impression of this complexity, see van Ess, 1991–97, chap. 3, passim; and Jad'an 1989.

cultural processes. The correlative discourse on *fasad al-zaman,* the corruption of the present time, the discontents of civilization, and preference for the elemental is in any case quite ubiquitous and pervasive universally. But scrutiny of such cases of deliberate disengagement from the state would reveal that this condition was in great measure correlated with an attitude of patrician piety and haughty aloofness on the part of divines who disposed of private incomes. For the rest, and as Ibn Khaldun realized long ago in a famous chapter of his *Muqaddimah,* the cultivation of learning of a religious nature *(ilm)* was always a manner of gaining livelihood. Very much unlike mendicant friars, the ulama generally engaged in gainful employment, occasionally in trade. Remuneration for judges and other ulama, their institutional organization, and their financial functions (supervision of *awqaf,* endowment properties) goes back to a very early period in Muslim history (Muʻayatah 2000, 230, 234ff.). What rudimentary social history of Muslim societies that exists tells us indeed is that there were veritable, long-lived dynasties of ulama in state service (for instance, Robinson 2003, 162ff.).

When this pietistic and theologically fideist (but by not of necessity literalist) tendency did come into prominence (but by no means to predominance), it did so when it crystallized as legal schools and theological creeds under caliphal patronage. This was a time, under the Buyid occupation of Baghdad in the late tenth and through the first half of the eleventh century, when the caliphate was under siege with varying degrees of severity, and in the face of Buyid encouragement of plebeian Shiʻism and the consequent civil disturbances in the caliphal capital, the caliphate tended to adopt increasingly less latitudinarian positions on matters doctrinal. Hanbalite patrician divines, favored by the caliphate at one point, produced official caliphal creeds and were integrated into court, like the celebrated divine Abu Ala' ibn al-Farra' (d. 1066), who acted as judge of the caliphal harem and produced a legal treatise on government in which the prerogatives of the caliphate were sustained fully.

And although Shiʻism developed as a coherent phenomenon in some but not all respects earlier than Sunnism, what has been said about the flowering of Sunnism under caliphal patronage would apply equally to Shiʻite patricians at the time, divines as well as litterateurs and Alid aristocrats, in Baghdad at least, although Shiʿism is, with Crone as well as others, regarded as the very quintessence of contentions that the caliphate is illegitimate and is to be shunned. One might mention here al-Sharif al-Radi (d. 1009–10) and al-Sharif al-Murtada (d. 1044), Shiʿite patricians who were appointed to high position—such as *naqib al-ashraf*, Syndic of the Ashraf (descendants from Muhammad through his daughter, who enjoyed a number of privileges, including tax privileges and state subventions) and leaders of the annual pilgrimage processions *(amir al-hajj)*—and wore the black cloaks and turbans of caliphal service. It is not surprising that Shiʿite patricians, like their Sunni counterparts, should maintain their connection with the most patrician of patrician families (the Abbasids) at a time when the caliphal and imperial capital Baghdad had been occupied by parvenu interlopers, that is, semibarbarian princes and their troops seeking a political foothold among the ragged, unwashed commoners and their semicriminal fraternities.

Yet Crone, although aware of some of these matters, clearly prefers not to draw historical conclusions that might be arrived at from them (conclusions that might have ameliorated her account) and favors the constricting simplifications and the summary polemical labels of medieval polemicists, pietists, and heresiographers. She insists that "critical distancing" from the state must be taken at face value. What "critical distancing" (2004a, 38) existed on the part of certain sections of traditionalist pietists cannot be legitimately overdrawn or construed as a total model. There is no evidence for the claim that the ulama—eminently practical men, here summarily reduced to unworldly pietism or pietist activism—were the "acknowledged moral and religious leaders of the majority of Muslims" (33), a corollary to the unfounded contention that they were estranged from the state. With regard to "critical distancing," one might usefully compare this theory in some respects to the reserve of even state secretaries toward dealings with the moody, arbitrary, disloyal, and hazardous life at court and to their construal of the uncertainties of courtly employment as a professional hazard and an affliction with sometimes mortifying and fatal consequences to which ulama, including Ibn Abi Du'ad and his sons, also fell victim.

The social, cultural, and ideological histories of the ulama across the vast scale of medieval Muslim polities is still to be written. Hourani already warned that the fact that the ulama were ulama is not sufficient to explain their historical roles, being groups of persons who held offices, enjoyed privileges, controlled massive endowments, and had specific links to various social groups (Hourani 1976, 119). The assertion that Islamic political thought was predominantly religious calls up naturally the question of its agents and carriers, mainly the ulama according to this conception. One needs in this case to discuss the question of the Muslim hierocracy, an institution that Crone for one prefers to neutralize by referring to its members as "scholars," thereby lodging them in a ponderous, logomaniacal ethereality that conjures up images of remote yeshivot or seminar rooms.

In studying the ulama, one might with very many qualifications liken them to a Rabbinate,[34] though I prefer the term "priesthood" because it indicates a certain historical development that started in the eleventh century and culminated in the state priesthoods of the Ottoman and Safavid states (a Shiʿite priesthood created almost from scratch, with personnel imported from eastern Arabia and south Lebanon in the later instance when the Safavids imposed Shiʿism as the state religion of Iran). Another consideration of primary salience is that this social category, cohesive or inchoate in different measures according to time and place, fulfilled specific functions assigned to priesthoods by the history of religions and

34. The analogy is quite common in the literature. The simple image of the Rabbinate as an autocephalous community leadership seeking to "rabbinise" the Israelites collectively (Neusner 1987, 189ff.) and transform them into a community devoted to the study of the Talmud in anticipation of deliverance seems to undergird the conception of the ulama. But the history of the medieval Rabbinate is a complex one. They performed a wide array of functions, social, devotional, legal, educational, and magical, and they were collectively and gradually professionalized in the course of the Middle Ages. There were significant differences between those under the authority of the Babylonian Geonim, the Spaniards, and the Europeans, all of which was a function of political arrangements under which they were active. The simpler image seems to derive principally from the Tosefists of France and Germany. Rabbinical autocephaly was highly mitigated by the varying degrees of central control, perhaps most pronounced among those subject to the Geonim, whose prerogatives included certification and ordination. See Halbertal 1997, 96ff. In contrast, the ulama represented imperial religion and its legal and other institutions.

by historical sociology, especially Weber's, constituting what he called a "sodality." No religion can persist, maintain its devotional arrangements and credal armature, and police its canonical integrity and continuity without a priestly class, a class of religious specialists and professionals. That Islam did not have a priesthood—understood as a social function, not exclusively as a sacerdotal group—is an idea that can be dated to Muslim Reformism at the end of the nineteenth century. In contrast, medieval Muslim divines were quite aware of their very distinctive corporate and soteriological status and were (and still are) distinguished by special dress. With Crone (2004a, 395) as well as others, the denial of a Muslim priesthood underpins the contention that Islam is entirely sui generis, lacking the Christian separation of church and state. This was a separation that was asserted despite the medieval European grafting of different measures of sacredness upon the *gladius* and with the royalization of the papal office, such that the *sacerdotium* acquired an "imperial appearance" and the *regnum* a "clerical touch" (Kantorowicz 1957, 193), despite the Byzantine experience (on which, see especially Dagron 1996). It is meant generically and rhetorically to demarcate Muslims and their history, rather than to scrutinize closely the actual and changing relations between religious institutions, sacerdotal or not, and the state.

What is demonstrable in this regard, moreover, is that the ulama lacked social, political, and corporate cohesion before being transformed by sultanic states between the twelfth and thirteenth centuries, in the central lands of Islam, into a professionalized and cohesive force. Their upper echelons were to some but not considerable extent distinct from local merchant patriciates with which they were socially intertwined and eventually felt entitled to claim that they, rather than political authorities, were collectively the true inheritors of Prophecy as a normative system after the waning of the caliphate—all the while affirming that the order chosen by God for the world could only be guaranteed by the state, be it caliphal or sultanic. The ulama were not only ulama; they were stratified, as was society, and belonged to a variety of social groups. They performed cultic, legal, educational, administrative, and cultural functions and fulfilled magical, mystagogic, and thaumaturgical roles as well. These functions were configured differently at different times and places. They were patronized by sovereigns who controlled the cultic and legal institution and by political and military grandees as well as by patricians who founded and funded educational institutions that qualified them, employed them, and gave them prominence. They were distinguished by dress and educational formation and controlled vast properties (*waqf* endowments). Their entry into political life and their contribution to political thought were correlated with these circumstances, and they cannot summarily be reduced to populists, pietists, and moralists. Ultimately they derived their official standing and authority from the caliphate, which was the ultimate authority that certified and legitimated the legal and devotional institutions, de jure and de facto to the extent that this was possible, given medieval conditions of control and communications. The sultanic successor-states of the caliphate perpetuated the function of political instance as the highest institutional authority in the legal and cultic systems.

Yet the anachronism and the confusion between times that regard the ulama as having been corporately constituted centuries before they were to be so do not seem to dent the tropes Black wishes to sustain, with contrafactual insistence on regarding the development of Muslim jurisprudence a successful act of establishing an authority alternative to that of the state and its imperialist and royalist ideology. For this to be possible, Muslim jurisprudence must be regarded more as a pietistic and moralistic corpus of commands and prohibitions, in which the ideological takes precedence over the legal and in which reference to the canon is taken as literalist rather than hermeneutical, symbolic, and traditionalist.[35] Correlatively, Black insists on a contrast between neotribalism and patrimonialism (2001, 350ff.). Thus, for all his wide reading and some fine observations on matters of detail, the overall picture painted by him forestalls the possible understanding of the Sunni theory of the caliphate and deals with this important subject on predictable traditional lines, which will be discussed below.

35. See esp. Legendre 1974, passim, and, for a perspective from experimental social psychology, Deconchy 1980, 7ff.

God's Caravan

Crone reproduces in more ample compass most of the arguments stated already and, following her, it would be appropriate to begin at the beginning and with the Beginning, indeed with Adam and Eve. She proposes that this might be seen as an ancestral time when, according to Muslims, a certain foundational "paradigm" for Islamic political thought was set. Crone composes an Islamic myth of creation from a variety of disparate sources, connects them in a specific narrative confected for this particular purpose, and declares this to be canonical and original, despite the interesting and complex variety of creation myths in circulation, which would require careful handling and could call up a variety of associations, contexts of deployment, and interpretive possibilities,[36] and not all of which were of old-testamental origin.[37] Be that as it may, Crone's myth overinterprets this supposed Beginning to make government an inescapable feature of the universe, perhaps more in the spirit of Calvin's *Institutes of the Christian Religion* (bk. 1, chap. 5) than in that of medieval Muslim divines. Crone sees this Muslim myth declare, definitively and once and for all, all government that is not God's to be deviant and ipso facto illegitimate, not unlike Black's assertion of a "contradiction" between "Islam" and kingship. It is curious that this argument from primordialism is made a point of contrast between Islam and Christianity: medieval Christian conceptions of politics are not generally seen to be overdetermined by such primordialism when a similar argument might be made for a similar Christian deduction of political authority from the Fall (Buc 1994, 71ff.),[38] or from the royal figure of Christ in the New Testament that, in the full-

36. An idea of these possibilities might be obtained from Ajina 1994, 1:170ff. On the creation of mankind, see Ajina 2:64ff. On Satan, see al-Saʿfi 2001, 83ff.; and Beck 1976. See also Beltz 1980.

37. For instance, see autochthonous Arabian myths deployed typologically to ground Muhammad's priestly-prophetic authority in Stetkevych 1996, 112, passim.

38. For a notion of God's government much closer in letter and spirit to that Crone infers from her myth than to medieval Muslim notions, see Bossuet 1990, 1, 39–40.

ness of time, was to become a political theology with Eusebius and others, a liturgical element under Theodosius, and indeed a constant iconographic motif of the Pantocrator from the fourth century onward (Beskow 1962, 33ff., 123ff., 261ff., 295ff., 313ff.).

On the face of it, Crone's assertion that medieval Muslim political thinkers believed government to be coeval with Creation might well be unobjectionable. I will not go into the question of how legitimate it might be to posit this version of Muslim myths of creation as the starting point of political thought rather than to regard it as an argument for pious Weltschmerz and a component of Heilsgeschichte with implications for eschatology. Nor can I inquire, as Crone might well have done, into precisely when and in what sorts of contexts or genres of writing this myth, and the notion that creation and political power are coeval, were deployed. Nor again can I discuss that other relevant question, that of the interfaces between Islamic mythology and Islamic political theory, most saliently the typological use made in Islamic political thought of the figure of prophecy in connection with the caliphate, and even more so with the Shiʿite imamate; this is a matter of capital importance for Islamic political thought that is nowhere explored in the books under consideration. Yet it would be well to be attentive to the conclusion the author draws from her assertions and into the way in which this conclusion is made to convey the overall argument of the book.

Crone's conclusion is that only tyranny and anarchy are to be had without God's sole government, as mediated by His Messengers, the last of whom was Muhammad. Right from the start, this conclusion renders almost entirely redundant the main preoccupations of Islamic political thought, which is that of political order in general and the myriad connections between the sovereign and divinity, rather than the question of legitimacy or rather problem of illegitimacy, which Crone's consideration of myth is intended to render central. For quite apart from commandeering the appropriate Qur'anic verse, that God was said to have set up Adam and by extension later prophets as His deputies on earth (and noting that this was often stated in works about politics to be the origin of polity), the solicitation by Islamic political theory of such myths, when in evidence, is due precisely to the fact that the principal preoccupation of Muslim political thinking was exercised by the problem of order rather than of legitimacy, order being equivalent to what Byzantine political thought termed *taxiarchia* (Al-Azmeh 1997, pt. 2, passim; Abd al-Latif 1999, 108ff.), and of the way in which God continued to govern beyond the time of Muhammad, through the caliphs and the imams.

This topic in its turn is related to the "strangely Hobbesian" pessimistic anthropology already mentioned, and the consequent need of humankind for the imposition of order in a manner indivisible, reminiscent of God's indivisible suzerainty, His *monarchia*. Prophets were sent to advert and warn, messengers to convey dispensations in the form of laws for the proper regulation of human sociality, and righteous monarchs to rule, at moments when the perennial human propensity to recidivism became unmanageable and humans were in danger of returning to their fractious and savage state of nature—a conception contrary to Crone's claim that the Muslims generally saw the state of nature as having come to an end when divine mercy provided them with the Muhammad (2004a, 263).

Yet overall, order of the prophetic type imposed by messengers was not the only serviceable one to humankind, and in this context prophetic order appears as at once an historical specification of the broader category of workable order, which was of necessity monarchical and absolutist, and which almost invariably has divine sanction despite the protestations of some marginal pietists. It was also a soteriological preference, although a prophetic order was, by the broad consensus of writers on politics and history, uncommon. Indeed, the Muhammadan moment itself was usually pronounced to be peculiar, exceptional, miraculous, and out of keeping with the normal course of things, to be replayed only with the advent of the Messiah. For the rest, the perennial question of the need for order to be imposed upon an unreceptive and incorrigible humanity was central to political thought under the caliphate and its successors. It is a question to which no perfect solution was possible, given that sociality was an unnatural union imposed upon mankind by unsocial means. This position was not unique to Islamic political thought but was also prominent, for instance, in Augustine's notion of violence as an instrument of salvation (Morrison 1982, 82–93). Most important of all, it seems that the conclusion Crone derives from the mythological "paradigm" she constructs is seriously skewed: the conclusion that might legitimately have been drawn, and which was continually drawn by Muslim writers on politics, does not have to do with legitimacy, nor does it claim that only God's government is legitimate, but rather that given the unregenerate nature of humankind, they must be ruled, and ruled continuously, by rulers who may not be God's anointed, but who are otherwise God's appointed, if human sociality is to continue, with legitimacy and salvation an optional extra that is not always available.

Nevertheless, Crone insists on the model of political thought whereby polity is conceived as an "all-purpose community" led by an "imam": this last is a very complex term historically and semantically, as complex as its cognates *princeps* and *pontifex,* but which in this book is left captive to pietistic or, in the case of Shi'ites, vatic resonances and implications it did have but under very determinate conditions and contexts of use. What makes Islam and the political thought it produced unique, according to this reading by Crone and Black, is that the primary and axial concern of Muslim political ideas was not the ubiquity of government—its forms, mechanisms, and origins—but the ubiquity of illegitimacy, including the illegitimacy, or the ambiguous legitimacy, of all Muslim governments except those at the very earliest period of Islam. And it should be added: in the messianic future to come, a point to which Crone does not do justice.

The theology of history, and salvation history in particular, gives great weight to typologies, and Muslim typologies deployed in political discourses are far broader in remit and salience than establishing Qur'anic relations, as Crone does, between Muhammad and Moses (2004a, 16), or indeed than taking account of the Shi'ite stress on the pairs Moses/Aaron and Muhammad/Ali, which she does not mention.[39] But this cannot be seen reasonably to lead to the conclusion that the main concern of Islamic political thought is the question of legitimacy, or rather of illegitimacy. Legitimism and theories of the nature and functions of government are

39. For a rich view of this, see Mårtensson 2001. On Muhammad and Moses, see Prenner 1986. On monotheistic political typologies, see Al-Azmeh 1997, 41ff.; on Muslim typologies in general, see Al-Azmeh 1995, chap. 3.

quite distinct matters, despite their occasional conjunctions. Crone is perfectly well aware that Muslim Sunni divines, and with some ambivalence in Shiʿites as well, regarded all but manifestly and determinedly impious and antinomian authority to be legitimate or at least necessary for the good order of the world, and it is vexing that she inhibits herself from drawing the appropriate conclusion from this, and rather implies this could be relegated to incapacity, timidity, hypocrisy, or worse, rather than to the very foundation of their political culture.

Nevertheless, the question of legitimacy, making reference to arguments of an historical or quasihistorical character, did exercise the early sectaries. But the inordinate space given to early politico-religious sectarianism, in this and many other works on Islamic political thought, tends to underline the hyperdoctrinaire character imputed to Islamic political thought and to the predominance, presumed to be real rather than virtual or symbolic, of its marks of origin over its actual history, topics, and concepts. In all, the two elements of this position, attributing to Islam and its political theory an autarchic character, and confining its definition of politics to pious heresiographic positions, singly and together provide a perspective that renders inaccessible and unthinkable both the major concepts that structure Islamic political thought and its actual history, which starts not with the Arabs and their Qur'an but with the Late Antique traditions of monarchy (Al-Azmeh 1997, passim).[40]

Thus taking sectarian self-narratives for objective historical reconstruction, sectarian political thought is removed from the history proper to political thought and reduced to a political history of sects forlornly or neurotically pondering origins, bemoaning their loss, and in some cases seeking irredentist restitution by force. In this regard, matters not manifestly apparent to a surface reading of the Muslim canon or irreducible to presumed Arabian beginnings, that is, most dramatically certain aspects of Shiʿite messianism, are explained in terms of extraneous contamination, by the malign Gnostic "virus," for instance (Crone 2004a, 81) so that the doxography in this book becomes construed as a heresiography,

40. In shorter compass, see Al-Azmeh 2004b.

clearly here in the spirit of the connoisseur rather than that of the censorious divine but to the same unhistorical effect.

Clearly the model of interpretation deployed is that of accretions to and subversions of a clear Beginning, while much analytical and historical clarity might have been obtained from a reversal of perspective. The contrast with historical scholarship might be illustrated by scholarship on early Christian dogmas, in which Neoplatonism and other elements are regarded as integral components in a process of growth, development, incorporation, adjustment, and differentiation, and not adjudged as primarily inauthentic and un-Christian. This contrast applies also, and most saliently for the purposes of this article, to Christian-Byzantine political conceptions in connection with their late pagan and Late Antique heritage.[41]

The locus classicus for the trope of Muslims as super-Muslims irrepressibly given to brooding over origins, subversions, and imperfections are two collateral questions. The first is, as we have seen, that of legitimacy as, according to Crone, no mere human had the legitimate right to impose obligations upon others (2004a, 315, passim), this being the exclusive prerogative of the Divinity. This first question makes the main preoccupation of political thought that of tyranny—defined as ungodliness or nongodliness—and how to avoid it, in presumed continuity with ostensible Arab habits, now that proud tribesmen have been transformed into miserable subjects (145).

Apparently as a consequence, political thought, contrafactually unless political thought be confined to heresiography, is said to have become dominated by ulama. This is the second question. Crone is well aware that a "civilian elite" of courtly literati was active in generating political thought, but this group is, contrary to evidence, said to have flourished only from the third Muslim century, in conformity with the story of atavistic Arab purity in decline. In all, Crone's discussion of the rise of "scholars" under the Umayyads (2004a, 42ff.) is impressionistic and unconvincing, with the issue prejudged rather than argued in terms of social history. The lettered

41. See Peterson 1935. More recently, and by way of example of the possibilities opened by such a perspective, see Beskow 1962, esp. 313ff.; and Wallraff 2001.

classes—the intellectuals—of the early centuries are identified by her with Muslim divines, and no incongruity is discerned in the assertion of a purely sectarian understanding of politics, by divines, in the first two centuries, and the simultaneous assertion that these early intellectuals also comprised philologists, antiquarians, and others (146–47), without due mention of poets who were such important spokesmen of sacral kingship, much like state secretaries, often with a literary bent, descendants of the *grammatikoi,* and indeed courtly theologians and jurists. Understanding the social history of political thought in Muslim polities would have been greatly aided by a discussion of three types of cultural production under the late Umayyads and the Abbasids: belles lettres *(adab),* "wisdom" (*hikmah:* medicine, philosophy and the natural sciences), and religious sciences (*ilm*). Such an understanding would have been enhanced by giving consideration to the social and political bearers of these three genres, their relations to court, the types of writings on politics they produced, and the areas in which such writings were disseminated and the pragmatics of their reception, in different times and places.

But Crone insists a priori on the presumed dominance of the ulama, and on the assertion that they were somehow congenitally opposed to the state, contrary to evidence that they cannot be understood apart from the state, even the most pietistic *ahl al-hadith,*[42] as we have seen. Such an insistence seems to be a desideratum of the historiographic model structuring this book, from which the idea arises, in the work of some scholars if not to the protagonists themselves, that the rulers in place, caliphs and sultans alike, had "no legal status," that they were not "intrinsically Islamic" now that government was no longer a "mere branch of religion" (2004a,

42. See, in particular, the convincing contrary conclusions of Zaman 1997 for an early period commonly regarded as the point at which the "divorce" between state and society and between caliphate and ulama occurred. Similarly, historical fact disproves the contention of a "triumph" of the literalist and pietistic party from this point onward, specifically, Melchert 1996. For later periods, see in particular Makdisi 1963, passim; Laoust 1959; 1960; 1968, reprinted in *Pluralismes dans l'Islam* (Paris: N.p., 1983), 177–258—this last reference is a crucially important study not mentioned by Crone and cited but not used by Black.

146). Without considering historically the question of what might have been "intrinsically" or "extrinsically" Islamic or if these categories were indeed of analytical or historiographic as distinct from polemical relevance—and resting content with presumed marks of origin and of authenticity—Crone makes the strange assertion that, by the tenth century, only among the marginal Zaydis and Kharijites was the "pan-Islamic heritage" of "multipurpose communities" still alive in its appropriate tribal environment (212).

It seems peculiar that the carriers of the "pan-Islamic heritage" should be identified with the ostensibly pristine reservation of outback sectarians, except that this manner of transforming a historical fragment into a total historical type is unfortunately all too common. Yet the historiographic and narrative purposes served by this world stood upon its head are quite clear. It is thus not unnatural that the more properly historical and central "pan-Islamic heritage," exemplified by imperial and urban Sunnism—for the Sunni, imperial ulama are nevertheless also said to carry this heritage—is construed along lines arguably more appropriate for marginal, isolated sectaries dwelling in this remote fastness or that.

This point brings our discussion to the second of the two collateral questions that constitute the locus classicus for the trope of Muslims as super-Muslims beholden to tribalist egalitarianism, that of self-regulating communalism, the cognate of Black's "Muslim post-tribalism." Crone believes, apparently but in all likelihood not entirely in a spirit of didacticism, that her "Western reader" will be best placed to understand the Muslim umma or community if he or she envisages it pictorially, as a stock scenario of Araby, according to a once apparently gorgeous, if by now musty, metaphor, that of the caravan (2004a, 21ff., passim).

For not only in the beginning are Muslims said to regard themselves to be primarily members of an umma, but much later, in the eleventh and twelfth centuries, they also saw themselves exclusively as such. All forms of social organization—kin groups, legal schools, mystical brotherhoods, doctrinal movements, and much more—were "simply" subdivisions of the umma. According to this conception, "Muslim society," in the singular, was "an assembly devoted to worship" (Crone 2004a, 397). No mention is made in this context of social stratification, status groups, professional groups, residential groups, urban or rural households, bureaucracies, armies, or subjects of various states, among very many other things or "identities."[43] In this ethereal world, Muslims are supposed to have set themselves up as an acephalic community, remote from the state, either brooding about the past as they worship or work with downcast eyes and broken spirits, or conducting themselves with exemplary piety, cultivating the dubious "long tradition" of reading the Qur'an in an antiauthoritarian vein (230), all the while vesting authority in nothing but religious knowledge.

This last, religious knowledge, was supposed to be dispersed equally among the believers at large, even among greengrocers from Kufa (128); it was this dispersal that constituted, according to Crone, the notion of consensus, *ijma'*.[44] I need not go into the intricacies of this notion of great conceptual, legal, and historical complexity or into its social histories and the social, political, cultural, and other uses to which it was put, topics that have not yet been attempted by scholarship that has not yet even occupied itself properly with the social mechanisms of consensus over the canonical variants of the Qur'an and traditions. What is salient, though, is not only that the notion of consensus presumes in historical fact a consensus on the fact of and, to some, the necessity of disagreement and of mutual acceptance within given parameters of such disagreement—the assumption is that the Muslim community is collectively guarded from error, not unlike Gratian's *concordia discordantium canonum*. While the latter is premised on an inner unity emerging from inspiration by the Holy Spirit (Schlüsser 1977, 11ff.), the former is self-ratifying, a Great Tradition

43. Such a notion has decided consequences for the study of the ulama. In light of it, these are seen as a socially nonspecific, all-purpose, fairly homogenous and protean social actor performing its all-purpose role by virtue of authority arising, naturally, from religion in a society seen as essentially unstructured by anything but "primary" relations and "primordial" loyalties and by definition estranged from the state and thus united by nothing except religion represented by the ulama. Thus, for instance, in the much-quoted work of Lapidus 1967 and in the postmodern expression of similar ideas by Chamberlain 1994.

44. An impression of the complexity of this important notion may be gathered from Mansour 1975 and Calder 1983.

socially constituted—unlike magical constitution and certification adumbrated by Gratian—although behind the self-constitution of Muslim consensus lurks distantly some form of inspiration or at least a vague notion of theodicy or of grace expressed in a well-known prophetic hadith.[45]

The notion of consensus, crucially for this argument, was also traditionally regarded not as that of the masses but as that of the ulama. The ulama generally held the common mass in disdain or at best with great diffidence and, not unnaturally given their social role and status, excelled themselves in advocating the withholding of religious knowledge—as distinct from ritual practices and the simple profession of faith—from the common run of humanity. The Qur'an itself was generally considered to be a text with varying grades of semantic accessibility, a fact that expresses a worldly hierarchy of knowledge and of differential capacities for understanding and does not suggest a diffused knowledge open to all and sundry.[46] Not unnaturally, the ulama also generally restricted the profession and discussion of dogmatic matters to those duly qualified and certified (by a formal license, *ijaza,* and peer acceptance[47]), and the saying was very common that he who has no proper instructor had the Devil as his instructor ("*man la shaikh lah shaikhah al-shaitan*"). The state as represented by the caliph was often called upon to suppress unlicensed preaching. Even with respect to knowledge of the very Qur'an, it must be stressed that, in legal terms, proper textual knowledge of it, its preservation and retention, was a collective duty incumbent upon the collectivity of Muslims, not an individual obligation incumbent upon Kufa greengrocers, however meritorious (al-Suyuti 1949, 101). The divines who asserted this included the great al-Ghazali (d. 1111), to whom Crone devotes a protracted discussion, who famously spoke in terms of "bridling" *(iljam)* the commoners

45. This collective self-ratification invites some comparison with the Rabbinate, which is similarly self-certifying and which is similarly sensible to internal diversity resulting from the "ultimate contingency of all truth claims." See Boyarin 2004, 152–53.

46. Possible citations are innumerable. See McAuliffe 2000, 61ff.

47. On certification, see Makdisi 1981, 140ff. This book will also give the reader an appreciation of the overall educational process in question, of its techniques, structures, and complexities.

and preventing their access to theology. Not unnaturally, Crone like many others confines this reticence, which is in fact more a determined position associated with a severely hierarchical vision of society and its associated proprieties and improprieties than a reticence toward the philosophers (2004a, 187). These last are said, without good reason but in line with the polemics of a medieval antiphilosophical current of opinion, to be "inauthentic" or insufficiently Islamic, alienated and rejected or at best marginalized "within Islam," and thus fearful of the purportedly cohesive and closed all-purpose community.[48] Generally speaking, Crone's treatment of the central topic of hierarchy in Islamic political thought (2004a, 334ff.) is patchy and unsatisfactory.

So even on Crone's assumptions, it would appear that this supposedly acephalic community turns out decisively to have a head in the shape of the priestly institution, and to be so headed in a manner that is authoritarian or at best paternalistic rather than populist. We might add that this priestly institution, in its various times and places, is unthinkable without the state, including tensions with and ambivalences toward the state by certain of its sections and indeed with ambivalences and ambiguities in the course of the lives of many individuals who belonged to it. It will not do at all simply to describe the situation as one in which the caliphs were "the arm" of the "scholars" (2004a, 133). Clearly, when Muslim divines spoke about the equality of Muslims, they could have meant no more and no less than what would have been intended by Christian priests, monks, bishops, popes, and kings when they spoke of brotherhood in Christ.

Such matters are only the tip of the iceberg of obscure social history of religion in the Muslim classical period and in the Muslim middle ages. One unexplored area of special pertinence is the degrees, modalities, and social and political settings of religious observance and personal behavior. It is not uncommonly asserted, and this is clearly and continuously reiterated by the books under discussion, that Muslims were and are obsessed with piety. The picture of society that emerges in works of law and other

48. This view reflects an extremely resilient prejudice in studies of medieval Arabic philosophy. For a systematic corrective, see Gutas 1998; 2002.

literature written by the ulama tend to construe society, prescriptively rather than descriptively, as being determinedly and almost exclusively religious, and regulated by the shari'a, such that "the burden of social obligations that a medieval Muslim had to bear for the sake of general welfare and public propriety far exceeds anything imaginable to a modern Westerner" (2004a, 184). But this is apologetic self-representation of, and special pleading by, the ulama, not social history.

Quite apart from the fact that such a burden is equally attributable to other communities, including substantial Christian communities today who would presumably count among Crone's "Western readers," the point made is never demonstrated with reference to social history and is in the nature of an a priori presumption: any study of medieval compendia of legal rescripts and responsa *(fatwa)*, of medieval contemporary history, of books of market inspection *(hisba)*, and any attempt to look into the actual competence and reach of the central and formal legal institution in an age of difficult communication and difficult central control, or of the complex relations between local customs and bookish regulations, would alert the reader to the fact that things could not conceivably have been as claimed and that the social history of religion is, to say the least, exceedingly complex and should be approached with very scrupulous care.[49]

If one were at this juncture again to join Crone in her appreciation of Islamic political thought, to behold the spectacle of her caravan, and to note with her that autocephalic people banding together in this way necessarily required guidance (2004a, 21), and if the caraveneer be the "scholar," then one would find paradoxically that the main disciplining instrument at the disposal of this caraveneer is a notion of communalist nomocracy, dispersed among Muslims, the prerogative of no one. Implicitly following a model of arid Judaic legalism, which spread with deleterious analytical

49. Apart from works of hisba and collections of concrete responsa (*fatawa*—most notably the North African and Andalusian collection of Wansharisi [d. 1508]—on which work is based Powers' book [2002]), a start might be made with medieval works by jurists that take up the iniquities of the ulama themselves, such as al-Subki 1908, and works that discuss common practices in terms of the fiqh, such as *al-Madkhal* [The preface] of Ibn al-Hajj al-Fasi (n.d., 4 vols.).

and scholarly consequences from earlier notions by Schleiermacher and Wellhausen,[50] and habitually, almost by somatic reflex, generalized to Islam, this nomocratic order, sometimes referred to in the literature as orthopraxy, is generally called the shariʿa of which the ulama, in this conception, would be not so much the movers or the agents as the vehicles of its demotic and autarchic self-regulation. Given the simplicity ascribed to this "Islamic post-tribal" situation, this shariʿa, "sealed in the past," can only be an all-purpose comprehensive codified "constitution" (2004a, 281ff.) to which adherence must in the very nature of things be blind.

Nomocratic Desires

It is regrettable that Crone's awareness of the complexities of Muslim theology (2004a, 219) does not appear to have produced a sensibility toward consequences of such an awareness and that it does not seem to extend to the internal complexity and diversity of Muslim law. The author gives preference to the assertion that all one needed from religion was the minimal knowledge contained in old wives' religiosity, the religiosity of the goodly but despised rustics, *idiotês* or *idiota* to antique and medieval European letters,[51] an attitude to religious doctrine occasionally praised by some Muslim theologians hankering after peace and uniformity in moments of disorder, just as some Fathers of the Church tended toward favoring apophatic theology and stressed the primacy of devotional practice in the face of endemic dialectical disputes (Lim 1994, 153ff., passim). Indeed, some jurists and divines, like Juwayni (d. 1085), al-Ghazali's teacher who is also much quoted by Crone, or Ibn Babawayh (d. 991) for the Shiʿa a century earlier, did write handbooks of basic devotions and dogmas to guide the perplexed in conditions where there was no central control and no correlative juridical system in regular operation. But such works in

50. See the comments of Chapman 2003, 43ff. It is little noted in this regard that whereas, in Rabbinical Judaism, the legal rulings of the Talmud do constitute part of the inspired canon, the same cannot be said for Muslim legal works.

51. The attitudes are comparable and ubiquitous. See Stock 1983, 28–30.

themselves presupposed that the demos was, on its own, incapable of self-regulation or of correct belief. There were even juristic debates about the very legality of holding congregational Friday prayers without the authorization of the caliphate (Calder 1986, 35–47).

These considerations are important for assessing the twin presumptions of internal homogeneity and of self-enclosure that undergird Crone's notion of shari'a to be examined in the paragraphs to follow. On these presumptions, crucial matters for Islamic political thought are summarily dismissed. One of these is the question of non-shariist regimes that nevertheless assure the proper workings of human sociality, the lack of salvific prospects notwithstanding. This topic is not uncommon in Muslim writings about politics, and it does contain much material for theories of political order. What might plausibly be described as a conception of natural law *avant la lettre,* obeyed by human societies not blessed by a divine dispensation, is said to be absent. But such a notion of a human condition innately regulated by dispensation innocent of revelation *[bara'ah asliyya, fitra],* indistinct in outline and substance but nevertheless implied as a concept, was clearly there.[52] It bears some comparison to traditions of Stoic natural law (and to some extent Old Testament pseudoepigraphical and later Talmudic references of an unwritten law) concerning the regulation of human societies before revelation, perhaps most famously expressed in St. Paul's reference (Rom. 2:12–15) to a period *ante legem* when a dispensation natural to humankind was inscribed in the *syneidesis.*[53] Indeed such a notion developed a variety of discussions pertaining to the general theory of legal purpose, especially in works of jurisprudence, *usul al-fiqh,* and including most coherently al-Ghazali's *Mustafa,* Averroes's (d. 1198) commentaries on Plato's *Republic* and Aristotle's *Rhetoric,* and al-Shatibi's (d. 1388) *Muwafaqat.* It is implicit in the ubiquitous discussions of rational polities *(al-siyasah al-aqliyyah)* as most decidedly

52. See esp. al-Shatibi 1922, 2:225ff., 3:7; and al-Ghazali 1937, 1:63, 174.

53. See particularly Bultmann 1980, 218–19; Funkenstein 1965, 78–79, 129–30n27; Forschner 1998, 16–17, 74. I am grateful to Matthias Riedl for directing me to these references.

distinct at once from the religious and the tyrannical, of which the best known is that of Ibn Khaldun. When Crone does mention such matters, these occur as afterthoughts (2004a, 268).

By way of amplifying the remit of aversion to everything non-shariist and "non-Muslim" she attributes to Muslims, Crone unfortunately resorts to rhetorical arguments for the obsessive introversion of Muslims—without qualification—in common currency. Thus, for instance, Arabic philosophy, fairly competently if selectively paraphrased in the relevant sections, is set at a distance as not having been sufficiently Islamic (for a corrective, see Murad 1999). This setting apart serves equally to highlight the division between what is "authentically" Muslim and what is not. In a way, Farabi (d. 950) seems to be disqualified from inclusion in Muslim political thought on account of having learned philosophy from Christians who, contrary to what we know about most of them and about the great philosopher himself, are said to have "worked on the margins of high society" (Crone 2004a, 188). Nevertheless, Farabi is quite correctly regarded as having worked in terms of important themes pertaining to Hellenistic theories of kingship (2004a, 193ff.). Yet no appreciation is evident of the salience of this theme, central, as has been suggested many times above, to Islamic political thought philosophical and otherwise, nor are appropriate conclusions, connections, and comparisons drawn (Al-Azmeh 1997, 190ff., passim).

These and other matters are declared extraneous to shari'a, and therefore of little relevance to Islamic political thought. They are to be assessed, according to the works under discussion, by the shari'a's simple functions of inclusion into the autocephalic community and exclusion from it, and to be, on behalf of medieval Muslim thinkers, accepted as valid or rejected insofar as they did or did not relate to the shari'a's alleged status as "a moral order" defining "the moral status of acts in the eyes of God" (Crone 2004a, 286–87, 9). Quite apart from the fact that Allah is not a moralist but an exacting and sometimes capricious yet compassionate judge and taskmaster, it is important to note that the presumption that the shari'a is a moral code is a very common misconception that plays an important role in defining Islamic political thought as conceived in the works under discussion.

The shari'a, however, is in fact not so much a code of law as a general title for good order and an ideological sign, like *nomos* or *dharma,* and neither of the authors of the books under discussion has gone beyond the ideological use of the term made by medieval sources and modern neo-traditionalism to look into the precise uses and possible senses in which it is used. *Shari'a* is a term best avoided in concrete historical discussions, where attention needs to be directed to concrete expressions of it, namely, in Muslim jurisprudence (fiqh), which is very much unlike a code. It is rather a corpus of precedents, many of them contradictory but all equally valid under the principle of consensus, and is a body of hermeneutical procedures for interpreting both precedent and canon. It is clear that attributing to this the character of a code is meant not to describe or inform but rather rhetorically to suggest Levitical precision, definitiveness, and immobility, all of which features are out of keeping with historical reality and which are indeed anachronistic.

As for morality, Crone's argument under review, which is quite common in Islamic Studies scholarship but not among Muslim divines and for which there is little evidence in the classical sources, tends to gloss over the problems presented by considering the relationship between law and morality in any legal or social setting, in none of which is there a uniform pattern, let alone a correspondence between the two. It appears, moreover, that the insistence that shari'a be a moral code is a topos used to connote—but neither to describe nor to illustrate—the communitarian and acephalous model of "Islamic society," a ubiquitous caravan uniform over time and space, in which social practice is construed as conforming to law and in which law is presumed to emanate from uniform "Muslim" social practice, the two arising out of a religion that is the sum total of social life, and that fashions society as no more nor less than a congregation. The social and institutional modalities of legal precepts, institutions, and practices; their geographical and social reach; and their relation to custom and to *mazalim* courts run directly by political authorities; and collateral matters including, most crucially, the political, institutional, and ideological relationship between the legal system and the state; and the complex interrelations between morality, law, and religion: all these need to be studied in historical terms rather than as archetypes passing for ideal types and studied historically rather than solicited through ideological statements that might convey the impression of a utopian order (Powers 2002).

Rather than being a moral code or a set of moral precepts, the shari'a as concretely expressed in jurisprudence is a technical repertoire of law, although this did in many instances, in medieval Muslim history and in other histories as well, have moral and social force whose incidence and mechanisms must be scanned historically rather than be taken for granted as a priori assumptions. Works of Muslim jurisprudence often open with an elaborate discussion of the nature of technical vocabularies intended to disallow the terms used in jurisprudence from being used in a commonsense way, and it might legitimately be surmised that one reason scholarship has not frequently enough addressed the distinction between law and morality properly but rather identified the two is the lack of technical expertise and of patience to read through treatises of law and legal method. It is curious that the very substantive advances in scholarship on classical Muslim law produced in the past two decades, which give little credence to the image in common currency, are not often noted enough, as if with a will to denial.

In the eyes of jurisprudence, including Muslim jurisprudence, acts may be adjudged legal yet be in themselves immoral, and the task of lawyers, professionals of practical intelligence, was to translate *norma normans,* considered in strictly legalistic terms, into *norma normata,* which mediates legalism and practical legality. Casuistical means of getting around the prohibition of interest, for instance, were perfectly legal, and marital repudiation, which may be unfair and immoral and is indeed generally classified by legists as reprehensible *(makruh)*, is nevertheless in its turn perfectly legal. Muslim divines in the Middle Ages, like lawyers everywhere, were well aware of the distinction between morality and legality.[54] As practical lawyers and casuists, Muslim divines did not conflate legality with righteousness, and worked by discrimination, not by generalization in the manner of moral philosophers overall.

54. See, for instance, Johansen 1988 and Chehata 1973, 19ff.

For their part, morality and ethics were discussed in a variety of medieval Arabic literary genres, including philosophy, sententious literature, and biography, which are of decided relevance to political thought. But they form no part of legal literature, in which the criteria of judgment are technical rather than moral. They do form an important component in Fürstenspiegel, where they are treated in a fashion neither homiletic nor legalistic but rather utilitarian, occasionally with a breath of philosophical ethics but altogether as a component in the art of politics, of human husbandry (Abd al-Latif 1999, 76ff., 186ff.; Subtelny 2002, passim). Fürstenspiegel authored by later ulama did enjoin rulers to take the counsel from the ulama, and reminded them of their mortality and their duties to God, but they did not conflate fiqh with morality.

This egregious simplification of Muslim law, both as to its structure and nature as a legal corpus and as social practice, the former simple, closed, and conclusive and the latter a simple matter of blind adherence, is clearly crucial to the image of the "Islamic post-tribal" caravan and all-purpose community as described. The denial of history—and claims for the prodigious stability of Muslim law over time[55]—lends metahistorical stability and coherence to this presumed community and lends a certain glib cogency to its discursive redaction, in legal, political, and other writing. It is therefore not unnatural that Crone should write of the functions and duties of government in Islamic political thought exclusively in terms of restrictive monocratic prescriptions arising from the shari'a or the absence of such prescriptions.

The specific division of governmental functions between those that are shariist and those that are not is almost entirely Crone's. Her account of them (2004a, chap. 18) is enumerative and involves neither conceptual nor historical analysis, nor does it look into the important matter of the sacralization of the public order that takes place in the genre of al-*siyasah al-shar'iyah,* where it properly belongs (Al-Azmeh 1997, 101ff.; Abd al-Latif 1999, 145ff.). Not much is made in Crone's discussion of manuals and

55. This claim is normally officiated by means of the trope of the "closure of the Gate of Ijtihad," repeated by Crone, Black, and many others. See Hallaq 1984 and Turki 2002.

other works of Muslim law (fiqh), nor indeed of al-Mawardi's systematic discussion of these matters. It is odd that a book that makes so much of Islamic law should refer hardly at all to legal literature, to manuals and collections of fiqh, or to the very important theoretical literature on the principles of jurisprudence. Crone's discussion amounts to a combination of prescriptive statements trawled from sundry sources and anecdotal accounts of certain practices randomly assembled from historical works.

Among shariist functions discussed by Crone are the validation of the community, the execution of law, jihad (a good discussion on pp. 369ff., rebutting many stereotyped conceptions[56]), *al-amr bi al-ma'ruf wa al-nahy an al-munkar*) (commanding righteousness and forbidding iniquity), the preservation of religion, and certain fiscal services: in short, matters that are of concern to shariism as defined by the author, although we have no explanation as to why fiscal services for instance are included here or in the original sources. Commanding righteousness and forbidding iniquity are only rarely mentioned in legal works, and the issue appears more frequently as a topic in theological or homiletic works. That this theme finds its place in this discussion of Crone's is likely to be connected rather with the author's vision of autarchic communitarianism, in which public prerogatives devolve into the demos, to such an extent that she can state, with little justification, that it was meritorious "or even obligatory for private citizens to take the duty of enforcing public morality upon themselves" (2004a, 301).

Historical works are replete with accounts of the bad ends to which many such persons came, but there is no evidence that they were so plentiful as to constitute a distinct social practice at any stage in the history of Muslims. In the sources, the performance of such acts is in stereotypical fashion attributed to the rare persons who founded states or movements of revivalism (such as Ibn Tumart [d. 1130], founder of the Almohad Empire in North Africa and Spain). The difference is that the former unfortunates acted quite often in the informal and habitual ways of public vigilantism in moments of disorder and anomie, an extraordinary circumstance given

56. For an historical approach, see Rahmuni 2002.

that social control was generally exercised in the standard way common to all societies, by social relations and conventions, personal example, and police action. In any case, traditions about enjoining the righteousness and forbidding iniquity are meant for what in contemporary terms might be called pietist self-awareness. But being the work of practical men, such traditions were always glossed with an eye to the public interest. Such traditions indeed generally call on the vast majority of people to act against iniquity not necessarily with their hands, nor necessarily with their tongues, but in their hearts; apart from exceptional cases (such as Wahhabism or Talibanism), the tradition in question incited the moderation of peaceable piety, not vigilantism and zealotry. Clearly, here as elsewhere in this and other books under discussion, textual fragments are made to yield total social histories and comprehensive ethnological types.

But all this, the overdramatization included, still does not satisfy the inquiry into what relation shar'ist duties might entertain with public authorities and with topics proper to political thought. Yet Islamic political thought cannot be legitimately conceived without them. Without inquiring into this relationship, what we will have is inevitably an arbitrary miscellany, as in chapter 18 of Crone's book, where "internal security" and charity, axial functions of government in Islamic political thought, including the Muslim juristic theory of the caliphate propounded by al-Mawardi, are for no apparent reason pronounced to be nonshariist, and they are lumped together with the provision of medical services, the construction of roads and other infrastructure, education, and culture, containing potted information on this or that aspect of these topics, all of them important for social and institutional history and for the public/private interface of philanthropy and public work but not to political thought. Public order is a prime component of Islamic political thought, juristic and otherwise, and cannot be dismissed as being merely a desideratum of "non-legal literature" (Crone 2004a, 305).

The Spectral Caliphate

Having discussed the notion of autarchic, acephalic communalism and its supposed legal and other manifestations, we must continue following

Crone's categorical assumptions. The shariist community is said to have existed in fact, with historical predominance, even in capital cities and metropolises far removed from the Kharijites and the Zaydis, although the latter are incongruously also seen as its only remaining repositories. But this was also a world of make-believe. The Abbasid Empire, the erstwhile repository of legitimacy, no matter how dubious to Crone's presumed actors and in her own estimation, is said to have come to an "effective end" in 861 (2004a, 88). With the empire no longer one vast all-purpose community incongruously modeled on a small tribal unit, Muslims had to "cope with a fragmented world" but without so much as a glance beyond the facts of political fragmentation to the idea of an ecumenical empire that the Abbasids embodied, despite myriad troubles, for nearly four hundred years after 861.

The story starts with the "end of simplicity," which came with the arrival of the Abbasids (2004a, 32): this was when caliphs were, according to Crone and against evidence, no longer vehicles of collective salvation or continuators of soteriological genealogy but merely guardians of the community, thus becoming quasicaliphs, unlike their Umayyad predecessors, the picture of whom as it appears here often lacks coherence and conviction (2004a, 30). The caliphate is said to have henceforth become "a surrogate institution." A surrogate institution being better than none, the disconsolate Sunni hierocracy, their supposed antipathy to the state notwithstanding, therefore opted for a discourse on the caliphate that was like an insurance policy "without the small print," consisting of rules without qualifications, "even though the qualifications are sometimes such as to undermine the rules altogether" (2004a, 224).

Framing the Sunni legal theory of the caliphate in this way eradicates altogether the imprint of history and simultaneously substitutes the small print of quotations from here and there for the overall theory of the caliphate: this theory is embedded in a conception of power, order, and authority in the context of which legal theory is a specific technical elaboration. And the small print of actual history consists in the practices and theories of the supreme office that cannot with any justice be confined to works of doxography, heresiography, and theology, the mainsprings of Crone's discussion. The small print of legal treatises on the caliphate, so important for Crone's topic, demonstrates moreover, and quite unambiguously, that these treatises consist, not of prescriptive and idealizing maxims and requirements animated by a supine attitude of piety, but rather of technical legal discourse, which has little to do with communalist moralism and which consisted largely of "small print" (Al-Azmeh 1997, 99ff., chap. 7, passim).

The most salient case in point of this technical discourse is the most representative and influential treatise of the caliphal counselor, diplomat, jurist, and judge, al-Mawardi (d. 1058). He takes up the various prerogatives and functions of the supreme office, in a manner that integrates both shariist sources of public authority, such as interpretations of the Muslim canon, and previous Abbasid practice in areas such as war and peace, the delegation of authority, and public order. It is clearly incorrect to claim that the caliphate had not been previously covered in legal handbooks: the caliphate in general had not been so covered, being preserved in Palatine institutes, in the administration, in works of history and belles lettres, in works on politics. Yet some aspects of its functions had been the subject of juristic elaboration, such as finance and taxation as treated in *Kitab al-amwal* of Abu Yusuf (d. 798) some three centuries before al-Mawardi. These topics were in both cases presented, not as "constitutional law" (Crone 2004a, 222ff.), but in the manner usual in works of jurisprudence: as a repertoire of texts, precedents, and practices relating to the thematic cluster that makes up the juristic topic of the caliphate, from which the sovereign might choose according to the small print of circumstances and according to his appreciation of the public interest. The public interest here is not that of an acephalic "Islamic post-tribal" community but of the Abbasid state and its subjects, a universal Muslim empire working toward both worldly order and salvation.

What al-Mawardi did was not to try and "preserve" the "constitution" (Crone 2004a, 223), which did not in fact exist. What al-Mawardi accomplished in effect was to draw up a systematic legal repertoire of possible procedures for discharging the duties of the caliphate, to state comprehensively the legal aspects of public authority in systematic compass. The structure and purpose of his oft-quoted *al-Ahkam al-Sultaniyah* (1996) is that of a technical legal treatise.[57] In line with genre-specific properties, to each topic treated (for example, taxation, non-Muslims, manumission, the fisc, public charity, and the delegation of authority) a number of different options, interpretations, and former practices and preferences are cited, and a number of analogies are made with a variety of contractual and other legal transactional forms. The final decision devolved to the caliph, here acting in his capacity as the head of the legal institution. Muslim jurisprudence has generally the character of judges' law.[58]

The treatise was moreover written under circumstances when the worst was about to be over for the caliphate and when it was about to embark upon renewing itself, benefiting from long historical experience, taking stock of Abbasid practice and of legal arrangements available, after two centuries of serious disturbance and varying degrees of military and political disempowerment. It was unsurprising that this was a time when the caliphate continued and indeed intensified the ceremonial and literary expression of the lofty and sacral and sometimes soteriological aspects that it has always had. These last are given very little or no attention in the books under discussion and most likely reflect an aversion to nontheological and nonhomiletic works, as reflecting their "un-Islamic" origin in the civilian rather than the priestly elite, although the priestly elite, including al-Mawardi, were more often than not fully complicit in this ecumenical and monarchical caliphal ideology and counted as members of court. After all, they were all equally believers in an ecumenical Muslim empire, unthinkable without its supreme office. There is no justification for claiming that al-Mawardi's enterprise was doomed ab initio and that his "solution" was undermined by the Saljuqs (Crone 2004a, 234): historical developments speak to the contrary, and the claim makes no sense

57. It never ceases to amaze me that most discussions of al-Mawardi's legal elaboration of the caliphate give the impression that his admittedly dry *Ahkam,* on certain passages from which most discussions of his political thought are usually based, had not actually been read through and that it is unusual to find reference to his legal compendium or his Qur'anic exegesis.

58. No reference is made here to Weber's notion of *Kadijustiz.*

except as an a priori supposition dictated by the historiography of malediction that has already been reviewed.

Al-Mawardi was a contemporary of the last Buyids (for a century or so the overlords of Baghdad) and of the early Saljuqs. After a short initial period during which some of their princes behaved like callow parvenus, they preserved and at times indeed elevated the caliphal office, no matter how symbolically; having been originally Condottieri, they were "used to keep their religious convictions private, so they allowed the Abbasid caliphate to continue" (Crone 2004a, 220). They were born and raised in an atmosphere of imperial ecumenism embodied by the caliphal office wherein resided legitimacy, without which the world would have been inconceivable and in the context of which their indistinct Shiʿism clearly seemed irrelevant. The vast majority of them purposefully nurtured and perpetuated the caliphal office, for such continuity was not necessarily premised on caliphal empowerment but on ecumenical empowerment. Indeed, they did support the caliphs "in return for legitimation," and this is precisely the point of importance, provided we understand by legitimation the conferment of legality within a technical system of law. The connection between legitimacy and legality parallels that between morality and law that has already been discussed. The caliph was the ultimate arbiter of legality. The Buyids rooted themselves in imperial institutions, their private courts apart, which in any case calqued the administrative and other apparatuses of the supreme office. The caliphs were not simply "high priests" in their pay, high priests who, Crone claims contrary to evidence, no longer had religious authority (Crone 2004a, 222).

It was participation in imperial, ecumenical, and Muslim legitimacy, drawing on the prodigious symbolic capital of Abbasid caliphal imperialism, that the Buyids (and the Saljuqs, as well as the distant Ghaznavids, Ayyubids, and others) sought, as did Serb, Rus, and Bulgar princes with regard to Byzantium. This is why Crone's claim and that of Gibb and many others, that all this was just pusillanimous legalistic genuflection, is quite beside the point. The famous *imarat al-istila'* of al-Mawardi, often highlighted in Islamic Studies scholarship, whereby overpowering princes were mandated by the caliph with a multiplicity of caliphal duties and prerogatives, was in technical juristic terms in line with a variety of previous

Abbasid precedents, including the office of the vizierate, and not the work of craven jurists in the service of desperately solicitous caliphs keen merely to cultivate a charade. Its legal basis was the juristic notion of delegation and representation common in legal transactions, which varied between the delegation of very specific tasks and a mandate of broader sweep. The caliph decided the extent to which his authority and functions were to be delegated in light of circumstances (including circumstances of his impuissance), and broadly conceived delegations of authority resulted not only from diminished caliphal circumstances but also from decisions of earlier, strong, and very effective caliphs, such as al-Ma'mun during the vizierate of al-Fadl b. Sahl. Whatever extent to which the caliphate at certain points in its very long history was a shadow of earlier moments of glory, this shadow still remained the shadow of God on earth.

It was, for Crone, just brute force, in the form of kingship, that became predominant at the end of the period she covers. She vastly overstates the "illegitimacy" of sultans and, as we have seen, vastly exaggerates and overdramatizes the importance, salience, and consistency of the negligible few who sustained such a position (Crone 2004a, 45ff.). She consequently inclines to the view that kingship reared its unseemly head and came into its own only toward the end of the period in association with the waning of religion (153ff.). She finds in the Fürstenspiegel[59] a sacralization of kingship, and concludes that "to early Muslims, kings were usurpers of God's power. To later Muslims, by contrast, they typified it" (2004a, 164). There is no justification in history for such a conclusion, quite apart from the question of which "Muslims" are indicated here; both caliphs and sultans were conceived generically according to conceptions of monarchy divinely sanctioned.

In point of fact, there was no "return" in later Muslim kingship to "local Persian traditions" like Zoroastrianism, Neoplatonism, and Gnosticism

59. Like Black, Crone dates Arabic mirrors for princes too late, and regards them with no good reason as being "overwhelmingly" communitarian (Crone 2004a, 152), thus excluding, among other things, the very early works of Ibn al-Muqaffa' and Abd al-Hamid b. Yahya al- Katib (d. 750), and texts such as Ahd Ardashir, all much earlier than the eleventh century, not counting later works.

(Crone 2004a, 164). This position can only be maintained if one were to suppose that, after the passage of five centuries of Muslim rule, Islamic traditions remained foreign to Persia and that traditions in place since the seventh century remained unchanged. The fact is that we know earlier Persian political writings only from later and reworked versions in Arabic, not from their Pahlavi originals. The caliphs were almost from the very beginning conceived in the Hellenistic mold of sacral kingship, unsurprising as Islam is a product of history as well as of geography, the history and geography of Late Antiquity in the Near East, and not a product of the early polity of Muhammad's Arabia, except insofar as this last is presented as a genealogical charter.

Crone does mention, almost as an afterthought, that Late Antique notions were active in the early claim by the Umayyads to sacral office without any sense of incongruity, as they were far more "tribal" and "Arabian" than their successors and would not therefore, according to the interpretative themes of this book, be expected to be so sullied. Nevertheless, it is maintained that these claims were ostensibly severed with the coming of the Abbasids and compromised by her assumption, unfounded as we saw, that the ulama thenceforth became the central social fact. Crone's discussion of the Umayyads is somewhat ambiguous and in part uncertain, portraying them as at once the end of early Muhammadan religious charisma and as continuators of Late Antique royalism and allowing them no legacy to later political thinking. This displays a characteristic reluctance to see the two—Muhammadan charisma along dynastic lines and Late Antique monarchism—as confluent and indeed correlative. Like the Umayyads, the Abbasids continued until the very end to be God's direct deputies and appointees, and Muhammad's legatees and kinsmen as well (Crone 2004a, 195n113). That some ulama objected to this mattered little and cannot legitimately be made into the centerpiece of "Islamic political thought." Similarly, that the pope is not St. Peter but his vicar does not prevent the former from carrying the keys to heaven, nor does the fact that an icon is a mere figure diminish its magical effectiveness.

For a proper appreciation of the history of Islamic political thought, a major shift of perspective is required, one in which it matters little conceptually whether the supreme political instance is occupied by a king or by a caliph: the two were grafted one upon the other as to their monarchical descriptions, prerogatives, epithets, and functions. Indeed, the caliphate was a technical juristic specification within the generic instance of monarchy, adding to it a genealogy of blood, of kinship with the Prophet, and the charisma of his apostolate. A technical specification is precisely what is explicitly offered: at the very beginning of his *Akham*, al-Mawardi mentions briefly the rational justification of monarchy, which we have seen to be grounded in the crooked timber of humanity, and the resultant problem of order and its maintenance, which can only be assured by overpowering authority. But he says that for his purpose, for the purpose of a legal treatise, these considerations are irrelevant, as legal institutes are derived from distinctive sources using particular procedural rules building upon traditions, not least because the imam has to fulfill certain obligations of a devotional nature that might not in themselves be called for rationally (al-Mawardi 1973, 3). By the same token, we find that salvation-historical arguments are absent from this account, except insofar as there is reference to Muhammad's prophecy. Such irrelevance is genre-specific: the purely rational, anthropological argument is not untrue, nor incorrect, certainly not false or otherwise irrelevant, but its place is not in legal treatises but in other genres, like advice literature, to which al-Mawardi himself contributed. The imperative of monarchy is an a priori ground for order in the world overall. The specification of the caliphal form of monarchy in terms of Muslim jurisprudence is a technical one, albeit the ground for the best of all possible worlds.

Conclusion

It may be said that if the study of Islamic political thought is to be pursued according to a way that is recognizably historical, and in order for it to be appropriate to the frame of historical inquiry, historical material pertaining to it needs to be configured, in its emphases, in a manner corresponding to what the present state of historical knowledge and historical method requires and allows. Otherwise the history of political conceptions under the Muslim empires would remain largely the *terra obscura* that we gather from the books under discussion. We have seen how certain matters are amplified beyond measure in order to fit a preconceived pattern and narrative of rise and decline, how marginal matters are overinterpreted, how central matters are registered as afterthoughts and underinterpreted, and how the history of Islamic political thought and of its central concepts are construed in a manner so contrafactual, improbable, and tendentious as to produce an image unrecognizable to the frame of history and resistant to the basic requirements of historical scholarship. That the books discussed above are meant to be textbooks and that textbooks are meant to simplify is something quite other than making them the occasion for uncritically and unreflectively restating and perpetuating an old *doxa*.

We have seen how claims for exceptionalism are used to justify an egregious disregard for both the normal equipment of the historical science and the usual workings of human societies, and how there is instead an insistence on a predictable, well-defined, stable *homo islamicus,* who may surprise but who must be prevented from speaking in any tongue but that of the shibboleth. "Islam" becomes thereby a denominative category that runs amok, calling up common clichés with which to fill itself. In this way, a paradigmatic grid of misapprehension, sometimes almost willful, is perpetuated in textbook form.

It has been suggested that this state of affairs with the current historiography of Islamic political thought is a function of overpatterning and of the primacy of clichés and stereotypes, untempered by an undeniable measure of historical knowledge. As a consequence, I should suggest that, in redressing the situation, historical scholarship needs to go beyond the name of Islam taken as a grid of historical categorization and a means of historical explanation. "Islam" appears in the literature surveyed as a categorical fallacy, as a vast error of historical categorization, and needs to be decomposed to other categories amenable to historical treatment. One could then avoid skewed emphases, repetitive clichés, and missed opportunities for proper historical narrative and interpretation afforded by the sources, and disallowed, as we have seen, by being simply ignored.

Above all, for the study of Islamic political conceptions to go forward, I hope that it is clear from the above that it would need properly to define its subject matter and the topics crucial for its understanding, and not to rest content with recourse to the paraphrase and the common cliché, which can only result when attempts are not made to go beyond the smoke screen of the medieval sources. And these topics would need to be integrated within the broader historical swell that gave rise to them and beyond divisions of East and West, Christendom and Islam—beyond an ideological and culturalist historiography that conjures up historical entities by naming them. In this connection, this broad historical swell is that of Near Eastern, Hellenistic, and Late Antique conceptions of monotheistic monarchy as inflected by ecumenical imperialism and wedded to Muslim genealogies—the double genealogy of the caliphate, at once directly connected to divine dispensation, and to Muhammad's dispensation, figuring at once as charisma, legal order, and blood relation, but also inserted in a universal history of salvation.

Clearly, an appropriate starting point here might be the imaginative, innovative, and erudite scholarship spawned in recent decades by studies of Late Antiquity, which has brought under critical scrutiny most of the commonplaces concerning late Rome and Byzantium, and early medieval Europe as well, and opened the way to a reconsideration of periodization in terms of a very fruitful comparativism, beyond the conjuration of labels and dewy-eyed classicism. Finally, the appeal to Late Antiquity is not yet another search in the quest for origins; it is an inquiry into conditions of possibility and the starting point of a comparativism and of a periodization.

WORKS CITED

INDEX

Works Cited

Abd al-Jabbar al-Asadabadi al-Qadi. 1966. *Tathbit dala'il al-nubuwwah.* Edited by Abd al-Karim Uthman. Beirut: Dar al-Arabiyah.

———. n.d. *Al-Mughni fi al-adl wa'l-tawhid.* Edited by Abd al-Halim Mahmud and Sulayman Dunya. Cairo: Al-Dar al-Misriyah lil-Ta'lif wa al-Tarjamah.

Abd al-Latif, Kamal. 1999. *Fi tashrih usul al-istibdad: qira'ah fi nizam al-adab al-sultaniyah.* Beirut: Dar al-Tali'ah lil-Tiba'ah wa al-Nashr.

Abd al-Raziq, Ali. 1933–34. "*L'Islam et les bases du pouvoir,* par 'Ali 'Abdurraziq." Translated by Léon Bercher. *Revue des Études Islamiques* 7(3): 353–91 and 8(2): 163–222.

———. 1972. *Al-Islam wa usul al-hukm.* Beirut: Al-Mu'assasah al-Arabiyah lil-Dirasat wa al-Nashr.

———. 1994. *L'Islam et les fondements du pouvoir.* Translated by Abdou Filali-Ansary. Paris: Éditions La Découverte.

Abdel Razek, Ali. 2012. *Islam and the Foundations of Political Power.* Edited by Abdou Filali-Ansary, translated by Maryam Loutfi. Edinburgh: Edinburgh Univ.

Abdullah, Sayyid Muhammad. 1968. *Mabahis.* Delhi: Kutub Khanah Naziriyah.

Abou el Fadl, Khaled M. 2001. *And God Knows the Soldiers: The Authoritative and the Authoritarian in Islamic Discourses.* Lanham, MD: Univ. Press of America.

———. 2004. *Islam and the Challenge of Democracy.* Princeton, NJ: Princeton Univ. Press.

Abu al-Fazl. 1863. *Insha'-i Abu al-Fazl.* Lucknow, India: Newalkishor.

———. 1965[1872, 2005]. *A'in-i Akbari, I.* Translated by Henry Blochmann. Delhi: Oriental Reprints. [Also 1872 edition. Edited by Heinrich Blochmann. Calcutta: Bibliotheca Indica. Reprint, 2005. Aligarh: Sir Syed Academy.]

———. 1873–86. *Akbar-namah.* Edited by Agha Ahmad Ali and Abdur Rahim. Calcutta: Bibliotheca Indica. [Also 1998 edition. Translated by Henry Beveridge. Delhi: Low Price Publications.]

Abu al-Majd, Ahmad Kamal. 1962. *Nazarat hawla al-fiqh al-dusturi fi al-Islam.* Cairo: Matba'ah al-Azhar.

Abu Ubayd al-Qasim ibn Sallam. 1988. *Kitab al-amwal.* Edited by Abd al-Amir Ali Muhanna. Beirut: Dar al-Hadathah.

Acar, Feride. 2002. "Turgut Özal: Pious Agent of Liberal Transformation." In *Political Leaders and Democracy in Turkey,* edited by Metin Heper and Sabri Sayarı, 163–80. Lanham, MD: Lexington Books.

Afsaruddin, Asma. 1999. "In Praise of the Caliphs: Recreating History from the *Manaqib* Literature." *International Journal of Middle East Studies* 31(3): 329–50.

———. 2006. "The 'Islamic State': Genealogy, Facts, and Myths." *Journal of Church and State* 48(1): 153–73.

Ahmad, Aziz. 1969. *An Intellectual History of Islam in India.* Edinburgh: Edinburgh Univ. Press.

Ahmad, Layla Abd al-Latif. 1987. *Al-Sa'id fi ahd Shaikh al-Arab Hammam.* Cairo: al-Hay'ah al-Misriyah al-Ammah lil-Kitab.

Aigle, Denise. 2005. *Le Fars sous la domination mongole. Politique et fiscalité (XIIIe XIVe s.).* Paris: Association pour l'avancement des études iraniennes.

Ajina, Muhammad. 1994. *Mawsu'at asatir al-Arab an al-jahiliyah.* Beirut: Dar al-Farabi.

Akif, Muhammad Mahdi. 2005. "Fi hiwar shamil: al-Murshid al-amm lil-Ikhwan al-Muslimin." *Afaq Arabiyah,* Dec. 22.

Akyıldız, Ali. 1993. *Tanzimat Döneminde Osmanlı Merkezi Teşkilatında Reform: 1836–1856.* Istanbul: Eren.

Alam, Muzaffar. 1996. "Assimilation from a Distance: Confrontation and Sufi Accommodation in Awadh Society." In *Tradition, Dissent and Ideology: Essays in Honour of Romila Thapar,* edited by R. Champakalakshmi and Sarvepalli Gopal, 164–94. Delhi: Oxford Univ. Press.

———. 2012. "Strategy and Imagination in a Mughal Sufi Story of Creation." *Indian Economic and Social History Review* 49(2): 151–95.

Algar, Hamid. 1990. "Political Aspects of Naqshbandi History." *Naqshibandis.* Istanbul: ISIS: 123–52.

Ali, Ahmed, trans. 1984. *Al-Qur'an.* Princeton, NJ: Princeton Univ. Press.

Ali Sirhindi, Nasir. 1872. *Diwan-i Nasir Ali.* Lucknow, India: Newalkishor.

Allievi, Stefano, and Jørgen Nielsen, eds. 2003. *Muslim Networks and Transnational Communities in and Across Europe.* Boston: E. J. Brill.

al-Amiri al-Nishaburi, Abu al-Hasan Muhammad ibn Yusuf. 1967. *Kitab al-i'lam bimanaqib al-Islam*. Edited by Ahmad Abd al-Hamid Ghurab. Cairo: Dar al-katib al-Arabi. Reprint, 1988. Tehran: Markaz Nashr-i Danishgahi.

Amuli, Talib. 1967. *Kulliyat-i ash'ar-i Malik al-Shu'ra Talib Amuli*. Edited by Muhammad Tahiri Shihab. Tehran: Sana'i.

Anderson, Benedict. 1992. *Imagined Communities: Reflections on the Origin and Spread of Nationalism*. London: Verso.

Anderson, Jon W. 2005. "Wiring Up: The Internet Difference for Muslim Networks." In *Muslim Networks: From Hajj to Hiphop*, edited by Miriam Cooke and Bruce B. Lawrence, 252–63. Chapel Hill: Univ. of North Carolina Press.

Anidjar, Gil. 2003. *The Jew, the Arab: A History of the Enemy*. Stanford, CA: Stanford Univ. Press.

An-Na'im, Abdullahi Ahmad. 2010. *Islam and the Secular State: Negotiating the Future of Shari'a*. Cambridge, MA: Harvard Univ. Press.

Anton, Hans Hubert. 1968. *Fürstenspiegel und Herrscherethos in der Karolingerzeit*. Bonn: Röhrscheid.

Aqili, Sayf al-Din Haji ibn Nizam. 1958. *Asar al-vuzara'*. Edited by Mir Jalal al-Din Hussein Urmavi. Tehran: Intisharat-i Danishgah-i Tehran.

Arjomand, S. A. 1979. "Religion and Ideology in the Constitutional Revolution." *Iranian Studies* 12(4): 283–91.

———. 1999. "The Law, Agency, and Policy in Medieval Islamic Society: Development of the Institutions of Learning from the Tenth to the Fifteenth Century." *Comparative Studies in Society and History* 41(2): 263–93.

———. 2001. "Perso-Indian Statecraft, Greek Political Science and the Muslim Idea of Government." *International Sociology* 16(3): 455–73.

———. 2003. "Medieval Persianate Political Ethic." *Studies on Persianate Societies* 1(1): 3–28.

Arnold, Thomas W. 1924. *The Caliphate*. Oxford, UK: Clarendon Press.

al-Arwi, Abd Allah. 1992. *Mafhum al-tarikh*. Beirut: al-Markaz al-Thaqafi al-Arabi.

Asad, Talal. 1986. "The Idea of an Anthropology of Islam." Center for Contemporary Arab Studies Occasional Paper Series. Washington, DC: Georgetown University.

al-Ash'ari, Abu al-Hasan Ali b. Isma'il. 1929–33. *Maqalat al-Islamiyyin*. Edited by Helmut Ritter. Istanbul: Devlet Matbaasi.

al-Ashmawi, Muhammad Sa'id. 1987. *Al-Islam al-siyasi*. Cairo: Sina lil-Nashr.

Assmann, Jan. 2000. *Herrschaft und Heil. Politische Theologie in Altägypten, Israel und Europa*. Munich: Carl Hanser.

Aubin, Jean. 1981. "Un chroniqueur méconnu, Sabankarai." *Studia Iranica* 10(2): 213–24.

———. 1995. *Emirs Mongols et vizirs persans dans les remous de l'acculturation*. Paris: Association pour l'avancement des études iraniennes.

Averroës. 2001. *Decisive Treatise and Epistle Dedicatory*. Translated by Charles E. Butterworth. Provo, UT: Brigham Young Univ. Press.

Al-Awadi, Hesham. 2004. *In Pursuit of Legitimacy: The Muslim Brothers and Mubarak, 1982–2000*. London: I. B. Tauris.

al-Awwa, Muhammad Salim. 1979. *Fi usul al-nizam al-jina'i al-Islami: dirasah muqaranah*. Cairo: Dar al-Ma'arif.

———. 1987. *Al-Aqbat wa al-Islam*. Cairo: Dar al-Shuruq.

———. 1989. *Fi al-nizam al-siyasi lil-dawla al-Islamiyah*. Cairo: Dar al-Shuruq.

———. 1998. *Al-Haqq Fi al-ta'abir*. Cairo: Dar al-Shuruq.

———. 1999. *Religion and Political Structures: An Islamic Viewpoint*. Occasional Papers no. 3. Birmingham, UK: Centre for the Study of Islam and Christian-Muslim Relations.

Azad Bilgrami, Mir Ghulam Ali. 1910. *Ma'asir al-kiram*. Hyderabad: Kutub Khanah Asifiyah.

al-Azm, Sadik Jalal. 1969. *Naqd al-fikr al-dini*. Beirut: Dar al-Tali'ah.

Al-Azmeh, Aziz. 1982. *Ibn Khaldun: An Essay in Reinterpretation*. London: Frank Cass.

———. 1986. *Arabic Thought and Islamic Societies*. London: Croom Helm.

———. 1993. *Islams and Modernities*. London: Verso.

———. 1994. "Chronophagous Discourse: A Study of Clerico-Legal Appropriation of the World in a Muslim Tradition." In *Religion and Practical Reason*, edited by Frank E. Reynolds and David Tracey, 163–212. Albany: State Univ. of New York Press.

———. 1995. *Al-Kitabah al-tarikhiyah wa al-ma'rifah al-tarikiyah*. Beirut: Dar al-Tali'ah.

———. 1997. *Muslim Kingship: Power and the Sacred in Muslim, Christian, and Pagan Polities*. London: I. B. Tauris.

———. 1998a. "The Muslim Canon from Late Antiquity to the Era of Modernism." In *Canonisation and Decanonisation*, edited by A. van der Kooij and K. van der Toorn, 191–228. Leiden: E. J. Brill.

———. 1998b. "Geschichte, Kultur und die Suche nach dem Organischen." In *Die Vielfalt der Kulturen: Erinnerung, Geschichte, Identität 4,* edited by Jörn Rüsen, Michael Gottlob, and Achim Mittag, 74–114. Frankfurt: Suhrkamp.

———. 2001. "Civilization, Culture, and the New Barbarians." *International Sociology* 16(1): 75–93.

———. 2004a. "Islam and the History of Civilisations." *Tidskrift för Mellanost-studier* 11(2): 61–87.

———. 2004b. "Monotheistic Kingship." In *Monotheistic Kingship: The Medieval Variants,* edited by J. Bak and A. Al-Azmeh, 9–29. Budapest: Central European Univ. Press.

———. 2006. *The Times of History: Universal Topics in Islamic Historiography.* Budapest: Central European Univ. Press.

Babur, Zahir al-Din Muhammad. 1970. *Babur-namah.* Translated by Annette S. Beveridge. Delhi: Oriental Reprints.

Bada'uni, Abd al-Qadir. 1865–69[1973]. *Muntakhab al-tawarikh.* 3 vols. Edited by Kabir al-Din Ahmad, Ahmad Ali, and W. N. Lees. Calcutta: Bibliotheca Indica. Reprint, Delhi: Oriental Reprints. [Also see English translations: Vol. 1 by G. S. A. Ranking; Vol. 2 by W. H. Lowe; Vol. 3, by T. W. Haig.]

al-Baghdadi, Abd al-Qahir ibn Tahir. 1970. *Kitab al-milal wa al-nihal.* Edited by Albir Nasri Nadir. Beirut: Dar al-Mashriq.

Baghdadi, Baha' al-Din Muhammad b. Mu'ayyad. 1937. *Al-Tawassul ila al-tarassul.* Edited by Ahmad Bahmanyar. Tehran: N.p.

al-Baghdadi, Isma'il Paşa. 1951–55. *Hadiyat al-arifin.* Istanbul: Tubi'a bi-inayat wakalat al-ma'arif fi matba'atiha.

Bahar, Muhammad Taqi. 1958. *Sabkshinasi ya tarikh-i tatawwur-i nasr-i farsi.* Tehran: Amir Kabir.

Baker, Raymond William. 1990. *Sadat and After: Struggles for Egypt's Political Soul.* Cambridge, MA: Harvard Univ. Press.

———. 2003. *Islam without Fear: Egypt and the New Islamists.* Cambridge, MA: Harvard Univ. Press.

al-Bakkay, Latifah. 2001. *Harakah al-Khawarij: nash'atuha wa tatawwuruha ila nihayah al-ahd al-Umawi.* Beirut: Dar al-Tali'ah lil-Tiba'ah wa al-Nashr.

al-Baladhuri, Ahmad ibn Yahya. 1866. *Futuh al-Buldan.* Edited by M. J. de Goeje. Leiden: E. J. Brill.

———. 1960. *Ansab al-ashraf.* Edited by Muhammad Hamid Allah. Cairo: Dar al-Ma'rif.

———. 1968. *Liber expugnationis regionum*. Edited by M. J. de Goeje. Lugduni Batavorum: E. J. Brill.

Balibar, Etienne. 1998. "The Borders of Europe." In *Cosmopolitics: Thinking and Feeling Beyond the Nation*, edited by Pheng Cheah and Bruce Robbins, 216–29. Minneapolis: Univ. of Minnesota Press.

al-Balkhi, Muqatil ibn Sulayman. 1969. *Tafsir muqatil ibn Sulayman*. Edited by Abd Allah Mahmud Shihatah. Cairo: Al-Mu'assasah al-Halabi.

Bamyeh, Mohammed A. 2000. *The Ends of Globalization*. Minneapolis: Univ. of Minnesota Press.

———. 2004. "Global Order and the Historical Structures of *Dar al-Islam*." In *Rethinking Globalism*, edited by Manfred Steger, 217–30. Lanham, MD: Rowman and Littlefield.

Barani, Ziya'. 1860–62[2005]. *Tarikh-i Firuz Shahi*. Calcutta: Asiatic Society. Reprint, Aligarh: Sir Syed Academy.

———. 1972. *Fatawa-i Jahandari*. Edited by Afsar Salim Khan. Lahore: Research Society of Pakistan.

Al-Barnamaj al-intikhabi lil-Ikhwan al-Muslimin. 2005. Cairo: N.p. Issued Oct. 15.

Al-Barnamaj al-intikhabi lil-Ikhwan al-Muslimin fi Majlis al-Shura. 2007. Cairo: N.p. Issued May 14.

Barnamaj Hizb al-Ikhwan al-Muslimin: al-isdar al-awwal. 2007. Cairo: N.p. Issued Aug. 25.

Bartold, Vasily Vladimirovich. 1963. "Caliph and Sultan." *Islamic Quarterly* 7:117–35.

Batou, Jean. 1991. *Escapes from the Periphery*. Geneva: Droz.

———. 1993. "Nineteenth Century Attempted Escapes from the Periphery: The Cases of Egypt and Paraguay." *Review (Fernand Braudel Center)* 16(3): 279–318.

Bayat, Asef. 1997. "Un-civil Society: The Politics of the 'Informal People.'" *Third World Quarterly* 18(1): 53–72.

Bayhaqi, Abu al-Fazl Muhammad ibn Hussein. 1989. *Tarikh-i Bayhaqi*. Vol. 1. Tehran: Sa'di.

Beck, Edmund. 1976. "Iblis und Mensch, Satan und Adam: Der Werdegang einer koranischen Erzählung." *Le Muséon* 89:195–244.

Beckingham, Charles. 1977. "In Search of Ibn Battuta." *Journal of the Royal Society for Asian Affairs* 8(3): 263–77.

Bellin, Eva. 2012. "Reconsidering the Robustness of Authoritarianism in the Middle East: Lessons from the Arab Spring." *Comparative Politics* (Jan.): 127–49.

Beltz, Walter. 1980. *Die Mythen des Korans. Der Schlüssel zum Islam.* Düsseldorf: Claassen.

Benford, Robert, and Scott Hunt. 1995. "Dramaturgy and Social Movements: The Social Construction and Communication of Power." In *Social Movements: Critiques, Concepts, Case-Studies,* edited by Stanford Lyman. London: MacMillan. Reprinted from *Sociological Inquiry* 62(1) (Feb. 1992): 36–55.

Berges, Wilhelm. 1938. *Die Fürstenspiegel des hohen und späten Mittelalters.* Leipzig: K. W. Hiersemann.

Berlin, Isaiah. 2000. *The Proper Study of Mankind: An Anthology of Essays.* Edited by Henry Hardy. New York: Farrar, Straus and Giroux.

Berman, Harold Joseph. 1983. *Law and Revolution: The Formation of the Western Legal Tradition.* Cambridge, MA: Harvard Univ. Press.

Bernier, François. 1972. *Travels in the Mogul Empire, 1656–1668.* Translated by A. Constable. New Delhi: S. Chand.

Beskow, Per. 1962. *Rex Gloriae: The Kingship of Christ in the Early Church.* Stockholm: Almquist and Wiksell.

Bianchi, Robert. 2004. *Guests of God: Pilgrimage and Politics in the Islamic World.* New York: Oxford Univ. Press.

Bidlisi, Amir Sharaf Khan. 1994. *Sharaf-namah.* Edited by M. Abbasi. Tehran: Hadith.

Bieler, Andreas, and Adam D. Morton. 2001. *Social Forces in the Making of the New Europe: The Restructuring of European Social Relations in the Global Political Economy.* Basingstoke, UK: Palgrave.

Bilgrami, Mir Abd al-Wahid. 1957. *Haqa'iq-i Hindi.* Translated by S. A. A. Rizvi. Aligarh: Aligarh Muslim Univ., Maulana Azad Library. [Also Bilgrami, Mir Abd al-Wahid. 1957. *Haqa'iq-i Hindi.* Translated by S. A. A. Rizvi. Kashi: Nagri Pracharini Sabha.]

Binder, Leonard. 1988. *Islamic Liberalism: A Critique of Development Ideologies.* Chicago: Univ. of Chicago Press.

Biruni, Abu Rayhan. 1879. *Al-Athar al-baqiyah.* Edited by C. E. Sachau. London: William H. Allen.

al-Bishri, Tariq. 1983. *Al-Haraka al-siyasiyah fi Misr, 1945–1952.* 2nd ed. Cairo: Dar al-Shuruq.

———. 1987. *Dirasat fi al-dimuqratiyah al-Misriyah.* Cairo: Dar al-Shuruq.

———. 1991. *Al-Dimuqratiyah wa nizam 23 Yuliyu, 1952–1970.* Cairo: Dar al-Hilal.

———. 2003. *Al-Wad' al-qanuni bayn al-shari'a al-Islamiyah wa al-qanun al-wad'i.* Cairo: Dar al-Shuruq.

———. 2004. *Al-Muslimun wa al-aqbat fi itar al-jama'ah al-wataniyah.* Cairo: Dar al-Shuruq.

———. 2005. *Manhaj al-nazar fi al-nuzum al-siyasiyah al-mu'asirah li-buldan al-'alam al-Islami.* Cairo: Dar al-Shuruq.

Black, Anthony. 2001. *The History of Islamic Political Thought: From the Prophet to the Present.* Edinburgh: Edinburgh Univ. Press.

Blochet, Edgar. 1905–34. *Catalogue des manuscrits persans de la Bibliotheque nationale.* Vol. 2. Paris: Imprimerie nationale.

Bloom, Allan. 1987. "Jean-Jacques Rousseau." In *History of Political Philosophy,* edited by Leo Strauss and Joseph Cropsey, 559–81. Chicago: Univ. of Chicago Press.

Bocock, Robert. 1986. *Hegemony.* Chichester, UK: Tavistock Publications.

Boroujerdi, Mehrzad. 1996. *Iranian Intellectuals and the West: The Tormented Triumph of Nativism.* Syracuse, NY: Syracuse Univ. Press.

Bossuet, Jacques Bénigne. 1990. *Politics Drawn from the Very Words of Holy Scripture.* Translated by Patrick Riley. Cambridge, UK: Cambridge Univ. Press.

Bosworth, C. E., and P. Jackson. 1997. "Shabankara'i." In *Encyclopedia of Islam.* 2nd ed., 9:158–59. Leiden: E. J. Brill.

———. 2004. "Hazaraspids." In *Encyclopedia of Islam.* 2nd ed., 12:93. Leiden: E. J. Brill.

Boullata, Issa J. 1990. *Trends and Issues in Contemporary Arab Thought.* Albany: State Univ. of New York Press.

Boyarin, Daniel. 2004. *Border Lines: The Partition of Judaeo-Christianity.* Philadelphia: Univ. of Pennsylvania Press.

Boyer, Pascal. 1990. *Tradition as Truth and Communication: A Cognitive Description of Traditional Discourse.* Cambridge, UK: Cambridge Univ. Press.

Boyle, John A. 1961. "The Death of the Last 'Abbasid Caliph: A Contemporary Muslim Account." *Journal of Semitic Studies* 6(2): 145–61. Reprint, 1977. In *The Mongol World Empire 1206–1370.* Vol. 11. London: Variorum Reprints.

———. 1968. "Dynastic and Political History of the Il-Khans." In *The Cambridge History of Iran.* Vol. 5, *The Saljuq and Mongol Periods,* edited by J. A. Boyle, 303–421. Cambridge, UK: Cambridge Univ. Press.

Bozkurt, Gülnihal. 1996. *Bati Hukukunun Türkiye'de Benimsenmesi.* Ankara: Türk Tarih Kurumu.

Bräunlich, Erich, 1934. "Beiträge zur Gesellschaftsordnung der arabischen Beduinenstämme." *Islamica* 6:68–111, 182–229.

Breckenridge, Carol A., et al. 2002. *Cosmopolitanism.* Durham, NC: Duke Univ. Press.

Browers, Michaelle L. 2006. *Democracy and Civil Society in Arab Political Thought: Transcultural Possibilities.* Syracuse, NY: Syracuse Univ. Press.

Brown, Nathan J. 2002. *Constitutions in a Nonconstitutional World: Arab Basic Laws and the Prospects for Accountable Government.* Albany: State Univ. of New York Press.

Brown, Nathan J., and Amr Hamzawy. 2008. *The Draft Party Platform of the Egyptian Muslim Brotherhood: Foray into Political Integration or Retreat into Old Positions?* Washington, DC: Carnegie Endowment for International Peace.

Brown, Peter, et al. 1997. "The World of Late Antiquity Revisited." *Symbolae Osloensis* 72:5–90.

Browne, Edward G. 1928. *A Literary History of Persia.* Vol. 3, *The Tartar Dominion (1265–1502).* Cambridge, UK: Cambridge Univ. Press.

Bruell, Christopher. 1988. "On the Original Meaning of Political Philosophy: An Interpretation of Plato's Lovers." In *The Roots of Political Philosophy: Ten Forgotten Socratic Dialogues,* edited by Thomas L. Pangle, 91–110. Ithaca, NY: Cornell Univ. Press.

van Bruinessen, Martin. 1992. *Agha, Shaikh, and State: The Social and Political Structures of Kurdistan.* London: Zed Books.

Brunschvig, Robert, and G. E. von Grunebaum, eds. 1957. *Classicisme et déclin culturel dans l'histoire de l'Islam.* Paris: Besson, Chantemerle.

Buc, Philippe. 1994. *L'ambiguïté du livre: Prince, pouvoir et peuple dans les commentaires de la Bible au moyen âge.* Paris: Beauchesne.

———. 2001. *The Dangers of Ritual: Between Early Medieval Texts and Social Scientific Theory.* Princeton, NJ: Princeton Univ. Press.

Bulliet, Richard. 1989. "Travel and Transport, Islamic." In *Dictionary of the Middle Ages.* Vol. 12, 379–80. New York: Scribner.

Bultmann, Rudolf. 1980. *Theologie des Neuen Testaments.* Tübingen: J. S. B. Mohr.

Bunt, Gary. 2003. *Islam in the Digital Age: E-Jihad, Online Fatwas, and Cyber Islamic Environments.* London: Pluto Press.

———. 2005. "Defining Islamic Interconnectivity." In *Muslim Networks: From Hajj to Hiphop,* 235–51. Chapel Hill: Univ. of North Carolina Press.

Burke, P. 2002. "Context in Context." *Common Knowledge* 8(1): 152–77.

Busse, Heribert. 1968. "Fürstenspiegel und Fürstenethik im Islam." *Bustan* 9:12–19.

Büyüktanır, Zeki. 2006. *Madımak Çığlığı.* Istanbul: Can Yayınları.

Cahen, Claude. 1958–59. "Mouvements populaires et autonomisme urbain dans l'Asie Musulmane du Moyen Age." *Arabica* 5(3): 225–50; 6(1): 25–56; 6(3): 223–65.

———. 1977. *Les peuples musulmans dans l'histoire médiévale.* Damascus: Institut Français.

Calder, Norman. 1983. "Ikhtilaf and Ijma' in Shafi'i's Risala." *Studia Islamica* 58:55–81.

———. 1986. "Friday Prayer and the Juristic Theory of Government: Sarakhsi, Shirazi, Mawardi." *Bulletin of the School of Oriental and African Studies* 49(1): 35–47.

Calmard, Jean. 1993. "Les rituels shi'ites et le pouvoir: L'imposition du shi'ism safavide, eulogies et malédictions canoniques." In *Etudes Safavides,* edited by Jean Calmard, 109–51. Paris: Institut Français de Recherche en Iran.

Cameron, Averil. 1983. "Eusebius of Caesarea and the Rethinking of History." In *Tria Corda: Scritti in onore di Arnaldo Momigliano,* edited by Emilio Gabba, 71–88. Como, Italy: Edizioni New Press.

———. 1987. "The Construction of Court Ritual: The Byzantine Book of Ceremonies." In *Rituals of Royalty: Power and Ceremonial in Traditional Societies,* edited by David Cannadine and S. R. F. Price, 106–36. Cambridge, UK: Cambridge Univ. Press.

Cameron, Averil, Lawrence I. Conrad, and G. R. D. King, eds. 1992. *The Byzantine and Early Islamic Near East: Papers of the First Workshop on Late Antiquity and Early Islam.* Princeton, NJ: Darwin Press.

Cantarino, Vicente. 1975. *Arabic Poetics in the Golden Age.* Leiden: E. J. Brill.

Cantineau, J. 1949. "Racines et schèmes dans les langues sémitiques." In *Actes du XXIe Congrès International des Orientalistes.* Paris, July 23–31, 1948, 93–95.

Caskel, Werner. 1953. *Die Bedeutung der Beduinen in der Geschichte der Araber.* Cologne: Westdeutscher Verlag.

———. 1962. "Der arabische Stamm vor dem Islam." In *Atti del convegno internazionale sul tema Dalla tribú allo stato,* 139–51. Rome: Accademia nazionale dei Lincei.

———, trans. 1966. *Ğamharat an-nasab: Das genealogische Werk des Hišam Ibn Muhammad al-Kalbî.* Leiden: E. J. Brill.

Çelebi, Hajji Khalifa Katib. 1943. *Kashf al-zunun an asami al-kutub wa al-funun.* Istanbul: Maarif Matbaası.

Chakrabarty, Dipesh. 2000. *Provincializing Europe: Postcolonial Thought and Historical Difference.* Princeton, NJ: Princeton Univ. Press.

Chamberlain, Michael. 1994. *Knowledge and Social Practice in Medieval Damascus, 1190–1350.* Cambridge, UK: Cambridge Univ. Press.

Chapman, Stephen. 2003. "How the Biblical Canon Began." In *Homer, the Bible and Beyond: Literary and Religious Canons in the Ancient World,* edited by Margalit Finkelberg and Guy G. Stroumsa, 29–51. Leiden: E. J. Brill.

Chaunu, Pierre. 1981. *Histoire et décadence.* Paris: Perrin.

Chehata, Chafik. 1973. "La religion et les fondements du droit en Islam." *Archives de Philosophie de Droit* 18(18): 17–25.

Chejne, Anwar G. 1962. "Travel Books in Modern Arabic Literature." *Muslim World* 52(3): 207–15.

Chishti, Abd al-Rahman. n.d. "Mir'at al-asrar." London: British Museum, Or. 216.

Cicero. 1928. *De Re Publica, De Legibus.* Translated by Clinton Walker Keyes. London: William Heinemann.

Clifford, James. 1992. "Traveling Cultures." In *Cultural Studies,* edited by Lawrence Grossberg, Cary Nelson, and Paula A. Treichler, 96–117. New York: Routledge.

Coller, Ian. 2011. *Arab France.* Berkeley: Univ. of California Press.

Commins, David Dean. 1990. *Islamic Reform: Politics and Social Change in Late Ottoman Syria.* New York: Oxford Univ. Press.

Connolly, William. 1999. *Why I Am Not a Secularist.* Minneapolis: Univ. of Minnesota Press.

Cook, Michael. 2000. *Commanding Right and Forbidding Wrong in Islamic Thought.* New York: Cambridge Univ. Press.

———. 2003. *Forbidding Wrong in Islam: An Introduction.* New York: Cambridge Univ. Press.

Cooke, Miriam, and Bruce B. Lawrence. 2005. *Muslim Networks: From Hajj to Hiphop.* Chapel Hill: Univ. of North Carolina Press.

Coser, Lewis. 1956. *The Functions of Social Conflict.* Glencoe, IL: Free Press.

Cowgill, George L., and Norman Yoffee, eds. 1991. *The Collapse of Ancient States and Civilizations.* Tucson: Univ. of Arizona Press.

Crone, Patricia. 1987. *Roman, Provincial and Islamic Law: The Origins of the Islamic Patronate.* Cambridge, UK: Cambridge Univ. Press.

———. 1994. "Two Legal Problems Bearing on the Early History of the Qur'an." *Jerusalem Studies in Arabic and Islam* 18:1–37.

———. 2004a. *Medieval Islamic Political Thought.* Edinburgh: Edinburgh Univ. Press.

———. 2004b. *God's Rule—Government and Islam: Six Centuries of Medieval Islamic Political Thought.* New York: Columbia Univ. Press.

Dabashi, Hamid. 1996. "The Philosopher/Vizier: Khwaja Nasir ad-Din Tusi and the Isma'ilis." In *Medieval Isma'ili History and Thought,* edited by Farhad Daftary, 231–44. Cambridge, UK: Cambridge Univ. Press.

Dagron, Gilbert. 1996. *Empereur et prêtre: étude sur le "césaropapisme" byzantin.* Paris: Gallimard.

Dakhlia, Jocelyne. 1998. *Le divan des rois: le politique et le religieux dans l'islam.* Paris: Aubier.

Danishpazhuh, Muhammad Taqi. 1962. "Editor's Introduction." In *Tuhfeh [dar akhlaq va-siyasat].* Tehran: Bungah-i Tarjumah wa Nashr-i Kitab.

Darling, L. T. 2008. "Islamic Empires, the Ottoman Empire, and the Circle of Justice." In *Constitutional Politics in the Middle East,* edited by S. A. Arjomand, 11–32. London: Hart.

Dawn, C. Ernest. 1991. "The Origins of Arab Nationalism." In *The Origins of Arab Nationalism,* edited by Rashid Khalidi, Lisa Anderson, Muhammad Muslih, and Reeva S. Simon. New York: Columbia Univ. Press.

Deconchy, Jean-Pierre. 1980. *Orthodoxie religieuse et sciences humaines; suivi de (Religious) orthodoxy, rationality, and scientific knowledge.* La Haye: Mouton.

Demandt, Alexander. 1984. *Der Fall Roms: Die Auflösung des römischen Reiches im Urteil der Nachwelt.* Munich: C. H. Beck.

Deringil, Selim. 1998. *The Well-protected Domains: Ideology and the Legitimation of Power in the Ottoman Empire, 1876–1909.* London: I. B. Tauris.

Digby, Simon. 1975. "'Abd al-Quddus Gangohi (1456–1537 A.D.): The Personality and Attitudes of a Medieval Indian Sufi." In *Medieval India: A Miscellany.* Vol. 3, 1–66. Bombay: Asia Publishing House.

al-Dinawari, ibn Qutaybah. 1986. *Uyun al-akhbar.* 2 vols. Edited by Y. A. Tawil. Beirut: Dar al-Kitab al-Ilmiyah.

Diouf, Mamadou. 2000. "The Senegalese Murid Trade Diaspora and the Making of a Vernacular Cosmopolitanism." *Public Culture* 12(3): 679–702.

Donner, Fred. 1981. *The Early Islamic Conquests.* Princeton, NJ: Princeton Univ. Press.

Downing, Brian M. 1992. *The Military Revolution and Political Change: Origins of Democracy and Autocracy in Early Modern Europe.* Princeton, NJ: Princeton Univ. Press.

Duara, Presenjit. 1995. *Rescuing History from the Nation: Questioning Narratives of Modern China.* Chicago: Univ. of Chicago Press.

Duby, Georges. 1978. *Les trois ordres ou l'imaginaire du féodalisme.* Paris: Gallimard.

Dunya, Sulayman, ed. 1958[1873]. *Al-Shaykh Muhammad Abduh bayna al-falasifah wa al-kalamiyyin,* 1–29. Cairo: Isa al-Babi al-Halabi. [For Abduh's original essay, see Abduh, Muhammad. 1873. "Al-Hashiyah ala sharh al-Dawwani." In *Hashiyatay al-allamah al-muhaqqiq Abd al-Hakim al-Siyalkuti wa al-allamah al-mudaqqiq fadalah al-shaikh Muhammad Abduh mufti al-diyar al-Misriyah kilahuma ala sharh al-imam al-fadil al-mawla Muhammad b. As'ad al-siddiqa al-shahir bi al-Jalal al-Dawwani ala al-Aqa'id al-Adudiyah.* Cairo: N.p.

Eaton, Richard Maxwell. 1978. *Sufis of Bijapur, 1300–1700: Social Roles of Sufis in Medieval India.* Princeton, NJ: Princeton Univ. Press.

Eickelman, Dale F., and James P. Piscatori, eds. 1990. *Muslim Travellers: Pilgrimage, Migration, and the Religious Imagination.* Berkeley: Univ. of California Press.

Elias, Norbert. 1987. "The Retreat of Sociologists into the Present." In *Modern German Sociology,* edited by Volker Meja, Dieter Misgeld, and Nico Stehr, 150–72. New York: Columbia Univ. Press.

Enayat, Hamid. 1982. *Modern Islamic Political Thought.* Austin: Univ. of Texas Press.

Encyclopedia of Islam. 2nd ed. Leiden: E. J. Brill.

van Ess, Josef. 1977. *Anfänge muslimischer Theologie: zwei antiqadaritische Traktate aus dem ersten Jahrhundert der Higra.* Beirut: Orient-Institut.

———. 1991–97. *Theologie und Gesellschaft im 2. und 3. Jahrhundert Hidschra. Eine Geschichte des religiösen Denkens im frühen Islam.* Band 3. Berlin: De Gruyter.

Euben, Roxanne L. 2006. *Journeys to the Other Shore: Muslim and Western Travelers in Search of Knowledge.* Princeton, NJ: Princeton Univ. Press.

Evans-Pritchard, Edward E. 1949. *The Sanusi of Cyrenaica.* Oxford, UK: Clarendon Press.

Faizi Fayyazi, Abu al-Faiz. 1983. *Diwan.* Edited by A. D. Arshad. Lahore: Punjab Univ./Tehran: Furughi.

Farabi, Abu Nasr. 1987. *Al-Siyasah al-madaniyah.* Edited by Fauzi M. Najjar. Tehran: Al-Zahra.

al-Fasawi, Sufyan. 1976. *Kitab al-ma'rifa wa al-tarikh.* Edited by Akram al-Diya' al-Asmari. Baghdad: Ri'asat Diwan al-Awqaf.

al-Fasi, ibn al-Hajj. n.d. *Al-Madkhal.* 4 vols. Cairo: Maktabah Dar al-Turath.

Ferster, Judith. 1996. *Fictions of Advice: The Literature and Politics of Counsel in Late Medieval England.* Philadelphia: Univ. of Pennsylvania Press.

Filali-Ansary, Abdou, ed. 2003. *Réformer l'Islam? Une introduction aux débats contemporains.* Paris: Éditions la Découverte.

Findley, Carter. 1989. *Ottoman Civil Officialdom: A Social History.* Princeton, NJ: Princeton Univ. Press.

Fischer, Jürgen, 1957. *Oriens-Occidens-Europa. Begriff und Gedanke "Europa" in der späten Antike und im frühen Mittelalter.* Wiesbaden: F. Steiner.

Fleischer, Cornell H. 1986. *Bureaucrat and Intellectual in the Ottoman Empire: The Historian Mustafa Ali (1541–1600).* Princeton, NJ: Princeton Univ. Press.

Forschner, Maximilian, 1998. *Über das Handeln im Einklang mit der Natur: Grundlagen ethischer Verständigung.* Darmstadt: Primus.

Foruzani, A. Q. 2000. "*Al-Tawassul ila al-tarassul,* majmu'ah-i geranqadr az Baha' al-Din Muhammad b. Mu'ayyad Baghdadi." *Kitab-i Mah: Tarikh wa Joghrafiya* 32:13–15.

Foucault, Michel. 1972. *The Archaeology of Knowledge.* Translated by A. M. Sheridan Smith. London: Tavistock.

———. 1977. "Nietzsche, Genealogy, History." In *Language, Counter-Memory, Practice,* translated by Donald F. Bouchard, 139–64. Ithaca, NY: Cornell Univ. Press.

———. 1991. "Governmentality." In *The Foucault Effect: Studies in Governmentality,* edited by Graham Burchell, Colin Gordon, and Peter Miller, 87–104. Chicago: Univ. of Chicago Press.

de Fouchécour, Charles-Henri. 1986. *Moralia. Les notions morales dans la littérature persane du 3e/9e au 7e/13 siècle.* Paris: Institut Français de Recherche en Iran.

Fowden, Elizabeth Key. 1999. *The Barbarian Plain: Saint Sergius between Rome and Iran.* Berkeley: Univ. of California Press.

Fowden, Garth. 1993. *Empire to Commonwealth: The Consequences of Monotheism in Late Antiquity.* Princeton, NJ: Princeton Univ. Press.

———. 2004. *Qusayr 'Amra: Art and the Umayyad Elite in Late Antique Syria.* Berkeley: Univ. of California Press.

Fraenkel, Pierre. 1961. *Testimonia Patrum: The Function of the Patristic Argument in the Theology of Philip Melanchthon.* Geneva: E. Droz.

Freimark, Peter. 1967. "Das Vorwort als literarische Form in der arabischen Literatur." PhD diss., Univ. of Münster, Germany.

Friedmann, Yohanan. 1971. *Shaykh Ahmad Sirhindi: An Outline of His Thought and a Study of His Image in the Eyes of Posterity.* Montreal: McGill-Queens Univ. Press, Institute of Islamic Studies.

Friedrich, Manfred. 1992. *Geschichte der Deutchen Staatsrechtswissenschaft.* Berlin: Duncker und Humblot.

Frye, Richard Nelson. 1965. "The New Persian Renaissance in Western Iran." In *Arabic and Islamic Studies in Honor of Hamilton A. R. Gibb,* edited by George Makdisi, 225–31. Cambridge, MA: Harvard Univ. Press.

———. 1975a. *The Golden Age of Persia: The Arabs in the East.* New York: Barnes and Noble Books.

———. 1975b. Preface to *From the Arab Invasion to the Saljuqs.* Vol. 4 of *The Cambridge History of Iran.* Cambridge, UK: Cambridge Univ. Press.

Funkenstein, Amos. 1965. *Heilsplan und natürliche Entwicklung. Formen der Gegenwartsbestimmung im Geschichtsdenken des hohen Mittelalters.* Munich: Nymphenburger.

Furuzanfar, Badiʿ al-Zaman. 1972. *Majmuʿah maqalat wa ashʿar.* Edited by Inayat Allah Majidi. Tehran: Dihkhuda.

Fustel De Coulanges, Numa Denis. 1956. *The Ancient City: A Study on the Religion, Laws, and Institutions of Greece and Rome.* Garden City, NY: Doubleday Anchor Books.

al-Futuh, ʿAbd al-Monʿam Abu. 2006. "Reformist Islam: How Gray Are the Gray Zones?" *Arab Reform Bulletin* 4(6) (July): 1–2.

Futuhi Nasab, Ahmad. 2004–5. "Editor's Introduction." In *Sharaf al-Din Fazl Allah Husseini Qazvini's "al-Muʿjam fi athar muluk al-ajam,"* xiii–xlix. Tehran: Anjuman-i Asar wa Mafakhir-i Farhangi.

Gallois, William. 2005. "Andalusi Cosmopolitanism in World History." In *Cultural Contacts in Building a Universal Civilisation: Islamic Contributions,* edited by Ekmeleddin Ihsanoglu, 68–74. Istanbul: Research Center for Islamic History, Art, and Culture.

Gangohi, Shaikh Abd al-Quddus. n.d. "Rushd-namah." Staatbibliothek, Berlin MS. Sprenger 827.

Gardet, Louis. 1967. *La cité musulmane; vie sociale et politique.* Paris: J. Vrin.

Gauchet, Marcel. 1985. *Le désenchantement du monde: une histoire politique de la religion.* Paris: Gallimard.

Geary, Patrick J. 2002. *The Myth of Nations: The Medieval Origins of Europe.* Princeton, NJ: Princeton Univ. Press.

van Gelder, G. J. H. 1998. "Ijaz." In *Encyclopedia of Arabic Literature,* edited by P. Starkey and J. S. Meisami, 1:390. London: Routledge.

———. 2004. "Poetry in Historiography: Some Observations." In *Problems in Arabic Literature,* edited by Miklós Maróth, 1–13. Piliscsaba, Hungary: Avicenna Institute of Middle Eastern Studies.

Gellens, Sam. 1990. "The Search for Knowledge in Medieval Muslim Societies." In *Muslim Travellers: Pilgrimage, Migration, and the Religious Imagination,* edited by Dale F. Eickelman and James P. Piscatori, 50–65. Berkeley: Univ. of California Press.

Geréby, G. 2004. "Carl Schmitt and Eric Peterson on the Problem of Political Theology: A Footnote to Kantorowicz." In *Monotheistic Kingship: The Medieval Variants,* edited by Janos Bak and Aziz Al-Azmeh, 31–61. Budapest: Central European Univ. Press.

Gerschenkron, Alexander. 1962. *Economic Backwardness in Historical Perspective: A Book of Essays.* Cambridge, MA: Belknap Press.

Ghani, Muhammad Abdul. 1941. *Pre-Mughal Persian in Hindustan: A Critical Survey of the Growth of Persian Language and Literature in India from the Earliest Times to the Advent of the Mughal Rule.* Allahabad: Allahabad Law Journal Press.

Ghanim, Ibrahim al-Bayyumi. 1999. *Tariq al-Bishri: al-qadi al-mufakkir.* Cairo: Dar al-Shuruq.

al-Ghannouchi, Rachid. 1993. *Al-Hurriyah al-ammah fi al-dawlah al-Islamiyah.* Beirut: Markaz Dirasat al-Wahda al-Islamiyah.

al-Ghashi, Mustapha. 2003. "Al-Rihlah al-Maghribiyah wa al-sharq al-Uthmani, muhawalah fi bina' al-surah." PhD diss., Univ. Muhammad V, Faculty of Arts, Rabat, Morocco.

al-Ghazali, Abu Hamed Muhammad ibn Muhammad. 1877. *al-Mustafa min ilm al-usul.* Baghdad: N.p.

———. 1937. *al-Mustafa min ilm al-usul.* Cairo: al-Maktaba at-Tijariyah.

———. 1956. *Streitschrift des Gazali gegen die Batinijja-Sekte.* Edited by Ignac Goldziher. Leiden: E. J. Brill.

———. 1964. *Ghazalis' Book of Counsel for Kings (Nasihat al-muluk).* Translated by F. R. C. Bagley. London: Oxford Univ. Press.

———. 1972. *Nasihat al-muluk.* Edited by Jalal al-Din Huma'i. Tehran: Anjuman-i Asar-i Milli.

———. 1982. *Ihya' ulum al-din.* 4 vols. Edited by Fazlul Karim. New Delhi: Kitab Bhavan.

Ghazlan, Mahmud. 2005. "Khamsah asbab ʻdat ila nijah murashahin fi Muʻatham al-Dawa'ir." *Afaq Arabiyah,* Dec. 10.

el-Ghobashy, Mona. 2005. "The Metamorphosis of the Egyptian Muslim Brothers." *International Journal of Middle East Studies* 37(3): 373–95.

Gibb, H. A. R. 1955. "Constitutional Organization." In *Law in the Middle East,* edited by M. Khadduri and H. J. Liebesney, 3–27. Washington, DC: Middle East Institute.

———. 1959. *The Travels of Ibn Battuta, A.D. 1325–1354.* Vol. 2. Cambridge, UK: Cambridge Univ. Press.

———. 1962. *Studies on the Civilization of Islam.* Edited by Stanford J. Shaw and William Roe Polk. Boston: Beacon Press.

Gillespie, Michael. 1999. "Liberal Education and the Idea of the West." In *America, the West, and Liberal Education,* edited by Ralph C. Hancock, 7–26. Lanham, MD: Rowman and Littlefield.

Gilmartin, David. 2005. "A Networked Civilization?" In *Muslim Networks: From Hajj to Hiphop,* edited by Miriam Cooke and Bruce B. Lawrence, 51–68. Chapel Hill: Univ. of North Carolina Press.

Ginzburg, Carlo. 1976. "High and Low: The Theme of Forbidden Knowledge in the Sixteenth and Seventeenth Centuries." *Past and Present* 73:28–41.

Goitein, Solomon D. 1968. *Studies in Islamic History and Institutions.* Leiden: E. J. Brill.

Goldziher, Ignaz. 1971. *Muslim Studies.* Vol. 2. Translated by C. R. Barber and S. M. Stern. London: George Allen and Unwin.

Grabar, Oleg. 1973. *The Formation of Islamic Art.* New Haven: Yale Univ. Press.

Graham, William A. 1987. *Beyond the Written Word: Oral Aspects of Scripture in the History of Religion.* Cambridge, UK: Cambridge Univ. Press.

Gramsci, Antonio. 1978. "Some Aspects of the Southern Question (1926)." In *Selections from Political Writings (1921–1926),* edited by Quintin Hoare. New York: International Publishers.

Gran, Peter. 1979. *Islamic Roots of Capitalism: Egypt, 1760–1840.* Austin: Univ. of Texas Press.

———. 1996. *Beyond Eurocentrism: A New View of Modern World History.* Syracuse, NY: Syracuse Univ. Press.

———. 1999. "Quest for a Historical Interpretation of the Life of Shaykh al-Azhar Ibrahim al-Bajuri (1784–1860): An Agenda Article." In *Islah am tahdith? Misr fi asr Muhammad Ali,* edited by Ra'uf Abbas, 59–93. Cairo: al-Majlis al-A'la.

———. 2001. "Modern Middle Eastern History Beyond Oriental Despotism, World History Beyond Hegel: An Agenda Article." *Cairo Papers in Social Science* 23(2): 162–99.

———. 2002. "'Passive Revolution' as a Possible Model for Nineteenth-Century Egyptian History." In *Money, Land, and Trade: An Economic History of the Muslim Mediterranean,* edited by Nelly Hanna, 84–100. London: I. B. Tauris.

———. 2004. "Upper Egypt in Modern History: A 'Southern Question.'" In *Upper Egypt: Identity and Change,* edited by Nicholas Hopkins and Reem Saad, chap. 4. Cairo: American Univ. of Cairo Press.

———. 2005. "Egypt and Italy, 1760–1850: Toward a Comparative History." In *Society and Economy in Egypt and the Eastern Mediterranean, 1600–1900,* edited by Nelly Hanna and Ra'uf Abbas Hamid, 11–40. Cairo: American Univ. of Cairo Press.

———. 2006. "Egyptian History." In *World and Its Peoples.* Vol. 8, 1060–65. New York: Marshall Cavendish.

———. 2007. "Modern World History as the Rise of the Rich: A New Paradigm." *History Compass* 5(3): 1026–49.

Grosrichard, Alain. 1979. *Structure du sérail: la fiction du despotisme asiatique dans l'Occident classique.* Paris: Seuil.

von Grunebaum, Gustave E. 1953. *Medieval Islam: A Study in Cultural Orientation.* 2nd ed. Chicago: Univ. of Chicago Press.

Gutas, Dimitri. 1998. *Greek Thought, Arabic Culture: The Graeco-Arabic Translation Movement in Baghdad and Early 'Abbasid Society (2nd–4th/8th–10th centuries).* London: Routledge.

———. 2000. *Greek Philosophers in the Arabic Tradition.* Aldershot, UK: Ashgate Variorum.

———. 2002. "The Study of Arabic Philosophy in the Twentieth Century: An Essay in the Historiography of Arabic Philosophy." *British Society for Middle East Studies Bulletin* 29(1): 5-25.

Habermas, Jürgen. 1998. "Remarks on Legitimation through Human Rights." *Philosophy and Social Criticism* 24(2/3): 157–71.

Habib, Irfan. 1960. "Political Role of Shaikh Ahmad Sirhindi and Shah Waliullah." In *Proceedings of the Indian History Congress.* Aligarh: Indian History Congress.

———. 1965. "Distribution of Landed Property in Pre-British India." *Enquiry* 2(3): 59–108.

———. 1998. "A Political Theory for the Mughal Empire: A Study of the Ideas of Abu'l Fazl." In *Proceedings of the Indian History Congress,* 59th sess., Patiala, 332–53.

Habib, Irfan, and Tapan Raychaudhuri, eds. 1982. *The Cambridge Economic History of India.* Vol. 1. Cambridge, UK: Cambridge Univ. Press.

Habib, Mohammad, and Afsar Salim Khan. 1961. *The Political Theory of the Delhi Sultanate.* Allahabad: Kitab Mahal.

al-Haddad, Muhammad. 2003. *Muhammad Abduh: qira'ah jadidah fi khitab al-islah al-Islami.* Beirut: Dar al-Tali'ah lil-Tiba'ah wa al-Nashr.

Hadot, Pierre. 1972. "Fürstenspiegel." In *Reallexikon für Antike und Christentum,* edited by Ernst Dassmann and Theodor Klauser, 555–632. Stuttgart: Hiersemann.

Hafiz [Shirazi]. 1967. *Diwan.* Edited by Qazi Sajjad Hussein. Delhi: Sabrang Kitab Ghar.

———. 1972. *Diwan.* Translated and edited by Sajjad Hussein. Delhi. Sabrang Kitab Ghar.

Hafiz-i Abru. 1999. *Jughrafiya-yi Hafiz-i Abru.* 3 vols. Edited by Sadiq Sajjadi. Tehran: A'ineh-i Mirath.

Ha'iri-Yazdi, Mahdi. 1995. *Hikmat wa Hukumat.* N.p.: Shadi.

Hakki, Ibrahim Paşa. 1889. *Hukuk-i idare.* 2 vols. Istanbul: Karabet Matbaasi.

Halbertal, Moshe. 1997. *People of the Book: Canon, Meaning, and Authority.* Cambridge, MA: Harvard Univ. Press.

Hallaq, Wael B. 1984. "Was the Gate of Ijtihad Closed?" *International Journal of Middle East Studies* 16(1): 3–41.

———. 1990. "The Use and Abuse of Evidence: The Question of Provincial and Roman Influences on Early Islamic Law." *Journal of the American Oriental Society* 110(1): 79–91.

———. 2005. *The Origins and Evolution of Islamic Law.* Cambridge, UK: Cambridge Univ. Press.

Hamadani, Mir Sayyid Ali ibn Shahab. n.d. *Zakhirah al-Muluk.* MS. 760. Paris: Bibliothèque Nationale de France.

al-Hamawi, Yaqut b. Abd Allah. 1982. *Irshad al-arib ila ma'rifah al-adib.* Edited by D. S. Margoliouth. 3 vols. New Delhi: Kitab Bhawan.

Hammam, Muhammad, ed. 2003. *Al-Rihlah bayn al-sharq wa al-gharb.* Rabat, Morocco: Kulliyat al-Adab wa al-Ulum al-Insaniyah bi al-Rabat.

Hamori, Andras. 1994. "Going Down in Style: The Pseudo–Ibn Qutayba's Story of the Fall of the Barmakis." *Princeton Papers in Near Eastern Studies* 3:89–125.

Hamzawy, Amr, and Dina Bishara. 2006. *Islamist Movements in the Arab World and the 2006 Lebanon War.* Carnegie Paper no. 75 (Nov.). Washington, DC: Carnegie Endowment for International Peace.

Hardt, Michael, and Antonio Negri. 2000. *Empire.* Cambridge, MA: Harvard Univ. Press.

Haridi, Salah Ahmad. 2004. *Al-Jaliyah fi madinah al-Iskandariyah fi al-asr al-Uthmani, 923–1213 H/1517–1798 M: dirasah watha'iqiyah min sijillat al-mahkamah al-shar'iyah.* al-Haram [Giza]: Ayn lil-Dirasat wa al-Buhuth al-Insaniyah wa al-Ijtima'iyah.

Harris, Hugh. 1927. "The Greek Origins of the Idea of Cosmopolitanism." *International Journal of Ethics* 38(1): 1–10.

Hasan, Agha Mahdi. 1963. *The Tughlaq Dynasty.* Calcutta: Thacker Spink.

Hashmi, Sohail H. 2003. "The Qur'an and Tolerance: An Interpretive Essay on Verse 5:48." *Journal of Human Rights* 2(1): 81–103.

Hasrat, Bikrama Jit. 1953. *Dara Shikuh: Life and Works.* Calcutta: Visvabharati.

Hegel, Georg Wilhelm Friedrich. 1956. *The Philosophy of History.* Translated by J. Sibree. New York: Dover.

Heinrichs, W. P. 1998a. "Metaphor." In *Encyclopedia of Arabic Literature,* edited by P. Starkey and J. S. Meisami, 2:522–24. London: Routledge.

———. 1998b. "Rhetorical Figures." In *Encyclopedia of Arabic Literature,* edited by P. Starkey and J. S. Meisami, 2:656–62. London: Routledge.

Helms, Mary W. 1988. *Ulysses' Sail: An Ethnographic Odyssey of Power, Knowledge, and Geographical Distance.* Princeton, NJ: Princeton Univ. Press.

el-Hennawy, Noha. 2006. "Around the Bloc: Mohammed Mehdi Akef." *Egypt Today,* Jan.

Henninger, Joseph. 1989. *Arabica Varia: Aufsätze zur Kulturgeschichte Arabiens und seiner Randgebiete.* Göttingen: Vandenhoeck and Ruprecht.

Hetherington, Kevin. 1998. *Expression of Identity: Space, Performance, Politics.* Thousand Oaks, CA: Sage.

al-Hibri, Azizah Y. 1992. "Islamic Constitutionalism and the Concept of Democracy." *Case Western Reserve Journal of International Law* 24(1): 1–27.

Hijazi, Mahmud Fahmi. 1974. *Usul al-fikr al-Arabi al-hadith inda al-Tahtawi, ma'a al-nass al-kamil li-kitabihi "Takhlis al-Ibriz."* Cairo: al-Hay'ah al-Misriyah al-Ammah lil-Kitab.

al-Hilli, al-Allamah. 1986. "Minhaj al-karama." In *Ibn Taymiyya. Minhaj al-sunna al-nabawiyah,* edited by Muhammad Rashad Salim. Saudi Arabia: N.p.

al-Hindi, al-Muttaqi. n.d. *Kanz al-ummal fi sunan al-aqwal wa al-af'al.* Aleppo: Maktabah al-Turath al-Islami.

Hinds, Martin. 1971. "Kufan Political Alignments and Their Background in the Mid-Seventh Century A.D." *International Journal of Middle East Studies* 2(4): 346–67.

Hobbes, Thomas. 1966. "Leviathan; Or the Matter, Form, and Power of the Commonwealth, Ecclesiastical and Civil." In *The English Works of Thomas Hobbes of Malmesbury,* edited by William Molesworth. London: John Bohn.

Hodgson, Marshall G. S. 1974. *The Venture of Islam: Conscience and History in a World Civilization.* 3 vols. Chicago: Univ. of Chicago Press.

Holt, Peter M., and Bernard Lewis, eds. 1962. *Historians of the Middle East.* London: Oxford Univ. Press.

Holton, Robert John. 2002. "Cosmopolitanism or Cosmopolitanisms? The Universal Races Congress of 1911." *Global Networks* 2(2): 153–70.

Horst, Heribert. 1964. *Die Staatsverwaltung der Grosselguqen und Horazmsahs, 1038–1231.* Wiesbaden: F. Steiner.

Hourani, Albert H. 1976. "History." In *The Study of the Middle East: Research and Scholarship in the Humanities and the Social Sciences,* edited by Leonard Binder, 97–136. New York: Wiley.

———. 1980. *Europe and the Middle East.* Berkeley: Univ. of California Press.

———. 1983. *Arabic Thought in the Liberal Age, 1798–1939.* Cambridge, UK: Cambridge Univ. Press.

———. 1991. *Islam in European Thought.* Cambridge, UK: Cambridge Univ. Press.

Hrbek, Ivan. 1962. "The Chronology of Ibn Battuta's Travels." *Archiv Orientalni* 30:409–86.

Huntington, Samuel. 1996. *The Clash of Civilizations and the Remaking of World Order.* New York: Simon and Schuster.

Husaini, Syeda Bilqis Fatema. 1988. *A Critical Study of Indo-Persian Literature During Sayyid and Lodi Period, 1414–1526 A.D.* New Delhi: CAAL/School of Languages, Jawaharlal Nehru Univ.

al-Husseini, Ikhtiyar al-Din. n.d. *Akhlaq-i humayuni.* MS. 768. Paris: Bibliothèque Nationale de France.

———. *Dastur al-vizarah.* MS. 768. Paris: Bibliothèque Nationale de France.

Huwaydi, Fahmi. 1995. "Didd kawkalat al-alam!" *Al-Ahram,* Oct. 10, 11.

Ibish, Yusuf. 1977. "Ibn 'Arabi's Theory of Journeying." In *Traditional Modes of Contemplation and Action,* edited by Y. Ibish and P. L. Wilson, 441–49. Tehran: Imperial Iranian Academy of Philosophy.

Ibn Abd al-Barr, Yusuf ibn Abd Allah. n.d. *Al-Isti'ab fi ma'rifah al-ashab.* Edited by Ali Muhammad al-Bajawi. 4 vols. Cairo: Maktabat Nahdah Misr.

Ibn Abi al-Hadid, Abu Hamid ibn Hibah Allah. 1963. *Sharh Nahj al-Balagha,* edited by Hasan Tamim. Beirut: Dar al-Ihya' al-Kutub al-Arabiyah.

Ibn Battuta. 1992. *Tuhfah al-nuzzar fi ghara'ib al-amsar [Rihlah].* Beirut: Dar al-Kutub al-Ilmiyah.

Ibn Hajar al-Asqalani, Ahmad ibn Ali. 1995–96. *Lisan al-mizan.* Edited by Muhammad Abd al-Rahman Mar'ashli. 8 vols. Beirut: Dar al-Ihya' al-Turath al-Arabi.

Ibn Hazm, Ali ibn Ahmad, Abd al-Rahman Khalifah. 1928. *Al-Fisal fi al-milal wa al-ahwa' wa al-nihal.* Cairo: Tutlab min Maktabah wa Matba'ah Muhammad Ali Subayh.

Ibn al-Jawzi, Abu al-Faraj Abd al-Rahman ibn Ali. 1986. *Al Du'fa' wa al-matrukin.* Edited by Abu al-Fida' Abd Allah al-Qadi. Beirut: Dar al-Kutub al-Ilmiyah.

Ibn Kathir, Abu al-Fida' Isma'il ibn Umar al-Shafi'i. 1966. *Al-bidayah wa al-nihayah.* Beirut: Maktabah al-Ma'arif.

Ibn Khaldun, Abd al-Rahman. 1958. *The Muqaddimah: An Introduction to History.* Translated by Franz Rosenthal. New York: Pantheon.

———. [1858]1970. *Muqaddimat Ibn Khaldun, Prolégomènes d'Ebn-Khaldoun, Texte Arabe, Publié, D'Après les Manuscrits de la Bibliothèque Impériale.* Edited by M. Quatremère. Paris: Benjamin Duprat. Reprint, Beirut: Maktaba Lubnan.

Ibn al-Maghazili. 1974. *Manaqib Ali b. Abi Talib.* Tehran: al-Maktabah al-Islamiyah.

Ibn Majah, Muhammad ibn Yazid. 1972. *Sunan.* 2 vols. Cairo: Isa al-Babi al-Halabi.

———. 1983. *Sunan Abi Abd Allah Muhammad ibn Yazid al-Qazvini ibn Majah.* Riyadh: M. M. al-A'zami.

Ibn Miskawayh, Ahmad ibn Muhammad. 1952. *Al-Hikmah al-khalidah: Javidan khirad.* Edited by Abd al-Rahman Badawi. Cairo: Maktabat al-Nahdah al-Misriyah.

———. 1990. *Tajarib al-umam.* Edited by A. Imami. Tehran: Surush.

Ibn al-Muqaffa'. 1966. *Athar ibn al-Muqaffa': Kalilah wa Dimnah. al-Adab al-kabir. al-Adab al-saghir. al-Durrah al-yatimah. Risalah fi al-Sahabah. al-Athar al-ukhra. Qaddama lil-tab'ah wa ashraf 'alayha Umar Abu al-Nasr.* Edited by Umar Abu al-Nasr. Beirut: Dar Maktabah al-Hayah.

———. 1976. *Conseiller du Calife.* Translated by Charles Pellat. Paris: Maisonneuve et Larose.

Ibn Sa'd, Muhammad. 1990. *Al-Tabaqat al-kubra*. Edited by Muhammad Abd al-Qadir Ata. Beirut: Dar al-Kutub al-Ilmiyah.

———. 1997. *Al-Tabaqat al-Kubra*. Beirut: Dar al-Sadir.

Ibn Tawus, Ahmad ibn Musa. 1990. *Bina' al-maqalah al-Fatimiyah fi naqd al-risalah al-Uthmaniyah*. Edited by Ali al-Adnani al-Ghurayfi. Qum: al-Mu'assasah Al al-Bayt li-Ihya' al-Turath.

Ibn Taymiyya, Taqi al-Din. n.d. *Al-Siyasah al-shar'iyah fi islah al-ra'i wa al-ra'iyah*. Beirut: Dar al-Katib al-Arabi.

Ibn al-Tiqtaqa, Muhammad b. Ali. 1980. *Kitab al-Fakhri fi al-adab al-sultaniyah wa al-duwal al-Islamiyah*. Beirut: Dar Beirut lil-Tiba'ah wa al-Nashr.

al-Iji, Adud al-Din. 1983. *Al-Mawaqif fi ilm al-kalam*. Cairo: Maktabah al-Mutanabbi.

Imara, Muhammad. 1979. *Al-Islam wa al-sultah al-diniyah*. Cairo: Dar al-Thaqafah al-Gadidah.

———. 1984. *Rifa'ah al-Tahtawi: ra'id al-tanwir fi al-asr al-hadith*. Cairo: Dar al-Mustaqbal al-Arabi.

İnalcık, Halil. 1998. *Essays in Ottoman History*. Istanbul: Eren Yayıncılık.

———. 2006. *Tanzimat: değişim sürecinde Osmanlı İmparatorluğu*. Ankara: Phoenix Yayınevi.

İnalcık, Halil, and Donald Quataert, eds. 1994. *An Economic and Social History of Ottoman Empire, 1300–1914*. New York: Cambridge Univ. Press.

Inglebert, Hervé. 2001. *Interpretatio christiana: Les mutations des savoirs, cosmographie, géographie, ethnographie, histoire, dans l'antiquité chrétienne, 30–630 après J.-C.* Paris: Institut d'études augustiniennes.

Iqbal, Abbas. 1962. *Tarikh-i mufassal-i Iran az istila'-i Mughul ta I'lan-i Mashrutiyat*. 2nd ed. Tehran: Amir Kabir.

———. 1981. "Editor's Introduction." In Nakhjavani, Hindushah ibn Sanjar ibn Abd Allah al-Sahibi, *Tajarib al-salaf*. Edited by A. Hasan Rawzati, 341–54. Isfahan: Nashr-i Nafa'is-i Makhtutat.

———. 1999. *Tarikh-i Iran pas az Islam*. Tehran: Namak.

Iran Chamber Society. 2010. *The Bostan of Saadi*. Accessed July 27. http://www.iranchamber.com/literature/saadi/books/bostan_saadi.pdf.

al-Isfahani, Hamzah ibn al-Hasan. 1921–22. *Tarikh sani muluk al-ard wa al-anbiya*. Edited by Javad Irani. Berlin: Kaviani Verlag. [Also published in 1961, Beirut: Dar al-Maktabah al-Hayah.]

Isfahani, Mahmud ibn Muhammad ibn al-Hussein. 1985. *Dastur al-vizarah*. Edited by Riza Anzabinizhad. Tehran: Amir Kabir.

al-Jabarti, Abd al-Rahman. 1880. *Aja'ib al-athar fi al-tarajim wa al-akhbar*. 4 vols. Cairo: Bulaq [Also see English translation by Thomas Philip and Moshe Perlman, Stuttgart: Steiner, 1994.]

al-Jabri, Mohammed Abed. 1999. *Arab-Islamic Philosophy: A Contemporary Critique*. Translated by Aziz Abbassi. Austin: Center for Middle Eastern Studies, Univ. of Texas at Austin.

Jacob, Christian. 1999. "Du livre au texte: pour une histoire comparée des philologies." *Diogènes* 47(186): 4–22.

Jad'an, Fahmi. 1989. *Al-Mihna: bahth fi jadaliyah al-dini wa-al-siyasi fi al-Islam*. Amman: Dar al-Shuruq.

Jahangir, Nur al-Din. 1864[2005]. *Tuzak-i Jahangiri*. Edited by Sayyid Ahmad Khan. Aligarh: Scientific Society. Reprint, Aligarh: Sir Syed Academy.

———. 1968. *Tuzak-i Jahangiri*. Translated by Alexander Rogers and Henry Beveridge. Delhi: Munshiram Manoharlal.

al-Jahiz. 1955. *Risalah al-Uthmaniyah*. Edited by Abd al-Salam Muhammad Harun. Cairo: Dar al-Kitab al-Arabi.

———. 1985. *Al-Bayan wa al-tab'in*. 4 vols. Edited by Abd al-Salam Muhammad Harun. Cairo: Maktabah al-Khanji.

Jajarmi, Muhammad ibn Badr al-Din. 1959. *Munis al-ahrar fi daqa'iq al-ash'ar*. Tehran: Ittihad.

al-Jarrahi, Isma'il ibn Muhammad al-Ajluni. 1979. *Kashf al-khafa' wa Muzil al-Ilbas*. 2 vols. Beirut: Mu'assasah al-Risalah.

Jaspers, Karl. 1959. *The Idea of the University*. Edited by Karl W. Deutsch. Boston: Beacon Press.

al-Jirjawi, Muhammad ibn Hamid al-Maraghi. 1998. *Tarikh wilayah al-sa'id fi al-asrayn al-Mamluki wa al-Uthmani: al-musamma bi-nur al-uyun fi dhikr Jirja min ahd thalathah qurun*. Edited by Ahmad Hussein al-Namki. Cairo: Maktabat al-Nahdah al-Misriyah.

Joas, Hans. 1996. *The Creativity of Action*. Translated by Jeremy Gaines and Paul Keast. Cambridge, UK: Polity Press.

Johansen, Baber. 1988. "Die sündige, gesunde Amme. Moral und gesetzliche Bestimmung *(hukm)* im islamischen Recht." *Die Welt des Islams* 28:264–82.

Jonsson, Einar Mar. 1987. "La situation du *Speculum regale* dans la littérature occidentale." *Études Germaniques* 4:391–408.

Juwayni, 'Ala' al-Din 'Ata Malik. 1958. *Genghis Kahn: The History of the World Conqueror*. Translated by L. A. Boyle. Manchester, UK: Univ. of Manchester Press.

Juwayni, Muntajab al-Din Badi' Atabak. 1950. *Kitab atabat al-katabah: majmu'ah-i murasalat-i diwan-i Sultan Sanjar.* Edited by Muhammad Qazvini and Abbas Iqbal. Tehran: Sihami.

Juynboll, G. H. A. 1983. *Muslim Tradition: Studies in Chronology, Provenance and Authorship of Early Hadith.* Cambridge, UK: Cambridge Univ. Press.

Kaleli, Lütfi. 1995. *Sivas Katliamı ve Şeriat.* Istanbul: Alev Yayınları.

Kantorowicz, Ernst Hartwig. 1957. *The King's Two Bodies: A Study in Mediaeval Political Theology.* Princeton, NJ: Princeton Univ. Press.

Karal, Enver Ziya. 1942. "Zarif Paşa Hatıratı, 1816–1862." *Belleten* 4(16): 443–94.

Karim, Karim H. 2002. "Muslim Encounters with New Media: Towards an Inter-Civilizational Discourse on Globality?" In *Islam Encountering Globalization,* edited by Ali Mohammadi, 36–60. New York: RoutledgeCurzon.

Kashifi, Hussein Wa'iz. 1774. *Akhlaq-i muhsini.* Lucknow: N.p.

Kashifi Bayhaqi, Kamal al-Din Hussein. 1965. *Al-Risalah al-aliyah fi al-ahadith al-Nabawiyah.* Edited by Jalal al-Din H. Muhaddis Urmavi. Tehran: Bungah-i Tarjomah wa Nashr-i Kitab.

Kazemi, Muhammad. 2011. "Andarz-namah-i siyasi dar adab-i farsi: ba mehwariyat-i barrasi shah-armani dar se kitab-i Shah-namah-i Firdawsi, Siyastnamah-i Khwajah Nizam al-Mulk Tusi wa Nasihah al-muluk-i Ghazzali." MA thesis, Shahid Beheshti Univ.

Keith, Ronald C., and Zhiqui Lin. 2003. "'The Falun Gong Problem': Politics and the Struggle for the Rule of Law in China." *China Quarterly* 175(1): 623–42.

Kemp, Anthony. 1991. *The Estrangement of the Past: A Study in the Origins of Modern Historical Consciousness.* New York: Oxford Univ. Press.

Kermani, Nasir al-Din Munshi. 1959. *Nasa'im al-ashar min lata'im al-akhbar: dar tarikh-i vuzara'.* Edited by Jalal al-Din H. Muhaddis Urmavi. Tehran: Intisharat-i Danishgah-i Tehran.

Kerr, Malcolm H. 1966. *Islamic Reform: The Political and Legal Theories of Muhammad Abduh and Rashid Rida.* Berkeley: Univ. of California Press.

Keshavdas, 1969. *Keshav Granthavali.* Edited by V. P. Mishra. Varanasi: NPS.

Khalidi, Tarif. 1995. "Islamic Views of the West in the Middle Ages." *Studies in Interreligious Dialogue* 5(1): 31–42.

Khan, Iqtidar Alam. 1977. "Shaikh Abdul Quddus Gangohi's Relations with Political Authorities: A Reappraisal." In *Medieval India: A Miscellany.* Vol. 4, 73–90. Bombay: Asia Publishing House.

Khan, M. A. Muqtedar, ed. 2006. *Islamic Democratic Discourse: Theory, Debates, and Philosophical Perspectives.* Lanham, MD: Lexington Books.

Khan, M. Ishaq. 1994. *Kashmir's Transition to Islam: The Role of Muslim Rishis, Fifteenth to Eighteenth Century.* New Delhi: Manohar.

Khatib, Sulayman. 1992. *Al-Din wa al-hadarah fi fikr al-Tahtawi: qira'ah Islamiyah.* Cairo: al-Markaz al-Islami lil-Dirasat al-Hadarah.

al-Khazin al-Baghdadi, Ali ibn Muhammad. 1961. *Lubab al-ta'wil.* Cairo: al-Maktabah al-Tijariyah al-Kubra.

Khomeini, Ruhollah. 1981. *Islam and Revolution: Writings and Declarations of Imam Khomeini.* Translated by Hamid Algar. Berkeley: Mizan Press.

Khusrau, Amir. 1950. *Nuh sipihr.* Edited by Wahid Mirza. Oxford, UK: Oxford Univ. Press.

Khwafi, Fasih al-Din. 1962. *Mujmal-i Fasihi.* Mashhad: Bastan.

Khwandamir, Ghiyath al-Din ibn Humam al-Din. 1973. *Tarikh-i habib al-siyar.* Tehran: Khayyam.

———. 1983. *Tarikh-i habib al-siyar.* Tehran: Khayyam.

———. 1993. "Qanun-i humayuni." In *Ma'asir al-muluk,* edited by Mir Hashim Muhaddis, 257–307. Tehran: Mu'assasah-i Khadamat-i Farhangi-i Rasa.

Khwarazmi, Muhammad ibn Ahmad. 1895. *Liber Mafatih al-olum, explicans vocabula technica scientiarum tam Arabum quam peregrinorum.* Edited by Gerlof van Vloten. Lugduni-Batavorum: E. J. Brill.

Kinra, Rajeev. 2006. "The Mirror Has Both Luminous and Blind Sides: Dara Shukoh's Conversations with Baba Lal Dayal." Paper Presented at the 35th Annual Conference on South Asia, Univ. of Wisconsin, Madison, Oct. 21.

Kleingeld, Pauline. 1999. "Six Varieties of Cosmopolitanism in Late Eighteenth-Century Germany." *Journal of the History of Ideas* 60(3): 505–24.

Knysh, Alexander. 1992. "*Irfan* Revisited: Khomeini and the Legacy of Islamic Mystical Philosophy." *Middle East Journal* 46(2) (Autumn): 631–53.

Kolff, Dirk H. A. 1990. *Naukar, Rajput and Sepoy: The Ethnohistory of the Military Labour Market in Hindustan, 1450–1850.* Cambridge, UK: Cambridge Univ. Press.

Koselleck, Reinhart, and Paul Widmer, eds. 1980. *Niedergang: Studien zu einem geschichtlichen Thema.* Stuttgart: Klett-Cotta.

Koselleck, Reinhart, et al., ed. 1972-2004. *Geschichtliche Grundbegriffe.* 8 vols. Stuttgart: Klett-Cotta.

Kraemer, Joel L. 1986. *Humanism in the Renaissance of Islam: The Cultural Revival during the Buyid Age.* Leiden: E. J. Brill.

Kramer, Martin S. 2001. *Ivory Towers on Sand: The Failure of Middle Eastern Studies in America.* Washington, DC: Washington Institute for Near East Policy.

Krieger, Leonard. 1973. “The Autonomy of Intellectual History.” *Journal of the History of Ideas* 34(4): 499–516.

al-Kufi, Ahmad b. Ali. 1980. *Al-Istighatha fi bida‘ al-thalathah*. Sargudha, Pakistan: Ihqaq al-Haqq.

al-Kulayni. 1990. *Usul al-kafi*. Edited by Muhammad Ja‘far Shams al-Din. Beirut: Dar al-Ta’aruf lil-Matbu‘at.

Kuran, Timur. 2004. *Why the Islamic Middle East Did Not Generate an Indigenous Corporate Law*. Law and Economics Working Paper Series, Paper 16. Los Angeles: Univ. of Southern California Law School.

———. 2010. *The Long Divergence: How Islamic Law Held Back the Middle East*. Princeton, NJ: Princeton Univ. Press.

Kurzman, Charles, ed. 2002. *Modernist Islam 1840–1940: A Sourcebook*. New York: Oxford Univ. Press.

Kymlicka, Will. 1995. *Multicultural Citizenship: A Liberal Theory of Minority Rights*. Oxford, UK: Clarendon Press.

Laissus, Yves. 2004. *Jomard: le dernier Egyptien (1777–1862)*. Paris: Fayard.

Lambert, Jean. 1995. *Le Dieu distribué. Une anthropologie comparée des monothéismes*. Paris: Cerf.

Lambton, Ann K. S. 1962. “Justice in the Medieval Persian Theory of Kingship.” *Studia Islamica* 17:91–119.

———. 1970. “Islamic Mirrors for Princes.” In *La Persia nel Medioevo*, 419–42. Rome: Accademia nazionale dei Lincei.

———. 1974. “Islamic Political Thought.” In *The Legacy of Islam*, edited by J. Schacht and C. E. Bosworth, 404–24. Oxford, UK: Oxford Univ. Press.

———. 1981. *State and Government in Medieval Islam: An Introduction to the Study of Islamic Political Theory*. Oxford, UK: Oxford Univ. Press.

———. 1984a. “The Dilemma of Government in Islamic Persia: The *Siyasatnama* of Nizam al-Molk.” *Iran* 22:55–66.

———. 1984b. “Dihkan.” In *Encyclopedia of Islam*. 2nd ed. Vol. 2. Leiden: E. J. Brill.

———. 1988. *Continuity and Change in Medieval Persia: Aspects of Administrative, Economic, and Social History, 11th–14th Century*. Albany, NY: Bibliotheca Persica.

Lammens, Henri. 1914. *Le berceau de l’Islam*. Rome: Sumptibus Pontificii Instituti Biblici.

Laoust, Henri. 1959. “Le Hanbalisme sous le Califat de Baghdad (241/855–656/1258).” *Revue des Études Islamiques* 27:67–128.

———. 1960. "Le Hanbalisme sous les Mamlouks Bahrides (658–784/1260–1382)" *Revue des Études Islamiques* 28:1–71.

———. 1968. "La pensée et l'action politique d'Al-Mawardi (364/450–974/1058)" *Revue des Études Islamiques* 36:11–92.

———. 1983. *Pluralismes dans l'Islam*. Paris: P. Geuthner.

Lapidus, Ira M. 1967. *Muslim Cities in the Later Middle Ages*. Cambridge, MA: Harvard Univ. Press.

———. 1975. "Hierarchies and Networks: A Comparison of Chinese and Islamic Societies." In *Conflict and Control in Late Imperial China*, edited by Frederic Wakeman Jr. and Carolyn Grant, 26–42. Berkeley: Univ. of California Press.

———. 1992. "The Golden Age: The Political Concepts of Islam." *Annals of the American Academy of Political and Social Science* 524 (Nov.): 13–25.

Larcher, P. 1995. "Où il est montré qu'en arabe classique la racine n'a pas de sens et qu'il n'y a pas de sens à dériver d'elle." *Arabica* 42(3): 291–314.

Laroui, Abdallah. 1976. "The Arabs and Cultural Anthropology: Notes on the Method of Gustave von Grunebaum." In *The Crisis of the Arab Intellectual: Traditionalism or Historicism?*, translated by Diarmid Cammell. Berkeley: Univ. of California Press.

Leask, Nigel. 2004. *Curiosity and the Aesthetics of Travel Writing, 1770–1840*. Oxford, UK: Oxford Univ. Press.

Legendre, Pierre. 1974. *L'amour du censeur: Essai sur l'ordre dogmatique*. Paris: Éditions du Seuil.

Lenker, Michael. 1982. "The Importance of the Rihla for the Islamization of Spain." PhD diss., Univ. of Pennsylvania.

Levend, Agah Sırrı. 1962. "Siyaset-nameler." *Turk Dili Arastırmaları Yıllıgı* 217:167–94.

Levtzion, Nehemia, and Gideon Weigert. 1998. "The Muslim Holy Cities and Foci of Islamic Revivalism in the Eighteenth Century." In *Sacred Space: Shrine, City, Land*, edited by Benjamin Z. Kedar and R. J. Zwi Werblowsky, 259–77. New York: New York Univ. Press.

Levy, Reuben. 1930–33. *An Introduction to the Sociology of Islam*. 2 vols. London: Williams and Norgate.

Lewis, Bernard. 1982. *The Muslim Discovery of Europe*. New York: W. W. Norton.

———. 2004. *From Babel to Dragomans: Interpreting the Middle East*. New York: Oxford Univ. Press.

Lim, Richard. 1994. *Public Disputation, Power, and Social Order in Late Antiquity.* Berkeley: Univ. of California Press.

Little, Lester K. 2004. "Cypress Beams, Kufic Script, and Cut Stone: Rebuilding the Master Narrative of European History." *Speculum* 79(4): 909–28.

Lockman, Zachary. 2004. *Contending Visions of the Middle East: The History and Politics of Orientalism.* Cambridge, UK: Cambridge Univ. Press.

Lubeck, Paul. 1999. *Antinomies of Islamic Movements under Globalization.* Center for Global International and Regional Studies Working Paper Series, WP#99-1. Santa Cruz: Univ. of California Press.

Luther, K. Allin. 1990. "Islamic Rhetoric and the Persian Historians, 1000–1300 A.D." In *Studies in Near Eastern Culture and History in Memory of Ernest T. Abdel-Massih,* 90–98. Ann Arbor: Univ. of Michigan.

Madigan, Daniel A. 2001. *The Qur'an's Self-Image: Writing and Authority in Islam's Scripture.* Princeton, NJ: Princeton Univ. Press.

Mahbubani, Kishore. 1993. "The Dangers of Decadence." *Foreign Affairs* 72(4): 10–14.

Mahdjoub, Muhammad Dja'farr. 1988. "The Evolution of Popular Eulogy of the Imams among the Shi'a." In *Authority and Political Culture in Shi'ism,* edited by Said Amir Arjomand, 54–79. Albany: State Univ. of New York Press.

al-Majdi, al-Sayyid Salih. 1958. *Hilyah al-zaman bi manaqib khadim al-watan; sirah Rifa'ah Rafi' al-Tahtawi.* Cairo: Maktabah Mustafa al-Babi al-Halabi.

Makdisi, George. 1963. *Ibn 'Aqil et la résurgence de l'Islam traditionaliste au XIe siècle.* Damascus: Institut Français de Damas.

———. 1981. *The Rise of Colleges: Institutions of Learning in Islam and the West.* Edinburgh: Edinburgh Univ. Press.

Mandaville, Peter G. 2002. "Reimagining the *Ummah?* Information Technology and the Changing Boundaries of Political Islam." In *Islam Encountering Globalization,* edited by Ali Mohammadi, 61–90. New York: RoutledgeCurzon.

Mansour, Kamil. 1975. *L'Autorité dans la pensée musulmane. Le concept d'Ijmâ (consensus) et la problématique de l'autorité.* Paris: J. Vrin.

Manzoor, Parvez. 1990. "Islamic Liberalism and Beyond." *American Journal of Islamic Social Sciences* 17(1): 77–88.

Mardin, Şerif. 1962. *The Genesis of Young Ottoman Thought: A Study in the Modernization of Turkish Political Ideas.* Princeton, NJ: Princeton Univ. Press.

———. 1973. "Center-Periphery Relations: A Key to Turkish Politics." *Daedalus* 102(1): 169–90.

———. 1978. "Youth and Violence in Turkey." *European Journal of Sociology* 19(2): 229–54.

Marlow, Louise. 1997. *Hierarchy and Egalitarianism in Islamic Thought.* New York: Cambridge Univ. Press.

Marrou, Henri Irénée. 1983. *Saint Augustin et la fin de la culture antique.* Paris: E. de Boccard.

Marsilius of Padua. 2001. *Defensor Pacis.* Translated by Alan Gewirth. New York: Columbia Univ. Press.

Mårtensson, Ulrika. 2001. "The True New Testament: Sealing the Heart in al-Tabari's Ta'rikh al-Rusul wa'l-Muluk." PhD diss., Dept. of Theology, Uppsala Univ.

al-Marwazi, Ahmad b. Ali. 1970. *Musnad Abi Bakr al-Siddiq.* Edited by Shu'ayb al-Arnaut. Beirut: al-Maktab al-Islami.

Masud, Muhammad Khalid. 1990. "The Obligation to Migrate: The Doctrine of *Hijra* in Islamic Law." In *Muslim Travellers: Pilgrimage, Migration, and the Religious Imagination,* edited by Dale F. Eickelman and James P. Piscatori, 29–49. Berkeley: Univ. of California Press.

al-Mas'udi, Abul Hasan Ali. 1893. *Kitab al-tanbih wa al-ishraf.* Edited by M. J. de Goeje. Leiden: E. J. Brill.

Masuzawa, Tomoko. 2005. *The Invention of World Religions; or, How European Universalism Was Preserved in the Language of Pluralism.* Chicago: Univ. of Chicago Press.

Matar, Nabil I. 1999. *Turks, Moors and Englishmen in the Age of Discovery.* New York: Columbia Univ. Press.

———. 2003. *In the Lands of the Christians: Arabic Travel Writing in the Seventeenth Century.* New York: Routledge.

———. 2008. *Europe Through Arab Eyes, 1578–1727.* New York: Columbia University Press.

Mattar, Philip, ed. 2004. *Encyclopedia of the Modern Middle East and North Africa.* 2nd ed. Detroit: Macmillan Reference USA.

Mauss, Marcel. 1930. *Civilisation. Le mot et l'idée.* Edited by Lucien Febvre, Émile Tonnelat, Marcel Mauss, Adfredo Niceforo, and Louis Weber. Centre International de Synthèse, Première Semaine internationale de synthèse. Paris: La Renaissance du livre.

al-Mawardi, Ali ibn Muhammad. 1973. *Al-Ahkam al-sultaniyah wa al-wilayah al-diniyah.* Edited by M. al-Saqq. Cairo: Mustafa al-Babi al-Halabi. [Another edition was published in 1978, edited by Isam Faris al-Harastani and Muhammad Ibrahim al-Zaghli. Beirut: Dar al-Kutub al-Ilmiyah.]

———. 1996. *The Ordinances of Government* (Al-Ahkam al-Sultaniyya w'al-Wilayat al-Diniyya). Edited by Wafaa H. Wahba. Reading, UK: Garnet.

McAuliffe, J. Dammen. 2000. "Text and Textuality: Q.3:7 as a Point of Intersection." In *Literary Structures of Religious Meaning in the Qur'an,* edited by Issa J. Boullata, 56–76. London: Curzon.

McDonald, Kevin. 2002. "From Solidarity to Fluidarity: Social Movements Beyond 'Collective Identity': The Case of Globalization Conflicts." *Social Movements Studies* 1(2): 109–28.

McGrath, Alister. 1987. *The Intellectual Origins of the European Reformation.* Oxford, UK: Oxford Univ. Press.

Mehta, Pratap. 2000. "Cosmopolitanism and the Circle of Reason." *Political Theory* 28(5): 619–39.

Mehta, Uday Singh. 1999. *Liberalism and Empire: A Study in Nineteenth-Century British Liberal Thought.* Chicago: Univ. of Chicago Press.

Meinecke, Friedrich. 1924. *Der Idee der Staatsraison in der Neueren Geschicte.* Munich: Oldenbourg.

Meisami, Julie Scott. 1991. *The Sea of Precious Virtues (Bahr al-Fava'id): A Medieval Islamic Mirror for Princes.* Salt Lake City: Univ. of Utah Press.

———. 1992. "Ravandi's *Rahat al-sudur:* History or Hybrid?" *Edebiyat* 5:181–215.

———. 1995. "Exemplary Lives, Exemplary Deaths: The Execution of Hasanak." *Actas, XVI Congreso UEAI,* 357–64. Salamanca, Spain: Union Europeenne d'Arabisants et d'Islamisants.

———. 1997. "Mixed Prose and Verse in Medieval Persian Literature." In *Prosimetrum: Crosscultural Perspectives on Narrative in Prose and Verse,* edited by J. Harris and K. Reichl, 295–322. Cambridge, UK: Cambridge Univ. Press.

———. 1998. "Artistic Prose." In *Encyclopedia of Arabic Literature,* edited by P. Starkey and J. S. Meisami, 1:105–6. London: Routledge.

———. 1999. *Persian Historiography to the End of the Twelfth Century.* Edinburgh: Edinburgh Univ. Press.

Meisami, Julie Scott, and Paul Starkey, eds. 1998. *Encyclopedia of Arabic Literature.* London: Routledge.

Melchert, Christopher. 1996. "Religious Policies of the Caliphs from al-Mutawakkil to al-Muqtadir, A.H. 232–295/A.D. 847–908." *Islamic Law and Society* 3(3): 316-42.

Melikian-Chirvani, Assadullah-Souren. 1997. "Conscience du passé et résistance culturelle dans l'Iran mongol." In *L'Iran face à la domination mongole,* edited by Denise Aigle, 135–77. Tehran: Institut Français de Recherche en Iran.

Melville, Charles. 1998. "Ebn al-Teqteqa." In *Encyclopedia of Islam*. 2nd ed., 18:58–59.

Metiner, Mehmet. 2004. *Yemyesil seriat, bembeyaz demokrasi*. Istanbul: Dogan Kitap.

Millar, Fergus. 1992. *The Emperor in the Roman World (31 B.C.–A.D. 337)*. London: Duckworth.

Miller, David, et al., eds. 1991. *The Blackwell Encyclopedia of Political Thought*. Oxford, UK: Blackwell Publishing.

Minorsky, Vladimir. 1986. "Lur-i buzurg." In *Encyclopedia of Islam*. 2nd ed., 5:826–28. Leiden: E. J. Brill.

Miquel, André. 1967. *La géographie humaine du monde musulman jusqu'au milieu du 11e siècle*. 2 vols. Paris: La Haye, Mouton.

Mirkhwand, Muhammad b. Khawandshah. 2001. *Tarikh-i rawzah al-safa*. Tehran: Asatir.

Mohiuddin, Momin. 1971. *The Chancellery and Persian Epistolography under the Mughals, from Babur to Shah Jahan, 1526–1658: A Study on Insha', Dar al-Insha', and Munshis Based on Original Documents*. Calcutta: Iran Society.

Morony, Michael G., Donald S. Whitcomb, and Irene A. Bierman. 1995. *Identity and Material Culture in the Early Islamic World*. UCLA Near East Center Colloquium Series. Los Angeles: Center for Near Eastern Studies, UCLA.

Morrison, K. F. 1982. *The Mimetic Tradition of Reform in the West*. Princeton, NJ: Princeton Univ. Press.

Morton, Adam. 2007. *Unraveling Gramsci: Hegemony and Passive Revolution in the Global Political Economy*. London: Pluto Press.

Mottahedeh, Roy. 1976. "The Shu'ubiyah Controversy and the Social History of Early Islamic Iran." *International Journal of Middle East Studies* 7(2): 161–82.

———. 2001. *Loyalty and Leadership in an Early Islamic Society*. London: I. B. Tauris.

el-Moudden, Abderrahmane. 1995. *Al-Badawi al-Maghribiyah qabl al-isti'mar: qaba'il inawan wa al-Makhzan bayn al-qarn al-sadis 'ashar wa al-tasi'ashar*. Rabat, Morocco: Jami'ah Muhammad al-Khamis, Kuliyyat al-Adab wa al-Ulum al-Insaniyah bi al-Rabat.

Mu'ayatah, Zarif Marzuq. 2000. *Nash'ah al-dawawin wa tatawwuruha fi sadr al-Islam*. Al-Ayn: Markaz Zayid lil-Turath wa al-Tarikh.

Mubadirat al-Ikhwan al-Muslimin hawwal Mabad' al-Islah fi Misr. 2004. Cairo: Dar al-Manarah.

Mubarakshah, Muhammad b. Mansur b. Sa'id. 1967. *Adab al-harb wa al-shuja'ah.* Edited by Ahmad S. Khwansari. Tehran: Iqbal.

Mubed, Zulfaqar. 1843. *Dabistan-i mazahib.* 3 vols. Translated by David Shea and Anthony Troyer. London: Oriental Translation Fund of Great Britain and Ireland.

———. 1983. *Dabistan-i mazahib.* 2 vols. Edited by Rahim Rizazadeh Malik. Tehran: Tahuri.

Muhammad, Mirza Khan ibn Fakhr al-Din. 1977. *Tuhfah al-Hind.* Edited by Nur al-Hasan Ansari. Tehran: Bunyad Farhang-i Iran.

Muhibb Allah. n.d. *Risalah-i taswiyah [Sharh-i taswiyah].* MS. India office, D.P., 1167B.

———. n.d. "Maktub Banam Mulla Jaunpur." Maulana Azad Library, Aligarh, Zakhira-i Ahsan, no. 297.7/37, Farsi Tasawwuf.

Mujahid ibn Jabr. 1977. *Tafsir mujahid.* Edited by Abd al-Rahman al-Tahir ibn Muhammad al-Suwarti. 2 vols. Beirut: al-Manshurat al-Ilmiyah.

Mujtabai, Fathullah. 1978. *Aspects of Hindu-Muslim Cultural Relations.* New Delhi: National Book Bureau.

Munawwar, Muhammad ibn. 1998. *Asrar al-tawhid fi maqamat al-Shaikh Abi Sa'id.* Edited by Muhammad Reza Shafi'i Kadkani. Tehran: Agah.

Munshi, Nasr Allah 1998. *Kalilah wa Demnah.* Edited by Muhammad Taqi Danishpazhuh. Tehran: Hirmand.

Munshi, Nur al-Din. 2002. *Wasa'il al-rasa'il wa dala'il al-faza'il.* Edited by R. Sami'zadah. Tehran: Anjuman-i Asar wa Mafakhir-i Farhangi.

Murad, Ali Abbas. 1999. *Dawlah al-shari'a: qira'ah fi jadaliyat al-din wa al-siyasa inda Ibn Sina.* Beirut: Dar al-Tali'ah.

Murphy, Walter F. 1993. "Constitutions, Constitutionalism, and Democracy." In *Constitutionalism and Democracy: Transitions in the Contemporary World,* edited by Douglas Greenberg, Stanley N. Katz, Melanie Beth Oliviero, and Steven C. Wheatley, 3–25. New York: Oxford Univ. Press.

[Sharif] al-Murtada, Ali ibn al-Hussein al-Musawi al-Alawi. 1967. *Amali al-Murtada: ghurar al-fawa'id wa al-durar al-qala'id.* Edited by Muhammad Abu al-Fadl Ibrahim. Beirut: Dar al-Kitab al-Arabi.

Musawi Bojnurdi, Kazem, ed. 1994. *The Great Islamic Encyclopaedia.* Vol. 6. Tehran: Center for the Great Islamic Encyclopaedia.

al-Musawi, Muhsin. 2006. "Pre-modern Belletristic Prose." In *Arabic Literature in the Post-classical Period,* edited by Roger Allen and D. S. Richards, 101–33. Cambridge, UK: Cambridge Univ. Press.

Muslim ibn al-Hajjaj. 1994. *Sahih Muslim* [bi sharh al-Nawawi]. Edited by Isam al-Sababiti, Hazim Muhammad, and Imad Amir. Beirut: Dar al-Ma'rifah [1995 version, Beirut: Ibn Hazm].

Mu'tamad Khan, Mirza Muhammad. 1865. *Iqbal-namah-i Jahangiri*. Edited by Abd al-Hay, Ahmad Ali, and W. Nassau Lees. Calcutta: Bibliotheca Indica.

Nafisi, Sa'id. 1984. *Tarikh-i nazm wa nathr dar Iran wa dar zaban-i Farsi: ta payan-i qarn-i dahum-i hijri*. 2nd ed. Tehran: Furughi.

Nagel, Tilman. 1981. *Staat und Glaubensgemeinschaft im Islam: Geschichte der politischen Ordnungsvorstellungen der Muslime*. Zurich: Artemis.

Najjar, Fauzi M. 1958. "Al-Farabi on Political Science." *Muslim World* 48(2) (Apr.): 94–103.

———. 1996. "The Debate on Islam and Secularism in Egypt." *Arab Studies Quarterly* 18(2): 1–21.

al-Najjar, Hussein Fawzi. 1987. *Rifa'ah al-Tahtawi, ra'id fikr wa al-imam nahdah*. Cairo: al-Hay'ah al-Misriyah al-Ammah lil-Kitab.

al-Najjar, Muhammad Rajab. 1981. *Hikayah al-shuttar wa al-ayyarin fi al-turath al-Arabi*. Kuwait: Al-Majlis al-A'la lil-Thaqafah.

Najm al-Din Razi, Abd Allah ibn Muhammad. 1986. *Mirsad al-ibad min al-mabda' ila al-Ma'ad*. Edited by Muhammad Amin Riyahi. Tehran: Ilmi wa Farhangi.

Nakhjavani [Sahibi], Hindushah ibn Sanjar ibn Abd Allah. 1965. *Tajarib al-salaf dar tarikh*. Edited by Abbas Iqbal. Tehran: Tahuri [1981 edition, edited by A. Hasan Rawzati].

al-Nasa'i, Ahmad ibn Shu'ayb. 1930. *Al-Sunan al-kubra*. Edited by Hasan Muhammad al-Mas'udi. Cairo: N.p.

———. 1984. *Fada'il al-sahabah*. Edited by Faruq Hamadah. Casablanca, al-Dar al-Baida': Dar al-Thaqafah.

Nasawi, Shahab al-Din Muhammad. 1991. *Nafsah al-masdur*. Edited by Amir Hasan Yazdgirdi. Tehran: Virastar.

Nasr, S. H., ed. 1977. *Isma'ili Contributions to Islamic Culture*. Tehran: Imperial Iranian Academy of Philosophy.

Natanzi, Mu'in al-Din. 1957. *Muntakhab al-tawarikh-i Mu'ini*. Edited by Jean Aubin. Tehran: Khayyam.

Nederveen Pieterse, Jan. 1995. "Globalization as Hybridization." In *Global Modernities*, edited by Mike Featherstone, Scott Lash, and Roland Robertson, 45–68. London: Sage.

Nelson, Janet. 1976. "Symbols in Context: Inauguration Rituals in Byzantium and the West in the Early Middle Ages." *Studies in Church History* 13:97–111.

———. 1977. "Kingship, Law, and Liturgy in the Political Thought of Hincmar of Rheims." *English Historical Review* 92(363): 241–79.

———. 1994. "Kingship and Empire." In *Carolingian Culture: Emulation and Innovation*, edited by Rosamond McKitterick, 52–87. Cambridge, UK: Cambridge Univ. Press.

———. 1997. "Review of Joseph Canning's *A History of Medieval Political Thought, 300–1450*." Institute of Historical Research. http://www.history.ac.uk/reviews/paper/jinty.html.

———. 1999. "Kingship and Government." In *New Cambridge Medieval History*, edited by Timothy Reuter, 3:95–129. Cambridge, UK: Cambridge Univ. Press.

Netton, Ian Richard, ed. 1993. *Golden Roads: Migration, Pilgrimage, and Travel in Mediaeval and Modern Islam*. Richmond, UK: Curzon Press.

Neusner, Jacob. 1987. "Rabbinic Judaism in Late Antiquity." In *Encyclopedia of Religion*, edited by Mircea Eliade, Charles J. Adams, et al., 12:184–92. New York: Macmillan.

Nietzsche, Friedrich. 1968. *The Will to Power*. Translated by Walter Kaufmann and R. J. Hollingdale. Edited by Walter Kaufmann. New York: Vintage Books.

Nishaburi, Razi al-Din Muhammad. 1962. "Makarim-i akhlaq." In *Du Risalah dar akhlaq*. Vol. 1, edited by Muhammad Taqi Danishpazhuh. Tehran: Intisharat-i Danishgah-i Tehran.

Nizam al-Mulk [Tusi]. 1962. *Siyasat-namah (Siyar al-muluk)*. Tehran: Bungah-i Tarjamah wa Nashr-i Kitab. [Also see the 1976 version.]

———. 1978. *The Book of Government or Rules for Kings*. Translated by Hubert Darke. London: Routledge and Kegan Paul.

Nizami Arudi, Ahmad b. Umar b. Ali. 1962. *Chahar maqalah*. Edited by Muhammad Qazvini. Tehran: Zawwar.

Nizami, Azra. 1972. *Socio-religious Outlook of Abu'l Fazl*. Bombay: Asia Publishing House.

Nöldeke, Theodor. 1920. *Das Iranische Nationalepos*. Berlin: De Gruyter.

Nu'man ibn Muhammad, Abu Hanifah. 2002. *The Pillars of Islam: Laws Pertaining to Human Intercourse/Da'a'im al-Islam of al-Qadi al-Nu'man*. 2 vols. Translated by Asaf A. A. Fyzee. New Delhi: Oxford Univ. Press.

Nur al-Din b. Shams al-Din. 2001. *Ghazan-namah*. Tehran: N.p.

Nussbaum, Martha, and Joshua Cohen, eds. 1996. *For Love of Country: Debating the Limits of Patriotism*. Boston: Beacon Press.

Oakley, Francis. 1973. "Celestial Hierarchies Revisited: Walter Ullmann's Vision of Medieval Politics." *Past and Present* 60:3–48.

———. 1996. "'Anxieties of Influence': Skinner, Figgis, Conciliarism and Early Modern Constitutionalism." *Past and Present* 151:60–110.

Okandan, Recai Galip. 1949. "Devletin Sahsiyeti." *Istanbul Universitesi Hukuk Fakultesi Mecmuasi* 15:483–523.

———. 1950. "Devletin Sahsiyetinin Muessese Fikriyle Izahi'." *İstanbul Universitesi Hukuk Fakultesi Mecmuasi* 16(1–2): 88–96.

Olender, Maurice. 1992. *The Languages of Paradise: Race, Religion, and Philology in the Nineteenth Century.* Translated by A. Goldhammer. Cambridge, MA: Harvard Univ. Press.

Olrik, Axel. 1965. "Epic Laws of Folk Narrative." In *The Study of Folklore,* edited by A. Dundes, 129–41. Englewood Cliffs, NJ: Prentice-Hall.

Omar, Irfan. 2005. "Dara Shukoh's Islamization of the Upanishads: An Exploration of the Qur'anic Notion of a 'Book Kept Hidden.'" Paper presented at the 34th Annual Conference on South Asia, Oct. 2005, Madison, WI.

Parham, Baqir. 1998. *Ba Nigah-i Firdawsi: mabani-i naqd-i khirad-i siyasi dar Iran.* 2nd ed. Tehran: Markaz.

Paul, Jurgen. 1995. "Insha' Collections as a Source on Iranian History." In *Proceedings of the Second European Conference on Iranian Studies,* edited by B. G. Fragner et al., 535–50. Rome: Istituto Italiano per il Medio ed Estremo Oriente.

———. 1998. "Ensha'." In *Encyclopedia of Islam.* 2nd ed., 8:455–57. Leiden: E. J. Brill.

Peterson, Erik. 1935. *Der Monotheismus als politisches Problem: Ein Beitrag zur Geschichte der politischen Theologie im Imperium Romanum.* Leipzig: Hegner.

Pickthall, Marmaduke William. 2000. *The Glorious Qur'an: Translation.* Elmhurst, NY: Tahrike Tarsile Qur'an.

Pitkin, Hanna Fenichel. 1972. *The Concept of Representation.* Berkeley: Univ. of California Press. [Also see the 1967 edition.]

Pollock, Sheldon. 2000. "Cosmopolitan and Vernacular in History." *Public Culture* 12(3): 591–625.

Powers, David Stephan. 2002. *Law, Society, and Culture in the Maghrib, 1300–1500.* Cambridge, UK: Cambridge Univ. Press.

Prenner, Karl. 1986. *Muhammad und Musa: Struktur-analytische und theologiegeschichtliche Untersuchungen zu den mekkanischen Musa-Perikopen des Qur'an.* Altenberge: Verlag für Christlich-Islamisches Schrifttum.

Qadduri, Abd al-Majid. 1995. *Sufara' magharibafi Urubba, 1610–1922: fi al-wa'y bi al-tafawut.* Rabat, Morocco: al-Mamlaka al-Maghribiyah, Jami'ah Muhammad al-Khamis, Kulliyat al-Adab wa-al-Ulum al-Insaniyah bi al-Rabat.

Qanungo, Kalika Ranjan. 1952. *Dara Shukoh*. Calcutta: S. C. Sarkar.

al-Qaradawi, Yusuf. 1997. *Min fiqh al-dawlah fi al-Islam*. Cairo: Dar al-Shuruq.

Qazvini, Hamd Allah Mustawfi. 1983–84. *Tarikh-i guzidah*. Edited by Abd al-Hussein Nava'i. Tehran: Amir Kabir.

———. 2001. *Zafar-namah: qism al-Islamiyah*. Edited by Mahdi Mada'ini. Tehran: Pizhuhishgah-i Ulum-i Insani wa Mutala'at-i Farhangi.

Qazvini [Naqib Khan], Mir Ghiyath al-Din. 1979. *Mahabharat*. Persian translation. Edited by M. R. Jalali Na'ini and N. S. Shukla. Tehran: Tahuri.

Qazvini, Sharaf al-Din Fazl Allah Husseini. 2004–5. *al-Mu'jam fi athar muluk al-ajam*. Edited by Ahmad Futuhi Nasab. Tehran: Anjuman-i Asar wa Mafakhir-i Farhangi.

Qumi, Najm al-Din Abu al-Raja'. 1985. *Tarikh al-vuzara'*. Edited by Muhammad Taqi Danishpazhuh. Tehran: Mu'assasah-i Mutala'at wa Tahqiqat-i Farhangi.

al-Qummi, Ali ibn Ibrahim. 1966. *Tafsir al-Qummi*. Edited by Tayyib al-Musawi Jaza'iri. Al-Najaf: Maktabah al-Huda.

al-Qurtubi, Muhammad. 1967. *Tafsir al-Qurtubi*. Cairo: Dar al-Katib al-Arabi.

Rafiqi, Abdul Qaiyum. 1972. *Sufism in Kashmir, from Fourteenth to Sixteenth Century*. Varanasi: Bharatiya Publishing House.

Rahman, Fazlur. 1983. "Some Key Ethical Concepts of the Qur'an." *Journal of Religious Ethics* 11(2): 170–85.

Rahmuni, Muhammad al-Sharif. 2002. *Al-Jihad: min al-hijrah ila al-da'wah ila al-dawlah: bahth fi mawaqif al-ulama al-Muslimin fi al-qarnayn al-rabi' wa al-khamis lil-hijrah*, edited by Abd al-Majid Sharafi. Beirut: Dar al-Tali'ah lil-Tiba'ah wa al-Nashr.

Ramadan, Tariq. 1999. *To Be a European Muslim: A Study of Islamic Sources in the European Context*. Leicester, UK: Islamic Foundation.

———. 2004. *Western Muslims and the Future of Islam*. Oxford, UK: Oxford Univ. Press.

Rashid al-Din, Tabib. 1945. *Mukatabat-i Rashidi*, edited by M. Shafi. Lahore: N.p.

———. 1994. *Jami' al-tawarikh*. Tehran: Alburz.

Rawzati, A. Hasan. 1981. "Editor's Introduction." In Hindushah ibn Sanjar al-Sahibi, *Tajarib al-salaf dar tarikh*. Isfahan: Nashr-i Nafa'is-i Makhtutat.

Razi, Abd al-Jalil. 1952. *Kitab al-naqdh*. Edited by Jalal al-Din H. Muhaddis Urmavi. Tehran: Sipihr.

al-Razi, Abd al-Rahman ibn Ahmad. 1994. *Kitab fada'il al-Qur'an wa tilawatuh: wa khasa'is tulatihi wa hamalatih*, edited by Amir Hasan Sabri. Beirut: Dar al-Basha'ir al-Islamiyah.

al-Razi, Fakhr al-Din Muhammad ibn Umar. 1980–89. *Mafatih al-ghayb.* Cairo: Dar al-Ihya' al-Turath al-Arabi.

Reichmuth, Stefan. 1998. "The Interplay of Local Developments and Transnational Relations in the Islamic World: Perceptions and Perspectives." In *Inter-regional and Inter-ethnic Relations.* Vol. 2 of *Muslim Culture in Russia and Central Asia from the Eighteenth to the Early Twentieth Centuries,* edited by Anke von Kügelgen, Michael Kemper, and Allen J. Frank, 5–38. Berlin: Klaus Schwarz.

———. 2004. "Murtada al-Zabidi (1732–91) and the Africans: Islamic Discourse and Scholarly Networks in the Late Eighteenth Century." In *The Transmission of Learning in Islamic Africa,* edited by Scott R. Reese, 121–53. Leiden: E. J. Brill.

Reis, Sidi Ali. 1975. *The Travels and Adventurers of Turkish Admiral Sidi Ali Reis.* Translated by A. Vambéry. Lahore: Al-Biruni.

Renan, Ernest. 1883. *L'Islamisme et la science: Conférence faite à la Sorbonne le 20 mars 1883.* Paris: Calmann Lévy.

Richards, John F. 1998. "The Formulation of Imperial Authority under Akbar and Jahangir." In *The Mughal State, 1526–1750,* edited by Muzaffar Alam and Sanjay Subrahmanyam, 126–67. Delhi: Oxford Univ. Press.

Richter, Gustav. 1932. *Studien zur Geschichte der älteren arabischen Fürstenspiegel.* Leipzig: J. C. Hinrichs'sche Buchhandlung.

Ricoeur, Paul. 1970. *Freud and Philosophy: An Essay on Interpretation.* New Haven: Yale Univ. Press.

Rida, Muhammad Rashid. 1999. *Tafsir al-Qur'an al-hakim al-mashhur bi-Tafsir al-Manar.* Edited by Ibrahim Shams al-Din. 12 vols. Beirut: Dar al-Kutub al-Ilmiyah.

Ridley, Ronald. 1998. *Napoleon's Proconsul in Egypt: The Life and Times of Bernardino Drovetti.* London: Rubicon Press.

Rieu, Charles. 1885. *Catalogue of the Persian Manuscripts in the British Museum.* Vol. 3. London: British Museum.

Ritter, Hellmut. 1948. "Irrational Solidarity Groups: A Socio-psychological Study in Connection with Ibn Khaldun." *Oriens* 1(1): 1–44.

Rizvi, Saiyid Athar Abbas. 1965. *Muslim Revivalist Movements in Northern India in the Sixteenth and the Seventeenth Centuries.* Allahabad: Balkrishna Book Co.

———. 1975. *Religious and Intellectual History of the Muslims in Akbar's Reign, with Special Reference to Abu'l Fazl, 1556–1605.* New Delhi: Munshiram Manoharlal.

———. 1978. *A History of Sufism in India.* Vol. 2. New Delhi: Munshiram Manoharlal.

———. 1986. *A Socio-Intellectual History of the Isna 'Ashari Shi'is in India.* Canberra: Ma'rifat Publications.

Robbins, Bruce. 1992. "Comparative Cosmopolitanisms." *Social Text* 31/32:169–86.

———. 1998. "Actually Existing Cosmopolitanism." In *Cosmopolitics: Thinking and Feeling Beyond the Nation,* edited by Pheng Cheah and Bruce Robbins, 1–19. Minneapolis: Univ. of Minnesota Press.

Robinson, Chase F. 2003. *Islamic Historiography.* Cambridge, UK: Cambridge Univ. Press.

Robinson, Francis. 1997. "Ottomans-Safavids–Mughals: Shared Knowledge and Connective Systems." *Journal of Islamic Studies* 8(2): 151–84.

Rodinson, Maxime. 1988. *Europe and the Mystique of Islam.* Translated by Roger Veinus. London: I. B. Tauris.

Roemer, Hans Robert. 1971. "Insha'." In *Encyclopedia of Islam.* 2nd ed., 3:1241–44. Leiden: E. J. Brill.

Rorty, Richard, and Gianni Vattimo. 2005. *The Future of Religion.* Edited by Santiago Zabala. New York: Columbia Univ. Press.

Rosefsky Wickham, Carrie. 2002. *Mobilizing Islam: Religion, Activism, and Political Change in Egypt.* New York: Columbia Univ. Press.

Rosenthal, Erwin Isak Jakob. 1948. "Some Aspects of Islamic Political Thought." *Studia Islamica (Hyderabad)* 22:1–17.

———. 1962. *Political Thought in Medieval Islam: An Introductory Outline.* Cambridge, UK: Cambridge Univ. Press.

———. 1971. *Studia Semitica.* Vol. 2, *Islamic Themes.* Cambridge, UK: Cambridge Univ. Press.

Rosenthal, Franz. 1968. *A History of Muslim Historiography.* Leiden: E. J. Brill.

———. 1970. *Knowledge Triumphant: The Concept of Knowledge in Medieval Islam.* Leiden: E. J. Brill.

———. 1990. *Greek Philosophy in the Arab World: A Collection of Essays.* Aldershot, UK: Variorium.

———. 1997. "The Stranger in Medieval Islam." *Arabica* 44(1): 35–75.

Rowson, E. K. 1998. "Saj'." In *Encyclopedia of Arabic Literature,* edited by P. Starkey and J. S. Meisami, 2:677–78. London: Routledge.

Roy, Oliver. 2002. "Soviet Legacies and Western Aid Imperatives in the New Central Asia." In *Civil Society in the Muslim World: Contemporary Perspectives,* edited by Amyn B. Sajoo, 123–48. London: I. B. Tauris.

Rudolph, Susan Hoeber, and James Piscatori, eds. 1997. *Transnational Religion and Fading States.* Boulder, CO: Westview Press.

Rumi [Jalal al-Din], Maulana. 1976. *Masnavi Maulana Rumi.* Edited by Qazi Sajjad Husain. Delhi: Sabrang Kitabghar.

Rutherford, Bruce K. 2006. "What Do Egypt's Islamists Want? Moderate Islam and the Rise of Islamic Constitutionalism." *Middle East Journal* 60(4): 707–31.

———. 2008. *Egypt after Mubarak: Liberalism, Islam, and Democracy in the Arab World.* Princeton, NJ: Princeton Univ. Press.

Rypka, Jan. 1968a. *History of Iranian Literature.* Edited by Karl Jahn. Dordrecht: D. Reidel.

———. 1968b. "Poets and Prose Writers of the Late Saljuq and Mongol Periods." In *The Cambridge History of Iran,* edited by J. A. Boyle, 5:550–625. Cambridge, UK: Cambridge Univ. Press.

Sabari, Simha. 1981. *Mouvements populaires à Bagdad à l'époque abbaside IXe–XIe siècles.* Paris: Librairie d'Amérique et d'Orient.

Sabzawari, Tahir Muhammad Imad al-Din Hasan. 1603. *Rawzah al-tahirin.* Bodleian Library, Oxford MS, Arch Swinton, Eliott 314.

Sa'di [Shirazi], Muslih al-Din. 1876. *Majmueh kulliyat-i nazm wa nasr-i Sa'di.* India: Odeh Akhbar.

———. 1906. *Sadi's Scroll of Wisdom.* Edited by L. Cranmer-Byng and S. A. Kapadia. London: John Murry.

———. 1917. *Kulliyat.* Bombay: Muzaffari.

———. 1949. *Kulliyat-i nafis-i hazrat-i Shaikh Muslih al-Din Sa'di Shirazi.* Tehran: Amir Kabir.

———. 1997. *Kulliyat-i Sa'di.* Edited by Muhammad Ali Furughi. 6th ed. Tehran: Quqnus.

Sadiki, Larbi. 2004. *The Search for Arab Democracy: Discourses and Counter-Discourses.* New York: Columbia Univ. Press.

al-Sa'fi, Wahid. 2001. *Al-Ajib wa al-gharib fi kutub tafsir al-Qur'an: tafsir ibn Kathir anmudhajan.* Tunis: Tibr al-Zaman.

Said, Edward W. 2000. "Orientalism Reconsidered." In *Orientalism: A Reader,* edited by Alexandar L. Macfie, 345–64. New York: New York Univ. Press.

Sa'id, Muhammad. 2005. *Al-Nasab wa al-qarabah fi al-mujtama' al-Arabi qabl al-Islam.* Beirut: Dar al-Saqi.

Saktanber, Ayşe. 2006. "Women and the Iconography of Fear: Islamization in Post-Islamist Turkey." *Signs* 32(1): 21–31.

Salah, Muhammad. 2006. "Murshid al-Ikhwan al-Muslimin: musta'iddun li-irsal 10,000 Mujahid ila Lubnan." *al-Hayat,* Aug. 4.

Salamé, Ghassane. 2005. *Quand l'Amérique refait le monde.* Paris: Fayard.

Saleh, Walid A. 2004. *The formation of the classical tafsir tradition: The Qur'an commentary of al-Tha'labi (d. 427/1035) by Walid A. Saleh.* Boston: E. J. Brill.

Salihpur, Jahangir. 1995. "Farayand-i urfi shudan-i fiqh-i Shi'i." *Kayan* 24 (Apr.–May): 17–23.

al-Samarqandi, Abd al-Razzaq Kamal al-Din ibn Ishaq. 1946. *Matla' al-sa'dayn wa majma' al-bahrayn.* Edited by Muhammad Shafi. Lahore: Chapkhan-ye Gailani.

Sarkar, Jadunath. 1919. *History of Aurangzib, Based on Original Sources.* 5 vols. Calcutta: M. C. Sarkar.

Sartain, E. M. 1996. "Medieval Muslim-European Relations: Islamic Juristic Theory and Chancery Practice." In *Images of the Other: Europe and the Muslim World Before 1700,* edited by David Blanks. Cairo Papers in Social Science. Vol. 19, monograph 2, 81–95. Cairo: American Univ. in Cairo Press.

al-Sayyid, Radwan. 1993. *Mafahim al-jama'ah fi al-Islam: Dirasat fi al-susyulujiyah al-tarikhiyah lil-ijtima' al-Arabi al-Islami.* Beirut: Dar al-Muntakhab al-Arabi.

Schimmel, Annemarie. 1973. "Islamic Literature in India." In *A History of Indian Literature,* edited by Jan Gonda. Vol. 7, pt. 5. Wiesbaden: Otto Harrassowitz.

———. 1975. *Mystical Dimensions of Islam.* Chapel Hill: Univ. of North Carolina Press.

———. 2004. *The Empire of the Great Mughals: History, Art and Culture.* London: Reaktion Books.

Schlüsser, Hermann. 1977. *Der Primat der heiligen Schrift als theologisches und kanonistisches Problem im Spätmittelalter.* Wiesbaden: F. Steiner.

Schulze, Reinhard. 1996. "Was ist die islamische Aufklärung?" *Die Welt des Islams* 36(3): 276–325.

Senellart, Michel. 1995. *Les arts de gouverner: du regimen médiéval au concept de gouvernement.* Paris: Editions du Seuil.

———. 1999. "Justice et bien-être dans les Miroirs des princes de Osse et Seckendorff." In *Specula principum,* edited by Angela De Benedictus. Frankfurt: Klostermann.

Sezal, İhsan, and İhsan Dağı, eds. 2001. *Kim Bu Özal? Siyaset, İktisat, Zihniyet.* Istanbul: Boyut Yayıncılık.

Shaban, Muhammad 'Abd al-Hayy Muhammad. 1971. *Islamic History: A New Interpretation.* Vol. 1. Cambridge, UK: Cambridge Univ. Press.

Shabankarah'i, Muhammad b. Ali. n.d. *Majma' al-ansab.* MS. (References to folio numbers are to Persian manuscript 15, Royal Asiatic Society [see W. H. Morley. 1854. *A Descriptive Catalogue of the Historical Manuscripts in the Arabic and Persian Languages Preserved in the Library of the Royal Asiatic Society,* London]).

al-Shahrastani, Muhammad. 1995. *Kitab al-milal wa al-nihal.* Edited by Amir Ali Muhanna and Ali Hussein Fa'ur. 2 vols. Beirut: Dar al-Ma'rifah.

Shaked, Shaul. 1995. *From Zoroastrian Iran to Islam: Studies in Religious History and Intercultural Contacts.* Brookfield, VT: Variorum.

Shalash, Hashim Taha. 1981. "Al-Zabidi fi kitabih Taj al-arus." PhD diss., Jami'ah Baghdad.

Shami, Nizam al-Din. 1984. *Zafar-namah: Tarikh-i futuhat-i Amir Taymur Gurkani, majara-i khunintarin qatl-i am-i shahrha-i Iran.* Tehran: Bamdad. [Also see the 1937 version published in Beirut.]

Sharif, Mian Mohammed. 1966. *A History of Muslim Philosophy.* 2 vols. Wiesbaden: Otto Harrassowitz.

Sharif, Mir Seyed. 1963. *Tuzukat-e Timuri.* Tehran: Asadi. [The Persian translation was provided by Abu Talib Husseini from the original Moghul language version, edited by Major Davy and published by India Office in 1773].

Sharma, Sri Ram. 1972. *The Religious Policy of the Mughal Emperors.* New York: Asia Publishing House.

al-Shatibi, Ibrahim ibn Musa. 1922. *Al-Muwafaqat fi usul al-ahkam.* Edited by M. Munr. Cairo: N.p.

Shaybub, Khalil. 1948. *Abd al-Rahman al-Jabarti.* Cairo: Dar al-Ma'arif.

Shayyal, Jamal al-Din. 1945. *Rifa'ah al-Tahtawi za'im al-nahdah al-fikriyah fi asr Muhammad Ali.* Cairo: Dar al-Ihya' al-Kutub al-Arabiyah.

Shea, David, and Anthony Troyer, trans. 1843. *The Dabistan or School of Manners.* London: Oriental Translation Fund of Great Britain and Ireland.

Sheikh, Samira. 2006. "Religious Difference and Political Institutions in Gujarat, c. 1400–1700." Paper presented at the 35th Annual Conference on South Asia, Univ. of Wisconsin, Madison, Oct. 20–22.

Sherwani, Haroon Khan, Ghulam Yazdani, and P. M. Joshi. 1973. *History of Medieval Deccan, 1295–1724.* Hyderabad [copies can be obtained from Director of Printing and Publication Bureau, Govt. of Andhra Pradesh].

Shichor, Yitzhak. 2003. "Virtual Transnationalism: Uygur Communities in Europe and the Quest for Eastern Turkestan Independence." In *Muslim*

Networks and Transnational Communities in and across Europe, edited by Stefano Allievi and Jørgen Nielsen, 281–311. Boston: E. J. Brill.

Shils, Edward. 1957. "Primordial, Personal, Sacred, and Civil Ties." *British Journal of Sociology* 8(2): 130–45.

Simidchieva, Marta. 2004. "Kingship and Legitimacy as Reflected in Nezam al-Molk's *Siyasatnama,* Fifth/Eleventh Century." In *Writers and Rulers: Perspectives on Their Relationships from Abbasid to Safavid Times,* edited by Louise Marlow and Beatrice Gruendler, 97–131. Wiesbaden: Reichert.

Skinner, Quentin. 1969. "Meaning and Understanding in the History of Ideas." *History and Theory* 8(1): 3–53.

———. 1978. *The Foundation of Modern Political Thought.* Cambridge, UK: Cambridge Univ. Press. [Also see 1987 edition.]

Smith, W. C. 1980. "The True Meaning of Scripture: An Empirical Historian's Nonreductionist Interpretation of the Qur'an." *International Journal of Middle East Studies* 11:487–505.

Spiegel, Gabrielle M. 1990. "History, Historicism, and the Social Logic of the Text in the Middle Ages." *Speculum* 65(1): 59–86.

Spuler, Bertold. 1971. "Hazaraspids." In *Encyclopedia of Islam.* 2nd ed., 3:336–37. Leiden: E. J. Brill.

———. 1985. *Die Mongolen in Iran: Politik, Verwaltung und Kultur der Ilchanzeit 1220–1350.* Leiden: E. J. Brill.

Starn, Randolph. 1975. "Meaning-Levels in the Theme of Historical Decline." *History and Theory* 14(1): 1–31.

Stetkevych, Jaroslav. 1996. *Muhammad and the Golden Bough: Reconstructing Arabian Myth.* Bloomington: Indiana Univ. Press.

Stierle, Beate. 1971. "Schriftauslegung der Reformationszeit." *Verkündigung und Forschung* 16(1): 55–88.

Stirling, Arthur Paul. 1965. *Turkish Village.* London: Weidenfeld and Nicolson.

Stock, Brian. 1983. *The Implications of Literacy: Written Language and Models of Interpretation in the Eleventh and Twelfth Centuries.* Princeton, NJ: Princeton Univ. Press.

———. 1990. *Listening for the Text: On the Uses of the Past.* Baltimore, MD: Johns Hopkins Univ. Press.

———. 1996. *Augustine the Reader: Meditation, Self-Knowledge, and the Ethics of Interpretation.* Cambridge, UK: Cambridge Univ. Press.

Storey, Charles A. 1953. *Persian Literature: A Bio-bibliographical Survey.* London: Luzac.

Strauss, Leo. 1991. *On Tyranny*, edited by Victor Gourevitch and Michaele S. Roth. New York: Free Press.

———. 1995. *Philosophy and Law: Contribution to the Understanding of Maimonides and His Predecessors*. Translated by Eve Adler. Albany: State Univ. of New York Press.

Streusand, Douglas E. 2006. "Sir Hamilton A. R. Gibb, Abu Yusuf, and the Concept of Islamic Civilization." In *History and Historiography of Post-Mongol Central Asia and the Middle East: Studies in Honor of John E. Woods*, edited by Judith Pfeiffer and Sholeh A. Quinn, 542–54. Wiesbaden: Harrassowitz.

al-Subki, Taj al-Din. 1908. *Mu'id al-ni'am wa mubid al-niqam*. Edited by D. W. Myhrman. London: Luzac.

Subrahmanyam, Sanjay. 1997. "Connected Histories: Notes Towards a Reconfiguration of Early Modern Eurasia." *Modern Asian Studies* 31(3): 735–62.

Subtelny, Maria. 2002. *Le monde est un jardin: aspects de l'histoire culturelle de l'Iran médiéval*. Paris: Association pour l'avancement des études iraniennes.

al-Suyuti, Jalal al-Din. 1949. *al-Itqan fi ulum al-Qur'an*. Edited by Muhammad ibn al-Tayyib Baqillani. Cairo: al-Maktabah al-Tijariyah al-Kubra.

———. 1979–81. *Jami' al-ahadith lil-Jami' al-Saghir wa zawa'idihi wa al-Jami' al-Kabir*. 9 vols. Damascus: Matba'ah Muhammad Hashim al-Kutubi.

Szombathy, Zoltán. 2002. "Genealogy in Medieval Muslim Societies." *Studia Islamica* 95:5–36.

al-Tabarani, Sulayman ibn Ahmad. 1995. *Al-Mu'jam al-awsat*. Edited by Tariq b. Iwad Allah b. Muhammad and Abd al-Muhsin b. Ibrahim al-Husseini. Cairo: Dar al-Haramayn.

al-Tabari, Abu Ja'far Muhammad ibn Jarir. 1879–1901. *Annales quos scripsit Abu Djafar Mohammed ibn Djarir at-Tabari cum aliis*. Edited by Michael Jan de Goeje. 12 vols. Leiden: E. J. Brill. [Also published as *The History of al-Tabari* ("Ta'rikh al-rusul wa'l-muluk"]. 40 vols. Albany: State Univ. of New York Press, 1989–2007.)]

———. 1987. *Tarikh al-umam wa al-muluk*. Vol. 2. Beirut: Dar al-Kutub al-Ilmiyah.

al-Tabarsi, Ahmad b. Ali b. Abi Talib. 1965-67. *Kitab al-ihtijaj*. Edited by Muhammad Baqir al-Khrasan. 2 vols. Najaf: Matba'at al-Nu'man.

Tabatabai, Javad. 1996. *Khwajah Nizam al-Mulk*. Tehran: Tarh-i Naw.

Tabrizi, Ahmad. "Shahanshah-namah." Unpublished manuscript in the British Museum, London.

Tageldin, Shaden. 2011. *Disarming Words.* Berkeley: Univ. of California Press.

al-Tahtawi, Rifa'ah Rafi'. 1834. *Takhlis al-ibriz fi talkhis Bariz aw al-diwan al-nafis bi-iwan Baris.* Egypt: Dar al-Taqaddum.

———. 1973. *Al-A'mal al-kamilah lil-Rifa'ah Rafi' al-Tahtawi.* Edited by Muhammad Imarah. Beirut: Al-Mu'assasah al-Arabiyah lil-Dirasah wa al-Nashr.

———. 1990. *A-Dawlah al-Islamiyah: nizamuha wa 'amalatuha: wa huwa al-mutammim li-kitab Nihayah al-Ijaz fi Sirah Sakin al-Hijaz.* Edited by Abd al-Rahman Hasan Mahmud and Faruq Hamid Badr. Cairo: Maktabah al-Adab.

Tainter, Joseph A. 1988. *The Collapse of Complex Societies.* Cambridge, UK: Cambridge Univ. Press.

Tavakoli-Targhi, Mohamad. 1998. "Modernity, Heterotopia, and Homeless Texts." *Comparative Studies of South Asia, Africa, and the Middle East* 18(2): 2–13.

———. 2001. *Refashioning Iran: Orientalism, Occidentalism, and Historiography.* New York: Palgrave.

Taylor, Charles. 2004. *Modern Social Imaginaries.* Durham, NC: Duke Univ. Press.

Tibi, Bassam. 2012. *Islamism and Islam.* New Haven: Yale Univ. Press.

al-Tirmidhi, Muhammad ibn Isa. 1965. *Sunan al-Tirmidhi wa huwa al-Jami' al-Sahih.* Edited by Abd al-Wahhab Abd al-Latif and Abd al-Rahman Muhammad Uthman. 5 vols. al-Madinah al-Munawwarah: al-Maktabah al-Salafiyah.

Todorov, Tzvetan. 1978. *Symbolisme et interpretation.* Paris: Seuil.

Toynbee, A. J. 1951. *A Study of History.* Oxford, UK: Oxford Univ. Press.

Trevor-Roper, H. R. 1959. "The General Crisis of the 17th Century." *Past and Present* 16 (Nov.): 31–64.

Trimingham, J. Spencer. 1971. *The Sufi Orders in Islam.* Oxford, UK: Clarendon Press.

Tripathi, Ram Prasad. 1998. "The Turco-Mongol Theory of Kingship." In *The Mughal State, 1526–1750,* edited by Muzaffar Alam and Sanjay Subrahmanyam, 115–67. Delhi: Oxford Univ. Press.

Troeltsch, Ernst. 1912. *Die Soziallehren der christlichen Kirchen und Gruppen.* Tubingen: J. C. B. Mohr.

Turki, Abdel-Magid. 2002. "Aggiornamento juridique: continuité et créativité ou fiction de la fermeture de la porte de l'Ijtihad?" *Studia Islamica* 94:5–65.

Tusi, Nasir al-Din. 1960. *Akhlaq-i Muhtashami.* Edited by Muhammad Taqi Danishpazhuh. Tehran: Intisharat-i Danishgah-i Tehran.

———. 1964. *The Nasirean Ethics.* Translated by G. M. Wickens. London: Allen and Unwin.

———. 1976. *Akhlaq-i Nasiri*. Edited by Mujtaba Minuvi and Ali Riza Haydari. Tehran: Khwarazmi.

Ullmann, Walter. 1966. *Principles of Government and Politics in the Middle Ages*. New York: Barnes and Noble.

Urfi Shirazi, Muhammad. 1915. *Diwan-i Urfi Shirazi*. Kanpur: Matba'i Munshi Naval Kishur.

Urry, John. 2000. *Sociology Beyond Societies: Mobilities for the Twenty-First Century*. London: Routledge.

Vassie, Roderic. 1988. "Persian Interpretations of the Bhagvadgita in the Mughal Period with Special Reference to the Version of Abd al-Rahman Chishti." PhD diss., School of Oriental and African Studies, Univ. of London.

———. 1999. "'Abd al-Rahman Chishti and the Bhagavadgita: 'Unity of Religion' Theory in Practice." In *The Heritage of Sufism*, edited by Leonard Lewisohn, 2:367–78. Oxford, UK: Oneworld.

van der Veer, Peter. 2001. *Transnational Religion*. Working Paper for the Center for Migration and Development. Princeton, NJ: Princeton Univ., July.

Voll, John. 1994. "Islam as a Special World-System." *Journal of World History* 5(2): 213–26.

al-Wahidi, Ali ibn Ahmad al-Nisaburi Abu al-Hasan, and Abd al-Hayy al-Farmawi. 1994. *Al-Wasit fi tafsir al-qur'an al-majid*. 4 vols. Beirut: Dar al-Kutub al-Ilmiyah.

Waldman, Marilyn Robinson. 1980. *Toward a Theory of Historical Narrative: A Case Study in Perso-Islamicate Historiography*. Columbus: Ohio State Univ. Press.

Waldron, Jeremy. 1995. "Minority Cultures and the Cosmopolitan Alternative." In *The Rights of Minority Cultures*, edited by Will Kymlicka, 93–119. Oxford, UK: Oxford Univ. Press.

Wallraff, Martin. 2001. *Christus versus Sol. Sonnenverehrung und Christentum in der Spätantike*. Münster: Aschendorff.

Walzer, Richard. 1963. "Aspects of Islamic Political Thought: Al-Farabi and Ibn Xaldun." *Oriens* 16:40–60.

Watt, W. Montgomery. 1973. *The Formative Period of Islamic Thought*. Edinburgh: Edinburgh Univ. Press.

———. 1999. "Idjara." In *Encyclopedia of Islam*. 2nd ed. Leiden: E. J. Brill.

———. 2003. *Islamic Political Thought*. Edinburgh: Edinburgh Univ. Press.

Watwat, Rashid al-Din Muhammad ibn Muhammad. 2004. *Namaha-i Rashid al-Din Watwat*. Edited by Qasim Tuysirkani. Tehran: Intisharat-i Danishgah-i Tehran.

Weber, Max. 1968. *On Charisma and Institution Building: Selected Papers.* Edited by S. N. Eisenstadt. Chicago: Univ. of Chicago Press.

———. 1978. *Economy and Society: An Outline of Interpretive Sociology.* Edited by Guenther Roth and Claus Wittich. Berkeley: Univ. of California Press.

Weismann, Itzchak. 2001. *Taste of Modernity: Sufism, Salafiyya, and Arabism in Late Ottoman Damascus.* Leiden: E. J. Brill.

Werbner, Pnina. 1999. "Global Pathways: Working Class Cosmopolitans and the Creation of Transnational Ethnic Worlds." *Social Anthropology* 7(1): 17–35.

Wheeler, Brannon M. 1996. *Applying the Canon in Islam: The Authorization and Maintenance of Interpretive Reasoning in Hanafi Scholarship.* Albany: State Univ. of New York Press.

Wiedenhofer, Siegfried. 1992. "Tradition, Traditionalismus." In *Geschichtliche Grundbegriffe,* edited by R. Koselleck et al. 4th ed. Vol. 6, 607–49. Stuttgart: E. Klett.

Ya'qubi, Ahmad ibn Abi Ya'qub. 1883. *Tarikh.* Edited by Martijn Theodor Houtsma. 2 vols. Lugduni Batavorum: E. J. Brill.

Yavari, Neguin. 2004. "Polysemous Texts and Reductionist Readings: Women and Heresy in the *Siyar al-Muluk.*" In *Views from the Edge: Essays in Honor of Richard W. Bulliet,* edited by Neguin Yavari, Lawrence G. Potter, and Jean-Marc Ran Oppenheim, 322–46. New York: Columbia Univ. Press for the Middle East Institute.

Yücer, Hür Mahmut. 2003. *Osmanlı Toplumunda Tasavvuf: 19. Yüzyıl.* İstanbul: İnsan.

Yunis Ali, Mohamed Mohamed. 2000. *Medieval Islamic Pragmatics: Sunni Legal Theorists' Models of Textual Communication.* Surrey, UK: Curzon.

Yusuf Ya'qub, Abu. 1985. *Kitab al-kharaj.* Edited by Ihsan Abbas. Beirut: Dar al-Shuruq.

Zahran, al-Badrawi. 1983. *Rifa'ah al-Tahtawi wa waqfah ma'a al-dirasah al-lughawiyah al-hadithah: ma'a tahqiq nass kitabihi al-Tuhfah al-Maktabiyah.* Cairo: Dar al-Ma'arif.

Zaman, Muhammad Qasim. 1997. *Religion and Politics under the Early 'Abbasids: The Emergence of the Proto-Sunni Elite.* Leiden: E. J. Brill.

———. 2003. "The Scope and Limits of Islamic Cosmopolitanism and the 'Discursive Language' of the 'Ulama." In *Muslim Networks: From Hajj to Hiphop,* edited by Miriam Cooke and Bruce B. Lawrence, 84–106. Chapel Hill: Univ. of North Carolina Press.

Zambaur, Eduard Karl Max von. 1927[1955]. *Manuel de généalogie et de chronologie pour l'histoire de l'Islam, avec 20 tableaux généalogiques hors texte et 5 cartes*. Hanover: H. Lafaire.

Zaydan, Yusuf. 1996. *Fihris makhtutat maktabah Rifa'ah Rafi' al-Tahtawi*. 3 vols. Cairo: Ma'had al-Makhtutat al-Arabiyah, al-Munazzamah al-Arabiyah lil-Tarbiyah wa al-Thaqafah.

Zeigler, Norman P. 1998. "Some Notes on Rajput Loyalties During the Mughal Period." In *The Mughal State: 1526–1750*, edited by Muzaffar Alam and Sanjay Subrahmanyam, 168–210. Delhi: Oxford Univ. Press.

Zubaida, Sami. 1999. "Cosmopolitanism and the Middle East." In *Cosmopolitanism, Identity, and Authenticity in the Middle East*, edited by Roel Meijer, 15–33. Surrey, UK: Curzon.

Index